PLANNING, POLITICS AND PUBLIC POLICY

PLANNING, POLITICS AND PUBLIC POLICY

The British, French and Italian experience

Edited by

JACK HAYWARD

Professor of Politics, University of Hull

and

MICHAEL WATSON

Lecturer in Politics, University College of Wales

CAMBRIDGE UNIVERSITY PRESS

Published by the Syndics of the Cambridge University Press
Bentley House, 200 Euston Road, London NW1 2DB
American Branch: 32 East 57th Street, New York, N.Y. 10022

© Cambridge University Press 1975

Library of Congress Catalogue Card Number: 74-82587

ISBN: 0 521 20570 0

First published 1975

Printed in Great Britain
at the University Printing House, Cambridge
(Euan Phillips, University Printer)

CONTENTS

CONTRIBUTORS

Editors

Jack Hayward, Professor of Politics, University of Hull

Michael Watson, Lecturer in Political Science, University College of Wales, Aberystwyth

Contributors

François d'Arcy, Senior Lecturer in Political Science, Institut d'Etudes Politiques, University of Grenoble

Attilio Bastianini, Lecturer at the Institute of Architecture, Torino Politecnico; Turin town councillor

Jean-Jacques Bonnaud, Chef du Service Industriel, Commissariat Général du Plan

Bernard Cazes, in charge of long-term planning studies at the Commissariat Général du Plan

John Corina, Fellow of St Peter's College, Oxford; Professor in Management Sciences, UMIST

Nigel Despicht, former Director, Transport Division, United Nations Economic Commission for Europe; currently Visiting Senior Fellow, University of Sussex

Rosita Donnini, Lecturer in Financial Science, University of Macerata

Gioachino Fraenkel, Assistant to the Director of Economic Services, Confederazione Generale dell'Industria Italiana, Rome

Pierre Grémion, Chargé de Recherche at the Centre National de la Recherche Scientifique (CNRS), Centre de Sociologie des Organisations, Paris

Bruno Jobert, Researcher at the Centre d'Etudes et de Recherche sur l'Administration Economique et l'Aménagement du Territoire, Institut d'Etudes Politiques, University of Grenoble; Grenoble town councillor

Isidoro Franco Mariani, Professor of Social Statistics, University of Bari; Editor of *Rassegna de Statistiche del Lavoro*

Lucien Nizard, Professor of Political Science and Director of CERAT, Institut d'Etudes Politiques, University of Grenoble

Gianfranco Pasquino, Fellow of the Istituto Carlo Cattaneo, Bologna; Managing Editor of *Rivista Italiana de Scienza Politica*

Umberto Pecchini, Editor of *L'Informazione Industriale,* Turin

Valerio Selan, Professor of Political Economy and Financial Science, University of Macerata; Member of Lazio Regional Committee for Economic Planning

Jim Sharpe, Lecturer in Public Administration, Faculty Fellow, Nuffield College, Oxford; Oxford City Councillor

Trevor Smith, Senior Lecturer in Politics, Queen Mary College, University of London

Jean-Claude Thoenig, Attaché de Recherche at the Centre National de la Recherche Scientifique (CNRS), Centre de Sociologie des Organisations, Paris

Yves Ullmo, former Chef de Service at the Commissariat du Plan; at present Directeur des Synthèses at INSEE, Ministry of Finance

Giuliano Urbani, Professor of Comparative Politics, University of Florence

Jean-Pierre Worms, Chargé de Recherche at the Centre National de la Recherche Scientifique, Centre de Sociologie des Organisations, Paris

Maurice Wright, Reader in Government, University of Manchester

Stephen Young, SSRC Research Fellow, Department of Government, University of Manchester

PREFACE

This book has had a long and laborious gestation, commencing in the spring of 1968. At the annual conference of the Political Studies Association, in the course of which a paper by Michael Watson on 'The Political Implications of Planning, the French case' was discussed, Professor Ghita Ionescu announced that a research project to study the relations between planning and politics in three East European countries had been launched. At his suggestion, supported by Professor Morris-Jones of the Comparative Politics Group of the PSA, Hayward and Watson initially intended to undertake a contrasting study of several West European countries and a preliminary outline of such an investigation was prepared in May 1968 and discussed at a CPG meeting in the following October. We decided quite quickly thereafter that we would probably wish to confine ourselves to Britain, France and Italy, countries attempting comprehensive, medium-term national planning, to allow a more searching investigation in which the diversity of assumptions and approaches among the contributors would be less likely to get out of hand. Although our investigation would be undertaken by a multinational and multidisciplinary team, the focus of interest would be planning as a political and administrative phenomenon, rather than emphasising the economic aspect as was customary, largely because those who had written on the subject were economists.

Because both the editors had previously worked on French planning, it proved relatively straightforward to collect together a well qualified group of French contributors to work alongside the British group. Unlike the predominantly academic and political science composition of the British group, the French team was more diversified, containing experienced economic planners and researchers in the sociology of organisation, as well as academic political scientists. (The more sustained French planning experience undoubtedly accounts in part for this contrast.) More difficulty was experienced in securing suitable Italian collaborators, so a mainly Anglo-French exploratory conference was held in June 1969 at Nuffield College, Oxford, which confirmed the interest in undertaking comparative research of the

[ix]

planning experience in the three countries. It was agreed that it would add immeasurably to the complexity of the task if it was to be conducted in conjunction with the East European studies, so it was decided to proceed independently. A provisional list of specific policy sectors and proposed contributors was drawn up, it being agreed that the main purpose was to investigate the impact of planning upon political and administrative decision-making relationships and the resistance of established relationships to the introduction of planning, both at the national and regional levels.

During the next eighteen months, a conference was held at the Planning Commissariat in Paris to discuss preliminary working papers; an Italian team was recruited with the help of Professor Sartori; separate meetings of the national teams met to discuss the project. The editors prepared two brief papers that were intended to serve as guidelines to all contributors: one clarifying the way in which the concept of planning was to be used and offering a simple model of planning as a form of governmental decision-making; the other setting out a checklist of the specific issues to be considered in the policy case studies, as well as laying the foundation for the overall comparative assessment. Three years of preliminary work came to an end in July 1971 when the Social Science Research Council agreed to offer the editors a grant to undertake the proposed work and the project proper was launched at a conference at St Peter's College, Oxford, in September 1971.

The final structure of the book emerged as a consequence of the methodological strategy adopted, so it is necessary to allude to this briefly. Our interest in planning as a political 'technology' for governmental decision-making concerned its use in the liberal democratic and mixed-economy context in Western Europe. We tried to establish propositions which were valid for this type of politico-economic system on a cross-national basis. We deliberately chose to limit the number of countries for consideration so as to enable us to explore comparisons between their experience in greater depth. We also chose to seek contributions by specialists on selected aspects of the question from *within* each country concerned. We wished to bring together people who had already done substantial work in one or more aspects of the subject, building upon an existing fund of research and extending it in a comparative direction, although more empirical work has been necessary to fill some gaps. The main effort was aimed at encouraging the contributors to think about the data in a broader context. To achieve this end, a process of interpersonal socialisation through a series of meetings was envisaged. Starting from replies to a questionnaire and reactions to a simple model prepared by the co-organisers, it sought to lead from a confrontation of separate standpoints towards a meeting of minds. The questionnaire was left behind as first national and then cross-national papers were prepared, exchanged, discussed and redrafted. The whole process developed pragmatically because it seemed appropriate to the work in hand. The successive stages in the process of interaction between contributors were: an initial effort at comparison, followed by national-sector papers, then by cross-national papers based upon them, culminating in an overall, comparative introduction and conclusion. The diversity of treatment is a reflection of the freedom which each contributor had within a very loose overall framework, allowing the specific nature of each national and sectoral experience to be fully expressed rather than strictly subordinated to a set of preordained premises. The number of contributors and our ignorance of each other's national and sectoral experience made it especially essential to increase the integration of approach and of analysis, which in the time available has been only partially successful.

Our main purpose has been to investigate the interrelationship between planning conceived as a technique of public economic policy-making and the working of political and administrative processes in three West European states. This has involved an examination of the formal and informal ways in which planning has been introduced and the responses of these political systems to the attempt to make planning an integral part of governmental decision-making. The studies of the French planning experience by several American scholars since the early 1960s have either been at too high a level of generality, inadequately underpinned by first-hand empirical work (such as S. S. Cohen's *Modern Capitalist Planning: The French Model,* 1969) or of a more limited kind (such as the admirable study of *Industrial Planning in France,* 1969, by J. H. McArthur and B. R. Scott) in which the firms rather than the political and administrative decision-makers are the focus of interest. Thus, even in the case of France, which has been most extensively studied, the planning process retains an unreality which has made it difficult for would-be imitators to learn from its successes and failures. As a result, the reasons for the transition from the optimism of the early 60s to the pessimism of the early 70s towards the planning venture remain to be explained at other than a polemical level.

The time span emphasised has been the 1960s, during which the prestige of the French model first waxed and then waned. (Andrew Shonfield's classic, *Modern Capitalism,* 1965, reflected the earlier mood.) Instead of studying planning primarily from the standpoint of the economist, assuming a given political context (as was done in the P.E.P. study of *Economic Planning and Policies in Britain, France and Germany,* 1968) our emphasis has been upon the interrelationship between the attempt to plan and the political and administrative institutions and processes of Britain, France and Italy at the national and regional levels. Who was involved and how was bargaining conducted? What changes were brought about by the intention to plan? What constraints did traditional practices, attitudes and values place upon the innovative tendencies associated with planning? How far were the form and content of planning themselves modified by the social, administrative and political context into which they are introduced?

In any attempt to answer such questions, some of the matters on which we have focused were unavoidable, while others were selected from a range of possibilities because they could be tackled by potential contributors. It was essential to examine the national context of planning in each of the three countries and have an evaluative description of the institutions established to undertake overall planning. Close scrutiny of industrial policy and manpower policy was also considered indispensable to an understanding of the processes through which planning was implemented. Land use policy and transport policy were important correctives to a tendency to envisage planning primarily from the macro-economic standpoint, a country like Britain finding them more congenial than comprehensive economic planning on the French model. The regional dimension, which has been such an important feature of the planning mood from the early sixties, could also not be excluded without gravely impairing the interest of the study. Despite the limited extent to which long-term planning has so far impinged upon public policy, it was considered desirable to include a gallocentric chapter on the subject. Some readers will turn to this book for information, while others will be more concerned with the interpretations offered. We hope that the final structure of the book, which has emerged from the problems selected for special investigation, provides a suitable balance between generalisation and particularisation.

The editors wish to emphasise both the collective nature of the project and the personal responsibility of each author for his own contribution. Although Hayward and Watson initiated the project and have had the function of guiding it from start to finish, they have not attempted to impose a methodological strait-jacket upon their fellow contributors, contenting themselves with trying to secure a minimum of comparative cohesion, as well as offering suggestions and encouragement. We hope that whatever has thereby been lost in rigour will be made up in the richness of the materials assembled. It has been very much a pioneering effort and as such suffers abundantly from many of the inadequacies of such a venture. If it prompts others to do better, we shall be content. Despite all the difficulties involved in international and interdisciplinary collaboration, the editors have found this an intellectually enriching experience and we believe all the participants will have benefited from having ventured outside the more or less parochial confines of their own specialism.

Since the completion of this book, the return of a majority Labour Government in October 1974, committed *inter alia* to the establishment of a National Enterprise Board and the conclusion of planning agreements, has given an apparently 'Italian' twist to British industrial policy. The French, after a pause to reconsider the future of planning, have appointed a new Planning Commissioner, Jean Ripert, committed broadly to the Monnet and Massé traditions. His other Italian equivalent, Planning Secretary Giorgio Ruffolo, has resigned in disgust at the political and administrative paralysis of planning in his country. Recent or forthcoming publications of valuable studies of French planning (*Planification et Société*, University of Grenoble Press 1974) and British planning (Jacques Leruez, *Economic Planning and Politics in Britain*, Martin Robertson 1975) to name just two, indicate that this subject continues to attract attention as the centrepiece of attempts at engineering changes in societies that are extremely resistant to change.

Finally, the editors wish to express their thanks to the Warden and Fellows of Nuffield College, Oxford and to the European Educational Research Trust for their support at the vital gestation stage of the project; to the Social Science Research Council, without whose financial support the project could never have been brought to completion; and to the Politics Department of the University of Keele from which Jack Hayward coordinated the project. We also wish to record our gratitude to M. Pierre Viot of the Cour des Comptes, formerly in charge of the Regional service of the Planning Commissariat, for the help, advice and encouragement he gave us in the early stages of the project. The Italian contributions were financed partly by the Consiglio Nazionale delle Ricerche. The Italian contributors wish to thank Professor Veniero del Punta, University of Florence, Dr Franco Mattei and Dr Giorgio Ruffolo for their help. They particularly wish to thank Professor Giovanni Sartori of the Centro di Politica Comparata, whose invaluable sponsorship led to their participation in the project.

Mr and Mrs Watson undertook most of the translation from French, the remainder of the French papers being translated by Jack Hayward, who also revised all the translations. We would like to express our particular gratitude to the project's part-time secretary, Mrs Sheila Pye, for the prodigies she performed in deciphering the illegible and to Miss Charmian Hall for her enthusiastic help with the preparation of the manuscript for publication.

1974

Jack Hayward
Michael Watson

Introduction

Change and choice: the agenda of planning

JACK HAYWARD

It has been persuasively argued that whereas 'underinstitutionalisation' might be a major cause of political decay in developing countries, in the developed countries a prime cause of the political stagnation afflicting them is the fact that they suffer from 'overinstitutionalisation', traditional institutions successfully stifling innovation. Past success has encouraged complacency and inertia, coupled with a capacity to resist pressures to change.[1] Whereas the main concern of those who were involved in or commented upon the planning experience of the 1960s and beyond in Western Europe (especially in Britain) has been with the economic causes of stagnation or development, our aim is to focus on the political and administrative factors inhibiting or facilitating economic policy changes and the adaptability of existing institutions to the challenge represented by an attempt at national economic planning. In comparing the experiences of the three polities selected, we shall need to make some preliminary distinctions between the contrasting national, cultural and institutional contexts, the varying situations, motivations and dominant forces that shaped public policy. First of all, the notion of planning as a non-traditional manner of policy-making must be explored.

Planning and the policy-making process: humdrum and heroic

Except in time of crisis, the fear of change is a pervasive phenomenon. Paradoxically, resistance to change by the underprivileged manual worker in the form of restrictive practices, which were such a feature of public discussion in Britain in the sixties, has received far more emphasis than comparable behaviour higher up the social hierarchy, although such comment was always much more trenchant when public officials rather than private managements were concerned. Disturbing the *status quo* is not merely an inconvenience but a threat to many people, some of whom are in a position successfully to defeat innovative intrusions. Change is usually controversial, proposed changes tending to become issues of dispute. In matters of public

[1]

policy this means that they become politicised. Although controversial
policies do not necessarily become the subject of party conflict, the
liberal democratic polity tends to divide the disputants along party
lines, infusing the issues with partisan significance. In the sixties, the
issue of planning was much more highly politicised in Italy than in
Britain, while in France – where planning remained depoliticised until
the sixties – it has usually been possible to achieve a greater measure of
consensus on the subject and thereby make it less of a political issue, at
least within the decision-making nucleus.

The agenda of government and the methods used to accomplish it
have changed dramatically in the twentieth century. In Britain, the
classic land of liberal *laisser faire*, the inter-war years witnessed a crisis
in the conception of a market economy run on capitalist lines, with the
government playing only a marginal role except in special cases or as a
short-term expedient. It is not surprising that in the 1930s the subject
of national economic planning was raised as a solution to this predica-
ment by people of very varying political views in Britain and France.
There were also exponents of a technocratic standpoint who thought
that national economic planning could be divorced from politics
because they conceived planning essentially as a matter of rational
and efficient management. This standpoint was sometimes combined
with a corporatist approach – which also existed independently –
according to which the interested parties, especially government,
business and worker organisations, should collaborate together in
the making of public policy. The motivations of such advocates of
economic planning might be either revolutionary, reformist, conservative or reactionary. Italian fascism, after being extremely anti-
interventionist in the early twenties, created, in the wake of the slump,
the expedient instruments of public entrepreneurship which were to
become such a salient instrument of public policy in the post-war
period. The highly politicised issue of planning was to disappear from
the agenda of government in Britain and Italy in the late forties, while
in France it was to survive unscathed the political swing to the right.
Despite the underlying trend towards government economic *intervention* of greater volume, range and duration, circumstances – partly
general and partly specific to each country – played a decisive part in
propelling the issue of *planning* to the forefront of public concern in
the early sixties.

Before attempting to characterise more precisely what type of
political and administrative policy-making process is involved in the
enterprise called planning, it should be made clear that we are
interested in a process that cannot be identified with a particular
document called a plan. The existence of a formal plan is not a
prerequisite of planning, which is constituted by a set of activities that

may not be described in any document. Such a formalistic approach encourages a distinction between planning and implementation fraught with conceptual and practical dangers. It obscures the fact that planning conceived as a set of procedures for making choices governing future action is a normative model of an efficient decision-making process and as such is an unrealistic description of the way organisations behave in practice. As Banfield put it in 1959,

in the real world we are struck at once by two facts: there is very little planning, and there is even less rationality. In general, organizations engage in opportunistic decision-making rather than in planning: rather than laying out a course of action which will lead all the way to the attainment of their ends, they extemporize, meeting each crisis as it arises.[2]

He went on to enumerate the factors that led organisational choice to diverge from the ideal of comprehensive planning: uncertainty of the future, likelihood of provoking opposition, limited choice, the 'preference for present rather than future effects' coupled with a concern about organisational maintenance, the absence of clearcut objectives, with no serious attempt being made to use resources efficiently in attaining objectives. So, while bearing firmly in mind the normative character of planning, at the same time, one should not divorce rational conception from irrational achievement.

Economists and politicians have been especially guilty of separating the preparation of a plan from its practical application, partly because they are more interested in the content of plans than in the planning process. Yet it is not only *what* but *how* and *who* that will decide whether or not a particular planning activity will be successful. Economists have often been inclined to assume that failures in planning are to be attributed to faults in preparation, whereas partial and inefficient implementation – owing to political and administrative action or inaction – are usually a much more important weakness than miscalculation. An economist, who was able to observe the mid-sixties British planning venture from inside a ministry, recognised that

The sustained and growing inability to manage our affairs suggests that the roots of our problems are not really economic at all. We must look for attitudes and institutions which are too rigid and inflexible to permit the adjustments we need to make...The really interesting question is whether there is any institutional change which would unlock the door to development.[3]

So, although Soviet and French experience have accustomed us to think of planning in terms of particular plans, British and Italian experience cannot be fitted into such a formalistic framework, while the USA engaged in its planning activities under the disguise of PPBS (planning-programming-budgeting-system).

In a study devoted primarily to the developing countries, 'the widening gap between promise and performance' was attributed in large measure to a failure to appreciate that not only economic potential but administrative capacity and political action were pre-requisites of planned economic development.[4] There are two major sources of unplanned decision-making. In the private sector, profitability as determined by the market is the dominant preoccupation, especially in industrialised societies. Decisions are taken in the light of the situation prevailing and anticipated in the market. Except where one producer is in effective control of the market, uncertainty makes forward planning by the individual firm hazardous. Those public corporations which are genuinely autonomous and operate along competitive lines might respond to market forces in the same way as private corporations. However, British public corporations tend to be subject to much greater government control than is formally supposed to be the case, and French attempts to give their public enterprises more autonomy have been unconvincing. Italy has achieved a type of public entrepreneurship that combines sensitivity to the market with responsiveness to public policy. Within the state sector proper, decisions are generally the outcome of discussion between a plurality of policy-making units, each pursuing separate objectives which, under the guise of the public interest, have more to do with organisational power struggles and the defence of sectional interests. The problem here will be less a matter of reducing uncertainty than reaching agreement by reducing intransigence.

What changes are necessary in the decision-making processes of government to make planning possible? In trying to answer this question, it is important not to regard planning primarily as the contrary of market decision-making but of the unplanned, 'muddling through' political and administrative policy process formulated by Lindblom.[5] The characteristics of this humdrum type of decision-making – in contrast with the heroic type represented by planning – are threefold. Firstly, there are no explicit, over-riding medium or long-term objectives. Secondly, unplanned decision-making is incremental. Action is undertaken *step by step*, change taking the form of marginal adjustments. Policies are adapted piecemeal as circumstances require, the range of policy comparisons being limited to alternatives that differ only slightly from existing policies. Thirdly, humdrum or unplanned decisions are arrived at by a continuous process of mutual adjustment between a plurality of autonomous policy-makers operating in the context of a highly fragmented multiple flow of influence. Not only is plenty of scope offered to interest-group spokesmen to shape the outcome by participation in the advocacy process, the aim is to secure, through bargaining, at least passive acceptance of the decision by the interests affected. The chief criterion of a 'good' decision is subjective acceptability rather than an objective one such as quantitatively measured efficiency.

In contrast to this humdrum decision-making process, characteristic of pluralistic liberal democracies, one may set up a model of what a political decision-making process with planning would be like. It would be heroic in the dual sense that it would be both an ambitious political exercise in rational decision-making and an ambitious assertion of political will by government leaders. The three basic features of such heroic policy-making would be, firstly, the setting of explicit objectives for future development, together with a government commitment to implement them in the medium and long term. Secondly, there is an explicit rejection of incrementalist improvisation in favour of a more or less comprehensive coordination of public policies. This would involve a systematic revision of existing programmes of action to secure conformity with policy objectives and a detailed examination of a wide and differentiated range of possible alternatives for future action. Thirdly, there is an attempt to rely less upon an agreed compromise between interested parties and more upon the analysis of alternative policy opportunities defined in advance, in the light of the government's priorities and available resources, backed up by an assertion of public power. What is often presented as an exercise in rationality is often more a matter of 'guesstimation', so that under the guise of reducing uncertainty there is plenty of scope for wishful thinking and public deception. As the junior partners in heroic policy-making, planners are very much at the mercy of politicians and administrators. Alongside the initial, public-relations benefits of heroic planning, its great weakness is that it is 'a most difficult activity with limited probability of clear-cut success and high probability of starkly visible failures at best.'[6]

Politicians, in particular, are naturally extremely reluctant to accept such risks and, along with administrative officials, they may well prefer a situation in which they would not have to assume public responsibility for attaining such problematic objectives. Consequently, they tend to prefer to stick to the traditional, case by case, piecemeal intervention, which can often be undertaken away from the public eye. Given the inherent difficulties of comprehensive planning, it is natural that governments should resort to more partial forms of planning activity. In countries such as France, with a long tradition of state intervention, assertive behaviour by government is taken for granted and provides the instruments for enforcing plan implementation although, as we shall see, piecemeal intervention may stop far short of planning as we have defined it. Lacking a strong state and administration, Italian governments have not been able to rely upon the same measure of acquiescence in state intervention, except by autonomous public enterprises, nor have they been as able to assert their sovereignty in the economic sphere. In Britain, deeply entrenched liberal attitudes have made it difficult to contemplate state economic intervention as a natural and permanent phenomenon, much less a form of planning that would upset traditional self-restraining methods of government. The tendency to rely upon short-term, piecemeal improvisation is so much a characteristic feature of the traditional humdrum style of decision-making in all three countries that tremendous obstacles must be overcome if a longer-term and coordinated view is to prevail. The agents of change capable of bringing about the transition to a planned type of decision-making have been rare, which accounts for the patchy record of the three countries examined.

National aptitudes for planning

Although the impact of the great slump in the capitalist countries and the apparent success of Soviet planning had led to discussion of the need to plan the economy in the 1930s, especially in left-wing quarters, it was not until the aftermath of the Second World War that an attempt was made to translate the slogan into reality. While Britain seemed far better equipped to engage in planning – inheriting a wartime organisation of comprehensive economic control and having a Labour government enthusiastically committed to planning – it was left to France to undertake this major innovation. Shonfield's characterisation of the British disassociation of private and public power as 'arm's length government' goes a long way towards offering a general explanation of the 1945 Labour government's failure to embark upon national economic planning.[7] A pluralistic conception of authority meant that a nominally sovereign government was inhibited about using its power without first obtaining consent to its actions from those over whom it was exercising power. The government bent its energies primarily towards consulting with a view to persuading those it was unwilling or unable to coerce. The initiative was thus surrendered to business organisations and trade unions who were elevated into corporatist veto groups, capable of frustrating public policy or at least modifying it so that it became acceptable. A preoccupation with tactical, short-term improvisation rather than strategic, long-term planning meant that urgent matters were dealt with to the neglect of important ones.[8] Both interministerial coordination and the centralisation of control in the Treasury were attempted. Both failed because of the entrenched departmentalism of British government and the reluctance of the Treasury to intervene positively, partly motivated perhaps by its lack of economic expertise. Having embraced Keynes-ian short-term economic management, the Treasury found it repug-nant to concern itself with problems of long-term investment.

Departmentalism is so central a problem to effective economic planning that it is worth pausing to consider it. Although the com-ments that follow refer specifically to Britain, similar problems also arise in an acute form in France and Italy, one of the purposes of national planning precisely being to overcome the consequences of departmentalism.

Within departments, it is associated with a strong and sometimes uncritical adherence to particular lines of policy, and attitudes of mind, which have become established as traditional...The prestige of the department as a whole, and of its minister in particular, depends on the success with which its pre-determined policies are defended and upheld in interdepartmental disputes. Between departments, it is associated with a disposition to regard issues of policy as being normally if not necessarily decided by a somewhat stylized process of quasi-diplomatic bargaining between ministries, in which the arguments presented are in no way impartial or disinterested...There is a danger that the economic considerations which are relevant to particular policy decisions, in so far as they are presented at all, will be treated as merely *ex parte* statements by the department from which they originate.[9]

While problems of interdepartmental coordination can be partially corrected by mergers into a small number of large ministries, this still leaves intact the difficulties associated with the problem of who should organise the coordination. In Britain, the Treasury traditionally operated by persuasion rather than command, even if this involved making concessions. It conceived its coordinating role essentially as incrementally reconciling the *ad hoc* initiatives of spending ministries within overall public expenditure limits. Vertical decision-making, based on clientelist collusion between sponsor ministry and trade association, predominated over horizontal coordination. It was not until the 1960s that the Treasury undertook medium-term forward programming of public expenditure, one of the areas in which genuine progress was made towards public sector planning. Inhibi-tions as far as the private sector was concerned were more tenacious.

Undoubtedly, successful mid-1940s business resistance towards ex-tending the industrial working parties into development councils in Britain, at a time when Monnet was making them an instrument for adapting a compliant private sector to the purposes of French econ-omic planning, was a significant indicator of the different post-war experience in the two countries. The contrast was apparent to atten-tive observers as early as December 1946, when *The Economist* drew the lessons of the First French Plan: 'It is the first time that a democratic state has ever given itself a set of authoritative signposts to guide its

economic policy making.' By comparison with the British working
parties, the French modernisation commissions 'were given a definite
part to play in forming a consistent policy to embrace all of them. The
parts consequently fit together into a whole and M. Monnet has an
industrial policy where Sir Stafford Cripps will have, at best, only a
collection of unrelated expedients.' Recalling this comment during the
British revival of interest in French experience in the late fifties, a
political and economic planning group dwelt also on the lack of
effective Treasury coordination of investment, whether public or
private. This remained the responsibility of public and private corporations, such *ad hoc* intervention as occurred being undertaken by
the sponsor ministry.[10] However, there is a world of difference
between sponsorship and *tutelle*, reflecting the different balance between private and public power in Britain and France. (Italy represents
an ambiguous case, depending upon whether the autonomous state-
owned corporations are regarded as public or private; if they are
treated as public, which seems reasonable, they are nevertheless not
subject to supervision and control by the central ministries.) In
Britain, the sponsor ministry has been the spokesman for its clientele
within government and the Treasury has traditionally avoided interfering in the policies of the sponsor ministries except to ensure
economy in public expenditure. By contrast, in France the Finance
Ministry has always intervened positively to the point of practically
dispossessing the spending ministries of many of their powers, so that
their advocacy of clientele interests has generally been ineffective
except when the Planning Commissariat has given its blessing, backed
ultimately by political 'arbitration'.

   In all three countries, the Marshall Plan requirement that recipients
of American assistance should prepare plans was acted upon. However, in Britain and Italy this took the form of a report to the OEEC,
forecasting the development of the economy in the next five years,
which passed almost completely unnoticed and certainly was not
treated as a guide to public or private action in the countries concerned. Although planning had been advocated on the left in Italy at
the end of the war, resistance by the bulk of the Christian Democrats
to anything more ambitious than particular plans limited to specific
geographical areas or sectors, coupled with a refusal or incapacity to
secure effective coordination of economic policy, ensured that intermittent and piecemeal improvisation was the order of the day. In
France, where national economic planning was a going concern, the
effect of the Marshall Plan requirement was to extend the duration of
the First Plan to 1952. The funds supplied also strengthened the hand
of the Commissariat against the Finance Ministry in the early days,
enabling the longer-term investment preoccupations of the planners

to achieve priority over the short-term concern with inflation. The Monnet strategy, which survived until the early sixties, was to keep a low political and administrative profile, avoiding controversy and conflict as much as possible, securing substantial consensus between the élite holders of economic power in the public and private sectors in the concerted pursuit of what were presented as self-evident ends: national recovery and modernisation to overcome the handicap of past economic stagnation.

While in Britain the restoration of a market economy was a feature of the early post-war years, in France the acceptance of competition was a more gradual matter. Yet a strength of French planning was that it avoided identification as being antithetical to the market economy, ideologically or practically. On the contrary, in a country notorious for its Colbertist *étatisme*, the stimulation of French competitive capacity in an international context was a feature of all her plans, although this aspect was only stressed particularly in the Fifth and Sixth Plans. After all, Monnet was not only the father of French planning but also the architect of the European Coal and Steel Community, which, while it provided for a measure of planning, involved an acceptance of competition which the EEC was to extend further. Although it would be wrong to reduce the so-called indicative planning merely to national market research, the stress on the more liberal aspects of French planning – prescriptive of the direction in which it was intended France should move rather than descriptive of the reality – helped to win acceptance from some potential opponents in France and to change the attitudes and behaviour of public and private decision-makers from opposition and suspicion to support and collaboration. Less felicitously, the public-relations presentation of French planning, selectively stressing the non-conflictual and depoliticised aspects of France's experience, were seriously to mislead British business-men, civil servants, politicians and journalists about the concomitant changes that the introduction of planning would require, although there was undoubtedly much self-deception and gullibility *outre Manche*.

The relative emphasis placed upon alternative objectives of economic planning have varied between countries and over time. It is not always easy to decide the order of priority between objectives, although one of the functions of a plan is to compel a clearcut choice. In Britain, the rediscovery of planning in the early sixties was closely related to the desire to give rapid economic growth a higher priority than it had previously enjoyed, while in Italy it was particularly associated with the policy of redirecing growth by encouraging the industrial development of the South. In France, from the early emphasis on economic modernisation of the country's basic industries

Table 1. *Growth in per capita GNP as % of USA, 1913–2000*

	1913	1950	1960	1970	1980*	2000*
UK	80	46	50	46	41	32
France	42	42	51	62	71	95
Italy	24	20	29	35	41	54

* Projections assume that the growth rates of 1960–9, i.e. France 4.8%, Italy 4.7% and UK 1.9%, will continue to the end of the century.

SOURCE: Adapted from E. Stillman *et al, L'Envol de la France, 1973, p. 63.*

to the current emphasis upon industrialisation in a context of international competition, it has been possible to infer a hierarchy of priorities in each plan. For example, whereas the early plans had placed great stress upon the anti-deflationary objectives of increasing productive investment and preserving full employment, the Fifth Plan switched the emphasis to the anti-inflationary aims of price stability and a favourable balance of payments. (The economic early warning indicators of deviations in implementation, used in the Fifth Plan but subsequently discontinued, were extremely sensitive to price increases and balance of payments deficits but relatively insensitive to failures to achieve the planned rate of growth in GNP and industrial investment or to an increase in unemployment.) The rate of increase in private consumption and the volume of investment in public services were targets of a lower order, while the number of houses for sale and foreign aid were even further down the hierarchy of priorities. The choices made reflect the prevailing ideological preferences and practical preoccupations of governments. France and Italy have never had the intense commitment to a stable rate of exchange which was so important a factor in Britain throughout the sixties that it involved sacrificing the National Plan and then full employment in an unsuccessful endeavour to preserve the pound's parity. The French were nevertheless extremely irritated when the Conservative government in Britain resorted to a floating exchange rate because, when other countries also followed a policy of deliberate undervaluation of the currency, the balance of payments benefits that accrued were reduced. Subsequently France decided to float the franc rather than sacrifice economic growth.

Given that maintaining a high rate of economic growth in France, attaining it in Britain and recapturing it for the purpose of geographically redistributing its benefits in Italy, have been salient features of national economic planning, it is of some interest to consider explanations of why their performance has been different. Table 1 indicates the dramatic nature of the change. Even if one discounts the projections to the end of the century, based on the experience of the sixties, it is clear that there has already been a catastrophic fall in the relative position of the UK. By 1960 she had already been overhauled by France, with Italy coming up fast and bidding fair to equal the UK in 1980. Comparing the relative performances of the three countries in the early fifties and in the mid-sixties, whereas the UK's economic growth was 27.8% (1950–4 to 1963–7), France managed 44.1% (1950–4 to 1963–6) and Italy attained 60.4% (1951–4 to 1963–7).[11]

However, when it comes to explaining why national growth rates have differed, the results have been extremely inconclusive. Denison's famous study placed a great deal of stress on relative gains from the reallocation of labour. He argued that 'in France the employment outlook, the large gains yet to be realized by curtailing agricultural and non-farm self-employment, the rapid extension of education beyond the compulsory level, and the apparent French ability to cut into the residual productivity gap, combine to provide an especially favorable prospect for future rapid growth of national income.' In contrast, 'the United Kingdom's uniquely small opportunity to gain by contracting agricultural employment and self-employment, coupled with continuation of small labour force increases, will continue to make it difficult to match continental growth rates unless and until the UK starts to curtail the gap in residual productivity'. As for Italy, 'The outstanding feature of the Italian position is the very large gain yet to be realized from contraction of agricultural and non-farm self-employment.'[12]

This potentially fatalistic assessment is undermined, however, by Denison's admission that the French – and to a lesser extent the Italian – high growth rate was due in large measure to an unexplained improvement in residual productivity and that the impact of planning upon resource allocation might have had a material bearing on this. An authoritative French study has stressed that this residual factor – amounting to 4% out of an annual growth rate of 5% – could be attributed as follows. Half the residue could be accounted for by three factors: better training of manpower, mobility of labour from low to high productivity occupations and the accelerated modernisation of plant and machinery. The other half was attributed to an intensification of workers' effort, technical progress, improved organisation of production and increased volume of production. The study refuses to single out any one factor as the explanation of post-war French economic growth. After reviewing other partial explanations, its authors consider that

planning facilitated growth in a diffuse but certain fashion. But its capacity and its impact within the productive system was much too limited to have been the *deus ex machina* as some people have believed. It can clearly only explain a small part of the sustained growth in industrial labour productivity. It would have been an empty framework if it had not been applied to an economy otherwise endowed with a genuine dynamism.[13]

So, the best economists having failed to account for differential growth rates conclusively or to identify the precise relevance of planning to growth, we are left to ascertain what aptitudes the three countries have demonstrated in the hazardous enterprise of national economic planning.

Cultural and institutional differences meant that the challenge of planning was approached with varying degrees of circumspection, from different quarters and with greater or less resolution. The French tradition of state intervention has been one of piecemeal, case by case, pragmatic response to events which the government cannot anticipate but with whose consequences it is expected to deal. The readiness to intervene in an *ad hoc* way, however, should not be confused with planning. Although there has been a transition from this policy of incrementalist improvisation in a short-term perspective towards medium and long-term attempts to anticipate developments and select policies in a rational and consistent manner, the extent of the change should not be exaggerated. Writing in the mid-sixties to persuade a British audience to accept more systematic state intervention as a condition of succesful planning, Shonfield asserted that 'Postwar French planning can be regarded as a device that mobilized a number of instruments of public enterprise and pressure, which had been lying around for some time, and pointed them all in the same direction', having earlier stated that 'no other nation has so self-consciously fought to make a coherent system out of the devices which have been adopted more or less haphazardly elsewhere'.[14] While it is salutary to stress this contrast with Britain and Italy, later chapters will indicate that the move from state intervention to planning has been both patchy and partial in France itself. Effective coordination has been extremely difficult to achieve within the public sector and consensus-building with the trade unions has been largely a failure, although their weakness has usually meant that this is not a serious handicap. The action of a few well-placed innovators, such as Monnet, Gruson, Bloch-Laîné, Massé and Delors, allied political administrative and economic skills with the capacity to exercise decisive influence, harnessing the cumulative effect of many propitious factors in favour of successful planning.

Despite the claim by the Labour secretary of state for economic affairs a year before taking office that, in contrast to Conservative-style planning, 'it will in fact have to have teeth in it somewhere' the British flirtation with planning throughout the sixties could be characterised as toothless tripartism. It has generally been agreed in retrospect that British planning in the 1960s was condemned to failure by the self-indulgent belief that painful choices between competing policy objectives could be evaded, thereby avoiding the conflicts that would arise and the need to enforce a decision against resistance. It was believed that consensus could be reached by compromise between government, business and the trade unions and that the centralised market research and consensus-building aspects of so-called indicative French planning would suffice. It was hoped that new institutions would enable incompatible objectives to be attained by eliminating the inconsistencies between them. The belief that a new nostrum was to hand that would ensure that Britain could also experience a rejuvenating economic miracle was strongest in certain industrial quarters, who were desperate to find a remedy to the stop–go governmental exacerbation of a business cycle that it was supposed to correct. A Conservative government, at its wits end, clutched at planning as one more expedient to evade unpopular policy choices.

The half-baked conversion of leading British businessmen and Conservative ministers to what they took to be French-style planning in 1960–1, predicated on its non-imperative character, was a fundamental cause of the subsequent fiasco. It is sometimes asked why Britain turned to the French rather than the German (or for that matter Italian) model as a guide to securing sustained economic growth. The answer is that the free market approach had been tried in the 1950s and had failed. In any case, British businessmen might applaud the rhetoric of competition but were not so keen on competition in practice. Also, it was at this time that de Gaulle, setting aside the discreet circumspection of the Fourth Republic, extolled the praises of the Plan as the centrepiece of French domestic policy and achievement. The small group within the Federation of British Industries (FBI) who engineered the revival of interest in planning believed that it would simultaneously increase business influence on public policy and actually reduce government interference in industry. They were encouraged in this belief by French planners who emphasised the 'indicative' aspects of their work so as not to frighten the British businessmen and civil servants who consulted them. Apart from the planning of public expenditure, the FBI only wanted 'a measure of coordination, based on uncoerced business calculation' in the private sector, to be undertaken by a tripartite body independent of government, the future NEDC. Yet the belief that national economic planning could be achieved by voluntary agreements between interested parties and the government was illusory, especially as the FBI itself had never hitherto had a properly planned policy, being content to react to each issue separately as it arose.[15]

The business inspiration behind British planning's advent and demise was reflected in the fact that between the FBI's Brighton conference of 1960, when it put planned economic growth first and its 1965 Eastbourne conference, when it gave priority to the balance of payments, the leading businessmen refused to face the consequences of their earlier choice. The heyday of planning in Britain lasted for five years. It was initiated under a Conservative government in the wake of a July 1961 financial crisis and it was destroyed under a Labour government by the financial crisis of July 1966. As both crises were precipitated by speculation against sterling, it could be claimed that what (inadvertently) the 'gnomes of Zurich' and the City of London had given in 1961 they took away in 1966. A pluralistic paralysis in which administrative and interest-group consensus was treated as a prerequisite of planning led one exasperated planner to exclaim that 'unless the parties to the discussion, government, management and trade unions, are prepared to sacrifice some of their sovereignty, then the present endless round of discussion without decision and activity without action is likely to continue indefinitely'.[16] It only seems paradoxical if one ignores the foregoing analysis, that after the demise of the National Plan in 1966, state intervention actually increased in Britain. This not only underlines the distinction between planning and state intervention but indicates that in Britain planning was envisaged as a painless substitute for government action and that when comprehensive planning appeared to have failed, further recourse was had to piecemeal intervention.

In Italy, planning also reemerged as an issue in 1961 but for very different reasons than obtained in Britain. It was not the lack of economic growth but its very rapidity in the fifties that had exacerbated the gap between the North and South, correction of which was to be the major objective of Italian planning. Admittedly, the Cassa per il Mezzogiorno had been set up in 1950 to plan Southern economic development on a long-term basis but it proved unable to overcome the characteristic problems of Italian coalition politics, piecemeal patronage and bureaucratic administration. Interministerial coordination was put in the hands of a Cabinet committee but ministers failed individually to give financial effect to the policies agreed collectively. In any case the average delay between the decision to spend and the release of funds is claimed to be 900 days, laborious traditional public expenditure procedures resulting in unspent funds being used for other purposes.[17] The Cassa was 'compelled to direct investments to places and projects whose sole claim to intervention lay in the degree of political support and influence with the Cassa that they succeeded in generating'.[18] From the mid-fifties the creation by the Christian Democrat-dominated coalition government of the Ministry of State Holdings, and the greater role accorded to the Institute for Industrial

Reconstruction (IRI) which was detached from Confindustria, were indicative of a desire to shift leftward, which in 1962 was to be realised in Fanfani's first Centre-Left government. This marked an historic acceptance by the Italian Socialist Party (PSI) of the desirability of seeking reform within the existing politico-economic system and involved the isolation of the Communist party. The nationalisation of electricity, the adoption of a programme of economic planning and a commitment to establish regional government were some of the concessions made by the Christian Democrats to obtain socialist support in 1962 and then entry into a coalition government in 1963.[19]

However, the right wing of the Christian Democratic party, the Liberals and in particular the peak business organization Confindustria, were bitterly opposed to national economic planning and its Centre-Left political connotations. Unlike its British counterpart, the mouthpiece of Italian industrialists was adamant that they were totally opposed to sharing economic decision-making power. They had a close clientelistic relationship with the Ministry of Industry and Commerce which, while it did not match the privileged access to government that they had enjoyed under fascist corporativism, nevertheless was a champion of their expedient new-found faith in pre-Keynesian economic liberalism, amounting to a desire to avoid state control. However, Confindustria did not speak for the giant firms like Fiat and Olivetti, who favoured 'programming', the euphemism business favoured because that term emphasised its support for *indicative* planning. Such firms did not fear state compulsion and wanted a situation in which they could rely on government policy and the trade unions not to upset their plans. They were content that Confindustria, which reflected the views of the multitude of tiny firms, should oppose planning because it gave them a better bargaining position in dealing with Centre-Left governments that were not especially well disposed towards private business.[20] As for the trade unions, they were conscious of their exclusion from economic decision-making. The non-Communist unions were especially willing to support planning if it involved their participation in a new decision-making process and the avoidance of a wage restraint policy. The subsequent failure of planning to tackle the problems placed on its agenda by Saraceno in 1963: the poor distribution of labour between North and South, the inadequacies of education, housing, public transport, the problems of urbanisation and the inefficiency of the civil service, led the unions to try to take matters into their own hands at the end of the decade.

It was common knowledge that the state machine was unable and disinclined to take on the new functions required by planning. Despite repeated calls for civil service reform,

Italian bureaucrats have demonstrated that their ability to avoid centralized and coordinated direction is extraordinary, born of almost a century during which each ministry became a feudal holding, jealous of its prerogatives and largely isolated from the rest of public administration...The most strongly held implicit value in the system is that no one will seriously challenge the freedom of each ministry to do essentially what it chooses.[21]

Bureaucratic legalism, addiction to precedent, sluggishness and out-right incompetence have encouraged Italian governments to use multipurpose public enterprises like IRI to carry out their economic planning objectives, notably the development of the South. However, there has been a tendency to employ such public agencies as trouble-shooters, dealing with *ad hoc* crises, although the planning of public sector investment has made some headway. Nevertheless, the pat-ronage power of such vast concerns has been used, like that of private firms, to provide party finance, and this enables enterprises like IRI and ENI to operate like private empire-builders rather than as agents of national policy. Italy has therefore been characterised by planning that is so disjointed and ineffectively coordinated that in a compre-hensive sense it hardly merits the name, although certain of its partial planning activities have excited lively interest elsewhere.

Planning within institutional constraints

What became clear in the sixties, as the planning experience in the three countries unfolded, was that if it was hoped that planning would bring about dramatic changes in the economy, polity and society, the preconditions of such success were drastic changes to make effectively devised and implemented plans feasible. We have seen that France, despite the problems which were to fuel the explosive events of May 1968, had the institutional and attitudinal aptitudes to facilitate the new task of planning. Helped by a rapid transition from a pre-industrial into a post-industrial society (a process which is patchy and still far from complete) such as Italy was also experiencing in the post-war period, France had the firm political and informed techno-bureaucratic leadership to steer this development rather than simply drift with it. Although many social and economic by-products of rapid development were either not anticipated or not dealt with, contribu-ting to the persistence and intermittent eruption of bitter class and regional resentments and conflicts, the chronic state of chaos afflicting Italy was avoided. While Italy seemed to lack effective government and administration, especially in the pre-industrial, underdeveloped, paro-chial South, Britain was caught up in the toils of an antiquated industrial structure, a powerful but immobilist administration and politicians preoccupied with short-term manoeuvres within a party framework. In the context of the impatient Italian consciousness of the need for reform and the incapacity to achieve it, and the frustrated British will to stem the post-imperial slide towards relative poverty and second-rate status by institutional engineering, planning in the French manner appeared to be an inviting but ever-receding mirage.

Both in Britain and in Italy, strengthening the policy-making capacity of the central, regional and local government appeared to be a prerequisite of planned public action, Britain making more progress at the central and local level, while Italy moved with greater determination at the regional level. The major Labour government innovation – the Department of Economic Affairs, which had the main responsibility for national and regional economic planning – having proved abortive, it was the Conservative government in 1970 that proposed and carried through a reorganisation of central government that represented some progress, although it stopped short of concentrating the power over economic policy at present divided between the Treasury and the Cabinet secretariat. It both tried to strengthen the centre's capacity to give strategic definition to the government's policy objectives, particularly through the creation of a small, multidisciplinary central policy review staff (CPRS) and by the establishment of two giant departments – the Department of Trade and Industry (DTI) and the Department of the Environment (DoE) – which would be better able to devise their own strategies without laborious interdepartmental bargaining and suggest clear priorities to the prime minister and chancellor of the exchequer who dominated collective decision-making. Furthermore, planning units were established in some central ministries, although they have been confined to a mainly research task rather than having the policy analysis and guidance function envisaged by the Fulton Committee on the civil service. Like the other innovations, this reform has been converted into an adjunct of the existing administrative practices rather than forming part of an overall public policy planning system.

The principal instrument for steering the public sector in Britain has been control over resource allocation. Public expenditure control is more pervasive in its range and more penetrating in its impact than any other weapon in the central government's armoury. Using the annually revised five-year public expenditure survey system developed in the early sixties under a Conservative government to systematise and rationalise the public allocation of resources, it was intended to fix objectives for each ministry within the context of a medium-term economic assessment. So, despite a claim that 'government has been attempting to do too much', the Heath government became committed to developing further a type of public sector planning which the Macmillan government had initiated under parliamentary pressure a decade earlier, following the 1961 Plowden Report on the control of public expenditure, itself based on a two-year dialogue with the permanent secretaries[22] that led to a reorganisation of the Treasury along functional lines in 1962. Given that Treasury control over public expenditure was the main instrument by which the public sector was planned if at all, the public expenditure surveys, representing decisions and not merely aspirations, were the one part of the National Plan that represented a real government commitment. As they are 'more an exercise in the allocation of resources than a way of increasing the amount of resources that exist to allocate',[23] their economic growth-promoting potential should not be exaggerated. However, to the extent that public expenditure planning has changed the traditional allocation of existing resources, it might have contributed towards such an increase in resources.

Authority over economic policy is even more dispersed in Italy, with a reliance upon interministerial committees to work out agreed policies. Although responsibility for economic planning was confided in 1962 to the budget minister in the hope that this would ensure harmony between the annual budget and the quinquennial plan, it was not until 1964 that an imperfectly unified budget replaced separate ministry budgets. The annual struggle between spending ministries, focussed on the budget, impairs attempts to secure effective, comprehensive, medium-term coordination of public expenditure. This has particularly serious effects upon the allocation of public funds to the three to five-year expenditure programmes of functional agencies. In any case, the Budget Ministry failed to secure control over the plan-related agencies and it had to compete with separate Treasury and Finance Ministries, as well as the immensely powerful Bank of Italy. The fragmentation due to the division of responsibility for macro-economic policy – with the traditional-style Treasury more powerful than the would-be innovative Budget and Planning Ministry – in addition to the rivalries of the numerous spending ministries, forms the largest rock upon which Italian planning foundered.[24] The establishment of regional government probably means a further diffusion of economic policy-making in the hope that functions which the central ministries have been unable to discharge effectively will be carried out in the regions. In sharp contrast, the French in the sixties developed a system by which the annual budget was closely related to both national and regional planning, to ensure that short-term policy would conform as far as possible to the medium-term guidelines and to retain central control over the territorial allocation of resources by regionalising public investment.

While parliaments have historically been supposed to have an

important say over budgetary policy, in practice the elected representatives in the three countries concerned have seldom been able to make
significant changes in their government's proposals. In the case of
planning, parliaments have had even less influence, although in the
sixties France did ensure that not only the functionally representative
Economic and Social Council (ESC) but parliament also would be able
to debate the plan before it went into effect.[25] Conscious of the need to
have a political legitimisation of the policy choices it embodied, the
representatives of the people were invited to give their blessing to plans
that they were not allowed to alter. In all three countries it is clear that
public sector planning is very much a matter for the executive
(although the House of Commons' expenditure committee has
attempted to increase scrutiny of medium-term policy), while private
sector planning is carried out by the government in conjunction with
organised interest groups. Although the views of bodies like the ESC in
France, NEDC in Britain and the National Economic and Labour
Council in Italy are indicative of the attitudes of the major interest
groups, such formal consultation is more a matter of window-dressing
than a serious channel of consensus-building.

   The difficulty of reconciling with planning the pluralistic view that
those in authority should not give orders but negotiate agreed solutions, emerges at its clearest in the field of incomes policy, where the
desire to retain free collective bargaining has proved a stumbling block
either to the attainment of an agreed policy at all (France and Italy) or
one capable of enduring beyond the short term (Britain). A percep-
tive British observer has pointed out that in a polity seeking to
accommodate the demands of powerful interests,

if the unions stick to an industrial strategy – of seeking piecemeal concessions
by damaging strikes – then there is little the government or society can do
unless these unions have a clear notion of what they want and if this is
economically and politically negotiable within the contours of the society. If the
unions do not know their mind they will simply drag the economy down. If they
know their mind, but the rulers are not prepared to compromise with them the
same result is likely to occur.[26]

If the national experiences studied are anything to go by, a comprehensive and coordinated type of planning worthy of the name presupposes a type of authority that is prepared to use its power when
it cannot strike a bargain, be relatively uninhibited about intervening
to back its judgement and not be too squeamish about acting in a
discriminatory fashion. Such prescriptions clearly go against the grain
in a country like Britain, whereas in France a rather authoritarian style
of government has meant that planning has been attractive because
it is expected to make a relatively despotic government more en-
lightened in the way it exercises power. An inability or a reluctance

to make such assertions of state sovereignty doubtless go a long way to explaining the failure to pursue a policy of comprehensive planning in Britain and Italy.

As we have argued earlier, the institutional constraints on innovation are extremely tenacious.[27] Consideration of particular aspects of the attempt by three nation states to plan their economies since 1960 should amply substantiate a truism that was seldom perceived by those involved at the time and should be taken to heart before the experiment is once again attempted in Britain. Planning is neither the prelude to totalitarianism nor the painless panacea for the ills of industrial capitalism. It requires changes not merely in public policies but in the way they are arrived at and carried into effect. Rather than improvising after the onset of a crisis, it would be as well to evaluate past experience and derive such insights as they have to offer, so that when the vicious circle comes around yet again, we shall be better prepared to try to break out of it. Consideration of the experience of the sixties is calculated to increase scepticism about the capacity of liberal democratic polities to engage successfully in comprehensive planning of an innovative and farsighted kind. The ensuing pages will shed some light on the political and administrative factors that partly account for the disillusionment with comprehensive planning in the early seventies.

NOTES

1 M. Kesselman, 'Overinstitutionalization and political constraint: the case of France', *Comparative Politics*, III, October 1970, pp. 24–6.

2 E. C. Banfield, 'Ends and Means in Planning', *International Social Science Journal*, XI, No. 3, 1959, p. 363, cf. pp. 365–8. See also, M. Meyerson and E. C. Banfield, *Politics, Planning and the Public Interest*, 1955.

3 D. Seers, 'The structure of power' in H. Thomas (ed), *Crisis in the Civil Service*, 1968, p. 84. See also B. Gross, 'Planning the Improbable', in B. Gross (ed), *Action under Planning*, 1967, pp. 10–11, and D. Seers, 'The prevalence of pseudo-planning' in M. Faber and D. Seers (eds), *The Crisis in Planning*, I, chapter 1.

4 A. Waterston, *Development Planning. Lessons of Experience*, 1966, pp. 293–4, 333–7, 348–9; cf. A. Waterston, 'An operational approach to development planning' in Faber and Seers, *Crisis in Planning*, pp. 88–94.

5 C. E. Lindblom, 'The science of "muddling through"', *Public Administration Review*, XIX, Spring 1959, especially pp. 80–6. See also C. L. Schultze, *The politics and economics of public spending*, 1968, chapter 3 *passim*. This reversal of the Lindblom criteria was suggested in a preliminary working paper by Bernard Cazes.

6 Y. Dror, 'Comprehensive Planning: common fallacies versus preferred features', in F. van Schlagen (ed), *Essays in Honour of Professor J. P. Thijsse*, 1967, p. 98.

7 A. Shonfield, *Modern Capitalism*, 1965, chapter 6 *passim*. See also A. A. Rogow and P. Shore, *The Labour Government and British Industry, 1945–51*, 1955, chapter 2.

8 R. Opie, 'The making of economic policy' in Thomas, *Crisis in the Civil Service*, p. 61, cf. pp. 56–7; cf. W. Plowden, *The Motor Car and Politics in Britain*, 1971, 1973 edn, pp. 435–6, 439–40.

9 P. D. Henderson, 'Government and Industry', chapter 10 in G. D. N. Worswick and P. H. Ady (eds), *The British Economy in the 1950s*, 1962, p. 374; cf. R. Opie, in Thomas, *Crisis in the Civil Service*, pp. 64, 71–4.

10 PEP, *Growth in the British Economy*, 1960, p. 223, cf. p. 222.

11 S. Kuznets, *Economic Growth of Nations. Total Output and Production Structure*, 1971, pp. 38–9.

12 E. F. Denison, *Why growth rates differ. Postwar experience in nine countries*, 1967, pp. 341–2; cf. S. Kuznets, pp. 144–6, 250–1, 290–1.

13 J-J. Carré, P. Dubois and E. Malinvaud, *La croissance française. Un essai économique causale de l'après-guerre*, 1972, p. 615, cf. p. 669; and Denison, *Why growth rates differ*, pp. 323, 340, cf. pp. 284, 315.

14 Shonfield, *Capitalism*, pp. 85, 73.

15 S. Blank, *Industry and Government in Britain. The Federation of British Industries in Politics, 1945–65*, 1973, pp. 168–9, 213, chapter 6 *passim*. On the inadequacies of British trade associations, see *Report of the Devlin Commission of Inquiry into Industrial and Commercial Representation*, Association of British Chambers of Commerce/Confederation of British Industry, November 1972.

16 R. Bailey, *Managing the British economy. A guide to economic planning in Britain since 1962*, 1968, p. 137. 'At no stage was there any machinery for ensuring that policy decisions and actions of particular Ministries were consistent with the aims of the NEDC growth programme.' (*Ibid.* pp. 37–8.)

17 P. A. Allum, *Politics and Society in Post-War Naples*, 1973, p. 26 note. But see below, p. 138.

18 J. LaPalombara, *Italy. The Politics of Planning*, 1966, p. 44, cf. pp. 36–48.

19 *Ibid.* pp. 33–5 and chapter 4 *passim*. See also M. Edelman and R. W. Fleming, *The Politics of the Wage–Price Decisions. A Four Country Analysis*, 1965, pp. 76–7.

20 Edelman and Fleming, *Politics of Wage–Price Decisions*, pp. 74–5, 293.

21 LaPalombara, *Italy*, pp. 106, 113. On Confindustria, see J. LaPalombara, *Interest Groups in Italian Politics*, 1964, especially pp. 266–71 and chapter 8 *passim*, and on IRI, S. Holland (ed), *The State as entrepreneur*, 1972, especially pp. 39–42, 81–92, 204–12, 218, 312–14.

22 Sir R. Clarke, *New Trends in Government*, 1971, p. 103, cf. pp. 3, 41–53, 57, 110. See also Plowden Report, 1961, Cmd. 1432, pp. 5–12; cf. U. K. Hicks, 'Plowden, planning and management in the public services', *Public Administration*, Winter 1961, pp. 300–10 and the special number of *Public Administration* on the Plowden Report, Spring 1963.

23 S. Brittan, 'Inquest on Planning in Britain' in PEP, *Planning*, XXXVIII, No. 499, January 1967, p. 31, cf. p. 30; and Sir R. Clarke, 'The Public Sector' in the special issue of *Public Administration*, Spring 1966, devoted to 'The machinery of economic planning', pp. 65–7. See also chapter 18 of *The National Plan*, September 1965, Cmd. 2764. For a more recent assessment, see H. Heclo and A. Wildavsky, *The Private Government of Public Money. Community and Policy inside British Politics*, 1974, especially chapter 5.

24 See G. Ruffolo's *Rapporta sulla Programmazione*, 1973 for a masterly analysis of the weaknesses in Italian planning by the man who was its planning officer since 1964 and general secretary of the Plan from 1969 to 1974. On the budgetary aspect, see especially pp. 64–75, and on the division of administrative responsibilities for economic policy see pp. 97–101.

25 See J. E. S. Hayward, *Private Interests and Public Policy. The experience of the French Economic and Social Council*, 1966, and P. Corbel, *Le Parlement Français et la Planification*, 1969.

26 S. E. Finer, 'The political power of organized labour', *Government and Opposition*, VIII, No. 4, Autumn 1973, p. 406.

27 See also K. H. F. Dyson, 'The world of the West European Planner: a view from inside', *Government and Opposition*, IX, No. 3, Summer 1974, pp. 323–60.

I

The national context

1. France

YVES ULLMO

The purpose, objectives and supports of planning

French planning underwent a pragmatic development, related to the successive problems which it had to resolve. It is not, therefore, the result of a body of doctrine. On the contrary, the formalisation of its practices, as far as this exists, occurred for the most part after the event. Two basic aims nevertheless remain permanent, to differing degrees: the development of 'rationality' and of 'transparency'.

The development of planning and the successive problems of French society from 1945

If one wished to outline the salient features of the successive plans, it might be said that they alternate between phases with an economic bias and phases with a social emphasis. The first three Plans had essentially economic objectives. The First Plan, christened the Monnet Plan after the founder of the Planning Commissariat (CGP), the creator of planning in France, covered the period 1946–53; the Second Plan, 1954–8; the Third Plan 1958–61. They can be briefly characterised as follows: the Monnet Plan was essentially a plan for the reconstruction of the French economy. It deliberately concentrated upon a certain number of bottlenecks christened basic sectors. While the pre-war period was characterised by a semi-stagnation of the French economy, the Second Plan, once reconstruction had been carried out, introduced the idea that growth could and should be sustained, thus producing a fundamental innovation in the socio-economic behaviour of the French. Like the Third Plan (which concentrated upon this objective) it sought to prepare the highly protected French economy to face international competition, which the planners anticipated well in advance. The Third Plan's partial programming of public investment prepared the way for the Fourth Plan (1962–5) and the Fifth Plan (1966–70). The Fourth Plan emphasised social objectives. In the words of M. Massé, then planning commissioner, planning sought to achieve a 'less partial idea of man'. This took the form essentially of an increase in planned public investment (housing, health, education, culture, transport, etc) which constituted what was then called 'the hard core of the Plan'. The initial steps towards deconcentration, rather than decentralisation, through the regionalisation of the Plan which made its appearance at the end of the preparation of the Fourth Plan and developed during the preparation of the Fifth Plan, was another reflection of the new approach. On the other hand, the ambitious aim of implementing an incomes policy that satisfied both the aims of regulation and redistribution was not attained. While the Fifth Plan contained an invitation to restructure industry, the Sixth Plan (1970–5) is above all one of industrialisation and the organisation of the French economy in response to international competition. However, it also expresses a wish to increase solidarity, reflected essentially by the increase in social benefits and in the quality of life to be met through public investment policy. It is doubtless risky to prophesy what form the Seventh Plan will take. Nevertheless it is likely that the demand for increased attention to the quality of life and to the reduction of inequalities will become dominant.

These successive phases involved what some people might regard as abdications of responsibility. Nevertheless they have reflected a continuous tendency towards ever more comprehensive planning. It must be emphasised that planning was dissociated from post-war *dirigisme* although the latter has far from disappeared. The instruments utilised in the implementation of the First Plan – Marshall Aid funds used for investment, licensing of imports and of industrial building – were examples of an administration exercising very strict control over the management of enterprises. Under the Second Plan, the dissociation occurred partly against the will of the Planning Commissariat, particularly because the instruments of intervention were controlled by divisions of the Ministry of Finance (budget, treasury, taxes, prices), and not by the Planning Commissariat, although the latter was then under the aegis of the Ministry of Finance. From that time on, the planners have tried to rationalise the use of these instruments. This occurred especially under the Fifth Plan, which proposed a new style of industrial policy based essentially on shaping the environment of business, the state only exceptionally intervening in specific sectors. Because the instruments of intervention are far from having completely disappeared and continue to be used in a dispersed and largely discretionary way by the Ministry of Finance, planning appears to a certain extent to be anti-*dirigiste*. Another abdication concerns incomes policy. The Sixth Plan included in this respect only very limited guidelines (guaranteed minimum wages, payment on a monthly basis). Forecasts of the evolution of the different categories of income were excluded from the Plan proper.

Throughout these vicissitudes the permanent thread is that of rationality and transparency. In this context rationality means seeking the most efficient combination of means to attain the goals at which one is aiming. Transparency means the application of these techniques in a public context, choices being made within a socio-political process. These aims have become an increasingly marked feature of French administration since the Liberation. It was increasingly realised that alongside the traditional ministries, characterised by legal regulation, has developed an economic and social administration seeking to achieve specific results by taking specific action. Planning also involves a systematic effort to move from a situation of compartmentalised administration towards a cooperative administration more suited to achieve synthesis. At the same time the fiction that the main task of French administration is the tutelage of the administered – a legacy of the authoritarian tradition – gives way to the recognition of socio-economic groups, which some would dub lobbies. Finally, the planning process is a powerful instrument forcing a secretive administration to put its cards on the table.

The planners' intention is similar in the purely political sphere. They aim above all to make economic and social matters subject to political decision, which in the nineteenth century was essentially limited to international relations and internal public order. The first half of the twentieth century was characterised by a shift of interest towards economic and social action. Government was the main beneficiary through a gradual weakening of parliament, without the government itself, for lack of a framework for ensuring consistent action, being able to appreciate all the practical implications of the day to day economic and social decisions which it took. Planning aimed (we shall see presently whether it succeeded) to provide the government with this framework; it also aims to establish a real consistency of governmental action in the economic and social sphere.

As one moves up the successive layers which constitute the history of French planning, the range becomes increasingly comprehensive. The starting point, we have seen, was private investment in selected areas. This was quickly extended into a 'physical' body of planning characterised on the technical plane by the projection of the industrial input–output table. From the Third Plan on, the physical study of growth was extended into the study of the distribution and redistribution of incomes (overall economic table) and from the Fourth Plan on, by the study of investment finance (financial operations table). Parallel with this, the planning of public investment, introduced for some sectors at the time of the Third Plan, was rapidly extended to cover them all. The Sixth Plan introduced the notion of collective functions, i.e. it considered operating costs and transfer costs as well as investment costs, with the implication that the analysis should cover the whole budget. Similarly, as far as redistribution is concerned, after the Fifth Plan had included social benefits, the planners began to examine the distribution aspects of the various collective functions, while a new 'target-groups' approach aimed at identifying and embracing all aspects of economic and social policy concerning certain particular social groups (old people, children, immigrants, etc). Lastly, the regionalisation of the Plan rapidly became an attempt to link regional and town plans with national planning, these plans being themselves linked with the general guidelines of the policy of balanced territorial development.

This tendency to comprehensiveness doubtless derived from a certain internal logic of planning. However, it also arises from the variety of problems with which successive Plans have had to deal, without these problems, once tackled, ever managing to appear sufficiently 'settled' to need any longer to be the concern of planning. The new requirements which have come to light during the last few years (quality of life, protection of the environment) also tend to enlarge the area of concern of planning. There have been calls for social planning, or better still societal planning, covering the whole of future development.

The attitude of socio-economic and ideological groups towards planning

The principle of the Plan does not itself appear to be the object of ideological debate. Discussion has focussed upon the matters to be covered by planning and increasingly about the effective content of successive Plans.

The attitude of the employers must be analysed in its historic development. At first support for planning was not very great. Public enterprises were a source of support, as was a limited part of the private enterprise sector, the steel industry, because it was the most concentrated and was, moreover, used to functioning in a not very competitive context. From the Third and Fourth Plans, trade associations generally became faithful supporters of planning, which provides them with information and perhaps above all a periodic opportunity to expound their demands. It must be stressed that we are referring to trade associations and not the mass of firms, mainly small and medium-sized, which these organisations are supposed to represent yet which know very little about the Plan. Although for a long time it reserved its position, the CNPF itself, which represents the whole of private enterprise, posed from the Sixth Plan as a partisan of planning but its position remains ambiguous. It continues to be very anti-interventionist. Its stand in favour of the Plan was linked largely to the tactical wish to see the Sixth Plan give priority to industrialisation and in this way to promote a new brand image of the CNPF. It expects above all from planning a more marked commitment by the government and greater rationality in public action. The CNPF has not itself been able to decide between the demand for an undifferentiated support of production, called for by the more developed enterprises of French industry, and the continuation of selective aid to sectors in difficulty, which a large proportion of small and medium-sized enterprises continue to demand. The special case of agricultural organisations must be mentioned. In the general context of very extensive intervention by the government (outside the context of planning) they have always shown themselves favourable towards planning.

The changing attitudes of the unions vary both as between the different confederations and between periods. Broadly speaking, they all shifted from a favourable attitude in principle to reticence or opposition. This is especially true of the CGT, which after participating in the planning commisions at the start of the First Plan was only readmitted for the Third Plan. The CGT has always rejected any sort of commitment arising out of participation in the planning process and has expressed its opposition to the decisions finally reached, but in the preparation of the Plan it is actively present as the spokesman for working-class demands. Force Ouvrière behaves in the same way for fundamentally different and rather ambiguous reasons. It declares itself in favour of planning in principle but against *étatisme* and particularly against any form of incomes policy. It supports the consensus-building work of the commissions but refuses to be bound by the resulting recommendations.

The evolution of the CFDT (formerly CFTC) confederation was characterised by a switch from a very extensive involvement in the planning process to outright boycott during the preparation of the Sixth Plan. At the time of the Fourth Plan's preparation, the CFDT was one of the principal supporters of planning, which it saw as a powerful instrument for the transformation of society. This was expressed in the theory of democratic planning, which also reflected a certain desire on the part of the representatives of economic and social movements to acquire political status. Similarly, during the preparation of the Fifth Plan, the CFDT was the only union which dared to declare itself in favour of an incomes policy, with the reservation that this policy should not only be a wages policy but encompass all incomes. Disappointed by the content of the Fifth Plan, the CFDT adopted a stance of radical confrontation, strongly influenced by post-1968 leftism. In contrast the CFTC, the remnant of Catholic unionism that survived after the 1964 split, maintains a favourable attitude towards a contractual wage policy and through this towards a continuing dialogue within the framework of the Plan.

Within the administration, supporters of planning have always constituted a restricted but active, not to say an activist, nucleus. Several different currents combine. First of all the economists, drawn by their profession to the practical application of rational methods to the preparation of decisions. However, within this group a distinction must be made between the micro-economists (mainly elite engineers of the Mines or Ponts et Chaussées corps) who represent a tradition of economic calculation in the administration and in public enterprises, and the macro-economists, who under the leadership of Claude Gruson instituted national economic accounting and have used it for short and medium-term regulatory policy. These macro-economists are to be found mainly at INSEE and the forecasting division of the Finance Ministry. Other faithful supporters of planning are the *ad hoc* 'missionary' bodies that deal with new tasks of an essentially temporary nature, or the horizontal agencies such as the DGRST that administers scientific and technical research. Whether it is because they have to carry their policies against the resistance of the established ministries and need support, or whether it is because they are trying to achieve partial consistency and so are naturally more sensitive to the requirements of planning, they willingly fit their programmes and their practices into the framework of the Plan. Recently, planning has found new support in the social welfare ministries which see in it an advantageous means of supporting their claims in a generally unfavourable administrative and governmental context. Likewise, the fate of the regional administration is closely linked with that of planning, the main functions of the regional bodies being concerned with the preparation of the Plan.

If one finally leaves the administration proper to consider the local authorities, despite a certain hesitant progress associated with a tendency to deconcentrate rather than genuinely decentralise town planning, local councillors are rather uninterested in planning, although the idea of 'inclusion in the Plan', i.e. the promise of financial help from the state for a public investment project during the course of the Plan, is the most practical method of implementing the Plan and so has a very favourable connotation.

Originally, planning was intended to be apolitical. Others might claim that it was a combination of contradictory ideas united by the need to reconstruct the French economy. In any case, the political implications of the planning process were very far from being perceived. For example, the first three Plans were not submitted for the formal approval of parliament.

Planning acquired a political status during the Fourth Plan, subject to two distinct but in fact connected ambiguities. On the one hand, under the influence of Planning Commissioner Massé and with the support of the President of the Republic General de Gaulle, there was the idea that the Plan should become a forum of national consensus and consequently an enthusiastic 'commitment'. This derived from the belief that the use of science for the preparation of decisions should make it possible to reach irrefutable choices because they were rationally based, thus excluding any strictly political choice. On the other hand, the doctrine of democratic planning, advocated by the CFDT and M. Mendès-France, was in fact based on a similar view, although politically slanted to the Left. No one imagined that from this socio-political process aimed at the conscious transformation of society, major conflicts could arise. On the contrary, it seemed obvious that once the facts were known, the march towards reform and a better life would be made with general accord.

From the Fifth Plan and especially from the Sixth Plan, the idea of consensus grew weaker and then disappeared completely. It has been replaced by a realisation that the Plan represents the government's medium-term economic and social policy and is thus a case of the majority imposing its wishes on a minority, even if in a politically liberal society this involves taking considerable notice of the minority's aspirations and claims. Ideological debates become concerned with the content of the Plan, especially on the Sixth Plan's industrialisation priority.

An analysis of the intellectual groups which support planning is complicated, for there is an overlap between groups of a mainly intellectual and those of a civic-cum-political nature. The first type consists essentially of economists, advocates of rationality, whether they are more concerned with applying efficiency norms (the micro-economists) or whether they are more concerned with the explanation of economic or even social behaviour (the macro-economists). Among the civic-cum-political groups, the supporters of European unity should be mentioned first of all. It was in fact from the Planning Commissariat that the idea of the Coal and Steel Community was launched and the consequences of France's entry into the European Economic Community made the French planners early champions of planning on a European scale and consequently of rapid integration. The supporters of Mendès-France in the 1950s and the Club Jean Moulin, which at the beginning of the sixties undertook extensive studies of planning, were part of this stream of ideas. At that time, the same was true of the CFTC and even to a certain degree of the PSU, which today occupies a position much further to the left. Still in the same ideological area, the links between planning and certain groups of left-wing Catholics should also be mentioned, although in actual fact these have always remained rather unstructured. Finally, the regionalists might also be included as supporters of planning because the impetus towards a certain amount of regional autonomy has very largely come about through the procedure of the Plan's preparation.

The institutions of planning

In analysing the French planning experience, three functions can be identified: information, dialogue and the definition of the government's programme.

(i) The information function is exemplified by former Commissioner Massé's work. He presented the Plan as national market research, providing the various economic and social agencies with comprehensive, detailed and consistent information about the perspectives for the growth of public and private demand, and of production. Moreover, it should be noted that this function was gradually extended from purely economic information to all social problems. This function can be broken down into the following phases: first of all, the diagnosis of the existing situation and its probable developments; then making explicit the problems brought to light; finally forecasting the most likely evolution of events, taking into account intended action. A fourth phase should consist of evaluating the results of the actions undertaken, but it has to be admitted that up to now this has hardly been carried out. This advance-information function applies to the medium-term and increasingly to the long-term, in contrast to short-term forecasting.

(ii) The dialogue function comprises two constituent elements. On the one hand, the planning process seeks to reveal the medium-term projects or preferences of the various interest groups, and so it has considerable importance in all those areas where the expression of preferences is not secured through the market mechanism. On the other hand, it enables the intentions of the administration and of the government to be tried out and 'sold' to the interest groups.

(iii) Finally, the definition of a governmental programme is associated with the organisation of a public socio-political process leading to 'decisions' (or rather to medium-term guidelines in the sense that a Plan never contains decisions in the strict sense but rather pre-decisions, almost all of which need to be confirmed in the actual conduct of economic and social policy).

The closely related character of these functions in the French experience should be emphasised, although other approaches are conceivable and indeed present. To proceed to its logical conclusion, i.e. making forecasts, the information function requires that solutions be found to the problems brought to light, at least as far as government action is concerned. Clearly, an outside observer with responsibility for predicting the future could work out what these solutions might be, allowing for the government's reactions, but this is to go outside the sphere of planning. Besides, it can easily be conceived that the definition of a medium-term government programme need not involve a public process; but in that case, in the absence of the dialogue function, it would be likely that the programme would only reflect the values of the bureaucratic elite and prove impracticable when faced with socio-economic reality. Moreover, because every government has a natural tendency to act only in response to the pressures of the moment and thus sacrifice any long or medium-term scheme to immediate requirements, there is a strong likelihood that if the planning process were not public it would not in fact exist. The fundamental difficulty which all consultants have in effectively impinging on policy decisions supports this view. Finally, the dialogue function can scarcely thrive if it is not intimately linked with governmental decisions. There is a kind of reciprocity with those consulted, who only supply information about their own schemes or preferences to the extent that they receive in exchange certain commitments from the government.

The governmental and administrative organisation of planning

The apparatus as a whole will be examined first, then how it works in practice. The present position, which is not necessarily the definitive one, is the outcome of a variety of considerations or approaches which indicate uncertainty as to the best place to locate the planning organisation. Thus at the Liberation a proposal was made to create a Ministry of the Economy with executive responsibilities separate from the Ministry of Finance. The planning organisation would naturally have been located within it, as evidenced by the existence for a number of years of a programming division within the economic half of the Ministry of Finance. The ideas canvassed by Bloch-Laîné at the end of the 1950s were similar. He suggested the transfer of the Ministry of Finance's budget division and that part of its treasury division responsible for the general financial balance, along with the CGP and INSEE, to the prime minister. Conversely, the initial location (until 1962) of the CGP within the Ministry of Finance reflected the view that rather than separate the economy from finance, it would be better to make finance more sensitive to economic considerations.

The present practice may be simply presented as follows: the CGP is a small-scale organisation, currently having a staff of some 60 senior officials. Its personnel is so small that it does not in fact have the capacity to conduct its own research (although it has funds for research), and it has to rely on other parts of the administration for the studies and projections required for the preparation of the Plan. Its essential role is to advise the government and – this is fundamental – to be involved, as of right, in every aspect of the preparation of the Plan, whose work it organises. Allowing for the exception of the First Plan, it has no powers of its own for the Plan's implementation and is not even compulsorily consulted, except in the preparation of the government's investment budget and for certain decisions involving incentives to private investment (FDES, Crédit National). It carries out its responsibilities primarily through its participation, in a purely consultative capacity, in the administrative process through which government decisions are made. It does this through bilateral relations with the ministries and membership of interministerial committees. Every year the CGP prepares a report on the implementation of the Plan, but it takes the form of a government report to parliament appended to the Finance Bill, so it is neither an internal Commissariat report in which the CGP could call for measures to ensure a better implementation of the Plan, nor a public report published by the CGP on its own responsibility which it could use to exert some pressure on the government. The CGP comes directly under the prime minister. The existence from 1967 to 1972 of a minister of planning did not really change this system of direct relations with the prime minister's personal office. Finally, with ups and downs, the CGP enjoys a fairly large measure of the independence necessary to enable it to carry on its task of promoting consensus-building, yet without being excluded from the governmental and administrative apparatus.

What judgement can be made on this way of working? First of all the ambiguity of the CGP's situation needs to be underlined, at one and the same time part of the administration and outside it, at one and the same time adviser to the government and promoter of consensus-building. It has often been proposed that this ambiguity should be removed by giving up the CGP's responsibility for consensus-building, making it a specialist adviser to the prime minister in the same way that the forecasting division advises the Ministry of Finance. Conversely, a separation of the CGP from the governmental and administrative structure might be sought to make it a kind of monitoring or watchdog institution, totally free in its studies, judgements and forecasts. The first formula would very probably have led to the abandonment of the open character of planning; the second formula would undoubtedly have led to the re-emergence of a new organ of planning within the governmental and administrative apparatus. Consequently, in the absence of a radical revision of the planning system, it seems likely that the ambiguity will remain.

The lack of its own resources means that the CGP has difficulty in giving practical form to its ideas, still more in getting them accepted and, even if the basic guidelines have been adopted, in ensuring their effective implementation by the Ministry of Finance and the other ministries. In the final analysis, it could be said that the CGP is completely powerless as far as the implementation of the Plan is concerned, and that formal procedures could be conceived for re-inforcing its position, such as the extension of those areas in which its advice is compulsory or even granting it a right of veto over certain decisions. But it has to be admitted that this implies giving power of a political nature to an administrative body, which would probably not be acceptable. It should be noted, on the other hand, that the CGP has been frequently requested by the prime minister to make suggestions on how to deal with particularly tricky matters or those involving several ministries. French industrial policy provides examples of this. Equally one may mention the special tasks given to the CGP to try to work out an incomes policy as well as a new employment policy.

On the other hand, the CGP's lack of executive powers gives it a permanent incentive to avoid isolation, notoriously a major threat to planning bodies. The CGP's capacity for independent action is limited, even as far as making proposals is concerned, although it can exert pressure in certain matters that it judges particularly important. However, the fact that it always has to contact the ministries forces it to remain permanently in touch with the on-going business of government, to formulate only those proposals which are likely to be acceptable to other parts of the administration, and not to introduce additional difficulties by superimposing its own responsibilities on those of the traditional ministries. On the whole, this system results in a relatively high probability that the Plan's guidelines will be implemented by the administration.

Finally, the separation of the CGP from the Ministry of Finance, while it leads to permanent conflict and cuts the CGP off from the chief resources for the implementation of the Plan (which are all too often used in the service of a non-planning logic), nevertheless constitutes an element of internal opposition, within the government apparatus, to the hypercentralisation of the Ministry of Finance. It may be thought that anything that introduces an element of pluralism into the governmental apparatus is eminently desirable.

The internal organisation of the CGP seeks both to ensure the possibility of integrative action and contact either with other parts of the administration or with the interest groups. The economic service, responsible for the overall organisation and for the synthesis of the planning work as a whole, has the most general task and is the most cut off, its relations with the socio-political environment occurring for the most part through the other CGP services. The same holds good, largely, of the financial service, responsible for public expenditure and revenue as well as the money market aspects of the overall synthesis.

But it has greater contact with the outside world to the extent that it is the interface with, on the one hand, the financial institutions – a particularly important role during the preparation of the Plan – and on the other, with the business firms, especially in so far as they make use of the government incentives which are granted on the advice of the CGP. Both the financial and economic services deal, within the administration, mainly with the Ministry of Finance.

The industrial service is responsible for the overall conception of industrial policy. It should be noted that, as with all the services of the Plan which are responsible for a particular sector, there is an inevitable competition between the partial synthesis undertaken by the CGP and that made by the relevant ministries. Besides, the industrial service is characterised by its contact with the industrial world, which, for reasons of ease of communication, is generally conducted with the trade associations and the big corporations rather than with other types of firm.

The social affairs service is responsible for manpower policy, for social investment and public services (education, health, housing) and for social transfer payments. Except for redistribution of income and employment, it does not really perform a synthesis function. It rather identifies social needs or at any rate demands, and acts as their spokesman *vis-à-vis* those responsible for the overall syntheses, especially the financial one. It is characterised by two types of outside relationship: one with the trade unions, the other with the representatives – in so far as they exist – of specific social groups: families, the handicapped, the elderly, immigrants, for whom representative organisations are virtually non-existent. The relationship with the unions occurs less at the highest national level than with the representatives of the relevant unions on particular planning commissions, who appear, rather inaccurately perhaps, as spokesmen of the users of public services. The ability of specific social groups to articulate their needs is directly linked with their capacity for organisation. The task of the social affairs service is in this respect particularly difficult when it posits new problems and needs without being able to find sources of support capable of giving them effective expression.

The regional and urban service (SRU) is responsible for the regionalisation of the Plan and for land-use planning. To the extent that the regionalisation of the Plan, notwithstanding a considerable measure of deconcentration, still consists essentially of the allocation of public investments between the regions, without any significant impact of the work of regional planning upon national planning, the SRU is more concerned with allocation than with synthesis. The SRU has a fundamental role of contact with the outside world, but the way regional institutions work at present means that it is more responsive to the small but active groups of regional civil servants than to the regional interest groups.

With regard, finally, to the various vertical services – energy, transport, agriculture – there is a double function as in the case of the industrial service: interaction with the relevant interest groups and working out a medium-term policy for the sectors, both activities being carried on in competition with the ministries. As far as sectoral medium-term policy is concerned, the CGP intervenes mainly in the absence of action by the ministries. As soon as a ministry effectively defines a medium-term policy, it is very difficult and perhaps pointless for the CGP to try to change this policy, except in so far as it relates to the policies of other ministries. Interaction with interest groups occurs, in almost all cases, mainly through the sponsor ministries, and the CGP service acts as an intermediary, or even mediator, between the ministries, the relevant modernisation commission (which is often dominated by the sponsor ministry) and the other services of the CGP. But it sometimes happens that the modernisation commission, especially as a result of the independent action of the interest group representatives, refuses to endorse the medium-term policy of the ministry, which restores some freedom of action to the CGP officials.

In addition to the internal organisation of the CGP, a number of points should be made about its relationships with the rest of the administration, especially those parts which explicitly or implicitly have a planning function. In fact, it is rather difficult to separate clearly the CGP from the other parts of the administration. In the first place, we must consider a broader category: the macro-economic evaluation specialists. Those who make projections at INSEE and the forecasting division, both located within the Ministry of Finance, contribute directly to the preparation of the Plan's economic syntheses, while the CGP itself only possesses a very small group of specialists. Moreover, the same groups of specialists at INSEE and the forecasting division play an equivalent role in the preparation of economic syntheses required for the conduct of short-term policy. On the one hand, then, it can be estimated that there is no discontinuity between the CGP, INSEE and the forecasting division, even though the roles performed are different. On the other hand, the CGP can be regarded as the outlet for the medium-term work of the macro-economic specialists, in the same way as the budget and treasury divisions or the ministerial *cabinet* of the finance minister are the outlets for the short-term work of these same specialists.

A less intimate but nevertheless important relationship exists with the sectoral planning specialists in the various ministries: statistical and research services, PPBS units, etc. In these cases it is no longer possible to talk of interpenetration but of a certain community of concerns due to the similarity of roles, which clearly does not exclude the use of different administrative tactics. In a few cases, senior officials (*chargés de mission*) of the CGP act as representatives of the ministries in the planning process. In the final analysis, the vertical services of the CGP cannot carry out their task satisfactorily unless they establish a close relationship with the relevant ministries.

Finally it is necessary to note the special character of the relations of the CGP with the other horizontal parts of the administration, those that consequently have a certain planning function. Relations with DATAR (Delegation for Regional Development and Planning) are characterised by a mixture of cooperation and competition, a relationship facilitated when the two bodies were united under the control of the minister responsible for planning and spatial development. The allocation of responsibilities decided in 1963, when DATAR was set up, under which the CGP was responsible for preparing spatial planning policy and DATAR for its application, was not really operational, as evidenced by the fact that DATAR gradually provided itself with its own means of research, whilst the CGP's Regional and Urban Service attempts to intervene in the regionalisation of the budget in order to ensure the correct implementation of the regional programmes drawn up as part of the Plan. The other bodies with a horizontal function, such as the General Delegation for Scientific and Technical Research (DGRST) or the Ministry of the Environment, have excellent relations with the CGP. They perform their own interministerial function by planning, and quite naturally they wish to link this with the general process of plan preparation. Lastly, the special character of the relations between the CGP and the budget division should be stressed, as in French government practice the latter fulfils in short-term decision-making the function of securing general consistency that planning seeks to exercise over the medium-term. The internal logic of the budgetary function has led the budget division to extend its traditional action by developing what has been called the 'rationalisation of budgetary choice' (called PPBS in the Anglo-Saxon countries) and in particular by the preparation of programme budgets. The articulation between these two types of planning will be one of the principal problems of the Seventh Plan's preparation.

It should be realised that the planners do not constitute a really homogeneous group. In the first place, a distinction is generally made between the specialists, i.e. the economists responsible for making projections and located for the most part at INSEE or the forecasting division, and the 'politicians', closer to decision-making, located in the CGP. This distinction accurately reflects a differentiation of roles, but it should be stressed that the true line of demarcation between the administrative system and the governmental system is found at the ministerial *cabinet* level which alone really forms part of the governmental system.

Another distinction separates the macro-economists, essentially responsible for synthesising tasks, from the micro-economists, responsible for tasks of analysis, located within the ministries with vertical responsibilities. Moreover, the regional planners constitute a separate group, much more concerned with institutional questions (promoting decentralisation) than with the traditional functions of planning. Even within the CGP, discussion between the SRU and the rest of the CGP sometimes involves insurmountable difficulties.

Finally, is a new cleavage not being created amongst the planners between economists and other social scientists? The relatively uncertain character of such social sciences often leads specialists in these fields into conflict with the economists. Moreover, perhaps under the influence of the May 1968 events, a certain view has developed according to which economics is associated with the Right and sociology with the Left, although this proposition is certainly open to attack by the Marxists.

The organisation of consensus-building

Only the organisation of consensus-building for national and not regional planning will be dealt with here. We shall consider in turn the modernisation commissions and the Economic and Social Council.

While French administration makes use of a large number of consultative committees, the modernisation commissions of the Plan are *sui generis*, having their own special rules of the game. The first rule is that the commissions are consultative. Participants are not bound by decisions reached. The second rule is that the commissions seek to be representative, but nevertheless do not seek to reflect the whole economic and social world. The criteria of such an attempt at accurate representation would, moreover, be highly questionable. Linked to this fact is the principle that voting ought to be avoided and that the work of the commissions should aim at unanimity, even if this involves minority opinions also being given a place in their reports. In practice, the expression of such minority opinions have become frequent.

A third principle is that the commissions should link the socio-economic groups closely with the administration. In contrast to other consultative bodies, they are not conceived as being outside the administrative system, with government officials making their intentions known to what are usually called the 'social partners'. On the contrary, they aim to make the representatives of these partners work with the administration, though this may be at the cost of a certain ambiguity. Finally, they are free in making their reports. The problem of bringing these reports into line with the government's Plan has been resolved in various ways in the past; in practice, the commissions are asked to spell out the solutions finally decided upon by the government, without in any way giving up the right to state their own positions.

Commission members are appointed by the prime minister after nomination by the planning commissioner. Every commission includes representatives of all the trade unions and farm organisations selected by their parent organisations, as well as representatives of the employers, either from the CNPF alone for commissions which do not deal with productive activities, or from both the CNPF and the relevant trade associations in the case of production commissions. Every commission also includes representatives of the ministries. A ministry division director in charge of matters dealt with by a commission becomes its vice-chairman *ex officio*. The other ministries concerned are either members by right or associate members, i.e. they are only called upon when subjects involving them are dealt with. During the preparation of the Sixth Plan, an effort was made to personalise the representation of the ministries by designating the civil servants by name, but this was very largely a failure. Finally, the commissions include various experts or well-known figures who attend in their own right, usually industrialists in the production commissions and scientists, academics or private experts elsewhere. The commissions do not include members of parliament, except when they are nominated in another capacity, e.g. as mayor.

The commissions are run by their chairmen, vice-chairmen, rapporteurs general and rapporteurs. The chairmen can come either from the public sector or the private sector. In the case of civil servants, they are not directly responsible for the areas dealt with by the commission, being generally members of one of the *grands corps*. Similarly, when someone from the private sector is selected, trade associations' spokesmen are not selected. Those chosen may, however, play an important part in these organisations.

Each rapporteur general is assisted by several rapporteurs, who are generally one of three types of civil servant, an official from the relevant ministry, a CGP *chargé de mission*, or independent civil servants, generally from the *grands corps*. Everything depends in practice on the power relationships between the administration and the CGP, as well as the degree of effective involvement of the administration in the process of Plan preparation.

Alongside the nominated members of the commissions, there is a wholly informal category of members of the working parties which commissions can set up at will. In fact, these working parties include members of the relevant commission, but anyone whose presence the chairman or rapporteurs think likely to prove useful can be called upon to participate.

The organisation of the modernisation commissions became more extensive and complex as planning concerned itself with more and more matters. There are three types of commission. The horizontal commissions are responsible for the work of synthesis. The General Economic and Financial Commission prepares the overall synthesis. The other main horizontal commissions are the Manpower Commission, the Social Services Commission, the Research Commission and the National Commission for Regional Development. The first of the two types of vertical commission includes those which involve productive activities. During the preparation of the Sixth Plan, they were: energy, industry, agriculture, agricultural and food industries, trade, tourism, transport, post office and telephone, artisans. The other vertical commissions are responsible for public services. When the Sixth Plan was being prepared, they included: housing, education, health, cultural affairs, social welfare, sport and socio-educational activities, as well as two land-use commissions, one for the towns and the other for rural areas.

The Sixth Plan created a new body, the committee. Some committees attached to the horizontal commissions themselves had a horizontal character, e.g. finance, foreign exchange, competition. The task of the others was to analyse the problems of particular sectors, e.g. the Industry Commission had about twenty industry committees attached to it. To add to the complexity of this machinery, some common groups were established. When an especially difficult problem was involved an intergroup was set up. At the time of the Sixth Plan, for example, there were intergroups for the handicapped, the aged, industrial training and so forth.

Since the Fourth Plan, the Economic and Social Council considers the guidelines report on the major policy objectives of the Plan, then the report on the Plan, before parliament discusses them. In practice, this examination is carried out by the Council's investment and planning section, which consults the other sections. Then the opinion of the Economic and Social Council is discussed in plenary assembly. In fact, the Council remains outside the planning process, since, unlike the commissions, it does not actually share in the preparation of the Plan and is only consulted after the government has made its choices.

The planning process

A few preliminary points need to be made. From the time of the Fourth Plan, the Plan's preparation has consisted of two phases: the guidelines or determination of the major objectives, then the preparation of the Plan itself, i.e. working out programmes sector by sector in the light of the major objectives. In fact, these two public phases are preceded by a preparatory phase confined within the administration. Altogether the preparation of the Plan lasts for about three years. This gives some indication of the scope of a process that is at one and the same time socio-economic and political.

Consensus-building with interest groups

The following remarks apply essentially to the preparation of the Plan. While the modernisation commisions meet each year to check on the implementation of the Plan, their consultation is, on this occasion, more formal. It is confined mainly to checking the divergences between forecasts and programmes on the one hand, actual achievements on the other. The Sixth Plan provided for its automatic re-examination at the halfway mark. This might allow the commissions to play a more effective part in the adaptation, even the revision, of the Plan during the course of its application. The strategy of the interest groups, that of the planners and the results obtained, will be examined in turn.

In the consensus-building process, interest groups appear to pursue essentially two aims: the collection of information, this being especially true of the trade unions, and the articulation of demands, which can sometimes go as far as proposing well worked out reforms. The interest groups have generally always shown great reluctance to enter into firm commitments arising out of the planning process. The employers, in particular, have been unwilling to accept that the commissions should be concerned with what might be called their private affairs, namely their own strategies and management activities. Linked to this, they rarely show any desire to influence the major economic and social decisions or, more precisely, they react to the choices proposed by the planners while refraining from formulating fully articulated counter-proposals, i.e. comprehensive alternative development schemes. There have been exceptions to this, those of the then CFTC in the Fourth Plan associated with the doctrine of democratic planning and that of the CNPF in the Sixth Plan during the debates on the industrialisation objective.

The planners expect a lot from the consensus-building process. In the early days of planning, because of the lack of statistics, they particularly sought information. This function has gradually declined in importance. In the early 1970s their concern has been with four themes: the sounding out and ordering of social preferences, especially as far as the commissions dealing with public services are concerned; preliminary testing of reform proposals; the 'apprenticeship' for change, the commissions in some ways simulating forseeable lines of development; finally, in the case of the horizontal commissions, debating the major economic and social choices, which, as we have seen, the interest groups have nearly always evaded.

For a long time one of the planners' objectives was to establish a consensus. Some even hoped that the work of the commissions could give rise to a sort of contract or rather quasi-contract, but the gradual recognition of the political character of the choices involved in planning has meant that this objective is hardly pursued any more. The results are satisfactory as far as information is concerned, even if this role of the commissions is tending to diminish. The first phase of the work on the Plan nevertheless constitutes an irreplaceable occasion to establish an inventory of the available knowledge in the areas covered, and in this way provides a powerful encouragement to the development of the statistical apparatus and economic and social information. Equally, the work of the commissions can be considered to yield satisfactory results on the sounding out of preferences, although their claim to representativeness is somewhat dubious. Especially in the case of the commissions dealing with public services, the ultimate users are not in general represented in a satisfactory manner, being unorganised, while the same is true of the consumers in the commissions concerned with production. To some extent, the trade unions perform this role, but it is far from being clear, for example, that the teachers' unions can be considered as satisfactorily representing the consumers of education. This fact has largely inspired the development of regional consultation. Besides, using the commissions for the articulation of social demands and needs leads to a very strong and inevitable tension between the guidelines phase, concerned with what is desirable and the Plan proper, concerned with the practicable. Finally, some consider that this system of consultation is necessarily demagogic, tending to build up demands; but conversely it can be argued that, even if the process is imperfect, the recipients of public spending have few other such opportunities to be heard. Likewise, the consensus-building process works fairly well in the testing of reform proposals and to a lesser extent in the apprenticeship for change,[1] but this is achieved at the cost of a certain prudence in 'reformism' and in tackling problems considered too controversial. It is true that the preparation of the Plan provides the opportunity to assemble and to arrange in order of priority all the schemes of reform, but only the acceptable ones are put forward, even if in some cases their authors overestimate their acceptability. Certain planners rather like to succumb to the myth of the innovator, the independent individual who promotes a change-making idea and is capable of getting it accepted through the process of Plan preparation. In fact, this happens only rarely. Furthermore, every time the planners have tried too strenuously to interefere in the strategy or activities of the socio-economic actors, these attempts have failed. This is especially true in the case of private enterprise, although not perhaps at the very beginning of planning. Thus, the attempts in the modernisation commissions to work out sectoral programmes for certain branches of industry have nearly always remained at a rather high level of generality, without succeeding in tackling in any detail the problems of industrial structure, nor *a fortiori* formulating recommendations concerning particular firms. This is certainly an inherent limitation of the public and tripartite type of consensus-building.

Lastly, the planners experienced a relative set-back when they tried to get a discussion of the major social and economic choices, even when, during the preparation of the Sixth Plan, the administration put all its cards on the table, at the cost of revealing its internal dissensions for all to see.

Planning and the administration

All the ministries and non-competitive public enterprises are involved in the process of planning, with two exceptions: the Ministry of Defence, which participates in the modernisation commissions but whose medium-term programmes are decided separately and are therefore virtually regarded as settled in advance, and the Ministry of Ex-Servicemen whose expenditure is considered unavoidable. There are some marginal cases: Civil Defence has asked, so far without success, to be included in planning. The same is true of the Ministry of Justice, though this public function will probably be covered in the preparation of the Seventh Plan. Conversely, the planners have always undertaken technical studies of development without these ever impinging on political decisions.

Two other preliminary remarks should be made. The ministries in general have a different approach during the preparation of the Plan as compared with its implementation. In addition, a distinction should be drawn between the administrators and the political decision-makers (the ministers and their personal staffs). Notwithstanding repeated efforts, the process of Plan preparation is on the whole beyond the control of the political decision-makers. The ministries decide their line in the modernisation commissions in substantially independent fashion. It might be maintained, moreover, that this autonomy is a precondition of the very working of the planning process.

The vertical ministries do not have the same attitude as the horizontal ministries. We have already touched on the competitive–cooperative relationships existing between the vertical ministries and their counterparts within the CGP, especially in the work of the modernisation commissions. The vertical ministries use the preparation of the Plan as an additional source of information, especially for macro-economic problems or those which cut across the responsibilities of several ministries. The Plan is used essentially as a mouthpiece for their own demands and the demands of the socio-economic sector with which they are most closely in contact. The intensity of the participation of the vertical ministries thus clearly depends on their own capacity for compiling information and on the support they expect to derive from the Plan in the day-to-day administrative and governmental process. On the other hand, during the implementation of the Plan, the most widespread tendency is for the vertical ministries to withdraw into themselves and relax their relations with the CGP. This may be either because, as effective executants of the Plan, they consider that this work is their own business, for which they only have to render account afterwards, or even because they believe they should resume complete freedom of tactical and even strategic manoeuvre. But often, particularly during the budgetary discussions, they once again use the Plan to justify their position.

For their part, the ministries with a horizontal function, primarily the Ministry of Finance,[2] use the Plan, to some extent, to pose medium-term problems of synthesis capable of improving their own activities, while declining, from the outset, any commitment to it. It is doubtless here that the conflicts between the constraints of day-to-day management and the requirements of medium-term objectives appear most marked, even if the former are partially influenced by the latter.

Planning and the political decision-making process

The attitude of the government towards planning seems to be the same whatever the party majority in power. First and foremost, planning, and particularly the preparation of the Plan, acts as a barometer of interest-group pressure, with the government being tempted to break the barometer. There is an intimate relationship between planning and socio-economic information: the logic of the planning approach entails that it is better, where possible, to make latent conflicts (including those which oppose the Ministry of Finance to everyone else) explicit in advance rather than indulge in a deliberately calculated delay which leads to secret decision-making. We might ask whether this logic does not presuppose a combination of conditions and whether these conditions in fact exist in the contemporary socio-political context in France, which is characterised by deep social and ideological divisions that challenge the most basic principles of the social system.

As a corollary, it should be emphasised that a necessary trade-off for the provision of information on the socio-economic environment through the planning process is a certain measure of commitment by government to the outcome of this process, and this may raise problems. In the first place, it is clear that the satisfaction of demands, the influence on decisions and ultimately on objectives that the participants in consensus-building seek, implies that the consultative process give rise to what can be called a decision-plan, whose scope and content remain to be determined. It is as if there was an exchange between the provision of information and the commitment required of the government, so that the preparation of the Plan is probably to be sharply distinguished from the other channels through which the demands of social groups are usually articulated. Faced with this requirement, the government is reluctant to commit itself, for it knows that it will be held to the commitments it makes even by those who do not accept the Plan. The contemporary socio-political context of France undoubtedly contributes to this reluctance. Besides, it is clear that the extension of the areas in which planning activity is carried on cannot lead to an extension of the number of commitments entered into within the context of the Plan without creating too may complications. This is partly due to the CGP's difficulty in setting priorities and making choices.

It may be asked whether the use made of planning by the government does not give rise to an even more fundamental difficulty, which any government has in defining an integrated strategy, faced with the permanent temptation of what has been called incrementalism – dealing with problems as and when they present themselves with sufficient urgency to necessitate a solution. It should, moreover, be noted that the president of the republic, better placed than the government *vis-à-vis* public opinion, if only because of his election by universal suffrage, has committed himself more fully in fixing the principal objectives of the Sixth Plan, whose duration coincides roughly with his term of office. Once again the current divisions of French society may explain this tendency. Furthermore, the undeniable difficulty of relating a process of four or five-year planning to an on-going system of decision-taking will be readily acknowledged.[3]

In a way, the Plan always comes ahead or after decisions, a point we shall return to later. Moreover, the question arises whether a more basic antagonism does not exist between managing, which is characteristic of day-to-day activity, and preparing schemes, which is what planning activity is about.

In legal terms, various methods have been used to secure parliamentary approval of the Plan. Generally, the government has resorted to the procedure of the *en bloc* vote, in keeping with the idea that the Plan is a consistent whole which represents a well-articulated governmental policy and that therefore any major amendments would destroy its overall balance.

Nevertheless, it is necessary to provide some safety valves, allowing for the possibility that discussion in parliament might lead to modifications in the government's project. Two techniques are used to this end. The first, which does not commit the government very far, is a declaration at the end of the debate referring to this or that point put forward. The government announces that it will take these points into account in the preparation of the Plan (in the case of the debate on principal policy choices) or in its actual implementation (when the carrying out of the Plan is discussed). This technique was used in the National Assembly for the debates on the Fifth Plan and in the Senate for the debates on the guidelines of the Sixth Plan. The amending *lettre rectificative* has a greater bearing because it is incorporated into the actual text which has been approved. Nevertheless, this second technique does not allow much influence to be exerted on the content of the Plan or its guidelines, and amendments introduced in this way have always been of a minor nature.

Beyond this, there is the matter of the significance of the parliamentary debates at which successive plans have been presented. If the debates on the major objectives have allowed certain speakers to make general assessments or criticisms of the logic of the major choices proposed by the government, they have never given rise to any well worked out counter-proposal.[4] As for the debates on the Plan, they have consisted essentially of the ventilation by the deputies of a series of sectional or local demands. Moreover, up to 1973, parliament has never had any serious discussion on the Plan's implementation. In particular, it has never tried in any systematic way to link the review of the Plan's application with the annual preparation of the Finance Bill. Against this, some people claim that the debates devoted to the Plan are on a higher level than the other parliamentary debates and allow members of parliament to study certain basic problems which they would not otherwise have a chance to examine. This is probably too optimistic a view of the matter.

What are the reasons for this relative failure? There are the practical explanations for it. Our constitutional system ensures almost total control by the government of the running of parliament and its legislative work. Moreover, the Fifth Republic has been characterised by the existence of a reliable parliamentary majority, so it is difficult to see how a Plan different from that proposed by the government could result from parliamentary discussion. There are also practical explanations: the economic ignorance of the members of parliament and parliament's lack of research staff. The first explanation is certainly not very complimentary and probably incorrect inasmuch as the essential choices of the Plan are more than a matter of economics and only require that one should be able to appreciate the real political implications of the proposed perspectives. On the other hand, the second explanation is undoubtedly valid, particularly because, in addition, the political parties themselves lack any research capability. Real progress could be made in this field by learning from the experience of other countries. Moreover, it would no doubt be possible to involve members of parliament earlier in the process of preparing the Plan, so that they would be more familiar with all aspects of the proposed decisions.

Other explanations stress the way in which parliamentary debate is organised. The belated timing of the debate was mentioned during the vote on the Fourth Plan. It was claimed that once the Plan had been prepared it was too late to change it, so if it was to play an effective part, parliament should be involved at an earlier stage, when the major guidelines were laid down. But the Fifth Plan innovation of a guidelines vote did not significantly improve parliament's effectiveness. In any case, it is clearly difficult for parliament to challenge a Plan that claims to be consistent, in which a part cannot be modified without affecting other parts, if not the whole Plan. Nevertheless, there are changes which are politically important but economically insignificant. Furthermore, the scope for discussion in stages and at different levels has perhaps been insufficiently explored.

It may be expected that the gradual development of programme budgets, which will accustom parliament to discussions relating ends and means, will quite probably have a beneficial effect on the discussion of the Plan. In fact, this touches on a fundamental difficulty. The discussion of a *project*, such as the Plan, is at odds with the normal parliamentary practice, which is to discuss legislation, i.e. *rules of the game*. Budgetary debates provide supporting evidence of this because the budget is in fact a project but is voted in the form of rules of the game, that is in the form of permission to raise certain taxes and carry out certain categories of expenditure. The fact that it is voted in 'rule of the game' form helps to make the budget very largely incomprehensible, at least when programme budgets do not make explicit the underlying schemes they represent.

In analysing the scope of the Plan, Nizard's distinction between the decision-plan, economic policy in practice and partial regulation, is useful. Planning is only very partially a decision-making process. The Plan is a guidelines document, whatever its commitment value may be. Every decision stated in the Plan needs to be confirmed by a later decision. The existence of a basically *contingent* process over time means that the idea that from the start a set of decisions can be taken once and for all is self-contradictory. It is because of uncertainty that decisions are in fact taken sequentially. The notion of strategy, formulated by the decisions theorists such as Massé, certainly seeks to integrate uncertainty within a set of sequential decisions, prepared in advance but taken step by step. It must be stressed, however, that no strategy would be able to meet all eventualities and that as a result every strategy must be supported by tactics.

Beyond these rather abstract considerations, some other points can be made. First and foremost, the effective decisional content of the Plan is closely linked to the number of detailed, or better still itemised, pieces of information which it contains. The enumeration of specific investment projects (X hospital or Y steel plant) or the announcement of measures (increasing the minimum wage at the same rate as the general wage level) undoubtedly gives greater practical backing to the decisional character of a Plan than does the fixing of macro-economic objectives (rate of GNP growth) or even of an expenditure total for the whole period of the Plan. This is because the growth rate is a result which can only be achieved through a set of unspecified actions whose consequences are not certain, while fixing a total figure leaves unsettled how such a sum is to be spent, once again because it is not sufficiently detailed. As a corollary, the Plan's effective decisional content is very closely bound up with its commitment value. Greater detail facilitates checking the extent to which the commitments have been carried out.

Leaving the difficult dialectic between contingency and commitment for more empirical concerns, recent developments have undoubtedly reduced the Plan's decisional content, restricting it to forecasts – which are often only a slanted way of stating commitments that one does not wish to make – and to guidelines or decisions to undertake research which are intrinsically only preliminary to decisions in a strict sense.

The Plan nevertheless influences effective economic and social policies. It would certainly be extrapolating too far from the actual content of the Plan to say that its preparation helps define a general strategy for the government. This would imply that as of now there is a generalised social planning, which in fact does not exist and would probably be Utopian. In fact, the preparation of the Plan provides an opportunity for the definition of a whole group of strategies – or, to put it more modestly, of policies – in various spheres.[5] These policies do not become consistent with each other until the Plan has finally been worked out, inasmuch as the Plan specifically aims at ensuring their consistency. To the extent that the state is not unitary and consistency can only be achieved by a reconciliation of often opposed aims, there is every likelihood that when the Plan is implemented, these various policies may diverge. So, even when they are each carried out as part of the Plan, it is probable that they may nevertheless evolve more according to their own logic than according to the logic of coordination and consistency. This is even more likely to hold true when the extent of the Plan's commitment is ambiguous, or, as often happens, when the course of the planning process has led the decision-makers to accept more commitments than intended.

On the other hand, it is noticeable that the Plan, or the preparatory work for the Plan, acts as a point of reference beyond its function of indicating real commitment. The specialist studies, which are kept confidential or whose hypothetical or forecasting character is under-lined if they are published, nevertheless influence the government's day to day actions, e.g. social benefits in the Sixth Plan. In the same way, the economic forecasts provided as information to the trade associa-tions are often brandished as objectives which have been assigned to them or which they assign themselves, and are used in the general bargaining between these industries and the government.

It should be stressed that, as a counterpart to the Plan's influence upon the actual conduct of economic and social policy, in some ways the Plan takes on increasingly precise form through the policies followed during the application of the *preceding* Plan. This raises the whole problem of the ability to make modifications or undertake reforms during the preparation of the Plan. It can also be surmised that this problem would be very different if one had to reconcile fixed-term planning with 'rolling' programme budgets, a by no means unlikely prospect.

Finally, a more general question must be asked about the develop-ment of planning practices in France and about the relationships which are established between the planning practices of the state as an agent – whether it is unified or multiple – and the planning practices of the other economic and social actors. It must be emphasised that plan-ning practices have spread very slowly in France. There seem to be two reasons for this. On the one hand, there is the centralised character of our society, which certainly discourages the development of indepen-dent schemes by the various social and economic actors in so far as the formulation of these projects in terms of a completely articulated strategy runs up against the major uncertainty: ignorance of the future behaviour of the state. On the other hand, we must confess to a certain intellectual backwardness compared with other countries of a similar level. Contrary to what certain people have thought, it is unlikely that the development of these planning practices is corre-lated with increasing social integration. The socialising function of the Plan seems, on the contrary, to be all the more effective when planning practices are less widespread in society.

Swedish experience provides evidence of a country where indivi-dual plans (public as well as private) are so widespread that integrat-ing them into a comprehensive project has been rejected, and general planning is limited to an exchange of information between the various planning groups. In fact, although social integration is very developed in Sweden, it is probable that planning has not contributed very much to it. In France, on the contrary, national planning has been compelled to act in advance of individual planning activities. According to an enquiry carried out a few years ago, the number of firms engaging in planning on their own account did not exceed about fifty and it is unlikely that the situation has changed much since then. Similarly, one of the major difficulties which the development of urban planning encounters in France is that there is hardly a single urban complex capable of effectively preparing its own plan. In fact, the progress of comprehensive planning is certainly dependent upon the development of specific plans, but it should be realised that this development, when it occurs, will very probably lead to a fundamental change in comprehensive planning.

Evaluation and perspectives

Two questions can be asked. Has planning achieved the purposes at which it aimed? Over and above these purposes does it play an implicit socialisation role?

It seems necessary first of all to eliminate certain false problems. As far as the role of planning on the rate of growth is concerned, it has been authoritatively argued that it is impossible to isolate the part played by planning in the acceleration of the growth rate noted since 1945.[6] It may simply be concluded that planning has contributed to a modification of expectations and more basically of the attitude of businessmen compared with the Malthusian behaviour (refusal to compete and innovate) which characterised the pre-war years. Planning certainly played a part in giving credence to the idea that sustained growth was possible. Has planning made possible a more efficient use of investments? Once again, this claim cannot be tested although, at the beginning of the sixties, international comparisons of marginal coefficients of capital showed that France was doing well, perhaps because of planning. Finally, has planning increased the percentage of rationally taken decisions? If one is of a lugubrious disposition, a list of the errors made in successive plans can be drawn up. Once again this sort of assessment is unlikely to yield convincing conclusions.

Setting aside these erroneous approaches, some propositions of a technical and political kind can nevertheless be formulated. Technically, planning was certainly the driving force in increasing and improving economic and social information. It has also definitely encouraged a more systematic consideration of the medium and long-term contexts in decision-making, even if, as we have seen, the adoption of planning practices still remains limited. Another positive aspect of planning is the increased, even if imperfect, awareness of new factors: transfer payments and redistribution policy, urban policy, industrial policy, are examples of this among others. On the whole, the pursuit of rationality has certainly contributed to the development of a new attitude, a new approach to decision-making. At a more political level, while planning has been able in general to identify the real problem, it has, paradoxically, not always succeeded in eliminating the false problems.

If the content of successive plans is examined, the subjects discussed generally deal with the most important problems of French society during the period under review. The solutions put forward, even if they have not always been implemented, clearly indicated the direction policy should take. No doubt there were errors. The Plan has always underestimated the needs of housing and telecommunications. No doubt there were also omissions. The Fifth Plan was not able to foresee the events of May 1968 but who did? On the whole the balance sheet is positive. Planning has also made it easier to distinguish those problems about which nothing can be done from those which are really susceptible to public choice, but here its success is certainly less clearcut, witness some of the political debates before the 1973 general election, which were calculated to inspire scepticism about the pedagogic virtues of the work done in preparing the Plan. However, it might be argued that it is the insufficient attention paid to this work which explains these miscalculations.

To the extent that it sought to modify the way in which French institutions worked, planning failed as far as parliament and the Economic and Social Council were concerned. It has not enabled a 'new politics' to emerge, as was postulated by the doctrine of democratic planning. This hope could be dismissed as illusory, whether its attainment was sought through the organised representative interest-groups, involving the risk of a kind of corporatism, or spontaneously, as was hoped by the supporters of workers' control. The growing reluctance of those in political power to subject their economic and social policy to medium-term *public* planning is indirect evidence that the French system of planning can be an effective instrument in the struggle against the oligarchic character of French society. However, there is obviously no decisive argument against those who think that in a divided society, power must shroud itself in secrecy.

Moreover, planning in France – paradoxically – has provided the most powerful support for decentralisation. The reasons for this may be circumstantial. However, it seems that the logical development of planning must lead it towards multi-level planning, i.e. a dovetailing of the central Plan and the plans made by organisations in the environment, the practical working of the Plan having shown that it is impossible to concentrate at the centre all the information which would make it possible to plan in both a centralised and a rational way.

Has planning an implicit socialisation function? Undoubtedly, the preparation of the Plan plays an apprenticeship role, especially in the context of change, subject to the reservations already expressed. At a deeper level, planning is synonymous with movement even if it very largely excludes brutal change. One no more plans a static society than one plans a revolution. Doubtless, planning also leads to a greater awareness of the interdependence of things. Many socio-economic problems constitute what have been called positive sum games, so that a realisation of the fact that it is possible to cooperate in order to obtain something more or better has a socialisation function. Conversely, there are also zero sum games, the work of the Plan showing that there are absolute losses for some. Even in positive sum games, the distribution of the gain may lead to what could be called relative losses. It has already been said that for some people planning exacerbates conflicts, even creates them. In such cases, planning has opposite results. It plays instead a desocialising role. It does not seem really possible to settle this dispute without a more thorough analysis than it has been possible to carry out here.

To sketch the perspectives of planning in France is certainly difficult. On the one hand, strong cross-pressures are exerted for the extension of the field of planning towards social planning, taking more notice of the environment, the quality of life, the reduction of inequalities. Conversely, we have seen that there is a permanent temptation for those in power either to have recourse to secret planning (which is perhaps impossible in a society like ours), or to strip planning of all operational content, reducing it to a ceremony. All of which does not mean that planning practices will not develop in any case, because they are a deep-seated requirement in the running of our society.

NOTES

1 Planners like to recall that it was in the Agriculture Commission that the farm organisations admitted that a decline in the active farm population was inevitable.

2 The case of bodies responsible for partial syntheses, e.g. the case of research, have been touched on previously.

3 This excludes the hypothesis of a rolling Plan, which, everything leads one to believe, would rapidly become a routine activity, excluding any medium and long-term analysis and perspective.

4 A counter-plan to the Fifth Plan was put forward by a PSU deputy but was not debated.
5 For example, general macro-economic policy, industrial policy, agricultural policy, health policy, social welfare policy and so on.
6 J-J. Carré, P. Dubois and E. Malinvaud, *La Croissance Française*, 1972, chapter 14.

SELECT BIBLIOGRAPHY

Atreize, *La planification française en pratique*, Les Editions Ouvrières, 1971.
Gruson, C., *Origine et espoirs de la planification Française*, Dunod, 1968.
Hackett, J. and A.-M., *Economic Planning in France*, Allen and Unwin, 1963.
Ullmo, Y. *La Planification en France*, Cours de l'Institut d'Etudes Politiques, 1971–3.

2. Britain[1]

TREVOR SMITH

The history of British economic policy over the past decade or so may be regarded primarily as a series of attempts by successive governments to move from a 'mixed' to a 'managed' economy. The foundations of the mixed economy had been consolidated by the nationalisation acts of the post-war Labour government, as a result of which there was a more or less clear structural delineation between the private and public sectors of industry. In the immediate aftermath of war strict and specific physical controls had been imposed on both sectors but these were later superseded by the use of general demand management techniques which were to be the main instrument of economic regulation throughout the 1950s. With the turn of the decade, in an endeavour to break out of the cyclical stop–go response to recurring sterling crises, recourse was again made to the use of micro-economic techniques to complement the existing Keynesian repertoire, and their adoption heralded the shift towards a managed economy.

Loosely defined, the term 'planning' is often used to describe the rationale of economic regulation in modern industrial society to differentiate it from that of earlier epochs. Accordingly, the shift from a mixed to a managed economy in Britain is seen as a question of degree – a change in emphasis rather than in fundamentals. If, with hindsight, one surveys the *results* of the shift it is tempting to accept such an interpretation. But planning is as much a matter of mood as it is of method, of temper as well as technique, and – if this is allowed – it is perhaps better to focus on to the *intentions* of policy-makers and to adopt a more parsimonious definition of planning. For the purposes of this chapter, then, planning will be restricted to one of two senses. First, it will be used to describe the attempts at developing extensive, national policy programmes, of which the period of directed planning from 1939 to 1949 and the period of indicative planning from 1961 to 1966 are the only examples afforded, so far, by British experience. Secondly, it will be used to describe specific, sub-national aspects of policy in the sense that we speak of sectoral planning, public expenditure programming, regional planning, incomes and prices regulation, manpower forecasting and training, etc.

Planning was intended, therefore, though not in so many words, to provide the means by which the transition from a mixed to a managed economy was to be induced. Clarity of purpose, however, did not make for ease of execution and, in the event, planning had a somewhat chequered history as the 1960s unfolded.

Before examining the recent experience of planning it is first necessary to sketch in broad outline the main phases of British economic policy of which it was a part. In the 1960s four main changes in the relative emphases of economic policy are discernible. First, the period up to mid-1961 was essentially a hangover from the predominant Keynesian modes of the previous decade, through which it had been hoped to hold the economy in reasonable equilibrium as between the competing goals of containing inflation, sustaining full employment, and maintaining a favourable balance of payments. The second period, from 1961 to 1966, was one in which the main objective of policy was the stimulation of economic growth by co-opting the methods of indicative planning. This, in turn, gave way to the third period, which spanned the years from 1966 to 1969, in which restoring both the trade balance and international confidence in sterling were accorded top priority. And, finally, from 1969 onwards government attention was concentrated simultaneously on the need to promote employment while reducing inflation.

A formal commitment to planning, in the sense of devising a national economic strategy, survived for the five years up to 1966. A tentative flirtation with the idea was renewed in 1969 with the publication of *The Task Ahead*, but was not pursued further. The influence of the planning episode lingered more substantively, however, in that the planning machinery remained intact and, following the abandonment of the National Plan in 1966, much sub-national activity – especially in the areas of incomes policy, industrial restructuring and public expenditure programming – was prosecuted with greater urgency.

New structures

The most visible evidence that Britain had embraced planning once more was to be seen in the unprecedented wave of institutional innovation in the machinery of economic policy-making which was inspired by the dramatic and almost overnight conversion announced by the chancellor of the exchequer on 26 July 1961. Institutional innovation and reform continued throughout the decade: it occurred within the machinery of central government; was manifested most clearly in the creation of a plethora of quasi-government agencies;

and was reflected – though to a lesser extent – in changes among employers' organisations and the trade unions.

The following is a chronological list of the main developments:

(i) *Within the machinery of central government*

1961 Treasury reorganised following the Plowden report.

1963 Board of Trade (BoT) functions extended to include responsibility for industry and regional development.

1964 New Labour government created Department of Economic Affairs (DEA) and Ministry of Technology (Min.Tech.). BoT and Treasury's functions reduced as a result.

1965 Government Economic Service formally constituted. Regional Economic Planning Boards (REPBs) set up in each region.

1968 Fulton report on the civil service published and accepted by government; Civil Service Department established.

1969 DEA abolished and planning returned to the Treasury; Min.Tech. enlarged to include Ministry of Power; Ministries of Housing and Transport regrouped under a new secretary of state for local government and regional planning.

1970 Conservative government assimilated BoT and Min.Tech. into a Department of Trade and Industry (DTI); a Central Policy Review Staff (CPRS) attached to Cabinet Office.

(ii) *Amongst quasi-government agencies*

1962 National Economic Development Council (NEDC), National Economic Development Office (NEDO) and National Incomes Commission (NIC) formed.

1964 Economic Development Committees (EDCs) formed for particular industries under NEDC aegis; Industrial Training Boards (ITBs) formed for particular industries.

1965 Regional Economic Planning Councils (REPCs) formed in each region; National Board for Prices and Incomes (PIB) appointed in place of the NIC.

1966 Industrial Reorganisation Corporation (IRC) formed.

1969 Commission on Industrial Relations (CIR) established.

1970 Conservative government abolished PIB, IRC and reduced num-
–72 ber of EDCs. Created Office of Manpower Economics (OME), National Industrial Relations Court (NIRC), enhanced role of CIR, and established Industrial Development Executive (IDE).

1973 Pay Board and Prices Commission created.

Many of the changes were inspired by the experience of other countries, particularly France, though most if not all had been anticipated in the writings of the British advocates of planning in the 1930s;[2] some of the changes, moreover, had much in common with previous arrangements.[3]

The decision to adopt indicative planning arose out of a disenchantment with the macro-economic techniques of demand management, which, in turn, was reinforced by envy of the economic performance of the EEC member-states (with the final eclipse of imperial power the international peer group was to become an important determinant of the nation's psychology). It was hoped that the economy would revive by harnessing the micro-economic methods of indicative planning to the existing Keynesian macro-economic ones. Indicative planning was necessary, it was argued, because of the nature of the modern industrial economy in which the intervention and role of the government played so great a part. Industry – both private and nationalised – the trade unions and government now stood in a much closer and more interdependent relationship with each other. The time had come for this to be properly acknowledged by a systematic formalisation of government–industry relations so that a more integrated and coherent framework for economic activity could be devised. This argument appealed to social democrat and capitalist alike: for the former it promised the possibility of making the private sector of industry more publicly accountable; while for the latter it held out the prospect of giving industry a larger voice in the formulation of policy together with longer periods of stable economic policy. (It was a desire for the latter that stimulated the Federation of British Industries to convene in 1960 a conference of leading industrialists to discuss the need for the adoption of indicative planning on the French model. This initiative, according to Samuel Brittan, directly influenced Selwyn Lloyd – the chancellor of the exchequer – in his decision to embrace Monnet-style planning a year later.)[4] And thus it came about that the NEDC was created.

The planning agencies

NEDC was to be a tripartite forum in which the three contracting parties to planning – unions, employers and government – would collectively participate in the determination of medium and long-term economic policy. From 1962 to 1964 it was composed of three ministers (the president of the BoT, the minister of labour, and the chancellor of the exchequer who acted as the NEDC chairman); six industrialists, including two from state industries; six representatives of the Trades Union Congress (TUC); two 'independent' academics; and the director-general of NEDO. Its terms of reference were:

(i) To examine the economic performance of the nation with particular concern for plans for the future in both the private and the public sectors of industry;

(ii) To consider together what are the obstacles to quicker growth, what can be done to improve efficiency, and whether the best use is made of our resources;

(iii) To seek agreement on ways of improving economic performance, competitive power and efficiency; in other words to increase the rate of sound growth.

During its first two years, until the Conservatives lost office, the NEDC published a plan for achieving a 4% rate of growth entitled *Growth of the UK Economy to 1966*, and a supplement, *Conditions Favourable to Faster Growth*.

The status of the NEDC as an independent body was explicitly acknowledged from the outset, with the government self-effacingly regarding itself as being no more than an equal partner alongside industry and the unions. Giving it its own research secretariat in the form of the NEDO was an additional endorsement of its independence.

NEDO consisted of an economics division and an industrial division. Initially the former was the larger of the two and comprised the greatest concentration of economic expertise in the country. The economists were primarily concerned with the macro-economic aspects of planning and with model building (most of them being transferred to the DEA in 1964), while the staff of the industrial division dealt mainly with the micro-economic implications of planning for particular sectors. Most of the NEDO staff were employed on short-term contracts, and many were seconded to it by their employers; it was estimated that about 80% came from industry, with the remainder being recruited from the civil service, universities and unions. The director-general provided the link between the NEDO and NEDC.

The first batch of nine EDCs were created in 1964. Their number was later increased to twenty-four, covering most of the private sector industries and one nationalised one – the Post Office – but had declined to nine by 1971. Their composition reflected the 'Noah's Ark' principle which had been applied to NEDC, and the task of husbanding their activities rested with the staff of the NEDO industrial division. (For a fuller account of the EDCs see my chapter 'Industrial planning in Britain').

With the change of government in 1964 the planning machinery was modified and extended. The formation of a planning ministry, the DEA, indicated that planning was to become primarily a government responsibility, but the NEDC/NEDO arrangements were to be maintained as a forum for consultation and as an alternative, non-governmental source of expertise. The planning agency network was completed by the appointment in 1965 of the REPCs and REPBs in the regions.[5]

The interventionist agencies

A distinction should be drawn between the agencies concerned with planning *per se*, discussed above, and the interventionist agencies which, while they could be subsumed under the umbrella of planning, could survive equally well without it; indeed, as it happened, they flourished rather better after the abandonment of the National Plan in July 1966. One, the Monopolies Commission (MC), had originally been created in 1948 to police those proposed mergers and takeovers referred to it by the BoT to establish whether or not they should be allowed to proceed in the public interest. It was expanded and recast first in 1956 and again in 1965. Its longevity relative to other such agencies is unique.

The ITBs were established under the 1964 Industrial Training Act to review manpower requirements and to formalise and develop training provision for their particular industries. Tripartite in composition with provision for educational representation, they were financed by compulsory levies and by 1971 numbered twenty-seven.[6] The regulation of incomes and prices was attempted first by the appointment of the NIC in 1962, as a successor to the Council on Prices, Productivity and Incomes set up in 1957, and secondly by the creation of the PIB in 1965.[7]

The formation of the IRC in 1966 and the CIR in 1969 completed the cycle of institutional innovation in the machinery of economic policy in the 1960s though, had the 1970 election not intervened, the Labour government had intended to merge the PIB and MC into a single Commission for Industry and Manpower. The incoming Conservative administration began to initiate a new wave of institutional reform.

The rationale behind the new structures

Very little thought was given as to how and in what ways the various agencies, planning and interventionist alike, were to operate or how they related to one another. The sudden, 'Damascus Road' conversion of the Conservatives to planning in 1961 set the pattern for subsequent decisions made during the decade. Any number of general statements were uttered by ministers and others but no clear guidelines were ever enunciated.

In part this lacuna was deliberate, being necessitated by the rubric of indicative planning, which stressed that government was engaged in equal partnership with the unions and management. The independence of the new agencies was continually emphasised and official spokesmen had to be somewhat circumspect, therefore, to avoid appearing to take too much initiative in elucidating how the machinery was to operate. This was also highly functional to the situation since little consideration was ever given to the problem; even within the Cabinet there was confusion over the role of the DEA.[8] It was clearly hoped, however, by co-opting various kinds of expert and by associating the unions and management more closely with the formulation of policy, that firmer ideas for operating the new agencies would emerge: such thinking epitomised the mushy ecumenicism which the age exuded in abundance.

Looking back it is possible, nevertheless, to tease out a broad rationale implicit in the arrangements devised under the Labour government's dispensation. The DEA was to have ultimate responsibility for constructing economic plans, a task which it discharged with the publication of *The National Plan* in September 1965 – eleven months after the creation of the DEA. In the production of plans the DEA was to try and integrate industrial, or vertical, planning with regional, or horizontal, planning and to co-ordinate both private and public sector programmes. Within the context of central government it was intended that the DEA would provide the longer-term policy backdrop against which the Treasury, with its short-term monetary and fiscal responsibilities, and other ministries would discharge their tasks. It was further expected that a beneficial 'spin-off' would emanate from the creative tension generated by the interaction of the Treasury and the DEA.

NEDC, for its part, was to symbolise the tripartite concordat on planning. It was to provide a forum for evolving a moving consensus on planning policy and to mobilise support for that policy. NEDO was to act primarily as a switchboard between industry, government and the unions, working for this purpose mainly through its industrial division and the EDCs; close liaison was to be maintained between NEDO, the DEA's industrial advisers, and the sponsoring departments (mainly Min.Tech. and the BoT) of each industry in Whitehall. NEDO also constituted an independent source of advice, additional to those stemming from the government departments, which moreover was intended to assist in the consensual evolution of policy by providing an objective factual basis for the deliberations of the NEDC.

Since a basic nostrum of planning is to complement macro-economic controls, which by their nature 'are general, universal, non-discriminating',[9] by the development of micro-economic techniques, it was necessary to assemble an extensive communications network to furnish the requisite detailed data about the economy. Accordingly, the EDCs were to form the vertical antennae, providing information from within and between industries, while the REPCs constituted the horizontal antennae, providing information from within and between the regions. Thus, the DEA, NEDC, NEDO, the

EDCs and the regional agencies together comprised the main institutional apparatus of planning. They were intended to be geared to the production of national economic plans and concerned with the long haul of economic policy formation; and they had few, if any, executive functions.

Their longer time horizons and lack of powers contrasted with the position of the interventionist agencies. The IRC was to induce desired structural changes in industry by encouraging mergers and takeovers with the low interest loans made available to it by the government. The ITBs were empowered to raise levies to finance their activities. Strictly speaking, neither the PIB nor the MC had any formal powers themselves (delaying price or wage increases, or disallowing amalgamations remained vested in the government), but their adjudicatory functions on the specific references sent to them by ministers made them an important influence. The CIR came late on the scene and had an inauspicious start; its formal position was enhanced by the 1971 Industrial Relations Act but its operational effectiveness was simultaneously reduced by the withdrawal of trade union co-operation because of their extreme opposition to the Act. The interventionist agencies, then, were not integral to planning but, in the context of the 1960s, may be regarded as adjuncts to it.

The foregoing description makes the economic machinery appear more coherent and better defined than it was. In practice there was a considerable blurring and overlap of function between the different agencies; and the various EDCs and REPCs revealed wide divergences in interpreting their tasks. For example, some EDCs encroached on the work of their corresponding ITBs; other EDCs, notably in the case of transformers, acted almost as an IRC; the Wool Textiles EDC overlapped with the concerns of the Yorkshire and Humberside REPC. The PIB, for its part, trespassed on the territory of the IRC, CIR and MC, while the *ex cathedra* statements of its chairman competed with those of the director-general of NEDO as they vied with each other to be the custodian of the nation's economic conscience.

The greatest confusion, apparent mainly among businessmen, came from the simultaneous presence of the IRC encouraging larger industrial formations and the MC's concern with trust-busting. But they were quite consistent with the bespoke, micro-economic approach of indicative planning and thus complemented each other; in some circumstances the public interest might be served best by concentration, in others not.[10] Overlap and confusion stemmed mainly from the lack of precise definition as to how the new agencies were to set about their tasks. They tended to be defined negatively in terms of what they were not, rather than positively in terms of what they were. In this way assurances were given that NEDC was not a parliament of industry, usurping the powers of the House of Commons, although it was clearly intended to be more than just another advisory committee; similarly, the IRC was said not to be a government merchant bank, nor were the REPCs to be seen as threatening the statutory planning powers of local authorities, but what exactly these agencies were was not elucidated. In the circumstances, then, the new economic agencies were left largely to their own devices to determine in practice what their roles and operational modes would be. If their creation violated the traditional British principle of adapting established institutions to perform new tasks, for the most part their subsequent development was in strict accord with the conventional protocol of 'muddling through'.

The processes of planning

The failure to specify precisely how the various elements in the new machinery were to operate stemmed partly, as stated, from lack of thought and partly from the constraints inherent in the difficult process of trying to establish planning by nurturing a consensus on the pace, direction and content of economic policy. The one premise which was fully explicated and acted upon was that the susceptibilities of established institutions, interests and procedures should not be affronted as a result of the new departures which the adoption of planning was meant to achieve. Indicative planning was seen essentially as a matter of inducing attitude-change and mobilising opinion along agreed lines by means of persuasion, exhortation, precept and incentives, and it was by recourse to such means that it was distinguishable from the coercive controls of directed planning. A measure of ambivalence, therefore, was built into the experiment from the start: the underlying model was 'organic' rather than 'mechanistic'. In short, the aim was to graft planning onto the existing framework of policy-making, rather than to replace it, though in the long run presumably planning was expected to overshadow and later supersede the earlier arrangements as they – or parts of them at least – became generally recognised as redundant and were allowed to atrophy. The net result of all this was that throughout the experiment two parallel policy-making jurisdictions co-existed uneasily with one another. Various means were established to co-ordinate and, as far as possible, integrate the two systems.

Firstly, a good deal of official exhortatory rhetoric was directed towards the lower tiers of management and the unions, and to the public at large. The Conservatives declared 1962 as National Productivity Year with supporting circuses being arranged by the British

Productivity Council. In 1964 the Labour government succeeded, where the Conservatives earlier in the year had failed, in getting a Joint Statement of Intent on Productivity, Prices and Incomes solemnly signed by representatives of the TUC, employers' organisations and the government. The Queen's Award for Industry was instituted as a spur to further achievement in technology and exporting. Following devaluation in 1967, the initiative of some Surbiton typists in working longer hours without payment launched a brief 'I'm backing Britain' movement which showed that symbol manipulation was not confined to the policy-making elites. But in so far as there was a widespread commitment to planning, the exhortations of ministers and others were far less influential than were the cumulative effects of the reformist literature which monopolised the intellectual climate of the 1960s and which started with the publication of Michael Shanks' *The Stagnant Society*.[11]

Secondly, it was expected that the introduction of new skills and the recruitment of more experts into the policy-making process would lead to a more effective system of co-ordination. Innovations to this end began with the re-organisation of the Treasury in 1961 and continued with the formation of the NEDO, the Government Economic Service, the implementation of the Fulton report on the civil service, the short-contract employment of outside experts, or 'irregulars', in both the civil service and the new quasi-government economic agencies, and the increasing use made of management consultants. These reforms were reflected in the development and implementation of a host of new management techniques which included cost-benefit analysis, output budgeting, and accountable management. These techniques were intended to assist in fostering greater rationality in decision-making particularly in areas of sub-national planning; on only three occasions was any overall attempt made to produce national plans which sought to integrate all aspects of the economy, viz: the NEDC plan, *The National Plan* and *The Task Ahead*. (Though there were discernible differences between the three documents: the first was by way of being a feasibility study with an assessment of possibilities; the second was intended as a fully-fledged plan, containing both a forecast and a guide to action; while the third was modestly presented as a discussion document based on a forecast.[12])

Thirdly, co-ordination and integration in economic policy-making was to to be facilitated by the institutional arrangements made within central government and outside it. The DEA was handicapped, as already noted, by ambiguity in its role *vis à vis* that of the Treasury and it was further disadvantaged during its brief five-year existence by a rapid turnover in both its ministerial and official hierarchies;[13] the prime minister took overall charge of it between 1967 and 1968, but this failed to reverse its diminishing credibility. Some commentators, too, argued that NEDC's performance had been impaired by the Treasury – DEA conflict which resulted in excluding the chancellor of the exchequer from the ministerial team on NEDC from 1964 to 1967. Thus, the lack of clear-cut definitions to guide the various elements in the economic policy-making machinery, the emphasis placed on formal equality as the basis of tripartism, and the rapid turnover among key personnel all conspired against the success of the planning experiment: available energies were too dissipated trying to cope with the amorphous situation for the requisite central direction and single-ness of purpose to be forthcoming.

In these circumstances it is not surprising that, left largely to their own devices, the quasi-government agencies developed hetero-geneously. Despite denials to the contrary, the IRC behaved exactly like a state merchant bank, which followed naturally from the compo-sition of its staff. The PIB, under the flamboyant chairmanship of Aubrey Jones, began its work in a fairly unstructured, off-the-cuff way before settling down and devising a more routine mode of operating, which was later emulated by the CIR.[14] The REPCs varied consider-ably in their approaches to their tasks: some acted as vociferous pressure groups (especially in the North, North-West and South-West); others, such as that for Yorkshire and Humberside, worked assiduously but with less publicity; while some, like those for the East Midlands and East Anglia, simply ticked over. The other regional agencies, the REPBs, tended to observe the conventional procedures of inter-departmental civil service committees exhibiting little overt dyna-mism: the ambivalent status of the DEA and the scepticism it aroused among other Whitehall departments circumscribed the extent to which REPB chairmen, who were DEA officials, could innovate.

The EDCs, for their part, revealed much disparity in their develop-ment, due partly to the differences between the industries they covered and partly to the personal propensities of their chairmen. In husbanding their activities the NEDO adopted two guiding prin-ciples – a carefully contrived style of stage management coupled with a policy of the parsimonious mobilisation of available resources (a fuller discussion of these principles will be found in my chapter 'Industrial planning in Britain'). The strategy of parsimonious mobilisation, however, had important consequences for the relative influence of the interest groups involved: while relying, wherever possible, on EDC participants to provide data and prepare papers was both cheap and likely to foster an increased sense of commitment, it very often meant risking the possibility that an EDC would become little more than an additional but highly legitimised channel for the expression of the views of the more powerful trade associations. It was a gamble, nevertheless, which the NEDO's industrial division was quite ready to take. The trade union participants rarely had the resources to feed hard data or position papers into the deliberative processes of the EDCs, either to support or oppose those of the trade associations. At the EDC level of planning, then, tripartism was largely myth: management and the NEDO technocrats were the main innovators, government was usually passive, while the unions were too overstretched to contribute much more than their physical presence – and even this seemed taxing enough, to judge from attendances. In the event, with the demise of planning, this imbalance of forces mattered little.

At the national level, on the NEDC and elsewhere, the unions were better placed, for they had long exercised their conjugal rights in the established *menage à trois* of bilateral, and occasionally multilateral, consultation between government, management and themselves. It was not that the TUC was stronger than the CBI so much as that the latter's position was relatively weaker than many of its constituent trade associations in terms of experience and resources. The CBI had only been formed in 1965.[15] A fundamental fault in the tripartite basis of the NEDC was the inevitable weakness of the two 'umbrella' representative organisations – the TUC and the CBI. It was hoped that by channelling the representation of both sides through them that their status, *vis à vis* their diverse and often self-interestedly stubborn constituent members, would be strengthened. But there are two kinds of opportunity cost to be paid for promoting this type of inclusive representation. First, there is the inevitable 'control loss' inherent in the insertion of an additional link in the communications system between the centre (i.e. government) and the periphery (i.e. individual industries, firms, unions and the shop floor).[16] And, secondly, there is the related problem that the greater the span of representation achieved by an organisation, the less able is it to harness the commitment of its members to collective decisions: very broad constituencies make for the formulation of policies based on the lowest common factors and even then, as the experience of both the TUC and CBI showed, it was difficult to sustain a common front among their members.

There was an element of legerdemain in NEDC tripartism; or, as one minister preferred to put it in an interview with me, 'it is not a confidence trick so much as a trick of confidence'. The hope rested in getting the experiment moving so that as it developed and produced results individual unions and firms would come to accept the value of planning. Although launched in the name of *participation*, planning and its NEDC framework was in practice an exercise in *mobilisation*, and it was a realisation of this which provoked dissent among the ranks of both employers and unions. The Industrial Policy Group was formed in 1967 to propagate the virtues of capitalist enterprise, which the chancellor called 'potentially sinister'. Among the unions the leftward shift in the leadership of the two largest – the transport workers and the engineers – the failure of the reforms initiated by George Woodcock when general secretary of the TUC and the increase in shop-floor militancy could all be interpreted *inter alia* as manifestations of disenchantment with the prospect of mobilisation.

At an early stage in the planning experiment the prime minister was aware of the need to secure support for it at the periphery. In September 1965, in a speech at Bristol, he floated the idea of creating factory production committees. Two months later *The Times*' labour correspondent reported that the proposal had caused consternation in Whitehall but, in supporting it, he went on to suggest that provision should be made for linking the factory committees with the appropriate EDCs.[17] In the event, though Mr Jack Scamp was asked to investigate the possibility of creating such committees, nothing more was forthcoming in this direction. Another attempt to build up support for the modernisation of industrial practices, which was one of the main planks of planning, was the convening of two National Productivity Conferences held in September 1966 and June 1967. Both were carefully prepared by the NEDO and the audiences were drawn from the highest echelons of business and the unions. They were chaired by the prime minister who referred to them as the 'parliament of industry' with NEDC forming the 'cabinet of industry'. At least a positive definition of NEDC's role was offered – any other results the conferences had were less visible.

Closely related to the issue of mobilisation and/or participation is the question of public accountability. Parliament showed little interest in planning as such; most MPs, apart from a vociferous handful of *laisser faire* Conservatives, seemed to go along with the fashionable view that planning was necessary, but there was no campaign for bringing it within the purview of the legislature. During the 1960s the reform of parliamentary committees went to unprecedented lengths culminating in the creation of a new Expenditure Committee.[18] This was seen by its proponents as a logical corollary to the use of output budgeting in Whitehall which had been developed as part of the Treasury's post-Plowden efforts to improve its forecasting of public expenditure. But though an integral part of it, there is more to planning than forecasting and, while parliament was necessarily involved in such planning matters as the passage of the Industrial Expansion Act in 1968 and debating the prices and incomes standstill of 1966, MPs showed no signs of wanting to be consulted in the process of devising plans or even to be given an opportunity to review the work of the planning agencies on a regular basis. (It is interesting to note that whereas the interventionist agencies – the PIB, IRC and ITBs – were obliged by statute to make annual reports to parliament, the planning agencies – NEDC, the EDCs and REPCs – were not.)

The quasi-government economic agencies existed in a state of constitutional limbo and it is a measure of the successful selling of planning that few, if any, voices were raised – in parliament or outside it – about how and in what manner they were held to public account. Since the question was not posed, no formal codification of their position was made available. It is possible, however, to divine three implicit assumptions about their accountability. First, the introduction of new skills and new expert personnel into the policy-making process provided a measure of control. Secondly, the administrative pluralism inherent within Whitehall in the creative tension between the Treasury and the DEA and among the new agencies introduced a system of checks and balances. And, thirdly, tripartism plus the presence of independents in the NEDC/EDC framework helped to safeguard the public interest.[19]

The outcomes of planning

Planning, in the sense of adhering to an extensive national economic programme, came to an abrupt halt with the announcement of the deflationary measures by the government in July 1966. But if the Plan was dead, planning activity of one sort or another continued. The planning agencies lost much of their *raison d'être*, with the EDCs and REPCs being the hardest hit in the long run, while the DEA began its lingering death. In the first flush of post-planning *tristesse* NEDO valiantly endeavoured to sustain the EDCs' activities and the secretary of state for economic affairs sought to reassure them of the value of their mission. NEDC fared better because the contracting parties were reluctant to discard its symbolism (though at one point the TUC became irritated with it) even if its substance had all but evaporated. Its neutral status – 'neutered' might be more appropriate – provided a forum of last resort for tripartite meetings to take place when other venues were politically unacceptable (e.g. three-way discussions on the economy took place under its aegis in 1972 when, because of its hostility to the Industrial Relations Act, the TUC would have found any other rendezvous embarrassing). With the advent of the Conservative government a steering committee, known as the Group of Four and consisting of the TUC's general secretary, the directors-general of the CBI and NEDO, and the permanent secretary of the Treasury, was formed to facilitate the work of the NEDC. Soon after the July measures the CBI made it quite clear that, however bruised it was by the Plan's failure, it wanted to continue with tripartism in a strengthened 'partnership'.[20] The CBI continued its attempts to consolidate and expand its span of representation, to broaden its concern beyond the self-interest of industry, and in 1971 seized the initiative from a government sceptical of such policies and persuaded its members to submit to a voluntary ceiling for price increases.

The interventionist agencies flourished with the abandonment of the Plan. The PIB, especially, came into its own, being used by the government as one of its major instruments for deflation. Industrial restructuring was also emphasised with a spate of IRC-sponsored mergers; Min.Tech.'s responsibilities burgeoned; and with the Shipbuilding Industry Act (1967) and the Industrial Expansion Act (1968) further government money was released for industrial reorganisation.

Within Whitehall the Fulton proposals to improve the management efficiency of the civil service were proceeded with, but only half-heartedly as it later transpired, and renewed efforts were made to improve the forecasting of public expenditure. The reform of public expenditure review had begun with a report from the House of Commons estimates committee in 1958. This prompted the appointment of the Plowden committee which reported in 1961 and which led to the Treasury reforms of the same year. Thereafter the impetus for reform slackened somewhat, though two White Papers were published – one in 1963 and the other in 1966 – which analysed the breakdown of public expenditure. The failure of the National Plan and the increasing need to curtail public sector spending gave a further spur to action: if the government could not plan the economy it could at least show that it had managed to improve the medium-term surveys of its own anticipated expenditure. In 1969 a new system of presenting public expenditure, based on the principles of output budgeting, was inaugurated.

Reflecting on the planning episode of the 1960s provokes the obvious question why, in view of the euphoria with which it was initially embraced, was planning abandoned? The simple answer, of course, is that when the government found it could no longer hold the ring between the conflicting claims of stimulating economic growth and maintaining the parity of sterling it opted in favour of the latter. But, then, this begs the more fundamental question of why it was that balance of payments considerations were allowed to dictate economic policy yet again and at a point when it involved sabotaging a planning programme specifically designed to rescue policy-making from the constraints imposed by recurrent sterling crises. The answer to this question is that, despite the heady rhetoric surrounding it, the planning experiment was severely handicapped from the start by the lack of thought and foresight given to it.

In the first place the resources available to government, or the extent to which it was prepared to make them available, were inadequate to the task of trying to operate two systems of economic regulation in tandem, i.e. the conventional system of Keynesian demand management and the newer kind of indicative planning. Moreover, given limited resources, the planning programme was hopelessly over-ambitious in attempting (1) to devise an incomes policy, (2) to begin industrial planning, and (3) to launch regional planning. In the event, resources were very unevenly distributed in favour of established practices and interests (i.e. the Treasury and balance of payments problems) and to those of the newer departures which were most closely related to them (i.e. the PIB and incomes policy). Industrial planning (the IRC excepted) and, even more, regional planning were accorded low priority in terms of resources and policy-making. Planning seems to be presented with a paradox: periods of economic boom do not engender a felt need for planning, when both resources and time are more readily available; economic crises, on the other hand, are more likely to arouse an interest in planning when time and resources are necessarily at a premium. Compounding the problem was the fact that the period from 1962 to 1966, when planning was being launched, was characterised by the weak position of government: half of it was presided over by the Tories, reeling under the successive blows of an unpopular pay-pause, the Profumo affair and the decline of 'Super Mac', while the other half was administered by the Labour government with a miniscule parliamentary majority. And when strong government was again possible after Labour's victory in 1966, the commitment to planning *vis à vis* sterling had already waned.

In the final analysis, perhaps, the failure of indicative planning to take root was that it was introduced too late on in the development of the economy. To be successfully implemented planning requires, in the initial stages at least, the protection of a relatively closed economy. By the 1960s, however, the pattern of world trade, and the extension of international oligopolies and the rise of the multi-national corporation had made serious inroads into the economic sovereignty of the nation-state; and, for Britain, the role of sterling as a reserve currency exacerbated the problem.

After 1966 planning became 'the love that dare not speak its name'. Despite the set-backs and disappointments, strong residues remained. In 1970 the Conservatives were returned to power apparently determined to transform the 'managed' economy once more into a competitive economy, with the government playing a very much reduced role except in the field of policing industrial relations. The PIB and IRC were abolished, and ailing industries were told not to expect government subsidies to prop them up. These intentions were short-lived. Faced with raging inflation, the government tried to restrain wage increases by every means possible short of resorting to a formalised incomes policy, but by 1973 it had to set up a Prices Commission and a Pay Board in the fashion of the Nixon administration. And in the previous year it had reconstituted the IRC in the form of the Industrial Development Executive. *Plus ça change...*

NOTES

1 This chapter is based partly on research carried out for the Acton Society Trust which was supported by a grant from the Social Science Research Council.

2 Oswald Mosley, Arthur Salter, Harold Macmillan, Barbara Wootton and particularly G. D. H. Cole in his *The Machinery of Socialist Planning*, 1938, anticipated the reforms of the 1960s.

3 For example, the National Production Advisory Council was a forerunner of NEDC; the three Development Councils set up under the Industrial Reorganisation Act of 1947 were similar to the EDCs; and the old Regional Boards for Industry were the immediate predecessors of the REPCs.

4 Of the three, the government was the last to be converted – or re-converted – to planning. The TUC, without ever developing what it meant, had annually called for more planning. Organised business, in the form of the FBI, bestowed its approval on indicative planning at the 1960 Brighton conference. Cf. Samuel Brittan, *Steering the Economy*, rev. edn 1971, pp. 238–45.

5 For a full discussion of these regional bodies see below, p. 238 f.

6 See below, p. 194 f.

7 See below, p. 178 f.

8 Evidently George Brown, its first minister, saw the DEA as a supreme economic overlord to which the Treasury was subordinate, while Harold Wilson, the prime minister, saw them as equal ministries, complementing each other in a relationship of creative tension. See Brittan, *Steering the Economy*, pp. 310–13; H. Wilson, *The Labour Government 1964–70: A Personal Record*, 1971, pp. 3–5 and p. 710; and G. Brown, *In My Way*, Penguin edn, 1972, chapters 5–6.

9 E. A. G. Robinson, *Economic Planning in the United Kingdom – Some Lessons*, 1967, p. 45.

10 Relatively late in the day this point was elucidated in *Mergers: A Guide to Board of Trade Practices*, 1969.

11 First published in 1961. For a critical assessment of the reformist literature and its impact see Trevor Smith, *Anti-Politics: Consensus, Reform and Protest in Britain*, 1972, pp. 11–18.

12 These judgements are taken from T. S. Barker and J. R. C. Lecomber, *Economic Planning for 1972*, 1969.

13 During its first three and a half years it had three secretaries of state, ten subordinate ministers, and three permanent secretaries.

14 Cf. A. Fels, *The British Prices and Incomes Board*, 1972, pp. 72–6.

15 It was born in 1965 out of an amalgamation of the former Federation of British Industries, the National Association of Manufacturers and the British Employers' Confederation. Cf. W. P. Grant and D. Marsh, 'The Confederation of British Industry', *Political Studies*, December 1971.

16 Cf. O. E. Williamson, 'Hierarchical Control and Optimum Firm Size', *Journal of Political Economy*, 1967.

17 'Production committees idea troubles civil service', *The Times*, 1 November 1965.

18 At one point in his period of reforming zeal as Leader of the House of Commons, Mr Richard Crossman flirted with the idea of forming a select committee to scrutinise private sector industry. See 'MP's committee plan', *The Times*, 13 July 1967.
19 I discuss the fallacies in these arguments in *Anti-Politics*, pp. 57–70.
20 Cf. John Davies, 'Industry and Government', *Three Banks Review*, June 1967, pp. 23–8.

SELECT CRITICAL BIBLIOGRAPHY

For a general account of recent economic policy see Samuel Brittan, *Steering the Economy*, Penguin 1971.
Wilfred Beckerman (ed), *The Labour Government's Economic Record 1964–70*, Duckworth 1972, offers a critical but sympathetic assessment of Labour policies, while Nigel Harris, *Competition and the Corporate Society: British Conservatives, the State and Industry 1945–64*, Methuen 1972, provides an excellent account of post-war Tory economics.
A very critical view of the National Plan has been written by Samuel Brittan in *Inquest on Planning*, PEP 1967, and T. S. Barker and J. R. C. Lecomber's *Economic Planning for 1972: an appraisal of the 'Task Ahead'*, PEP 1969, suggests how planning might best be continued.

3. Italy

GIANFRANCO PASQUINO AND
UMBERTO PECCHINI[1]

The objectives and supports of planning

Economic planning was actually started in Italy after some ten years of debate, essentially as part of a political bargain involving the entrance of Socialists, for the first time in the history of united Italy, into a coalition government. Nevertheless, the political alignment that had supported planning was much broader than the Socialist party, as it also included the Republicans and the Christian Democratic Left.[2] Planning was not just a political act. It was a response to economic developments in the period of post-war reconstruction and the 'economic miracle'. However, since there were marked divergences in the judgements of the causes and consequences of these events, the ultimate goal of planning was conceived differently by the Socialists and the Christian Democrats. As a matter of fact, most Socialists thought that planning was the best and the most modern instrument for the transition from a mixed economy to a decentralized and flexibly controlled 'socialist' economy (especially if the related regional reform, brought forward by the Socialists and embodied in the Constitution, were implemented rapidly). The Christian Democrats and, above all, the Republicans, deemed planning to be an important instrument for incremental reforms to facilitate the working of a neo-capitalistic economic system. Such explicit or implicit differences of opinion jeopardized, to some extent, both the identification of objectives and their achievement.

Four documents can be considered the theoretical and empirical bases of the Italian experience in planning: La Malfa's *Additional Note* (1962), the Giolitti Plan (1965), the Pieraccini Plan (1966–70), and the Giolitti Document (1971). The specific economic and social objectives set out in the first five-year plan remained significantly unchanged, despite the fact that the version of the plan approved in the end, the one presented by the Socialist Pieraccini was, in the vision of the society it outlined, much vaguer than the one proposed by the Socialist Giolitti. The primary objectives of the first plan were: the continuation of a high growth-rate – from 5.5 % to 6 % per year – and the achievement of full employment; the correction of *sectoral* imbalances between agriculture and industry as well as the remedying of *regional* disparities between North and South; lastly, correcting the imbalance between private and public consumption. As far as the first objective is concerned, the maintenance of a high growth-rate was a prerequisite for the achievement of the other two goals, while full employment would itself be the result of successful planning.

At the beginning of the 1970s, however, the planners became aware of the basic changes occurring in the Italian economy. This awareness was reflected in the preliminary document to the second plan. First of all, the planners adopted a more sober stand towards the general objectives of planning, stressing that their achievement required a long-term perspective. Secondly, they emphasized that

today's most immediate task is to remove the obstacles to the resumption of short-term expansion, through the activation of public expenditures and the creation of general conditions favourable to the renewal of investments. However, emergence from the present depression would not be lasting if expansion were not, from its inception, devised to eliminate the severest *structural bottlenecks* which have more than once interrupted the growth process in the past.[3]

As a famous Italian economist remarked: 'The problem of increasing the growth rate...thus appears for the first time among the acknowledged problems of the Italian economy. The first task of planning becomes, therefore, to point the way out of depression and stagnation.'[4]

The civil service necessarily had to play a part in all planning activities, but its adaptation to this new task seemed to represent a primary objective for the plan only on paper. This was so despite the fact that the government itself (in the 1965 report attached to the Bill on the reform of the Budget Ministry) denounced the lack of necessary qualified personnel and also complained about 'the lack of adequate means for studying the problems concerning planning itself, and for the inquiries, research and data-collecting necessary to the preparation of documents and to the elaboration and up-dating of the program'. Bitter attacks upon the decisional slowness, political conservatism and technical misinformation of the Italian bureaucracy had become more than the prerogative of the extreme Left. As will become clear, planning was looking, on the one hand, for the co-operation from the bureaucracy which was indispensable to it, while on the other hand trying, through the creation of separate bodies, to escape from its grip. It never forced the civil service into a direct confrontation or made precise attacks which, taking into account the resilience of traditional administrators, would probably have had counterproductive effects.

Some additional comments are necessary concerning the changes in the objectives of planning. Apart from the resumption of rapid growth, the original goals have not changed, because they have not been achieved, for various reasons, among which were the two economic crises of 1964–5 and 1970–4. When national planning was introduced, the Italian economy was developing very rapidly. Had it maintained that level, the achievement of the other goals would have been a relatively easy matter. Therefore, the initial goal, all things considered, was not so much economic growth as the *regulation of growth* and an attempt to direct it towards certain sectors rather than others.

One of the most pertinent and fundamental criticisms of the economic planning experience of the 1960s has been of its assumption of a consistently and rapidly increasing GNP after this had ceased to be a reality. The 1964–5 economic crisis brought the goal of growth to the fore again, while the measures taken to deal with the large deficit in the balance of payments were clearly short-term monetary and fiscal measures, outside the context of planning. The main goal in the seventies seems to be not only growth but a new type of growth, to be achieved through the increase of productive investment (with growth being an important and direct consequence of it) and *not as an indirect consequence of social investment*. Meanwhile, the state administration has proved to be a severe handicap by allowing the amount of funds budgeted for, but not utilized (especially for house and school building), to rise to unprecedented heights. Small wonder, therefore, that the investments of private enterprises are alone considered immediately productive, while the investments of public enterprises seem to play a subordinate role except insofar as they are entrusted with the task of rescuing firms from bankruptcy to prevent an increase in unemployment. Scientific research is not considered to be a productive investment. Far from appreciating the interdependence between economic development and scientific research in a technological era, Italian politicians continue to consider scientific research as a luxury and the financing of it as an underpaid fringe activity.

Undoubtedly, the subject of economic planning as an instrument for the creation of a juster and more efficient society has been widely discussed within both the non-Communist and Communist Left. It is, however, difficult to maintain that we have gone so far as to make a new ideology out of planning, owing to the cleavages existing within the Left on the very way of conceiving the implementation of planning and since, especially on the part of the Republicans, planning was often associated with *incomes policy*. Since the trade unions, from their relatively weak starting positions, considered and still consider incomes policy exclusively as a sophisticated way of controlling wages, planning lost the possibly essential support of the trade unions. They ended up by directing their energies towards the formulation and implementation of a politics of reform outside the planning framework.

Another basic change occurred in the attitude taken by planners towards the necessity and feasibility of an incomes policy. The *Progetto 80* quietly undermined not the theoretical validity of such a policy but its actual feasibility, by stating that

the possibility of predetermining the limits of bargaining, within an agreed framework, among the government, the trade unions, and firms, so that it will not provoke situations incompatible with planning, appears scarcely realistic, not only because it clashes with the principle of free bargaining between the parties...but also because, in so far as the trade unions will accept such agreements, they will no longer fulfil their function of transmitting the impulse and the pressures coming from the grass roots.[5]

This attitude is further strengthened by the preliminary planning document (1971–5), which, after declaring the political and technical unfeasibility of an administrative regulation of incomes, points out the possibility of coming to an open confrontation between the objectives of wage claims and those of planning.

In order to analyse realistically and adequately the relationships between planning and the trade unions, we must clearly separate three aspects: the role conferred by planning upon the trade unions; the trade unions' attitude towards planning; and the effects of the introduction and existence of planning upon trade unions. As far as their role is concerned, the trade unions were considered participants only in the consultative phase but there always lurked in the mind of public and private entrepreneurs the desire to involve them in the fulfilment of some general objectives of planning. Since monetary stability was a major prerequisite for the achievement of the objectives of planning, to most trade unionists the demands for their involvement seemed to imply a sort of tacit agreement on social peace.

The positions adopted by the various trade unions on planning as an instrument of economic policy were not identical. It is important to stress that almost all CGIL trade union MPs decided to abstain on the final vote on the five-year plan, while their fellow parliamentary party members in the PCI and PSIUP voted against it.[6] The secretary-general of the confederation, Agostino Novella, explaining the reasons behind his group's abstention, declared:

CGIL thinks that a planned economic policy represents a higher plane for the initiative and strengthening of the trade unions' functions and activity, but the constructive support for this approach does not mean either approval of any economic program, in abstraction from its contents, or systematic opposition or, finally, scepticism towards any plan whatsoever. It implies, on the contrary, a strong commitment to criticism and support according to the evaluations made on the contents of the plan, particularly with reference to the problems of working-class conditions. We think this autonomy of judgement to be the fact which must characterize a unitary trade union organization wishing to express the interests of workers, regardless of their party affiliation and their ideological orientation, and the condition indispensable to give new impetus and renewed strength to the politics of trade union unity and autonomy.[7]

To complete the picture, we must add that CISL and UIL members voted in favour. Scalia (CISL) announced his union's willingness to collaborate

because planning is meant not only as a necessary instrument for the achievement of a better socio-economic organization of the country, but also as an instrument of greater awareness in social relationships, insofar as it can and must aim at overcoming particularistic interests and at the support of the national community's general interests.[8]

Finally, the neo-fascist trade union, CISNAL, motivated their negative vote by underlining the need for a better system of participation and consultation, perhaps through the creation of a neo-corporative chamber.

The positions adopted by the trade unions on incomes policy were clearly distinguished at the outset: an open refusal by the CGIL, acceptance with many reservations by the CISL and acceptance with some qualifications by the UIL. Through the impact of the unification process between unions and the victorious labour contract renewals of 1969, the opposition to incomes policy hardened on the part of all trade union federations and sectors, coinciding with the reduced inclination on the part of the government to press for it. Putting the emphasis upon a better utilization of existing resources and a greater production of new resources, planning had a strong appeal for the trade unions. Theoretically, it seemed the right instrument to overcome an unacceptable dilemma: growth of employment *or* increase of wages. Practically, however, Italian trade unions, while taking a favourable stand on the main objectives of planning, could easily, and rightly, criticize its parameters – that wages had to be anchored to the average increase in productivity of the system – as misleading, and its instruments inadequate.[9]

Little is known about the attitudes of public holding companies towards planning. Article 2 of the procedural rules states that the planning document 'defines the policies adopted by the State and public agencies for the achievement of the plan's objectives, with an indication of the timing and the amount of the intervention as well as general directives on the implementation measures'. To some, this article seemed too carefully worded, to others it appeared sanctionless. Through their authoritative spokesmen, IRI and ENI paid lip-service to the planning goals but were anything but deferential in implementing them. Only a careful assessment of forecasts and results could give us a balanced picture of the actual behaviour of public holdings (which has been and is much criticized, it is fair to add), but they certainly did not strive to fulfill their assumed role.[10]

As a matter of fact, economic planning was never widely supported either by economic groups – small, medium or large firms, either private or public – or by the civil service, even if, verbally, the principle of the necessity of planning for a mixed economy was accepted almost universally. Whatever little support planning enjoyed came from some PSI and DC factions, from the secretary of the Republican party and from certain groups of intellectuals, together with their journals. The greatest failure of the planning technocrats has doubtless been their inability to mobilize the support of other politically relevant groups. Let us recall, for instance, that even within the PSI there were significant differences of opinion between Pieraccini, Giolitti and Lombardi on this subject, and that one of the promoters of the Centre-Left government, Fanfani, dismissed planning as a 'dream book'. The insurmountable obstacle was represented, however, by the fact that Christian Democrats and Socialists aimed at different types of society, whose foundations were to be built by planning, but they did not dare to express their models openly for fear of jeopardizing their cooperation. Thus, the ideological call for a 'socialist' society, or one based on collaboration between classes, lost its appeal, and planning became a mere instrument for creating a welfare state.

There was no discernible evolution of support and opposition to planning on the part of the various groups. Instead, we might identify a progressive disillusion, even on the part of the groups which in principle were most favourably disposed to planning, due to its scanty achievements.[11] The groups that, from the very beginning, were opposed to planning, especially Confindustria, which had roundly denounced it as an attempt to destroy private initiative and to collectivize the Italian economy, kept up their opposition.[12] Theirs was an intransigent opposition, in which constructive criticisms were substantially absent. The Liberal party proposals consisted, on the one hand, of the possibly coercive implementation of an incomes policy and of the regulation of the trade unions and the right to strike and, on the other hand, were based on the return to private ownership of ENEL (the state electricity corporation) and on the reduction of the public sector of the economy in general. An authoritative spokesman of private enterprise took a more flexible stand some years later in a revealing article when the fears of coercive planning had completely disappeared.

If today's social contract is to be kept alive, leaving to the enterprises their own function in a market economy, the 'political contract' will have to have purely functional goals, that is to aim at informing and reducing the uncertainty of factors impinging upon the decisions and the behaviour of the State as well as on those of the workers and enterprises.[13]

The large industrial firms, either private or public, never felt tied to the choices of planning and showed an overt indifference towards this extraneous body inserted into the economic life of the country. Investments and locations went on as if nothing had happened, taking advantage of the lack of statutory powers to enforce the priorities indicated by the plan. Finally, the Communists (upon whom a great deal of the behaviour of the trade unions depended) even if they were in principle in favour of planning, proved to be lukewarm supporters in practice, since they judged the choices made as not incisive enough, and because they thought that its procedures were not sufficiently democratic.

Planning institutions

We must first of all make a distinction between the institutions created *ad hoc* and the legal and political instruments which were at the disposal of the planners, or those which they considered indispensable. In order to proceed to planning, three kinds of bodies were set up: political, specialist and consultative. Apart from the transformation of the Budget Ministry into a Ministry of the Budget and Economic Planning (BEP) with greater functions and powers, the other political bodies concerned are CIPE (Interministerial Committee for Economic Planning) and the state under-secretariat for BEP.

CIPE is at present composed of the ministers of the treasury, of finance, of industry and trade, of agriculture, of foreign affairs, of foreign trade, of state holdings, of public works, of labour and social security, of transport, of the merchant navy, of tourism and of the Cassa per il Mezzogiorno, under the chairmanship of the prime minister and the vice-chairmanship of the budget and planning minister.[14] CIPE's main functions consist of:
– preparing the guidelines of national economic policy;
– indicating, on the basis of a report prepared by the BEP minister, the

general directives for the elaboration of the national economic plan and, on the basis of a report prepared by the Treasury minister, the general directives for the formulation of an estimate for the state budget, together with the general directives for the implementation of the plan;

– examining the general economic situation in order to adapt short-term measures;

– promoting the necessary coordination of the activity of the central administration with that of the public holdings, in order to implement the plan and to harmonize national economic policy with the economic policies of the EEC countries;

– carrying out the tasks formerly assigned to the abolished Interministerial Committee for Reconstruction (CIR);

– approving the annual program of the Institute of Statistics;

– receiving information from the BEP minister.

The functions of the BEP Ministry are, firstly, the traditional tasks of:

– cooperating with the Treasury Ministry in preparing the draft budget estimates;

– presenting to parliament by March the report on the country's economic situation during the previous year;

– presenting to parliament by September, together with the Treasury minister, a forecast for the next year;

– presenting to parliament by the beginning of October a statement on the economic and financial situation;

– collaborating with the ministers concerned in expenditure plans amounting to a billion [milliard] lire or on capital account for any amount, but lasting more than one fiscal year and for the provisions modifying revenues;

– participating in ministerial committees dealing with economic or financial matters.

The new economic planning tasks conferred on the BEP minister are:

– preparing the outline of an economic plan to be submitted to the Cabinet;

– taking part, with the prime minister, in the presentation to parliament of the bill on the economic plan;

– giving his prior opinion on the actions required by the implementation of the plan and on changes in the budget;

– seeing to the implementation of the plan, about which he keeps the prime minister informed;

– checking on the application of the plan's directives by the ministers;

– periodically reporting to the prime minister and to CIPE on the implementation of the plan;

– participating in interministerial committee meetings on economic planning matters;
– presiding over the Interministerial Consultative Committee for Economic Planning and the Interregional Consultative Committee.

In order to adapt the internal organizational structure of the BEP Ministry to its new roles, the specialist secretariat for planning, the general division for the implementation of economic planning and the general affairs division were created. The secretary for planning is responsible for the preparation of the planning documents and issuing the detailed directives concerning the activities of inquiry, research and data collection to be undertaken by the Institute for Economic Planning Studies (ISPE). The importance of the secretary's office is symbolized by the fact that he is appointed by the president of the republic on the nomination of the BEP minister, and approved by the Cabinet. The secretary for planning is the key figure in the planning functions of the BEP Ministry. To increase the ministry's planning capacity the post of economic adviser was established with a staff of thirty, the ministry being authorized to employ further specialist personnel whose total number was not to exceed 270 people. The BEP Ministry can also call on the research services of a number of institutes. These are – besides ISPE – ISCO (National Institute for Short-Term Economic Studies), and ISTAT (Central Institute for Statistics). Together with other private or public agencies, non-official associations and experts – to whom the carrying out of particular studies can be entrusted[15] – these bodies appear to have become extensions of the BEP Ministry.

Subsidiary consultative roles are played by the Economic Planning Advisory Council (EPAC, composed of nine experts chosen by CIPE), the Interministerial Consultative Committee for Economic Planning (ICCEP) and the Interregional Consultative Committee (ICC). The ICCEP is presided over by the BEP minister and composed of the secretary for planning, the general director for the implementation of planning and by representatives of the Cabinet and of each ministry. Its task is to ensure coordination between the views of the various ministries at the preparatory stage in planning. Finally, there is the ICC, which is also presided over by the BEP minister and is composed of the chairmen of the various regional councils. It has consultative functions concerning the regional aspects of planning. The BEP's general division for the implementation of economic planning provides the secretariat for CIPE, ICCEP and ICC. It examines relevant draft legislation, checks whether the proposals prepared by other ministries correspond to the plan's directives, and considers the budgetary implications. The BEP's general affairs division deals with international economic problems, the short-term economic situation and the preparation of the general report on the country's economic situation.

It should be stressed that the Bill for the organization or reorganization of all the above mentioned bodies only became a law on 1 April 1967, by which time the five-year plan had already been prepared three times, with the informal but effective help of the Planning Office, whose director was to become the secretary for planning.

In the 1960s, the BEP Ministry essentially worked on two tasks: the draft of the first five-year plan (followed by the Giolitti paper that would have probably been the basis of the second five-year plan, had the Centre-Left government not fallen in February, 1972) and the draft of *Progetto 80*. The elaboration of annual plans was an additional function.[16]

There is no doubt, however, that planning did not seek or could not play a role of publicization of medium-term socio-economic choices among the socially and politically relevant groups, and has not been able to involve them in the consultative process, as we will see below. Finally, planning as an attempt to *bind* the public sector of the economy to the pursuit of a coherent set of goals has clearly failed. Even if we consider as planners all those who in any way take part in the formulation and implementation of the plan at the administrative level, they do not form a dominant group in the economic policy process. They are unable to coordinate the economic policies of the large state corporations such as IRI or ENI, owing to the lack of any system of control over them or the ability to take sanctions against them. Furthermore, there is a conflict between the planners, headed by the minister and secretary for planning, with left-wing political preferences and the traditional bureaucratic personnel, with a legal training and Centre-Right political preferences. This has been especially serious because planning was recognized as implying the need for a general administrative reorganization and a change from the usual bureaucratic procedures. The contrast between the achievement-oriented style of the planners and the legalistic style of the bureaucrats led to a clash, the dimensions of which are not easily ascertainable, but which ranged from outright opposition to non-compliance by the bureaucrats. In addition, some of the important data-collecting functions for the formulation and the revision of the plan escaped the planner's control, being entrusted to ISTAT and to ISCO, while matters concerning the actual application of the plan were entrusted to the two general divisions for the implementation of economic planning and for general affairs. So the planners often failed to get the government machine to respond to their initiatives. The secretary for planning is not a career official of the BEP Ministry. His tenure depends on the minister's confidence, so much so that on the occasion of the Social Democrat Preti's accession to the Ministry in June 1969, the first contact between the two men led to the resignation of the secretary for planning. Endemic conflicts continued for the whole period of the first plan between the BEP Ministry and the Treasury. Overlapping of functions and conflicting policies ended up by making clear the need for a complete restructuring of the economic ministries, a matter discussed in 1972. It is suggested that a superministry for the Economy, to be entrusted to the BEP Ministry, should aim at a general coordination and direction of the whole sector. In order to further strengthen his position, the superminister for the economy would also become vice-president of the Council of Ministers. This proposal undoubtedly had its roots in the problems of the 1962–72 decade but also, of course, in the need for a better overall control of economic policies.

From preparation to implementation of the plan

The planning process is formally divided into three parts. The first is devoted to the discussion by parliament of a preliminary document – not having legislative status – proposed by the government and embodying the general goals and directives that the government proposes. The second part consists of the elaboration of the plan itself by the government, on the basis of the choices approved by parliament during the first stage, followed by the final approval of the programme in parliament. The third part concerns the plan's implementation.

The initiative throughout in the planning process is in the hands of the government, the plan being the most comprehensive expression of the government's policy. Although parliament is entrusted with the final examination and approval of the plan, it cannot affect the basic choice of objectives. The insertion of the regions into the process of planning takes the form of proposals to be integrated into the plan. However, the regions have not been given freedom of action because of the desire to keep them subject to the central planning authorities under the control of government and parliament. In order to increase the articulation, some regional planning laws are foreseen, which will be used for the approval of the interventions that the regions wish to carry out during the five-year term, in the matters in which they have the power to act. As far as the local authorities are concerned, their involvement occurs through the regions. They are consulted in the preparation of the various *frameworks for regional economic development.*[17] The regional challenge to the state-centralized organization has been modest. The central government delays delegating powers to the regions as well as the funds necessary to carry them out, passively absorbing and limiting the pressures for change. The same tactics were also adopted in the preparation of the 1971–5 national economic plan that assigns to the regions a role of merely applying the planning choices made at the centre. The regions participated exclusively in a consultative and non-decisional capacity, notably through the Interregional Consultative Committee. We cannot, therefore, agree with the ecstatic assessments of the process of consultation that took place during the drafting of the 1971–5 plan: 'for the first time in Italy, an extensive network of communications arose that included the central administration, the regions and the major organized interests'.[18]

The process of plan preparation actually commences in the BEP Ministry working to the directives of CIPE. After having consulted the Interregional Committee, BEP prepares the guidelines to the plan and submits it to the Cabinet for approval, whence it passes on to parliament, which discusses and approves it (not in statutory form) by January of the year previous to the completion of the current plan. For the elaboration and approval of the plan, two years are allowed.

Within a month of the approval of the initial planning document, CIPE consults the Interregional Committee and formulates the criteria and guidance necessary to the articulation of regional and national economic planning. Within the parameters fixed by such criteria and guidance, each region – having consulted the local authorities – prepares a framework for the economic development of its own area and presents it to CIPE by 30 September of the year prior to the expiration of the current plan. This regional development framework is accompanied by observations and proposals concerning the final formulation of the national plan and the projects that it wishes to undertake. CIPE and the BEP minister examine the framework regional development plans, using them for the elaboration of the national plan and for its regional articulation. Either the prime minister or the BEP minister consults the main trade unions and the main business organizations, reporting back to CIPE, which gives to the BEP Ministry its directives for the detailed preparation of the national plan. Certain specified companies and public bodies are required to supply, at the request of the BEP Ministry, secret information on their investment and other plans.

At this point, the BEP Ministry, on the basis of the planning document, in compliance with the directives of the CIPE and taking into account the advice received, prepares the plan. It then submits the plan to CIPE and the National Economic and Labour Council (CNEL). The latter should receive the plan by March of the final year of the current plan and give its opinion within two months. By June, the Cabinet approves the plan and presents it to parliament, which approves a short Bill to which the plan is appended.

To acquire as precise and up to date as possible a view of the country's economic situation, the government requires the submission of certain reports at fixed times, around which the planning choices and policies are expected to revolve. During the political debates on these reports, possible modifications to the criteria used and objectives pursued may be carried out. In particular, by the end of April each year, the Treasury minister and the BEP minister present to parliament a general report on the country's economic situation in the previous year, while the minister for the Mezzogiorno presents a report on the plan coordinating intervention in the South. By the end of September each year, the Treasury minister and the BEP minister present to parliament the planning forecast for the coming year, attaching a report which explains the criteria on the basis of which the national economic plan will be adapted. The Mezzogiorno minister presents a forecast on the plan coordinating intervention in the South for the next year. With the same deadline, the relevant ministers present reports on scientific and technological research in Italy, a forecast of the activities of the state electricity corporation (ENEL) and reports forecasting the activities of the autonomous state shareholding corporations such as IRI. All these reports are first submitted to CIPE.

In order to implement the national economic plan, besides the approval of the Regional Planning Acts and the presentation to the Chambers of the various reports mentioned, it is foreseen that there will be a series of further consultations of the regions and of the main trade unions and business organizations, carried out by the prime minister or by the BEP minister. After having informed the CIPE about the results of these consultations, the competent ministers, jointly with the Treasury minister and the BEP minister, present to parliament the Bills concerning the plan's implementation. The same procedures apply to Bills for the revision of planning legislation.

Anxieties have been expressed over the inadequately democratic nature of Italian planning. The preliminary analysis by parliament of the planning document prepared by the government is not considered to be sufficient. Parliament's control over the executive's proposals is superficial, since it lacks the necessary information and is unable to debate alternative proposals. Some deputies have maintained that the plan should be a parliamentary task, while others have regarded the French Planning Commissariat as an alternative model to be imitated. The consultation of organized interests affected by planning, it has been suggested, should take place before the elaboration of the preliminary document and not afterwards.

Present procedure does not seem to satisfy anybody. In particular, the Communists have stressed the necessity that

Parliament should really *amend* the programme (and not only *propose* amendments) and then supervise its application and development. Hence the need that the parliamentary debate on the planning Bill should include a stage in which it is possible to intervene in the *drafting* of the plan, in the light of the regional plans and of the essential proposals put forward by the regions and that every year a stage of reports, supervision and updating should occur. Hence the need that Parliament be equipped with the means for the acquisition of information and exercise of supervision and in its procedures to enable it to keep up with the country's economic development and to carry out its function of control over the Executive.

The left wing of the Christian Democratic party has also pointed out that

...apart from any acknowledgement – more formal than real – of the need for a consultation of social forces and of autonomous territorial agencies, and apart from the stress placed – in an almost mystifying way – upon the participation of Parliament (which is not, however, given the necessary means for the enforcement of such participation) [legislation] substantially renders the government, in its entirety or in its parts (Cabinet, CIPE, BEP Minister) the only body endowed with effective decision-making powers.[19]

Application of the plan depends upon the government's political will alone. It is only through the legislation implementing the plan that it acquires reality, yet it is at the mercy of an unsolved political problem: the commitments that planning can effectively impose on the activity of parliament. The experience of the first plan shows, however, that the achievement of the plan's goals has been attempted not only through the planning legislation but through the usual instruments used by the state for economic policies. Their limited efficacy is due to the fact that fundamental reforms have so far proved impracticable. The picture is the same at the level of regional implementation of the plan.

What role has planning actually played and what have been its effects? The first experiment seems to have had less influence on the economic actors than on the planners themselves. This is suggested by the new arrangements proposed for the second five-year plan: a general framework, planning actions and annual plans. The general framework is represented by the whole of the planning hypotheses concerning the development of the economic system on the basis of trends foreseen in the long term and of their comparison with planning's general choices. The *planning actions* indicate behaviour that the central administration expects both in the field subject to its own authority, and by the other actors, notably public and private enterprise. They are of three types: general planning actions, concerning comprehensive intervention; sectoral programmes, aimed at the economic activities of whole industries (according to the conventional national accounting categories); and projects concerning more specific operations. In a number of cases, it was proposed that operational pilot-projects be devised, located in predetermined areas, designed in such a way as to be rapidly carried out. Of course, all these projects are not a starting point but the end point of a planning process, preceded by fixing politically coherent choices (the so-called 'compatibility framework' or 'central goal system') to which public intervention in the various sectors is linked. The *annual control plans*, that represent the need for flexibility of the plan, are intended to link current economic policy with the long-term perspective and with the planning actions. The annual plan must therefore check whether planned development is taking place; introduce new planning actions; check on whether the evolution of the economic situation conforms with the framework adopted at the beginning; take the necessary short-term corrective measures; and if necessary modify the timing of planning implementation action. The annual plan is the instrument for the supervision of the working adaptation and up-dating of the national economic plan.

The planning process in practice

We can broadly distinguish three stages in the planning process: preparation of the plan by experts; consultation with the socio-economic organizations and parliamentary debate. Probably the preparation by experts has up to now received most attention. As far as the first plan is concerned, after La Malfa's *Additional Note*, 'the guidelines for a plan of the country's economic development' were outlined in the so-called Saraceno Report by the National Committee for Economic Planning composed of twelve experts and by the representatives of nine industrial and trade union organizations. Quite soon, however, an inner nucleus within the committee developed, represented by a small team of experts who had a particularly close and co-operative relationship with the BEP Ministry. They constituted the planning office that existed until 1967, when its functions passed to the Secretariat for Planning.

The stage of consultation with social and economic forces does not seem to have been of great significance. As a matter of fact, the three trade unions were only *informed* about the first draft, which was prepared by the planning office and then submitted to the ministers of the economic departments and to the governor of the Bank of Italy. (The second and third drafts respectively included the remarks and amendments of the economic ministers and then of the Cabinet.) Afterwards (in January 1965) the opinion of the National Economic and Labour Council (CNEL) was requested, on the basis of which new modifications were introduced. Then, the BEP minister pointed out that because of the passage of time it was necessary to revise the quantitative framework of the plan.[20] The parliamentary debate began in the budget committee. It then passed to the floor of the Chamber of Deputies where some amendments were introduced and, finally, to the Senate, which approved the text coming from the Chamber of Deputies without modification, so that the Pieraccini Plan completed its parliamentary itinerary on 25 July 1967 (over thirty-one months after the draft of the initial document).

It should be stressed that the five-year plan was substantially the work of a small team of experts. The BEP Ministry's consultative bodies (the EPAC and ICCEP) worked entirely under the minister's direction. Despite the provisions (in the April 1965 decree establishing CIPE) for periodic consultations with the country's main trade unions and business organizations on the problems of implementing and up-dating the economic development plan, almost all observers agree that these consultations have been exceptional and have had no impact on the formulation of the plan's basic choices, so much so that some have proposed the creation of a mixed worker–entrepreneur delegation, of a *permanent* nature, attached to the planning bodies to provide a channel of communication.[21]

So, it cannot be said that in Italy economic planning aimed at establishing even an occasional debate on a national economic development project. In this sense, even the limited work of education and information about the country's economic problems by an important and relevant group of economic and social actors has clearly not been achieved. The attempt to set up a dialogue between trade unions and business organizations on the goals of economic development did not fare better since, if the trade unions were totally unwilling to allow their freedom of action in the labour market to be restrained, Confindustria was not at all willing to give in on choices such as those regarding the amount and location of investment.

It is, however, important to underline that, while the trade unions were not unfavourable towards economic planning, Confindustria took up and has since maintained a firm stand of opposition in principle to any plan that might allow the government either more effective or increased control over the country's economic activity. (It has castigated the 'immorality' of incentive policies and policies of planned bargaining![22]) It should be added that the large private firms, such as Fiat and Pirelli, have continued to act without interference, informing the government – if at all – only after the event. As for public enterprises, they used their acceptance of some governmental directives only as a bargaining counter to obtain concessions, rejecting other directives as part of the same blackmail tactics. To a certain extent, public enterprises have, in fact, viewed planning as a threat to their traditional way of taking decisions through privileged access to certain ministries or party factions, or even as an obstacle to the possibility of acquiring further influence.

Planning has not been able to collect and use fully reliable information, a great weakness in a plan that was visualized as essentially quantitative. The planners' data have often clashed with that provided by Confindustria (which is often unreliable) without it being possible to resolve the conflict. Nobody in Italy ever thought of planning as an experiment in the collection and use of data in a neutral, apolitical manner. Nevertheless, planning was often presented by a press owned by private economic groups as an attempt to control the economic dominance of such interests, the reliability of the data being a secondary consideration. The clashes that took place were kept secret because, through planning, the aim was to defeat not only the political forces that had advocated it, but the formula of the Centre-Left government itself. In this context the transfer of the BEP Ministry from Giolitti to Pieraccini in 1964 was clearly a success for the opponents of *dirigiste* planning in contrast to *indicative* planning. Malagodi and the Italian Liberal party, the leading critics of *dirigiste* planning, had very close ties with Confindustria and particularly with Northern industrial milieux. Malagodi was appointed Treasury minister in June 1972, following a post-electoral shift to the Right-Centre.[23]

One of the most significant differences between the Giolitti and Pieraccini Documents consists in the stand taken towards the large industrial companies, in particular over the control of investment. The third chapter of the Pieraccini Plan says:

In relation to private firms, the action of the plan will develop through the coordinated exercise of the powers allotted by the existing legislation to public bodies and the formulation of policies to influence the evaluations of the economic actors. Furthermore, within the general system of consultation, legislation on the procedures for the elaboration and approval of the plan will give the planning agencies the *power to request* [author's emphasis] from the industrial associations information on the development plans of the various sectors and, in particular, to ask larger firms about their multiannual investment plans; since advance information of the intentions of the large firms will permit discussion of the implications of such programmes with their executives, both as far as their compatibility with the plan's general goals and their adaptation to public investment is concerned.

This formulation replaces that of the Giolitti Plan which envisaged the establishment of a watchdog committee, acting on behalf of CIPE, and the *obligation* was to be placed upon the larger companies to 'communicate their biennial investment plans to the planning bodies' so that the public authorities might themselves formulate their policies in such a way as to harmonize the actions of the large private firms with the plan's general goals. The approach adopted was ineffective since it did not define clearly the great enterprises' obligations, it was not supported by sanctions and did not dispose of effective instruments for implementation by the other decision-making centres – the civil service or the enterprises and public agencies endowed with organizational and financial autonomy. The Pieraccini Plan declared:

The government departments are active subjects of the plan. Their field of responsibility is clearly defined by their institutional functions. They have the task of coordinating their activities to secure the plan's implementation. The autonomous public enterprises and agencies, as well as the firms they control, are responsible for taking their decisions in accordance with the plan's goals. This implies prior examination of their specific programmes and the monitoring of the results.

Furthermore, there was no mention of the instruments through which the planning authorities could assert their choices over government departments and firms. Bearing in mind that in Italy public enterprises often represent powerful pressure groups linked to some factions of the majority party, it is very difficult to make them 'shape their decisions in conformity with the plan's goals'. Therefore, the only real instruments were the ones available to influence the choices of the private firms. Far from being a *dirigiste* form of planning, as was maintained in the parliamentary debates by the spokesmen of the Right and as Confindustria wished to accredit for reasons of propaganda, Italian planning was less than indicative. It was only suggestive. We can only concur with the severe but well-documented left-wing Socialist judgement:

From all the governmental initiatives – text of the plan, reform of the BEP Ministry, Bill on planning procedure – we can infer the role attributed to the plan's authorities: a formal coordination function, powerless in the private sector, and without real impact even in the public sector; with obstacles to overcome, due to the dualism of powers in relation to the Treasury.

A last point must be stressed. Many, above all the Leftists, stated that it was necessary to carry out some preliminary reforms to ensure successful planning.[24] The Communists particularly emphasized the reform of all forms of public enterprise (still an important issue), the Socialists and the Leftist Christian Democrats fought for town planning reforms and Stock Exchange reform, the latter having worked very badly over the last six or seven years. Lastly, many pointed out the need for a coordination of important policies enacted at the same time as the five-year plan, such as the Second Green Plan for agriculture and the legislation transforming the role of the Cassa per il Mezzogiorno.

Despite all the difficulties encountered in the making of the plan and the obstacles which it was anticipated would hinder its implementation, Italian planners never considered the problem of distinguishing between a *desirable* and a *possible* form of planning. One may speculate that the desirable function of planning is now fulfilled by *Progetto 80*, a way of popularizing forecasts, hopes and objectives and stimulating responses before proceeding to planning proper. This seems to be the case even though the publicization of *Progetto 80* only took place after a leak and the theft of the document from the minister's desk.[25]

It must be stressed that the changes in planning procedure have concerned the planners and not the other socio-economic actors. In particular, business and trade unions have preferred, and still do, to work *outside* the context of the plan, even if *not always against* the plan's choices. Industrial executives, faced by the stagnation crisis of the Italian economy, have sought short-term financial aid outside the plan's context. The trade unions base their demands on some fundamental principles of the plan – above all on full employment and on the reduction of the imbalance between North and South – jointly with the so-called politics of reform, for schools, houses and hospitals, aimed at allocating an increased share of the national income to social consumption. Nevertheless, the politics of reform as proposed by the unions is unrelated to planning. The steps taken both in favour of industry and the demands of the trade unions are, therefore, related mainly to contingent situations.

As to the effects of planning on Italian trade unions, they cannot be easily ascertained. The seventies will be recalled as the decade of the unification attempt, and certainly planning contributed to a *rapprochement* among the three main democratic trade unions. Obliged to participate in the consultation process, the trade unions slowly developed a united front on many matters. However, other events had a great impact on the unification process: the most important social conquest of the sixties – the Workers Statute – and the celebrated 'Hot Autumn'. However, it may not only be a coincidence that the diminishing role of planning has been accompanied by great tensions between and within the trade unions. Without underestimating the part played by the general political situation, it seems fair to conclude that planning has started a unification process among trade unions, and autonomy from political parties. Though slow and with contradictory features, this change may prove to be one of its positive unintended consequences.

There is a significant, probably role-determined, discrepancy between the enthusiastic evaluation of the impact of planning upon public administration made by the budget minister and extra-governmental observers. According to the minister, planning has thoroughly modified the coordination of public action at the governmental and public administration level: 'never before have the contacts among the various ministries been so close. For the first time departmental relations based upon the formal allocation of responsibilities are replaced by cooperative relations based upon the problems to be solved'.[26] A paragraph in the planning document having declared that in order to give the administrative apparatus the capacity to intervene in the economic process with great rapidity, flexibility and effectiveness, it was above all necessary to organize adequately the office for the reform of the public administration, a Ministry for the Reform of the Bureaucracy was set up, which should have abolished innumerable useless agencies but whose actions ended up in a complete fiasco. If we add that, even in the planning document, the emphasis was put upon a *gradual implementation* of the reform and that the regions only began their activity after June 1970, it is fair to conclude that planning did not work in such a way as to modernize public administration.

We cannot say, in conclusion, that the quality of Italian economic and social decisions has improved following the introduction of planning, even if it has not worsened. Since planning has not been able to provide a meaningful frame of reference for the political forces that have most to gain from a better allocation of national resources, few struggles have been fought on its behalf. The limited support attracted by planning implies no greater success in the future.[27] As with most reforms attempted in Italy, planning appears to be a durable institution if for no other reason than the fact that the creation of bodies such as as ISPE have given birth to strong vested interests. It is not possible to forsee what shape planning will take because, for a start, it has never had a well-defined shape. A more optimistic view is, however, provided by an authoritative economic periodical:

Planning has been up to now a first effort: uncertain, inconsistent, if you will, but an effort. In the first phase, it has been a symbol around which an ideological battle took place concerning the restriction of freedom which might result. Then it has been an attempt to create a habit of reasoning about economic matters in different terms: a habit of emphasising the interdependence between problems; to consider general issues rather than sectoral and partial aspects. In this sense, one cannot legitimately say that the first plan has been a fiasco: it could not but be a first approximation and some results can be foreseen. It could not miraculously solve the ancient ills of bureaucratization, of the compartmentalization of state intervention, of the corporative inclinations of individual businessmen or of social groups. But *something has been done*: something more and something less than the nonexistent operational instruments and the insufficient political momentum permitted.[28]

NOTES

1 The sections on 'The objectives and supports of planning' and 'The planning process in practice' were written by Pasquino, the sections 'Planning institutions' and 'From preparation to implementation of the plan' by Pecchini.

2 The best and most detailed account of the first attempts at planning in Italy is given by P. Barucci, 'Il programma economico nazionale 1966–1970: precedenti storici ed aspetti economici', in AA.VV., *Il programma economico 1966–70*, Giuffré, Milan 1967, pp. 157–231. See also J. La Palombara, *Italy: The Politics of Planning*, Syracuse University Press, Syracuse 1966.

3 Ministero del Bilancio e della Programmazione Economica, *Documento programmatico preliminare. Elementi per l'impostazione del Programma economico nazionale 1971–1975*, Roma, 1971. It contains the explicit premise that all objectives are to be seen in a long-term perspective.

4 A. Graziani (ed), *L'economia italiana: 1945–1970*, Il Mulino, Bologna 1972, p. 84.

5 On this point see also L. Frey *et al, Politica dei redditi e programmazione*, Franco Angeli, Milan 1967 and the article by B. W. Headey, 'Trade Unions and National Wages Policies', in *Journal of Politics*, XXXII, May 1970, pp. 407–39, who imposes two very stringent conditions for the feasibility of a wages policy in a democracy: 'first, the working class must be sufficiently united politically to elect a Socialist government that will administer the wages policy in such a way that workers, or at least their leaders in the trade unions, are convinced that the policy is not simply a way of depressing their incomes relative to those of the rest of the population; second, the workers must be sufficiently united to form a strong centralized union movement that can help administer the policy without imposing excessive strain on the cohesion and loyalty of its own organization' (p. 407).

6 The CGIL is controlled by Communists and Socialists, CISL is Christian Democrat inspired and the UIL is controlled by the Social Democrats. Vittorio Foa, of the PSIUP, voted against the plan 'because abstention would have had a positive meaning only if all trade union MPs – including the CISL and UIL ones – had abstained'. See also his article 'Il sindacato e la politica economica', in *Problemi del socialismo*, IV, No. 15, 1967, pp. 147–54.

7 Quoted by V. Valli, *Programmazione e sindacati in Italia*, Franco Angeli, Milan 1970, p. 246.

8 *Ibid.* p. 248. On these problems see also F. Momigliano, *Sindacati, progresso tecnico, programmazione economica*, Einaudi, Turin 1966. Valli, following Momigliano, puts it well: 'trade unions must be present at every phase of planning without accepting binding commitments which might excessively curtail their freedom of action' (p. 87).

9 See the excellent analysis by Claudio Napoleoni (unsigned article) 'Programmazione economica e azione sindacale in Italia', in *La Rivista Trimestrale*, IV March–June 1965, pp. 3–41. The theoretical debate, however, did not go on. The limited impact of planning quickly brought it to a halt. It is noteworthy that the polemical journal *Politica del Diritto*, which systematically reports on trade union activities and whose collaborators include the best experts on labour law, has not devoted a single article to themes like 'planning and trade unions' or 'planning procedures and collective bargaining'. Planning as a framework for collective decisions has faded away even if Gino Giugni states that 'the natural place for checking "compatibilities", after all, cannot but be that of planning'. 'I sindacati dalla politica delle riforme all'autunno rivendicativo", in *Politica del Diritto*, III, April 1972, p. 181.

10 Some information is contained in an interesting book by M. Pacini, *Programmazione e società. Le istituzioni, la programmazione economica in Italia negli anni '70*, Etas-Kompass, Milan 1969, especially chapter 15. However, see S. Holland (ed), *The State as entrepreneur*, pp. 205–8, 312–13.

11 One may illustrate this change by reference to one of the forerunners of Italian planning, the Republican party's secretary Ugo La Malfa who, from the great hopes and the rosy optimism of 1962–3 moved to a sceptical, almost defeatist, view. In *La Voce Republicana* of 10–11 August 1966, he states: 'Why should one speak of planning? In Italy, for one reason or another, nobody wants planning, even if everybody pretends to want it'. More recently, La Malfa proposed a plan, to be

implemented in the five-year period of the parliament's mandate and binding the coalition parties, still insisting upon the link between planning and incomes policy.

12 Declaration by the Liberal party's rapporteurs Alpino and Goehring, spokesmen of the medium and small firms, on the occasion of the parliamentary debate of 3 October 1966. They added that 'Center-Left planning is not coercive if the private decision-making centers comply with the program, otherwise they will be coerced. Moreover, the large enterprises will *even* have to debate their future investment programs with the plan's representatives.' (Author's emphasis.)

13 G. Manca, 'La "contrattazione politica" e il punto di vista degli imprenditori', in *Mondo Economico*, XXIII, 13 January 1968, p. 19. The emphasis was placed upon a renewed confidence in the irreplaceable role of private enterprise and planning was reduced to an exchange of information. Supporting evidence can be found in a statement by the budget minister in 1968, when a *rapprochement* with private entrepreneurs was sought. Pieraccini had to admit that 'the planning experiment was born in a climate of profound distrust, if not of open hostility from a substantial part of the Italian entrepreneurial world'. Pieraccini, 'Dalla programmazione anno zero alla programmazione anno '70'.

14 A bill recently presented aims at reducing the number of ministers that compose CIPE, by eliminating the ministers of foreign affairs, foreign trade, transport, the merchant navy and tourism, who would be called upon only for matters pertaining to them.

15 For example, CENSIS (Study Centre for Social Investment) prepares reports that are of great relevance, particularly in the field of education.

16 It is probable that five-year plans will be replaced by yearly indicative ones, whose form, however, is still to be defined.

17 See the report by the BEP undersecretary, 'L'articolazione regionale della Programmazione', in *Mondo Economico*, XXIII, 16 March 1968, pp. vii–viii.

18 See the observations on the role of the regions in *Proposta di parere della Regione Emilia-Romagna sul 'Programma economico nazionale 1971–75'*, Ufficio Stampa della Regione, Nos. 27–8, 13 November 1972, pp. 17–18. Above all, consult 'Documento dei Presidenti delle Regioni' formulated in the Bari meeting, 20 June 1972, published in *Esperienze Amministrative*, XIV, Nos. 4–5, 1972, pp. 135–44.

19 F. Bassanini and B. Tomai, 'Procedure della programmazione, poteri del Parlamento e competenze delle Regioni', in *Relazioni sociali*, IX (May–June 1969), pp. 382–3, propose the creation of an Interparliamentary Committee for Economic Planning. See also D. E. Apter's general statement: 'Parliaments should become forums of open debate on planning, participate in priority setting through legislative decision-making, and serve as agents of popular and technical review and revision'. 'The Premise of Parliamentary Planning', in *Government and Opposition*, VIII, No. 1, Winter 1973, p. 11.

20 The revision was entitled 'Further note to the 1965–69 programme for economic development covering the five-year period 1966–70'.

21 See in particular G. Lizzeri, who states: 'Economic planning, insofar as it pertains to the decisions taken by the existing entrepreneurial centers, is a topic that cannot be dealt with any more, as in the past, through meetings and hearings at the BEP Ministry...This Ministry is a typical superstructure for passive political mediation with regard to the autonomous economic decisions taken by entrepreneurial groups, above all big public and private groups. The opposition to these decisions (volume and type of investment, industrial policies, location and so on), acquire a political meaning only if it is made where the decisions are taken; it has no meaning if it is expressed verbally at the level of the planning bodies. 'Sindacati e strategia delle riforme', in *Relazioni sociali*, X, July–August 1970, p. 552.

22 See below, pp. 134–6, 139.

23 See Malagodi's general report to the Liberal party's tenth National Congress, Rome 1966. Additional material for the evaluation of the PLI's stand on economic planning can be found in *Problemi economici e giuridici del programma quinquennale*, Sansoni e Fondazione Luigi Einaudi, Rome 1966. This book contains an interesting debate between economists and politicians of the Liberal party held in April 1965.

24 A very accurate and long list of these reforms, some put into practice later – notably the Workers Statute – but most of them still not passed, can be found in the minority report by Valori and Passoni (PSIUP) of the Standing Committee on the Budget and State Holdings, to the Chamber of Deputies, 29 September 1966, pp. 18–22.

25 On long-term planning, see below, pp. 424 f.

26 Pieraccini, 'Dalla programmazione anno zero all programmazione anno '70', in *Mondo Economico*, XXIII, 16 March 1968. For more restrained and critical assessment by a scholar who is sympathetic to planning, see G. Pastori, 'Riforma della Pubblica Amministrazione: risultati e prospettive', in *Relazioni Sociali*, VIII, May 1968, pp. 560–1.

27 For an alternative view, see the optimistic article by P. Ranci, 'Il piano è morto, viva il piano', in *Relazioni sociali*, X, November–December 1970, p. 740, who states that: 'in a political situation where one is accustomed to hear only the voices of the strongest sectoral interest – that of the Bank of Italy aiming at the maximum strengthening of the lira, that of the Treasury aiming at the maximum containment of public debt – it is important to introduce systematically a timely voice speaking for the medium-run objectives chosen by the community'.

28 E. Massacesi, 'Programmazione e procedure', in *Mondo Economico*, XXIII, 2 November 1968, p. 10 (author's emphasis).

SELECT BIBLIOGRAPHY

Graziani, A. (ed), *L'economia italiana (1945–1970)*, Il Mulino, Bologna 1972.
Lombardini, S. *La programmazione. Idee, esperienze, problemi*, Einaudi, Turin 1967.
Predieri, A. *et al, Il programma economico 1966–70*, Giuffré, Milan 1967.
Ruffolo, G. *Rapporto sulla programmazione*, Laterza, Bari 1973.
Valli, V. *Programmazione e sindacati in Italia*, Angeli, Milan 1970.

II

Industrial policy

4. Planning and industry in France

JEAN-JACQUES BONNAUD

The object of this paper is to show in what way, to what extent and in which direction planning has influenced public policy in the field of industrial development in France throughout the 1960s.

Industrial policy may be defined as all the actions whereby the central government and other public bodies – regions, local authorities and public enterprises – exercise influence on the environment and the behaviour of industrial firms. These actions may consist simply of information or forecasting, the authoritative fixing of objectives, rules and prohibitions, providing incentives or negotiating. If such a broad definition is accepted, every state has an industrial policy, although the differences are very great.

The introduction of planning in France, as elsewhere, results in new concepts, new institutions and new instruments of policy in the various spheres of economic policy. For these reasons, it changes the economic policy mechanisms and decision-making processes. It is especially interesting to see how this applies to industrial policy, as planning from the start in 1946 accorded a very large place to the problems of industrial development. This is a first and major difference between French industrial policy and the policy pursued in Britain and Italy, where there has been no such longstanding attempt to fix medium-term development objectives for industry as part of a national plan. Its importance has been subject to wide fluctuations, according to the economic environment of industrial activity in France, and the present situation cannot be clearly defined until the historical background is recalled: this will be the subject matter of the first part of this chapter. The second part will examine the Plan's influence upon industrial policy through the application of new concepts, new institutions, new instruments and new power relationships. The third part will try to identify the limits of the real influence of planning on industrial policy, which will doubtless make it possible to arrive at a better definition of their respective natures.

The Plan has been concerned with industrial policy from the very beginning of French planning. Three main factors have determined the relationship between planning and industrial policy: the inheritance of a tradition of great administrative centralisation, the introduction by Jean Monnet of 'concertation' (consensus-building) and the evolution of industry's economic 'environment'.

After 1946, the Plan was grafted onto a civil service which had inherited – in industrial policy matters – traditions of state intervention and centralisation of decision-making that one can trace back to Colbert in the seventeenth century. Having developed during the war economy of the First World War and then the 1929 slump, the central administration engaged in a long and compulsory interventionist phase during the Second World War and had developed a large machine for supervising and directing the economy. Furthermore, the government – by virtue of the very principles of the new constitution and the large number of nationalisations enacted – found itself running many firms in the fields of energy, transport, credit and even manufacturing industry (cars, trucks, chemicals, petroleum).

Concertation (consensus-building) involved consulting in each sphere the relevant businessmen and trade unions (management and workers). This innovation played an important role throughout the existence of planning, thanks to its institutionalisation in the modernisation commissions. They continually increased in number between 1946 and 1965, incidentally reflecting a gradual extension in the matters planned, often at the request of the interested parties. But once again the limits of this innovation should be precisely demarcated. It involved firstly, the regular presence of trade unionists; secondly, the very vast area open to discussion, that of medium-term industrial policy. But dialogue with and consultation of the interested parties is a longstanding tradition within French administration and in 1960 one could enumerate about 4,000 commissions, committees and higher consultative councils attached to the central administration, which shows that alongside the Plan, a true 'consultative administration' had continued to develop in France.

Finally, industry's economic environment has played a determining role in as much as the content and ambitions of each Plan were linked with the situation at each period. From this viewpoint, three periods can be distinguished covering the first five Plans. The First Plan was conceived as a reconstruction plan and concentrated on the development of a small number of basic industries. In these six industries, the Plan did not only fix targets, as it did for other industries. On the one hand, it gave these targets an imperative character as against the indicative character of the other targets, while on the other hand it included 'production and modernisation programmes'. The Second, Third and Fourth Plans sought to plan the implications of sustained economic growth. From the industrial policy standpoint, the previous strategy of directing development in certain directions was replaced by an emphasis upon consistency. Planning involved increasingly detailed market research, and horizontal policies covering all firms were adopted, notably through export, investment and research policies, rather than the First Plan's industry-by-industry approach. The main criteria of state intervention were the rate of growth, profitability, export efforts, innovation efforts and the effort to transfer the location of firms outside the Paris area. Concern about the balance of payments alongside economic growth remained that of classic state control at the frontier over goods, men and capital. In the industrial field, the Plan fixed 'indicative objectives' which were in fact merely forecasts.

The Fifth Plan (1965–70) initiated an important change in the conception and content of French planning. The economy, industry in particular, felt the full impact of international competition, with consequential changes in the objectives and methods of implementing industrial policy. The objectives increasingly took the form of a strategy, i.e. a set of priority targets and the best ways of achieving them. This led industrial policy to stress structural problems, firstly the structure of firms, then the structure of each industry. At the level of the methods to be used in carrying out the Plan, the government gradually lost, owing to the application of the Rome Treaty, its complete freedom to use the many types of incentive that had been developed and applied previously. It had to give greater attention to the constraints of a balanced budget and the search for policy instruments that exercised a distorting effect on the competition between firms. The appearance of the present conception of industrial policy can be dated from the Fifth Plan.

The influence of planning on industrial policy in the 1960s

The preceding historical background shows that the conception of industrial policy was characterised by great change in the 1960s, largely through the influence of increased exposure to international competition. The Plan's contribution is unequally found at three levels: conceptual; methods of preparation and institutional level; application of industrial policy.

It is no exaggeration to assert that the new conception of industrial policy owes a great deal to planning, broadly conceived, not only in the preparation of the Plan itself but as a continuous process of reflection and advice to government under the stimulus of the planning commissioner. Three stages were necessary to move from a conception of industrial policy regarded as the sum of consistent industrial forecasts and interventions judged to be 'in conformity with the Plan' by

Planning Commissariat experts (whose judgement owes more to their assessment of the schemes than to the Plan's content) to an integrated conception in which industry's place is defined overall in the context of the whole economy, followed by a hierarchy of objectives drawn up in a consistent way.

Two innovations were introduced through the Fifth Plan. The definition of an industrial merger policy was coupled with the stipulation in the Plan of the mainly fiscal means necessary to achieve it, as set out in the July 1965 Act, passed after the Guidelines Act but before the final vote approving the Fifth Plan. The 'national champions' policy which is a characteristic of the various European industrial policies, was in France in some sense planned and is inspired by a certain kind of diagnosis. Three 'industries especially exposed' to international competition – aluminium, chemicals and electrical and mechanical engineering – were made the subject of special policies. But this was done outside the traditional modernisation commission consultative framework, and the three industrial programmes were not published, although the experts making up the three working parties were chosen by the government on the recommendation of the planning commissioner. They included officials of the Planning Commissariat in key posts and their reports were sent to the government by the planning commissioner. In this way industrial planning was directed at attaining certain (unpublicised) ends.

During the Plan's implementation, and in accord with a decision made public when the government approved the draft text of the Fifth Plan at a Cabinet committee meeting on 20 July 1965, two committees were set up by the prime minister. The first one, the Industrial Development Committee was set up in March 1966. Its terms of reference were as follows:

To assess the desirable direction of development that French industry should take in the medium and long term.

To define the guidelines and policies to be followed in the various industries, as well as the means necessary to achieve them.

To coordinate the means at the government's disposal to assist initiatives taken by industries or by firms acting in accordance with these policies.

To create general conditions favourable to industrial development and in particular to help eliminate those civil service and major public enterprise practices which inhibit the rationalisation of firms.

To organise and supervise the work of specialised industry groups (agricultural industries, shipbuilding, machine tools, public works raw materials, chemical firms in which there is a state shareholding) assess their conclusions and make appropriate proposals to the government.

The Industrial Development Committee's rapporteur general was the planning commissioner. Its rapporteurs general were successively

F.-X. Ortoli (former planning commissioner, minister of finance, minister of industrial development and then president of the EEC Commission) and René Montjoie, planning commissioner. Its staff consisted of Planning Commissariat experts and its work was done at the rue de Martignac. The committee's 14 members consisted of 5 industrialists (2 public sector, 3 private sector), 2 bankers (1 public, 1 private), 5 civil servants and 1 trade unionist. Its report – except for the work of the special industry groups – was published in April 1968, providing a sort of charter of industrial development that can be briefly summarised as follows:

The objectives of industrial policy are the highest and most regular rate of industrial activity. The key principle is respect for the laws of a competitive market. The government's role is, through the Plan, to illuminate those decisions by firms that have long-term consequences; intervene when competition is incapable of preventing monopolies, promote innovation and avoid industrial or regional disequilibria; as far as possible, respect the principle of true costs in the management of the public sector.

This programme of action was reiterated with a few additional points in the Sixth Plan Guidelines Report, which defined industrial policy as having three parts. Firstly, a policy to deal with industry's environment (sources of finance, industrial training and research, forward looks); secondly, a policy to adapt firms and industrial structures to fit general objectives and the definition of the necessary means (financial and fiscal incentives, training and information); thirdly, a corrective industry-by-industry policy, whose success requires either an indication of the action that the government should take or action programmes negotiated between the government and the trade associations.

The government had also set up a Public Enterprises Committee (its rapporteur general was Simon Nora, from 1969 to 1971 the prime minister's right-hand man) whose 1967 report has led to the acceptance of a new conception of public enterprise and new rules of management. Public enterprise should be conceived primarily as a business whose main function is to provide goods and services at the lowest cost. The government confined itself to laying down a general framework. If the directives it fixes in the public interest diverge from the firm's interest, the cost should be borne by the state. The Nora Report also recommended increasing the autonomy of public enterprise through the conclusion of programme contracts between the state and each firm for the Plan's duration, fixing the multiannual objectives and commitments of both sides. For public enterprises in the competitive industrial sector – petroleum, chemicals, cars, aircraft, sea and air transport, banks – the Nora Report suggested a more active participation in management by the state through public holding companies, but the committee was not unanimously in favour of this proposal.

The Sixth Plan includes a great many indications of this kind and undoubtedly constitutes a turning point in the way in which the contribution of planning to industrial policy is conceived. The present conception of industrial policy might be presented in the following way. At the plan preparation stage, the government attempts to define its industrial policy in as integrated and exhaustive a manner as possible, within the Plan's medium-term perspective and its institutional framework. At this level, one may speak of a search for greater centralisation of the decision-making process. At the implementation stage, the government abandons *dirigisme*, using the Plan to secure the centralised definition of objectives and seeking increased decentralisation in favour of private firms (freedom in principle and – when there is an industrial programme – consensus-building to achieve contracts), increased autonomy for public enterprises (commercial management and multiannual contracts) and increased deconcentration of the administration (intervention is only laid down in principle, allowing greater discretion).

At the same time the tasks which the government allotted to the Planning Commissariat changed. Each time that state intervention became important, the government tended to ask the Commissariat to work out an industrial policy for that sector. We have already mentioned its role concerning industries exposed to foreign competition. With the application of the Fifth Plan in 1965–7, the Commissariat was very closely associated with the definition of industrial programmes (steel agreement, computer plan, shipbuilding restructuring plan, state chemical firms, parts of the food industry). It was also asked, as part of the preparatory work for the Industrial Development Committee, to make detailed studies (which did not lead immediately to a plan for a particular industry) of the public works and machine tools sectors. In 1967–8, the government asked the Planning Commissariat to make recommendations in the very important fields of manpower and research policy, some of which influenced government policy as late as 1970–1. Finally, in 1969 the government asked the planning commissioner for a report evaluating the policy applied in the avant-garde industries: nuclear power, aircraft, space and computers. The decisions to slow down the development of 'graphite-gas' nuclear power stations and launch the Airbus project to compensate for the commercial uncertainties of the Concorde project, were taken at that time. The Commissariat's reports were not published, but they constitute a very important aspect of its function within the administration. The government's desire to integrate its industrial policy within the economic planning process is clear, but it did not extend to the public and concerted preparation of planning decisions.

With this change at the conceptual level is linked a significant change in institutions and techniques. Industrial policy's institutions and procedures are modified to facilitate the centralisation and integration of the way in which industrial policy is defined. First of all, the innovations concern the planning apparatus. This has been constituted since 1946 by the modernisation commissions. Few in number at the beginning, they increased with successive extensions of the Plan's coverage. In the industrial sector, at the time of the Fifth Plan's preparation, there were seven commissions (energy, agricultural industries, chemicals, non-ferrous metals, manufacturing industries, engineering, electronics) and numerous working parties attached to other commissions (shipbuilding and aerospace in the Transport Commission, building and public works in the Housing Commission. Altogether, two hundred industries were involved). In addition, a working party of the National Commission for Regional Development was devoted to industry, and many horizontal commissions dealt with the so-called industrial environment policies – investment capital, taxation, foreign trade, research – although industry's particular problems were not specifically examined by specially constituted bodies. This institutional apparatus was well suited to an industrial policy in which – in the competitive sectors – the policy for each industry consisted of market research plus mere 'recommendations'. Only in the case of public enterprise industries (energy) did real programmes involving both objectives and the means of achieving them actually exist. Furthermore, the industrial environment policy and most of the industrial structure policy were submerged in general policies concerned with financing investment, employment, etc.

With the Sixth Plan in August 1969, the apparatus was reorganised to distinguish the specifically industrial aspects in all spheres of economic policy. The fundamental innovation was the creation of a grand Industry Commission, replacing almost all the others. The exceptions were the Energy Commission, which retained the public service or state monopoly industries (coal, electricity, gas) and for traditional reasons, petroleum, half of whose refineries are run by firms with public shareholdings; the Agricultural Industries and Food Commission, which remained independent because of the Ministry of Agriculture's resistance and the specific political implications involved in this sector's decisions; finally, the Plan's permanent Electronics Commission. The Industry Commission brought within one framework industries that come under the supervision of various ministries (Industry, National Defence, Transport, Equipment). The industries concerned are dealt with in twenty-two vertical committees plus a horizontal committee to examine the specific problems of medium and small firms. In addition, intergroups, chosen in the same way as the members of the commissions and committees, deal with industrial finance, industrial employment and industrial research. In practice, there was also a common working party of the Industry and Regional Planning Commissions to examine the regional aspects of industriali-sation. On the other hand, no special institutional links, apart from the exchange of information, were created between the Industry Commission and the newly established Competition Committee.

The techniques used in preparing the Plan show the same desire to integrate and centralise the way in which industrial policy is worked out, while at the same time reducing the Plan's detailed forecasting function. Detailed projections are made for twenty rather than a hundred categories and the results are not published in the Plan but separately. Furthermore, during the Guidelines phase, the presenta-tion of the preliminary projections sought to treat as a whole all the manufacturing industries exposed to international competitition. It was on this basis that simulation studies of the sensitivity of industry to different hypotheses of government economic policy (in the spheres of industrial training, regulation of working hours, tax policy and finan-cing investment in particular) were undertaken with the help of an economic model, called the medium-term physical–financial model.

The new institutions and associated techniques seem to have had two effects on the real circumstances in which industrial policy is defined. Firstly, there has been what might be called an 'apprenticeship effect' on all the participants, officials (including planners), business repre-sentatives and trade unionists. They have become accustomed to consider all aspects of industrial policy as they interact on each other and have achieved – in greater or lesser measure according to the industry concerned – the substitution of an 'economic policy' ap-proach for the older, detailed 'market research' approach. Secondly, arising out of the Plan Guidelines debate, the theme of accelerating industrial development definitely acquired greater simplicity and persuasive impact. The new institutions and methods of plan pre-paration powerfully contributed to this theme's success, first in the choice of the Sixth Plan's priorities and then with public opinion. In the event, the CNPF (French peak business organisation) grasped more quickly than the trade unions – which in the previous Plans had advo-cated a high rate of growth – the opportunity of using planning to give maximum weight to its own conception of industrial development.

On the other hand – and it was an important weakness – all the Planning Commissariat's efforts, in the course of preparing the Sixth Plan, to develop a public enterprise policy that was not simply the sum of sectoral policies, especially in the matter of financing investment and prices, failed. Subsequently, programme contracts were negotiated with three public enterprises: electricity, railways and radio-television. No contracts were signed in coal, gas and Paris transport. There has therefore been only partial implementation of the Nora Report in the public service sector and none at all in the competitive sector.

The modifications and innovations introduced into the governmental and administrative machine for the purpose of improving the implementation of industrial policy are a logical extension of this new conception. At the beginning of the decade, the situation was as follows. There was intense centralisation based on the ministries located in Paris, especially as far as all decisions about tax or financial incentives were concerned. There was a dispersion of functions between many ministries or agencies: the Ministries of Industry, Transport, Armed Forces, Housing for specific industries; the Finance Ministry for fiscal and financial incentives, prices policy, export promotion and public purchasing policy. Also involved were the Ministries of Scientific Research and of Labour, as well as major financial bodies such as the Crédit National, the Central Fund for Hotel Finance and the Bank of France (especially for medium-term loans); finally, public enterprises whose purchasing policy could be decisive in certain industries. Coordination and the search for consistency in administrative action were secured by either temporary or permanent bodies. Of the latter, the most important in the industrial field was the Economic and Social Development Fund (abbreviated to FDES in French) and particularly four of its specialised committees which advised the Finance Ministry. Committee No. 1 was responsible for all subsidies, tax exemptions, assistance for firms being decentralised or reorganised (if industrial). It had as its chairman the planning commissioner, and included representatives of all ministries (other than Defence) and the aforementioned financial bodies. Committee No. 5 was responsible for public financial intervention in the agricultural and food industries, secretarial staff being provided by the Planning Commissariat, while Committees 4 and 6, responsible for defining and implementing the investment programmes of the energy and transport public enterprises, were both presided over by a member of the Planning Commissariat. In addition, the planning commissioner gave his advice directly on the major medium and long-term loans of the Crédit National (a public bank channeling public loans to private industry) and belonged to the Bank of France's Medium-Term Committee.

This system had a rather striking feature: lacking a charter of industrial development – neither the Fourth nor the Fifth Plans could be considered to have provided such a charter – decision-making power and the definition of policies were dispersed among the various ministries and agencies concerned. On the other hand, implementation was partially coordinated, planning experts playing a role that owed more to their personal skill than to their ability to invoke the letter or spirit of the Plan, the Finance Ministry remaining firmly in overall control.

As a result of the work of the Industrial Development Committee, and over and above the impetus it gave to various policies limited to particular industries through the creation of temporary working parties, the end of the decade was characterised by a number of institutional innovations. In 1969, the creation of a Ministry of Industrial and Scientific Development was an important step in collecting hitherto dispersed responsibilities under one authority. In November 1970 an Industrial Policy Interministerial Committee was set up to coordinate the activities of the various ministries concerned. In addition to the relevant ministers, the committee includes the planning commissioner, while the chairman is the industrial development minister by delegation from the prime minister. Its work is prepared by an interdepartmental committee of officials which includes a Planning Commissariat representative. The 1969 creation of the Industrial Development Institute (IDI), a state merchant bank which, like the British IRC, was not part of the central administration, reflected a desire to counterbalance the increased centralisation and precision in the definition of objectives with greater flexibility in the implementation of policy. But discussion about its role very quickly led to the adoption of a different kind of institution than either the British IRC or Italian IRI, IDI's funds being used mainly to assist small and medium-sized firms and IDI not administering state shareholdings. Furthermore, the funds at the Ministry of Industrial Development's disposal were increased in the 1970, 1971 and 1972 budgets at the expense of the FDES which is controlled in practice by the Finance Ministry.

With regard to infrastructures, which play an increasing role in the application of regional industrial development policy, a decentralisation of responsibility was launched in favour of the regions. As far as the localisation of some infrastructures is concerned, this is merely an application of the Sixth Plan's general aim of promoting the autonomy of regional planning. Regional prefects have acquired increased powers in allocating industrial development subsidies to firms that are established or are transferred to the provinces.

The objectives of these new decisions are three-fold. Firstly, they seek a transfer of power in the implementation of industrial policy from the Finance Ministry to the Industrial Development Ministry. Secondly, financial decentralisation has been attempted, the creation of IDI being followed by measures, inspired by Sixth Plan recommendations in 1971, to give another state bank, the Crédit National, increased funds and to reduce Finance Ministry supervision over its day to day management. Finally, there has been an attempt to decentralise certain decision-making powers to regional bodies, reinforced by the government's decision, following the Sixth Plan's preparation, to present annually to parliament (from 1971 for the 1972 budget) an official regionalisation of public investment funds.

On the other hand, the FDES remains the essential point of government policy coordination in matters of public enterprise. However, in practice, while the FDES plays an important part in financing investment on an annual basis, it does not integrate the policy of each enterprise into multiannual programming.

The limits of the influence of planning on industrial policy

Planning – in a market economy exposed to international competition – does not seek to fix in advance and in a precise way all industrial policy decisions, but to define the rules of the game and see that they are respected. The growing ambition of governments and the related role assigned to the Plan in the sixties are significant. They seek to compensate for the diminishing effectiveness of the traditional instruments of direct administrative intervention stemming, on the one hand, from the freeing of international trade, on the other from the growing diversification of the various elements of industrial activity.

The limits to the role of planning stem from three basic factors: the omissions in the content of the Plan itself; the slowness in the transformation of power relations in the process of industrial policy-making; the resistance of the traditional administrative structures.

Planning does not establish sufficiently operational procedures in a certain number of important areas of industrial policy. One should, nevertheless, bear in mind that from the beginning industrial planning was limited to the industry as a whole and not the firm; general intervention was preferred to selective intervention. As far as content is concerned, the Sixth Plan initiated – as the government intended – very substantial progress, compared with the Fifth Plan, in the analysis of the interdependencies between the various elements of economic policy affecting industry. But all the consequences of this analysis were not followed to their logical conclusions. For example, a matter as important as competition is not the object of a detailed policy concerning the various industrial activities. Price policy is stated firmly in the Plan's Guidelines Report but this is not followed up in the final Plan by any precise details on the objectives or the implementation methods envisaged. So, although the Plan wanted to allow more freedom to industrial prices – for which foreign competition provided a minimum constraint – and recommended that the cost of services should be controlled (trade, hotels, professional fees, etc), the reverse policy was followed at the start of the Sixth Plan. It was modified in June 1972, more for short-term reasons than to implement a planning recommendation. Similarly, cyclical policy, whose importance was underlined by both the Industrial Development Committee and the Sixth Plan Guidelines Report, both for industry as a whole and especially for certain industries (building, public works, investment goods) for which precise implementation measures were to be stipulated, disappeared almost entirely from the final text of the Sixth Plan. Yet again, notwithstanding the analyses and the expressed intention to develop regional planning, the references in the Plan to the location of industry are very weak. Regional industrial policy remains largely outside the Plan, partly because of the inability to define an appropriate industrial policy in each region, and doubtless because of the reluctance of the relevant central ministries to see inroads made into their sphere of responsibility. Even in a sphere where there is so much effort and so many decisions such as financing investment to be made, astonishing gaps remain: no financial programming of public enterprises, nothing either on the programming of the state's financial interventions in industry, vague references to IDI. Likewise the notion of a sectoral programme has been clearly weakened in the Sixth Plan: of course these programmes entail the fixing of clear and sufficiently precise objectives, but the means to achieve them have not been mentioned. This defect is linked with a more general weakness: the inability to achieve a thorough programming of public expenditure.

The gaps in the Plan – in contrast with matters such as taxation, programmes for industrial research or actions in certain industries where very precise directives are provided with an indication of priorities – not only reflect a lack of analysis, but, in almost every case, they correspond to the government's unwillingness to make a political choice when faced by a conflict between the interests of rival power groups. To assess the extent to which planning has influenced traditional power relationships in matters of industrial policy is not easy. This influence was exerted in two stages. The creation of the Plan in 1946 allowed the introduction, in a permanent way, into the already long-established cooperation between administration and business, of a third 'partner', the unions, and for this enlarged cooperation to be given a broad framework and more ambitious objectives. This first stage has been the object of numerous analyses in recent years.

The innovation introduced in the sixties results from the fact that the changes in the conception of the Plan have brought to light new problems and cleavages, not only between the three main traditional partners, but also within each of them. These cleavages are the consequence – in the industrial sphere in particular – of the fact that industry is affected by the international context (the reduction of tariffs) and the technological context (acceleration of innovation and changes in the nature of competition). To these specific evolutionary factors can be added the repercussions on industry of the structural transformations seen throughout French society (urbanisation, qualitative aspirations of the population once the advance to a living-standard measured in terms of per capita income has been assured for the majority, desire for a change in the models of authority), and the growing awareness of the interdependence between industrial development and social advancement, whether positive (contribution to full employment, occupational mobility of labour, expansion of the regions, increases in skill and income), or negative (pollution, mendacious advertising, alienation in work, creation of monopolies or oligopolies restricting competition...).

Planning does not start the power conflicts which are caused by these structural factors, but, to the extent that the government has tried (in industry as well as in other areas of economic and social policy) to use planning as a favoured channel both for dialogue between the different 'social spokesmen' and for the expression of its medium and long-term policy, planning has without doubt revealed and accelerated certain forms of awareness. From this point of view, it is worth examining the differences between the analyses made within the framework and at the prompting of planning[1] – almost exhaustive analyses, given limited present knowledge – and the actual content of the Plan. Space prevents a study of the analyses and work of the planning bodies which would show that industrial planning has raised and debated, if not all, at least a certain number of important questions.[2] The report of the Industry Commission, at the first stage of policy choice, shows traces of recommendations which subsequently disappeared from the final document spelling out the government's decisions. It raised problems such as the improvement of working conditions, the faster growth of the incomes of the lowest-paid workers, the introduction of a minimal levy on companies to rationalise industrial structures, the necessary cooperation between all the 'social partners' to organise redeployment of resources into new activities, the need to encourage the creation of new firms and to change investment arrangements (especially to allow savings hitherto allocated to sectors like agriculture or housing to be devoted to industry). Other issues were not taken up in the Commission's recommendations but references can be found either in the reports of certain industrial committees or in the unpublished minutes of the Commission discussions.

Three examples are significant. Firstly, the nature of the means for implementing priority programmes in industry. Here, the minister of finance resisted the pressure of those industrialists who favoured including supplementary low interest loans in the budget or simply wanted the possibility of using interest subsidies to be considered. It was also impossible to secure a multiannual government financial commitment in the Plan's priority sectors, such as mechanical engineering, chemicals, agricultural and food industries, civil electronics. On the other hand, the government did enter into financial commitments in non-priority industries such as steel, and also where the initial decisions were taken outside the planning process, such as the Concorde programme. Thus, in practice, the notion of industrial priorities was abandoned. Secondly, the limitation or possible reduction of the privileges granted to Crédit Agricole (an agricultural investment bank) which enables it to compete with the banks in attracting savings, was not, under the pressure of farming interests, recommended, notwithstanding pressure to the contrary from the civil service and industry. Thirdly, ways of changing price policy were not defined in the Plan, despite the pressure of industrialists. Apart from statistical and administrative inadequacies, the reason was the pressure from shopkeepers, who felt threatened by industrial growth. In practice there was even a decline in the influence of planning compared to the 'planning contracts' of 1967–70, which were related to the Plan's implementation.

In general, the debates on the objectives and the means to achieve them brought into play different coalitions. In the first part of the decade (roughly the Fourth and Fifth Plans), the objectives were general and simple enough not to provoke strong conflict between the three principal partners; it was rather the inadequacy or absence of certain choices that were attacked. On the other hand, the study of means was particularly developed: attention was focussed on methods of financing, and the plans spelt out in detail the financial and fiscal measures (in the form of fiscal advantages accorded on a case-by-case basis) to be applied. The split became clearer between the administration (itself seldom divided and then largely only on points of detail) and an important section of the employers on the one hand, as well as of the trade unions on the other. The latter opposed unsuccessfully the stress on increased self-financing. A temporary coalition broke up at this time between the unions and the minister of industry. They had attempted to get the idea of a State Industrial Bank incorporated into the Plan, an idea floated in 1961 by the minister of industry and touched on very discreetly in the Fifth Plan, but without any operational commitment, after a prolonged conflict between the interventionist minister of industry and the minister of finance. The latter was not himself especially non-interventionist, but wanted to avoid the loss of power which such an industrial bank would involve and was forced by general budgetary policy to limit the amount of public financial support for industry.

Starting with the setting up of the Industrial Development Committee, from about 1964 and still more with the preparation of the Sixth Plan, the nature and spheres of conflict changed. The three partners were not only divided over the choice of objectives but took up strongly opposed positions. At the Guidelines stage, of the unions – all of whom contested if not the principle of priority for industrial development in the Sixth Plan, at least the way in which it was presented – one (CFDT) withdrew from further discussions and, moreover, from the whole machinery of consensus-building; the others, while remaining, took a more reserved stance. Certain fundamental questions, such as whether to maintain or reduce salary/wage differentials, split the unions, both inside and outside the planning bodies. In contrast, the employers' and the administration's views on the Guidelines were fairly close. Amongst the employers, however, differences of emphasis have appeared between the representatives of the large firms, liberal and relatively flexible in relations with the trade unions, and the representatives of the smaller firms, more conservative and desirous of further public assistance. Nevertheless, although an issue divides the civil service and employers, the line of cleavage passes through each of them. The issue concerns the desirability and possibility of proceeding, in the context of the Plan, to the choice of priorities between sectors and of defining, within priority sectors, genuine programmes of action. The Planning Commissariat, the Ministry of Finance – anxious to limit and channel the request for financial aid – and the horizontal divisions of the Ministry of Industrial Development, were among the advocates of the definition within the framework of the Plan of two sorts of objectives, intersectoral and sectoral; the Ministry of Finance differing from the other ministries over the problem of financial assistance, as indicated previously. This 'maximalist' position was, in general, supported by the unions who approved it in principle, but contested either the nature of the choices actually made, or the vagueness of the content, or the 'clandestine' character of the programmes.[3]

The CNPF had, contrariwise, come out in a doctrinal assessment of planning at the end of 1967, against the principle of discrimination between industries, while approving the principle of the definition of general strategies in certain sectors. Similarly, while the specialist divisions within ministries, which are responsible for the supervision of a particular industry, welcomed the formulation of policies in their own sector, they did not bother about the definition of intersectoral priorities. Furthermore, administration and businessmen frequently differed over how policy should be applied. The result was that the range of measures drawn up by the Industry Commission did not work to the same extent in all policy areas. Horizontal policies and sectoral policies were the object of very open debates, decisions being taken within the consensus-building processes, usually along the lines proposed by the civil servants in horizontal groups, or along the lines advocated by the business spokesmen in vertical groups. (This last assertion should be modulated according to the industry considered.) However, intersectoral choices or priorities, which upset business as much as the civil service, would have been neglected without the efforts of the planners.

The main lesson learned during the preparation of the Sixth Plan in this sphere is that, for the adoption of the Plan itself – rather than for that of the Guidelines – the debate has shifted and has extended beyond the traditional bodies responsible for consensus-building, to spread into three new spheres. Firstly, that of interadministrative cooperation, even before the launching of the Plan, which is very largely dominated by the Finance Ministry. Secondly, that of inter-ministerial cooperation, where the finance minister has been quite strongly opposed by the spending ministries, the prime minister and even the president of the republic, when he intervenes.[4] In this phase the role of parliament, if it was not purely formal (especially as far as the information given to parliamentary committees is concerned, a real effort having been made to improve this at the time of the vote on the Sixth Plan), remained very marginal with regard to industrial policy. The same is true of the Economic and Social Council. Thirdly, as far as public opinion was concerned, one must bear in mind the exceptionally wide interest which the debate on industrialisation attracted in 1969–70. Public opinion was also kept informed of the policy debate among ministers conducted in the various interministerial committees which punctuated the preparation and the final decisions taken on the Plan in March and April 1971.

The main limitation to the influence of planning on the industrial policy which the government wished to establish through the institutional innovation described above, undoubtedly stems from the resistance of the traditional administration to the efforts of integration and coordination. First of all, some ministries seek to avoid having their activities subjected to any outside pressure, even that of the government, through the Plan (or through programme budgeting procedures). Hence their acceptance and sometimes even their repeated requests for discussion of the objectives, while resisting discussion of their application. In practice, institutional innovations have petered out. The government's attempt to put the minister of industrial and scientific development, by delegation from the prime minister, in control of the industrial policy process, has not really succeeded as yet. This emerges very clearly in two measurable phenomena. On the one hand the Industrial Policy Interministerial Committee meets very rarely (four times since its creation) and most of the industrial policy decisions made at the governmental level are on the agenda of the Economic Interministerial Committees as well as, quite often, those of the Regional Development Interministerial Committee meetings. On the other hand, apart from some fairly limited funds for direct intervention – smaller even than the Delegation for Regional Development's budget for that purpose – the bulk of public resources (excluding, however, research expenditure) comes under the FDES and is subject to the vicissitudes of the budgetary discussion controlled by, or under the predominant influence of, the minister of finance (and the prime minister).

Within the Ministry of Industrial Development itself, the efforts to develop a division to oversee all policy (the Industrial Policy Division in 1967) failed, partly because of the opposition of the specialist divisions. A step backwards had to be accepted in 1970 with the substitution for the Industrial Policy Division of a Research Programming Division with more modest aims and means at its disposal.

The new system of coordination not having really functioned, the system in operation at the beginning of the decade has remained in force. Certainly, references to the Plan being very much more precise and numerous, the information of the government departments about governmental objectives is better. Likewise, the opportunities for the Planning Commissariat experts to raise conflict to a political level are greater and the grounds for argument better based. On the other hand, the system remains weak because it does not include all public action that has repercussions on industrial policy. Moreover, the Planning Commissariat lost some of its political stature between 1967 and 1972, when it was under a minister delegate to the prime minister, before being brought once again directly under the prime minister in June 1972. Finally, the vicissitudes of the international monetary system and the development of inflation have multiplied at the end of the period the possibilities of open conflict between the achievement of the Plan's objectives and the necessities of cyclical policy: the policy of encouraging investment abroad as against the short-term management of foreign exchange reserves, and the freedom of firms to fix industrial prices as against the short-term necessities of the fight against inflationary price increases.

NOTES

1 These analyses appear in various preparatory reports. For industrial policy these analyses consist essentially of the report of the Industrial Development Committee, the Guidelines Reports, the work of commissions and committees.

2 In this connection, the reader should refer to specialised studies. Amongst the most recent concerning industry: J. P. Pagé and J.-J. Bonnaud, 'L'utilisation du modèle physico-financier dans les choix du VIe Plan', Commissariat Général du Plan. On the Sixth Plan as a whole, see G. Mignot, 'La concertation dans la préparation des Plans', and J.-J. Bonnaud, 'Le VIe Plan et la prise des décisions de politique économique à moyen terme' in *Droit Social*, Special Number, April–May 1972.

3 Parliament joined in this criticism. It is significant to note that the sectoral work of the Committee of Industrial Development was not published nor brought to the attention of parliament, despite pressure applied repeatedly in 1967, 1968 and 1969 during the discussion of the Planning Commissariat budget.

4 See references quoted in note 2.

SELECT CRITICAL BIBLIOGRAPHY

The March 1968 report of a committee of experts on *Le Développement Industriel*, La Documentation Française, expounds the philosophy of industrial policy applied by the government since the Fifth Plan, when it became aware of the consequences arising from the exposure of the French economy to foreign competition. See also the 1970 report of the Sixth Plan Industry Commission, also published by La Documentation Française, which was responsible for giving detailed application to the principles laid down in the 1968 expert committee report. Jean-Jacques Bonnaud's article on 'Les instruments d'exécution du Plan utilisés par l'Etat à l'égard des entreprises', *Revue Economique*, XXI, No. 4, July 1970, pp. 554–96, describes in detail the administrative machinery through which state intervention in industry occurs and the criteria by which it is used to implement the Plan.

J. H. McArthur and Bruce R. Scott, *Industrial Planning in France*, Harvard University Press, Boston 1969, have made an important critical study of the extent to which the Plan is used by firms, of the state's influence over the economy and of the planning process's influence upon the policies pursued by the state and the firms. They conclude that there is only an indirect and rather feeble influence at the level of the industry or firm. Finally, Erhard Friedberg's paper on 'Internationalisation de l'économie et modalités d'intervention de l'Etat: La "politique industrielle"', in *Planification et Société*, Colloque d'Uriage, Grenoble University Press 1974, describes the consequences of the choice made in favour of international competition on the increasing interpenetration of the administrative system and the industrial system, which are respectively dominated by the Ministry of Finance and by big business. The author argues that their relationships are becoming increasingly politicised, being subject to the arbitrament of the para-political ministerial *cabinets*, which are more responsive to pressures from industry than was traditional administration.

5. Industrial planning in Britain[1]

TREVOR SMITH

During the 1950s British government policy towards industry was generally low-keyed. For the most part government saw itself as trying to create an economic climate in which industry could prosper. The role of the state was to be more limited than it had been under the post-war Labour administration; one symbolic manifestation of this was the denationalisation of the steel industry in 1953 together – though somewhat abortively – with that of long-distance road haulage. The government, however, intended to keep a watchful eye on the spread of monopoly control and restrictive practices, to which end it strengthened the Monopolies Commission (MC) in 1956 and later, prior to relinquishing office in 1964, passed the Resale Price Maintenance Act which outlawed price-fixing agreements.

Around the turn of the decade the government became more interventionist. It forced the aircraft manufacturers to rationalise themselves into two main groups, Hawker Siddeley and the British Aircraft Corporation. In 1959 the Cotton Industry Act provided state money for modernising the Lancashire textile mills. Additional funds were made available for the more depressed regions,[2] and in a White Paper the nationalised industries were enjoined to adopt a more commercial approach in their activities.[3] In 1961 the government's new stance towards industry was formalised with the adoption of 'indicative' planning, which led to the establishment of the National Economic Development Council (NEDC) and its Office (NEDO), the National Incomes Commission (NIC), and the Industrial Training Act (1964) provided for the formation of Industrial Training Boards (ITBs).

With the advent of the Labour government in 1964, the pace of institutional innovation quickened perceptibly: Economic Development Committees (EDCs) were formed, together with new regional planning agencies (REPCs and REPBs). These were followed by the appointment of the National Board for Prices and Incomes (PIB) in 1965 and the MC's role was further expanded. In the next year the Industrial Reorganisation Corporation (IRC) was created, followed by the Commission on Industrial Relations (CIR) in 1969. The ingenuity of the new government was not confined to institutional change and reform; in its fiscal policy, too, it endeavoured to intervene positively in the industrial sector in the form of a Corporation Tax, a Selective Employment Tax, and a Regional Employment Premium. In 1967 another White Paper sought to enhance the commercial efficiency of the nationalised industries.[4] During the 1960s, therefore, government policy towards industry marked a strong contrast with the practice of the previous decade. But this was not the only difference, for industry itself was undergoing fundamental changes: the decline of older industries, the development problems of newer industries and – most visibly, perhaps – the unprecedented rate of amalgamations, all contributed to the creation of a highly dynamic industrial milieu.

An attempt will be made to trace and assess the main developments in industry/state relations which occurred in the 1960s. The substantive results will be outlined *en passant*:[5] the main focus of attention will be concentrated on the interaction of the various sets of participants involved in the conduct of industry/state relations in general, and in the industrial planning experiment in particular. Finally, an analysis will be made of the further twists and turns in government policy which followed the Conservatives' return to office in 1970.

The aims of industrial policy

British industrial policy in the 1960s was an amalgam of diverse and often conflicting aims. In principle the over-riding goal was to promote faster economic growth, though in practice – when a choice had to be made – balance of payments considerations were accorded first priority. The intention was to stimulate economic growth in two main ways: behaviourally and structurally. The former consisted largely of bringing industry, the unions, and government into a more formal relationship (via the NEDC/EDCs network) in an attempt to foster a climate of opinion – to which, ostensibly, all three parties would contribute and to which, it was hoped, all would subscribe – within which agreed industrial policies could be formulated. The latter aimed to bring about the modernisation of industry by encouraging, initiating or even compelling desired structural changes. Inducing changes in attitudes and behaviour was the main method of the Conservative government from 1962 to 1964, while structural modification was more a feature of the Labour administration which followed it. Although this difference of emphasis reflects the ideological preferences of the political parties it also reflects the sequence of events in the planning experiment. Cooperation and consensus were seen as a basic prerequisite to the formulation of specific interventionist policies, although sustaining and developing tripartite agreement was regarded as a continuing concomitant necessity.

Looking back over the decade, and examining the Labour government's record in particular, it appears that industrial modernisation involved the controlled running down of supposedly obsolete industries (e.g. coal), supporting basic but essential industries (e.g. steel and shipbuilding), and husbanding new technologies (e.g. natural gas, computers); the Shipbuilding Industry Act (1967) provided £400 million for financing the modernisation of shipyards, and the Industrial Expansion Act (1968) made £100–150 million available for underwriting general industrial modernisation. Additionally, other, no less important, considerations contributed to industrial policy-making. Firstly, attempts were made by means of the Selective Employment Tax (SET) which was introduced in 1966, to shift excess labour from the 'unproductive' service industries into manufacturing.[6] Secondly, through the Regional Employment Premium (REP), increases in development area grants, and the introduction of new grants for the intermediate – 'grey' – areas, the government sought to attract new industry (thereby raising employment levels) into the more depressed regions of the economy.[7] And, thirdly, a number of policies were promoted with the expressed purpose of improving Britain's international economic position: these included the encouragement of exports; a search for ways of producing indigenous substitutes for imported goods, and offsetting foreign influence in certain strategic sections of the economy, whether it came in the form of competition (e.g. IBM's computers) or outright ownership (e.g. Skefco's bid for a major ball-bearings producer).

Thus British industrial policy revealed many similarities with that of France, with one significant difference: if the aims were often identical, the time periods in which they operated were very different. In France, promoting economic growth, exports and regional balance were the main considerations behind the Second, Third and Fourth Plans which covered the years from 1950 to 1965. The Fifth and Sixth Plans were concerned more with effecting changes in the structure of industry and with warding-off foreign competition and ownership. British policy, on the other hand, endeavoured to encompass all these aims, more or less simultaneously, within the confines of a single decade.

Government–industry relations in practice, 1964–70

Within the machinery of government the Department of Economic Affairs (DEA), the Ministry of Technology (Min.Tech.), the Board of Trade (BoT) and the Ministry of Labour were the main ministries concerned with industrial planning at the outset of the Labour government in 1964. In the next six years these arrangements were modified. Some of the changes were relatively minor, such as the decline of the BoT's influence or the re-naming of the Ministry of Labour as the Department of Employment and Productivity (DEP).[8] The slow decline of the DEA, however, coupled with the gradual and related enhancement of Min.Tech., were of greater significance. Indeed, the relationship between government and industry over the period can be discussed largely in terms of the development of Min.Tech., the operations of the various EDCs, and the activities of the IRC.

The Ministry of Technology[9]

The creation of Min.Tech. symbolised the new government's intention to effect a technological renaissance in industry, to which it had committed itself in the run-up to the 1964 general election. In its initial phase it was relatively small and politically weak (for example, neither of its two ministers had parliamentary experience). Like the DEA, Min.Tech. was conjured up from scratch; but unlike the former, which had elements of other ministries transferred to it, it had to poach staff on a piecemeal basis from other ministries. Moreover, apart from a very general instruction to encourage the development and application of advanced technology, its specific remit was limited to overseeing the computer, machine-tool, electronics and telecommunications industries as well as the government's industrial research establishments. It was essentially a promotional rather than a regulatory ministry.

By the end of 1965 'sponsorship' for the mechanical and electrical engineering industries had been added to its tasks. But 1966 was the year which saw the consolidation of Min.Tech.'s position: it was made responsible for shipbuilding and took over most of the Ministry of Aviation, including responsibility for the aircraft production industry; it acquired a new minister and permanent secretary, both of whom were to remain in their posts until 1970; and it gained in status *vis à vis* the DEA as the main ministry for conducting industrial policy following the abandonment of the National Plan. Three years later it was expanded still further into one of the giant 'federal' ministries by the absorption of the Ministry of Power, together with many of the BoT's functions (including regional industrial policy and investment grant administration) and some of the DEA's responsibilities such as the formal supervision of the IRC. Min.Tech.'s remit now covered all the major private sector industries and it was in direct control of nearly all the nationalised industries – coal, electricity, gas, atomic energy and steel. The one apparent anomaly was that the duty of policing mergers and monopolies was given to the Department of Employment and Productivity. This occurred presumably because of a desire to maintain a separation of ministerial powers between a merger-fostering Min.Tech. with its IRC, and a merger-investigating Monopolies Commission operating under the aegis of the DEP. Thus in the space of five years Min.Tech. had emerged, after a faltering start, into one of the major departments of state. Its staff had grown nearly eight-fold to almost 40,000 and its ministerial team had been enlarged from two to seven, two of whom sat in the Cabinet. Min.Tech. was also one of the pioneers in adopting a unified staffing structure whereby senior posts were open to scientists, engineers and other specialists and not kept as the exclusive preserve of the general civil servants of the administrative class; in this innovation it anticipated one of the main recommendations of the Fulton Report.

However remarkable, in a period of considerable institutional turnover, its staying power proved to be, its policy achievements were less impressive. It failed in its efforts to put shipbuilding on a sound footing partly, as Sir Richard Clarke has pointed out, because the purely *industrial* problems could never be analysed in isolation from *employment* considerations. In the field of aircraft production, the continuation of Concorde and approval for the development of the RB 211 engine for the Lockheed Tristar hardly suggest that Min.Tech. made any significant steps in the evaluation of costly, high-risk, advanced technology projects. It did bring about a rationalisation of computer production with the formation of a single company (ICL) in 1968 although, as events quickly showed, a single national economy could not sustain a viable computer industry. But, in assessing Min.Tech.'s not very auspicious record, it must be remembered that it was called upon to act in some of the most difficult industrial terrain, which has thrown up some of the most intractable policy problems for governments, both in Britain and elsewhere. Min.Tech. did succeed in institutionalising the principle of discriminatory intervention at the level of the firm, notably in machine tools. Whatever reservations the Conservatives had about specific items of its policy, they took it over with little change and used it as the main foundation of their own Department of Trade and Industry (DTI) when they were returned to office in 1970.

The Economic Development Committees

NEDC was established in 1962, but the first EDCs did not appear until two years later. Their terms of reference were:

Within the context of the work of the NEDC and in accordance with such working arrangements as may be determined from time to time between Council and the Committee, each Committee will:

(i) examine the economic performance, prospects and plans of the industry and assess from time to time the industry's progress in relation to the national growth objectives and provide information and forecasts to the Council on these matters;

(ii) consider ways of improving the industry's economic performance, competitive power and efficiency and formulate reports and recommendations on these matters as appropriate.

The first litter included chemicals and the distributive trades, most of the engineering industries, woollen textiles, paper and confectionery. To these were later added other industries, so that by 1967 twenty-one EDCs had been spawned which together covered four-fifths of the private sector labour force as well as the Post Office (the one state industry to be subsumed under the EDC framework).

On average the EDCs consisted of up to 18 members: 8 industrialists, 4 trade unionists, 2 independent members (usually academics or management consultants), a NEDO staff member, an official from the appropriate sponsoring ministry, a DEA representative, and an independent chairman from outside the industry; the EDC secretary was supplied from the NEDO staff. The EDC members were formally appointed by the director-general of the NEDC, though in practice the trade associations furnished him with lists of industrialists from which he made his selection; while the TUC – in consultation with the appropriate unions – nominated the union members. The chairmen were appointed after preliminary soundings had been taken with the relevant industries to see whether or not they would be acceptable. Ostensibly, the governing principle behind the appointment of the industrial members (who were seen as the key figures) was to try and secure the services of the most influential personalities from among the leading firms in each industry. Their endorsement, it was hoped, would legitimise the EDC in the eyes of its industry, and their contribution would help to galvanise the EDC into becoming a useful vehicle for planning and developing the fortunes of the industry. Whatever value their symbolic commitment may have had, their substantive contributions must, in general, have been fairly slight, given that the inroads into their time rarely exceeded three days a month. The real motive power for the EDCs was provided by the staff of the NEDO industrial division.

The NEDO industrial staff developed their own methods of 'stage management' for the EDCs, based on the principle of what might be called 'the parsimonious mobilisation of available resources'. Apart from the 'across-the-board exercises', in connection with such tasks as gathering data for the *National Plan* and the *Task Ahead* in which the NEDC required all EDCs to participate, the NEDO staff saw their job as encouraging certain tendencies and restraining others. Put baldly, this was to persuade the EDCs to concentrate on identifying the main problems of their industries and indicating possible solutions, and to refrain from overmuch lobbying of government on behalf of industry. As far as possible they sought to put the burden of eliciting data and views about industries' problems on to the relevant trade associations rather than providing special facilities for the purpose. And to this end they urged the rationalisation and consolidation of trade associations where it was felt that representation in an industry was too fragmented. From the NEDO point of view the ideal milieu for an EDC was an industry in which two or three efficient and representative trade associations were operating. Where an industry was dominated by a single trade association, as in the case of chemicals or electrical engineering, it became extremely difficult to prevent the EDC concerned from being an appendage of the trade association. At the other extreme, as evidenced by the distributive trades where some 150 trade associations operated, NEDO found it almost impossible to discover any expression of common interest; the distributive trades' EDC set about providing a central focus for the industry which eventually led to the formation of the Retail Consortium in 1967.

The NEDO staff's main instrument of stage management was by manipulating the role played by the EDC chairmen. Each chairman was a substantial industrialist in his own right and the NEDO staff sought to steer the direction of the EDC by operating through him. Before each EDC meeting they would brief the chairman on the items of agenda. At such briefings the relevant DEA industrial adviser (himself a businessman on secondment to the civil service) would be present together with the trade association and TUC officials who respectively serviced the industrial and union members of the EDC. Sometimes the independent members would also be in attendance. If necessary, prior to the chairman's briefing, the NEDO staff might have consulted with the trade association or TUC officials if it was felt desirable to try and present a common front on the part of the officials. By providing background material and presenting, where possible, a consensus of 'the back-room boys' the NEDO staff endeavoured to prevent the EDCs or their chairmen running off in all directions. In addition to these devices, undesirable diversity was restrained by quarterly plenary meetings between the EDC chairmen and the NEDC director-general, and by the creation of a steering group to coordinate liaison between the DEA and NEDO. Thus both above and below the level of the EDC members, as it were, a number of interlocking caucuses were established to keep the EDCs on the lines prescribed, in the main, by the NEDO staff. But while NEDO staff displayed considerable ingenuity in shepherding the activities of the EDCs on a day-to-day and month-to-month basis, they could not by themselves elaborate on the longer-term development of the EDCs. The demise of the National Plan in 1966 cut much of the ground from under the EDCs and this put an added premium on the technocratic pragmatism which underlay the NEDO stage management.

Even if the Plan had been persevered with, the EDC experiment would still have laboured under a number of difficulties. In the first place, little if any thought was given to the life-span of the EDCs. Were they to be of permanent or short duration, or were they to be assembled at periodic intervals to conduct an audit of the industry? In the event some, like those for chemicals, the distributive trades and most of the engineering ones, soldiered on; some, including the EDCs for knitwear, printing, building and civil engineering, broke up with varying degrees of acrimony; while others, such as those for rubber, paper and the Post Office, seemed to peter out. In the judgement of Tom Fraser – the NEDO industrial director – the main cause of these differential survival rates was a general lack of consistency on the part of government, coupled with 'the variability of departmental approach to the work of the EDCs'.

Secondly, there was the problem of securing effective communication between an EDC and the constituent firms in its industry. The circulation of published reports was universally undertaken, though not apparently universally read.[10] To facilitate communication three EDCs, those for chemicals, distributive trades and mechanical engineering, arranged conferences for their constituent firms. By mid-1967, however, a mood of disenchantment was detectable amongst industrialists, who complained of the amount of time being consumed by requests for information from official committees including the EDCs. Unilever took exception to answering a NEDO questionnaire on exports. In the following year some trade unions began to be disillusioned with the EDCs.

Thirdly, despite the formal rubric, tripartism – in the sense of equal participation – was, as in France, something of a sham. The trade unions did not have the same opportunities as the industrialists: on the EDCs their representation was half that of the industrialists; there were no trade unionists among the EDC chairmen; and only a handful of unionists were taken on to the NEDO staff. For the most part, the unions' position was largely of their own making, for they were reluctant to release their officials for duty either as chairmen or as seconded staff members – not as a matter of principle but because of their limited manpower; indeed, to judge from attendance records, they found it difficult enough to muster a full complement for the regular EDC meetings. The enthusiasts of tripartite indicative planning argue that the unions' attitude towards the EDCs was short-sighted and indicated the need for modernising them by enlarging their staffs and improving their research facilities. But such a view reveals more about the simple-minded evangelical zeal of the supporters of planning than it does about the nature of the unions' response to tripartism.

The zealots are the prisoners of their own rhetoric, drawing naive parallels between organised business and organised labour and ignoring the fundamental differences which exist between the two. To point to the initiating propensities of an efficient and well-organised trade association in contrast to the essentially defensive and reactive stance of a trade union is not to demonstrate that the latter should emulate the former; rather it is to define their intrinsic differences and also to expose a basic fallacy in the underlying assumptions of tripartism. Changes in the organisation and attitudes of trade unions, which would enable them to make a more positive contribution to such tripartite agencies as the EDCs, are more likely to come from creating a system of representation and communication up from the factory floor to the EDCs than from improving the facilities of union head offices.[11]

A further problem, and one endemic to EDC-type bodies, is that of sustaining the interest and commitment of participants over an extended period of time. It is complicated by the volatile and dynamic nature of the processes by which individuals seek to optimise their psychological gratification, and the effects these have on participant behaviour. Tripartism is based not only on the principle of equal contributions from the contracting parties (about which doubts were expressed above), but also on the assumption that the individual participants will maintain a fairly high level of enthusiasm and involvement during their term of membership. Graham Turner has suggested that the reasons why businessmen appear to be very willing to sit on official bodies, such as EDCs, include the relatively low status accorded to industry in Britain *vis à vis* public service and the related pursuit of titles; and doubtless these cultural factors assisted in the EDC recruitment process. There seems, on occasions, to be a detectable progression of gratification thresholds whereby businessmen who have achieved director status within their companies move on to participate in the affairs of trade associations, the CBI and official bodies: the business career, that is to say, can be seen as a pyramid of gratification thresholds extending well beyond the confines of a company or, for that matter, a number of companies (gratification, after all, can be sought laterally through amassing outside director-ships as it can be vertically through the acquisition of representational or official posts). For tripartism this is something by way of a bonus, for it helps to secure the services of the more achievement-oriented businessmen from the ranks of leading firms with a participatory tradition. But the drawback to this is that alternative and better sources of gratification can arise which may compete for the energies of such men. Arguably, the EDC experiment suffered from this kind of competition.

Initially, there seemed to be a mood of goodwill towards the experiment which later receded. Sir Arnold Weinstock's reactions illustrate the point being made: he was a member of the electrical engineering EDC for two years 'but then walked out because he could not see the point of the exercise', according to Turner.[12] Now the faltering pursuit and final demise of the National Plan may well have contributed to his decision, but of much greater significance surely was the fact that his company, GEC, was searching around for takeover possibilities, which led successively to the acquisition of AEI and later English Electric[13] (both, incidentally, with strong IRC support). Although Sir Arnold's merger activities were amongst the most spec-tacular they were hardly unique in a decade of which the latter half, especially, was characterised by an unprecedented spate of company mergers and takeovers. This unusually dynamic industrial and com-mercial milieu may well have diverted some of the time and attention on the part of top businessmen which might otherwise have been retained by bodies such as the EDCs. At least Weinstock resigned; how far the EDCs suffered from participants who reduced their commitment to token levels it is difficult to assess.

But neither the Weinstock example nor speculation about reduc-tion in commitment levels exhaust the permutations in the process of gratification 'trade off'. The relative attraction of the EDCs declined, not only in relation to that of the participants' own firms and industries, but also as a result of the competition of other planning agencies, most noticeably from the IRC. The switch in emphasis away from the EDCs towards the IRC as a major instrument of industrial policy was a consequence of abandoning the National Plan in 1966. This objective reality was most visibly mirrored, perhaps, by the appointment of Sir Frank Kearton and Sir Donald Stokes (now both ennobled) to the IRC board; both were also leading EDC participants.

The Industrial Reorganisation Corporation

The creation of the IRC, however, was not received with universal acclaim by industry. The board of ICI condemned it at the outset as an undesirable means of extending state interference and as being created 'to further the policy of the public ownership of the means of production which the government is committed to implement in one form or another'. Similarly, the CBI said it would watch to ensure that the government's proposals did not envisage nationalisation by the back door, while the Institute of Directors called it 'trap door nationalisation'.

The idea of the IRC was first publicised in January 1966 in a White Paper which had been formulated within the DEA. Its formal terms of reference were:

(a) to promote or assist the reorganisation or development of any industry; or

(b) if requested so to do by the Secretary of State, establish or develop, or promote or assist the establishment or development of, any industrial enterprise.

In particular, it was meant to encourage exports, reduce imports, and assist in the realisation of the government's regional policy for industry. To this end it was enjoined to consult with the City, industry and the relevant government departments (mainly the DEA, BoT and Min.Tech.) and agencies (the EDCs and the National Research and Development Council). The IRC board was to consist of a chairman and between seven and fourteen members, though in practice it did not exceed eleven members in all. They were drawn from the ranks of industrialists, merchant bankers, and included a lawyer and a trade unionist. Its staff was always kept below thirty, of whom about ten were executives. Whereas the board consisted of eminent figures, the full-time staff consisted of younger pioneers with a zest for modernisation; most of them were in their thirties. In accordance with the independent, free-ranging, entrepreneurial status and ethos of the IRC, they were not given titles: they were to survey the terrain and propose courses of action subject only to the collective wisdom of the board.

Its open-ended remit and the considerable freedom extended by the government made the precise role of the IRC difficult to define. Although the Italian IRI provided a kind of precedent as a governmental interventionist industrial agency, the IRC was explicitly not to be a state holding company on the Italian model. Nor, apparently, was it to be regarded as a state merchant bank. In its second report it declared:

IRC is not a banker, though on occasions its ability to deploy funds is crucial. It is not a holding company though the capacity to own shares for a limited period is essential. IRC's main job is to improve the international performance of our manufacturing industries by promoting structural reorganisation...IRC's client is the national interest where this is identifiable.

(IRC Report and Accounts 1968/69, pp. 7–8)

This kind of rhetoric was doubtless deemed necessary to allay the fears of those who suspected the IRC was an instrument of full-blooded socialism. By the time of its next report, however, the IRC felt bold enough to state:

An important area of IRC operations has been acting as *the government's merchant bank* in a range of assignments dealing with industrial/financial problems where there is an interface with government.

It also reported:

The board of IRC has more than a banker's responsibility in respect of its investments. It is not enough to know that an investment is secure. IRC must also concern itself with the purpose for which the investment was made...

(IRC Report and Accounts 1969/70, p. 12, author's italics)

Thus, whatever it was or was not, the banking model served as a kind of lodestone to determine whatever definitions were currently on offer. The activity it most approximated, perhaps, was that of a game of real-life *Monopoly* with an initial stake of £150 million provided by the government.

It began, like the PIB and some of the EDCs, by commissioning reports and surveys from outside experts and consultants, but soon became dissatisfied with them as a basis for action (though they may have helped to secure a greater measure of acceptance for the IRC). The IRC quickly came to the view that: 'There are already enough reports of industrial investigations collecting dust in neglected files.'[14] The IRC made extensive use of existing data but it relied in the main on the visits it made to companies and the discussions it had with management; within its first eighteen months it had committed about a third of its initial finance to projects in seven sectors of industry and had made confidential contacts with some four hundred other companies. In addition to taking soundings in the City, in industry and among government departments, the IRC also set up 'about half a dozen teams of only one or two men each, culled from top-level industrialists, merchant bankers and accountants, to try to solve specific bottlenecks to greater industrial efficiency.'[15] Two such teams looked at the heavy transformer industry and the telecommunications industry. Reflecting their parent body's remit, they were 'given the vaguest possible terms of reference'. Unlike EDCs and royal commissions, they had the advantage of acting quickly; they did not have to attempt to balance rival interests, and if their missions proved fruitless or their proposals were rejected, the secrecy with which they conducted their tasks would ensure that unfavourable publicity was avoided.

Apart from the annual reports it was required to present to parliament, the IRC cultivated its relations with Whitehall (which pressed it to finance the Rootes–Chrysler merger), with the City financial community which welcomed the IRC's activities (unlike the proposal for a City EDC which was successfully resisted for more than five years), with the TUC, with whom it initiated talks on redundancies and with the CBI. The IRC monitored its own operations either by appointing a director to the boards of companies in which it had invested, or by instituting a system of twice-yearly follow-up visits to recipient firms. In 1970, however, its chairman thought it would be another four or five years before an overall assessment could be made of the IRC's work. In the event, the IRC was not subjected to any stringent conditions of public accountability. It was exempted from the direct effects of the checks and balances of administrative pluralism by seeking BoT approval, at an early stage in any of its proposed schemes, thus avoiding possible reference to the Monopolies Commission.

At the end of its five years of existence – the Conservatives abolished it in 1971 – the IRC reported that it 'has been substantially involved in about 90 projects at least 75 of which are turning out as expected. Rolls Royce is a special case. The remainder, though labouring to some extent, are still operating in the direction intended.'[16] During its life it had weathered the resignation of its first managing director and another board member,[17] successfully reversed the initial hostility of the CBI, and had been emulated by the French IDI.

Government and industry in the early 1970s

With the return of the Conservatives to office in 1970, an abrupt change in industrial policy was announced. The new government intended to 'disengage' by reducing the depth and scale of government intervention in industry. Accordingly, the IRC was abolished (along with the PIB and the Consumers' Council) and the Industrial Expansion Act repealed. The new government hoped to increase the competitiveness of the economy by pursuing a more vigorous anti-monopolies policy and, above all, by refusing to 'subsidise incompetence' with government grants. In addition, industrial relations were to be reformed and brought more effectively within the framework of the law. If the Labour government had developed a technocratic style of administration, its successor appeared to prefer legalism and *laisser faire*. Within two years, however, the Conservatives performed a total *volte face*, similar in many respects to the one which resulted in them adopting indicative planning in 1961. The bankruptcies of Rolls Royce and Upper Clyde Shipbuilders in 1971 severely tested the government's avowed aim of refusing to bail out inefficient firms. Considerable American pressure in the case of Rolls Royce (because of its contracts to develop the RB 211 engine for the Lockheed Corporation, which was itself in financial difficulties), and the militant 'work in' tactics of the union shop stewards at UCS, were enough to break the government's resolve. This capitulation, coupled with continuing massive unemployment and a low rate of economic growth, led to a return to a policy of selective government intervention in industry.

The Industrial Act 1972 provided an unprecedented amount (£550 million) of public money for industrial development, particularly in the depressed regions, which was to be channelled through the Industrial Development Executive (IDE) – a resurrected IRC with regional offshoots. The IDE resembled the IRC in certain respects. Its staff was recruited on short-term secondment from the City and industry; and its work was to be assisted by an Industrial Development Advisory Board of nine members, drawn from the private sector, plus the customary trade unionist. The new machinery was to advise on the best means of stimulating industrial development and to supervise the allocation of government grants. But if there were obvious similarities with the IRC, there were also differences. In the first place, the IDE was located within a government ministry – the DTI – under its own minister. This, the government stressed, made it fully accountable, unlike the IRC. Secondly, the IDE was given its own outposts in the depressed regions (Scotland, Wales, Ulster, and the Northern, North-Western, South-Western and Yorkshire regions of England). The regional machinery replicated the central system: regional industrial-development directors were appointed along with regional advisory boards. Thirdly, a central development unit was set up, and manned by recruits from the City and industry, to identify the development needs of industry and to monitor the results of the IDE's work. But perhaps the most significant difference between the IRC and the IDE emerges from their approaches: the former identified its own priorities and frequently took the initiative; the latter has probably adopted a more passive stance, and has tended to wait for industry to come forward with its own suggestions for consideration. Industrialists have had to wait months for their applications for assistance to be processed by the IDE.

The Conservative emulation of their Labour predecessors was by no means exhausted by the creation of the IDE. In mid-1972 the government imposed a ninety-day freeze on incomes and prices and set up a Pay Board and Prices Commission which shared between them the functions performed by the defunct PIB. In the same year it introduced the Fair Trading Bill under which the policing of mergers and monopolies was further formally strengthened. Whether the machinery will be used any more than the minimal amount achieved by Labour is very doubtful, but the Bill broke new ground by making provision for an Office of Fair Trading to improve consumer protection. In the field of industrial relations, the government rapidly backpedalled, in the face of strong trade union antagonism, by not resorting to the National Industrial Relations Court which had been created in one of its first enactments; and the CIR, one of the few Labour inventions to survive the election, limped along busying itself with uncontentious matters.

Meanwhile, through all the dramatic changes in government policy, industry itself was reviewing its own situation regarding its relationship with government. If the EDC experiment had not achieved the results which had originally been expected, the need to formalise government and industry relations remained in the forefront of CBI thinking. Together with the Association of British Chambers of Commerce it appointed a commission, under the chairmanship of Lord Devlin, a former judge, to inquire into the state of industrial and commercial representation and make recommendations for improvement. The subsequent Devlin Report[18] proposed the formation of a single peak organisation to be called the Confederation of British Business (CBB). Its creation would come from an amalgamation of the CBI and ABCC, to which, it was hoped, other major representative bodies like the Retail Consortium and the Chamber of Shipping would belong. Apart from providing a single spokesman for industry and commerce, it was felt that a merger of the two would be complementary in that the CBI organisation was strong at the centre but weak in the regions, while the ABCC had a strong regional network but was weak at the centre. The report suggested a drastic reduction in the number of existing trade associations from over 2,000 to about 100; ideally it hoped to see the creation of one effective organisation at the top of each industry. The main idea behind the Devlin proposals was to bring about a hierarchical system of representation consisting of three tiers: the bottom end would consist of product associations; these would affiliate to their appropriate industry associations, which would comprise the middle level; and these, in turn, together with the largest companies, would affiliate to the new CBB. Small firms, it proposed, should be catered for by a separate Smaller Business Council which, like the Retail Consortium, would belong to the CBB.

The main policy-making function of the CBB would be vested in a Heads of Sector Council of about forty members.

In the event the ABCC accepted the Devlin proposals, but they were rejected by the CBI. What is particularly interesting to note, however, is that the motives behind the creation of the EDCs – and the adoption of planning in the 1960s – are the same as those which prompted the appointment of the Devlin committee, which guided its deliberations and shaped its conclusions. This is not surprising given some of the personnel involved: T. C. Fraser, the former industrial director of NEDO was secretary of the Devlin committee; Campbell Adamson, the current CBI director-general had previously been head of the DEA's industrial advisers; Michael Clapham, the 1972 CBI president had been a director of the IRC; while Alex Jarratt, chairman of the CBI's influential economic committee, was the first secretary of the PIB. George Brown's body may now be languishing in the House of Lords but his soul goes marching on.

NOTES

1 This paper is based partly on research which was supported by a grant from the Social Science Research Council and carried out for the Acton Society Trust.

2 In three acts: Distribution of Industry Act (Industrial Finance), 1958; the Local Employment Act, 1960; and the Local Employment Act, 1963.

3 *The Financial and Economic Obligations of the Nationalised Industries,* 1961 Cmnd. 1337.

4 *The Nationalised Industries: a review of economic and financial objectives,* 1967 Cmnd. 3437.

5 The reader is referred to the following works for detailed descriptions of recent policy: S. Brittan, *Steering the Economy,* rev. edn, 1970, chapters 6–10 and W. Beckerman (ed), *The Labour Government's Economic Record 1964–70,* 1972, chapters 5, 7 and 9.

6 Samuel Brittan, *ibid.* pp. 324–8, suggests that SET was also intended to act as a disguised export subsidy which would help to avert devaluation, as a means of spreading the tax wider to cover services, and to damp down consumer demand.

7 The Industrial Development Act (1966) re-arranged the system of development grants; REP was introduced in 1967; and grants for the 'grey' areas were announced in 1969. See 'Regional Policy' by J. Hardie in Beckerman (ed), *Labour Government's Economic Record.*

8 For a different view of the change in the Ministry of Labour, see Corina's comments p. 185 (Ed).

9 I draw heavily on Sir Richard Clarke, 'Min.Tech. in Retrospect', Parts 1 and 2, *Omega,* I, Nos. 1 and 2, 1973.

10 See 'Deaf ears for NEDO', *The Guardian,* 3 February 1971, which reported that eleven weeks after the circulation of a report on agricultural machinery to manufacturers 'half the top executives of these businesses appeared not to have heard of it and only a quarter had seen a copy'.

11 An elaborate and extended system of functional representation had been urged by G. D. H. Cole in the 1930s as a necessary requirement if economic planning was to be democratically responsive. See, in particular, his *The Machinery of Socialist Planning,* 1938.

   Soon after becoming prime minister, Harold Wilson flirted with the idea of creating joint production committees at factory level to parallel union–management consultation at EDC level.

12 Cf. Graham Turner, *Business in Britain,* rev. edn, 1971, p. 354.

13 Graham Turner, *ibid.* pp. 344–5.

14 IRC Report and Accounts 1968/69, p. 8; cf. Turner, p. 77.
15 This paragraph, including quotations, is based upon Richard Casement, 'IRC probes in secret', *The Times*, 28 March 1967.
16 IRC Report and Accounts 1970/71, p. 10.
17 Ronald Grierson resigned for 'personal reasons' apparently connected with his opposition to the Industrial Expansion Act 1967 which provided for state shareholdings in private sector firms. Sir Charles Wheeler, chairman of AEI, resigned in protest over IRC support for GEC's successful bid for AEI.
18 Report of the Commission of Inquiry into Industrial and Commercial Representation, ABCC/CBI, November 1972.

SELECT CRITICAL BIBLIOGRAPHY

Graham Turner, *Business in Britain*, Pelican 1971, provides a good journalistic account of the developments in British industry and commerce during the 1960s. Sir Richard Clarke has written a good insider's account of the origins and subsequent rise of the Ministry of Technology in 'Min.Tech. in Retrospect', Parts 1 and 2, *Omega*, I, Nos. 1 and 2, 1973. For a discussion of the formation of the CBI, see W. P. Grant and D. Marsh, 'The Confederation of British Industry', *Political Studies*, XIX, No. 4, 1971 and Stephen Blank, *Industry and Government in Britain. The Federation of British Industries in Politics, 1945–65*, Saxon House 1973. Edmund Dell's *Political Responsibility and Industry*, Allen and Unwin 1973, provides a former Labour government minister's assessment. For a comprehensive parliamentary review of the subject, see the Sixth Report from the Expenditure Committee, *Public Money in the Private Sector*, H.C. 347 of 1971–1972, HMSO. More generally, see Stephen Young (with A. V. Lowe), *Intervention in the Mixed Economy. The Evolution of British Industrial Policy 1964–72*, Croom Helm 1974, of which Part 2 is devoted to the IRC.

6. Italian industrial policy in the framework of economic planning

GIOACHINO FRAENKEL

The background

Planning policy was adopted in Italy with the deliberate purpose of imparting to public action a more homogeneous and integrated character and in order to bring about a more efficient and extensive coordination of all forces which contribute to social progress. In particular, planning policy was designed to solve satisfactorily a set of basic problems of the national economy, stemming from the fast industrialisation process, from the manpower migration away from the farms and persistent high rates of structural unemployment, from the increasing demand for social infrastructures (such as schools, hospitals, low-cost housing, sports facilities, public transport), from the modernisation of agriculture and so forth.

This policy has had to deal with political, social, economic and administrative structures strongly attached and responsive to specific practical problems. Because it has not brought about changes in these structures it has been frustrated by their general resistance to all pressures from the outside. This has been the overriding factor conditioning the working of planning policy, both in its approaches and in its achievements. To arrive at a correct analysis and assessment of Italian industrial planning, we must first consider the background against which planning developed.

In the first place, in Italy the political will to formulate a medium-term economic policy was expressed by the parliamentary majority as late as 1962 when the Centrist coalition was replaced by the Centre-Left.[1] The new majority, however, while numerically secure, was internally torn by a multiplicity of ideological positions, some profoundly different, which resulted in a lack of consistency and cohesion. In particular, while there was broad agreement on the need to make planning an instrument for the rationalisation of the system, there was disagreement over the desirability of making it also responsible for changing the system itself. In consequence the formulation of a planning document met with many persistent difficulties: the first outline of a five-year (1964–8) economic plan was not approved by parliament, and Italy's first National Economic Plan – covering the period 1966–70 – was not officially approved until July 1967.

Furthermore, a serious economic recession developed in 1963 and 1964. Some of the measures adopted by the new Centre-Left government, in particular the nationalisation of electricity and repeated threats of similar actions, ended by discouraging saving and investment. Thus, in those years, the growth of the Italian economy suffered its first serious setback since the end of the Second World War. In this climate of political tension and economic difficulties the solution of the country's real problems was necessarily delayed. To reverse the unfavourable economic trends and restart the growth mechanism, the government adopted in 1964 emergency measures cast in the form of law-decrees. This was the first recourse to such emergency economic measures which in the late sixties were used with increasing frequency, even though in the meantime a five-year National Economic Plan had come into existence which should have made it unnecessary to resort to short-term improvisations.

Finally, the administrative machinery of central government showed its inability to implement legislative decisions. Italian public administration still reflects the strongly centralised and bureaucratised concepts of the 1865 legislation on administrative unification. Since that time, far from the system being modernised, it has become increasingly ponderous and fragmented. The very creation of the planning bodies has resulted in an expansion of the administration without increasing its flexibility.

In the 1960s, the autonomy of the political, socio-economic and administrative forces *vis-à-vis* the planning authorities seriously hampered the latters' action, as the results of the planning policy showed. Indeed, as the planners themselves have admitted, these results were rather insubstantial and fell short of what had been expected of the planning policy. Bearing this in mind, we shall consider briefly the guidelines of industrial policy laid down by the First National Economic Plan, the structure and instruments of industrial policy-making and planning, the reactions of the main socio-economic groups to the industrial planning-oriented policy and, finally, the procedures for industrial policy implementation in the Italian economy. We end by making a brief evaluation of the planning policy's impact on industrial policy and how planning activity may be adapted to suit the Italian context more appropriately.

The objectives of industrial policy

In the fifties the climate of economic policy in general, and of industrial policy in particular, was permissive, characterised by a pragmatism which, even though sometimes apt to lead to improvisation, enabled the government to avoid trying to impose unrealistic ideological principles. However, even during the fifties, but above all later, this pragmatism was sharply criticised on the grounds that it reflected an *absence* of any kind of economic policy and, in particular, of industrial policy. These criticisms reflected the familiar contention that any industrial policy is worthy of that name only if firmly framed in an ideology, and if it reserves for the state strong powers of intervention, guidance, choice, control and regulation. It should be recognised, however, that at least in the Italian case, such assertions proved to be on the whole erroneous. Not only was there striking qualitative and quantitative progress by industry in the fifties; in addition two basic choices were made, which have had and still have an impact on Italy's industrial development: the renunciation of protectionism (which in practice resulted not only in trade liberalisation but above all participation in the European integration process) and the start of industrialisation in the country's depressed areas. These policies, no matter how questionable, have ultimately prevailed, as evidenced by the fact that the planning policy had the purpose, even if not the effect, of harnessing industrial policy into predetermined and rigid patterns.

A review of the industrial policy guidelines set forth in the First National Economic Plan suggests that it proposed a whole series of actions designed to strengthen, directly and indirectly, the industrial structure from the viewpoints of efficiency, competitiveness and financial soundness. As regards efficiency, the proposals concerned first of all the actions designed to develop the external economies of production through an improvement of economic and social infrastructures. Provision was also made for measures aimed at the improvement of the competitiveness of the enterprises on the domestic and foreign markets. In this area, mention should be made of the Plan proposals designed to encourage – through mergers – the formation of adequate corporate structures. This objective, however, was to be reconciled with the need to safeguard competition on the domestic market, preventing the occurrence of distortions caused by the emergence of monopolistic and oligopolistic positions. The Plan's proposals concerning the smaller enterprises also fit into the framework of this effort to stimulate the competitiveness of enterprises by inducing them to optimise the size of their structures. The Plan calls for 'vigorous' action in support of these enterprises by the public powers, in recognition of the substantial efforts which they had to make to adjust their productive and organisational structures to current economic conditions, particularly since the abolition of customs barriers within the EEC.

The planning document also took into account the problems created by the 'challenge of technological progress'. It made the state responsible for providing an adequate 'technical assistance service concerned with making all industrial enterprises share the results of research' and financially supporting industrial research through a suitable policy of tax and financial incentives. The declared purpose of these actions was to increase industrial productivity and strengthen business by encouraging the development of advanced and high-technology enterprises in the context of a general research policy. The Plan also called for the establishment of a Department of Scientific and Technological Research to 'play a planning, coordination and promotion role in this sector'. These objectives, of course, could not be achieved without an adequate measure of financial support. In dealing with this subject, the Plan laid down the principle that public authorities would have to be concerned with 'ensuring an adequate capital flow into investment programs and providing financing in such forms and ways as to ensure a high degree of corporate financial stability'. This would necessitate a reform of the system of social insurance and of the taxation system, two reforms that were presented as urgent necessities to make these claims on business resources more consonant with the needs of a modern economy.

It must be said, however, that in the planning document the problems raised by public action for the promotion of industrial activity were dealt with piecemeal. Even though there was a chapter on industrial policy, part of the basic guidelines came, directly or indirectly, from other parts of the document (Southern Italy, energy, transport, public works, scientific research, vocational training). This disjointed treatment affected industrial policy as it took shape in the five years covered by the 1966–70 National Economic Plan. It undermined, at least in part, the supposedly unitary approach adopted towards the problems.

The structures and instruments of industrial policy-making and planning

The advent of planning induced profound changes among the government bodies responsible for formulating and implementing the guidelines of economic policy in general and of industrial policy in particular. Prior to planning, the decisions concerning industry were made, apart from parliament, by the various ministers (of industry, state holdings, public works, etc). On major decisions, opinions were obtained from the functionally representative National Economic and Labour Council (CNEL), the only body institutionally responsible for advising parliament and the executive on economic and social matters. However, in addition, certain ministers, and in particular the minister of industry, have obtained the advice of business and professional experts on specific problems.

With the advent of planning there were no significant changes in the areas of parliamentary decisions and of consultative functions. Negligible practical effects followed from the only noteworthy innovation: that concerning the 'fact-finding hearings' which the parliamentary committees on industry have held on several occasions with the industrial associations, the unions and representatives of individual concerns. Of major importance, however, were the innovations in the government's decision-making processes. A new institutional system was created, in which responsibility for industrial policy decisions was assigned to the new planning bodies. Although the latter are examined in greater detail elsewhere,[2] they must be touched on here because of their importance and major relevance to the framing of industrial policy.

In this connection, mention should be made of the Interministerial Economic Planning Committee (CIPE), created by Law No. 48 of 27 February 1967, even before the planning policy was given official sanction by parliament with the passing of Law No. 685 of 27 July 1967, approving the First National Economic Plan. CIPE, charged with laying down the guidelines of national economic policy and giving directives for the formulation of the subsequent National Economic Plans and other planning documents, is therefore also the main governmental decision-making body in the industrial planning area. CIPE is chaired by the prime minister, with the minister of the budget and economic planning serving as deputy chairman. Its *ex officio* members include the ministers having jurisdiction in the area of industrial policy (industry and state holdings, particularly). In the performance of its functions, CIPE utilises the documentation made available by the Budget and Economic Planning Ministry, prepared either under the direction of the secretary of planning or by the ministry itself, as well as by the Economic Planning Institute (ISPE). These papers also cover the industrial policy guidelines, both general policy and in relation to specific issues. An advisory function on various subjects is performed by the expert Technical-Scientific Committee on Economic Planning.

These institutions at the national level have their counterpart at the regional level. When the Ordinary Charter regions[3] were still at the formative stage, the Economic Planning Committees had been established, charged with surveying the regions' economic structures and formulating a set of guidelines for their economic development and consequently for their industrial structures. Industry was represented on these committees. Once the regions started working, these committees were dissolved and the regional executives assumed responsibility for the economic policy decisions within their jurisdiction. The law establishing CIPE also created the Interregional Consultative Committee to harmonise the policies adopted on the central and regional levels. The general consensus is that, with the creation of the Ordinary Charter regions, a solution to the problems raised by central–regional tension is well underway. Industrial policy problems, however, are touched upon only indirectly by the new institutional arrangements, because under the Italian constitution such matters still fall within the jurisdiction of the central government.

In the 1966–70 National Economic Plan, provision is made for a set of action instruments to be used in pursuing the Plan's objectives. The Plan imposes specific obligations on the ministries and public enterprises. The Plan respects the freedom of action by private enterprise and therefore relies on its voluntary cooperation. Government intervention assumes various forms: it can directly influence business decisions by steering them in certain directions (for instance, through incentives), or it may directly promote reciprocal consultation and negotiation. This lays the foundation upon which can be developed a non-hierarchical cooperative relationship between public and private planning, respecting their individual areas of independent and discretionary decision-making.

As far as firms in which the state has a controlling shareholding (such as IRI, ENI) or public corporations such as the National Electric Power Agency (ENEL) are concerned, they fit into the planning picture with specific operational tasks that are politically determined. The 1966–70 National Economic Plan, for instance, lays down that such enterprises shall develop their activities in the basic and service sectors, in manufacturing, in sectors involving a high degree of technological innovation, in Southern Italy and so on. It is worth mentioning in this context that the law imposed on the state enterprises certain minimum levels of investment in the South, specifically 60 % of all new plants and in any case not less than 40 % of their total investments. (In 1971 these rates were increased to 80 % and 60 % respectively.) It should also be noted that special procedures are prescribed to harmonise the activities of the state enterprises with the Plan's industrial policy guidelines. In particular, they are required to obtain CIPE's approval for their investment plans. Nevertheless, notwithstanding such procedures, the norms have not always been respected. Cases have in fact been established where the mixed-capital firms – with the evident agreement of the minister of state holdings – have not complied with the obligations imposed upon them. The prescribed percentages of investment in the Mezzogiorno by state enterprises have been achieved only sporadically.

The only real innovation in the relations between government and industry that has come out of adopting a planning policy is the procedure of 'planned bargaining'. Such a procedure, introduced in early 1968, is intended to establish a constructive dialogue between state and industry with the aim of examining and harmonising their respective programmes of action. It consists, in particular, of an exchange of information between the government and industry on their respective investment plans, so that their projects can be effectively harmonised. This arrangement, in theory at least, should be based largely on considerations of economic rationality, and geared towards the best utilisation of the available resources.

The planned bargaining procedure is based on the provisions of a Bill, introduced in February 1967 but never passed, on economic planning regulations. It provided that:

Corporations whose shares are listed in the Stock Exchange, their controlling corporations as well as Government-controlled corporations and public utility concessionary companies, and in any case all incorporated companies whose capital stock amounts to not less than five billion [milliards] Lire, shall be required to supply to the Budget and Economic Planning Ministry such information as may be required of them for economic planning purposes with respect to their investment programs and the related sources of financing.

Even though the Bill never became law, the government chose to go ahead with this consultative procedure. Its main objective was to promote an exchange of information on corporate plans for investments in the South and on the programmes planned in that area by the ministries. The purpose is to facilitate – through a timely provision of the infrastructures required and a more flexible operation of the incentive system – the implementation of integrated schemes of industrial investment, suitably proportioned and concentrated in the sectors and areas which both sides feel to be susceptible to effective development.

To implement the planned bargaining consultation programme, the government set up, within CIPE, a smaller ministerial committee to supervise such consultations and a technical committee of officials, formed by representatives of the respective ministries, to maintain direct contact with the enterprises. It was also announced that this planned bargaining method would not be limited to the major firms but would also extend to smaller ones. To this end, an Institute operating under the Cassa per il Mezzogiorno (Southern Italy Development

Fund) was to identify, with the cooperation of industrial associations, the smaller firms which are capable of being coordinated and forming organic investment systems, to which the planned bargaining procedures would be applied.

The main socio-economic groups and 'planning-oriented' industrial policy

The reactions of the main socio-economic forces to the introduction of planning were divergent and have shown over time a gradual critical change in the initial positions. When the first National Economic Plan was being drafted, the representatives of business had been very critical of it as they could not ignore the fact that the document had come into being in an atmosphere of marked hostility to the logic of neocapitalism. The Plan had become for the majority political parties a sort of end in itself, rather than a mere instrument of harmonisation and coordination. Criticisms from the business world did induce the political parties in power to make some revisions, and this in turn caused industry to tone down its critical attitudes considerably. As a matter of fact, the 1966–70 Plan's discussion of industrial policy shows that the planners:

(a) were fully aware of the most serious difficulties which Italian industry was facing in its struggle for survival and growth or which it would be facing in the medium term;

(b) were clear-minded enough in indicating the most effective ways and means to deal satisfactorily with such difficulties;

(c) showed clear indications – in outlining such ways and means – of their intent to move along classic and tested roads, those that had permitted Italy's fast and extensive growth of the fifties, naturally corrected and supplemented in the light of the subsequent development of the domestic and international markets.

For their part, the Marxist-inspired unions and, more generally, the forces of the extreme Left, which at first had strongly supported the moves for the adoption of a planning policy, ultimately rejected the Plan when they realised that, in its successive formulations, stress had increasingly shifted from the rejection of the existing system towards its simple rationalisation.

Finally, the civil service experts responsible for the drafting of the Plan clearly revealed the government machine's inexperience and its inability to come to grips with an integrated and consistent medium-term economic policy. The very political and administrative bodies responsible for the formulation of the planning policies have failed to promote the harmonisation process and to establish satisfactory and productive relations with the business organisations and unions. In the period considered, only two government–industry–labour conferences were held (on the problems of employment in general and female employment in particular and, therefore, indirectly on industrial development), while bilateral contacts on particular industrial problems were of a desultory and non-institutional nature, becoming more frequent and practical only during the drafting of the Second Five-Year Plan for 1971–5.

Furthermore, very little attention was paid to the task of informing the social partners about the industrial policy objectives pursued by the government and the related decisions by the planning bodies which, in fact, adopted extremely secretive working methods. In particular, as far as the planned bargaining method is concerned, the announcement of this innovation got a mixed reaction in industrial circles. Some enterprises indicated approval in principle, hoping that the method might prove effective in solving the old problem of coordinating industrial plans and projects with public provision of associated infrastructures. Others, on the contrary, sharply criticised this approach from the very beginning, arguing that it would delay rather than accelerate investment in the South; that it would encourage corrupt practices whereby financial contributions were exchanged for favourable political decisions rather than recognising rights under the existing laws, which would leave no room for discretion by the authorities; that it would further weaken the position of smaller enterprises *vis-à-vis* the big ones and make their survival even more precarious. In any event, despite the perplexities created by the planned bargaining method and in view of the limited and questionable results that it has produced, it was ultimately accepted – at least tacitly – by the industrial organisations. This clearly indicates that the parties concerned, the large firms and the government, have come to see in it more benefits than pitfalls. On the other hand, from the standpoint of planning technique, it cannot be denied that the experience deriving from this new method has proved very useful in starting joint working groups of planning bodies and enterprises, and in studying how to undertake specific programmes of sectoral industrial policy, which were initiated in the latter part of the 1966–70 period and which formed an integral part of the Second National Economic Plan for 1971–5.

The outcome of the planning policy

Industrial planning policy has fallen far short of its chosen objectives. In particular, its adoption failed to give a new dimension to public action consistent with that aimed at by planning itself – the strengthening of industrial structures. The causes are to be found mainly in the political and administrative spheres. The Plan approved by parliament was the product of a disparate set of ideas, which did not fix any scale of priority for the things to be done in the five years with the estimated resources available. It gave no indication of the operational instruments to be used in implementation. It did not make clear for whom and to what extent its standards were to be regarded as either binding or purely indicative.

The implementation of the principles set forth in the Plan has largely remained in the realm of pious hopes. This was due to the lack of a firm political will, as shown in the following examples. There has been no reform of the social security system with a view to lightening the burden imposed on industry by social security contributions (among the heaviest in Europe). Although approved in 1971, tax reform has still not been applied, so businesses have continued to labour under an extremely complicated, burdensome and obsolete taxation system. No new measures, other than those existing prior to the Plan, have been adopted to promote the export of Italian products, especially by the smaller firms. No restoration has been achieved of the basic financial equilibrium of firms, in particular a correct balance between self-financing and borrowing. This latter failure is particularly serious, since many experts feel that it was one of the decisive causes of the rapidly accelerating deterioration of Italian industrial structures during the late sixties and the early seventies. In this period industry has seen the source of self-financing practically dry up, while access to the stock market has been precluded because the cost of money thus raised is higher than that of other sources of financing, and because public and quasi-public agencies have drained off most of the available resources, in flagrant contradiction to the provisions of the Plan.

By the end of the period covered by the First Economic Plan the support to technological research in industry, which was to be one of the cornerstones in the industrial structural policy, had proceeded no farther than a single measure concerning research loans. In addition, in various schemes within the framework of medium-term industrial policy, the civil service had either taken no practical action or acted so tardily as to make such schemes ineffectual. In public finance, this state of affairs has resulted in the so-called 'carryovers', i.e. a widening gap between public investment budget appropriations and actual spending by the end of the fiscal year. The main reason for such shortcomings is that since the political adoption of the planning policy, the necessary consequences have not been fully drawn by the government and administration, as is confirmed by the following examples. The establishment of CIPE did not result in the simultaneous dissolution of all the other longstanding ministerial committees whose activities have a major impact on industrial policy (credit and savings, South and depressed areas of the Centre-North, prices). No action was taken to harmonise the activities of ISPE with the traditional ones of particular ministries, which has led to friction, delay and work duplication. Nothing was done to reorganise the traditional ministries and controlling administrative bodies on a modern and efficient basis or to set up new ministries (e.g. one for scientific and technological research, even though its establishment was envisaged in the Plan) or to transfer traditional administrative responsibilities to new organisations of an entrepreneurial type. Many industrial policy schemes of a general, sectoral or territorial nature therefore ended up by being entrusted to government-controlled corporations or state holdings.

In particular, the provision of public services planned to improve the external economies of industrial firms took place only in the sectors entrusted to government-controlled corporations or similar bodies (e.g. ENEL), while it was utterly inadequate in the areas of responsibility of central and local government, resulting in a volume of infrastructure provision far short of that envisaged in the Plan. The unsatisfactory performance of the government agencies was admitted by the planning bodies themselves. For instance, the Forecasting and Planning Report for the year 1969 states that the percentages of social programme fulfilment during the first three years (1966–8) were as low as 11% for urban transport, 16% for hospital building, 22% for school building. Only in three sectors did they exceed 50%: public health, land reclamation and telecommunications. The same report also complained that the time elapsing between the enactment of a law calling for the provision of infrastructural projects and their actual implementation averaged 500 days and could be as long as 900 days. Yet another example of bureaucratic slowness is provided by the procedures for the establishment of an industrial area consortium in the South. These include checking minimum requirements by the Committee of Ministers for the South, approval of the rules and publication of the relevant presidential decree, approval of the master plan of the consortium, and normally take at least four years.

As for the major firms in which the state has a controlling interest (such as IRI and ENI) it must be said that there have been cases in which these organisations, obviously with the concurrence of their minister, have failed to carry out certain specific obligations imposed on them. For instance, only in a few sectors have the percentages of investment in the South been respected. A flagrant case of violation by a state corporation of the 1966–70 National Economic Plan is the use of the Alfasud plant at Pomigliano d'Arco to build medium-size passenger cars, while under the Plan it should be making diesel engines and commercial vehicles.

In other aspects of industrial policy planning the results have also been largely unsatisfactory. The technical committee charged with promoting planned bargaining has operated largely in a perfunctory manner. There have been cases of consultation with large-scale industry, but there is no doubt that several investment programmes have been seriously delayed while waiting for the conclusion of these consultations. Furthermore, even though the industrial associations have helped by reporting all the lesser projects of which they are aware, the method has proved a complete failure with respect to small and medium enterprises, thus creating among the latter further causes of frustration due to a feeling of being excluded from all participation in the country's industrial strategies.

An appraisal of the results of the first planning experiment leads to the conclusion that it failed to achieve to any material extent the goals for which it had been adopted. Failing to take into sufficient account the resistance of certain forces and the excessive vitality of certain others, planning has not succeeded in harnessing the multitude of drives and pressures and in channelling them towards agreed goals, merging them into a single overall planned design. Should we then conclude that all of these experiences were entirely negative? Certainly not. They produced a wealth of clear and specific indications as to how Italian planning should *not* be set up. It should not be too far removed from Italian reality, not too vague, not too ambitious for the real possibilities of consensus and achievement. The new National Plan being drafted takes into account, at least in part, such considerations, and seeks to steer clear of the pitfalls encountered by the First National Economic Plan.

NOTES

1 The Centrist majority was composed of Christian Democrats, Social Democrats, Republicans and Liberals. The Centre-Left majority substituted the Socialists for the Liberals.

2 See G. Pasquino and U. Pecchini, pp. 77–80 above.

3 In some of the Special Charter regions (Sicily, Sardinia and Friuli–Venezia Giulia), *ad hoc* bodies have been formed to formulate the medium-term economic policy guidelines.

SELECT BIBLIOGRAPHY

Di Fenizio, F. *La programmazione economica*, Utet, Turin 1965.

Forti, G. B. *Appunti per una storia della programmazione in Italia*, Biblioteca della liberta, No. 36, January–February 1972.

Holland, S. (ed), *The State as Entrepreneur*, Weidenfeld and Nicolson, London 1972.

Ministero del Bilancio e della Programmazione economica, *Programma di sviluppo economico per il quinquennio 1966–70*, Instituto Poligrafico dello Stato, Rome 1967.

  La programmazione economica in Italia, Rome 1967.

Saraceno, D. 'Il programma quinquennale non è forse uno strumento superato?', *Mondo economico*, 22 November 1969.

  'La formazione del programma alla luce dell'analisi dei sistemi', *Mondo economico*, 17 January 1970.

7. A comparison of the industrial experiences

STEPHEN YOUNG

Industrial planning or policies for industry?

A comparative discussion of the different industrial experiences of Britain, France and Italy must recognise the existence of a clear distinction between 'industrial planning' and 'industrial policies'. The use of the word planning, on the one hand, implies the establishment of objectives, the creation of means of achieving them, and the implementation of an integrated programme covering inputs that affect the development of sectors such as manpower and investment policies. Industrial policy, on the other hand, is a much wider term including, for example, a swift response to events and the uncoordinated implementation of policies related to very specific fields like training or exports. It also covers the implementation of measures with much less definite aims than is the case with industrial planning.

The three national chapters show clearly that in the 1960s there have been five main types of policies and plans formulated by governments to affect public and private industry. Firstly, there have been attempts at national economic planning. Secondly, there has been the continuing process of altering the legal framework within which firms operate, in such spheres as company law, patents and competition. Thirdly, there have been occasions when governments have had to respond to what might be termed unexpected crises. The rapid escalation of expenditure on a development programme in which the state is heavily involved, a major bankruptcy or a takeover bid for an important firm are the most frequent examples. Fourthly, governments have tried to develop programmes covering problems that are dealt with elsewhere, such as manpower and regional policies, involving subjects within the field of industrial policy, like exports, research and development, or the advisory services identified below. Finally, there have been policies or plans designed to identify obstacles to growth or to restructure individual industrial sectors such as computers or shipbuilding. In this field, the French adopted policies developed by the British for their own use. In the 1960s in all three countries, the emphasis in practice was on largely uncoordinated policies for industrial problems rather than on industrial planning.

Government action to change the legal framework within which firms operated comes within the sphere of industrial policy, but it has been divorced from industrial planning as such. Although changing the law on competition policy would involve the establishment of objectives and the creation of means of achieving them, the implementation would, by contrast with active intervention of the type associated with, for example, a merger promotion policy, be a passive process with the scope for initiative lying entirely with the firm. With regard to a crisis, its very unexpectedness has meant that a government's response was unplanned in the sense that it was forced to react to events rather than take the initiative and implement policies to achieve a previously decided aim. Only in rare cases did governments have a plan ready which could be made to accommodate a crisis when it came.

It is with the last two types of measure that the possibility of referring to industrial planning *per se* arises. With programmes to encourage different patterns of research and development, exports, capital investment or training at the level of the firm, objectives were established and the means of achieving them were drawn up. Because the initiative in these matters lay with the firms, the extent to which plans were implemented was both varied and limited. Lastly, governments have frequently singled out individual industries for attention. The criteria used to pick them out, the establishment of objectives for the desired development of those industries, and the preparation of means of achieving those aims all involved planning. In the case of such sectoral programmes, however, industrial planning went further than with other types of industrial policy-making in that governments took more extensive steps with regard to policy integration and active implementation.

The overall emphasis of measures for industry was thus placed on policies for industry rather than on industrial planning. Comprehensive coordination of policies and programmes was largely absent. It is only with regard to the final type of measure, and to some extent with the fourth, that the phrase 'industrial planning' is relevant. However, this does not mean that all measures for individual industries were part of coherent sectoral plans. Governments frequently developed links with individual firms in an *ad hoc* fashion, especially where the proposal for government support came from the firms or where sectoral plans broke down. Nor was there industrial planning in the wide sense that governments implemented schemes to alter the way available resources were distributed between sectors. In practice, where government decisions affected the expansion of one sector or the contraction of another, such decisions were taken on an *ad hoc* basis.

The pattern of industrial policy

Attempts at industrial planning in the 1960s have to be seen against the previous experiences of the three countries emphasised in the national chapters. Despite increased state intervention in Britain in the 1930s and 1940s, governments during the 1950s had concentrated on providing a favourable climate in which industry could run its own affairs. By contrast, in France the tradition of a strong centralised state, involved to varying degrees with the affairs of industry and with an expanding public sector, went back at least as far as the seventeenth century. In the 1950s there was no denationalisation, and the development of indicative planning meant that the state became more involved, in an active and positive rather than negative and regulatory sense, with the private sector. Italian governments were closely connected with the private sector before the rapid expansion of the public sector began in the 1930s. As a result of this, and of the unemployment problems of the Mezzogiorno, great stress has since been laid on developing a large public sector which in turn has helped create many new, autonomous enterprises. These different traditions exerted a strong influence on the nature of industrial policy in the three countries and, to some extent, the manner in which the entrepreneurs behaved. They also help explain the divergent experiences of the three countries in the 1960s. In Britain, and to a certain extent in France, attempts were made to put a greater proportion of the available public funds into private industry, rather than into the public sector, while in Italy emphasis has continued to be laid on the expansion of the public sector. Of the three countries, France, under de Gaulle's influence, probably laid the most stress on prestige projects, whether in the public or private sectors, as with the development of an independent colour TV system and the magnox reactors.

During the first half of the 1960s in France and Britain, and during the second half of the decade in France and Italy, the results of national economic planning measured against the original targets proved disappointing. What emerged was the partial implementation of some sectoral plans rather than the application of a comprehensive set of programmes. With shipbuilding and fuel in France, computers and nuclear power construction in Britain and chemicals and electronics in Italy, plans were drawn up and in varying degrees implemented. However, these are comparatively isolated examples. All the national papers show how the authorities permitted deviations from the plans, sometimes – as with CIPE – very extensive ones. The nature of the relationship between national economic planning and sectoral planning changed during the 1960s. Initially, sectoral planning was seen in Britain and France as a means of implementing national economic plans. However, what emerged in Britain after July 1966 and in France during the Fifth Plan, and particularly after the Industrial Development Committee report, was the approach that had been present from the start of the decade in Italy. Governments in all three countries began to develop detailed policies for individual sectors that were not related or were only loosely related to wider national economic plans. By the end of the decade, it was clear that trying to implement detailed programmes for individual sectors had become an end in itself and not a means of implementing a wider national economic plan. This was clearly the case in Britain, and in Italy and France to the extent that some sectoral plans deviated from national plans.

In all three countries the development of sectoral programmes led to two main approaches being adopted towards the private sector. In Britain and France and to some extent in Italy, this was based on experience which, it was felt, showed that for all the efforts of governments, firms were still able to resist measures designed to make them behave in new ways. These two approaches were outside the economic and legal framework which governments had traditionally sought to provide. As the French experience shows, policies within that framework were generally more interventionist in the sense that the firm's freedom of action was more restricted. The most important approach was selective intervention. Governments channelled public funds to picked firms within previously selected industries. The outcome was the forging of direct links between the government or its agents and individual companies on what was, in Britain and Italy but not so much in France, an unprecedented scale. Whether the initiative came from the state or the firm, the state's purpose was always to provide finance so that events took a different course than they would have done if market forces had held sway. Examples include support for development in high technology industries like aerospace or computers, measures to induce rationalisation in industries like ship-building that suffered from overcapacity, and finance to speed up the reorganisation following a merger or for a capital investment project. Governments in Britain and Italy were more ready to rescue firms that were liable to go bankrupt for the social reason of saving jobs in poten-tially non-viable enterprises. In such circumstances French govern-ments applied more strictly economic criteria. The extent to which resources were allocated between expanding and contracting indus-tries differed between the three countries. Selective intervention was used both to keep multinationals out of key sectors and to develop national champions in key industries, especially in France where this policy was pursued more singlemindedly than elsewhere. In Italy the public sector was more commonly the vehicle for developing national champions, opposing multinationals and averting bankruptcies. How far the application of sectoral programmes can be described as industrial planning varies according to the extent to which governments were able to implement programmes. Often it was a case of isolated links with only a few of the firms in an industry.

The second main approach was to provide a range of advisory services and inducements on a variety of subjects stretching from research through investment and production to training and marketing. The aim was again to encourage firms to pursue new lines of action. Thus they were exhorted, for example, to make or install advanced equipment, to spend more money on research and development, to pay more attention to retraining and to relocate in the less prosperous areas. Much of the work of the French modernisation commissions and the British EDCs falls into this category. In Britain, because of the continuing importance of the balance of payments, successive governments sought to encourage industry to export more and to adopt more sophisticated overseas marketing operations. Such services had been widely available in France in the 1950s. In Britain and Italy, a great deal of government-inspired energy was devoted in the 1960s to following the French approach. Selective intervention was thus firmly based on the less discriminatory policy of providing a range of advisory services and inducements.

As regards policies towards the public sector, the French and British experiences had more in common than the Italian. In both France and Britain limited expansion took place mainly in public utilities, and repeated efforts were made to increase managerial autonomy, to promote efficiency, and to prevent regular financial losses. In Italy, by contrast, similar attempts had an extremely limited impact for most of the decade. Although there was some important indigenous expansion, the public sector, in line with historical tradition, was frequently used to rescue firms from bankruptcy. The distinction between the public and private sectors became increasingly hard to define. The nature of the state's financial involvement in British industry widened to include a range of minority equity holdings outside the nationalised sector. The latter was based on total ownership or majority shareholdings. Minority holdings ranged in size from the 10 % taken when The Nuclear Power Group was formed in Britain up to 47 % with the Ulster shipbuilders Harland and Wolff. Similar joint ventures between public and private enterprise took place in Italy and France, as for example in computers. Most of such public investments were meant to be permanent, although the IRC holdings in Britain were designed to be temporary. A connected change that further blurred the distinction was the increased involvement of private capital in public enterprise in France. In Britain this trend took the form of very limited denationalisation in the early 1970s, while in Italy market sources provided a decreasing share of public sector finance. For our purposes these minority holdings are regarded as being in the private sector.

The basis of government policy towards the private sector in all three countries has been to adapt capitalism to the context of the mixed economy by developing increasingly detailed policies. In doing this governments have been responding to the intensification of international trading conditions, both inside and outside the EEC, the expansion of highly competitive multinational enterprise and the bluntness of their macro-economic policies. They have worked on the basis of the market, of the profit motive and, in the overwhelming majority of cases, of firms that obtained most if not all their funds from internal or market sources rather than from the state. Governments have taken action designed to overrule or accelerate market forces in order to correct emerging imbalances. They have been prepared to intervene to subsidise jobs and where the market mechanism has not been sufficiently powerful to ensure that the industrial structure was adapted to meet changes in technological and international trading conditions. In Britain and France, governments have supported the creation of single product groups. Although governments have become more involved at the level of firms, the emphasis, especially in Britain and France, has been on leaving management to the managers.

A similarly non-ideological approach affected government attitudes towards the public sector. There was no question of using the nationalised industries as a powerful 'socialist instrument'. In both France and Britain, governments resisted pressures for more extensive nationalisation. The Nora Report and the 1967 White Paper were examples of the attempt to apply more commercial principles to public enterprise, especially in the competitive industrial sector. Italian governments, with limited success for most of the decade, tried to take a similar line, as for example in much of manufacturing. GEPI (Gestoni e Partecipazione Industriale) inspired by the IRC model, was established in 1971 to prevent further outright expansion of the public sector. Even in the few isolated cases where extension of the public sector was partly due to socialist political pressures, the organisation after nationalisation fitted the wider pattern of state-supported capitalism.

Attempts by governments in the 1960s to stimulate firms into acting in new ways took them into the world of the unknown. Whereas it had been relatively easy to forecast the broad impact of macro-economic policies in the 1950s, it was much more difficult to predict the full effect of more detailed policies in fields like discretionary employment taxes and subsidies, and the widescale promotion of mergers. Decision-makers were presented with debates and not the agreed views of economists. Some policies produced unexpected side effects. Preventing some bankruptcies in Italy, for example, made it difficult to resist political pressures to rescue other firms. The net effect was to limit the resources available for expanding sectors. A further difficulty was that detailed sectoral plans were often based on outdated information. The 1963 census of production was widely used in Britain in the late 1960s. Selective intervention often became more an act of faith than a calculated prediction proved true by events.

One of the outstanding features of industrial policy in the 1960s was the apparent inability of nationalised industries to respond flexibly to changing market conditions and government directives. Three main causes can be identified. First there were some instances in France, and with the IRI in the early 1960s, where financial independence enabled public corporations to resist political pressures, as for example over some patterns of expansion. Secondly, governments' attempts to influence the development of publicly owned industries in a positive, creative sense could be opposed, because the moves towards increased managerial autonomy within the public sector meant that political pressures could more readily be resisted. The limits of political influence are further shown by the lack of planned development of the public sector as a whole in Britain and France, or even in Italy where there actually was a Ministry of State Holdings. Finally, in complete contrast, the practical ability of governments to act negatively and veto proposals was extensive. The easiest way for governments to influence the public sector was through negative supervision, as when wage and price rises or capital investment plans were prevented or limited. In some instances the power of this negative approach enabled governments to restrict the commercially oriented plans of public corporations. Political pressures, for example, led governments to oppose the full rationalisation of some nationalised industries because of the redundancies that would have resulted, as was the case with the British Steel Corporation. On the one hand public corporations were prevented from responding to market conditions as they wanted to, while on the other they were able to resist some government directives. The more dynamic elements in the public sector appeared, as in some parts of the IRI and ENI, to be those that, as a result of their comparative success, were left to their own devices to operate commercially. The erratic performance of the public sector thus appears to have been largely the result of political or bureaucratic interference when it was made on a day to day basis rather than when it was directed at strategic decisions.

It is often assumed that companies in the public sector can more easily be influenced by governments in a positive and creative rather than in a negative and preventive sense. Paradoxically enough, it seems that in the 1960s in France, and to some extent in Britain and Italy, the reverse was the case. Although there were of course many instances where nationalised industries acted partly in accordance with their assigned role in the context of national, sectoral and regional plans, they also proved themselves to be slow-moving, inflexible policy instruments. They were allowed to deviate, sometimes extensively from previously defined roles in national, sectoral and regional plans. The most flexible elements in the public sector, in terms of responding positively to a government directive or market forces, were the more independent, entrepreneurial ones that most resembled the more dynamic parts of private industry.

Firms in the private sector also could ignore the state's efforts to influence them positively, as for example with planning targets. However, the extension of the government's role in industry, particularly through selective intervention, usually meant that it was to the firm's advantage to respond to the government's suggestions or put proposals to the government. As private sector policies were based on an adaptation of capitalism, it was *in the firm's interest* to cooperate speedily because it would probably lead to expansion and increased profits. For the most part, the firm's essential autonomy was not affected, although their patterns of behaviour and sometimes the direction in which they were moving were altered by government action. This was the case when, for example, the initiative for a project came from the firm and the state provided the finance enabling the firm to proceed where it might not otherwise have done so, because the finance or time scale were unattractive; also when an advisory service acted as a catalyst persuading the firm to alter its internal attitudes towards, for example, investing in more up to date machinery. However, there were instances of a new development where inroads were made into the firm's autonomy and firms were compelled to act against their will. This happened, for example, when a government intervened in a takeover battle, imposing its will on the objecting firm, or in the situation where the government moved in to change the top management of a firm to which it had, for example, lent money. In such circumstances the aim of the government was to maximise the use of that firm's resources.

It must be stressed that it was still very hard to influence those private sector firms that wanted nothing to do with government, so long as the government took the view that the issue was not so critical that it should impose its will on the firm. However, it does seem that to some extent – particularly with large firms in both expanding and contracting sectors – governments were able positively to influence private sector firms more easily than in the case of public corporations. The developing issue at stake here is how far the concept of Galbraith's 'mature corporation' will become a common phenomenon outside the defence industries where governments already had extensive influence by the start of the 1960s.

The changing nature of the relationship between government and industry

By the end of the 1960s the state in Britain, France and Italy had become more intimately involved with the affairs of the public sector, but more especially with the private sector than before, apart from periods of war and post-war reconstruction. This was largely due to a switch of emphasis away from indicative planning towards working out policies designed to improve the performance of specific industries. The sectoral approach led, even more than with indicative planning, to the forging of direct links between government bodies on the one hand and firms on the other. This development had begun to take place in France in the 1950s, but went further in all three countries in the 1960s in terms of both the numbers of firms involved and the increasingly detailed nature of the contact. The purpose of these links was not just to supply government funds but also to obtain detailed information to help assess needs and frame future policy, especially with regard to selective intervention and advisory services. In the late 1960s, links were forged through the 'planned bargaining' approach in Italy, while a combination of contractual devices and informal links were used earlier in Britain through the Ministry of Technology, the NEDO complex and their offshoots. In France 'programme contracts' were concluded with the Finance Ministry through the good offices of the Ministry of Industrial Development and the Planning Commissariat.

Although many factors were involved, some of which have already been mentioned, it seems with hindsight that there were four main reasons why the extension of the state's role changed the nature of the relationship between government and industry. The first two reasons concern the changing nature of industrial policy. By the end of the 1960s, it seemed clear that several factors had combined to make selective intervention a self-generating process. Once governments had begun to use such policies as a counter cyclical tool to help alleviate the bluntness of macro-economic policies, they tended to go on doing so. The very fact that firms knew governments were liable to provide help removed, or at least reduced (as in British shipbuilding, French steel and Italian textiles), the traditional threat of bankruptcy.

Conventional financial sources were liable to be discouraged by any projects that did not provide a safe return. In the private sector, projects that involved risks or high technology or huge sums, as with prestige projects, were left by conventional financiers to governments. National champions often returned to the government for further financial assistance. The examination of the needs of a whole industry when helping part of it and frequent reports on specific sectors from various organisations, led to the emergence of further problems that called for attention. Once some firms or industries had received assistance, others were liable to ask for it, especially if foreign competitors were being helped by their governments. The constant need to make advisory services of as much practical use as possible to firms of all sizes meant that policies in this field also developed self-generating characteristics. In the public sector, something of the same type occurred when disappointing performances led to increased political interference, which then tended to recur.

Secondly, although policies were becoming more detailed, governments in all three countries sought to make industrial policies more flexible so that they could be adapted to the needs of individual firms and to changing economic conditions. Efforts in this direction appear to have been most successful in France. With the Sixth Plan, there was an attempt at the implementation stage to move away from *dirigisme* towards greater decentralisation, in which a firm that was supported by the state was given greater freedom to operate under the influence of market forces. This was part of the wider attempt to exploit the virtues of capitalism while seeking to correct the less desirable imbalances it produced. In Britain and Italy, movement in this direction was less pronounced and it was also combined with an attempt to subject firms to tighter legal controls. Developments in this sphere were both a major difference from the 1950s and one of the crucial differences between the three countries.

The third factor contributing to the changing relationship was the modification of the institutional structures in the three countries associated with the development of both national economic plans and sectoral programmes. New bodies, often independent of government departments, were established to deal with specific problems in all three countries: ITBs and the NEDO complex in Britain, the ISPE in Italy and the Ministry of Industrial Development in France, directly inspired by Min.Tech. in Britain. Min.Tech.'s successor, the DTI, managed to break down the old non-intervention of the Board of Trade more successfully than the Italian Ministry of Industry has been able to temper its bureaucratic approach or the French Industrial Development Ministry its weakness *vis à vis* the Finance Ministry. There was some financial and executive decentralisation for example with GEPI, IRC, and IDI. The British experience shows this to have been a temporary innovation, reversed by the Conservative government's changes in 1970 and 1972. However, the industrial element of regional policy had been decentralised to some extent in all three countries by the start of the 1970s.

The outstanding institutional feature was the resilience of the established power structures of the centre. On the one hand, the British Treasury and French Finance Ministry were able to retain control of their traditional functions, and gain control of new functions in the planning sphere, while in Italy the customary division of power continued to prevail. On the other hand, many planning-oriented bodies lacked power in practice, even though they had formal responsibilities; examples include the DEA in Britain, the CIPE in Italy and the Ministry of Industrial and Scientific Development in France. This was partly because of the conflict between the established civil servants and the new planners. A further reason that emerged was that new institutions needed strong political support if they were to function properly. Lack of political strength limited the effectiveness of the BEP Ministry in Italy and, when it ceased to be directly under the prime minister, the Planning Commissariat in France; while firm political backing led to the replacement of the Board of Trade by the more 'interventionist' Ministry of Technology in Britain. The abundance of new organisations posed complex problems of coordination. Politically strong, centralised bodies like the FDES in France and the DTI in Britain proved more successful coordinators than new bodies like the DEA in Britain, the ICEEP in Italy, and the Industrial Policy Interministerial Committee and the Industrial Policy Division within the Ministry of Industrial Development in France.

Finally, there was an unprecedented increase in the personnel involved in the process of formulating and implementing policy. It was not just a question of an increase in the numbers of civil servants, accountants, scientists, and other academics involved within government organisations. The process of making detailed policies meant that employers' organisations and trade associations with their specialised knowledge became an even more indispensible source of information to government than before. In some circumstances the influence that employers' organisations had over their members encouraged governments to bring them more into the policy-making process. Close relationships were developed with many business organisations to which outsiders had no access. In the 1960s not only were more members of the industrial and financial community involved in an advisory capacity than before; they were given executive jobs, often with wide scope for initiative, in government agencies. By the end of the decade, developments in Britain and Italy appeared not just to emulate the pre-1960s experience in France but to match subsequent developments in that country.

The evolving nature of industrial policy, changes in the size and scope of government organisations involved with industry, and the establishment of a wider circle of policy-makers, combined to alter fundamentally the nature of the relationship between government and industry during the 1960s in the three countries. Industrial policy, and industrial planning where it existed, had become a more complex affair than before. It was now the result of interaction between a bigger government machine and an increasing number of firms against a background of swiftly evolving technologies and changing world economic conditions. In all three countries governments were becoming more financially involved with a growing number of industrial enterprises. The 1972 retreat from the British 'disengagement' experiment in favour of increased intervention, suggests that these features were fairly permanent. It remains to be seen how far it proves possible to reconcile efficient systems of appraising individual projects, industrial policies and sectoral programmes – as opposed to national plans – with the democratic desires, increasingly expressed, for accountability and control through elected representatives. The 1960s showed that it was very easy for ministries to shelter behind the cloak of 'commercial secrets' and reveal minimal amounts of information when supporting a project both at the start and throughout its course. The attempts of parliament and the public to get at all the facts were frequently frustrated. Galbraith's technostructure may have been widened in these three countries during the 1960s, but it remained highly elitist and undemocratic.

Two major emerging problems

By the end of the decade, two very important problems had emerged from the three countries' separate experiences. Firstly it had become clear that there was a significant omission in the institutions that had been evolved. Intervention solved nothing by itself. It was merely the end of the beginning. If the state's funds were to be used as efficiently as government institutions on the one hand, and parliament and the public on the other, had been led to believe, and if its involvement in other ways was to have the desired outcome, then ways of monitoring schemes, and particularly the use of funds, had to be developed. In the public sector the follow-up process took on some of the characteristics of political interference, which tended to be counter-productive. In the private sector there was systematic monitoring. But only occasionally were governments prepared to act decisively with regard to strategic decisions or changing the management during the course of the monitoring process, if things began to go wrong. This happened, for example, temporarily in Britain through the IRC and in France where governments have been more prepared than elsewhere to exert the influence gained from being a substantial shareholder in a firm. Potentially, this inclination to act while monitoring schemes runs counter to the moves (outlined in the previous section) towards giving a firm greater operational freedom. However, its importance lies in the fact that the way in which a policy measure is implemented over time at the level of the firm has a significant bearing on the extent to which the intended aim is achieved.

Secondly, the process of implementing industrial policies and sectoral plans in the 1960s seemed to release forces that collectively worked against consistent industrial and national economic planning. The first contributory factor was that the implementation of sectoral and national plans is totally dependent on a multitude of decisions at the level of the firm. Although governments found, in the face of an unexpectedly inflexible public sector, that it was in some respects easier to try to plan via the private sector, it was still very difficult to implement coordinated industrial programmes. This was because firms were free, for the most part, to ignore most of what the state did. Only rarely did governments force firms to act against their will. The 1960s showed there were clear limits to the extent to which political and administrative instruments, as opposed to economic factors, could influence firms. In addition, frequent policy changes, unpredictable intervention and waiting for the conclusion of consultations between government agencies and firms helped, with other factors, to create a new climate of uncertainty in industry. This worked against planning because it encouraged decisions to be short term, 'safe', and often altogether different from the generally optimistic projected decisions on which national and sometimes industrial plans seemed always to be based. Thirdly, both alteration of the patterns of public expenditure as a means of managing the economy and the direction of limited public funds away from financing expansion into the *ad hoc* treatment of crises militated against the limited attempts to plan the allocation of resources between industries, in both the public and private sectors. Finally, the self-generating nature of industrial policy and the development of unintegrated sectoral programmes encouraged a piecemeal, uncoordinated approach. Some of these factors – such as the creation of an additional element of uncertainty for industry – made it more difficult fully to implement sectoral plans.

Thus a paradox emerged whereby the process of implementing national and sectoral plans produced side-effects which, collectively, worked not in favour of successful planning but against it. This sustains the argument advanced at the outset: that many policies were implemented on an *ad hoc* basis and that there was in fact very little industrial planning *per se* in the 1960s in Britain, France and Italy.

III

Employment and incomes

Comparative preliminaries

JACK HAYWARD AND JOHN CORINA

All those economists who have attempted to explain national disparities in economic growth have attributed great significance to manpower factors: the percentage of the population employed, the hours worked, manpower training, the mobility of labour from agriculture to industry and services, immigration and so forth. So, manpower planning necessarily formed an important part of any attempt at growth-oriented macro-economic planning. Before considering the contrasting emphases and priorities in employment policy in France, Britain and Italy, some attempt must be made to explain these differences by reference to both the longer-term trends and the disparate situations that existed in the sixties in the three countries.

In the early sixties, the major contrast in the distribution of the labour force between agriculture, industry and services, unites France and Italy as against Britain. By 1961, only 3.7% of the British labour force was employed in agriculture, as against 55.0% in industry and 41.3% in services. Over the preceding century, there had been no net gain to industry, only a net shift of 16% from agriculture to the service sector. While, in 1962, 20.0% of the French labour force was still employed in agriculture, the drop in the farm population of 31.7% in the preceding century was distributed almost equally between a net increase of 15.1% in industrial employment (43.6% in 1962) and 16.6% in services (36.4% in 1962).[1] As for Italy, 25.2% of the labour force continued to work in agriculture as late as 1964, with 46.4% in industry and 28.4% in services. The shift in farm population was once again almost equally divided between the other two sectors, though in the Italian case, industry gained more than services. The most dramatic increases in productivity since the beginning of the twentieth century occurred in Italy, thanks to the shift from underproductive agriculture into industry.[2]

If we turn to the post-war period, Denison, who has particularly stressed the increases in productivity secured by reallocation of labour,[3] calculated that in the period 1955–62, the contribution to the increase in national income of a shift of labour from agriculture was (in %): UK, 0.38; France, 4.85; Italy, 8.44.[4] Kuznets has more recently documented in depth the dramatic differences in productivity between agriculture on the one hand and industry and services on the other in France and Italy, whereas in Britain the gap has been very small. A belated agricultural revolution in the Latin countries has been, therefore, one major factor promoting dramatic differences in per capita rates of growth in production over recent decades. Contrasting the early fifties with the mid-sixties in the three countries, the percentage increase in per capita product was: UK, 27.8; France, 44.1; Italy, 60.4.[5] Finally, Table 1 underlines the contrast between UK performance and that of the other two countries, while indicating a weakening in the Italian position and a strengthening in that of France.

Table 1. *Growth rates of output, employment and investment–output ratios in Italy, France and the UK, 1951–70**

	1951–5			1955–9		
	Out.	Emp.	I/O ratio	Out.	Emp.	I/O ratio
Italy	5.07	1.49	18.33	5.11	0.55	22.05
France	4.37	—	18.73	4.06	−0.34	21.80
UK	2.67	0.72	13.98	2.45	0.36	16.6
	1959–63			1963–70		
	Out.	Emp.	I/O ratio	Out.	Emp.	I/O ratio
Italy	6.05	1.58	24.35	5.08	−0.33	22.81
France	5.91	0.64	24.98	5.35	0.47	29.06
UK	2.97	0.79	18.86	2.35	−0.46	21.23

* Adapted from T. F. Cripps and R. J. Tarling, *Growth in Advanced Capitalist Economies, 1950–70*, 1973, pp. 47–8, 56.

Despite the dramatic shifts in the labour force from the primary to the secondary and tertiary sectors, Italy is still bedevilled by a chronic problem of mass unemployment, particularly in the rural South. It is natural, therefore, that insofar as planning has impinged upon employment policy, it should have been directed primarily at reducing the level of unemployment and towards regional policies that were similarly inspired. In Britain, commitment remained strong to the preservation of full employment in the early sixties and the main emphasis was upon a desire to limit the labour-market power of the trade unions through introducing wage restraint disguised as incomes policy, coupled with a desire to improve labour mobility through generous redundancy payments and better industrial training and retraining provision. In France, the chronic shortage of labour meant that manpower planning as such was a crucial part of national economic planning; and the relative weakness of the trade unions meant that, as in Italy – until the end of the sixties – it was possible to manage without a formal wages policy. The increased demand for skilled labour, as industrialisation gathered momentum, assisted the formalisation of an industrial training policy. The rising demand for semi-skilled and unskilled labour added a further dimension. Immigration inflows of labour became a sensitive issue, first in Britain and then in France, restrictions on such inflows hampering British economic growth in the sixties and threatening future French expansion, should the supplementation of the natural growth of population be curtailed under zenophobic pressure. The political context of labour-market planning is nowhere more obvious than in the controversial matter of migration,[6] but irrational prejudice rather than rational calculation has triumphed.

Neither Britain, France nor Italy succeeded in developing manpower policies as key components of counter-inflationary programmes during the sixties. Consequently, chronic inflation was an experience common to all three economies. But, if the explosive accelerations in prices and incomes during the early seventies were already foreshadowed in the failings of the sixties, it is striking that the sixties demonstrated a new contrast between rates of inflation in the UK, France and Italy. Table 2 illustrates that, over the decade as a whole, France experienced the largest increase at the domestic price level. However, between the two halves of the decade, there was a significant change, a relative acceleration in British consumer prices compared with French price changes, and a marked slackening in the average rate of increase for Italy; a change masked by the price record of France over the sixties as a whole. But by 1973 Britain and Italy rather than France were exhibited as prototype inflationary societies. The inflationary upsurge of the seventies has outlined more sharply the singularly poor price performance of Britain against a background where price movements in all three countries have become more synchronised in a general acceleration towards levels unprecedented in post-war market economies.

Table 2. *Rise of consumer prices in France, Italy and the UK*
(% change at annual rate)*

	1969/1959	1964/1959	1969/1964
France	3.9	4.0	3.8
Italy	3.6	4.5	2.8
UK	3.5	2.8	4.3

* Adapted from OECD, *Inflation. The Present Problem. Report by the Secretary General*, Paris, December 1970.

By the end of 1973 the defects of traditional-type manpower/wage control policies were reflected in the defects of anti-inflationary programming in Britain, France and Italy. Even before the energy crisis, the problem had developed into one of containing inflation (preventing the pace from speeding up) rather than moderating it. The dilemma is that the economic imperative for incomes restraint can become stronger while its social feasibility becomes weaker. Let us look at the experience of each of the three countries before attempting a comparative assessment.

NOTES

1 See OECD, *Agricultural Policy Reports: Low Incomes in Agriculture*, 1964.
2 S. Kuznets, *Economic Growth of Nations. Total Output and Production Structure*, 1971, pp. 144–6 and 250–1.
3 See above, Introduction, p. 11.
4 E. F. Denison, p. 211.
5 Kuznets, *Growth of Nations*, pp. 38–9, cf. pp. 290–1.
6 For a major British investigation of the dynamics of migration, see E. J. B. Rose *et al. Colour and Citizenship. A Report on British Race Relations*, 1969.

8. Planning and the French labour market: incomes and industrial training

JACK HAYWARD

Because of its politically sensitive nature, it has proved impossible to secure agreement about precisely what the concept of 'full employment' means. The associated concept of 'unemployment' seems at first sight to be capable of being defined more precisely but it too proves to be an extremely slippery notion, with a wide-ranging battery of statistical measurements according to the criteria selected. Owing partly to the slowdown in its population growth in the nineteenth century and stagnation prior to the Second World War, coupled with the existence of a largely pre-industrial economy protected from foreign competition, France did not suffer the kind of mass unemployment connected with the trade cycle that afflicted Britain, or the chronic unemployment and underemployment of the Italian South. Nevertheless, the only aspect of the labour market that really interested either the government, parliament, trade unions or public opinion in France was securing a level of employment at which virtually anyone seeking a job could find it in a relatively short space of time. It was conceived as part of 'social' rather than 'economic' policy, exemplified by the fact that the Ministry of Labour has sometimes formed part of a Ministry of Social Affairs, together with Health and Social Security. However, with the post-war development of the French economy and its increasing exposure to foreign competition, while lipservice has continued to be paid to full employment as an objective of public policy, it has become a subordinate and to some extent expendable part of an economic strategy in which industrialisation has come to occupy pride of place. Thus, in the Sixth Plan, full employment was only part of the objective of increasing the well-being of Frenchmen, which itself took third place to the prime objective: 'Guarantee France the mastery of its destiny', particularly by 'enabling France to cross the threshold of real economic power'.[1]

While manpower is a vital factor in securing maximum economic growth and has accordingly been given an important place in French planning, capital investment has occupied an even more central place. This is reflected both in the greater influence of business compared to the trade unions in determining priorities and in the much greater

importance and influence of the General Economic and Financial
Commission compared to the Manpower Commission in shaping the
final report. However, in the 1960s, attempts were made to deal with
inflation by tackling manpower cost-push. Firstly, the government
tried to secure agreement on an incomes policy; then it deliberately
allowed unemployment to increase while relying on price control to
compel employers to hold down wages; and finally it stressed industrial training and retraining as a way of eliminating the bottleneck of
shortages of skilled labour at a time when industrialisation was
pursued even at the cost of tolerating inflation. However, the Sixth
Plan did not follow the CNPF's November 1969 call to 'preserve the
mystique of investment growth, the positive heritage of our first
Plans' to the extent of embracing the target of 8 % growth. (It was not
clear whether this referred to gross domestic product or to industrial
production alone.) The belated conversion of the 'modernist' wing of
French big business to the virtues of rapid expansion did not overcome the prudence of President Pompidou, who was well aware that
his political support derived decisively from those elements – the
farmers, small shopkeepers and craftsmen – whose survival was most
threatened by a ruthless policy of uninhibited economic growth. It
should become clear, as we proceed, that French manpower policy has
always, in practice, been a subordinate accompaniment of other public
policies and not the centre-piece of governmental concern, as is
sometimes claimed.

Manpower policy and planning

Until the late 1960s, it could be authoritatively asserted by French
manpower experts that 'Of all industrial countries, France has the
most defectively organized labour market.'[2] A major cause was that,
despite its inflated ambitions, the government's employment exchanges were in 1959 responsible for only a minimal share – 8 % in
France compared with 20 % in Britain – of the business of bringing the
buyers and sellers of labour together. This in turn was partly due to the
fact that the number of officials responsible for this work was only 8 per
100,000 in France (compared with 37 in Britain). Yet in 1945, the
government's authority to control the labour market with a view to the
rational allocation of manpower was evident from the fact that it held
an employment bureau monopoly, controlled dismissals and strictly
regulated immigration. However, the government was too poorly
informed and equipped to carry out a *dirigiste* manpower policy.
'Behind an *étatiste* façade, the labour market was in reality left
to private initiative.'[3] Nevertheless, the pre-1968 unwillingness of

business to negotiate with trade unions meant that the government was frequently brought in to settle disputes and to make up for the lack of collective bargaining by state intervention.

In contrast to the British Ministry of Labour, which greatly extended its role in the 1960s as the Department of Employment and Productivity, the French Ministry of Labour proved incapable of such institutional innovation, even with the help of a much stronger planning impetus. It clung on nostalgically to its legalistic functions, primarily the regulatory enforcement of factory legislation and conciliation during industrial disputes. However, as in Britain, this role was no longer regarded as adequate by a government less concerned to restore industrial peace and maintain order than to plan economic development. In both countries there was a tendency to bypass the traditional ministries, but whereas the PIB worked closely with the strengthened DEP, the weak French Ministry of Labour was dispossessed of major functions, such as industrial training, in favour of new *ad hoc* agencies. Its unwillingness or inability to adapt to changing circumstances meant that it became increasingly marginal as far as manpower policy-making was concerned. It was displaced even from its prized role of intervention in industrial crises, the trade unions preferring to take the matter to the prime minister. Its weakness thus led its own clientele to bypass it, thereby further enfeebling its standing and influence. It is a notoriously 'under-administered' ministry, disproportionately feminine in recruitment and shunned by the best ENA graduates. Chaban-Delmas' attempt to correct this problem in 1970 by requiring all *grands corps* ENA graduates to spend their first year in either the Ministry of Labour, Education or Health, was quickly defeated. Ultimate and decisive indignity, the minister of labour is low in the political pecking order. In Cabinet making, the person selected is often a stop-gap required to secure the correct political balance.

An attempt was made to rejuvenate this sclerotic ministry in association with the creation in December 1963 of the National Employment Fund, aimed at facilitating the mobility of labour.[4] Instead of attempting to impose innovation from above, a small team of outsiders, including planners, were drafted in as agents of change, using the National Employment Fund and the studies required by planning as the thin end of the wedge. However, as in Britain, outsiders brought in on short-term contracts were no match for the ministry's permanent staff, who saw them as a threat, but one that could be frustrated and survived. The insiders were content to rule a shrinking and lacklustre domain rather than risk a loss of power if the changes were successfully implemented. Having relied simply on carrying out instructions from above, the majority of traditionalist officials were worried that they were now not merely allowed to contact the Planning Commissariat but encouraged to do so. Freed by a new approach that was profoundly repugnant to them and expressed in a language with which they were unfamiliar, the Ministry of Labour was even more unfitted to play an influential part in the planning process. Most of its officials were resigned to defeat in interadministrative battles and longed simply to be left in peace to carry out, in routine fashion, decisions taken by others. A minor ministry, lacking political weight and reluctant to acquire the expertise that would give it bargaining power in negotiations with other departments, its senior officials did not aspire to any role in the field of incomes policy nor try to use to the full the opportunities offered by the government's desire to pursue a more active manpower policy.

Most senior Labour Ministry officials were not interested in the Planning Commissariat and its Manpower Commission, according to a study conducted in 1965.[5] Over a third were ignorant about the activities of these bodies; the knowledge of a quarter was limited to their own specific sphere of action; while over a third were relatively well informed on the subject. The hostility of many officials was expressed in the judgement that manpower planning was a waste of time as far as they were concerned, which, given their reluctance to master the new techniques involved, it may well have been. They were reduced to the role of spectators in the commissions and working parties. Others were frightened that the planners would replace their protective concern with the workers' welfare by a narrowly economic view. When a sample of senior officials at the ministry were asked what they expected from the Plan, their answers fell into three categories. The first group of replies might be described as 'innovation and coordination' and covered 33% of respondents. They regarded the Plan as a way of achieving a more dynamic manpower policy, raising new problems and facilitating interadministrative cooperation. These functions were very much what the advocates of planning had in mind as major purposes of the enterprise, and not surprisingly were cited by those best informed. Secondly, the expectations of 38% of respondents were more traditional. They regarded the Plan as a way of improving the information available to officials, even educating them, or as a strategic weapon in the perennial battle against the Finance Ministry. The Ministry of Labour was regarded by the latter as a beggar and the support of the Planning Commissariat was a great help in the struggle for more money, e.g. for employment exchanges and industrial training, until Delors – at first the social affairs (including manpower) expert at the Planning Commissariat and then the prime minister's personal adviser in these matters – relieved the Ministry of Labour of functions it was incapable of discharging with a proper sense of their importance and urgency. Finally, 29% of respondents regarded the Plan as damaging to the work of the ministry, either because they disagreed with its approach and objectives or because they anticipated that it was a prelude to a deprivation of functions.

The negligible importance attached to meeting labour and business representatives – with whom its ties were relatively poor – also suggests an attitude of retreat *vis à vis* the challenges posed by planning. The cadres of the Labour Ministry clung to a secretive, backward-looking and verticalist approach, whereas planning required a more open and overall attitude by officials who were capable of presenting a case with a modicum of forward-looking statistical sophistication. The exclusion of the Ministry of Labour from the major policy decisions on manpower was due in large measure to the unwillingness of most of its senior officials to adapt to the need for change. This behaviour can be explained as a function of the ministry's weakness. Far from a feeble ministry seeking to use the Plan as a way of strengthening its position within the administration, the evidence suggests that it tends to become defeatist, and accepts that it is fated to be ignored by those equipped by their power and expertise to carry the day. Thus the Finance Ministry, after being somewhat suspicious of the Planning Commissariat as a threat to its traditional dominance, accepted the challenge and adapted itself to the new rules of the administrative game. The incapacity of the Ministry of Labour to play its part in a public policy process within a planning context meant that it was left to others to undertake the work or to impose changes upon it from outside.

The prime minister (especially Pompidou from 1966 to 1968 and Chaban-Delmas from 1969 to 1972), the planning commissioner (Ortoli and then Montjoie) and a member of the Planning Commissariat staff who became a close collaborator of the prime minister from 1969 to 1972 (Jacques Delors) played the key roles in overcoming the paralysis that afflicted French manpower policy. Pompidou was, above all, sensitive to the need to deal with the employment consequences of the Fifth Plan's commitment to industrialisation, mergers and adaptation to foreign competition, with the increased unemployment yet scarcities of skilled labour which they threatened. He had ready to hand a 1966 confidential report from the planning commissioner (drafted in large part by Delors) who recommended that because of the inadequacy of the Ministry of Labour, the task of running employment exchanges, industrial training and the National Employment Fund (responsible for facilitating the mobility of labour) should be confided to an autonomous public corporation. Pompidou was not prepared to implement so radical a proposal. Instead, he created a National Employment Agency by ordinance in 1967. It has been described as a 'Compromise between logic, the necessities of manpower policy, the interests of the users on the one hand and the sheer inertia of existing structures and habits on the other...'[6] The new agency did not have the overall management of manpower policy and it was less free from Ministry of Labour tutelage than envisaged by Delors and Ortoli. Nevertheless, the agency became the centrepiece of the Sixth Plan's attempt to improve the labour market, in terms of better information, guidance and job placement. Thanks to the 'finalised programme' – only one of six provided under the Sixth Plan – guaranteeing funds to achieve a fundamental objective over the duration of the Plan, the agency would by 1975 increase its share of total job placement to 30%.[7] The Ministry of Labour gave priority – within the limits of its exiguous budget – to increasing the agency's staff and a manager replaced a civil servant at its head. The agency's higher status particularly helped dissipate some of the employers' reluctance to use official services.

Pompidou also attempted in 1967 to overcome the employers' unwillingness to negotiate with the trade unions by exhorting them in a letter to deal directly with the workers' representatives on four issues. Firstly, a joint employment commission should be established in every industry. Secondly, works committees should receive advance warning of redundancy. Thirdly, the procedure for dealing with the employment consequences of mergers should be examined. Lastly, the financial arrangements during short-time working should be improved. At the time, the CNPF expressed opposition to all but the last of these suggestions. However, the Grenelle negotiations of May 1968 led the business spokesman to give way on all the other points and conclude an agreement in February 1969 with the trade unions. This agreement heralded a new era in French industrial relations, in which the CNPF attempted to acquire greater authority to enter into negotiations with the trade unions on a whole range of issues. The man who played the greatest part in this development, François Ceyrac, became the new CNPF president in 1972. His view was that 'French employment policy is the fruit of joint consultation. The Plan is more a record of the action carried out by the interested parties than a stimulus coming from above.'[8] His unspoken assumption was that the CNPF could dominate a tête à tête with the unions.

Even when the trade unions were not acceptable to business as partners in collective bargaining, the modernisation commissions – and in particular the Manpower Commission – offered an opportunity for their confederal leaders to meet and discuss labour market policy in a medium-term context. Having calculated – with the help of information supplied by the vertical commissions, INSEE and the Finance Ministry's forecasting division – the prospects for the size, occupational and regional distribution of the working population, it defines the limits of manpower policy and suggests the way in which a policy acceptable to the government and interested parties could be implemented. It has relied upon projections from past trends. As the chairman of the Manpower Commission from the Second to the Fifth Plan inclusive asserted:

The basic idea of which Jean Monnet was always clearly aware, that inspired the creation of the (Planning) Commissariat, is that the fundamental economic situation of a society depends on deepseated factors that only change slowly. Being masked by short term fluctuations, they are naturally neglected by the government and its officials, always subject to the pressures of the moment. The Manpower Commission, like the Planning Commissariat, was therefore established to take the measure of the deepseated preconditions of economic development and social progress and to attempt to make them prevail despite the short-term ups and downs.'[9]

As an acknowledgement that it is the Ministry of Labour that formally has the main responsibility for carrying out manpower policy, the commission's vice-chairman is *ex-officio* the ministry's director-general. Senior civil servants tend to dominate the Manpower Commission's work, forming a large part of the membership and sharing with the Commissariat staff the key task of acting as rapporteurs for the Manpower Commission and its sub-committees.[10] Freed from the cramping effects of the traditional bureaucratic ailments of hierarchy, formality and departmentalism, the Commission could support the more go-ahead elements which had tried unsuccessfully to reorganise and revitalise the sluggish Ministry of Labour. Of the trade unions, it was the CFDT that made the greatest effort at participation during the Fifth Plan in the mid-sixties and withdrew in disgust from all the modernisation commissions after the Guidelines phase of the Sixth Plan at the end of the sixties. All the unions made it clear that they did not regard participation in the work of the commissions as involving any compromise or commitment to official policy decisions. They are less well equipped or strategically placed than are the business spokesmen to pass off their policy preferences as an integral part of their 'technical' submissions. The union spokesmen are resigned therefore, either to follow in the wake of the rapporteurs with only marginal reservations; or they try to broaden the whole discussion into a challenge levelled at the government's policy, at which point they are ruled out of order for exceeding the commission's terms of reference. Union exasperation at such treatment, coupled with their mid-sixties experience (in which, for example, a massive run down in the steel labour force was decided by bilateral agreement between business and the government six months after the Fifth Plan Manpower Commission had reported), together with the post-1968 change in the political and industrial situation, accounted for the CFDT boycott of the second phase of the Sixth Plan. This gesture of protest was the only way that the trade union most deeply committed to using the planning process to the full could express its frustration. In the name of planning rationality, the unions were being denied concessions, e.g. in the rapid reduction in the workweek, that they partially extracted thanks to the May–June 1968 general strike.[11] Militancy seemed a better bet than statesman-like discussions at the Commissariat.

'Full employment', which had been considered to be equivalent to an unemployment (in the broad sense of people looking for work but not necessarily registered as unemployed) of 1¼ % in the Fourth Plan and 2 % in the case of the Fifth Plan, was equated with 1½ % for the Sixth Plan. The further demotion of full employment as an objective of public policy was evident in the Sixth Plan; there was no longer even a generously defined unemployment warning indicator system to encourage corrective action. The Manpower Commission would merely examine each year how the employment situation was developing by comparison with the Plan's forecasts, allowing the trade unions and business representatives to express their views prior to a report being prepared by the Planning Commissariat, on the basis of which action might be taken. Industrialisation rather than full employment was of primary importance, so the Sixth Plan Manpower Commission's recommendations were focussed on the former objective. Insofar as full employment was to be achieved, this would depend upon the attainment of industrial employment targets and the restraint on immigrant workers, whose influx had hitherto been so important a factor in France's economic growth at a time when the domestic working population was not growing. Although the industrialisation effort would increase the industrial labour force by a quarter of a million between 1970 and 1975, it would merely hold the proportion of the working population in industrial employment at 25 %, the main counterbalance to the declining farm population being the expanding service sector. The other major preoccupations of the Sixth Plan Manpower Commission were to improve the working of the labour market, centred on the National Employment Agency, to make the greater mobility of labour tolerable and to suggest ways in which the conditions of industrial work could be improved, particularly for the lowest-paid workers. To provide a minimum of coordination between the departments concerned with manpower matters, an Interministerial Employment Committee was set up in 1971. It included representatives of the Planning Commissariat, DATAR, agriculture, industry, education and labour, some of whom hitherto had little contact with each other on manpower matters.

The vicissitudes of incomes policy

Before turning to France's attempt to deal with structural labour market problems through a reorganisation of industrial training arrangements in the late sixties, we must examine the reasons for her failure to get a planned incomes policy off the ground in the early sixties. For, while in Britain the most ambitious efforts at a planned incomes policy (aimed not merely at restraining inflation but at promoting equity, improving productivity and reducing industrial conflict), were made in the years after 1964, by that date the French government had already conceded defeat. Both in Britain and France in the early sixties, incomes policy and economic planning were seen as interrelated. However, it proved impossible to secure an agreed incomes policy through the planning institutions, largely for political reasons. The presence in both countries of governments that did not enjoy the confidence of the trade union movements proved of itself an insuperable obstacle, over and above all the difficulties involved. The 1964 change of government allowed Britain to achieve the 'Joint Statement of Intent on Productivity, Prices and Incomes' that proved impossible to attain in France.

In France, the attempt to secure a concerted incomes policy was weakened from the start by the ambiguity which allowed proponents with conflicting aims to seem to be in agreement until the moment of truth when the policy was made sufficiently explicit to reveal the divergences. It was initially based upon an alliance between the government and the planners, both mainly concerned to secure the resources necessary to enable France to industrialise without succumbing to foreign competition owing to inflationary pressure, and the CFDT. The latter, as an extension of its 1959 conception of 'democratic planning', sought to compensate the trade unions' inability to engage in collective bargaining with the employers by a tripartite wages policy in which agreements would be made giving the workers a fair share in the fruits of economic growth. It was Jacques Delors, then a CFTC (now CFDT) section member of the Economic and Social Council's planning section, who helped to bring the two sides together. In a 1960 report, as part of the preparation of the Fourth Plan, Delors tried to reconcile the concern to preserve French planning's traditional industrial investment preoccupation with the need to plan public and private consumption. This involved, in particular, a modification of the income structure in favour of the lower-paid and large families, and was calculated to appeal particularly to the left-wing Catholics. A very impressed planning commissioner recruited him to the staff of the Commissariat but the idea of an incomes policy made only a sketchy appearance in the Fourth Plan, the government being more interested in securing what a senior official incautiously referred to in 1961 as a 'wages police'.[12]

Pompidou, the new prime minister in 1962, chose to proceed prudently by setting up a working party on incomes statistics, to explore the problem of inadequate data, particularly on non-wage incomes. (This work has continued slowly and discreetly in the Incomes and Costs Study Centre, set up in 1966 and attached to the Planning Commissariat.) However, in 1963, a bitter coal strike and the finance minister's anxiety over inflation thrust incomes policy very firmly to the fore. The agreed solution to the miners' strike by 'three wise men' (one of whom was the planning commissioner, advised by Delors) prepared the way for an Incomes Policy Conference in October 1963 under the planning commissioner's chairmanship. However, the atmosphere was poisoned, as far as the trade unions were concerned, by the July 1963 Act restricting the right to strike and the finance minister's September 1963 wage and price 'stabilization plan'. In this unpropitious situation, an attempt was made to explore the implications of an incomes policy with the major trade unions, business and farm organisations. The latter, who had been promised parity with the industrial sector in the Agricultural Guidelines Act of 1960 and whose income depended upon government decision, were the strongest advocates of incomes policy. While the CFDT was willing to accept wage restraint in return for a government commitment to replace unilateral decisions by contractual agreements covering public sector wage settlements, minimum wages and social transfer payments, the CGT and Force Ouvrière refused to accept any interference with collective bargaining. Big business was discreetly hostile to an incomes policy while the small and medium firms represented by CGPME came out vociferously against such a policy. The planning commissioner's proposals were overwhelmingly defeated in the Economic and Social Council, where it was clear that the trade unions and business were intensely hostile towards an incomes policy. Still, this did not stop the government imposing a limited wages policy in the public sector while relying upon price control to force employers to keep down wages in the private sector.

Thus the failure of the planning commissioner left the Ministry of Finance in charge of enforcing wage restraint on employers and workers indirectly through a prices policy. After an initial freeze, it sought a more flexible instrument of price control and developed first the 'price stability contract' and then the 'programme contract' – a bilateral agreement with a firm or trade association linked to the implementation of the Fifth Plan. In return for freedom to raise prices, business accepted a biannual examination (by the Finance

Ministry's price control division and the Planning Commissariat) of the extent to which a firm or industry had acted in conformity with the government's wage norm as well as their investment, production and export record. This policy proved relatively successful in restraining wages and prices until the general strike of May–June 1968. Thereafter price control was eased and private sector wages have outstripped those in the public sector, including the civil service, where the government exerts direct control.

A more limited form of contractual public sector incomes policy was developed in 1969 under the inspiration of Delors. The *contrat de progrès* formula derived from the *salaire de progrès* notion formulated by the CFDT and Force Ouvrière in the early sixties. It involved a tripartite conception of wages: partly a uniform share in national growth, partly a variable increase related to the performance by each specific industry, partly a disproportionately large increase for the lower-paid. This policy was strongly supported by all unions other than the CGT, especially in the electricity corporation. After a trial of strength with the CGT during the electricity strike of 1969 which was won by the government, a number of *contrats de progrès* were signed in the public sector, although until January 1971 the CGT boycotted them. From 1972, however, the CGT and CFDT – largely for political reasons – decided to boycott the public sector contractual policy and the dismissal of the Chaban-Delmas government in July 1972 meant the departure from office of his right-hand man, Delors, who had been the heart and soul of the policy. The *contrat de progrès* did not spread either to the civil service or to the private sector. Nevertheless, the lowest-paid workers have benefited from a 1969 Act which transformed the SMIG (guaranteed minimum wage) into the SMIC (growth minimum wage). This has meant that the poorer paid have done better in the 1970s than they did in the 1960s. Still, the overall verdict on French incomes policy is that it has been an excellent example of the paralysing power of the French *société bloquée*, whereas industrial training demonstrated that the stranglehold could be broken.

The industrial training breakthrough

In contrast with the highly charged incomes policy problem, the development of industrial training has been relatively uncontroversial, because government, business and trade unions all stand to gain something. Nevertheless, no agreed scheme was achieved until 1970 owing to divided responsibilities between ministries, the reluctance of most employers to take their responsibilities seriously and the disinterest of most workers. To achieve a decisive break with the immobilism of an omnipresent but powerless state administration, the refusal of employers to have face to face dealings with the trade unions and the latter's reluctance to appear to be engaging in collaboration with the class enemy, new circumstances and an agent of change were necessary. The rapidity of the industrialisation process made industrial training a more relevant issue than ever before, but the role of Jacques Delors as *deus ex machina* was to elevate it into an ambitious strategy for changing French society so that it no longer conformed to the Crozierian bureaucratic socio-cultural model. He was to use his position as Prime Minister Chaban-Delmas' right-hand man to take a decisive step in this direction, while remaining lucidly sceptical about the difficulty of his task and acknowledging that such efforts might be doomed to defeat.[13]

In a collection of essays by an elite group consisting mainly of public officials (including a number of planners such as Delors) that was prepared just before May 1968 but published after the 'events', the chapter devoted to 'The state and employment problem' showed many traces of Delors' handiwork and clearly foreshadowed the role he was subsequently to play. 'If one considers the state of labour relations in France at present, one has to admit their *stalemate nature* [*le blocage du système*]' which implied the need for a 'government strategy really intended to "unblock" the situation'.[14] It was essential to take advantage of the economic changes brought about by the need to adapt to EEC and international competition, as France became an industrial society. This task could not be left to the business and trade union organisations. They condemned state intervention only to invoke it to resolve the problems with which they were incapable of dealing by collective bargaining as, for example, occurred in Britain. However, the dangers of relying upon state regulation were clearly exemplified in the manpower field where

Law remains the main driving force of social progress. Administrative regulations are so detailed that they risk being too rigid and remain dead letters as a result. The administration have responsibilities thrust upon them which they cannot carry out...Manpower policy cannot be run, in all its details, from Paris, nor can it be carried out solely by government officials. For such a policy to succeed, there must be an atmosphere of mutual confidence between the employment officials, the employers seeking skilled labour and workers looking for jobs.[15]

The urgency of the task was stressed – 'the implementation of an active manpower policy must be achieved within the next three to five years' – but it was recognised that, given the intractability of French socio-cultural patterns of behaviour, rapid results could not be expected 'unless a new political atmosphere produces a miracle...such as our history has sometimes engendered, although they have generally been of short duration'.[16] The 1968 events were perhaps such a 'miracle' and the Chaban-Delmas government enabled Delors to meet his 'three to five years' deadline.

We have seen that even before 1968 the problem had been recognised and Prime Minister Pompidou had begun to deal with it in his characteristically piecemeal and circumspect manner, partly in response to business pressure. The CNPF had recently begun to take the problem of industrial training seriously by appointing to its staff the director of Manpower Research from the UIMM, the very powerful metallurgical industries trade association. In January 1966, he asked the government about the possibility of devising jointly financed training programmes. Finance Minister Debré played an active part in reaching an agreement with the CNPF that was given statutory expression in the December 1966 Industrial Training Act. As prime minister, Debré had established in 1959 a Coordinating Committee for Improving Social Opportunity (Promotion Sociale) to bring the ministries concerned into contact with trade unions and business organisations, backed up in 1961 with a secretariat and a small fund, but little progress was made. The 1966 Act recognised the workers' right to training, created an Interministerial Committee on Industrial Training under the prime minister's chairmanship, supported by a Permanent Committee of senior officials. The 1966 Act's arrangements for making industrial training agreements were extremely complex and bureaucratic, with only scanty financial support, so although the national and regional institutions to promote industrial training existed in embryo before 1968, the practical achievements were modest.

The 1968 'events' were partly a revolt of students and young workers against the threat or reality of unemployment, as well as the bleak career prospects. The employers' leaders, for their part, were worried at the consequences of importing disorder into industry by allowing state education to deal with industrial training. Following the Grenelle Agreement, whose sixth point referred briefly to the need to develop industrial training with government assistance, a December 1968 Act simplified the financing of industrial training grants by centralising the funds for trainee remuneration in the prime minister's budget, while the Ministry of Labour became responsible for paying out all non-agricultural grants. However, the real breakthrough came in the wake of the 1969 agreement with the July 1970 industrial training agreement between the CNPF and the trade unions, covering about 10 million workers. Firms self-excluded from this agreement were mainly in the leather, textile, clothing and furniture trades, employing about 600,000 workers. Discussions began in May 1969 with Delors – who was then only secretary-general of the Interministerial Committee for Industrial Training – stressing that the government hoped for a voluntary agreement between the employers and unions. He also made it clear that he was prepared to coordinate their proposals with what the government was doing, but if no agreement materialised the government would legislate. Delors' position was quickly strengthened by his appointment in June 1969 as the new prime minister's personal adviser on 'social affairs'.

Despite the bait of government money and the threat of statutory substitution in the event of failure to reach voluntary agreement, it took fourteen months to achieve consensus. The CNPF's social affairs negotiator, Ceyrac, had to deal with cross-pressures from certain large firms in the petroleum, chemicals and steel industries, who were already undertaking ambitious training programmes and the mass of small and medium-sized firms who were petrified at the thought of having to accept increased financial burdens. The trade unions were divided. The CGT wanted state control of industrial training, while the CFDT stressed the need for workers control and Force Ouvrière advocated tripartite control. In the event, the CNPF managed to keep control largely in its own hands, taking advantage of the unions' disunity and the knowledge that there was no likelihood of a strike on this issue. The employers obtained the full benefit of abandoning their traditional defensive attitude *vis à vis* government and the trade unions, minimising their influence over industrial training.[17] Whereas Delors and the planners had hoped for a genuinely tripartite control over industrial training, so that it was not restricted to a narrowly economic function but would lead to a blossoming of the human personality and a redistribution of power, the CNPF have – at least for the time being – been able to confine this innovation to its most prosaic interpretation. Trade union suspicions, by compelling the government to lean more on the employers for support, not merely on industrial training but for their general economic policy, have meant that the employers have been able to prevent serious inroads into management prerogatives.

The July 1971 Industrial Training Act laid down the new official institutional structure and imposed certain financial obligations on employers. At the centre, in addition to the Interministerial Committee and consultative National Council, which seldom met more than once a year, there were the Permanent Committee of senior officials and the Management Council of the Industrial Training Fund. All four bodies had a common secretariat – the General Secretariat of the Interministerial Committee on Industrial Training – headed until 1973 by Delors. The secretariat was responsible for the formulation and implementation of industrial training policy in cooperation with the ministries concerned; it provided a preliminary assessment of applications for funds made to the Management Council; and it coordinated regional industrial training schemes. The secretary-general, attached to the prime minister, was therefore in a strong position to control the overall development of industrial training. The policy followed is also influenced by the Commissariat's Manpower Commission, and in the case of the Sixth Plan an industrial training 'intergroup' composed jointly of members of the Manpower and Education Commissions.

The employers having been reluctant voluntarily to accept a share of the cost of industrial training, the 1971 Act made the following provisions. Employers would be required to spend 0.8 % of their wage bill in 1972, rising to 2 % in 1976, on industrial training. They could either finance their own schemes through industrial training agreements or make payments to training insurance funds or approved national/regional organisations. Otherwise, employers would pay to the government any difference between their own training expenditure and their liability. In 1972, the actual share of expenditure borne by the firms was 47 %, public funds accounting for the remaining 53 %. In 1971, the Ministry of Education spent half the public funds used in industrial training, the Ministry of Labour about 5 %, while about 17 % was spent through regional programmes, especially in the Nord and Brittany, under the aegis of the regional prefect. The number of people attending industrial training courses rose from three-quarters of a million in 1968 to nearly a million in 1971 and this was only a beginning.[18]

Industrial relations in a 'new society'

The reform of industrial relations, thanks partly to the new arrangements for industrial training, was a pillar of the 'new society' programme presented to parliament in September 1969 by Prime Minister Chaban-Delmas. However, the authors of *Pour Nationaliser l'Etat* had given an advance warning that the persistence of ideological conflict was a major factor, alongside centralised *étatisme*, in France's *société bloquée*. They therefore ridiculed 'those who dream of a "new society" dominated by a general consensus on the purposes of collective action, such as exists in other major countries. Their disillusionment risks equalling their utopianism, for it would be vain to try and impose on the French a model that neither corresponds to their temperament or to their traditions.'[19] This scepticism did not stop a number of the authors working with Chaban-Delmas to try and change the French model in a pluralistic, bargaining direction, with only limited success.

In a speech made five weeks before he left office with Chaban-Delmas (although he remained secretary-general of Industrial Training) Delors suggested how the government, business and trade unions might be able to live together. Within industrial relations, three areas could be distinguished which should each be dealt with differently. Firstly, there were matters affecting the day-to-day material interests of workers other than wages on which contractual agreement could be reached, such as employment, industrial training, health and safety. Secondly, there was an inevitable conflict between employers and workers over the share-out of the fruits of economic expansion. Thirdly, there was the conflict over the distribution of power in society, which naturally escalated into ideological conflict. Delors regarded it as essential that different rules of the game should be recognised as appropriate in these three areas, rather than allowing them all to become engulfed in the ideological battle.[20] However, all of these areas involve a power struggle, so it was not surprising that the attempt to establish an incomes policy, which belongs to the second category, became a victim of ideological conflict. We have seen that even in the case of industrial training, employers made sure that they emerged as the effective masters under the new arrangements. François Ceyrac gained promotion to the CNPF presidency partly on the strength of the prestige he had acquired as the chief architect of this victory.

The late 1960s and early 1970s have witnessed intriguing contrasts in the way industrial relations have been handled by the governments in Britain, France and Italy. In Britain, the trade unions have been considered to be so powerful that despite a strong twentieth-century tradition of *laisser faire* towards industrial relations, legislative enactment to discipline the workers has been a popular nostrum and was effected by the Conservative government, albeit with little success. In France, where state control was nominally both extensive and intensive, in fact government policy has been directed to securing greater contact between employers and workers with a view to reaching agreements without necessarily involving the state. This, too, has so far only yielded limited results. Finally, in Italy, government equanimity during the phase of business domination of industrial relations has not survived into the period when the trade unions have been able seriously to challenge that supremacy. In none of these countries has it been possible to subordinate the labour market to planning because governments have been ill-organised for the purpose and they have not been able to win the voluntary cooperation or effectively coerce both business and the trade unions so that their conduct conforms with public policy. Isolated successes, such as that achieved in French industrial training, seem to owe more to the entrepreneurial and political skills of agents of change such as Jacques Delors than to the planning process as such.

NOTES

1 *VIe Plan*, 1971, p. 11.
2 Jean-Phillippe Maillard (a collective pseudonym), *Le Nouveau Marché du Travail*, 1968, p. 58, cf. chapter 3, *passim*.
3 *Ibid.* p. 66, cf. pp. 57, 115–18.
4 This discussion relies heavily on the study by J. Lautman and J.-C. Thoenig, *Planification et Administrations Centrales*, 1966, Part 3.
5 *Ibid.* pp. 109–11 and chapter 6, *passim*.
6 Maillard, *Le Nouveau Marché du Travail*, p. 120; cf. J. Bunel and P. Meunier, *Chaban-Delmas...*, 1972, pp. 63–5.
7 B. Dassetto, 'La Commission de l'Emploi du VIe Plan' in *Droit Social*, April–May 1972, Special Issue on 'Aspects Sociaux du VIe Plan'; pp. 94, 102–3; cf. *VIe Plan*, p. 133.
8 In the same issue of *Droit Social*, p. 226.
9 J. Fourastié, preface to C. Vimont: *La population active*, 1960, p. 7.
10 J. E. S. Hayward, 'Le fonctionnement des Commisions et la préparation du Ve Plan. L'exemple de la Commission de la Main-d'Oeuvre', *Revue Française de Sociologie*, VIII, 1967, pp. 460–2.
11 See J. E. S. Hayward, 'The reduction of working hours and France's Fifth Plan', *British Journal of Industrial Relations*, VII, March 1969, pp. 110–12, cf. p. 84f.
12 For a more complete discussion of the origins and development of French incomes policy, see J. E. S. Hayward, 'Interest groups and incomes policy in France', *British Journal of Industrial Relations*, IV, July 1966, especially pp. 173 ff; J. Boissonnat, *La Politique des Revenus*, 1966, pp. 80 ff. and J. E. S. Hayward, 'State intervention in France', *Political Studies*, XII, September 1972, pp. 289–94.
13 Interview of 'Jacques Delors, le père de la formation permanente', *L'Express*, 12 June 1972, p. 78.
14 C. Alphandéry *et al*, *Pour Nationaliser l'Etat*, 1968, pp. 110–11, cf. pp. 126–8. The implicit reference to the bureaucratic model of French social – including industrial – relations, came naturally, as Michel Crozier was a member of the group. In 1970 he published a collection of essays under the title *La Société Bloquée*. Among other members of the group were Bloch-Laîné, Simon Nora, Jean Ripert (appointed planning commissioner in 1974) and Yves Ullmo.
15 *Ibid.* pp. 118–19, 122.
16 *Ibid.* pp. 139, 124.
17 Bunel and Meunier, *Chaban-Delmas...*, pp. 73–82, 87–9.
18 See 'La Formation Professionnelle continue et la promotion sociale', *Notes et Etudes Documentaires*, 3 March 1972, Nos. 3864–5. An abridged version in English, entitled 'Continuous Vocational Training and Social Promotion in France' was published by the French Embassy in London, reference number B/71/11/72.
19 Alphandéry *et al*, *Pour Nationaliser l'Etat*, p. 117.
20 Unpublished lecture to the Christian employers club, CFPC, on 31 May 1972 on 'Les relations professionnelles dans la société industrielle'. See also J. Boissonnat: 'Face à face avec Jacques Delors', *L'Expansion*, September 1972, p. 183.

SELECT CRITICAL BIBLIOGRAPHY

The factual background to French manpower policy is discussed descriptively in M.-F. Mouriaux, *L'Emploi en France depuis 1945*, A. Colin 1972, and critically in J.-P. Maillard, *Le Nouveau Marché de Travail*, Le Seuil 1968.
A penetrating analysis of the attitudes of senior French Ministry of Labour officials in the

context of national economic planning is to be found in J. Lautman and J.-C. Thoenig, *Planification et Administrations Centrales*, Copédith 1966.

On French incomes policy see J. E. S. Hayward, 'Interest groups and incomes policy in France', *British Journal of Industrial Relations*, July 1966, and on industrial training an informative account is provided by J.-M. Belorgey, 'La formation professionelle continue et la promotion sociale en France', *Notes et Etudes Documentaires*, Nos. 3864–5, La Documentation Française, 3 March 1972.

9. Planning and the British labour market: incomes and manpower policy, 1965–70

JOHN CORINA

British incomes policy: institutions and processes

For the purposes of comparing economic planning experiences, incomes policies may be defined in a broad way: to include all systems of pay settlement which are subject to some degree of influence or control at a level above that of the industry, with the state taking an interventionary role in the process. Nevertheless, it is useful to distinguish between the three incomes policy aims usually circumscribed within the planning process: the *anti-inflationary* short-term aim of slowing down the rate of income increases to reduce the pace of price increases; the longer-term aim of improving the distribution of earned incomes in the interests of *equity*; and the equally longer-term aim of improving pay structures in the interests of *efficiency*, productivity and more stable industrial relations. Explicitly or implicitly these aims are all present in incomes policies and are often in conflict. Most of the political programming has placed primary emphasis on the anti-inflationary aim, a certain weight of emphasis on efficiency, but rather little on equity since agreement on what is 'equitable' prejudges profound problems both in the theory of social justice and in the practice of regulating conflicts between interest groups. The stability of any set of institutions or rules for implementing an incomes policy may well depend on the weight attached to those three types of objective. The crucial feature in prices and incomes policy is to change the expectations of the two sides of industry. Employees, and their representative institutions the trade unions, are required to form different expectations of the size of wage increases and of the size of price increases they might expect to occur in the future. This is essential both in order to induce change in expectations about wage movements, and to guarantee participants that their restraint would not lead to a redistribution of income through price increases, which would be contrary to union beliefs about what is fair or contrary to their views as to what is attainable from 'free' collective bargaining.

Economies exhibiting centrally co-ordinated negotiating institutions have been generally regarded as prime examples of an institutionalized incomes policy. Surprisingly, the UK with a system of bargaining institutions probably more decentralized than anywhere else in Europe, has operated an incomes policy, and indeed a more elaborate one in principle, if not in practice, than anywhere else except perhaps the Netherlands. Britain especially stands out for the variety of institutional experiments during the post-war period, veering between crude confrontation and the most complex system of control perhaps seen in a market economy, operating at its peak between 1965 and 1970. Originally conceived as being dependent upon systematic planning of the domestic economy, UK incomes–prices policy developed momentum almost as an isolated sub-system of its own. The extent of sustained activity, even after abandonment of the National Plan in 1966, was as great as, or perhaps greater than, that in most other areas of structural change in the economy. The policy was pursued without highlighting the major problems of functional income distribution, without close analysis of the underlying national structure of employment income differentials, without cost of living compensation guarantees and without a clear depiction of the role of reserve legal powers. Yet the administrative mechanism, while it lasted, possessed at least one unique feature: the National Board for Prices and Incomes (PIB). As an example of innovation inducing a changing emphasis in administrative balance, the gathering of formal and informal powers after 1966 by the PIB showed a singular trend. There was a fundamental development in the surveillance relationship between the PIB and the public industries, in which the PIB became the 'efficiency auditor' for the whole of the public sector. Ultimately, extension of the PIB's functions became frustrated by the criss-cross of traditional departmental responsibilities and by the development of government 'backtracking' which inhibited the flow of references upon which PIB activity largely depended. But, at its peak, the established significance of the public agency concept was clear: legislation was prepared, in 1970, for the expansion of the PIB into a Commission for Industry and Manpower intended to embrace market power problems by absorbing the Monopolies Commission. Equally striking was the impact of prices and incomes policy upon the union–employer sub-strata of formal apparatus and informal relationships at industry and company level. The intensity of commitment to varied policy declarations, over five years, induced extensive medium-term effects upon the organization and behaviour of unions, employers and the departments (especially in the Department of Economic Affairs and later in the re-styling of the Labour Ministry as a Department of Employment and Productivity), quite apart from a deepening problem-focus upon the central areas of conflict: departmental co-ordination, basic relationships between government, unions and employers, changed relationships between the Trades Union Congress and its affiliates, and tensions within the governing Labour party and its trade union base. In all, the experiment in incomes policy displayed many characteristics unique to the UK industrial relations system.

This experiment may be viewed as a *search process*, concerned with many initially unknown variables and relationships, into the group dynamics of a fragmented industrial relations system. Whatever the changing economic context of an incomes policy, the set of institutional innovations, practices and rules introduced through fundamental policy decisions, and the means for implementing them, represent adjustments in the workings and balances of power relationships in the labour market. This dimension of *political* activity is inescapable because incomes policy is a focused effort, channelled through government, public agencies and labour market organizations, to express and preserve what is thought to be the public interest in a social situation of decentralized wage–price decision-making which (if left to complete autonomy) carries market disequilibrium disadvantages through high exposure to conflicts between group interests. Since the joint search for measures of agreement upon social norms is initiated and articulated at a level above the immediate loci of wage income and price determination, the ideal-type 'national' characteristic of such a framework should imply a higher degree of reconciliation between interlocking expectations than would otherwise be the case. Since social conflicts are interrelated, the social management of incomes and prices through a national framework is more than a specific bargain arrived at to check many income increases, and is only one part of any anti-inflationary policy which requires a more comprehensive approach. That approach was not yielded by the short-run conduct of demand management from mid-1966 to 1970.

Incomes policy, in the British context, may thus be said to have involved a concerted effort to promote *continuous* public responsibility for the short-run movement and longer-term development of incomes (including non-wage incomes), with the corollary – which was unfulfilled – that general economic policy and specific labour market policies should be conducted in such a way that their impact would not be inconsistent with this objective. Despite the 1964 *Declaration of Intent*, the notions of harmony through consensus or 'social contract' were not invoked as the major precondition for incomes–prices policy. It was recognized that the exercise of power to induce change in the labour market ultimately rested upon winning and maintaining consent at a variety of levels, but the policy was not based upon traditional centre–periphery concepts since it was also understood that the central labour market organizations could not adequately provide transmission links through which central recommendations on the timing and size of wage (or price) movements could be passed down to enterprise level. If 'consensus' is taken to imply a high degree of agreement upon goals and means, then if the British experience of incomes policy in the 1960s is to be viewed as more than a temporary truce in the orthodox behaviour of collective bargaining, consensus has to be seen through the stance of the participants: more as a changing product of political activity (the outcome of explicit views, disagreement, conflict and compromise) than as a stable condition. The *Declaration* and the 1965 WHITE PAPER establishing machinery and criteria, represented a national framework only in the sense of a first-stage agreement between the central parties: recognizing that special third-party institutions should be established to structure the processes of decision-making in the labour market. Although such a concept seemingly implied the step-by-step construction of a self-regulating wage policy – on the voluntaristic principle characteristic of the UK industrial relations system – this became increasingly overshadowed by the introduction and maintenance of external regulation in the form of legally enforceable sanctions. Where the system experienced greatest stress was not so much within the *administrative* machinery of the PIB, as stemming from the fluctuating commitment to consistent incomes-policy strategy at Cabinet level. The government demanded too much in too short a time from the labour market parties, and then retreated from the ostensible commitment to *develop* an incomes policy once some of the contingent conditions began to crumble. In short, incomes-prices policy was used more as an expedient to meet recurrent emergency balance of payments problems than as part of a long-term plan.

Planning for change in a decentralised wage–price determination system involves a number of obvious components: forecasting the required scale of change and estimating the timespan; reaching public agreement centrally on the broad principles to guide the pattern and growth of incomes; establishing agreement upon the area of regulation and a purview of the relationships between and within tiers; creating appropriate institutions to function as external and internal change agents; and not expecting the system in the short run to be highly sophisticated, consistent or resistant to ephemeral political factors. Here the central role became that of the external change agent – PIB – which was neither an external regulatory agent rigidly imposing outside standards nor a public consultant in disguise. The sources of power and influence which an external change agent can utilize are different from those of traditional government institutions, but they also depend heavily on government support. To sustain voluntary support, and especially to preserve the momentum of the internal change agents (chiefly the Trades Union Congress and the Confederation of British Industry), an external change agent became confronted with multiple functions: chiefly having to strike a shifting balance between a short-run investigatory function and a longer-run 'education' function, while facing the possibility of its own inhibition or destruction through sudden changes in government policy. The acid test of British incomes policy is what happens to any major strike threat in defiance of the 'rules of the game', given little direct influence by labour and employer organizations over affiliates. The traditional role of mediation, remarkable for its tenacity, presented an insoluble dilemma to the extent that there existed divergences between those portfolio-holders, departments and government attitudes concerned with the settlement of disputes and those concerned about stabilization and inflation. If the mid-1960s genuinely revived hope in the transformation of domestic economic policy through the general attempt at indicative planning, for incomes policy decision-makers this dissolved into dismay after mid-1966 as demand management reverted to the very pattern of stop–go which the new economic strategy had intended to break. As a consequence, current economic policy was split into two general streams of activity, which were neither entirely co-ordinated nor consistent: tactics for dealing with short-run crises and for attaining equilibrium in the balance of payments, and measures to achieve medium-run efficiency and long-run growth. Incomes policy was caught in between.

Institutional innovation

In Britain, general conceptions of incomes restraint had earlier promoted the establishment of 'specialist' and 'authoritative' bodies (operating without trade union approval): first, the Council on Prices, Productivity and Incomes (1957–61), and then the National Incomes Commission (1962–5). Indeed, the establishment of the NEDC reflected one conception of British planning, as a *political* venture, to make incomes, prices and productivity declarations more acceptable to trade unions. But after 1965, a more intricate semi-voluntary apparatus was built up for producing guidelines, for notifying price and income increases, for special investigations and general monitoring, and for stimulating productivity and efficiency improvement. Between 1966 and 1970, an inherent bias towards reserve statutory powers tended to colour the system.

The major institutional innovation was the creation and activity of the PIB as a statutory body, operating in collaboration with the incomes–prices strategy set first by the Department of Economic Affairs and later by the Department of Employment and Productivity. (This contrasted strongly with the 1960–5 era when incomes strategy had been completely dominated by the Treasury.) Only a subsidiary, sometimes duplicating, role, was undertaken by the unions – in the creation of the TUC's 'wage vetting' system – which rested largely upon the thrust of the TUC Incomes Policy Committee and the special pre-budget TUC conferences on incomes policy guidelines. There was marked change in the 'moral' powers of the TUC *vis à vis* affiliated unions; a certain shift away from attachment to the 'voluntary' doctrine which had been so strong that for over twenty years the TUC had failed to achieve major steps towards centralization within its existing constitution.

The other major institutional innovations, associated with incomes–prices policy, occurred within the employers' sphere. In 1965 several employer organizations merged into the Confederation of British Industry, which accepted far less *operational* responsibility than the TUC since it remained unprepared to undertake dividend surveillance or to assume a price-vetting function paralleling that of the TUC in the field of wages. This was partly a reflection of internal CBI weakness, and partly reluctance to accept any contractual relationship with the Labour government since in 1971 the CBI produced a (unilateral) voluntary price stability pledge from affiliates under a Conservative government. The other major innovations were the assumption of price-notification and price-vetting functions (diffused among fourteen departments with little co-ordination), and the assumption of responsibility by the Labour Ministry of wage increase notification and vetting functions (after 1968 this became pronounced) and of a major function in vetting the validity of productivity agreements.

Nevertheless, the key institution was the PIB (which retained close 'informal' relationships with the Labour Ministry). For five to six years, it established an *unprecedented* position of independent power and influence in wage and price determination processes. As an administrative body, the PIB had more in common with the organic than the mechanistic model (to use the Burns–Stalker approach[1]), and in this respect it was unusual for an official organization. It was cheaply run (costing over its life some £4 million), utilized on average four full-time Board members with a total average membership (including part-timers) of twelve, and employed a small nucleus of specialist staff and generalists. The Industrial Relations Branch was the most influential specialist division. (It is striking for its combination in staff working parties of specialists which antedated some of the findings of the Fulton Committee on the civil service.) As a seemingly permanent investigating body, one distinctive feature of the PIB was that it sustained an ethos, enthusiasm, and thrust of its own. Investigation and report production was a major concern. The PIB produced 170 reports, 5 of them general. Of the 165 cases referred to the Board and reported upon, 79 concerned incomes, 67 prices, and 10 both. The remainder were studies of productivity, prices and incomes applying to whole industries or sectors. The institution gathered its own information, operated *informally* although in conditions of secrecy, and its main self-conceived intention was not repressive but how to suggest practical ways in which industrial operations could be done more efficiently.[2] As a *modus operandi*, the Board discovered that incomes, prices, management structures, investment policy, etc, were inextricably bound together, and its recommendations became increasingly moulded by a 'package' analysis of problems. In consequence, the Board became the largest and most expert user of management consultants (more so than all government departments combined) in the history of British public administration. This raised problems of safeguards over the power given to consultants as agents of the Board, although the Board's procedures in utilizing consultants as 'fact-finders not policy-influencers' seems to have been effective in practice. A number of advisers – the 'marginal floaters' – also filled in some of the interstices in the formal relationship net with departments, linking the Board to the Labour Ministry, Cabinet Office, Monopolies Commission, Royal Commission on Trade Unions and Employer Associations, Department of Economic Affairs, etc, while the chairman also sat, by right, on the NEDC. The main gaps on the horizontal plane lay in the areas of fiscal policy, monetary policy, and international monetary policy. Although conflicts did occur within the Board, on certain wage issues of significance to members having trade union affiliations, it operated on the principle of collective responsibility, and unlike Royal Commissions made no provision for the splintering of recommendations through minority reports.

The PIB did not select its references, and had no enforcement powers on implementation of recommendations; and yet it moulded the *content* of incomes–prices policy through its practice of interpretation. With the strategy and broad principles set out in a series of government norm pronouncements (which during April 1965–December 1970 changed from a 3.5 % voluntary guideline, 3.5 % guide under the Plan, a statutory freeze, severe restraint, nil norm, 3.5 % ceiling, and a range of 2½ to 4½ %), the PIB's role was ostensibly subsidiary. It was its task, upon reference from the government, to consider proposals for raising prices or for increasing pay above the norm, and to report whether they fell within the criteria for exceptional treatment. The area and functioning of surveillance, and the taking of day to day decisions stayed with the departments (chiefly the DEA and the DEP), with a few cases selected for reference to the Board. The flow of investigation references fell more heavily on the wage than on the price side (price references for the private sector being relatively minor compared with those for the public sector), with a marked decline in the flow of all types of reference from mid-1969 to mid-1970. This tended to deflect attention away from issues of 'political' significance (as viewed in traditional role terms of regulating industrial conflict through mediation, conciliation, arbitration and Cabinet intervention), towards general policy references on broad 'educational' issues: notably productivity agreements, payment by results, job evaluation, salary systems and low-paid workers.

The progressive weakening of the PIB was influenced more by Cabinet decisions than by reaction from 'clients' to reports of the Board. The newly-avowed objectives of labour policy failed to dislodge industrial peace from its pre-eminent position as the practical goal of public intervention in the labour market. (Strike activity accelerated from 1968 to 1970 although the pursuit of incomes restraint does not seem to have been a major factor in this process.) So, in terms of total impact upon the continuous reformulation of incomes policy, the Board became a relatively weak agency, working neither in close detailed liaison, nor in close co-ordination, with the conduct of monetary and fiscal policy. It became increasingly functionless as an instrument, as the 'election cycle' began to unfold in the development of the wage explosion of 1969–70.

The general looseness of price restraint policy made the Board's highly restricted role in private pricing investigations even more negligible. The PIB did not succeed in its attempts to remedy its own weakness as a change agent. There were abortive bids to bring, first all arbitration tribunals and, later, the new Commission for Industrial Relations, under its wing. The Board, however, did succeed in becoming the 'efficiency auditor' and pay reviewer for the public sector. The problems of administering economy-wide prices policy, and the growing political sensitivity towards negative notions of 'incomes restraint', finally produced a solution during 1969–70 of transforming the PIB into a larger organisation with wage functions carried on behind a wider facade. On prices, there were two older institutions (the Monopolies Commission and the Restrictive Practices Court) and two contemporary institutions (the Industrial Reorganisation Corporation and the PIB), which overlapped since they were sponsored by different departments, and at times led to conflicting policies (especially over the effects of mergers) on the dimensions and effect of market power. The solution, a proposed Commission on Industry and Manpower (dropped after the June 1970 government change) was to bring restrictive practices, monopolies and mergers within an enlarged market-power horizon, and perhaps to capitalize upon the newly-acquired DEP image of promoting the efficient use of manpower. This development is of extraordinary interest. It suggests that pursuit of a prices, incomes and productivity policy carries so many ramifications that expansion occurs through conflicts with adjacent agencies and departments. For example, responsibility for monopolies and restrictive practices (including the Restrictive Practices Court) was transferred to the DEP (a non-traditional role for a Labour Ministry), and the CIM, while taking over the function and the personnel of the PIB, was to include the functions of both the PIB and the Monopolies Commission. At the same time, the legal delaying powers over wage and price increases were to be diminished, although the reserve powers for early-warning arrangements were to remain.

Over the five-year effective span, the PIB developed its own rationale, which became partly one of trying to tie wage increases more closely to productivity performance at enterprise level. Since it became extremely reluctant to use any public criteria other than that of productivity improvement, it was driven into a consultancy stance, especially upon the negotiation and application of productivity agreements. (Since the Cabinet took the lead in loosening interpretations of the declared criteria, this was followed by the DEP in its vetting activities, and although the PIB's interpretations were generally restrictive, these too began to stretch the criteria.) But the DEP independently created its own consultancy service (1969), to promote efficiency in the widest sense while centring the service upon industrial relations problems; and this became overloaded with requests from companies for help in productivity bargaining and in reconstructing pay structures. Some of this unexpected excess demand may be attributed to the fact that although the PIB captured attention as an advocate of productivity improvements, its own consultancy work was not universally successful. PIB productivity proposals had been ignored in a number of industries. The attempt to implement incomes–prices policy through heavy reliance upon engineering change in management ideology proved insufficient, without machinery to modify union attitudes at plant level towards the revision of pay structures. The weakness in the whole system was vulnerability to political decisions. The Cabinet and DEP occasionally signalled a firm stand where it was believed that pay increases could be postponed, if not prevented, without major strikes. On the other hand, the Cabinet also took the lead in stretching the criteria of prices and incomes policy, and the vetting decisions of the DEP (especially laxity over productivity agreements) and other departments (on prices) were clearly governmental responsibilities.

Legal powers as an innovation

The introduction of legal powers, in the field of prices and incomes, played a significant part in loosening the support of unions. Deterioration in union–government relations was also accelerated by the government response to the Royal Commission's report on trade unions and employer associations (1968), which placed the unofficial strike problem at the top of reforming priorities. The extension of legal powers envisaged in the Labour White Paper *In Place of Strife*, combined with the imminence of the election, destroyed the re-generation of a union–government dialogue on the distribution of the national income between pay and profits and upon the distribution profile of employment income. The Conservative government in turn repeated the same pattern of events.

Since the history of legal reserve powers is unusually entangled, it is worth isolating a broad generalization: that the British industrial relations system has been traditionally hostile to legal intervention, with an intensity almost unknown in other industrial societies. The introduction and renewal of legal reserve powers (the Acts of 1966, 1967 and 1968) increasingly undermined union support for incomes-prices policy, divided the mass of the Labour party, and produced divisions within the parliamentary Labour party and the Cabinet.

Briefly, the impetus began *before* the July 1966 sterling crisis, when in December 1965 the government (with the PIB in support) announced it would carry out its earlier decision to introduce legislation for a statutory early-warning system. The CBI preferred legislation rather than instituting its own arrangements for notification and vetting. Thus the original Bill (February 1966) appeared harmless to the TUC, since it neither altered the existing early-warning arrangements nor modified collective bargaining. At this stage, the legislative concept was merely an Enabling Act, and before any ministerial order could be made there would have to be consultation with both the TUC and the CBI. A further complication, however, appeared with the onset of the sterling crisis and the announcement of emergency measures, in-cluding an incomes standstill and the strengthening of the provisions of the Prices and Incomes Bill. The TUC acquiesced, from political loyalty, and the Standstill White Paper was explicit on the new statutory powers. The only part of the 1966 Act which was permanent was Part 1: placing the PIB on a statutory basis. Part 2, which incorporated the White Paper and the early-warning proposal, was intended as 'permanent' legislation which could only be activated by an Order in Council. The general standstill on prices and incomes was temporary (one year); and enforcement powers (as in the case of Part 2) could only be invoked by an Order. However, in October

1966, because of ambiguities in the Act, the government announced it would bring Part 4 into force. The immediate effect of the subsequent Order was to activate Section 30 (which, at that time, it was thought would protect from legal proceedings any employer who, in the context of the standstill, withheld a pay rise to which his employee was entitled under his contract of employment); and authorise Orders preventing price increases and pay increases. (Only 15 Orders – 14 on incomes and 1 on prices – were used against increases during the twelve-month period from mid-1966 to mid-1967.)

Faced with a swing towards militancy among major unions (led by the two largest ones, the Transport and General Workers Union and the Engineers), the TUC urged that Part 4 of the Act should be allowed to lapse in August 1967, and that the controversial Part 2 should not be implemented. But the government, confronted with a deteriorating balance of payments situation (which under the impact of the dock strike was to develop later into devaluation) was caught in a dilemma: something had to be done about the loopholes revealed in the existing legislation. Their overriding argument was that if Part 4 were allowed to lapse, the economy would have to grapple with the accumulated backlog of settlements and deferred pay rises, with deleterious effects on the exchange rate. So the Prices and Incomes (No. 2) Bill was produced on 5 June 1967: to supplement temporarily the powers of Part 2, and to offer a firmer legal defence for employers who had withheld increases in the past year of combined standstill and severe restraint. In June 1967, the government announced to the TUC their intention of bringing into force Part 2 of the 1966 Act (i.e. on the lapse of Part 4); and it was this declaration which set the scenario for serious internal division within the Cabinet and parliamentary Labour party during 1968. Whereas the case for legal powers had been urged in 1966 and 1967 to prevent the onset of a devaluation, the case for keeping legal powers was urged in 1968 and 1969 to reap the benefits of devaluation.

Alienation of individual unions was therefore matched by shrinking parliamentary support for legal powers. The 1968 Prices and Incomes Bill was fiercely debated, receiving a majority of 35 on second reading. (After the March 1966 election, the government's majority had risen from three to ninety-seven.) When further controversy arose over an Order on intervention in the bus industry negotiations (July 1968), the government's majority fell to twenty-four. The 1968 Act allocated new reserve power to the government until the end of 1969: to require the *reduction* of prices on recommendation from the PIB and to require notification of dividends and the restriction of excessive dividends. Whereas before, under the standstill and severe restraint phases, the government had the power to short-circuit references when imposing standstills, afterwards (1967–8) the power to delay pay or price increases was linked with reference to the PIB. The powers under the 1967 Act had given the government opportunities to order a delay of up to three months *while the Board examined the proposals*, and for a further three months if the Board came out against them: a maximum delaying power of seven months. Under the 1968 Act, the government still had the power to enforce a delay of up to three months, while the PIB examined a proposal, but if the PIB came out against a proposal, the government could, if it decided, *extend* the period of delay for up to another eight months, yielding a maximum total (including the initial investigation month) of twelve months.

Armed with a facade of legal powers – which could not be utilized because they were politically intolerable to the unions and which were more relevant to the psychology of international monetary confidence than to the actual domestic development of incomes and prices – the government gave ground. This was not in response to internal TUC pressure, since the General Council, as distinct from Annual Congress, consistently regarded legal reserve powers as 'irrelevant' to incomes policy. Far more important were the mobilization of block trade union votes and militant constituency groups at the Labour Party Conference (September 1968), where despite fervent appeals from the chancellor and the DEP secretary of state, a resolution demanding repeal of the Prices and Incomes Acts was passed by a majority of approximately five to one.

Having introduced a fundamental problem of duality – with incomes–prices policy administrators veering towards wage and price lags introduced through the retention of legal reserve powers, while union incomes policy supporters conceived of incomes policy in its original form as a system of voluntary continuous self-regulation – the government now retreated. At the end of 1969, in the White Paper *Productivity, Prices and Incomes Policy after 1969*, it was declared that improvement in the balance of payments 'made it possible to remove the more stringent controls of the 1967 and 1968 Prices and Incomes Acts'. The government was returning full circle to the notions of voluntary incomes policy, and the less stringent criteria, embedded in the 1965 statements (without the National Plan context but with a looser vision, in *The Task Ahead*, of growth goals). On the other hand, faced with the prospect of an incomes explosion, the government decided to continue in force (though these were not utilized) the powers under Part 2 of the 1966 Act: to hold up a pay or price increase for up to three months while the PIB examined it, and to require early-warning notification of proposed pay or price increases. A statutory order continuing the operation of Part 2 for a further twelve months was introduced in December 1969, and most reluctantly approved by a majority of twenty-eight in the House of Commons. These provisions were allowed to lapse naturally after the change of government in mid-1970, when legal concerns became channelled in the direction of the 1971 Industrial Relations Act.

Legal reserve powers thus modified the *formal* pattern of authority relations between government and the industrial relations system, by introducing the possibility of external regulation of labour market institutions. But their underlying significance was doctrinal – legal powers represented a centralization of normative regulation repugnant to the social values of the British collective bargaining system. They diverted attention away from the task of reconstructing normative systems at plant level. Beyond the context of the one-year freeze, legal power, as such, had little effect upon wage and price behaviour. If their existence can be interpreted as an indication of government commitment to incomes–prices policy, the ability to use them became severely curtailed by political sensitivities. Of course, legal powers were an issue for which there had been no mandate, and with a general election in sight together with Conservative hostility towards the existence of the PIB, they were unlikely to have been invoked during the period of disarray of 1969–70. Yet the deeper sensitivity lay elsewhere. The resort to legislation, however nominal its use, undermined union confidence in the government's incomes policy. The growing development of dissent is only weakly revealed in TUC resolutions. At first, the 1966 TUC very narrowly approved the government's July measures by 4,567,000 to 4,223,000 votes. Then, at the 1967 TUC, the General Council only just carried the day against repeal of the Prices and Incomes Act by 4,227,000 to 4,109,000 votes. When the final opinion shift came, it was dramatic; at the 1968 TUC, an all-embracing motion demanding repeal of 'existing legal powers' and rejecting any further legislation, was carried by 7,746,000 to 1,022,000 votes. The General Council seriously pressed the government to repeal Part 2 (1966) together with the 1967 and 1968 Acts. The rift was not closed as TUC–government relations worsened. By the 1969 TUC, voting opinion had gathered such force that despite the advice of the General Council (now alienated from the delegates), Congress demanded repeal of the 1966 Act *in full* – including the statutory basis of the PIB – and the motion was narrowly approved. The revolt of the militants, as in 1948–57, resulted in only the third defeat of the General Council's leadership over twenty-five years.

If the post-1966 experience suggested that the law could play a small role in reinforcing incomes policy, there was a marked contrast between the use of legal power during the freeze and the use of powers when the policy was disintegrating. By the selective use of powers (busmen, December 1967 and builders, 1968), public confidence in 'fairness' was undermined because these were not the most flagrant examples of norm-violation. The government itself became more concerned over the principle of legal enforcement than over policy content, and neglected other forms of sanction. There are very narrow limits to the support the law can give an incomes policy: its main functions in Britain being to symbolize government determination and to assure the public that 'equity' is to be maintained.

Incomes policy and the integration of decision-making

The problems attending these innovations – the PIB and legal reserve powers – were exacerbated by the lack of integration in *general* policy formulation. Within the total decision process, the continuous adaptation of policy orientation to short-run stresses on the balance of payments, without bridging the gap between short-run expedients and long-term horizons, meant that performance can only be assessed in terms of costs and benefits in individual circumstances and bargaining situations. But, in more general terms, the incomes–prices policy continuum moved towards a critical phase by 1969. On the organizational surface, there developed an extensive apparatus for social intervention in incomes and prices decisions, and for encouraging productivity and efficiency in resource allocation, with the long-run aim of structuring radical change in the collective bargaining system and the re-ordering of pay structures at company and plant level. Underneath, among the rank and file, the social stresses of restraint commitment (in the *absence* of rapidly rising real wages, lowered unemployment and balance of payments transformation) produced destructive union anxiety over the social costs (largely upon union cohesion) incurred, and over the intangible returns for the institutional effort put into incomes–prices policy since 1964.

The fundamental problem was the acceptability of incomes restraint, in a system where withdrawal from integrated economic planning had given way to traditional forms of demand management. Originally, the restraint objective was seen to occupy a socially subordinate role in incomes, prices and productivity policy: where its strategic efforts and viability stemmed from the fulfilment of a set of contingent conditions promoting faster economic growth and faster consumption. After 1966, however, to the extent that such contingent conditions remained unfulfilled, restraint became diverted into a progressively dominating role, so that it led to a 'degenerated' incomes policy where restraint became continuous and almost an end in itself. The system therefore became over-sensitized to short-run pressures – for weakening the payments constraint, for exchange rate stability, for bolstering foreign loan capacity, for reinforcing temporarily lowered relative export costs, and for aiding the rephasing of debt repayments. Yet at no visible point did incomes policy (given that other economic measures appeared ineffective at operating with unknown lags) mark a transitional stage towards the short-term goal of a balance of payments surplus, until late 1969–70 when policy had become effectively inert.

The founding of what was thought to be a voluntary and (hopefully) self-regulating system of incomes restraint was a large-scale *negotiating achievement* between government and interest groups in an era of planning optimism. Harmonization was assumed to be able to develop on two planes: harmonization in the formulation of the objectives of an incomes policy and harmonization in the implementation of an incomes policy. The major problem on the objectives plane was never confronted squarely (although the NEDC purportedly acted as the forum for overall distributive decisions). The parties were forced to choose between two principles of incomes policy and incomes growth in an economic policy context where their reconciliation became increasingly difficult. The first was the economic principle of a market-oriented short-run outlook which considered wage incomes as labour costs or price components, and made incomes growth dependent on the productivity of the enterprise. The other was the principle of community-sharing – that is, the principle of the indivisibility of income levels, consumption standards, and future incomes growth in real terms. The principle implied that it was neither possible nor equitable to confine pay increases to employees in enterprises with rapid productivity growth, but that the benefits (whether reaped through productivity bargains or not) should be shared amongst the wider community. Harmonization in the implementation of incomes policy was equally formidable. The national parties in the collective bargaining system comprise only the base component of an incomes policy system: the implementation of policy aims is both more extensive and intensive than the formal collective bargaining system itself. The coverage of incomes policy necessarily extended outside bargaining organizations to embrace quasi-bargaining organizations (as in the professions), unorganized workers and other groups. The penetration of incomes policy was ideally to move down into 'domestic bargaining' and micro wage-productivity relationships at plant level.

Certain facets of these problems may be illustrated. On the problem of objectives, the apparatus attempted to reduce the traditional role of comparability in incomes negotiations. The notion of comparability is deeply embedded in fair procedures of fixing pay and is fundamental to trade unionism. For a time, the PIB tempered the influence of 'crude comparability' while emphasizing the factor of productivity;

but the tenacity of comparability became more evident (and the PIB was increasingly forced to recognize it) once price instability and continuous above-norm wage change became visible to the labour market participants. While the PIB failed to reverse the legitimization of comparability, and provided no acceptable substitutes, it should also be noted that the whole incomes policy and procedures represented a serious challenge to pay-settlement in the public service (national and local government) which rested upon a variety of comparison devices. Between 1965 and 1970, the public service sector was successful in evading the full rigours of incomes policy criteria because, in effect, the public service still maintained the force of comparability and productivity was never a major factor. On the general problem of low pay, the PIB also found itself in a tangle of ends and means. After stating that the improvement of the position of the low-paid was a major goal of policy, the PIB first held that 'the position of the low-paid could be subsumed in the general problem of improving efficiency', and then retreated to the view that 'there was no single set of factors which was responsible for low pay'.

The problems of implementation lay in the dynamics of organizational adaptation and growth. Incomes policy, since it increasingly expanded through wider dimensions than wage-bargaining activity, into profits, rents, interest rates, manpower utilization, manpower allocation, investment criteria, pricing policy, efficiency and productivity, was viewed as a far wider operational concept than wages policy. The increasing recourse to improvizations, and many of the deficiencies attached to these, may be attributed to the fundamental problems of reorganizing departmental responsibilities and functions. These were exposed in the tensions created by the DEA–Treasury–Labour Ministry triad, in the semi-autonomy of the Board of Trade, and above all in the gap produced by the demise of the DEA. The final solution adopted was the unsuccessful attempt to elevate permanently the status and transform the functions of the Labour Ministry.

The main deficiencies in the administration of incomes–prices policy, during the 1965–70 period, may be highlighted briefly. Although an organization model of synchronized decision-making cannot be applied to the British labour market, where there was a lengthy gestation period for structural union changes and collective bargaining reform, it is clear that too much opportunity for communication conflict was provided by the piecemeal system. The processes of innovation produced imbalances. For example, the novel union guideline conferences were not synchronized with national wage negotiations, the CBI accepted far less voluntary responsibility on behalf of affiliates than the TUC, PIB liaison with the Treasury and Central Bank was exceptionally weak, merger policy remained completely unco-ordinated with DEP and PIB pricing-policy proposals, and the duplication of wage-vetting through the coexistence of statutory and voluntary (TUC) systems aided conflicts. The major defects, however, derive from the absence of a clear 'centre' for the incomes–prices policy system, rather than the accumulated tensions between the centre and the periphery. The lesson may be drawn that, from the start, the PIB concept should have been based upon centralized activity within one public agency – the agency providing a central locus for wage and price notification, with power to initiate its own references, to call for implementation, and to pursue vetting and investigations upon one set of standards. Because the apparatus remained diffused throughout 1967–70, the problem of devising a representative structure for high-level decisions on incomes–prices policy was never seriously raised. 'Co-optation' (to use Etzioni's term) remained the principle of PIB composition; and while the relationship between the PIB and government was never made explicit, responsibility for some of the *detailed* twists in incomes–prices management passed by default to the economic committee of the Cabinet. The NEDC (originally envisaged as the locus where incomes–prices policy became integrated with growth decisions through tripartite participation) never seriously undertook this function.

The existence of the PIB (and statutory powers) became an issue in the 1970 general election, in which the Conservatives made great play with the post-devaluation inflationary movement in prices. The PIB was highly vulnerable, in any event, since a change agent exists for the chief purpose of disrupting the conservative norms of the clients, thereby generating dynamic conservative resistance. Despite a reversion to non-interventionary economic policy, the new Conservative government remained undecided for some months, but dismantled the PIB in 1971; leaving an organizational residue in the truncated form of the new Office of Manpower Economics, with functions largely confined to the review of certain public-service pay elements, and the provision of services for *ad hoc* enquiries into pay disputes of national significance. From 1971 to 1972, the major emphasis was placed upon introducing a legislated change in the balance of power in the labour market (the 1971 Industrial Relations Act), while accepting confrontation (in the form of major disputes in the public sector) as a method of de-escalating the rising trend of pay settlements during the 1971–2 wage explosion.

While, during 1970–2, the government reverted to demand policies reminiscent of the early 1960s, it also faced a combination of labour market circumstances similar to those which, in 1962, had led the Conservatives towards the concept of increasing the growth rate and to the creation of the NEDC. Although the early 1970s repeated the pattern of the early 1960s – with the pursuit of wage restraint through the exertion of government influence upon the public sector, and the increasing alienation of national unions – there was a new feature. The CBI was induced to launch a 'price stability pledge' in 1971, and the renewal of the pledge in 1972 was utilized by the government. The NEDC was revivified as a forum for negotiating a package deal based on the notion of an absolute 'national norm'. This was the most revealing legacy of the preceding years of formal incomes policy: the distributive principle of elevating the lower-paid, unsuccessfully pursued by the PIB, had apparently become accepted as a legitimate social aspiration.

Manpower policy and industrial training

Manpower policies in Britain have been traditionally concerned with one major problem: the correction and avoidance of labour market imbalances over the growth cycle. But from 1960 to 1970 (particularly during the last half of the decade), manpower policies became increasingly viewed as elements of a strategy for changing an economy which had lost some of its adaptability and power of progress: as instruments to ensure future supplies of skilled labour, to overcome rigidities and resistance to technological change, and to encourage a more optimal utilization of manpower resources, not just across industries, but also within the place of work. Active manpower policy thus became elaborated as an incentive or cushion for the acceptance of change in the labour market. There were a number of innovations. A Selective Employment Tax was introduced (1966) primarily to shift the demand for labour away from the distributive and service sectors. One major innovation (the Redundancy Payment Act, 1965) and one reform (earnings-related unemployment benefit) were designed to compensate individuals for the personal costs of changes in the employment structure. Efforts were also made to improve the image and efficiency of the Public Employment Service, including a vocational guidance service for adults and strengthened assistance towards geographical mobility.

Disregarding SET (except for the regional differentiation element) and the costs of industrial training reimbursed by the Industrial Training Boards, the total resources devoted to these manpower policy institutions and programmes by 1970 were approximately 1¼ % of GNP. If the ITB costs are included, the total is nearer 2 %: roughly a doubling in real and relative terms since 1960. While the largest appropriations were those for regional employment creation, redundancy payments and industrial training, mobility measures and the Public Employment Service accounted for only a small proportion (less than a tenth) of total resources devoted to manpower policies. The Government Training Centres (with a capacity of under 10,000 places) mainly functioned as a supplement to the larger Industrial Training Board system. During the 1960s however, the volume of unemployment expanded (varying between 250,000 and 750,000); and so Britain, like many other economies, was far from possessing a machinery which could meet local or general variations in unemployment with immediately available opportunities for training.

Although manpower policy has involved many components, attention may be concentrated upon the most significant segment: the industrial training system as it developed since 1964. The system was introduced (under a Conservative government) after long and frustrated efforts to achieve an adequate volume and quality of industrial training through persuasion. In terms of enterprise-by-enterprise coverage, it represented one of the largest-scale attempts at structural change in the British economy. The inducement theory was 'catalytic action' but the practices have leaned continuously towards statutory obligation and the introduction of economic penalties on a selective basis. By 1970, the new approach – the independent collectivization of a great part of training costs under tripartite Boards for about thirty branches of industry covering over 18 million workers – had only limited parallels outside the UK. The Boards have authority to raise levies from all employers in their branch, and use these to pay grants to those who undertake training of an approved quality. The payment of a high proportion of approved training costs, through cross-firm subsidization, undoubtedly spurred many individual employers to expand on-the-job and off-the-job training. By 1968, it was estimated that, every day, some half a million workers received some ostensible training; that 25,000 training officers had been created in industry; and that total grant payments under the Industrial Training Act were about £130 million annually (of which only £3 million were paid by the state). The operational size of the Act, covering a million registrable establishments, was thus formidable. To some extent, the Boards have become bureaucratic structures enjoying substantial autonomy from the Labour Ministry and the industrial base; i.e. they symbolize *industrial* centres of influence more powerful than trade associations or large firms, and are often more influential than some employer associations.

The formal intention of the 1964 Act, which gave considerable discretion to Training Board operations, was (1) to ensure an adequate supply of properly trained men and women at *all* levels in industry; (2) to secure an improvement in the quality and efficiency of industrial training; (3) to share the cost of training more evenly between firms. The basic principle of 'collectivization' in training costs, and the ensuing concentration of power in ITBs, was thus not one of common financing for the whole manufacturing economy without branch differentiation (as in the French *taxe d'apprentissage* or in any country which finances an important part of vocational training via the general tax system). The advisory Central Training Council is responsible to the secretary of state (DEP and later DE) and hence parliament, while the CTC also advises the Boards via the secretary of state (without having any decision-making or supervisory role *vis à vis* the Boards). The minister alone is responsible for supervising, guiding and supporting the activities of the system. Despite the implied preference for voluntary advisory association on the national level, with executive power in the ministry, it was maintained that the strength of the system was the extent to which it obliged each industry to work out its own training schemes and needs through the ITBs. The actual organizational pattern brought a very high degree of decentralization and delegated decision-making, even upon important policy questions, to the ITBs. Thus one of the central issues in Britain became the adequacy of central powers, not only with respect to legal authority vested in the CTC and the minister, but also with respect to administrative resources.

Since industrial training was regarded as belonging to industry, with the role of the state as advance identification of major inter-industry manpower changes and very loose guidance of the ITBs, manpower policy evolved no central set of guidelines and remained curiously detached (apart from productivity bargaining) from incomes policy development and the general stream of educational expenditure. There were two reasons for this hiatus. First, the initial ideology which emphasized that, since individual training needs could only be expressed by *individual* enterprises, the function of the state was that of support and not initiation. Second, there were self-defined limits to union–employer co-ordination at *national* level: national unions and employer associations, long reluctant to accept anything more than a national advisory relationship to the Labour Ministry on highly general matters, were also unwilling to accept the dominant responsibility for manpower policies at enterprise levels. The government itself, after the National Plan, remained also within self-imposed limits, since it was discovered that the newly established Manpower Research Unit (Department of Employment and Productivity) could not produce detailed forecasts of sectional, occupational and total manpower which could be useful to the individual firm.

The interpretation of the aim of the ITBs thus became difficult in the absence of any coherently stated national labour market policy.

National interpretation of medium-run labour supply requirements between small and large firms and the incidence of costs and returns, became obscured by the wide variation in Board practices. The efficiency of Boards was, to some extent, governed by their size and influence: with large and rich Boards for certain sectors (engineering being the most outstanding case) coexisting with others having tiny resources and staff. As a rule, however, most Boards were dominated by the larger firms, who were called upon to subsidize training for the smaller enterprises in their industry. The levy practices became extremely variable across Boards, growing up in a haphazard way because the organizational pattern, envisaged under the Act, was designed to respond to bottom-level pressures. Thus a fundamental question was evaded from the start. What was the optimal way for costs of training and retraining to be shared between the state, each industry branch represented by the ITB, the individual employer and the individual worker?

With the grants seen as an 'incentive' and 'contribution' rather than a reimbursement of training costs to employers, the problems of launching the system became obvious during the first few years of installing the ITBs. Some Boards pitched their levies at a high level from the start, on the grounds that they could quickly set up training organizations and offer substantial grants for schemes to co-operating firms. Others kept levies low on the grounds that until firms became adjusted to the burden, they would remain unaware of the new benefits. At first, the scale of levy was usually charged to member firms on a common basis – a certain sum per worker employed or a fixed percentage of payroll. Later, the tendency developed to vary the levy on an occupational basis – making it marginally higher to firms with relatively expensive training requirements. Towards the end of the decade, differential rates became generally established for small and large firms, with some Boards exempting the very small establishments altogether. The flexibility of the ITB system was devised on the principle that manpower practices and management–worker attitudes varied widely between industries, occupations, areas and enterprises. But the lack of uniformity across industries has highlighted the necessity for adjusting the balance from the centre, thus yielding a more direct role to government. Up to 1971, however, this problem was approached largely in terms of voluntarily establishing industry-by-industry liaison links: most Boards now explicitly recognize the need to pool experience and to gain scale economies through the extension of horizontal responsibility as a subsidiary function. Where the same craft is common to a group of industries, demarcation agreements have been reached to determine which Boards should have responsibility for the craft. Thus despite its self-restricted advisory purpose, the Central Training Council (CTC) has functioned more as a co-ordinating body: especially co-ordinating training in the large employment categories common to all industries, such as clerical and commercial work, and management and supervisory training. Despite these efforts to reduce overlapping, by allocating broader competence to some Boards covering related industries, substantial differences remain. Most of these stem from the frame of industry-by-industry organization, since many occupations are dispersed extensively throughout very different industry branches or are even represented in all of them.

This highlights the question of whether the most rational organizational solution is to maintain some thirty largely independent Boards operating side by side. The minimal solution, long advocated by the union participants, would be a radical change in CTC functions and redefinition of its role with government. On this argument, the CTC would be strengthened, with its own staff and powers to administer public funds for the development of industrial training. Another alternative would be a 'centralist' solution on the pyramid model: a single, central ITB as a specialized authority under uniform management with sections for the various industrial branches, on the grounds that this would make it possible to create a tighter structure, more closely-knit implementation and probably more uniform management. But this centralist solution is strongly disliked: both by the craft unions (protecting apprenticeship practices and wishing to avert 'dilution agreements' promoted through any central sponsoring apparatus) and by the employers (unwilling to see funds channelled into a central organization which might redistribute them beyond their industrial-source boundaries). The ministry itself has long suspected that, given vast outnumbering of its own *technical* staff by the Board staffs (which in engineering and construction alone number nearly 400), detailed central control of the training machinery would be virtually impossible without government sanction for a great expansion in the specialist resources of the Department of Employment. In some countries, the promotion of vocational training is partly combined with the public employment service and its local agencies. In the UK, the problem is how, in an undercentralized system, the Boards can guarantee, to the minister and parliament, implementation of ITA measures at regional and local levels with employers' and workers' organizations, education authorities and individual firms, and how the Boards can provide adequate advice and supervision to their client. Sometimes the proposal has been advocated that the Board should be reconstituted on a regional rather than an industry branch basis, to secure the Boards' local communications with the employment service and with enterprises. A last alternative would be to base the system totally on occupations instead of industries. These last two alternatives are heavily weighed down with disadvantages, given the existing craft-union structures and practices in the UK, where one prime need is to lower the existing barriers between different crafts within each industry and enterprise unit. The pattern of craft representation in union structures and policies is extremely complicated in the UK and has been a potent force for conservatism to an extent unparalleled in other European economies.

The ITA system has produced a large and productive upheaval in British industrial training practices, while the organizational form has stimulated a conflict of group interests which has effectively constrained any 'jump' towards centralization and any benefits which might stem from a stronger government role. While the old system directly initiated training decisions which were irrational from the viewpoint of the economy, although often rational to the individual firm, the new system comprises a large step towards the allocation of costs in relation to training revenues on more rational criteria. The new system provided for a great variety of experiments, under various ITBs, with the usual learning-costs involved in approaching different optimal fits. The underlying principle was not one of establishing Boards as proxy institutions for the government collection and disbursement of training expenditures; it was a principle of delegating fiscal powers to semi-autonomous industrial bodies. By 1971, the government's review of the six-year development revealed that an impasse had been reached in which the system could neither be modified piecemeal nor could it be radically restructured without destroying the elaborate series of balances and compromises built into the previous structures of Board practices and attitudes. In the long run, the Boards were seen as disengaging from the levy/grant system, becoming 'training consultants' to their industries. In the short run, Boards had become increasingly aware that relations with their industries might become permanently damaged if they increased their levies. Conversely, levy reduction might be seen as an abrogation of the public responsibilities of certain Boards. Like the Labour government, the post-1970 Conservative government recognized, as an *aspiration*, the case for a national manpower commission (independent of the DEP) which would have overall responsibility for the employment service and all training facilities. But this aspiration has so far remained unfulfilled.

The significance of manpower policy in Britain is that it exemplifies the difficulties of government delegation of functional powers to new industrial bodies. Such bodies, through initiating schemes, necessarily conflict with their constituents and threaten the established employer associations in their traditional spheres of influence; while the government cannot assist them through adopting a mediatory (minimal) role or a co-ordinating (maximal) role. The process also exemplifies the changing power relationships between firms within each industry: the conflict between large and small firms has become more visible than in most other parts of the British planning system. The early idea of maximizing the social returns from training by spreading the cost incidence between firms in an industry tended to neglect this obstacle. While the power structure of Boards has tended to become oligopolized, strongly reflecting large firm interests, the result has been to produce resistance and a fall-out of smaller firms. The general problem posed by the experiment is how far can a planning instrument, conceived on these lines, permeate downwards into the mass of small firms?

Conclusion

Both the British experiments in incomes–prices–productivity policy, and in manpower policy, demonstrate a singular change in emphasis. Increasingly, the British emphasis has swung away from the industry-wide surface of the labour market and industrial relations down toward the depth determinants of the behaviour at company, plant and workplace levels. But can it lead us anywhere *concretely* in the short run, apart from pinning hopes on reforming collective bargaining through a change agent like the Commission on Industrial Relations or the PIB, or on transforming the co-ordination roles and elevating the responsibilities of the Department of Employment? The lesson of the decade of 'partial planning' in the labour market was that acknowledging inconsistency in the piecemeal British system could be quite different from living with contradiction, since the first can lead to evolution while the second leads to continued ossification.

The decade identifies clearly the weakness of the centre/periphery model for 'planning' or guiding the labour market parties. Union and employer structures and the bargaining forms around them approximate far more to 'shifting-centre' concepts than to simple bureaucratic forms capable of being subsumed within a hierarchical planning structure. This forces the social interest to face the realities behind 'centralization' where, once the control limit is reached, the system becomes dysfunctional to change while appearing functional to departments of state. If government wishes to introduce an incomes policy, national guidelines have to be transmuted into the decision-making parameter of the enterprise, where the reality is that managers have lost some (often large) parts of remuneration control to the work groups. If government wishes to eradicate sub-optimal labour utilization, this can only be pursued at the company and plant level through instituting joint regulation. If government wishes to avert some of the contributory causes of strikes, the industrial relations system must be rebuilt from the bottom upwards by tackling those domestic procedures and irrational pay structures which are factors in unofficial disputes. If the unofficial strike is the 'British disease', which Britain may have communicated to France and Italy, the more positive features of the British experiments in incomes and manpower policies may throw some illumination upon the future of planning processes and political institutions in other European countries.

NOTES

1 See T. Burns and G. M. Stalker, *The Management of Innovation*, 1966.
2 On 50 price increase references, the PIB recommended smaller increases in 20 cases and rejection in 7 cases; on 51 wage references, it recommended against in 17 cases and sought smaller increases in 24 cases.

SELECT BIBLIOGRAPHY

Blackaby, F. (ed), *An Incomes Policy for Britain*, Heinemann, 1972.
Corina, J., 'Incomes Policy: Retrospect and Prospect', *Monitor* (Institute of Manpower Studies), March 1974.
Fels, A. *The British Prices and Incomes Board*, Cambridge University Press, 1972.
Mitchell, Joan. *The National Board for Prices and Incomes*, Secker and Warburg, 1972.
OECD, *Manpower Policy in the United Kingdom*, 1970.

10. Incomes and employment policies in Italian economic planning

ISIDORO FRANCO MARIANI

EDITORIAL FOREWORD[1]

Until Italy began to suffer the balance of payments problems that have been a chronic feature of the British economy, Italian governments did not feel called upon to have an incomes policy, particularly as the weak and divided trade unions, in conditions of chronic unemployment, were in no position to contribute to cost-push inflation. Italy was content to rely upon indirect control through Central Bank management of monetary policy. Such control was more discreet, more easily exerted and more easily enforced than a formal incomes policy. There were a number of factors which, until the sixties, enabled Italy to rely almost entirely upon monetary policy in controlling inflation. More important than the advantages of a negligible national debt and low military expenditure, rapidly increasing Italian productivity kept well ahead of wages, while consumer prices – restrained partly by EEC entry – rose less than wages, so that workers' living standards improved. The modernisation backlog was a major stimulant to the rapid technological progress and investment opportunities of the early sixties, reflected in an average rise in annual growth of output per man hour in manufacturing of 8.9% in Italy over the period 1961–4. (In the same period, productivity increased by only 3.5% in the United Kingdom and by 4.9% in France.) However, the sixties witnessed a drastic change in the labour market situation, which in turn was reflected in a decline in Italian productivity – 6.9% in 1965–8 and 2.8% in 1969–72 – at a time when Britain was modestly improving its performance to 3.9% and then 4.8%, while France was moving on to rates of 5.8% and 8.3%.

Until the early sixties, Italian industrial relations were characterised by management's domination over labour. The latter had been subordinated to the strategies of the political parties, leaving it at the mercy of the employers in matters of collective bargaining. The interests of the mass of micro-firms represented by Confindustria and of the avant-garde giants like Fiat – which at least until 1962 played a pilot role in Italian wage policy comparable to that of Renault in France – were reconciled by combining a national bargaining straitjacket to keep down wage increases to what the marginal firms would accept, with flexible upward adjustments by the efficient firms. Helped along by a cost of living sliding scale, the centralised national system of bargaining guaranteed 'a minimum standard of living that will minimize social and political protest while it makes only minimal demands upon industry'. Meanwhile, the capital-intensive, advanced firms were able to engage in a policy of 'planned wages drift', which in return for higher earnings, secured the capacity to 'maximise labor docility, minimise strikes, and even exert considerable control over the development and political complexion of the labor movement'.[2] By playing off the divided unions against each other, in a context of underemployment, firms like Fiat had the workers at their mercy.

The creation of a public enterprise employers' organisation, Intersind, in 1956, separated off from Confindustria, was part of the political preparation within the Christian Democratic party for the emergence of the Centre-Left coalition. Until 1962, it did not challenge the Confindustria opposition to plant bargaining, although, like the pace-setting big private corporations, IRI was able to pay higher wages. Helped by the willingness of Intersind to undertake separate negotiations from Confindustria in 1962, the non-Communist unions – which had become disenchanted with the subordination of their economic functions to political ends – decided that selective union push would achieve more than discriminating managerial pull and the movement away from centralised national bargaining, via industry-level bargaining towards decentralised plant-level bargaining, began in earnest.[3] The more assertive role of the unions was sometimes helped by intervention from the Ministry of Labour, which tended to side with the unions in order to secure their political support and to avoid the unrest connected with strikes. The realignment of Italian political and economic forces that took place at the start of the sixties was associated with the venture into economic 'programming' but in the field of incomes and employment policy the record is not impressive.

The particular economic and social conditions in Italy have had a considerable influence on the manner and pattern of economic planning. Ever since the achievement of national unity, more than a century ago, Italy has been afflicted by a structural disequilibrium between resources and needs, between productive potential and population. That is why, traditionally, Italy has always been one of the countries with the highest incidence of emigration, predominantly to countries across the ocean (United States of America, Argentina and other South American countries) prior to the First World War and, in more recent times, to other European countries. Italy remains the only industrialized country which still has vast resources of labour and where under-employment, if not complete unemployment, still exists on an enormous scale. In recent decades, however, the situation has changed considerably: it has been realized that emigration is not the sole remedy for this disequilibrium and that, instead, adequate economic growth can lead to a complete absorption of the labour supply. This objective has in practice already been realized in the more industrialized areas, in central and northern Italy. Nevertheless, even in certain pockets of those areas, and above all in the southern mainland and islands, a vast quantity of labour is still idle.

This situation is evidenced in particular by the ratio between the working population and total population. This ratio (or employment rate) steadily diminished from 43.8% in 1959 to 36.6% in 1970, and has fallen further subsequently. The reduction is attributable to a series of favourable factors, such as the increase in the number of young people attending school (thereby delaying their entry into the labour force) and the improvement of pensions legislation (which induces many older workers to retire early, or at least not to continue working after reaching retirement age). Many people, however, believe that these factors are not sufficient to explain a reduction of such large proportions. In any event, the fact remains that the employment rate in Italy is one of the lowest encountered in the industrialized countries, and it is significant that the rate is particularly low for the female population, of which less than 20% number among the labour force. This phenomenon is nowadays attributed to a qualitative shortfall in the supply of labour rather than in demand. The situation is largely hidden, in that people tend not to seek employment if they know that they do not possess the requisites, above all education and training, demanded by the market.

This combination of factors explains why Italian economic planning, in its various configurations over recent decades, has always emphasized employment policy, leaving the question of an incomes policy in the background. Indeed, the primary objective stated in the 'Scheme for income and employment growth in the decade 1955–64' (otherwise known as the Vanoni Plan, the first attempt to introduce an organic development policy), was the provision of greater opportunities for more stable employment, in order to eliminate unemployment and to reduce the incidence of under-employment.[4] The Papi committee of economists appointed in March 1961 to draw up a new planning scheme (representing the second attempt), also included the attainment of full employment (together with maximization of income and narrowing of the gap between developed and underdeveloped areas) among its prime objectives.[5] The report presented at the end of 1963 by the National Commission for Economic Planning, which constituted the practical manifestation of the official launching of a planning policy, declared the principal objectives to be solution of the Southern Italy problem and improvement of productivity in agriculture. It contended that the attainment of full employment would be achieved through the elimination of the disequilibria of the nation's structures.[6] The related objectives contained in the 'Economic Development Programme for the quinquennium 1966–1970', the first document in which planning was formally embodied, were stated as 'the removal of sectorial, territorial and social disequilibria...through a policy constantly aimed at full employment and to the maximum and humane utilization of the labour force, which constitutes a permanent planning commitment'. The objectives of the 1966–70 Plan included an increase of the order of 1,400,000 jobs in extra-agricultural sectors. Agriculture was, and still is, an overpopulated sector, accounting at present for approximately 19% of the total labour force, despite the fact that the decrease in the number of farmworkers between 1965 and 1970 was more than double the 600,000 envisaged in the Plan. (See Table 1.) So the approach adopted in Italy has been contrary to that usually followed in countries in which, once a state of full employment has been reached, the situation calls for particular attention to incomes policy as an instrument for preserving that state in the framework of economic growth and monetary stability. It is symptomatic, in this connection, that in Italy there is explicit talk of incomes policy during periods of faster economic growth, namely, at times when the ease with which the unemployed, under-employed and new entrants to the labour force can find work appears to diminish the urgency of the need to create new jobs.

To understand the present Italian situation, a further factor has to be considered. Over the past four years the roles of employers' and labour organizations, especially the trade unions, have changed considerably. For many years – from the immediate post-war period until towards the middle of the sixties – negotiations were both intense and highly centralized. Until 1954, for example, in industry minimum contractual wages were negotiated directly between the major central employers' and labour organizations established at national level, which fixed the minimum wage-rates for almost all industrial workers, who were classified in certain fundamental categories, within which wages were completely standardized. The years subsequent to 1954, however, saw the development of negotiation on an industry basis, including the question of wages, while during the sixties there emerged negotiation at plant level, despite the opposition of employers and their organizations, who wished to limit the extent and content of negotiation.

Thus, whereas originally the principal trade union role was played by the national central inter-sectorial organizations, in recent years their importance has been gradually diminishing, due to the mounting autonomy of the organizations established at industry level and of the workers' representative organizations at plant level.[7] This development has not been without its consequences in the implementation, albeit empirical and not institutionalized in Italy's case, of an incomes policy. Once a collective bargaining agreement has been reached at sector level, negotiations are often immediately re-opened at plant level for adaptation (obviously with greater advantages for the workers) of the terms and conditions agreed at sector level. As a consequence, there are many centres at which decisions regarding wages may be taken, and the number of such centres has been increasing in recent times. This proliferation of new groups representing specific interests, and their assumption of decisional powers, has been accompanied by their increasing autonomy *vis-à-vis* other groups and government authorities.

However, an incomes policy figures among the essential conditions for implementation of planning policy. The policy was stated essentially in two propositions: (1) 'earned incomes must not rise at a rate very different from the growth of productivity'; (2) 'incomes policy cannot consist solely of a wages and salaries policy, but also of a prices policy, on which profits depend'.[8] Nevertheless, while employment policy and incomes policy are included as salient features of Italian economic planning, the link between the two is only indirect, in that employment policy is included among the objectives of economic planning, whereas incomes policy is included among the means. Both policies are, however, stated at the macro-economic level and have not, therefore, directly affected the individual enterprise.

However, in Italy a planning policy was never really introduced in practice. The failure to respond to stated objectives, or postulated conditions, is particularly evident precisely in the area of employment and incomes. As regards employment, the exodus from agriculture has occurred on an enormous and uncontrolled scale, its magnitude being, on aggregate, twice that envisaged in the Plan (1,275,000 between 1965 and 1970, against the assumed 600,000). However, the number of jobs in extra-agricultural sectors has increased in an extremely irregular fashion, following the peaks and troughs of economic activity, with uneven movements between industry and the service sector. The employment vacuum caused by the exodus from agriculture has not been filled, with the result that the total number of employed persons has diminished and, as observed earlier, the employment rate has fallen from 38.8% in 1965 to 36.6% in 1970.

The growth-pattern of earned incomes has not been very similar to that of productivity: earned incomes have often increased at a faster rate and only occasionally, in phases of economic recovery, has productivity outpaced incomes. During the period 1966–70 inclusive, the average annual growth of earned incomes was at least one point higher than that of gross national product (10.6% against 9.6%). Thus, the earned income share of national income without doubt rose, but certainly not as a result of planning, the objectives of which, moreover, included an increase of that share insofar as it had the effect of reducing the disequilibria in the distribution of national income.

Responsibility for implementation of these incomes policy directives, in particular, was to be assigned to what in Italy are the natural decision-making centres, namely the organizations representing em-

Table 1. *Italian employment by sector* ('000)

	Agriculture			Industry			Services			All sectors			Employment rate (%)
	No.	Variation from preceding year		No.	Variation from preceding year		No.	Variation from preceding year		No.	Variation from preceding year		
		No.	%		No.	%		No.	%		No.	%	
1959	6,847	—	—	7,176	—	—	6,146	—	—	20,169	—	—	43.8
1960	6,567	−280	−4.1	7,388	212	3.0	6,181	35	0.6	20,136	−33	−0.2	42.8
1961	6,207	−360	−5.5	7,646	258	3.5	6,319	138	2.2	20,172	36	0.2	42.5
1962	5,810	−397	−6.4	7,810	164	2.1	6,330	11	0.2	19,950	−222	−1.1	41.6
1963	5,295	−515	−8.9	7,986	176	2.3	6,349	19	0.3	19,630	−320	−1.6	40.3
1964	4,967	−328	−6.2	7,996	10	0.1	6,618	269	4.2	19,581	−49	−0.2	39.7
1965	4,956	−11	−0.2	7,728	−268	−3.4	6,515	−103	−1.6	19,199	−382	−2.0	38.8
1966	4,660	−296	−6.0	7,621	−107	−1.4	6,603	88	1.4	18,884	−315	−1.6	37.8
1967	4,556	−104	−2.2	7,782	161	2.1	6,769	166	2.5	19,107	233	1.2	37.8
1968	4,247	−309	−6.8	7,890	108	1.4	6,932	163	2.4	19,069	−38	−0.2	37.4
1969	4,023	−224	−5.3	8,048	158	2.0	6,800	−132	−1.9	18,871	−198	−1.0	36.8
1970	3,683	−340	−8.5	8,209	161	2.0	7,064	264	3.9	18,956	85	0.5	36.6

ployers and workers, leaving to government authorities the function of intervention to correct possible approaches conflicting with those directives.[9] The draft Bill containing the planning procedures which govern, among other regulations, the intervention of the two sides of industry by defining the functions, objectives and modalities of such intervention, has never been approved by parliament and therefore its provisions have never become binding. Above all, what has been missing is the unhindered collaboration of both sides of industry. This lack of collaboration was due – especially within the Socialist–Communist led CGIL – to the rejection, as a matter of principle, of any form of indicative planning and to the fear of assuming responsibility within the framework of a planning policy. It was believed that such participation would subordinate the trade union movement to the government and induce it to accept choices, and abandon other choices, with detrimental effects upon the condition of the working class.[10] This attitude did not change substantially when planning assumed a concrete form, with the government's presentation, and the subsequent approval by parliament, of the first five-year Economic Development Plan. However, they changed their opposition from one of principle to objections to the Plan's content. For example, as regards incomes policy, CISL was opposed to the principle stated in the programme of wages growth linked to the average productivity increase of the economy, namely a two-tier, industrial and plant-level, form of wages policy.[11] For its part, CGIL firmly repeated the need for 'negotiating autonomy' in the hands of the trade union leaders.[12] It should be observed that the negative attitude of the trade union leaders was influenced, albeit unconsciously and in varying degrees, by the experience of the fifties: as we have seen, during that period wage-bargaining was very centralized and incomes policy, as such, was conditioned by central decisions, with the result that only a relatively modest improvement in the conditions of workers was possible.

Beyond the institutional planning framework, incomes policy has in practice been managed, *de facto*, by the traditional protagonists, trade unions and employers' organizations, with occasional intervention, in more important cases, by government authorities as arbiters or conciliators. Incomes policy has, therefore, developed under the stimuli of the power relationships which condition the labour market. The underlying trend that emerges is the constant increase of the share of national income obtained by wage and salary earners: but, as we have seen, it is a trend determined by events, and registered *a posteriori*, rather than as the consequence of a premeditated choice. The dialogue between the parties has always seen the trade union leaders on the attack and the employers' representatives on the defensive. On the rare occasions when the latter have attempted to take the initiative and put forward proposals, they have been met with diffidence and hostility on the part of the trade union leaders.

An aspect worthy of separate discussion would be the behaviour of the government as representative of an employer, namely the state, towards its own employees (about 1,500,000, inclusive of teachers, railwaymen, police, etc). The government's attitude in this field, however, has never followed a clearly defined policy, but has been one rather of adaptation to circumstances and to the needs of the moment. As regards the State Holdings enterprises – which have their own representative organization, since by law they are not permitted to join private enterprise employers' organizations – it is readily evident that they are more exposed to trade union pressure, partly because they are more subject to political influences. Thus, in recent years, several major disputes with the unions have been settled much more quickly, and perhaps on more costly terms, in the public sector of industry than in the private sector. This was the case, for example, of the dispute regarding abolition of area-related wage levels (settled in December 1968 in the public sector and in March 1969 in the private sector) and of the renewal of the national collective bargaining agreements for the engineering industry in 1969 and 1973.

Government intervention in industrial disputes, which occurs frequently, is politically motivated. However, the role of the minister of labour has changed considerably over the years. Roughly until 1968, this role took the form principally of mediation or, in extreme cases, of arbitration. Since 1968 – that is roughly since the central labour confederations lined up against the industrialists' confederation over the issue of territorial-related wage levels – the government has adopted openly declared, partisan positions, with explicit support of workers' demands. Its intervention in labour disputes has thus changed from one of neutral mediation to one of 'oriented' mediation.[13] Evidence of the strengthening of this attitude was provided in Autumn 1969, during the protracted negotiations for renewal of labour contracts in major industrial sectors, when it was precisely with the labour minister's intervention that agreement was reached. This attitude of non-neutrality now represents a constant characteristic of government intervention in labour disputes, whether motivated by renewal of labour contracts or by employment problems arising, for example, when an enterprise is obliged to close or to reorganize. It is particularly in evidence when the dispute is with State Holdings enterprises. The purposeful and frequent intervention by the government, through the minister of labour, in labour disputes has become an authentic, if informal, instrument of incomes policy.

What has been said about incomes policy also applies to employment policy. A special, horizontally structured agency for the economic and social development of Southern Italy, the Cassa per il Mezzogiorno, does not have a function of direct stimulation, but one of creation of the environmental conditions necessary for the development of productive activity and, thereby, for increasing employment. In other fields, the individual ministries have retained their respective responsibilities, exercised with varying degrees of dynamism, according to the political ideologies and strength of personality of the minister concerned. In particular, there has been no diminution, much less solution, of the problem of the competitition between the Labour Ministry and the Education Ministry. The overlapping of responsibilities, in the area of vocational training, recognized to be one of the principal instruments of any employment policy, especially in the case of a country such as Italy (where under-employment is widespread, particularly in farming areas where unskilled labour abounds) is particularly serious.

In this respect it should be noted that vocational training in Italy is structured on four fundamentals: apprenticeship with enterprises, Labour Ministry centres and courses, Education Ministry vocational training institutes, and various other initiatives (courses organized by the civil service, public agencies and private enterprises).[14] An idea of the scale of this vocational training effort is provided by the following figures referring to 1968–9: 88,000 apprentices were trained, 48,000 students passed out from vocational training institutes, and 31,000 students obtained diplomas after attending two-year initial training courses financed by the Ministry of Labour. Of the other initiatives, the following merit particular mention: those promoted by IRI (Industrial Reconstruction Institute, the principal state industrial holding corporation), which runs six centres, frequented by approximately 10,000 trainees each year; the vocational training centres established by the Cassa per il Mezzogiorno and run by the Cassa in collaboration with local government authorities, industrial associations and enterprises; the inter-firm schools (approximately 50) established by private industrial enterprises; and the schemes provided under the terms of the labour contracts for the building and printing industries, run jointly by the employers' organizations and the trade unions. However, the fundamental fact is that these schemes do not come within the framework of economic planning, are run independently of one another and are not coordinated. Furthermore, they are insufficient to provide industry with the new skilled labour required each year.

In the field of employment policies there have also been two attempts to institutionalize a form of collaboration between government, trade union leaders and enterprises, but once again outside the framework of any planning scheme. The first was the tripartite conference on employment, held in 1967 and 1968, and the second was the national conference on female employment problems, held in March 1968. The purpose of both conferences was to make possible the joint study of the various aspects of employment with a view to devising specific measures which would increase the labour force. In the event, the attempts progressed no further than the study stage, both because of the difficulty of dealing with employment problems independently of those of economic growth and because of the clearly propagandistic purpose of the initiatives, with a general election scheduled for Spring 1968.

The union leaders adjudged the experience of these tripartite meetings to be particularly negative, and from then on always refused to participate in other similar conferences, even when they plied the government with demands to proceed with major social reforms (health, transport, housing, social security, etc). The results were perhaps more positive, insofar as the enterprises were concerned, in the context of *contrattazione programmatica* (planned bargaining) as an employment-policy instrument. This is a formula, adopted by the government in recent years, providing for an exchange of information on the investment programmes of the large industrial enterprises and on the interventions contemplated by the government for the development of Southern Italy. On the occasion of these meetings the question of employment, for the purpose of deciding upon the location of investment projects, assumes considerable importance, but it is still only a particular aspect of a more general policy.

EDITORIAL POSTSCRIPT

Coming after the period of rapid but unbalanced growth up to the early sixties and the economic crisis of 1963–5, the Italian government sought to promote a better-balanced growth by persuading business to invest in the underdeveloped South through the device of 'planned bargaining'. The aim was to substitute in part the southward mobility of capital for the northward mobility of labour. Treasury Minister Colombo declared in 1967 that the government:

> was willing, in exchange for a global commitment of entrepreneurs to invest (in Southern Italy) to correlate the timing of the building of the necessary infrastructures, as well as the provision of funds to finance the whole set-up, to the timing of the building of the plant...The government must use incisively its political bargaining power which, while respecting the entrepreneurs' freedom of choice can guide it, by means of the instruments at the government's disposal, at least in the field of public expenditure and the financing of undertakings.[15]

Such cooperation and coordination between government and business was fostered by the planning mood of the period, although firms were worried that planned bargaining would increase the discretionary authority of the government, while the trade unions felt as excluded as ever from the key national economic decisions. In any case, incentives to capital mobility have meant that investment in the South has been capital-intensive and has not had the hoped-for impact upon unemployment.

The 'Hot Autumn' of 1969 affected the position of the Italian trade unions much more significantly than the May events of 1968 had done in France. The Communist-aligned CGIL, the Christian Democrat-aligned CISL and the mainly Social Democrat-aligned UIL have all not only gained in strength and self-confidence but have gained a measure of independence of the political parties and have partially taken over their role as advocates of change in housing, social security, education and transport. However, the attempt at political party disengagement to achieve unity between the three confederations and thereby create a more effective instrument for political and industrial action, has so far failed to materialise. Militancy having paid in the industrial sphere, non-wage demands have been made and won involving the reduction of working hours and more say in the working of factories. The employers are very much on the defensive and Confindustria itself went through a serious crisis in the early seventies. The Centre-Left was restored to power in 1973 in the hope that it would win a respite from trade union militancy and enable the government to get to grips with the problems of stagflation. The unions, however, have supported the short-term, piecemeal, crisis intervention by the government to preserve jobs by rescuing private businesses threatened with bankruptcy, rather than more systematic attempts to deal with unemployment and inflation through reinvigorated economic planning. The lack of emphasis given to the problem of retraining agricultural labour for industry is a glaring weakness in matching the demand and supply of labour. Not merely have Italian growth and productivity declined, but the pattern of growth has not increased employment, which remains Italy's main preoccupation. Although the 1971–5 draft Plan restated its main target to be the correction of a 'persistent underutilisation of human resources',[16] there is little evidence that the government will be able to achieve this end.

NOTES

1 A brief foreword and postscript have been added by Jack Hayward to this contribution, sketching in some aspects of the political and industrial relations context.

2 M. Edelman and R. W. Fleming, *The Politics of Wage–Price Decisions*, pp. 32, 36, cf. pp. 41, 49.

3 *Ibid.* pp. 47–8, 51; cf. W. Kendall's chapter on labour relations in S. Holland (ed), *The State as Entrepreneur*. More generally, on the contrast between the response of large and small businesses to increased trade union bargaining power, see P. A. Allum, *Italy – Republic without Government?* 1973, pp. 29–32, cf. pp. 25–35.

4 The Vanoni Plan was not implemented for various reasons, not wholly disassociated from the hostile attitude of the major trade unions. The Socialist–Communist oriented CGIL in fact adopted a policy of intransigent opposition, deriving from the rejection of any form of indicative planning. Much more interesting for our purposes was the position adopted by the Christian Democrat-oriented CISL. Its attitude was largely conditioned by the inability to understand that the achievement of the general objectives outlined in the Plan, including the attainment of a

higher level of employment, would require the satisfaction of certain indispensable conditions (such as containment of consumption and of wage increases) which would have constituted an authentic incomes policy. See Giovanni B. Forti, *Appunti per una storia politica della programmazione in Italia*, in Biblioteca della liberta, No. 36, 1972, chapter 16.

5 *Ibid.* chapter 18.

6 *Ibid.* chapter 22. As this work points out, the industrialists' representatives observed that it is not only a matter of creating new jobs, but also of training the already existing labour force in more productive skills.

7 See AA.VV, *Movimento sindacale e contrattazione collettiva 1945–1970*, F. Angeli, Milan 1971.

8 Ministry of the Budget and Economic Planning, *Economic Development Programme for the Quinquennium 1966–1970*, Section 4, para. 51.

9 'A policy aimed at ensuring compatibility of income distribution with planning objectives obviously involves a sense of responsibility not only on the part of government but also of the employers' and labour organizations, which wield a direct influence on the level of prices and wages. The Programme is developed on the supposition that it is neither possible, given the nature of our institutions, nor advantageous...to impose quantitative constraints and limits on negotiation, which must be unrestrictedly conducted between the various economic categories.' (Economic Development Programme, para. 52.)

10 See G. B. Forti, *Appunti per una storia politica...*

11 'Letter sent by CISL to the Prime Minister, Aldo Moro, dated 11.10.1965', Section 3 of *Economic Development Planning and CISL Wages Policy*, CISL, Rome 1966.

12 See M. D'Antonio, 'Commento al programma economico nazionale', Cappelli, Bologna 1967, quoted by Forti, *Appunti per una storia.*

13 In this regard, see G. Giugni; 'Les tendances récentes de la négotiation collective en Italie', in *Revue Internationale du Travail*, July 1971, p. 339.

14 See Confederazione generale dell'industria Italiana, *Una nuova politica di formazione professionale*, Quaderni di studi e documentazione, No. 23, Rome 1973.

15 Quoted in M. Barbato, 'Planned bargaining in Italy' in Banco di Roma, *Review of the Economic Conditions in Italy*, XXII, No. 3, May 1968, p. 161, cf. p. 169. See CIPE, *Contrattazione Programmata*, 1968, p. 37.

16 Ministry of the Budget and Planning, *Programma Economico Nazionale 1971–75*, 1972, p. 113.

SELECT BIBLIOGRAPHY

AA.VV, *Movimento sindacale e contrattazione collettiva, 1945–1970*, F. Angeli, Milan 1971.

Edelman, M. and Fleming, R. W. *The Politics of Wage–Price Decisions. A Four Country Analysis*, University of Illinois Press, Urbana 1965, chapter 2.

Forti, G. B. *Appunti per una storia politica della programmazione in Italia*, Biblioteca della Liberta, No. 36, Turin 1972.

Giugni, G. 'Recent Trends in Collective Bargaining in Italy' in ILO, *Collective Bargaining in Industrialised Market Economies*, Geneva 1974, pp. 273–94.

Kendall, W. 'Labour Relations', chapter 10 of S. Holland (ed), *The State as Entrepreneur*, Weidenfeld and Nicolson, 1972.

Comparative conclusions

JACK HAYWARD

An underlying feature of manpower policy in the three countries, particularly its wage policy aspect, has been the attempt by governments and employers to curb the bargaining power of trade union movements. Traditionally, workers and their representatives were not regarded, in relation to employers and governments, as joint partners in the industrial relations decision-making process. In the sixties, however, anxieties that unions might further encroach upon management prerogatives, in a full-employment situation which greatly strengthened the bargaining power of organised and unorganised labour, were expressed in all three countries. It is not surprising that Britain should have been the first to feel the impact of this pressure because it was both the country with the most sluggish economic growth and the strongest trade union movement. (It is estimated that at the end of the sixties some 42 % of the working population were unionised in Britain, compared to about 32 % in Italy and 22 % in France.) If in Britain there was the greatest capacity to extract wage increases, there was the least capacity to concede them without exacerbating inflationary pressures. Despite the traditionally negative approach of the British labour movement towards collective bargaining, seeking to obtain material benefits and security of employment rather than a share in control of the enterprise, the unions' capacity to secure wage improvements in excess of increases in productivity contributed to rises in unit labour costs and balance of payments constraints upon growth. This in turn led to government intervention through incomes policy to supplement the relatively low resistance offered by employers. Despite efforts to disguise wage restraint as 'the planned growth of incomes', the failure of successive attempts to conclude or effectively implement portentous tripartite summit agreements set the scene for increasingly politicised industrial conflict between government and the more militant unions, with the TUC and CBI making well-meaning but ineffectual gestures towards pacification.

In France, failure to compel the coalminers in 1963[1] to accept a modest wage increase was a contributory factor to the attempt, in the autumn of that year, to work out an acceptable incomes policy, and to the imposition of a deflationary 'stabilisation plan' at de Gaulle's personal instance. Both of these attempts to reduce trade union pressure miscarried. The attempt by Planning Commissioner Massé to secure a concerted incomes policy among the interested parties quickly foundered. While the stabilisation plan had some short-term success, it materially contributed to the increased unemployment, particularly among the young, that fuelled the general strike of May–June 1968. However, this crisis, far from exacerbating class conflict in France, eased matters by yielding substantial immediate benefits for the workers, and the subsequent boom increased employment and profits. The more modernist wing of the employers movement, in contrast to what had occurred in 1936, saw the need to accept collective bargaining with the trade unions; while the tactical alliance between the two largest and most militant unions, the CGT and the CFDT, suffered from their contrasting attitudes towards the 1968 'events'. So, despite the spectacular general strike that seemed to some at the time as heralding the collapse of capitalism or at least the demise of Gaullism, the socio-political disturbance was absorbed and the Fifth Plan was even able to turn the 'events' to account, getting closer to some of its targets than it would otherwise have done.

If the French unions have not acquired much more power as a result of the 1968 crisis, though they have a firmer foothold in the larger private sector firms than they enjoyed heretofore, in Italy the 'Hot Autumn' of 1969 had consequences that were less spectacular but were more sustained. As in France, the turning point may have come in the early sixties, when the unions began openly challenging managerial domination on the wage front. However, the triennial negotiation of wage contracts in 1969 prompted an outbreak of strikes that led to a number of major concessions by the employers. Wages and their associated cost of living adjustments increased by over 20 % in 1970. Regional wage differentials (phased out in France) were abolished. A number of measures to improve working conditions were agreed, notably the reduction of the working week and of overtime, which in France had been achieved by legislation as well as by collective bargaining in the wake of 1968. In Italy, new labour laws tilted the balance in favour of the workers, who could furthermore usually rely on the minister of labour's tacit support. In the economic recession of 1970–2, increased unemployment was largely avoided by the threat that workers would occupy factories that were closed down unless they received generous severance pay. The reduction of working hours, in conjunction with longer school attendance and earlier retirement, curtailed the supply of labour, while the Cassa di Integrazione made up the earnings of those on short-time. Although attempts to unite the three largest trade unions failed, they now comprise, alongside the large industrial corporations, the Communist party and the Roman Catholic Church, the fourth dominant group in the Italian political economy. As such, they have broadened the scope of their consensus to include political pressure to secure reforms in pensions and health insurance, education, housing and transport. While attempts to unite the French trade unions have been bedevilled by ideological quarrels, in Italy the emphasis on practical issues of social reform has facilitated joint action.

In all three countries, the problem of how power should be related to responsibility has been raised without being effectively resolved. Collective bargaining has not been reinterpreted as an exercise in the gradual extension of joint regulation over wages, working conditions and the production process. The conservative response of governments has generally taken the form of an attempt to discourage managements who, they believe, should exercise responsibility, from conceding any power of substance to the unions.

However, the inability of many managements in Britain and Italy, as well as a few in France, to preserve workplace managerial prerogatives unscathed, has raised the question of whether the approach should be experimentally reversed. Should more industrial responsibility be shifted to those who have the power, not merely the unions but the shop stewards and even the rank and file? Talk of 'workers control', however, poses the problem of whether the workers' organisations have either the inclination or the capacity to exercise increased responsibility. Those (such as the British unions) who might have the bargaining power, seem to have neither the inclination nor the capacity to exercise increased responsibilities; while those (like the French CFDT) who have the inclination and perhaps the capacity to do so, clearly do not have the power to put such claims to the test. Unions have both the negative power to resist change and the latent, positive power to promote it. The industrial divorce of power from responsibility has so far resulted in a stalemate. In Britain and Italy, it has been a critical factor in preventing the collaborative pursuit of economic growth; while in France, despite the glaring inequalities with which increasing wealth is shared, the unions have not been able to become a veto group in matters of national planning for rapid economic expansion.

NOTE

1 In 1972 and 1974, the British coalminers played a comparably important role, in the latter case receiving the credit for creating, through strike action, the conditions in which the Conservative Government called a general election that led to its defeat.

IV

The regional dimension

11. The French regional planning experiments

PIERRE GRÉMION AND JEAN-PIERRE WORMS

Until the Second World War the regional question was the subject of major ideological clashes, without any effect on the country's political and administrative organisation. What is called in France local administration is based on two territorial authorities: the commune and the *département*. The system rests on two essential elements: the fragmentation of the communal structure, with nearly 38,000 authorities; and the double nature of the *département*: both local authority in its own right and deconcentrated area of management of the state's administration. In this system the Prefect plays a determining role in that while an official of the Ministry of the Interior, he is supervisor of the communes, executive of the departmental council and hierarchical head of the local services of the state. This constitutional structure has not been touched during the last twenty-five years: if the region has emerged as an extra level, it is as an appendage to this classical edifice. The main innovations occurred during the 1960s. However, before examining the French experience of regionalisation during the last decade, it is necessary briefly to review the characteristics of the preceding period: that is to say, the 1950s.

The 1950s, in effect, were characterised by the abandonment of the ideological debate and a new awareness of regional problems which occurred under the twin headings of industrial decentralisation and regional development. 1947 had seen the publication of a book which took up the conclusions of studies undertaken under the Vichy regime at the National Delegation for Public Works. Its title struck home and became a catchword: *Paris and the French desert*.[1] A little later, the then minister of housing, Claudius-Petit, took a vigorous stand in favour of a national plan of regional development, in which he called on the state to intervene in favour of industrial decentralisation, of agricultural modernisation, of the promotion of tourism and of cultural decentralisation. The first measures taken of this nature were introduced under the Mendès-France government in 1954 and that of Edgar Faure the following year.

This awareness of the problems of regional development did not bring about a modification of administrative structure. The state's

action in favour of regional development remained compartmentalised between the Ministry of Housing (responsible for controlling
permits for industrial building) and the Ministry of Finance (responsible for low interest loans, interest subsidies, and investment grants).
The Planning Commissariat (CGP) still hardly intervened in matters
of regional development. The first *plans of regional action* (1957)
were only academic documents bringing together information that was
for the most part already known. It was the CGP, however, which
during this period initiated the delineation of the regional boundaries
which, a few modifications apart, remain the same today. Locally, the
main feature was the appearance of Committees of Expansion in the
years following the war. These committees are voluntary associations
whose aim is to promote economic development. At the outset they had
a local or departmental base. A 1954 decree gave them official
recognition as bodies dealing with problems of economic development and able as such to perform a representative function *vis-à-vis* the
authorities.

With the coming of the 1960s, and under the influence of various
factors (change of regime, evolution of planning, and end of the
colonial period), the preoccupation with industrial decentralisation
and regional development gave rise to a vigorous interest on the part
of the central authorities in promoting a regional articulation of the
National Plan and a policy of regional development and planning.

Institutional changes

The pattern of the decade

There is no simple relationship between regional planning and institutional innovation. It is difficult to derive the institutional modifications at the regional level from the requirements of planning alone. For
the Fourth Plan (1961–4), the Planning Commissariat was the real
master of the regional decision-making process. Institutional adaptations were discreetly derived from the planners' requirements. This
formed part of a wider political context. French-style planning was
then advocated as a brand new way of bringing about social change.
The method's credibility was still intact, the 'myth' of the plan was at its
apogee. The planners' demands were supported by a reforming prime
minister, Michel Debré, keen to restore to the administration its
command function and imbue it with a concern for efficiency. In
addition to these factors, we should add that at the start of the sixties
the regional structure was modest and inconspicuous, which facilitated incremental innovation. From that period dates a series of
modifications of the administrative machine: the creation of co-

ordinating prefects and the interdepartmental conferences in 1961, as well as the sub-prefects responsible for economic affairs. This period was also characterised by collaboration between the authorities and the Regional Expansion Committees, voluntary associations 'approved' by the government, such approval being conditional on the composition of their membership.

The 14 March 1964 regional reform marks the beginning of the second stage, more or less coinciding with the period of the Fifth Plan, which one can end either in May 1968 or on 27 April 1969. The characteristics of this period are as follows. If planning helped bring about regional reforms, the 1964 regional reform was not due to the planners' demands. On the contrary, the planners were reluctant to see the creation of rigid structures. The reform was largely achieved against the will of the Planning Commissariat. The motive force was the Delegation for Regional Development (DATAR), especially in the creation of the Regional Economic Development Commissions (CODER), the most important institutional innovation of this second period. Thus the Planning Commissariat lost the leadership which it had exercised in the preceding phase: its contacts with the regions being limited to the expert level, the regional prefects and Regional Economic Development Commissions being controlled mainly by DATAR and the prime minister.

The third period starts with the defeat of the 27 April 1969 referendum and the election of Georges Pompidou to the presidency. It also coincides with the preparation of the Sixth Plan. The new president of the republic was personally unsympathetic towards the idea of a bold regional reform. He clearly advocated a region conceived as a federation of *départements*. Furthermore, an important change of emphasis occurred in leading government circles: local government reform was given priority while regional reform was played down. This change was accompanied by giving the *département* (the traditional level of administrative and political life) a more important place in the planning process.

To understand the mechanism and results of the regionalisation experiment, we must bear in mind some of the essential characteristics of the French political and administrative system. The Constitution recognises the existence of two types of local authority, freely run by elected councils: some 38,000 communes and 95 *départements*. However, the *départements* have the curious feature that the executive of the General Council is the prefect, i.e. an agent of the central government. Although these local authorities freely run their own affairs, their decisions are nevertheless subject to state supervision (*tutelle*) in political, technical and financial matters. The central administration checks both the appropriateness and the legality of decisions taken by the communes and the *départements*. These local authorities, together with the central government, provide the non-market goods and services in France. Regionalisation involves using the levers of supervision to obtain a rationalisation of such non-market public investment as roads, schools and so forth.

The institutions of 1964

France was divided into twenty-one districts of regional action, or planning regions. The reform of 1964 did not alter the pre-existing divisions in any way. Each of the twenty-one regions was composed of a number of whole *départements*; in 1970 the *département* of Corsica was made the twenty-second region. Some were formed from two *départements* (Alsace and Nord for example). Others on the other hand were made up of more imposing administrative groups: the Rhône–Alpes region covering seven *départements*, Midi-Pyrénées eight. Nevertheless all the regions, whatever their size and physical shape, were endowed under the reform with an analogous institutional structure. (The Paris region constituted the only exception to the rule but will not be discussed here.)

The new regional level was endowed administratively with a regional prefect, a Regional Administrative Conference, and a Regional Mission (see Fig. 1). The prefect of the *département* of the chief city of the region also became the regional prefect. He thus remained a classical territorial prefect endowed with new functions. For the regional functions which were entrusted to him, however, he was made responsible directly to the prime minister. The regional prefect constituted the pivot of the new institutions: he presided over the Regional Administrative Conference, and consulted the CODER (see below). He was required to inform Paris of the opinions of the region on the major national investments which concerned it; to pass on to Paris the region's suggestions in matters of regionalised investment; and to decide on the programming, within the region, of individual investments at the departmental level.

The Regional Administrative Conference (CAR) was the consultative body within the regional administration. Under the chairmanship of the regional prefect, it comprised the prefects of the region's departments and the regional service chiefs of the various ministries. One civil servant was given special status *vis-à-vis* the regional prefect, namely the treasurer and paymaster general of the region representing the Ministry of Finance. He had to advise on the economic and financial viability of all investments over which the regional prefect had the power of initiative and decision. The Regional Mission was created as, in a way, the *cabinet* (personal staff) of the regional prefect. An administrative nucleus consisting of four

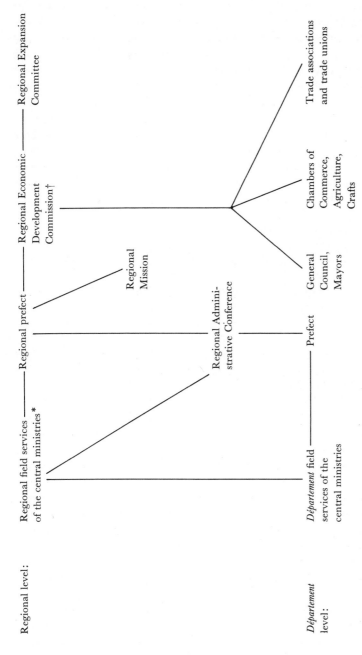

Fig. 1. *Organisation chart of French regional planning in 1972**

* Some ministries are not subject to prefectoral supervision over some of their functions but remain subject to the prefect as far as their investments are concerned.

† Replaced in October 1973 by two bodies: a Regional Council and a Regional Economic and Social Committee.

to eight young higher civil servants, some working full time, the others part time, the Regional Mission also provided the secretariat of the CODER.

The 1964 reform did not create any new regional field services of the ministries. The central ministries had always had regional districts charged with extremely varied functions according to their nature. Under the reform, each ministry was obliged to make the territorial limits of its regional services coincide with the limits of the planning regions. Nevertheless, the creation in 1964 of a regional prefect endowed with important powers led the ministries to expand their regional services, to balance the prefect's power. This was the case with the Ministry of Finance where, in the larger regions, the paymaster general was provided with an embryo of a regional mission. This was equally the case with the Ministry of Housing and Public Works.[2]

As a whole, these measures did not seriously modify the structures of state administration. The expense of running the new level has been borne in part by the chief *département* of the region. With regard to the career patterns of civil servants occupying regional posts the situation has varied. Undeniably, the creation of a regional level changed the balance of the prefectoral corps. The post of regional prefect could only be given to a prefect of a certain standing. It has proved, moreover, a way of promoting the more dynamic elements of the corps. The situation of the external services of the ministries has been different in as much as certain regional posts in them have been regarded as end-of-career posts.

The Regional Mission merits separate treatment. The authors of the reform were hoping that young higher civil servants from the *grands corps* (Inspectorate of Finance, Council of State, Court of Accounts) would choose to leave for the provinces to fill posts in the Regional Missions. This did not happen at all. The rivalries between corps would not allow the slightest innovation in this area. The aim of the Ministry of the Interior and the prefectoral corps was that the sub-prefects should become the heads of the Regional Missions: an objective achieved in three-quarters of the cases. Once filled in this way, the post became a corps preserve and could no longer be sought by the more brilliant elements of other corps. As for the situation of part-time members of the Mission, it did not lead to any fundamental modification in so far as it was more like a loaning of one's services.

The second stage of the regional reform of 1964 consisted of the creation of a Regional Economic Development Commission (CODER) of fifty members. The exact number of members of the CODER provided for under the reform varied slightly from one region to another. Its composition was made up as follows:

25 % were local representatives, nominated by the General Councils of *départements* in the region from among the councillors themselves and the mayors;

50 % were designated by Chambers of Trade, Chambers of Agriculture, Chambers of Artisans, farm and trade union organisations;

25 % were qualified personalities designated by the government on the suggestion of the regional prefect.

The president of the Regional Committee of Expansion and the mayor of the chief city of the region were made *ex officio* members.

From the point of view of its functions, the CODER was a consultative committee which could only give its opinions. It had no independent power of enquiry or debate. The agenda of its meetings was drawn up by the regional prefect. It did not have an investment budget. Neither had it any budget with which it could finance its own research. It was reduced to a purely consultative dimension. By order of the government the CODER generally met briefly twice a year.

The Regional Expansion Committees, which are voluntary associations approved by the public authorities, were deprived of the consultative functions which they had previously performed in favour of the CODER. On the other hand, they retained their research functions and it was by the indirect means of these that they often continued to be officially associated with the affairs of the region. Moreover, in a certain number of cases, the presidents of the CODER were presidents of the Regional Expansion Committees. This constituted a harmonising factor between the two institutions.

The CODER did not have permanent sub-committees at its disposal. On the other hand, the regional prefect set up working parties in his region charged with the preparation of the regionalisation of the National Plan. Generally these groups were tripartite in composition. They comprised members of the CODER, civil servants and experts. In this way the circle of consultation was enlarged to include two categories of participants: departmental officials and some personalities or experts not having a seat in the CODER.

The creation of the regional institutions did not lead to a modification of the power of local political bodies, whether *départements* or communes. The philosophy underlying the setting-up of the regions in 1964 was based on notions of specialisation and cooperation. Specialisation of powers because they were concerned only with economic and social planning; cooperation, since the region was not given any power of its own over lower-tier authorities. Nevertheless, by very reason of this absence of definition, it seems that the relationships between the region, the commune and the *département* were to be regulated by the mediation of the prefectoral corps. The prefects, acting both as supervisors of the communes and the executives of the General Councils, constituted the pivot between all these levels. This was in conformity with the French administrative tradition.

Still, one of the innovations of the 1964 texts remained that the regional prefect henceforth enjoyed hierarchical authority over his fellow departmental prefects through the Regional Administrative Conference. However, while the regional prefect possessed a certain freedom of action relative to his peers, all the agreements made by a prefect within the CAR entailed a mediating intervention from Paris. The relationship between the regional level and the centre was one of complete subordination. In fact, the region had no autonomy at all. Not even, as we have seen, in the case of regional research. It remained merely concerned with consultation and programming.

An understanding of the nature of the regionalisation of planning under the reform can be acquired by an enumeration of the tasks which had to be accomplished by the regional level. The first series of tasks dealt with forecasting and anticipating regional development, set within the national context. These tasks were carried out in cooperation with the Planning Commissariat (CGP) and the Delegation for Regional Development (DATAR) at the centre. An advisory body played an essential intermediary role: the National Commission for Regional Development (CNAT). Chronologically these were the first tasks which the regional level had to fulfil during the preparation of the Plan. These were the tasks of matching national forecasts and expectations with regional forecasts and expectations.

The second series of tasks allotted to the regional level concerned studies of a regional nature. Research on the regional urban structure represented a good example of this type; likewise the setting up of a regional housing index. These tasks constituted an attempt to gather purely regional information over and above the traditional administrative territorial divisions.

The third type of task was the planning of public investment during the second stage of the regionalisation of the Plan. It represents without doubt the most original stage of French-style planning. This programming operation required the establishment of a timetable and financial allocation for operations concerning infrastructure and social capital financed by the public authorities (state, *département*, communes, etc). These investments were classified in three categories: A, B and C.

(A) The major investments (motorways, universities, for example) on which the regions were consulted.

(B) The investments labelled 'regional' for which the regions (through the regional prefects, after the advice of the CODER) could make proposals concerning the relative priority of operations and of their localisation, within the limits of a financial sum specified by each ministry.

(C) The residual investments of purely local interest, for which the central government's financial contribution was to be allocated by the regional prefect between the *départements* of the region.

The regional public investment programmes did not signify a budgetary commitment. They did, however, represent an obligation in as much as they sought to establish regional priorities. Such programming could be defined as a regionalising intervention in public investment over whose financing the region had no power. The region was thus defined as a place at which synthesis and mediation took place.

The regionalisation of planning and the administrative process

The central administration played a decisive role in the control of research undertaken to contribute to the regionalisation of the Plan. As the region had no budget, studies of a regional nature were financed by central government. The expansion committees themselves could only continue to play their informative role as long as the government signed contracts with them. Although the administration controlled the choice of studies it did not carry them out itself. Planning has been accompanied by the development of the system of contracts made with expansion committees, with universities, but especially with commercial or para-public research organisations. The growth of contracting with research organisations was especially important for urban problems. The only administrative service which developed a level of regional expertise of high quality was INSEE, the National Institute of Statistics and Economic Studies (a division of the Ministry of Finance possessing a certain autonomy within the Ministry). On the initiative of INSEE, regional economic 'observatories' were established. The two fields of expertise in which INSEE specialises are demographic and employment studies.

The preparation of the regional segments of the National Plan's public investment programmes, i.e. programming activity proper, was carried out primarily by the Regional Mission. This had to work with the departmental services of the central administration on the one hand and the working parties set up by the regional prefect on the other. The rationalisation activities for which the Regional Mission was responsible owed nothing to techniques such as PPBS, never as yet used at regional level to determine regional priorities. Regional rationalisation involved the search for key criteria for allocating government funds between the local authorities. In the first, inventory stage a list of needs in respect of infrastructure and social capital was drawn up. This done, the programming stage of establishing regional priorities could get under way.

From a strictly institutional point of view, expertise was monopolised by the Regional Mission. The expertise function of the Mission very much depended, however, on the information possessed by others and notably the departmental services. The transmission of information thus became an arena of bureaucratic conflicts between the different levels of the administrative apparatus; the regional level being seen as a threat by the departmental bureaucracies to their own networks of influence. However, while a major conflict occurred in respect of regional expertise, it remained confined to the administration. Attempts to create centres of counter-expertise outside the administration either failed or were reintegrated through clientelistic relations, e.g. the policy of research contracts.

What has just been said of the obstacles faced by the Regional Mission is a principal explanatory factor of the limited changes produced in administrative practice. The weaknesses of the consultative procedures, which will be examined, reinforced this tendency.

What were the results expected of a regional planning articulated on national planning?

1. A horizontal *coordination* of the investment programmes of the different administrative services.

2. A *rationalisation* of the allocation of resources, putting an end to the dispersal of public funds across the map.

3. An *impregnation* of administrative decision-making by economic criteria instead of administrative criteria favouring distributive justice.

4. A *deconcentration* of the decisions of the central ministries and a *weakening* of the departmental administrations in favour of the region, defined as most suitable to obtain this coordination, this rationalisation and this impregnation.

These objectives were never made explicit in this way. They were rather a collection of ideas 'kicked around' in reformist circles in the higher civil service. These ideas sought to give practical expression to the change in social attitudes towards the state. To the extent that the state seemed to be responsible for the geographical sharing out of resources, it was necessary to apply in the regions the methods that had proved their effectiveness at the centre to gain a better mastery of the situation. It was necessary, in other words, to secure an administration which in its attitudes and behaviour was far more suffused with the presuppositions of economic reasoning.

With regard to these objectives, one can say that the changes in administrative practices have been slight. Regional planning was experienced as a supplementary procedure. The vocabulary changed but beneath the words it is not certain that the decisional mechanisms were really transformed. Unquestionably, greater coordination was obtained, but it did not take place at a regional level. The regional integration effort met with strong resistance from the prefectures and field services of the central ministries, i.e. from both horizontal and vertical administration. Resistance was no less strong in the environment of the administration, both among local authority representatives (mayors and general councillors) or from business and farm organisations (Chambers of Commerce, Chambers of Agriculture). The situation can be summed up by saying that planning failed to break the close relationship between the specialised branches of the administration and their 'partners', a relationship which tends to maximise sectoral interests in the process of decision concerning public investments. A mutual reinforcing occurred between administrative resistance and the resistance of local political leaders to attempts at integration, clarification and rationalisation of the decisions. This explains why the function of expertise devolving completely onto the Regional Missions was quickly converted into the classical administrative function of preparing dossiers.

The regional institutions resulted in a considerable strengthening of the preeminence of the general administration (prefectoral administration) by comparison with the specialised ministries and their field services. This effect was in fact expected and desired by the authors of the 1964 reform. However, an indirect effect was to lead some spending departments, particularly the Ministry of Housing and Public Works, to ensure their own development by playing off, against the region, the systems of administrative decision not linked to the Planning Commissariat. The ministry undertook a considerable development of its own instruments of intervention in matters of urban planning and action directed primarily towards the DATAR. Hence, the regionalisation of the Plan, which was already limited in practice to the programming of public investment, found the whole sphere of urban planning linked to land-use planning progressively passing from its control. The preeminent role of the prefectoral corps, whose status and legitimacy are linked with the capacity to operate marginal and incremental adjustments, made the central spending ministries especially worried about the 'irrational' consequences which this introduced in the management of their expenditure and in their forecasting and programming capability. They reacted by considerably recentralising their own decisions and notably in expanding the investments classified in category A.

The desire to ensure an effective regional level integration failed as a result of a double process: the reinforcing of departmental solidarities (horizontal coordination at a lower level) linked to a direct access to the centre (short-circuiting of the regional level); the strengthening of intrasectoral vertical communications which took the form of a systematic policy whereby the field services of the spending ministries primarily used their own channels of information with their central services. The administration's attempt to embrace all expressions of social demand and its satisfaction led to the transformation of most social conflicts into bureaucratic conflicts. A second result was the increasing refusal to provide information on regional development, and the development of parallel networks to gain access to this information and thereby acquire the influence associated with it.

The pre-planning situations in France and Britain can be regarded as opposite to each other. In Britain the administration arose from what Weber termed a traditional type (custom and precedent) and planning represented an attempt to adopt a 'rational–legal' model. In France, the state had been constituted from the beginning of the nineteenth century on the rational–legal model and planning can be seen from this point of view as an attempt to break with routine and bureaucratic obstruction, not by having recourse to a charismatic leader, but by calling for social mobilisation around new modes of collective action (the Plan as 'ardent obligation') fulfilling equivalent functions.

It was characteristic of the French approach that the failure of this attempt to break with routine took the form of a process in which the administration remained the essential pivot. Furthermore, the diminution of the role of regional planning institutions in long-term prospective study was significant, reflecting the transfer of this prospective function to other parts of the Planning Commissariat and especially outside the Planning Commissariat to DATAR.

The regionalisation of planning and the consultative process

The growth of consultative procedures is not a specifically regional phenomenon. It is linked to the intervention of the state in the economy, within the framework of a liberal political system. The development of consultation multiplies the association of economic participants in the administrative decisional process. It is a phenomenon which can be seen at a national level (the Planning Commissariat), at a territorial level (the region) and in the case of each ministry.

There were two salient characteristics of the 1960s French regional system. Firstly, in each region a consultative structure was created without there being a previous structure of political representation at this level. Secondly, within this structure, there was no differentiation between political representation and the representation of economic interests. In fact, political leaders of lower territorial authorities (*départements* and communes) and economic leaders were associated in one joint structure of representation, the CODER. In this sense, the CODER represented a unique institution in the evolution of French consultative administration.

Why was such an institution as the CODER created? The peculiar significance of the regional problem in French political life must first be recalled. Regional devolution was regarded as synonymous with the break-up of the unity of the national state. Regionalism had been associated with extreme right-wing or traditionalist movements, hence the impossibility at the end of the fifties and the beginning of the sixties to create regional authorities. Moreover, there was hardly any demand for them. If the region did develop, it was under the influence of the Plan. The Planning Commissariat pushed for the creation of a regional consultative system. But this system made use of a pre-existing structure: that of the Expansion Committees.

The creation of the CODER can only be explained within a political framework: the wish to extract political advantage from the development of a regional consultative system. It is this reason which explains the importance of the intended institution. It is this which explains the structure: a mixture of elected representatives from the local authorities and representatives of various economic interest groups. The region thus became less than a level of government but more than a level of consultation.

This political choice was not made in a social vacuum. It was an attempt to draw advantage from a dynamism which was showing itself locally, and which had culminated in the experience of the regional segments of the Fourth Plan's public investment programmes. This dynamism was based on the appearance of new economic forces which were unable to express themselves through the local government process. The creation of the CODER was directed towards these new forces (young farmers, young employers, trade union representatives, especially the CFDT) to offer them participation in regional development.

It is in the light of this political motivation that one can understand the strategies of the different groups and their greater or lesser 'investment' in regional action. Firstly, support, then deep disappointment among these new 'active forces' when they saw that their capacity to influence decisions through the consultative system (CODER and working parties) was, in the final analysis, feeble, a weakness linked to the nature of the structure itself and to the type of representation sought by the prefects. Secondly, initial distrust then active resistance from local representatives, whose participation at the regional level, supported by the defensive strategies of the local administration, aimed at neutralising the regional level. Therefore, very quickly, the CODER showed themselves incapable of being the focus of a new dynamism, because in dealings with the administration, and notably with the regional prefect, their scope for independent action was severely circumscribed. In the French case, regional debates were not politicised and partisan affiliations did not constitute the regulating principles of the behaviour of the participants. Traditional geographical solidarities and the close relationship between the administration and local political leaders explain the strategies of the participants much better.

As far as the regulation of societal behaviour is concerned, the weakening of administrative action based exclusively on the law is indisputably a phenomenon which is observed through the experience of regionalisation. At the same time, there has been the institutionalisation of other rules of action governing the relations between the state and socio-economic groups. The peculiar feature of French regional experience is, it seems to us, the contradiction between, on the one hand, prospective and forecasting activity undertaken essentially by state representatives and representatives of economic interests outside the classical political system, and on the other hand, resort to the traditional local government system for the implementation of the programme. This explains the artificial character of the connection between forecasting and programming.

The results of regionalisation in terms of public policy-making

In theory, the regionalisation of planning was carried out so that policies of regional development could be defined which would be neither academic documents nor catalogues of claims on the central authority. In fact, the reality was quite different. Firstly, the content of regional demands resulted from the competition among *départements*, between which the regional level should have arbitrated. The regionalisation of the Plan failed to disaggregate departmental demands in order to obtain new configurations of the expression of needs. On the contrary, because of all the institutional mechanisms which we have described, a sort of vicious circle developed which tended to strengthen the systems of departmental alliances based on the departmental aggregation of interests. Secondly, the regional level tried with all its might to prevent regional plans from being nothing more than a simple summation of departmental demands, but did not have the capacity to do this. Consequently, when all these demands, half-filtered by the regions, converged on Paris, their inconsistencies (for example, in forecasting population) were starkly revealed. At the same time, it exposed one of the weaknesses of the regional level; namely that for many participants, the region had been nothing more than an extra way of exerting pressure on Paris.

Given that the regional institutions and the procedures for the regionalisation of planning did not really reduce the powers of decision of the Parisian authorities in matters of allocating public expenditure to the local authorities, since the regions were not given their own resources, the possibility of putting pressure on Paris, that is access to the centre of the administrative system, has remained the essential factor around which local power is built. It is thus pivotal to an explanation of the rules of the game in the exercise of this power. In principle, for matters within the sphere of regional responsibility, the regional prefect has a monopoly of access to the centre, as much for the transmission of regional needs and suggestions on sharing out the corresponding funds, as for the negotiations which follow, and for supervising the implementation of the regional operations finally decided upon.

In fact, this monopoly by the regional prefect was strongly contested and circumvented. First of all, within the administration, departmental prefects sought to resist the ascendancy of the regional prefect by reactivating their Parisian networks (which was often well received by the central administrations, for whom the existence of close particularist relationships is an important condition of their own autonomy). For their part, the services of the spending ministries, departmental and regional, strove to escape from prefectoral authority by maintaining the strength of their own parallel networks of communication with their respective centres. Secondly, within the administration's environment, leaders of national repute, political as well as economic, cleverly exploited the progressive dispossession of the Planning Commissariat with regard to regional policy in favour of other parts of the administration, such as DATAR and the Ministry of Housing and Public Works, in order to recover a wide margin of autonomy in specific negotiations in Paris.

The regional institutions aimed at an important transformation of authority relationships at a local level. These were formerly characterised by a sort of egalitarian yet paternalist authority and proceeded by incremental adjustments. This was the dominant model of prefect–local political relationships. The ideology of 'consultative administration', which is part of the regional reform of 1964, aimed at substituting for this model of relationships between an all-powerful administrative authority and weakened local partners kept under tutelage, a more open system of relations, allowing the interest-group agents of change to appear both more dynamic and less exclusively concerned with making demands. For this, it was thought that the 'partners' of the administration should be chosen by them and not elected by constituents and should have no power of decision, which, it was thought, would make them more free to participate rationally in decisions for which they would not have to assume responsibility. This theory of irresponsible participation completely failed. Powerless, the 'partners' of the administration either adopted an attitude of withdrawal, or else they sought to recreate for themselves a true power of negotiation within the consultative structure. They have, therefore, quite simply reproduced at a regional level the previous system of authority relations, made up of maximum claims and administrative egalitarian arbitration. The logic of distributive justice (dispersal of funds), which governed these prefect–local political relationships at a departmental level, was extended to the regional level. The struggle to bring into local authority relationships a planning logic (forecasting, choice of priorities, etc) failed, and, in reaction, this reinforced centralisation.

At the end of this assessment of the functioning of the regional planning institutions set up in the sixties in France, there remains the question of the structural factors which help to explain their relative failure. If one confines oneself to the French case, the situation can be summed up in a phrase. Planning did not transform the traditional institutions or administrative practices; it is these institutions and practices which transformed the regionalisation of planning.

The word failure ought, however, to be used circumspectly. Failure in relation to what? To the intentions of the reformers? But a study of the decision process which ended in the creation of these institutions clearly shows that the intentions were multiple and contradictory. Failures with regard to a 'true' regionalisation of the Plan? But given that no regionalisation existed before, it is difficult to know what a true regionalisation of the Plan would be.

The only correct angle of attack from the point of view of political sociology is to place this experience in the framework of the evolution of the French political and administrative system. In this perspective, the experiment of the regionalisation of planning in the sixties appears indicative of the tensions which affect this system. It does not, however, constitute a political solution of these contradictions. Thus it appears as a transitory stage and the problems are no longer posed in the same terms at the beginning of the seventies. The regional institutions no longer have the strategic character which they possessed ten years ago.

The sequel to the 1960s experience

For France, the sixties ended in May 1968. For the history of regionalisation, this date is equally significant. Following the May crisis, the French were asked to pronounce on an important regional reform project. De Gaulle's scheme was rejected by the electorate in a referendum in April 1969. Since then, it has no longer been possible to analyse the evolution of regionalisation in continuity with the preceding experience. There are three reasons for this. Firstly, there was the change in political orientation following the replacement of de Gaulle by Pompidou as president of the republic. Secondly, there has been a restructuring of the strategies of the social groups on a new basis after May 1968. Thirdly, the accelerated evolution of the administrative system has modified the context within which French regionalisation has operated.

The working of the institutions of regional planning was accompanied, as has already been stated, by a reassertion of centralisation, which ended by emptying regional institutions of a large part of their content. Nevertheless, it can equally be asked whether the existence of a mechanism, which has been much discussed and which has partially functioned to no purpose, has not contributed to an increase in regional consciousness, which is at the outset awareness of frustration. From this could emerge the politicisation of the regional problem which we have indicated, politicisation which involved President Pompidou himself and which sought to defuse the social conflict dimensions of regional frustration. Opposition forces and political leaders have both participated in such politicisation, as Servan-Schreiber showed at Nancy in 1971. Thus, on the political level, the regional debate has moved much closer to the centre of the political system.

The double movement of administrative and political centralisation has led to elevating the definition of major objectives of regional policy and the particular choices which operationalise them to the highest organs of the governmental apparatus: the central divisions of the ministries are increasingly supplanted by the ministerial *cabinets* and the presidency. However, this elevation is a general phenomenon which is far from being explained simply by the ins and outs of regional policy. Rather one should reverse the order of cause and effect and see in the reinforcement of the central power and of the area of control of the political executive (at the expense as much of parliament as of the autonomy of the ministries), one reason for the regional institutions' loss of substance.

The setbacks to the rationalisation of choice in respect of regional policy and the reflux of problems and solutions to the summit of the state has contributed to the centralised politicisation of regional problems. In practice, this has been accompanied by a recognition on the part of the population of the regions of the specificity of its problems (notably in terms of employment) and the shifting of the negotiation for the solution of problems to a confrontation sought directly with the head of state. Thus, on the level of the play of political forces, regional policy is more and more the result of a negotiation between the president and 'the Bretons', 'the Alsatians', etc, etc…This accounts for the regional tours of Presidents de Gaulle and Pompidou.

Alongside this there has occurred a dissociation of regional and urban planning. Since 1964 urban problems have given rise to a multitude of institutional innovations or reforms: creation of the Ministry of Housing and Public Works, of the OREAM, legislation on land use, urban communities and the amalgamation of communes. A fully fledged system of urban planning has been progressively set up and made independent of the region, itself too dominated by the pressure of preponderantly rural *départements*. At the centre, this evolution has been reflected in the growing influence of the DATAR and minister of housing and public works – to the detriment of the Planning Commissariat.

This evolution tends to underline the incapacity of the regional level to achieve a planning which is able to integrate the problems of rural society with those of urban society. The region thus becomes a federal expression of the departmental interests represented by the General Councils. (This was the orientation given to it by President Pompidou after his Lyon speech of 1970.) This emphasis goes hand-in-hand with the refusal to establish the region as a political authority, with an assembly elected by universal suffrage and disposing of a budget. It is in this context that the Regional Reform Bill introduced by the government in 1972 must be understood.

Passed by Parliament on 5 July 1972, the Regional Reform Act is less radical than the regional proposals put to the referendum in 1969 by de Gaulle, reflecting the cautious views of President Pompidou. It is too soon to undertake an analysis of the way the 1972 Act has worked, but it contains a number of very clear political choices. The first and the most important is the refusal to give the region the democratic status that an assembly elected by universal suffrage would provide. Under the 1972 Act the region is a public corporation (*établissement public*) acting within the boundaries of the planning regions. Secondly, the CODER is replaced by two bodies: a Regional Council, composed entirely of political representatives (MPs, mayors, local councillors), and an Economic and Social Committee, composed of representatives of the region's organised interests (economic, social, educational, etc). Thirdly, the Regional Council is made up of three categories of member: the deputies and senators of the region, who account for 50 % of the membership; the representatives of the General Councils in the region, who must occupy not less than 30 % of the seats; and the representatives of the urban communes (i.e. whose population is more than 30,000) according to a system of weighting based on the size of their population. Fourthly, the Regional Council takes over all the CODER's responsibilities in respect of planning. But as a public corporation it can either undertake public investments of a strictly regional character on its own account or participate financially in local or central government projects within the region. Financial resources are provided for by the transfer to it of a central government tax (on driving licences) and by the option given to the Council of introducing an additional levy on a number of other central government taxes. Lastly, the regional prefect continues to supervise the work and carries out the decisions of the Regional Council. The model adopted here is that which governs the relations of the prefect and the General Council in the *département*. The Act does not provide for the functions of the regional prefect to be separated from those of the departmental prefect. The modest character of the modifications introduced by the 1972 Regional Reform Act merely serve to emphasise the point that regional planning has had only an insignificant impact upon the traditional French politico-administrative system.

NOTES

1 J.-F. Gravier, *Paris et le désert français*, Flammarion 1947.
2 The ministry was constituted in 1966 by merging the Ministries of Housing and Public Works.

SELECT CRITICAL BIBLIOGRAPHY

Many books have been published in France on regionalism in the 1960s but most of them are political polemics rather than analyses of the political and administrative system. One should consult, firstly, the book edited by J. L. Quermonne, *Administration traditionelle et planification régionale*, 1964, CERAT, Grenoble: the basic introduction to regional planning problems in the 1960s, expressing the hopes inspired by 'functional regionalism'. The CERAT also published *La réforme régionale et le réferendum du 27 avril 1969*, 1970, which covers the situation at the end of the decade, and a series of informative annual volumes on *Aménagement du Territoire et Développement Régional* from 1964 onwards.

Between 1965 and 1968, research by Pierre Grémion and J. P. Worms of the Sociology of Organisations group was published in two reports: P. Grémion, *La mise en place des institutions régionales*, Copédith, 1966, and P. Grémion and J. P. Worms, *Les institutions régionales et la société* locale, Copédith, 1968. They endeavour to elicit the social dynamics of the regional institutions during the Fifth Plan, concentrating upon the relations between the local and regional administration and their environment.

Pierre Viot's *Aspects régionaux de la planification française*, Commissariat du Plan, November 1966, is the best explanation of the central planners' objectives at the time of the Fourth and Fifth Plans.

The place of the region in the 1960s atmosphere of administrative reformism can be ascertained from the Association Française de Science Politique symposium on *La Région*, Fondation Nationale des Sciences Politiques, 1963.

12. Regional planning in Britain

MAURICE WRIGHT AND STEPHEN YOUNG

At the end of the 1950s the machinery available for regional planning in England and Wales[1] was highly centralised in both policy-making and implementation. The duties of the departmental regional offices and the non-departmental bodies involved with the regions were mainly confined to inspection and administration. Local authorities were mainly the agents of Whitehall. Decentralisation was more advanced in Scotland[2] where the machinery differed fundamentally in that the secretary of state had, through the four constituent parts of the Scottish Office (SO), a greater degree of authority in matters relating to the land-use planning side of regional planning.

Since the end of the Second World War, administrative responsibility for industrial location had been separated from that for land-use planning, housing and local government. By the beginning of the 1960s the division of functions between the Board of Trade (BOT) and the Ministry of Housing and Local Government (MHLG) at the centre had become an important institutional tradition and was subsequently to influence the re-organisation of governmental machinery at the centre and in the regions.

The main purpose of the institutional changes introduced under the Conservatives between 1962 and 1964 was to ensure more effective inter-departmental co-ordination. In June 1962 the Scottish Office was reorganised.[3] One of the main aims was to give the new Scottish Development Department (SDD) responsibility for all physical planning functions. In addition the secretary of state was given a new responsibility to draw up and implement regional plans. In January 1963 the Scottish Development Group (SDG) was established to help produce a plan for Central Scotland. This was a committee chaired by the SDD with senior representatives from all interested departments. It remained in existence to co-ordinate the work of all organisations involved with the implementation of the plan, and to undertake similar surveys in four other Scottish sub-regions.

More effective departmental co-ordination for the rest of Britain was one of the main aims behind the appointment in October 1963 of Mr Edward Heath as president of the Board of Trade and secretary of state for trade, industry and regional development. During 1963 and 1964 a Regional Development Division was established and a top level inter-departmental steering group began work to prepare regional planning documents for other regions along the lines of those which had been published for the North East and for Central Scotland.[4] In the North-East a Development Group (NEDG), closely modelled on the SDG, was set up to co-ordinate the activities of central and local government in implementing the plan. The regionalisation of White-hall departments was begun, and the MHLG offices were given land-use planning functions.

Local government co-operation on regional issues increased during the first half of the 1960s. The previous informal co-operation on land-use planning in some areas gave way to a more formal arrange-ment of Standing Conferences of local planning authorities. In the North-West, the North-East, and in Scotland, local government co-operation had been a strong force behind the creation or rejuvena-tion of the early Industrial Development Associations (IDAs). In these and other areas government departments had to take more notice of IDA activity during the second half of the 1960s.

After the formation of a Labour government in October 1964, attempts were made to structure the regional planning machinery more comprehensively.[5] Overall responsibility for regional matters was given to the Regional Policy Group at the newly created Depart-ment of Economic Affairs (DEA). In 1965 England was divided into eight planning regions. Regional Economic Planning Councils (REPCs) and Regional Economic Planning Boards (REPBs) were ap-pointed for these eight, and for Scotland and Wales as well. The REPCs were to promote regional planning in the context of the National Plan, and to advise on the regional consequences of national policies. The Council members were drawn from both sides of industry, from local government, and from among those with special knowledge of the region; they were appointed as individuals, not as delegates. The REPBs were established to co-ordinate the work of the regional offices of the central government departments concerned with regional development, along similar lines to the SDG and the NEDG. The pattern that had been established in the North-East in 1963–4 of each central department setting up regional offices was repeated through-out all English regions with all departments being brought together in one building. However, there was very little decentralisation of power to the regional offices, and the REPCs were given no executive powers. The establishment by local planning authorities of Standing Conferences throughout the country did not alter the balance of power between Whitehall and the local authorities. There were only two moves under the Labour government that can really be seen as shifting power away from Whitehall. A secretary of state for Wales was appointed and given a seat in the Cabinet. In Scotland a Highlands and Islands Development Board was set up. It was quite unlike any other regional body, charged not only with preparing a regional strategy, but provided with the finance and wider executive powers to implement that strategy: it was in fact a regional development authority. Between 1966 and 1973 it provided financial assistance totalling £14.2 million.[6]

The DEA was at the centre of the new regional planning machinery. On the one hand it had to knit together the competing claims of the different regions, while on the other it sought to co-ordinate the regionally oriented measures of the Whitehall departments. Thus, it organised meetings of the REPC chairmen, and reacted, or more accurately, avoided reacting to the REPC planning strategies, while sending representatives from London to the REPB meetings, and organising inter-departmental meetings on *ad hoc* and on-going issues at the centre. At the regional level it chaired the REPB meetings and its research staff supported both the Councils and the Boards. However the BOT and the MHLG retained executive powers over the main issues of industrial location and land-use planning. These and other departments, like transport, established their own means of co-ordinating their relationships between their central and regional offices, and with the local planning authorities. Thus at different times in different regions it was possible for departments to effectively by-pass the DEA. In Scotland this did not happen because of the accumulation of decentralised executive powers in the hands of one minister within a single department, and because that department had practical experience of co-ordinating several different policy areas.

In October 1969 the DEA was abolished, the Ministry of Technology was greatly enlarged, and a new post of secretary of state for local government and regional planning was established. The Ministry of Power and parts of the BOT and DEA were merged into Min.Tech. As far as regional planning was concerned, the minister of technology was now responsible for the nationalised industries, most of the private sector, for administering the Industrial Development Certificate (IDC) process, leasing advance factories, managing industrial estates in the development areas, and issuing the various grants and loans available for plant and machinery. Under the new secretary of state for local government and regional planning were the Ministries of Transport, and of Housing and Local Government, the regional research staff of the DEA, and the REPCs and the REPBs. These changes underlined the fact that although in England and Wales the 1960s had seen greater centralisation and in some respects improved co-ordination within the two main policy areas of industrial location and infrastructure, little impact had been made on the problem of knitting the two policy areas together, either within the context of regional plans, or on a more *ad hoc* basis.

The regional planning process

The regional planning process in Britain during the 1960s was characterised by a separation of power from responsibility. By the middle of the decade there were several central government departments with statutory functions and powers immediately relevant to regional planning, e.g. location of industry, land use, housing, transportation. One department, DEA, had been given a general responsibility for regional planning but possessed no statutory powers with which to discharge that responsibility directly itself, or indirectly by the co-ordination of other departments. Separation of power from responsibility at the centre was paralleled by the arrangements for REPCs and REPBs in the regions.

As 'intermediate governments' the Planning Boards were 'squeezed' by local authorities with statutory powers and executive responsibilities for land use and by a central government reluctant to relinquish executive power for economic policy-making to the regions. Lacking formal collective power, nevertheless the Boards had been given a collective responsibility for the preparation of an economic plan for the future development of each region, and for its reconciliation with national objectives. This was not a statutory duty. If departments at the national or regional level chose to ignore this responsibility or to denigrate it, or to interpret it differently, the DEA nationally and regionally had no power of coercion.

To discharge its responsibility at the regional level, the DEA attempted to co-ordinate the activities of the different departments directly through formal meetings of the Board and its sub-committees, and informally through contact with regional controllers and their staffs. While the superior rank of the Board chairman, the DEA under-secretary, was a potentially coercive instrument, the conditions for its use were limited by the personality and temperamental disposition of the individual, and his determination to pursue a particular course of action. If the government asked for the Board's recommendation or advice on a particular policy issue affecting his region, such as the introduction of the Regional Employment Premium, a determined and resourceful under-secretary could, by virtue of his superior rank, seek to impose his own views upon the members of the Board. He could also appeal to DEA headquarters to bring pressure to bear upon headquarters departments in Whitehall to instruct their regional offices. The limits of such action were very narrow, given the DEA's own lack of formal executive power.

The Scottish Economic Planning Board enjoyed several advantages denied to its English counterparts. First, its members had had a much longer experience of collaboration in the preparation of regional plans, e.g., the 1963 White Paper on Regional Development and Growth, and the 1966 Plan for the Scottish Economy. Secondly, it had the support of the Scottish Office and its minister, the secretary of state for Scotland, who had a seat in the Cabinet. Thirdly, it was supported by the Regional Development Division (RDD) of the Scottish Office, the body responsible for advising the secretary of state on economic planning in Scotland; the chairman of the Board was a senior official from the RDD. Finally, the Board comprised officials from four departments (agriculture and fisheries, education, home and health, and development) whose jurisdiction was confined to the region, unlike the English Boards where all the official representatives were drawn from departments with national jurisdictions and hence Whitehall headquarters. 'Its task of getting all relevant departments to think in terms of the region was therefore correspondingly lessened.'[7]

Despite these apparent advantages, in practice the Scottish Economic Planning Board did not work very differently from those in the English regions. Many important issues never reached it; and the same constraint upon those regional controllers whose authority derived from headquarters in Whitehall (Board of Trade, Department of Employment and Productivity, Ministry of Transport) was observable: they would not or could not commit their departments in certain matters which came before the Board and, as ever, the financial implications of any commitment were decided bilaterally between an individual department and the Treasury at the headquarters' level in Whitehall.[8] The Welsh experience was very similar.[9]

The potential capacity of the DEA to influence other departments was greater when the department was in the hands of the deputy prime minister, George Brown, but both he and his immediate successor were obliged by political and economic circumstances to pay more attention to the department's main tasks of national planning, prices and incomes policies, and the promotion of industrial productivity and rationalisation. Within the broad range of DEA's responsibilities, regional planning had a low priority until at least 1968. Ironically, the disillusionment with national planning which followed the abandonment of the National Plan in July 1966, and the transfer of responsibility for prices, incomes and productivity to the new Department of Employment and Productivity (Ministry of Labour) in 1968, denuded the DEA of much of its former responsibility, thereby elevating regional planning to the status of a principal rather than subordinate function. But, with the emasculation of its former functions, the department's status in the ministerial hierarchy declined. Thereafter the DEA's position *vis à vis* other headquarters departments, never very strong, noticeably weakened.

Despite these limitations of authority and status, and the comparative neglect of regional planning in the department itself, more might have been achieved at the regional level had the DEA been more certain, initially, what exactly it was trying to do: if it had been clear what it wanted the Planning Boards to do, and what the role of the Planning Councils was expected to be. From both ministers and civil servants issued countless variations on the vague theme of 'reducing regional imbalance' as the main aim of regional planning. While there was a marked reluctance to refine the concept of imbalance, it was obvious that individual regions could not be entrusted with the diagnosis of their own imbalance *vis à vis* other regions and the prescription of what each felt to be appropriate levels of population, employment, public investment etc. And yet, the central government's failure initially to provide inter-regional guidelines for the distribution of population, employment, etc, positively encouraged a piecemeal regional approach, in which each region competed with every other region for more population, more jobs, and a larger share of public investment.

At the regional level, departments such as labour, transport, trade, housing and so on, had carefully defined statutory duties, largely of a day to day kind, although some worked within a longer time-horizon, for example housing, which had to co-ordinate local authority plans for overspill housing. These were their staple diet and provided their *raison d'être*. To all departments in the region, other than DEA, regional planning was adventitious. Work specifically related to, say, the preparation of a medium-term or long-term plan of economic and social development had a very low priority compared with the urgency of the day to day work which derived from established statutory responsibilities. They were not obliged to take regional planning seriously; or, failing general direction from the centre, could give to it such meaning as was consistent with their own objectives.

The DEA's co-ordinating task at the regional level was thus a difficult one. Where the policies or decisions of regional officials conflicted, the DEA had no effective adjudicatory powers. Where compromise was impossible – and frequently departments were bound, or chose to be bound, by tightly drawn headquarters' briefs – reference to headquarters departments for instruction or guidance was the normal response of regional offices invested with no great administrative discretion. This procedure tended to harden the lines of the conflict rather than resolve it. The weakness of the DEA's position is revealed in this comment made in the late 1960s by a senior official in DEA headquarters:

Both regionally and at HQ the role of DEA with its limited staff must be largely that of co-ordination and stimulating Departments to tackle problems of regional importance. Wherever possible we probe Departments on their proposals, both in committee and in direct contact with them...but we are certainly not equipped to participate in the working out of the programme.

The problem of effective, horizontal co-ordination of departments organised hierarchically was exacerbated by the different degrees of authority delegated to regional offices, and by their willingness to use the authority delegated to them. Much depended upon the attitude of the regional controllers towards regional planning, and upon their personalities and those of the Board chairmen. The importance of personality and 'gentle persuasion' in the new regional institutions was a function of the lack of DEA's intrinsic executive power. The effectiveness of the machinery, and the relations between departments and between Board and Council, depended greatly on the ideas, attitudes and determination of the civil servants and laymen filling new and established positions. If the relationships between departments, and between them and the Council, had been made more explicit in terms of authority and responsibility, personality might have been a much less critical determinant of effectiveness.

In fact, the task of co-ordination at the regional level is much more difficult even than this. Land-use planning, the provision of housing, education and social services, are the statutory responsibilities of local authorities. Other 'field services' such as transport and communication are partly the responsibility of local authorities and partly the responsibility of public corporations and central departments. Public utilities, with the exception of water, are provided by nationalised undertakings; the hospital service, by local hospital management committees responsible to regional hospital boards.

The future economic, social and physical development of a region is, therefore, a task which involves the co-ordination of three levels of government with a multiplicity of inter-related and shared functions. The reconciliation of the future plans of central and local governments and statutory regional bodies, and their day to day decision-making and the reconciliation of both with an overall strategy for the development of the region, was a daunting task for a Board with no executive powers, and an advisory Council. Before 1968, no English Board or Council succeeded in enlisting the support and co-operation of these various local and regional bodies in the preparation of a plan, let alone its implementation. A study of the West Midlands concluded that the 'administrative machinery of the Planning Council/Board, therefore, has not been able to influence decisions substantially enough to promote a coherent regional strategy'.[10]

Regional bodies with statutory responsibilities continued to discharge them without paying too much attention to the planning exercises mounted by the Boards and Councils. For example, schemes for the expansion of existing towns on a large scale were negotiated between the local authorities concerned and the Ministry of Housing and Local Government in Whitehall, for the central government provides funds for such schemes. Yet these and other schemes for the creation of new towns were critical decisions influencing the distribution of population and employment in the region for many years to come. As has been said elsewhere, it is essential to integrate regional planning within a direct line running from Whitehall to town hall. Similarly, the response of local authorities to other new demands, of land use, communication, higher education, etc, have tended to be on an *ad hoc* basis without reference to a regional framework. Where they have needed guidance or financial assistance, they have tended to ignore the Boards and Councils, even by-pass the regional offices, and deal directly with the Whitehall departments. In the West Midlands 'the position of local government *vis à vis* the Planning Council has generally been one of conflict, the former fearing the regional machinery would trespass on its planning functions'.[11]

In Scotland, the Scottish Office found the task no easier. In implementing the growth area policy introduced in 1963, and in carrying out the regional plans for the Lothians and the Central Borders, it was dependent almost entirely upon the co-operation of the local authorities. Despite the Scottish Office's endorsement of the Central Borders Regional Plan, certain major proposals were not approved by the local authorities in the area and it had to be modified. In *The Scottish Plan 1965–70*, three areas were specified for 'out-county' overspill in West Central Scotland. While the Scottish Office took the initiative and, where necessary, showed a willingness to compromise, the basic decisions rested with the local authorities. As a result, two of the overspill projects were substantially modified and a third produced no action. One commentator concluded from this and other evidence that the Scottish Office had only a very limited authority to pursue regional development, and that local authority participation and co-operation was essential. None of the mechanisms to join the two levels of government – joint working parties of local authorities and the Scottish Office (growth area implementation), economic planning consultative groups (implementation of the regional plans for North-East Scotland, Tayside, the Borders, and the South West), or the joint planning advisory committees with direct representation of elected local councillors – none of these proved very effective.[12]

The new Town and Country Planning Act (1968) provided both an incentive and a sanction for closer co-operation between local authorities and the Planning Boards and Councils. Each local planning authority is required under the Act to prepare a 'structure plan' (with an economic and social as well as land-use basis) for its area which is consistent with a 'strategic plan' for the future development of the region as a whole. This has led to the setting up in several regions of Joint Planning Teams in which local authorities are collaborating with Planning Councils and Boards and the central government in the preparation of strategic plans.

Administrative practices and behaviour

Authority relationships within British central government departments, and in particular the formal lines of communication between different levels of authority, have tended traditionally to be vertical: regional planning requires a horizontal dimension. Thus there was the need at the regional level not merely to co-ordinate a number of discrete strands of policy-making in the hands of separate departments, but to integrate them in a unified and concerted whole before ends were foreclosed. But without major institutional innovation, or even much adjustment, the traditional response was a co-ordinating rather than an integrating one. In the regions the task was even more difficult where there was no existing basis even for a co-ordinating relationship between departments, let alone the integration of policy formulation and implementation which the concept of regional planning implies. Some departments like the Ministry of Labour and Board of Trade, had worked independently in the regions (though not at a regional level) for some years; they were asked in the mid-1960s to work closely both in the conception and implementation of policy with other departments, some of whom were newly arrived. Tensions and conflict were inevitable initially, and much turned on the personality, commitment and ability of the regional controllers. Departmentalism and compartmentalism were broken down only gradually.

Throughout the 1960s there was little conflict between central government and the Planning Boards. The main reason for this was simply that the Planning Boards (with the possible exception of that for Scotland) were only in a very limited sense unified regional administrations. Only on rare occasions did a Planning Board speak with one voice, and then usually on matters which had very few important policy implications for individual departments. The scope for regional–central conflict was very greatly reduced by the subordination of the region to the centre. The custom of taking most of the important decisions at the centre, and the need for regional departments to refer back constantly to the centre for direction and guidance, whether that need was real or assumed, made it more difficult in the mid-1960s to achieve an integration of attitudes and objectives at the regional level. At that time regional controllers exercised only a limited delegated authority to settle matters at their own discretion, so that the tendency was for policies decided centrally to be applied regionally, rather than for regional policies to be decided and implemented in the region within the context of broad national policy objectives. This was so because 'under the present centralised system of Departmental control, regional representatives of Departments play little part in Departmental decisions. Regional considerations are certainly taken into account by Departments, but this usually happened at an earlier stage of the Departmental process rather than as a result of regional consultations.'[13]

While in the making of substantive policy there was very little delegation of executive power, departments in the regions had a greater influence than before, separately, and collectively as the Regional Economic Planning Board, on the shape and content of policy made in Whitehall. Major policy issues were often referred to them for advice, although this usually occurred when the issue was manifestly a regional one with implications for particular regions. The degree of reference and its frequency varied from one department to another. The influence of the Planning Board on substantive policy tended to be *ad hoc* and piecemeal, mainly limited to those regional issues which became politically important or sensitive, or where decision became imperative. One effect of the introduction of regional planning in the 1960s which was observable towards the end of the decade was the greater freedom given to regional controllers to make decisions in their regions without reference to superiors in Whitehall.[14] Nevertheless their role was not primarily one of policy-making; they were and still are, managers. This is especially true of those controllers (Department of Employment, Department of Health and Social Security) who are responsible for a network of local offices throughout a region. Controllers do not regard themselves as initiators of policy; they are concerned more with the implementation within their regions of centrally determined policy. Because of this, it has been difficult for them to accept the role demanded by regional planning which requires initiation, or the re-thinking of existing policy and the approach to policy.

A traditional characteristic of British administration has been the dominance of the generalist administrator and the subordination of the professional/specialist. This dominance was as marked in the field of regional planning as elsewhere, despite the increasingly technical nature of the subject-matter. In the regions, the generalist administrator maintained a pre-eminent position throughout the decade. The senior civil servant, the chairman of the Regional Economic Planning Board, was invariably a member of the administration group, supported by a small secretarial staff of generalist administrators. While senior staff employed in other central government departments in the region reported to superiors in Whitehall headquarters and not to him, nevertheless he had a general responsibility for co-ordinating their work in the region. Some of them were professionals, like the regional controllers of the Department of Employment and (old) Board of Trade, and in his co-ordinating role towards them the generalist administrator's position was little different from that in Whitehall.

The dominance of the chairman within his own regional department was again a reflection of the traditional relationship between generalists and professionals. The research staff, employed as research officers but used increasingly as economists and statisticians, reported directly to him. Their numbers grew towards the end of the decade. In 1966 the research staff employed in the regions by the DEA totalled seven for the eight English regions. By 1969 there were twenty-five. Very few professional staff were employed at headquarters on regional planning research, a symptom not of the predominance of the generalist administrator but of the shortage of specialists and the relative neglect of regional planning in the early days of the DEA. Difficulties of recruitment have certainly contributed to the slow growth of the professional staff in the regions, but the ill-defined nature of regional planning and its low political priority made ministers and their senior advisors reluctant to use scarce staff in the regions on these tasks. Another factor was the political/administrative resistance of ministers and generalist administrators towards rational analytical decision-making systems and research in general.[15]

Bureaucratic style was not much affected by regional planning. The Whitehall administrator has tended traditionally to be problem-oriented, and analytical and research functions have not been well developed, partly because they were felt to be unnecessary or impracticable. With the introduction of regional development programmes for Central Scotland and the North-East in 1963, in which an attempt was made to shape the future, information about the past and the present and its relation to the future became essential prerequisites. This implied a shift away from the short to the medium and long-terms and a consideration of anticipated future problems as well as those currently exercising the minds of ministers and senior administrators. However, there was no profound change in the attitudes of generalist administrators: the traditional *ad hoc*, piecemeal approach with its associated 'crisis mentality' persisted in the handling of

regional problems. Preoccupation with the politically urgent or critical issue made it difficult to give adequate time or thought to future
problems. The persistance of this approach, even in those departments (such as DEA, DOE) with prime responsibility for regional
planning, fed the general disbelief in many other departments of the
need for, or possibility of, planning ahead. It also contributed to the
neglect of research, to the slow development of planning techniques
and expertise where the pay-off was problematic and distant in time.
Additionally there were those demands of the political system which
derived from the accountability of ministers to parliament; they
remained unchanged, and ministers continued to be occupied with the
short-term urgent problems by which their effectiveness as ministers
is still mainly judged.

Consultation and the consultative process

It is not easy to generalise about the effect of the introduction of
regional planning and the setting up of Planning Councils and Boards
on interest groups and their activities. To judge by what has happened in the North-West and the North-East regions, it seems that
there was an increase in the activity of established interest groups
rather than the formation of new groups in previously unorganised
sectors.[16] The Civic Trust for the North-West, the North-West IDA
(Industrial Development Association) and the North-East Development Council, had all been formed by 1961, but as a result of the
central government's greater concern with regional problems from the
mid-1960s, these and other groups became steadily more active on a
broadening range of regional and local issues. For example, the Civic
Trust for the North-West has a variety of different roles: as planning
consultant and research unit; and as a source of advice and pressure
upon government urging it to adopt new policies, and upon local
authorities to take advantage of government schemes. The North-
West IDA's pressure-group activities have been primarily related to the
capital investment cycle, but the increase in the range and intensity of
government activity at the regional level has given it more to react to
and to press for on a regular and continuing basis. As the capital
investment cycle slowed down at the start of the 1970s, new IDAs
sprang up.

The impact of the introduction of regional planning on the consultative process is a little easier to assess. The institutional and policy
innovations of the mid-1960s were exploited by established regional
interest groups for their own purposes in several ways. First, they were
able to use the new regional institutions as an additional means of
putting their case to central government. Although it was not intended that members of the Planning Councils were to act as represen-

tatives, some of them found it difficult to forget their group or local authority interest when they attended meetings of the council and its committees. Painter has shown how a clear 'inter-meshing between the Planning Council and (local) groups' followed the establishment of the REPCs.[17] Although his case-study concerns only the West Midlands, the point would appear to be valid for all other regions. On various industrial, environmental, local government and new town issues, Planning Council members have been able to use the Council as an extra means of bringing pressure to bear upon the government, always provided that they were able to convince the Council as a whole of the value of their ideas.[18]

Secondly, the establishment of regional branches of the main Whitehall departments led to the forging of close links between some groups and regional civil servants. But such groups have tended to approach regional offices mainly on administrative details rather than substantive policy issues, partly because of the lack of delegated authority in most regional departments. In some cases, however, where very close personal relationships have developed, policy issues have been discussed. If the regional controller of a department agrees with the view of the interest group leader, then the group's interest may be partly or even wholly represented to the centre through the medium of the controller. This was, on occasions, very useful indeed for a group: where, for example, a headquarters department asked its regional office for advice about how to react to a group's formal request or about a group's memorandum to the centre before a meeting with the minister. It has become established as part of the consultative process and groups like IDAs and the Civic Trusts spend time cultivating links with regional offices. Sometimes regional offices will also advise a group informally how best to make an approach to the centre; by concentrating on 'non-political' subjects, like the provision of infrastructure, for example. The crucial factor in a relationship between a group and a regional office is generally the character and convictions of the regional controller.

The increased concern of the central government with the problems of the regions has resulted in more policy activity and more financial assistance. It has thus left itself more open to pressure for still more and different government intervention and for more and different patterns of public and private expenditure. It is obliged, therefore, to explain, defend and justify those actions it takes. When government is concerned about the regions or a specific regional problem, and is contemplating some action and the commitment of resources, a situation arises in which there is a continuous process of policy-shaping and policy decision. Regional groups then have the opportunity to influence the emergent decisions if they can initiate or share in a dialogue with the central departments concerned. This can be done in several ways: through formal and informal correspondence with ministers and senior civil servants, by responding to a ministerial approach for advice or information, or by reminding ministers of promises made by their predecessors. In such circumstances a deputation to the minister assumes great importance, apart from the formal statement of views on both sides. First, before the meeting takes place, the group's proposals will have been fully examined by the minister and his senior advisers. Because of this, a group will try to arrange to see the minister once or twice a year to try to ensure that its views are injected into the on-going policy-making process at the highest level. The second reason is that at such a meeting a group will aim to state its formal, prepared view quickly, get the minister's reactions to it as speedily as possible, and then to come back at the minister in the hope of eliciting an extempore reply. From the minister's performance the group-leader can better judge whether he knows the subject well and has firm views on it, or whether he relies on the guidance of his civil servants. The value of this to the group is that it will know for the remainder of the meeting, and of that minister's tenure of that office, whether tactically it should concentrate pressure on the minister through his party or on his civil servants directly at the centre and through the regional office.

The involvement of a group in such a continuous dialogue with the centre does not of itself guarantee results. Despite a lot of pressure, the North-West IDA achieved nothing of their objective of securing amendments to the 1966 Industrial Development Act, or the 1970 Local Employment Act, and the Birmingham Chamber of Commerce failed to get IDC policy reversed.[19] However, the essential point is that involvement in a continuous consultative process gives a group greater opportunity to influence the outcome, especially on relatively small issues like the location of industrial training centres. To be successful, active political support at the centre is indispensable. It was vital to the concessions given to north-east Lancashire as safeguards from the potential economic and social disadvantages to it of a new town close by in central Lancashire, and to the decision to locate the National Exhibition Centre at Birmingham, both before and after the 1970 general election.[20]

Another result of institutional and policy innovation at the regional level is that interest groups have had access to more information than in the past. This is especially true of those groups with members serving on the Planning Councils, who, having signed a declaration under the Official Secrets Act, see some restricted and confidential papers. A close working relationship with the centre and/or the region can also mean access to information not otherwise generally available.

But in any case, much more information is now published, partly the result of pressure from bodies like the Planning Councils and the Economic Development Committees ('Little Neddies'). Since 1967, the Central Statistical Office has published an annual *Abstract of Regional Statistics* which has helped groups and Planning Councils to make comparisons of the need and the extent of government assistance in different parts of the country. The Ministry of Transport also publish much more detailed information about road improvement plans, and the criteria upon which they are based.

Access to the consultative process for an influential group can rarely be refused outright; after refusing twice, the prime minister was still obliged to meet the North-West IDA in October 1971. Some groups seem to have been invited by the government specifically to give their views, for example, the Civic Trusts and the national CBI. This implied, at least in the case of the CBI, an element of encapsulation of a department by the group.

Public procedures are emphasised in the relationship between groups and the government, but the existence of the Planning Councils and the regionalisation of departments has provided a means by which a group can press discreetly behind the scenes while continuing with public campaigns. The balance between the two types of pressures exerted by different groups depends on the extent of the links with the regional and central departmental offices, both directly and through the Planning Council, and in the case of industry, through the CBI to the centre.

The government's response to the increased activity of interest groups in the mid-1960s was one of paralytic inactivity, itself partly a reflection of the lack of political commitment to regional planning. For example, it refused to amend schemes; the CBI secured only marginal changes in the administration of investment grants; and the Regional Employment Premium was introduced and implemented, despite wide criticism, after extensive consultation. Nor was the government very willing to alter decisions: pressure to change the policy for the issue of IDCs was resisted, while its response to pressure to widen the development areas was to set up a committee of inquiry in 1967.[21] The government seemed to have adopted a policy of divide and rule: to those regions and sub-regions pressing for special treatment, the government replied by arguing that it could not discriminate further without risking demands from other regions for similar favour.

While maintaining steady pressure on government, for direct and indirect assistance, groups also pressed for the provision of more infrastructure. In turn, the government attempted to appease them in three ways, all of which afforded the groups little means for making a meaningful comparison of the different treatment handed out to them. First, the government attempted to buy-off opposition by the selective use of public expenditure, examples of which are the introduction of the Regional Employment Premium, the opening of a coal-fired aluminium smelter in the North-East, and the decision not to rationalise the structure of the British Steel Corporation. Secondly, it gave way on some issues, for example roads, diverting the argument into one about starting dates. Thirdly, it initiated some regional measures which did not discriminate geographically between development areas and the rest: examples include schemes for increasing mobility of labour and for the clearance of derelict land, and grants for the modernisation of industrial and domestic buildings. Because they were widely available, they afforded less opportunity for groups, in particular regions, to complain about government discrimination. In their turn, groups searched for issues that did not entail any reversal of government policy. Once the groups in the West Midlands had failed to reverse government IDC policy, they concentrated on putting the idea of a National Exhibition Centre to Whitehall.[22]

Governments have also reacted to the increase in group activity by using the groups to help, formally and informally, to prepare and implement particular policies. For example, since 1963 successive governments have given the North-East Development Council a financial grant to assist it in promoting the attraction of industry to the region on the grounds that the Council is helping to implement government policy.

Preparation of plans and studies

A characteristic feature of regional planning in the UK in the 1960s was the production of surveys, studies and strategies as putative guides to action by government and its partners.[23] The attempt to predict and alter future events is a novel departure for British government. All regions have undertaken surveys of their resources, their needs and demands, and discussed the policies which are thought appropriate to them. The planning documents published by the Planning Councils, with the notable exception of that for the South-East, were very coolly received by the government, and almost all the proposals for government action were ignored or rejected. As exercises in plan preparation they had two fundamental weaknesses, one methodological, the other political. The planning documents differed widely in both the approach adopted and in their subject-matter. For this, the central government in general, and the DEA particularly, must bear much of the responsibility by failing to provide adequate guidelines for the Councils and Boards to ensure that what emerged proceeded from the same national premises about the distribution of population and employment, and that similar methods of analysis were used by all regions. Without such a common basis it was virtually impossible for the government to co-ordinate the very different planning documents submitted to it, and to make rational decisions on the priority to be accorded industrial development, housing, communications, etc, between the ten regions. Secondly, the published plans and studies lacked a firm and obvious political authority, which meant that the central government could ignore them almost with impunity. This reaction by government meant that interest groups in the regions, including the local authorities, had little need to take them seriously; thus they continued to regard regional planning as a series of short-term *ad hoc* issues.

In preparing studies and surveys, increasing use was made of quantified and analytical techniques, and in the preparation of regional strategies some Regional Planning Councils and Boards even began to consider and to cost alternative strategies (South-East, East Anglia).[24] While the better surveys and studies have been based upon research and the preparation of statistical material, there are in practice a number of limitations to the use of analytical techniques in regional planning. Some of these are: the age and validity of raw data, e.g. all the censuses of population distribution and production taken in the 1960s were badly out of date when they were published; the lack of adequate time-series; the lack of comparability, due to changes in the method of collection, geographical area, etc; the inadequacy of certain basic data, e.g. on income, which is available from inland revenue sources only for the geographic area of the administrative county; the restrictions on the use of data under the Trade Statistics Act which makes it difficult for data collected by one department for a specific purpose to be used by another for regional planning. There is also a further difficulty which arises from the elementary state of national income accounting and economic forecasting. There are national accounts and (with a time-lag) national input/output tables; but there are no regional accounts or regional input/output tables. Attempts to construct the latter entail the disaggregation of data collected and analysed on a national scale. In fact, much of the data which has to be used for regional planning is obtained by the disaggregation of national data; for planning by sub-region and even region this is notoriously unreliable.

There have been a number of attempts to use cost/benefit and cost/effectiveness techniques in the analysis of particular regional problems. Most obviously, in studies connected with the conservation of estuarial water (Morecambe Bay Barrage),[25] the improvement of transport communications (the Dee Crossing;[26] the Furness Peninsula), and the development of Severnside and Humberside. Technically, the boldest attempt has been the study associated with the development of the central Lancashire New Town at Preston/Leyland/Chorley, in which techniques pioneered by Italconsult in the Taranto Bay Study were used to examine the possibility of building up an industrial complex.

The perceived utility of rational analytical decision systems is very much a function of the inherent difficulty in undertaking and producing credible work. The enthusiasm of the specialists for the use and refinement of planning techniques, for the collection and use of basic data necessary for the employment of those techniques, and generally for regional research, has been blunted by the indifference and hostility of some departments, without whose active co-operation little can be done, and by the scepticism of some senior administrators. One symptom of this was the few people engaged professionally in departments on research for regional planning in the middle of the 1960s; the situation began to improve towards the end of the decade.[27] Some departments, the Department of Employment, and the (old) Board of Trade, for example, tended to take a gloomy view of what could be done with *their* data for purposes other than for which it was specifically collected.

Resistance of a political/administrative kind to the adoption of rational analytical decision systems has tended to reflect the different values of ministers and administrators from those of the specialist regional planners. Cost and time have tended to be critical. Only limited funds have been made available for research; in the early years of the Regional Economic Planning Councils the total annual budget was in the order of £25,000 for the eight English regions. The time factor has tended to weigh heavy in the minds of ministers and administrators, where the political time-scale is traditionally short term. Research which relates to the medium and long term, and which may not point unequivocally to a particular course of action, has tended to be accorded much less priority than the short-term study of an immediate and pressing problem with which the minister and the department are faced. Here and there towards the end of the decade this resistance was beginning to be broken down as government found itself unable to answer basic questions, such as the costs and benefits of providing assistance to industry in the development areas.

During the 1960s there was also considerable resistance to the adoption of rational analytical decision systems, especially the preparation of regional plans and strategies, from local authorities and private industry. Regional planning was often viewed by them as an irritant, and regional departments as superfluous, an additional layer of administration between local and central government. Further, local authorities had no prescribed role in regional economic planning (until the passing of the new Town and Country Planning Act in 1968); they participated only as executive authorities in the discharge of duties statutorily entrusted to them, such as the preparation of land-use plans under the Town and Country Planning Acts, or as housing authorities under the Housing Acts. This made some of them reluctant or unwilling to collect or furnish essential data for the Regional Economic Planning Councils and Boards.

There have been examples, however, of co-operation between central government departments, local authorities and Regional Economic Planning Boards and Councils; in the studies of the Dee Crossing, Severnside and Humberside, for example. Earlier, central government and local authorities co-operated on land-use/transportation studies in Merseyside, in south-east Lancashire and north-east Cheshire, and in Tyneside, sharing finance and contributing staff on secondment and professional expertise and information when necessary. However, central government has usually taken the lead in such ventures. In the preparation of the regional studies, surveys and strategies, the local authorities have been consulted but have not participated on a joint or team basis. The initiative here has been with the Planning Councils and Boards; while cost-benefit studies have been invariably initiated by central government.

Regional planning and budgeting

Recommendations such as those made in many of the published regional planning documents, if accepted and acted upon, would have entailed the reallocation of considerable sums of public money already committed in public investment programmes for roads, schools, hospitals etc, drawn up by the Treasury after negotiation at the national level with individual departments. Expenditure plans of central government departments are prepared annually on a five-year forward-look basis. There is no specific regional element, although a categorisation of expenditure by spending authorities recognises both *local* and *central* government spending. Regions are recognised indirectly through the special aid programmes for the development areas, the intermediate areas and the special development areas, and in the commitment of funds for industrial investment. Expenditure plans are formulated centrally. Bids are made by spending authorities: local authorities through their parent departments; nationalised industries through the submission of capital investment programmes to the Department of Trade and Industry; and central departments. What emerges are national/global totals of expenditure. Regional expenditure budgets can be deduced, with considerable difficulty, by the disaggregation of these totals. It is not possible to distinguish priorities for expenditure as between one region and another, but there are discernible priorities for types of programme, and sometimes even specific localities, e.g. the urban aid programme and primary school programmes which were designed to have a great impact in areas with poor or obsolescent social capital, mainly the North and North-West regions.

Expenditure plans tend to be formulated centrally, department by department, programme by programme, in a series of bilateral agreements with the Treasury. Thus the road programme for the next five years is decided by the minister of transport industries (within the Department of the Environment) after the submission of bids from the regional divisional road engineers, who in turn have consulted and been advised by the local authorities in their divisions. Decisions on individual road schemes are then taken in the light of national road planning and the plans of other departments for, say, a new town, a rail closure, the development of an airport. Specific projects with more than local significance, which have regional and/or national implications, such as a new town, a port improvement scheme, or a large industrial development by a nationalised industry, require close co-ordination with other departments at the stage of formulating tentative expenditure plans. But there is no *regional plan* which requires inputs of transport region by region, although to some extent this has been attempted for conurbations, where the central government and local authorities have co-operated in the preparation of long-term land-use/transportation studies.

Expenditure plans are, then, *sectoral*, with co-ordination of other sectoral plans where this is obvious and inescapable. Such plans provide for so many *local* houses, roads, ports etc, but not for so many *regional* houses, roads, ports. Forward planning for the regions does not exist. In the first and crucial stage, programmes of expenditure are drawn up and negotiated on a sectoral basis, based on criteria applying to the country as a whole. As the control of each programme lies in the department, any modification to meet a regional requirement has to be fed in centrally to be effective. It is, therefore, almost impossible to change the distribution of public investment between, say, roads, houses and schools in a particular region to reflect the relative priorities accorded them there. In fact, the consideration of the level and distribution of public investment within a region by the investing departments scarcely exists. 'Although the programmes can be broken down on a regional basis we are a very long way from regional budgets, giving the regions any say in the allocation of funds between programmes.'[28] In the short and medium term there is little scope for influencing the distribution of public investment within a region, or between regions. Although both Central Scotland and the North-West were given larger shares of public investment in 1963, there are very obvious economic and political limits, and the exercise has not been repeated.

Neither Scotland nor Wales has a regional budget. Expenditure plans are sectoral and decided ultimately in Whitehall by the Treasury and the major spending departments. Paradoxically, it has been argued that the centralisation of the budget has worked to Scotland's advantage.[29] Because the secretary of state is a Cabinet minister with direct access to the chancellor of the exchequer and the Treasury, the Scottish case can be urged at the highest levels. The Scottish Office acts as a built-in pressure group arguing the case for Scotland's special needs. It is claimed that a specifically Scottish budget with the allocation of funds left to the Scottish Office would produce a smaller total for Scotland. In any case, something of the flexibility that would result from complete discretion to vary allocations between services and programmes within a total budget occurs in practice. During the final stages of preparing the annual Public Expenditure Review, the Treasury have allowed the Scottish Office to shift as much as £1 million from totals agreed sectorally. It is therefore possible at this stage for the secretary of state to make marginal adjustments in the allocations between services to reflect priorities as perceived in Scotland.[30] The Welsh Office appears rather more circumscribed – 'just a bit around the margin perhaps' – but at least there is some element of discretion, denied to all English planning boards, to vary the sectoral allocations.[31]

Increasingly in the 1960s, governments have tended to protect depressed and developing regions from the full effects of deflationary policies introduced to correct imbalance in external payments. Cuts in public expenditure which have invariably accompanied such measures have been made more selectively: special development, intermediate and development areas have been absolved from the requirement that local authorities reduce their spending on houses, roads, schools, hospitals and other social capital. While the incidence of short-term adjustments in the regions to *national* unforeseen circumstances has diminished, unforeseen *regional* circumstances still give rise to familiar short-term adjustments. Heavy and persistent unemployment in the late 1960s and early 1970s induced the government to increase public expenditure programmes throughout the country, but with special emphasis on those regions where the incidence was greatest: Northern Ireland, Central Scotland, the North and North-West. In the development and intermediate areas, the government has committed hundreds of millions of pounds on capital works and housing. Such adjustments have tended to be made piecemeal without much conception of an overall strategy, and unrelated to existing five-year expenditure programmes.

Conclusions

The traditional pragmatic approach of British governments and their administrations was obscured momentarily by the flirtation with regional planning in the mid-60s. In fact no regional planning (i.e. plan-formulating and implementing) was done, with the exception of Scotland, where even so the task of carrying out plans emphasised the difficulty, and occasionally the impossibility, of securing effective collaboration between the Scottish Office and local authorities. Governments continued to follow a mainly *ad hoc* approach to regional problems. Throughout the 1960s policies were made and unmade for the regions, largely centrally inspired and directed, the objectives of which tended to be unrelated to any integrated and consistent picture of the future.

Regional planning is more appropriately regarded as a part, or perhaps no more than a phase, in the development over the last forty years of regional *policy*. Since the return of the Conservative government in 1970 this seems even clearer. The seriousness of regional unemployment has stimulated new and bold policy-making, and the allocation of considerable additional resources. But the initiatives are classically *ad hoc* and piecemeal.

If expectations of what the Planning Councils and Boards might achieve in a strictly planning sense were disappointed, this was largely inherent in the limited concept of regional planning adopted by the Conservative and Labour governments in the early 1960s. Regional planning was not conceived by them as a new, radical function of government requiring new economic and social policies, new institutions and a new style of administration.

From their inception, neither the government nor the administration intended that Councils and Boards should exercise autonomous powers, independently of the centre, to deal with problems as they arose in the region. Still less was it intended that Councils and Boards should formulate and then implement plans for future economic and social development. While local authorities retained their traditional statutory responsibilities for land-use planning, for housing, for transportation and for urban planning, Councils and Boards could not make or carry out regional plans without the active support and collaboration of those local authorities. Until the passage of the new Town and Country Planning Act in 1968 there was no effective means of providing for that. Moreover, while initially in 1965 the Labour government apparently intended that regional plans should be produced within the framework of a national plan, it was by no means clear what the precise roles of the Councils and Boards were to be in the preparation of such plans. Confusion of functions and responsibilities between the Councils and Boards may have been deliberate, or simply a reflection of the government's own uncertainty about what it wanted them to do. The rationale offered in explanation of the first is that as the new bodies were something of an experiment, the government wished them to feel free to proceed in whatever way they thought most suitable.

The explanation of the disappointment of expectations is therefore to be found, not so much in an account of what the Councils and Boards failed to do, as in their inability to do so from the start. The existing constraints in the political and administrative system meant that the advent of regional planning was more apparent than real. These constraints were of four main kinds: first, inadequate statutory powers both at the centre and in the regions. In Whitehall, statutory power was denied to the department (DEA) given overall responsibility for regional planning, while those departments with statutory functions and powers immediately relevant to regional planning had no responsibility for it and little inclination to share that of the DEA. Administrative arrangements at the regional level reflected a similar divorce of statutory power from responsibility. Even in Scotland, despite the creation of the Scottish Development Department in 1962, the Scottish Office had no formal authority to ensure that decisions made on steering industry were integrated and consistent with those made on other related issues over which it exercised a direct control, such as housing. The BOT regional controller continued to exercise a jurisdiction independent of the SO and the SDD under the general authority of his headquarters in Whitehall. The composition and functions of the Planning Councils were carefully circumscribed from the beginning: they were advisory bodies, nominated only, not elected, and therefore representative of no clearly articulated political force, either local or regional. While they could exhort, urge and even protest, they had no sanctions to impose if the government chose not to seek their advice, or having asked for it, did not accept it. The Scottish Economic Planning Council could not even do that much; while it appeared to enjoy the advantage of direct access to the government through its chairman, the secretary of state, his presence constrained the Council's independence.[32] Without an electorate, all regional councils lacked political authority. This was one of the issues dealt with by the Royal Commission on the Constitution which reported in 1973. Although its members disagreed about how it should be done, all felt that there should be some degree of decentralisation and devolution for England, and more especially for Wales and Scotland.[33]

The second main constraint was inherent in the existing power structure. Policy-making power was geographically centralised, with

Whitehall departments holding a monopoly of both statutory and political power relevant to regional planning. Among those central departments power was functionally diffused: a confusion of departments and agencies whose objectives rarely coincided, whose policies often conflicted, and who competed with each other for a larger share of national resources. (Each power centre conducted its own separate negotiations with the Treasury.) The implementation of policies formulated largely at the centre was done at a sub-regional level through the local planning authorities and the regional branches of the Board of Trade, Ministry of Housing and Local Government, and the Ministry of Labour.

Thirdly, throughout almost the whole of the decade there was a lack of deep political commitment to regional planning. Until the occurrence of heavy and persistent unemployment in 1970 and 1971, no government afforded it a very high political priority. Until 1969, governments of both Left and Right were unwilling to initiate institutional changes to remove those obstacles in the existing departmental power structure described above, although the creation of the Scottish Development Department in 1962 had pointed the way forward. A concentration of policy-making functions in fewer central departments, and the delegation of some greater authority to the regions, would have been such a radical step, administratively so difficult to accomplish in the mid-60s, that a real political commitment would have been needed to innovate on the scale required. Its absence was apparent, also, in that time and again government chose to ignore or reject proposals and advice tendered by Councils and Boards, and to postpone or delay its reaction to submitted plans.

Within the DEA, regional planning had a very low political priority where it was in competition with more important claims on ministers' time and energy. Only with the emasculation of the department's functions after the abandonment of the National Plan in July 1966 did it begin to receive a special emphasis. This relative neglect was an important contributory factor in the failure to formulate clear objectives for regional planning, and to provide policy guidelines for the regions in the preparation of their plans. In other departments, regional planning was often seen as potentially conflicting with existing statutory functions, and seen by some as a nebulous, ill-defined extra function *not* integral to their work. Moreover, almost all departments evinced a marked distaste for the DEA's distinctive approach and abrasive administrative style. The lack of general direction from the centre and the absence of clear unambiguous and acceptable objectives, meant that for most departments regional planning had a very low political priority: they were not obliged to take it seriously, or could give it such meaning as was consistent with their own objectives.

Local authorities had little reason to pay much serious attention to the plans and studies produced by the Councils and Boards which central government departments had chosen either to ignore or reject. Each fresh round of plans served only to widen the credibility gap, and to make progressively difficult the collaboration of local authorities in the preparation of such plans, and their commitment to the broad economic and social aims contained within them. For most of the 1960s, the statutory responsibilities of local authorities in such fields as land use and housing were unaffected by putative regional plans prepared by the new regional bodies, and their traditional lines of communication with Whitehall departments were undisturbed.

Finally, an additional constraint in the political system was the failure to develop a regional consciousness. The planning dynamism of the early and mid-60s was largely national and economic in its orientation: the regional dimension was relatively neglected in the National Plan of 1965 and its 'roll-forward' – *The Task Ahead*, which appeared four years later. In the regions, a regional consciousness was at best intermittent. No regional political force emerged. (The Welsh and Scottish movements were *nationalist* in character.) When a regional issue became politicised it was largely because regional, sub-regional and local groups' interests coalesced on an *ad hoc* problem. Such coalitions tended to be reactive rather than innovative. With little real power in the regions, and with no electorate to whom they were accountable, Planning Councils did little to encourage the formation of a regional consciousness.

Even had those constraints inherent in the existing political and administrative system been absent or removed, the slow growth of the economy meant that the additional wealth created was small. Apart from the many competing claims from different parts of the public sector for these very scarce and limited additional resources, for new schools, hospitals and so on, and from the private sector for investment and consumption, there was an enduring political commitment to maintain a fixed exchange rate for the pound and to achieve and then maintain a surplus on the trade balance. It is true that, in the latter part of the decade, assistance to the depressed regions increased very considerably (tenfold between 1964/5 and 1969/70), but this was to finance new or expanded regional *policies*, whose purpose was not to implement regional plans (though they could be used for such a purpose) but to deal in the short term with acute regional problems of unemployment and under-investment. While those policies represented a diversion of existing real resources to particular regions, no government contemplated a similar re-allocation of existing resources favouring some regions at the expense of others to underwrite those plans, studies and strategies produced by the Councils and Boards.

The knowledge that in the prevailing economic climate there were insufficient additional resources to finance plans (all of which called for still more public expenditure in the regions), and the government's unwillingness to alter the existing allocations between regions except in response to short-term *ad hoc* and largely political pressures, contributed to the lack of credibility with which all regionally produced plans and studies were invested. Confidence in the credibility of regional plans is to a large extent a function of the expectation in the minds of the participants that government is prepared to contemplate a re-allocation of existing resources to reflect a judgement about relative regional priorities, or that additional public funds are available and will be forthcoming; neither of these conditions was met for the greater part of the 1960s.

It is difficult to estimate the direct results of the disappointment of expectations. Disillusionment with the efficacy of the new regional bodies was progressive. Changes in traditional institutions and administrative practices subsequently were not made as a direct consequence. In two respects, however, the failure of the mid-60s experiments has produced change: the first of these was institutional, the second processual.

The inability of the Councils and Boards to produce coherent and consistent plans for the economic and social development of their regions which commanded the support of the government on the one hand (and hence a commitment of re-allocated or additional resources), and the local authorities on the other (and hence a commitment to discharge their statutory functions in accordance with agreed plan-objectives), led the administration at the centre to assume the initiative. Plan preparation has entered a new and more promising phase with the setting up of Joint Planning Teams. Since 1969 local authorities and the central government have been collaborating in the preparation of strategic plans for the regions (so far, the South-East, the North-West, the West Midlands, West Central Scotland, and the North).[34] While the origin of this institutional innovation can be traced to the government's response to *A Strategy for the South East*, prepared and published by the South-East Economic Planning Council, the willingness of local authorities to participate in regional planning exercises is due more to the statutory obligations which they incurred under the 1968 Town and Country Planning Act. Land-use planning authorities designated under that Act have to produce structure plans for their areas which include estimates of future levels of employment, population, and industrial growth consistent with the plan for the region as a whole.

The failure of the Councils as plan-makers has emphasised their potential as advisory and consultative bodies. While the growth of their advisory function is not solely attributable to the atrophy of their plan-making function, Councils have been obliged to rethink their positions.

Changes in the consultative process were limited as interest groups continued to go to the centre. However, groups were able to exploit the new regional machinery and build up close links with regional civil servants. These factors, together with the availability of more infor-mation, meant that groups could supplement their pressure on the centre by bringing their influence to bear in new ways. The develop-ment and introduction of several new regional policies meant that the government laid itself open to pressure to alter the shape or applica-tion of those policies. The central government found it more difficult to respond directly and unequivocally as it became subject to pressure brought to bear upon it from all quarters at once. Groups were thus encouraged to make much more specific sets of proposals and to develop private procedures in their links with policy-making depart-ments at the centre; this supplemented the public pressure that they had traditionally used. To a certain extent they became built into the process by which policy was formulated and carried out. Links with the Cabinet, through individual ministers or to strong regional groups of MPs, were of great assistance.

The increase in unemployment in the early 1970s exacerbated the problems of areas that had not previously been regarded as depressed and led to the emergence of new interest groups. Within both the new and established groups there was a notable sinking of political dif-ferences. Elected and non-elected representatives sought to work together for the benefit of a particular area. This led to the develop-ment within regions of a number of different sub-regional conscious-nesses which were partly incompatible. This helped to prevent the emergence of a regional consciousness as a basis for EPC activity.

It is, of course, impossible to predict whether the general economic climate will be more favourable in the 1970s than it was in the previous decade. But, as in the past, if regional planning is to be more than the co-ordination at the centre and in the region of existing interventions by autonomous public sector bodies, then a lot will turn on the scale of additional resources made available to the public sector; also upon the degree of the government's political commit-ment to re-allocate existing resources in accordance with a set of priorities drawn up after careful consideration of the aims set out in the regional strategies which are currently being formulated by the Joint Planning Teams.

In several respects both the machinery and the process of regional planning are now better adapted for regional planning. Responsi-bility and executive authority for regional planning have been concentrated both at the centre and in the regions as a result of the extensive changes in the machinery of government made in 1969 and 1970. For most of the 1960s there were seven major departments at the centre, with representation in the regions, whose responsibilities were directly relevant to regional planning. Since the re-organisation, this number has been reduced to three: the Department of the Environment (DOE) the Department of Trade and Industry (DTI) and the Department of Employment (DE). It is not yet clear what role the Department of Energy will play in the regions. The DEA has disappeared; housing, transport, public building and works, and the oversight of local government, have been brought together within one department, the DOE; and the new DTI has responsibility for the whole of industry, both public and private, including location policy. Responsibility for regional planning is now shared largely between these two giant departments, although it is the DOE which has responsibility for the work of the Planning Councils and Boards and which provides the chairmen of the latter at the under-secretary level.

The inherent political and functional weaknesses of the Planning Councils persist but, whatever their future, the Planning Boards have become bodies with greater potential power to influence the economic and social development of the regions. Through time they have become more cohesive, with fewer members and with a chairman who is also the head of a large executive department. The habit of working together over nearly ten years, in the same building, should make it easier in the future than it has been in the past, at some times, in some regions, for the Board to function as a unified body rather than as a collection of independent departments with different and often conflicting values and roles. It should now prove easier for the Boards to take a collective view, not only about current problems but about future possibilities, which represents an integration rather than a summation of their interests and values.

In this the Boards will derive strength from the continuing process of decentralising executive power to regional departments. While this occurred on a small scale very gradually and reluctantly in the 1960s, since 1970 both the DOE and the DTI have been invested with much more substantial discretion to determine matters finally at the regional level. Moreover, partly as a result of the re-organisation of government machinery, and partly as a result of experience and the habit of closer collaboration, regional departments have become better able and more confident in making decisions without reference to the centre for guidance. Regional controllers not only have more discretion to commit their headquarters departments, they now feel more confident in doing so. Further, their potential power has also been strengthened by the growing dependence of local authorities since 1968 on the views which regional departments individually, and the Board collectively, take about the likely future economic and social development of the region.

As yet there is very little evidence of any growing political commitment by either major party to the broad concept of regional planning, without which the future efforts of Boards and Councils are likely to remain marginal, at least in so far as their work relates to the implementation of medium and long-term regional plans. More optimistically, it could be argued that the Conservative government had willed the means for the implementation of such plans. The 1972 Budget, and the Industry Act which followed, both provided policies for the economic development of the assisted areas backed up by a considerable commitment of resources. £1,013 million has been allocated for 1972–7 for cash grants, and £210 million has been allocated for selective regional assistance to help firms within the designated assisted areas. The latter will also benefit substantially from the £80 million set aside in 1972–7 for the shipbuilding industry, and to an unpredictable extent from the £150 million (which may be extended by up to a further £100 million) for selective assistance anywhere in Britain.[35] Within DTI an industrial development executive has been set up, with a minister advised by an industrial development advisory board of businessmen. In the regions, DTI regional directors, with the assistance of newly created regional industrial directors and regional industrial advisory boards, can authorise grants to firms of up to £500,000 without reference to the centre. Together with its responsibility for IDC policy, and assistance to firms under the Local Employment Acts, decisions on all of which now rest much more in the hands of the DTI regional directors, the DTI has, at the regional level, a powerful battery of weapons which could be used to influence the future economic and social development of a region as a whole. Whether they will be so used, and in conjunction with other policy instruments in the hands of the DOE (housing and transport, for example), within the terms of an overall strategy for the region provided by the Joint Planning Team, is as yet uncertain. What is significant is that there is for almost the first time in the regions an enormous potential for influencing (or retarding) the development of regional planning. Much will depend on the relationship between the chairman of the Board and the regional director of the DTI (also of under-secretary rank); and on the speed with which the Joint Planning Teams can complete their work and a *regional* strategy be agreed between the principal participants at the local, regional and central levels. If the DTI's weapons were to be used to influence the location and size of future economic development, prior agreement between all the principal participants on the fundamental strategic issues, such as the location of new or expanded towns, the selection of industries for assistance and encouragement, road and rail communications, would have to be obtained quickly if the provision of assistance for industry under DTI policies is not to take place on an *ad hoc* and short-term basis which may have the effect of pre-empting certain options and foreclosing others.

It remains to be seen whether the administration of the Industry Act by the DTI in the regions (and from the centre too) is more than the familiar response of central government to acute political problems, on this occasion high unemployment, and a failure or unwillingness on the part of industry to invest in new capital equipment. If it is more than this, if government becomes more firmly wedded to regional planning, then a precondition will be some change in the traditional attitudes of governments and their advisers with their preference for short-term, *ad hoc* solutions. Any deeper political commitment to regional planning in the 1970s would entail at least some renunciation of the 'issue-oriented' approach which characterised the attitudes of all governments towards the regions in the 1960s.

Two developments of the 1960s will make it harder for the government to do this: first, the discriminatory effects of regional policy have been progressively diluted by the elaboration of more and more areas with different status qualifying for greater or lesser amounts of government assistance. To the development areas designated in 1966 have been added the special development areas, the intermediate development areas and, until 1974, the derelict land-clearance areas. Secondly, the increased activity of problem-oriented interest groups at the regional and national levels will make it at least as difficult in the future as in the past for governments to try to resist or ignore pressures for short-term action to deal with current regional problems.

Even if the operation of the Industry Act in the 1970s were to breathe fresh life into regional planning, it seems unlikely, at least in the English regions, that planning would be done in the immediate future under the direction and control of regionally elected authorities. The absence of a clear and compelling recommendation in 1973 from the Royal Commission on the Constitution, the coolness of both the Conservative and Labour parties towards regionalism, and the new structure of English local government, combine to make it improbable that any government, Left or Right, will contemplate more in the immediate future than a further measure of self-government for the Scots and the Welsh.

NOTES

1 For details of the formal organisation and analysis of the practical experience in England and Wales prior to 1960 see J. B. Cullingworth, *Town and Country Planning in England and Wales*, 2nd edn, chapter 3; G. McCrone, *Regional Policy in Britain*, pp. 106–25; G. Denton, M. Forsyth and M. MacLennan, *Economic Planning and Policies in Britain, France and Germany*, pp. 299–311; and B. C. Smith, *Regionalism in England*, 3 vols. Acton Society Trust, I, chapters 2–4. Details of the organisational structures relating to Wales are described in F. M. G. Willson, *The Organisation of British Central Government 1914–64*, ed. D. N. Chester, pp. 34, 37, 355, 361, 441.

2 For more detailed description of the Scottish experience before 1960 see Willson, *British Central Government*, pp. 26, 37, 116, 356; and J. P. Mackintosh, 'Regional Administration – has it worked in Scotland?', *Public Administration*, Autumn 1964.

3 On the 1962–3 changes see Willson, *British Central Government*, pp. 469–78; Mackintosh, 'Regional Administration', pp. 255–7; T. D. Haddow, 'The Administration of Re-Development', *Public Administraton*, Autumn 1964; and *Central Scotland: A Programme for Development and Growth*, Cmnd. 2188, para. 160, HMSO 1963.

4 *The North East: A Programme for Regional Development and Growth*, Cmnd. 2206, HMSO 1963; *Central Scotland: A Programme for Development and Growth*.

5 See Sir Eric Roll 'The DEA', and A. W. Peterson 'The Regional Economic Planning Councils and Boards', both in *Public Administration*, Spring 1966; and Parliamentary Debates, H. C. vol. 703, cols. 1829–34. The new Ministry of Land and Natural Resources was absorbed by MHLG in February 1967, and a Land Commission set up.

6 See T. L. Johnson, N. K. Buxton, and D. Mair, *Structure and Growth of the Scottish Economy*, pp. 334–7; J. G. Kellas, *The Scottish Political System*, pp. 227–31; and the Board's annual reports.

7 C. R. Tindal, 'Regional Development in Scotland and Ontario', p. 281, unpublished Ph.D. thesis, University of Glasgow, 1972.

8 *Ibid.* pp. 290–3.

9 See E. Rowlands, 'The Politics of Regional Administration: the Establishments of the Welsh Office', and P. J. Randall, 'Wales in the Structure of Central Government', *Public Administration*, L, Autumn 1972, pp. 333–72.

10 C. Painter, 'The Repercussions of Administrative Innovation: The West Midlands Economic Planning Council', *Public Administration*, L, Winter 1972, pp. 474–5.

11 *Ibid.* p. 476.

12 Tindal, 'Regional Development', chapters 4 and 5.

13 DEA internal memorandum, 1967.

14 See J. A. Cross, 'The Regional Decentralization of British Governments', *Public Administration*, Winter 1970.

15 See above, p. 254.

16 What follows on the North-West region is based partly on a series of interviews with the principal interest groups in 1970–1.

17 Painter, 'Repercussions of Administrative Innovation', p. 470.

18 E.g. *ibid* pp. 475, 478.

19 *Ibid* pp. 475–6.

20 On the National Exhibition Centre lobby, see Painter, *ibid* pp. 479–83.

21 *The Intermediate Areas* (the Hunt Committee) Cmnd. 3998, HMSO April 1969.

22 Painter, 'Repercussions of Administrative Innovation'.

23 For an analysis of these, see M. B. Gahagan, 'Regional Economic Planning in Great Britain', chapter 5, unpublished M.A. thesis, University of Manchester, 1973.

24 *A Strategy for the South East*, HMSO 1967; *East Anglia: A Study*, HMSO 1968.

25 *Morecambe Bay: Estuary Storage*, report by the Economic Study Group, HMSO 1972.

26 *Dee Estuary Phase IIa*, report by Binnie and Partners, HMSO 1971.

27 See Gahagan, 'Regional Economic Planning', chapter 3.

28 DEA internal paper, 1968.
29 Select Committee on Scottish Affairs, *Minutes of Evidence*, pp. 173–4, H.C. 397 (1968–9), HMSO 1969.
30 *Ibid*; and Commission on the Constitution, *Minutes of Evidence 2*, p. 24, HMSO 1970.
31 Commission on the Constitution, *Minutes of Evidence 1*, para 448, HMSO 1970. See also the *Report of the Royal Commission on the Constitution*, Cmnd. 5460, HMSO 1973.
32 To emphasise its purely advisory role, its name was changed in December 1970 to the Scottish Economic Council.
33 *Report of the Royal Commission on the Constitution*, 1969–73, I–II, Cmnd. 5460/5460–1, HMSO 1973.
34 Those for the South-East and the North-West have already reported; a team for the Northern Region was appointed in 1973. Co-operation has taken on somewhat different forms in the West Midlands where the initiative was seized by the Standing Conference of local authorities.
35 *Public Expenditure 1972–77*, Table 2.7 and pp. 35–6, Cmnd 5178, HMSO 1972.

SELECT CRITICAL BIBLIOGRAPHY

No published work examines in any detail either the organisation of government for regional planning or the regional policy process. The literature is dominated by economists whose focus has been regional economic policy. Gavin McCrone, *Regional Policy in Britain*, Allen and Unwin, London 1969, analyses and comments on the economic and social causes of the regional problem, and has a full and balanced account of the development of government policies to deal with it up to 1968. Regional policy for the period 1964–72 is summarised fairly and succinctly by J. D. McCullum, 'UK Regional Policy 1964–72', in *Cities, Regions and Public Policy*, edited by G. C. Cameron and L. Wingo, Oliver and Boyd, Edinburgh 1973. A short, polemical critique of regional policy is Graham Hallett, Peter Randall and E. G. West, *Regional Policy for Ever?*, Institute of Economic Affairs, London 1973. Both the latter two books have useful short bibliographies.

13. Regional planning in Italy[1]

VALERIO SELAN AND ROSITA DONNINI

Historical and socio-economic background

An analysis of regional planning in Italy must be based on the observation of the two interconnected trends of regionalism and planning which chronologically have overlapped in different ways, according to whether one considers institutional and constitutional developments, the introduction of new processes or their actual working. We shall briefly outline the evolution of the two trends which in historic origin had different motivations and have only coincided, both formally and substantively, since 1970.

The need for a regional organisation was felt at the time of the formation of a united Italian state, when it was debated whether Italy was to have a federal or a unitary structure. The latter choice eventually prevailed. Certain socio-economic and political-cultural differences, however, have remained. This accounts for the fact that the regional boundaries established in the Republican Constitution of 1948, and which today define the operational scope of planning on a territorial level, coincide with the historic boundaries of many pre-unity states. There had been a very heated debate concerning the need to adapt such boundaries to changed socio-economic conditions, but it was eventually decided to leave the boundaries unchanged.

As for planning, this originally emerged as a typically sectoral necessity. It should not be forgotten that from 1922 to 1943 Italy was governed as a totalitarian state, in which economic planning from the top reflected specific requirements of a political and military nature (autarchy) and was typically carried out by sectors ('corporative' structure of the state). Even in the immediate post-war period, planning was initially sectoral (railway reconstruction plan, Sinigaglia plan for the steel industry) and concentrated in sectors largely in government hands. The establishment of the Cassa per il Mezzogiorno (Southern Italy Development Agency) in 1950 was the first example of large-scale territorial action which, while not involving a comprehensive economic and social plan for the Mezzogiorno[2], did require the Cassa to implement, under the aegis of a special Commit-

[269]

tee of Ministers, a set of priorities for public investment in agriculture and infrastructure in this vast area, for which it can draw on a special fund established on a five-yearly (originally ten-yearly) basis.

The Vanoni Plan (1954) was the first real attempt at laying before public opinion the problem of comprehensive planning. The political forces supporting this experiment were diverse. The far Left saw in planning something akin to the Soviet model or, to adopt a more sympathetic interpretation, one way of bringing about, in the interest of the working class, a condition of greater political control over the economic process. Certain political and business groups, remembering the experience of the corporative state, which had not been entirely negative for them, saw in planning an instrument for security and certainty in the implementation of production plans and a guarantee of state intervention on a larger scale. This was in keeping with a tradition of complementarity between private and public action which, despite formal polemics, re-emerges in Italy whenever the economy is in trouble. Other forces, finally, were apparently opposed to any kind of overall planning (for instance, the General Confederation of Italian Industry), regarding it as a limitation on productive efficiency which, in their view, was maximised by free private enterprise. Such forces reflected the interests and opinions of the industrialists operating in the expanding sectors.

The idea of regional planning was present in the Vanoni Plan, as it included among the basic objectives of Italian development that of the elimination of North–South disparities. This obviously called for an orientation of action not only by sectors but also by regions. We were thus on the eve of the introduction of regional planning proper which, in any case, as we have suggested, had found its first partial operational expression in the Cassa per il Mezzogiorno. The Cassa carries out multi-sectoral and multi-annual intervention programmes, which are additional to those of other government departments and based on proposals drawn up by the Committee of Ministers for Southern Italy, as the body responsible for the intervention policy guidelines. Through long-term planning and the multi-sectoral formulation of its interventions, the Cassa is able to adopt a unitary approach to the interdependent development requirements of the whole of this vast area, with a view to its integration into the nation's economic system. With the creation of the Cassa, the traditional criterion of allocating expenditures among the various economic sectors and the respective ministries was replaced by a completely novel method, which attributes to a single agency powers of administrative and financial autonomy. These special characteristics confer on the Cassa that degree of operational flexibility which is indispensable to an effective special-intervention policy aimed at a radical transformation of the social and economic structures of a vast area. The Cassa's innovative way of working has also provided a practical example of programming, later to constitute valuable experience for use in economic planning at the national level.

The Cassa has its own management body as well as executive organisation. The former consists of a board of directors, composed of a chairman, two vice-chairmen and ten members, chosen by the prime minister. The executive body consists of a directorate general which supervises the divisions operating in the various sectors, currently comprising: water supply and drainage systems, land reclamation and transformation, credit and finance, industry, industrial areas and centres, vocational training, tourism, handicrafts and fisheries, roads and construction. Its horizontal divisions include an overall planning and programming division and a research unit.

In 1957 new types of intervention were provided for in the fields of education, vocational training and social welfare. The Cassa was also authorised to grant subsidies in the sectors of fisheries and handicrafts, and to small and medium industrial enterprises, as well as to assist in the establishment of industrial areas with grants towards the cost of the creation of essential service facilities. The tasks assigned to the Cassa were thus extended to all productive sectors, and the function of public intervention in Southern Italy – to be the propulsive factor establishing an autonomous growth mechanism – was becoming increasingly explicit.

A review of the results produced by the foregoing policy of intervention in the Mezzogiorno reveals certain continuing inadequacies in its development; above all the lack of growth compared to Central–Northern Italy and the accentuation of the disparities within the Mezzogiorno itself. As a consequence, new development proposals were made in a number of official government documents, the first of which, known as *Progetto'80*, provides the basis for five-year economic plans in the current decade. In such documents the primary objective is stated to be, on the one hand, spreading industrialisation more widely with a view to achieving a better balance among the various regions; and on the other, organising development on a regional basis, reflecting a type of development based on ever-increasing participation by economic and social forces.

In pursuit of this twin objective, the Cassa's operations were further extended in 1972, with an increased emphasis on industrial development, involving notably loans for new plant and technical assistance to small and medium-sized firms. At the same time public enterprises were required to increase the proportion of their investment in new plant in the Mezzogiorno from 60 to 80% of the total. Meanwhile, the participation of decentralised authorities in planning was given practical force by the establishment of regional governments. This means that the development plans and specific projects sponsored by the Cassa for the industrial areas are no longer submitted for approval to the Committee of Ministers for the South but to the appropriate regional authorities.

Aside from the experience of the Cassa per il Mezzogiorno which, strictly speaking, cannot be considered a *regional* planning body, the period of regional planning falls into two parts: from 1965 to 1970 with the establishment of the Regional Committees of Economic Planning (CRPE) and post-1970, with the establishment of regional government. Until 1970 Italy's political-administrative structure, on a territorial level, was organised in the following manner:

(a) The communes, numbering about 9,000, are elected local government bodies with specific powers including land use (detailed master plans), local roads, certain types of infrastructure;

(b) The provinces, numbering 98, constituting the next level of elected local government bodies, have powers in the areas of provincial roads, technical and vocational education and certain types of infrastructure.

Prior to the establishment of regional government, control over both communal and provincial budgets was exercised by the Provincial Administrative Board, a body composed of representatives of communal and provincial governments and chaired by the prefect, an official from the Ministry of the Interior charged with representing the national government in each province.

The first phase of regional planning (1965–70)

The Regional Economic Planning Committees (CRPE)

The first National Economic Plan, approved in 1967 after a long and difficult progress through parliament, called for a territorial articulation of the Plan, using a complex procedure for formulating priorities at national level, regional consideration of these, followed by central control of the resulting regional plans for compatibility and coordination.

Considerably in advance of the establishment of the regions, the CRPE were given the task of cooperating with the central planning bodies on the territorial breakdown of the National Economic Plan. They met according to a programme fixed by themselves, usually for one or two days from eight to twelve times a year, though in a few regions they met more frequently. The members of the Committees were appointed by the Budget and Economic Planning Ministry. Their membership included representatives of the larger territorial units of the regions (communes with over 30,000 population and provinces), of Chambers of Commerce, of the field services of central government (agricultural inspectors, public works superintendents), and of labour and employers' organisations, as well as four experts, almost always representing the major political parties. The percentage figure for each category varied between regions and over time, but tended to reflect the political make-up of the region. In fact, during their period of operation the Committees behaved more like political than specialist advisory bodies. Institutionally, the role of the CRPE was that of advisers and consultants to the Ministry of Economic Planning. They had no direct links with the Cassa, other government departments, or the prefects. Although they were not able, therefore, to participate directly in the executive decision-making process, the Committees were consulted during the preparation of the National Plan and, through an attempt to establish regional development models, they did exercise a certain degree of indirect influence on central planning. Pressure was brought to bear, although not always successfully, in the field of infrastructure policy and large-scale industrial location.

The consultative system applied not only to the higher level – central planning – but also *vis-à-vis* the local authorities. The establishment of the CRPE did not affect the powers of local government, but since their representatives participated in Committee debates, the local authorities did, to a certain extent, feel bound by the conclusions gradually reached in such debates. Initially at least, the Committees were viewed favourably at the local level, with the result that they became heavily 'politicised'. But this interest was weakened, in many regions, by the very long delays in the formulation of the regional plans – due to political divergences and the lack of technical back-up – and by a feeling that the CRPE had little influence on specific economic policy decisions. The Committees, however, did play the useful role of bringing out, through wide-ranging debate, echoed in the daily and trade press, certain points of imbalance typical of each region. This publicity associated with the CRPE provided leverage on the central government's field agencies and on local governments, notably by groups of industrialists and trade unions, usually supported by allied political parties. In the final analysis, formal subordination to the central power remained almost total, including preliminary investigation and research activity. In effect, each CRPE in its planning work had to conform to a methodological framework prescribed by the Ministry of Economic Planning; approved study projects were paid for by the ministry; while the staffs of the CRPE secretariats were paid by the ministry, although Committee members served without remuneration.

The 1965 decree setting up the Committees envisaged the following duties and responsibilities.

(a) Ascertaining the economic resources and social conditions of each region.

(b) Identifying the major problems of regional economic development and proposing development objectives and means of intervention in the region to the central authorities.

(c) Preparing a draft plan for the economic development of the region, within the limits of the territorial breakdown of the national economic plan, in the light of the Economic Planning Ministry's directives.

(d) Upon request, assisting local government and local development consortia in planning their respective actions in the region and providing such bodies with guidelines for action.

(e) Giving advice to the Ministry of Economic Planning concerning the multi-annual coordination plans for government investment in the South.

(f) Supplying the Ministry of Economic Planning with all the information it required concerning regional economic activities and the implementation of the national economic plan within the region.

By the end of 1970, all but one of the regional plans had been prepared by the CRPE. Their common features have been:

(a) The statement of tendencies and hypotheses of regional development which had already been overtaken by actual developments at the time when the plans were submitted to the Interministerial Committee for Economic Planning (CIPE). For example, C. Beltrame writes:

...Let us consider two cases, those of Piemonte and Liguria. The central idea underlying Piemonte's regional plan is that of curtailing the industrial growth rate in the Turin area, where the bulk of the Region's industrial potential is now concentrated, by 'decentralizing' development to a number of lesser 'poles'...Instead, substantial investments have been made in the Turin area, while certain areas (for instance Verbania and Casale Monferrato) are unable to reverse their economic decline. As far as Liguria is concerned the argument about the coordination of the Ligurian ports (in particular Genoa and Savona) and the creation of organic links with the immediate Piemontese hinterland, through areas of port and industry decentralization (Ovadese, Valle Scrivia, Bacini delle Bormide) has not only made no actual progress on an operational level, but there have been no preliminary choices of basic importance...[3]

(b) A broadly similar choice of instruments was proposed for the implementation of regional plans. These include: (i) development finance agencies, qualified to acquire equity shareholdings and to engage in leasing activities; (ii) technical assistance centres; (iii) intercommunal transportation authorities; (iv) data banks; (v) territorial ecological plans (Piemonte); (vi) farm amalgamation zonal plans; (vii) regional educational coordination; (viii) public ownership of 'green areas'.

The more enduring value of some of these instruments compared with overall plans derives partly from the difference between comprehensive planning and specific measures. Furthermore, in the preparation of overall plans, the clash between radically opposed political and economic groups often took a demagogic form, while specific intervention proposals, generally the work of experts, appeared relatively non-controversial.

Certain regional plans, mostly in Northern Italy, have gone beyond the boundaries of a single region in considering development problems, these being viewed not only in relation to the adjoining regions but even in a European context. Typical examples of this approach are the plans proposed by Umbria and Emilia-Romagna, which call for the development of lines of communication capable of vitalising the entire surrounding area. So far none of these proposals have been accepted by the central planners.

The most advanced position, in its extra-regional scope, is that taken in Piemontese regional planning, such as it emerged from the report of the Istituto per le Ricerche Economiche del Piemonte (IRES), whose principles were accepted by the CRPE. In seeking to integrate Piemonte with Europe's 'strong' areas, IRES considered that Piemonte and the Po River Basin (including the Ligurian ports) should seek above all an organic integration with the Marseille–Lyon growth areas. This would represent the creation of a European 'strong' area in the south to serve as counterweight to the Paris–Amsterdam–Strasbourg triangle in the north. To this end, competition between Genoa (or the Ligurian port system) and Marseille for a position as Europe's only great port in the south should be avoided. The latter should instead be conceived as a great integrated port system, stretching from Genoa to the farthest western appendage of Marseille (Fos).

It should be emphasised finally, however, that there was no direct articulation between the regional plans and the actual programming of public investment. The latter remained a completely separate process in which the CRPEs were not directly involved, except in so far as their opinions were requested in some specific cases.

The CRPE and the political process

The CRPE did not in themselves, as purely consultative bodies, create a new structure of authority relations within the state. This was deliberate in so far as they were considered as a prelude to the establishment of the regional government system. In practice, however, there has been some tendency to encourage the communal and provincial governments concerned to coordinate their expenditure policies and their tactics *vis-à-vis* central government. Especially in the Northern regions, this development assumed significant proportions. It is hard to tell, however, whether this has involved any fundamental change in governmental practices, or represents merely a new way of dressing-up what has remained a substantially traditional line of conduct.

In the matter of regional economic research and analysis, the employment of experts by the CRPE by no means guaranteed them a monopoly in expertise. Most notably, the Chambers of Commerce created in this period a number of Regional Research Centres, which even went so far as to create a jurisdictional dispute between two ministries: the Ministry of Industry, which supervises the Chambers of Commerce and the Ministry of the Budget and Economic Planning, which was responsible for the CRPE. What happened was that the Ministry of Industry allocated to the Regional Research Centres a number of expertise functions to which the CRPE laid claim. In addition, the Research Institutes, financed for the most part by the provinces and communes, while sometimes doing research work for the CRPEs, have in other cases conducted independent research projects and have reached conclusions which, especially as regards the spatial pattern of development, have disagreed with those of the CRPE. In this way, the immediate impact of the CRPEs' conclusions on the authorities was weakened, though it helped to encourage the debate on the guidelines of regional development. However, once the regional authorities were instituted (see next section), most of them accepted the plans established by the CRPE as a starting point for their own planning activity.

In addition to their primary plan-making tasks, many CRPE acted as contractors for central government in carrying out specific research projects. Although formally required to complete such work by predetermined deadlines, the resulting documents were, like the planning proposals, discussed point by point in the Committees, which sometimes involved very considerable delays. Generally speaking, it can be said that in certain regions – mostly in the North – the studies conducted were of considerable interest and called for major research efforts. Their common fault was the failure to state how proposals were to be financed, so they never formed the basis for action.

Nevertheless, the long debates that have taken place in the CRPE have made some contribution towards the adoption of a more uniform methodology for the establishment of development needs and the creation of a more rational attitude on the part of local administrators. Some informal coordination of the actions of local authorities occurred as a result of the exchange of information and experience.

Relations between levels of government were mediated by the CRPE to some extent. The activity of the CRPE also gradually created in central government a closer attention to the 'regionalisation' of sectoral interventions. It should be noted, however, that this tendency had already begun to emerge after the creation of the Cassa per il Mezzogiorno.

The pattern of relations between central government, on the one hand, and local authorities and interest groups on the other, was not substantially changed by the operation of the CRPE. This was partly due to the fact that the national planning process, of which the CRPE were formally a part, itself lacked specific executive instruments. Contacts continued to be focussed on individual ministries. However, the establishment of a regional consultative body in fact increased the articulation of local authority and group demands at a political level in national policy-making. This might seem to contradict our previous statements about the formal and practical role of the CRPE, but this is not so. Two aspects of the problem should not be forgotten:

(a) the members of the CRPE, although appointed by governmental decree, were overwhelmingly political representatives from the local authorities;

(b) from their inception, the CRPE were regarded as transitional instruments, pending the introduction of regional government.

Turning to the regional level, the CRPE succeeded in most cases in mediating and coordinating a variety of local demands, through a difficult and laborious process leading to the establishment of the regional plans. In some cases, as we have seen, partially inter-regional plans were formulated and proposed. But because this coordination was with reference to the plans, it remained in the event largely ineffective. Moreover, at the central level, the sum total of the regional proposals was found to be far in excess of the total amount of available resources, two to three times as large in the case of investments. Thus, the identification of regional problems and demands has proved of some use on a qualitative level but of little practical use in quantitative terms.

Because of their very composition, part political and part 'corporative', the CRPE functioned to a substantial extent as political rather than specialist advisory bodies. As a result, while certain broad priority objectives for a region were accepted in some cases by all participants, their opinions differed, often along party lines, as to the means of fulfilling these objectives. For instance, in all the CRPEs the Communists fought for development through government-controlled enterprises in preference to private enterprise. They also tended to subordinate economic considerations to the demands of distributive justice. Moreover, electoral concerns induced the representatives of certain provinces to defend, within the region, locations of industries and infrastructures which could scarcely be justified on economic grounds.

In conclusion, it cannot be said that the CRPE performed in a wholly satisfactory manner. This was due in the first place to a congenital institutional weakness: they were basically intended as specialist advisory bodies to the Ministry of Economic Planning, from which they obtained their operating funds. But in reality their character was not markedly 'expert', in the sense of supplying information and advice to underpin decisions, since their ability to contribute directly to the elaboration of the First National Plan proved practically non-existent. Above all, the slowness in framing the regional plans and also in furnishing the Ministry of Economic Planning with the requested advice, made it virtually impossible for the work done by the CRPE to have any practical influence on the decisions of the central planners. In this connection, a particular difficulty was the problem of language: the local political representatives, at least in an initial stage, did not seem familiar with the use of economic terminology. Furthermore, a markedly autarchical tendency manifested itself in almost all regions, calling for the establishment of all kinds of industry within each region. This was particularly characteristic of the poorer and more depressed regions of Italy, and was also associated with demands for financial support by the central authorities.

In other respects, however, the activity of the CRPE, despite all the reservations that we have made, was an extremely important educational experience. In conditions of serious national and international economic and financial problems, many of the initial proposals have had to be held in abeyance. And yet the comparison between people's expectations and the quantitative limits, the need to balance objectives and resources rather than draw up simple lists of grievances, and the very contact with economists and experts at a local level, have formed a generally positive experience. Moreover, the hopes aroused among small and medium businessmen, and their increased awareness of the macro-economic realities, have established the foundations on which regional planning proper could be built up.

In the final analysis, the CRPE proved an important bridge to the post-1970 fusion of the two trends noted at the outset of this paper, regionalism and planning. Born in the shadow of a government commitment to implement the Constitution's regional provisions, the CRPE succeeded in generating a debate on the *regional* bases of development which itself made any possible withdrawal from that commitment less likely, certainly less easy. Initially part of a movement which insisted that the Constitution's regionalism be taken seriously, they contributed to its culmination by their own politicisation. They functioned as the precursors of political regions and not simply as instruments of the planning region apparatus. But in so far as the immediate apprenticeship for regional government was in a regional *planning* setting, regional government was itself inevitably marked from the outset by this experience, as will be seen in the next section. The emergence of a regionalised political system would, indeed, have been much less thinkable without the existence of a planning framework already incorporating a regional dimension, which the CRPE had helped to render acceptable. Conversely, when a country embarks on such a regionalised political system, the national level has increasingly to take into account the spatial as well as the sectoral dimensions of policy, and planning becomes more urgent. The CRPE, along with the Cassa, had already pointed to this need and provided experience in its satisfaction. The regional planning experience of the second half of the 1960s thus mediated the interaction between planning and regionalism, leading up to its mutation into an interdependent, organic relationship in the early 1970s.

The post-1970 phase of regional planning

The establishment of regional government

Regional organisation was described in detail in the 1948 Constitution. Basically this seeks to reconcile two separate requirements: on the one hand, conferring on the region its own 'personality' and autonomous decision-making power, limited to a clearly defined range of responsibilities, and on the other, state control, which is exercised in advance by parliament's approval of the charters (Constitutions) of each region. As in the case of the provinces and communes, there is no change in the principle that the overall decision-making power is vested in parliament. Continuing state control, however, is limited to the 'legitimacy' of the regional bodies' activities, interpretation of which is still a matter of controversy and is bound to give rise to conflicts between the regions and the central authorities until agreed practices have become established.

In 1968 and 1969 the constitutional provisions concerning the regions were implemented by statute and in May 1970 the regional councils were elected. The regional council chooses the members of the regional executive and department heads. The region has autonomous powers of direct intervention in a good many sectors (agriculture, trade, tourism, land use, regional transportation). Other important sectors are left out of its jurisdiction, such as credit, insurance and industry. The problem of regional policy-making in these sectors is still unresolved.

Immediately after the establishment of the regions, the transfer of functions from central to regional government began. This has been accompanied by a shift of personnel and, of particular importance for planning, of expertise. For instance, the Ministry of Public Works has lost more than half its staff. The same, but on a substantially smaller scale, has happened to other ministries. The law establishing the regions laid down that their civil servants should be recruited by transfer from other government employment, with the intention of avoiding an exceptional expansion of officialdom. As regional salary standards are also, for the moment at least, somewhat higher than those prevailing in the national civil service, this has made it possible for the regions to recruit trained specialist and other personnel.

The relations with the communes and provinces are regulated by the Constitution, which attributes to the regions the function of coordinating the activities of local government, formerly vested in the provincial administrative board. In this respect, the regions exercise not only the generic function of regional planning, but also more specific functions, directly or indirectly connected with regional planning, including the final approval of development plans for industrial areas, and more generally of local land-use plans, as well as control over the budgets of communal and provincial government. The regions have thus absorbed those executive functions relevant to planning previously held by the prefects, who have become – contrary to what has happened in France – purely executive arms of the central government in matters of police and public safety. The relations between regions are not formally organised in any way. Inter-regional agreements are simply made on a case-by-case basis because of the regional authorities' autonomy.

The regions are thus now the political organs of regional planning. Specialist regional agencies are in part provided for in the individual charters, and in part will be created in the implementation stage. These organs differ from region to region. Generally speaking, current experience suggests that such organs will be limited to four main types, not all necessarily operating in each region at the same time.

(a) The head of the responsible executive department (which is often that of the Budget and Economic Planning, but in other cases may be that of Industry and Planning or Land Use and Planning). It is important to note that functions are vested in the department heads from time to time, as the individual regional governments are formed.

(b) Such committees as may be appointed by the regional council to deal with economic planning.

(c) The region's research department, which is primarily responsible for short-term research activities. Most Italian regions think that they need to create their own autonomous data-collecting centres, duplicating the work of the Central Statistical Institute.

(d) The Institute for Regional Studies, whose function is to undertake the investigations necessary for the preparation of the Plan, including the sectors not within the specific jurisdiction of the regional authorities.

The regions are called upon to participate, in a consultative capacity, in the framing of the National Plan, making their proposals as regards not only the regional components of the Plan, but also its general guidelines. This takes place primarily through the Inter-Regional Consultative Committee set up in the Ministry of the Budget and Economic Planning. It is clear that, because of their power of autonomous action in a good many sectors, their participation has a significance for national planning radically different from that of the CRPE.[4]

In the relatively short time that has elapsed since the installation of the regional councils, and while the technical and organisational structures are still in a stage of adjustment, the regions have scarcely yet done any systematic comprehensive planning. However the planning tasks which they have chosen to undertake emerge fairly clearly from the provisions of the regional charters. We shall confine ourselves to summarising, by way of example, those set forth in two such charters.

Lazio Region devotes to planning the entire 'Title Seven' of its charter. It stresses its autonomy, contributing through its own independent initiatives and proposals to the determination of the objectives and instruments of national planning and formulating general economic development plans for its own territory. The region is committed to a coordinating function with respect to the local authorities and the public economic agencies at the regional level. More especially it collaborates with the central planning authorities in the formulation of the plans for government-controlled enterprises within the framework of the National Plan. It will also share in the choice of central public investment projects to be undertaken in the region.

The policy concerns of *Campania Region* are substantially the same: stress is placed on the utilisation of water resources, on vocational training and on emigration problems. The specification of the general purposes of planning is more advanced than in the other regions, especially as far as social objectives, elimination of disparities and relations with other regions are concerned. It proposes to establish, with the participation of the local authorities and of social, economic and cultural groups, the regional development plan, aimed at eliminating the region's internal imbalances. It includes among its action guidelines the continuing pursuit of inter-regional cooperation required for the fullest utilisation of resources and for a combined effort to eliminate wider social and economic imbalances.

After three years in operation, the experience of regional government appears radically innovative, constituting the terminal point of the regional devolution of national planning. Two interesting features stand out from a first cross-regional analysis:

(a) Despite a substantial identity of major objectives, regional variations arise because of differences in economic structure and the contrasting political complexions of the regional councils.[5] This leads to differing emphases placed on the treatment of private property, on the priority given to public action, on social objectives, on the elimination of disparities.

(b) There is also a significant difference in positions as to how the region's role in the framework of the national planning process is envisaged, depending on whether the charter refers to the region's 'autonomy' or to its being a 'subject' in that process.

The prospect for regional planning

Although regional government has resulted in a considerable decentralisation of decision-making power impinging on planning, it has not led, at least so far, to a more economical use of resources. Amongst a number of reasons for this, two perhaps stand out:

(a) The insertion of a new bureaucratic apparatus in the progress of various projects connected with planning has very substantially slowed down their attainment. A typical case in point is that of the development plans for the industrial areas in the South, which were previously approved by the Interministerial Committee for the South and by the specialists of the Cassa per il Mezzogiorno. Some of these plans, which were almost ready for final approval, had to await the further ratification of the regional authorities.

(b) As politically decentralised bodies, the regions are much more sensitive to local pressures than was the case with the central administration. This may in the long run have considerable advantages, but meanwhile it is slowing down the pursuit even of many of the objectives which the regions have written into their own charters.

As compared to the previous CRPE experience, consultation has sharply decreased. Although, in theory, the individual economic or social groups have ample opportunities to participate in the formulation of the regional planning guidelines, in practice this is taking place only in desultory fashion. In other words, the region, a sovereign political body, has not yet seen fit to create its own permanent consultative bodies. For the time being, the preparatory planning research and studies are in general entrusted to experts hired as consultants, but in the longer term most regional authorities should have built up sufficient specialist staff of their own, or established official regional research institutes. There is one other aspect of relations with economic and social organisations which should be emphasised. While, in the past, sub-national groups often had to exert pressure on central government from outside through lobbying, today they can do it in a more official way, by tailoring their approach to suit an individual region's socio-economic or prestige interests, so that their demands will be included as part of the region's planning proposals to the central government. They may achieve this by obtaining a sufficient degree of political support in the regional council.

For their part, the political parties are now directly represented in the regional decision-making process. Generally speaking, the Communist party is very active, both in the regions where it forms the majority and in those where it is in opposition, in stimulating and promoting planning actions. The other parties appear more hesitant, some of them because of their ambiguous position at the national level, notably the Socialist party.

It is clear that the coordination of regional plans, already difficult under the previous system, will become even harder. In effect, in the areas within their jurisdiction, the regional governments can condition the regional articulation of national planning, even if this conflicts with the central guidelines established by the Economic Planning Ministry. However, the central government, which formally has had to surrender many prerogatives to the regions, is resisting the operational consequences through its remaining powers of overall economic and financial management. The central administration thereby endeavours to oppose the strong political overtones which the regions are introducing into regional planning. In the case of sectoral plans drafted by the central authorities (such as, for instance, the Chemical Industry Plan), the regions are supposed to participate in the research work, at least as far as the location of industry is concerned. Up to now, however, the participation of the regions has in practice been limited to giving advice *after* the formulation of such plans. For their part, the regions are trying to acquire a more effective part in the development process by creating their own independent instruments of economic intervention, such as regional financing agencies which seek to influence industrial investment, so far without much success.

The establishment of the regions has been too recent to allow us to reach any final conclusion as to the prospects for this experiment as far as planning is concerned. Certain positive aspects can be reported, such as a more active concern of citizens, of local authorities, industrial groups and trade unions in the solving of *regional* problems. This is reflected in the attention paid to regional planning questions at elections, in the press and in representations to regional councillors. Many organisations, notably the Chambers of Commerce, the Confederation of Industry and the trade unions, have set up regional headquarters. Once the transitional stage is over, certain administrative procedures may well be simplified. It is also the case that certain objectives, given a minor rating on the national level, can now be singled out and figure in regional planning. The crucial problem, however, is still that of creating a leading class of civil servants in each region competent in the economic field and capable of coping with the new tasks, in a situation which (Federal Germany apart) constitutes a radical innovation in the European political context.

NOTES

1 Michael Watson has made a substantial number of modifications in presentation and content, after consultation with the authors.
2 This comprises the mainland south of Rome and the Islands of Sicily and Sardinia, embracing 8 regions, 38 provinces and 2,685 communes.
3 C. Beltrame, 'Realtà e prospettive della programmazione regionale', in *Esperienze Amministrative*, September–October 1970.
4 For an examination of the regional aspects of the national planning process since the establishment of the regions, see above, Pasquino and Pecchini, pp. 78, 80–1.
5 The first regional elections produced Socialist Communist governmental majorities in three regions and coalitions centred on the Christian Democrats in the remaining thirteen.

SELECT CRITICAL BIBLIOGRAPHY

Part 1 of K. Allen and M. C. MacLennan, *Regional Problems and Policies in Italy and France*, London 1970, provides a useful account and analysis of development policy for the Mezzogiorno since 1945, approached primarily with an economic assessment in mind. For consideration of the administrative aspects of the Mezzogiorno policy, including the role of regional government, see M. M. Watson, *Regional Development Policy and Administration in Italy*, London 1970.
Relevant Italian references are as follows:
Pasquarelli, G. 'Regioni e programmazione', in *Le Regioni*, ERI, Edizioni Radio-Televisione Italiana, Rome 1971, pp. 32–42.
Programmazione economica e Regioni – Atti del Convegno dell'Associazione Nazionale per la Programmazione Economica, Rome 1968: see, in particular, Allione, M., 'La pianificazione regionale nell'esperienza italiana'; Ferrara, G., 'Programmazione economica nazionale e rapporti Stato-Regione'; Talamona, M., 'Problemi di teoria e di metodo nella construzione dei piani regionali'.
Ruffolo, G. 'La programmazione nazionale e i rapporti con i piani regionali', in *Programmazione nazionale e regionale*, Boringhieri 1967.
Serrani, D. 'La lenta nascita delle regioni', in *Politica del diritto*, July 1971.

14. The regional dimension of planning

MICHAEL WATSON

What the country accounts show clearly is that the regional planning of the 1960s represented simply a phase within a continuous experience in all three countries. Given this conclusion, one is prompted to enquire into the dynamic of the respective experiences, those elements in them or accompanying them which crippled the 'experiment' and those helping to shape subsequent developments.

What emerges is that there are certain key pre-requisites for regional planning in terms of the formal political system. It then all depends upon how seriously a country wants to take regional planning or has to, and this latter is a function essentially of the political dynamics associated with regionalism. It should be made clear, however, that we are concerned with planning *at* the regional level, with the allocation of resources according to regional criteria as opposed to local or national sectoral ones. What is ultimately called for is not only a coordination in the implementation of policies and programmes occurring within a region but also their integrated formulation on a regional basis involving choices between policies. The term regional planning is sometimes used to refer to the planning of inter-regional development. This is a misleading usage, however, since the balance between regions is necessarily a function of national planning. Just as sectoral planning does not signify inter-sectoral planning, so regional planning does not, strictly speaking, signify inter-regional planning. Relationships between regions or sectors can only be dealt with under national planning, while regions and sectors as such can be planned separately.

The approach to regional planning in Britain, France and Italy in the 1960s involved no hint of devolution of political power to the region and very little deconcentration of administrative power. The use of the term *regionalisation* is significant in this respect, with its strong overtones of a re-organisation of administrative responsibilities, especially those of central government. What the country accounts show, however, is that this approach proved unsatisfactory in all three countries. The defects can be listed as follows:

Plans were frequently slow to be formulated, unevenly researched,

[285]

including a simple catalogue of requirements without a time-scale or priorities.

Planning proposals once formulated made little or only an unpredictable impact on central and local government policies.

Plans did not establish an allocation of public resources within the region on the basis of *regional* criteria, but as a 'pooling' of local and central priorities. Resources have continued to be dispersed according to local requirements or national sectoral evaluations.

Policy-makers and development agents remained dominated by short-term considerations and an *ad hoc* approach.

Accompanying these deficiencies, the procedures envisaged to carry out planning fell considerably short in practice of fulfilling the organisational requirements of a planning process, in particular the insertion of a horizontal dimension. To what extent this can be said to be due to their inappropriateness as procedures is clearly of major concern.

Can any general explanation be found for the inadequacy, for planning purposes, of regionalisation? What the inadequacy reflected above all was that the approach failed to cut through the existing pattern of relations of a vertical and sectoral nature. The regional activity of government departments remained compartmentalised, with lines of communication still running direct to the centre; while local authorities and interest groups continued to concentrate on links with government departments at the centre and (more particularly in France and Italy) with their principal field offices. In this situation, the regional planning bodies were used simply as an extra, secondary channel for the articulation of demands. Sometimes consensus could be achieved in the preparation of planning documents in so far as these appeared marginal to the real, on-going business of politics and administration. But for this very reason the output was not regarded as committing participants in the on-going business. It was noticeable in France, where the new procedures had greater statutory backing, that in so far as a potential threat was perceived to the existing position, there was a tendency to undermine the exercise by playing a double game if necessary.

The failure of regionalisation in these terms can be generally explained, it seems, by the lack of statutory powers to back up the planning responsibilities, as stressed in the British account. The key certainly lies in the inability of the regional planning authority to impose its influence on the relevant aspects of government policy. This is not so surprising when the 'authority' is simply an advisory committee, as in the case of the CRPE in Italy. Where it includes a major administrative component, such as the regional prefect and the REPB, the explanation is less obvious. A major factor seems to be less the possession of formal executive powers, which the regional prefect has not altogether lacked, than the ability to attract the close cooperation of groups and local authorities in preference to their other, more specialised links with government. It is clear that regional planning largely failed to evoke such cooperation. What this meant was that in terms of communication and compliance from government's 'partners', regional planning had little new or additional to offer the rest of government. In other words, the regional planning administration did not acquire the strength in relations *within* government that derives from the importance for policy-making and application of relations with 'the outside'. Yet it was the very fact of the resulting lack of impact on policy decisions that was a crucial factor in discouraging groups and local authorities from developing a priority commitment to regional planning. Regionalisation was thus caught in a vicious circle: vertical links between government and its partners in the regions reinforced administrative compartmentalisation, which in turn justified these links. Regional planning was either incorporated, as an adjunct, into the established decision-making pattern, or relegated to a politico-administrative vacuum. In this way its potential for change in terms of policy choices was neutralised.

If local authorities and groups had invested more politically at the outset in regional planning, this mobilisation would undoubtedly have created the conditions in which the new procedures could have imposed themselves more successfully in governmental decision-making. Such an investment, it should be stressed, would necessarily have involved weakening already proven ties with government of a sectoral and vertical (i.e. centralising) nature and also in France with the lower level of horizontal administration, the local prefect. This the local authorities and groups were evidently unwilling to do. Why, then, did the new arrangements not appear initially a likely profitable investment compared with the existing ones? The underlying explanation is surely that what 'authority' there was, in an institutional sense, was a purely bureaucratic one, moreover well removed from the centres of political power, and as such presenting itself simply as an extra, low-priority point of access. In other words, the change represented by regionalisation was viewed as only marginal to the system, and not as a major restructuring of it, which in the event confirmed its actual marginality. An important difference in the Italian case, for reasons that we shall see, was that it was widely regarded as the forerunner of just such a restructuring. In the final analysis, the failure to develop a close and primary network of relations under the 1960s regional planning can be attributed to the lack of the necessary medium of exchange for any such system of reciprocal influence, namely a relatively free-floating sum of power to be divided up via the political network of relationships and not the simple delegation of certain responsibilities. A crucial element in such power is undoubtedly the allocation of financial resources on a broad and discretionary basis.

A similarity can thus be identified in the regional planning systems set-up which accounts for a common lack of impact in re-orienting policy. This was their emphasis on purely administrative and consultative deconcentration, with the responsibility for working the new procedure being consequently entrusted to a part of the central government apparatus. Theoretically, a special ministry might be established in each region with powers and funds to perform a horizontal role, as exemplified, at least potentially, by the Welsh and Scottish Offices; but these are clearly special cases and to generalise the practice of regional ministries alongside national ones cannot be considered administratively practicable. It would produce even greater complexity in central government and congestion, in political decisions at least. The alternative is a regional devolution of power, as has taken place in Italy. The crux of the matter is that resources available within a region can either be allocated in a *regionally* planned fashion or not. Under regionalisation, resources have continued, effectively if not altogether in form, to be allocated piecemeal through the pre-existing central–local system, which regionalisation never succeeded in fundamentally modifying. In fact, the conception of a regionally planned allocation undoubtedly contains within it the prior notion of a regionally determined allocation, although the reverse does not, of course, follow: a regionally determined allocation may in practice be based on disjointed, incremental decision-making rather than planned.

What of the relationship of regional planning to national planning? In France, the existence of a well-established national planning system, occupying a large place in the governmental process, made little contribution to enhancing the effectiveness of regionalisation. On the other hand, the difficulties of national planning in Britain and Italy were certainly no stimulant to the progress of regional planning, especially as it was operated essentially as a sub-category of the former; indeed, the misfortunes of national planning inevitably rebounded on it. The basic feature of national planning has been its sectoral basis. Yet sooner or later the problem has been posed of its spatial basis, pointing unerringly to the region as the framework in which this can best be approached. But the pressure on government sectors to plan, increasing the forces for centralisation inside departments, cuts across the efforts of planners to regionalise national planning. In Italy a major pressure towards national planning has stemmed from the prior moves towards regional planning of the Special Statute regions and a central agency, the Cassa per il Mezzogiorno, as well as the post-1962 commitment to setting up the Ordinary Statute regions. However, when regional planning is strengthened by a separate political base, as in Italy after 1970, it can no longer be treated as a sub-category essentially subordinate to nationwide sectoral considerations. The spatial coordination function of national planning then becomes critical and primordial, rather than residual after sectoral programmes have been established. In other words, national planning has to become regionally as much as, if not more than, sectorally based, as the Second Italian Plan indicates in a preliminary way. Moreover, where there is regional government, the case for national planning virtually ceases to be open to dispute in so far as the national government accepts responsibility for the balanced spatial development of the country as a whole.

The sequel in each country to the regionalisation experience of the 1960s was affected by differences in the way it functioned and in its political context. The most notable difference relates to the greater politicisation of the process in Italy compared with the other two countries. Whatever the practical inadequacies of the CRPE in affecting policy, they were the focus of a significant regional discussion of development questions. Contributing largely to this state of affairs was the fact that they were widely considered as a prologue to regional government proper. As such, they had a political 'angle', unlike the purely bureaucratic consultative character of the CODER and REPC. This arose primarily from the pre-existence of the regional/federal issue in Italy. Parties were thus generally active, if not officially represented, in the CRPE, in contrast to their aloofness from the British and French experiences. The breadth of the ideological competition further added to the dynamic of the debate; so did the strength of the competition in expertise between the CRPE's secretariat and other regional research bodies, contrasting with the reliance on the central supply of information in Britain and France. Moreover, lacking an immediate administrative counterpart, the CRPE's scope for debate and investigation was much enhanced. In comparison, the influence of the regional planning administration weighed heavily on the proceedings of the REPC and especially of the CODER.

The consequences of generating a greater political dynamic, whose origins lay in the nature and circumstances of the CRPE, appear to have been two-fold. In the first place, it helped to ensure that regionalisation was indeed a 'warming up' for regionalism proper. The fact that the CRPE functioned in a more political, less technical-administrative way than the REPC and CODER, meant that they contributed to the politicisation of the regional issue in the second half of the 1960s (in other words to that momentum towards regional government which had its origins in the 1948 Constitution but which had lain dormant for so long). Beyond this, the effect of the CRPE's activity on what followed is to be seen, perhaps even more importantly, in the alacrity with which the new regional governments have committed themselves in their charters and in their organisation to economic and social planning, generally using the work of the CRPE as a basis for their own efforts. In the second place, the operation of the CRPE evidently produced some educative spin-off, in the sense of increasing the awareness of questions of regional development and of the possibilities for their solution, not least, as just noted, including the need for planning itself. The importance in this respect of a politically motivated debate, grounded in alternative facilities for research, is thus emphasised; the more so since the CODER and REPC, in contrasted debating and research situations, showed less potential for acting as a kind of educator in respect of regional problems of development. Yet such a capability is crucial for any planning approach seeking to function in an essentially non-imperative way.

While in Italy regional planning has become associated with regional government, in Britain and France the regional dimension of policy and planning has moved closer, indeed very close, to the centre of national political concern. A cumulative spiral seems to be operating: increased government attention – and regionalisation could be viewed as at least representing this – provokes a local and group reaction to demand still 'better' attention, usually measured in financial terms. The regional planning experience has, indeed, enhanced an important species of regionalist interest group, that employing specialists in regional development problems, the IDAs in Britain, Expansion Committees in France. This situation is compounded by the increased degree of competition between regions that regionalisation has, if nothing else, helped inspire. Yet for the reasons discussed earlier, this pressure continues to flow inexorably to the centre. In view of this a rationalisation of central and local structures has been undertaken. Essentially, the approach is to share regional planning between central and local government, and moves to reorganise both sides into larger units are relevant to this; it is expected that improved coordination and a more effective local participation will result.

Traditionally, national economic policy and planning has treated the regional dimension as subordinate to nation-wide sectoral considerations, but *politically*, problems of regional development have tended to become coordinate or even super-ordinate to many other policy matters. Regionalisation was really an attempt to relieve this pressure, without decentralising any power for dealing with the problems. Its failure in these terms is clear, itself adding to the demand for more effective treatment. In this situation central government is finding itself hard pressed, not just to reorganise internal administrative responsibilities but also to decentralise some power under the heading of regional policy and planning. It is doing this partly by transfer to its regional offices, but also to modernised local authorities. Faced with the reflux of responsibility, and the increased seriousness of the problem, central government has assumed a cooperative stance, giving more scope to its deconcentrated administration to deal with certain problems on the spot, and bringing local government more into the regional picture in power-sharing bodies such as the Joint Planning Teams in Britain, the OREAM[1] and the new Regional Councils in France.

Ultimately, however, over-riding central control looms more or less large in the background, if mainly for financial reasons. But the basic fact is that the political system remains a dual one. As such it remains centrifugal at the regional level. Whether this pressure is more powerful upwards or downwards depends on the balance of forces within the particular structure, e.g. upward in the case of the OREAM, downward in the case of the Joint Planning Teams, at least as far as effective execution is concerned. Essentially, the weakness of regionalisation remains, with no means whereby the regional dimension, as such, can impose itself. The power base is still not there to cut across the vertical local–central sectoral links and thereby integrate the disparate elements which determine regional development. Central government regional action for its part, even after the considerable bout of rationalisation, is still fundamentally divided between the DOE and DTI in Britain. However, in 1972, DATAR was brought under a Ministry of Regional Planning, Public Works and Housing in France, though this was not an enduring arrangement. In any case, the continuous subordination of major sectors at the centre to the requirements of regional planning is clearly not feasible; in particular, the sectional pressures exerted at the centre by national interest groups cannot be overlooked. There is little chance that sectoralisation will be broken down where regional planning remains primarily something attempted from the centre. Above all, the centre has continuing *national* responsibilities for industry, transport, education, etc.

There is, indeed, no evidence that a regional dimension can be forged by administrative deconcentration from central ministries or by bringing together local authorities. Even where there is a special regional planning administration with certain executive powers, as now exists with the regional prefect and REPB director, responsibility is still bound ultimately to revert to the location of political accountability: the centre. Since government's 'partners' know this, vertical relations continue to predominate, undermining the effective exercise of the regional administration's planning functions. On the other hand, bringing local authorities together characteristically produces a pooling of their proposals, an agreement to divide up the cake, or a degree of conflict which the centre is called on to resolve. This it cannot easily do except on the basis of custom, established interests and, above all, not favouring or offending anyone too much. The result of this national and/or local-dominated regional planning, as regionalisation has indicated, is inevitably that the dispersal of resources according to local and sectoral criteria continues to predominate, undermining their more effective *regional* employment. It is also noticeable that the greater emphasis given since the late sixties to the local role in regional planning has introduced into it a preponderance of land-use cum urban-structure considerations, as opposed to economic development considerations, which are fundamental to the political problem.

The key question that remains is whether the authorities in Britain and France, above all the central ones, can now rest content with the present stage. They have been forced since the late sixties towards some dispersal of power but have still kept it entirely within the existing (dual) governmental system. Clearly, there is not the same support within government that there was in Italy in the sixties for taking the regional dimension really seriously or simply believing this to be necessary. Yet given the basic contradiction that remains between the aims, e.g. regional programmes and strategies, and the organisational means chosen, the dynamic remains potentially in the situation. It may well be, however, that both governments, unwilling to contemplate a devolution of political power – and this has been a primary motivation behind their innovations so far – will, if permitted, accept as irreducible the insufficiencies of their policy-making for regional development. However, the political centrality the issue has acquired has elevated regional development from the status of a national economic policy and planning sub-category to a functionally autonomous field of public activity. Lack of success is thereby more readily identifiable, with its clear implications in terms of political pressure. There does, indeed, seem little chance that the latest procedures will relieve the pressure on central government for a solution to the regional development problem any more than the regionalisation of the sixties did, particularly since pressure since then has tended to mount, illustrated by the crucial place the problem now occupies in the EEC debate. In these circumstances the desire to decentralise power to the regions for organising their own development can be expected to grow, while the EEC begins to assume some responsibility for the balance between regions.

This has already been happening in Britain in the case of Scotland and Wales, where there are accompanying historical and cultural factors to speed the process. Once you have something like the Welsh and Scottish Offices, however, then the question of a decentralised political authority is posed more acutely. But until you have such a multi-purpose administrative authority at the regional level, there is little chance of planning a region's development except in name, i.e. as a collation and coordination of local and national sectoral plans and policies. The crucial aspect in the effectiveness of such an authority undoubtedly lies in its scope for allocating funds between competing uses. Moreover, its funds must clearly be at least similar to those available at local level, if regional planning is to aggregate local projects according to regional criteria. In France this scarcely happens at all yet; there is nothing really comparable to even the Welsh and Scottish Offices, which themselves remain restricted in practice in their allocative ability. Yet, with the political centralisation of the regional development issue, in terms both of ultimate responsibility and of debate, there is a continuing political dynamic in the French situation. Noteworthy in this respect is the fact that regional devolution has become an important facet of opposition politics, not to say a continuing point of discussion between the partners within the government majority. More crucial at the present stage, however, is that the organisational pressures for further administrative deconcentration remain strong – as evidenced by the 1972 regional reform.

In so far as central government in Britain and France continues to meet considerable difficulties in its organisation of regional development, the momentum for policy-making in this field will be to move it outwards to the regions as has already tentatively been happening. Given the nature of the post-1970 modifications examined above, there is little reason to suppose that such difficulties, as manifested in the 1960s regionalisation phase, will diminish in the current neo-regionalisation period. Whether this situation will encourage moves in favour of regional devolution, as opposed to deconcentration, is certainly another question. The development of regional administration, however, is likely to be accompanied by an increase in political debate about devolution. It certainly enhances the political case for it. Moreover, when the sole authority with a direct regional 'mandate' is administrative, there is little chance that it will be able to assert the regional standpoint strongly enough to secure effective planning at that level. In the face of representative authorities with locally or nationally defined responsibilities, a critical power resource is absent: political legitimacy. This, it is often held, can only follow political consciousness which, with a few exceptions, is weak in British and French regions. Political support for regionalism may exist, however, not only within regions but also, or alternatively, within national political and governmental bodies, as was the case in the early 1960s in

Italy when the commitment to establish regional government was made. The regional development and planning issue has increasingly enhanced this sort of regional consciousness. Thus not only is regional devolution a necessary step along the road to effective regional planning but more and more a seriously considered step. However, at present, cross-pressures to resist this remain very strong, ranging from arguments of economic indivisibility to ones of political indivisibility, sometimes combining the two. Behind them lies the basic fact that the centre holds the political power and will have to be very strongly persuaded to relinquish any of it to regional governments, which would clearly be 'partners' more to be reckoned with than are local authorities, not least in the planning sphere.

NOTE

1 See below, p. 303.

V

Land-use policy

15. Urban planning in France

FRANÇOIS D'ARCY AND BRUNO JOBERT

Urban problems and town planning were especially in vogue at the beginning of the sixties. In the context of the dominating ideology of modernisation which characterised this era, they became one of those 'real problems' about which a discussion illuminated by specialist analyses would make possible debates in which the exchange of genuinely rational arguments and of values would replace the sectarian quarrels of the past. The fact is that French society has not escaped from that complacent belief in the future which maintains that continual growth constitutes in itself a solution to social problems. This was true to such an extent that it seemed possible for a technicised planning subordinated to the industrial imperative to be substituted quite easily for an outmoded political game.

If discussion of the issue was still possible, it was on a very general normative level. For example the Club Jean Moulin asked

Do we want a society characterised amongst other things by: greater comfort for the ever-increasing middle-classes, compared with the discomfort and poverty of a large part of the population; behaviour increasingly characterised by recourse to gadgets and the satisfaction of individual rather than collective needs? If we aim at objectives other than the standard of living and the American way of life...it remains for us to define our political and social objectives. The Plan ought to help us to define these objectives in a realistic way, taking into account the possibilities of growth, then deciding on the way they can be achieved.[1]

It is with regard to this general choice that the Fourth Plan had claimed to give priority to public investments, an echo of which is heard in the debates on urban planning.

Urban problems at last became obvious: continuing after reconstruction, the inequalities of regional development and an increasingly massive rural exodus resulted first and foremost in a lasting lack of housing in spite of the ZUP policy and the large housing-estates policy at the end of the fifties. It was forecast that within a quarter of a century 10 million dwellings would be built in urban areas where 30 million men and women would live.[2] This shortage was not confined solely to housing. Thus the large suburban agglomeration seemed for a while to crystallise certain of the faults of urbanisation at this time:

the high rise housing estates at the heart of our cities or in the suburbs are nothing but a cancerous excrescence, born of insufficiently mastered techniques, not controlled and coordinated by men for men. It is a matter of urgency to create in its place a real urban fabric, in keeping with the fundamental needs of contemporary human communities.[3]

Alongside this, some people were beginning to criticise the splitting up of urban areas into semi-rural groupings given over to the cult of the motor-car and the individual dwelling and were questioning the capacity of France to preserve urban values when confronted with invasion by the Anglo-American way of life.[4]

The upsurge and transformation of urban planning in France seems, on the ideological plane, to be linked to a conception of life according to which plans would embody a national ambition. They would be the instruments of a mastery over the whole of social development. In a way, the story of urban planning over the last ten years has been that of unfulfilled ambition. As the practice of planning was progressively developed and institutionalised, so the contradictory elements which had presided over its creation became clear. But before a clear conception of these limits could be formed, urban planning developed in an extraordinary abundance of enactments and new institutions concerning not only urban policy but also regional development policy and land-use planning. The end of the Fourth Republic had prepared the way, incubating most of the texts which appeared in 1958. Another peak of activity occurred as soon as the Algerian war was ended, during the years 1962-7.

We shall commence by sketching in this legal and institutional evolution, postponing for the moment generalised reflections on the changes which arose in the very conception of urban planning.

The development of urban planning

We shall trace first of all the evolution of urban planning in the strict sense. We shall see subsequently how this planning is conditioned equally by considerations going beyond it relating to national planning and regional development policy. This breakdown is not only inspired by a concern for greater clarity. It is also to be explained by the fact that in France urban planning continues to juxtapose different concerns without integrating them.

Urban planning in the strict sense

The fifties was marked in France by important reforms in favour of industrial reconstruction, and the building of new housing underwent very rapid expansion between 1953 and 1958. The problems of the creation of associated public infrastructures and the control over land arose rapidly.

The new legislation of 1958 had two aims. In the first place, it substituted for the old plans called 'development projects' (created by a 1943 Act) the new 'urban plans'. These were henceforth established at the level of the 'agglomeration' and no longer of the commune.[5] They were intended to be guidelines for action, rather than merely to prevent action. Finally, in distinguishing between 'master town plans' and 'detailed town plans', they were expected to be simpler and easier to draw up. At least in so far as the last two points are concerned, the objective has not been achieved.

In the second place, the new legislation created the legal instruments of what was henceforth to be called 'operational town planning': major coordinated urban planning operations of which the most important were the priority urbanisation zones (ZUP). In fact, the expansion of the towns, in this period, was shaped much less by the town plan than by the ZUP created *ad hoc*, in response to particular needs.

In intellectual background the town planners, having for the most part received their initial training as architects, retained a dominant role, whether they operated within the administration or remained independent members of the profession intervening on demand.

At the administrative and political level the Ministry of Housing was the most important body, the local authorities still playing only a small role. But it was a weak ministry, over-centralised, its personnel being of high average age and of rather low quality. In the case of operational town planning, it let itself be relieved of a part of its prerogatives by a body created by the Caisse des Dépôts et Consignations (a public bank) peripheral to the official administrative services: the Central Office for Territorial Investment.

In fact, the reforms of 1958 came too soon to take into account the major changes which occurred in urban planning at the end of the fifties. The limitations of a planning based on urban expansion, on the deployment and spatial separation of functions, on the mechanical application of administrative and technical norms, began to be better understood ('crisis' of the large housing estates, neglect of the problems of development). Another conception emerged which saw in planning the instrument of multi-functional mastery of urban development. The ideological connotations which accompanied the spread of this new conception are characteristic of the beginning of the 1960s: Gaullism saw in planning the instrument for furthering an ambition, a collective project.

On the intellectual level, the transformation carried out represents the transition from a mechanistic to a structural and systematic mode of thought. Henceforth, the town is considered as a system of socio-spatial interactions, in which each action, each intervention, must be studied as a function of its impact on the whole urban structure.

It should not be forgotten, however, that this change corresponded also to a transformation in the way in which towns were built that characterised the early 1960s in France. From 1958 the new governmental policy was that of replacing public financing of housing by private investment and substantial tax advantages granted to property investment companies, thus encouraging the entry of large financial groups into the house-building market. The consequence, from 1962 to 1965, was a building boom whose effects on property speculation, urban disorganisation and lack of social infrastructure in the suburban areas, explain in some part the setting-up of new planning institutions.[6] Industrial development for its part was increasingly taken over by firms of national or international size, which are not tied structurally to a region but can provoke competition between various towns to secure the most advantageous location. At the same time there was a change in the nature of industrial production, and it became not so much a matter of technical connections as of the variety of possible exchanges, accessibility to multiple sources of information, and the quality of the labour force, which made the siting of a factory economically viable. The town as such became an economic instrument which the local authorities, anxious to keep their level of employment and revenue as high as possible, would have to adjust to meet the new demands of production. It thus became necessary for urban planning to take into consideration the role of these new economic actors.

Consequently, starting in 1964, projects modifying the system were worked out. They did not reach their culmination until the 1967 Land Guidelines Act. According to this Act, the fundamental town planning document is the Urban Development Master Plan (SDAU). In this document, the public authorities propose the major development guidelines for the agglomeration over the next thirty years. In contrast with the earlier master town plans, it does not establish a legal regulation of land use which, as such, would be binding on private interests, but only a document which 'guides and coordinates' public authority programmes. Only these, then, are directly affected by the SDAU and bound by its provisions.

With regard to private interests, the SDAU is given practical application in the land-use plan (POS), which lays down the regulations to be applied in the use of land: the limitation on the right to build, notably by the setting of a maximum density ('coefficient of land occupation'), zoning, the siting of public investments, etc.

Only the land-use plan, in that it contains legal provisions applicable to private persons with powers to overrule their interests, is the object of a public enquiry before its final approval. Moreover, it should be noted that the public enquiry in France is a much less developed procedure than it is in Britain, notably in that it is not quasi-judicial. This is an example of the extent to which the possible intervention of individuals in the process of town planning is badly provided for. (As far as the role of local councillors is concerned, see below.)

The POS do not apply to the whole of the area covered by the SDAU. There is another way of establishing the rules for land use where the SDAU proposes an important urban scheme: namely, the zones of coordinated development (ZAC). In these zones, in fact, the legal regulation of land use is not fixed in advance, but is left undefined until the projected urban development scheme reaches the stage of implementation. At this point, its architectural, financial and legal characteristics are determined by those concerned. If the scheme is entrusted to a private developer, its features are specified in a formal agreement between the developer and local authority.

This procedure, which was only made possible by the Land Guidelines Act, has since been widely adopted. In fact, this development has corresponded with a new stage in urban planning which appeared after 1968. So the most recent conception of urban planning is characterised, it seems, less by concern with norms than by an increase in operational concerns. It is less a matter of proposing a project to a community than of making the projects of private and public actors compatible, to preserve the widest possible range of choice for the future, to optimise the distribution of available resources. (See below, pp. 306f.)

These changes in the content of urban planning have corresponded with the appearance of new agents of innovation in this sphere and with a new institutional allocation of responsibilities.

The agents of innovation. The organisation of civil servants in 'corps' remains a basic feature of the French administration. In the sphere of urban planning, the new element has been the interest shown by the Ponts et Chaussées corps of engineers. For various complex reasons, analysed by J-C. Thoenig, the Ponts et Chaussées engineers have sought to become the new urban planning experts and have imprinted it with their own type of rationality. (See note 3, p. 389.)

This has been paralleled by a decline of the urban planning

architects, who have ceased to be the prime movers and urban planning experts. Yet they have not been totally replaced by the Ponts et Chaussées engineers, for over the same period (the early sixties) the need to establish multi-disciplinary teams, involving social science specialists, was recognised.

Thus multi-disciplinary study and research units were created within the administration. The creation of these units necessitated the recruitment on a contractual basis of numerous specialists who did not belong to the civil service (economists, sociologists). The entry of sociologists into the administration, which characterises this period, is also marked by the influence which sociological ideas about towns began to have on administrators. From this period, sociology has been seen as capable of providing answers to a certain number of problems. Its influence was to remain limited, however, notably because sociologists who entered the research services found it impossible to gain recognition for their skills. (A research service created in the Housing Ministry, in which they played an important role, was wound up at the end of 1968.) The status of this new personnel and its career possibilities have posed numerous problems which have often received only a temporary solution. Moreover, the work patterns within these units could not be established on the traditional basis of a hierarchical organisation. It should be noted, however, that it is nearly always career officials (generally Ponts et Chaussées engineers) who are directors of these units. One may suggest the hypothesis of a division between the management level and the specialists, whose work and terms of reference are defined by the former. The imbalance sometimes appears enormous between a directorate that remains deeply embedded in the state and the specialists with a precarious status on the periphery of the traditional administration.

Administrative organisation. The increasing importance of urban problems in economic development, the weakness of the Ministry of Housing and the new role played by the engineers of the Ponts et Chaussées (who had at their disposal a very effective administrative instrument through the Ministry of Public Works) brought about an important administrative reform in 1966: the merger of these two ministries into a single one, the Ministry of Equipment, a ministry specifically for urban areas, dealing thenceforth with housing, urban planning and the whole of civil engineering, and responsible for defining an urban policy.

One of the effects of this merger was the creation in each *département* of an Equipment departmental division, superseding the two divisions which had existed up to that time, the building division and the Ponts et Chaussées service. These amalgamations at the local level resulted in an increased preeminence of the Ponts et Chaussées engineers in the new administration.

It is interesting to note that one of the first actions of the new ministry was to provide itself with urban study units over which it had complete control: in each *département* a 'Study and Planning Group' was created, a body responsible for control over urban planning studies undertaken in the *département* and in certain cases for carrying them out itself. When this group carries out its own studies, it is generally composed of a multi-disciplinary team, always placed under a Ponts et Chaussées engineer.

It should finally be mentioned that the former services of the Ponts et Chaussées, and now the Equipment departmental divisions, not only carry out civil engineering works, but very often also those of the local authorities, at their request. This is especially true of road works. Furthermore, they supervise these selfsame local authority schemes. Thus they have very great power with regard to the local councillors to whom they are at the same time advisers, agents and supervisors...This ambivalence in their role recurs in urban planning.

However, during the sixties, the local authorities showed a growing interest in the problems raised by urban growth and sought to intervene more and more and to influence decisions in this sphere. A political repercussion of this development was observable at the time of the vote on the Land Guidelines Act: whereas the text proposed by the government stated that the SDAU and the POS would be drawn up by the central administrative services in consultation with the local authorities, the many mayors who were also members of parliament had a new draft drawn up stating they would be established *jointly* by the central and local authorities.

This point is clearly essential, and the influence the local representatives can hope to exercise depends on the degree of their commitment and the frequency of their interventions throughout the planning process. This is because planning appears to be a semi-continuous process of partial negotiations, of multiple compromises within which the maintenance of a certain overall consistency is attempted. When the point of overall decision is reached, the elected representative often finds himself faced with such a system of concessions and partial compromises that he cannot alter anything without upsetting the whole project. The sooner he intervenes in the process prior to the final decision, the more he can make his views count.

It has proved extremely important in practice that the capacity to intervene is largely a function of the mastery which the elected representatives have of the language of planners. In this respect it is possible to distinguish between two types of elected representative: the members of the communes' executives whose participation in the preparation of plans is variable, and the ordinary members of local councils who are only involved occasionally. Often a project is already worked out, leaving them with little more than veto power.

In practice, the joint elaboration (of projects) is institutionalised in committees which periodically bring together the planning specialists, local elected representatives, and civil servants. This is notoriously inadequate if the planning specialists are completely under the control of central administrative officials. To forestall this eventuality, the Land Guidelines Act provided for the creation of 'agglomeration agencies', responsible for drawing up the town plans and placed partly under the control of the local authorities. In fact, the Ministry of Housing and Public Works has slowed down the creation of these agencies, which exist only in a small number of agglomerations. It has preferred to set up its own research services which continue, as in the past, to draw up the town plans on behalf of the local authorities. And even where some towns have succeeded in establishing their own research units, the Ministry of Housing and Public Works has generally succeeded in having them headed by one of its own officials.

The extensions of urban planning

The development of a town cannot be considered in isolation; it is dependent on the place that the town occupies in a wider geographical setting. Efforts to plan it lead, therefore, to the introduction of considerations which in France are called *aménagement du territoire* (more centralist a term than regional development). Moreover, the link between urban growth and economic development, the burden of public investments upon local and national finances, also necessitate combining urban planning and economic planning. These apparently banal assertions are nevertheless the result of a long process which is far from complete and which we are now going to examine.

The notion of *aménagement du territoire* was born in the Housing Ministry at the start of the fifties. It was thus at the outset closely related to urban planning. It gave birth notably to the idea that there was a hierarchy of towns, the function fulfilled by them varying according to their size right up to the largest, which alone fulfilled all urban functions. A policy of regional development thus aimed not only at an optimal distribution of economic activities across the country but also at ensuring that the urban hierarchy should be established in a satisfactory manner in every region.

In 1958, the Ministry of Housing was given the responsibility for regional development: in this sphere it had to coordinate the action of all the other ministries. But this was too ambitious an undertaking for a relatively weak ministry of low prestige, and its role remained limited.

In 1962 various circumstances gave a new urgency to the problem of regional development: the repatriation of French people from Algeria, a crisis arising from the contraction of the farm population and a reduction of employment in the mining and traditional industrial regions. Except in the case of the Algerian repatriates, these developments were related to fundamental structural changes: the acceleration of rural depopulation, a growing industrial concentration and the increasingly important role played by finance capital. Given these conditions, a new administrative service was created, responsible directly to the prime minister – the Delegation for *Aménagement du Territoire* and Regional Action (DATAR). This inherited notably all the responsibilities of the Ministry of Housing concerning *aménagement du territoire*.

The control that it has endeavoured to exercise has taken two directions. On the one hand, it has tried to reduce the social tensions arising in the agricultural west and in the declining industrial regions, by creating new employment and by expressing the state's concern. On the other hand, it has been necessary to provide the expanding industrial sectors with the infrastructure necessary for their development: the policy of developing public investment in the major cities (the counter-magnets to Paris), the development of major transport arteries and of the eastern half of France, have all contributed to this policy. But it is probably the policy of industrial location by direct negotiation with private groups which has been the most original aspect of DATAR's policy.

Preoccupation with these issues has quite naturally led the DATAR to oversee urban planning, at least in the most important towns. This supervision is exercised at two levels.

(a) On the one hand, over the urban planning documents themselves: regulations lay down that the SDAU must be approved either by the prefect for small and medium-sized towns or by the government for large towns. For the latter, DATAR has brought about the creation of a 'Central Urban Planning Group' in which it participates jointly with the representatives of the ministries concerned, and which examines the SDAU before passing them on to the government for approval.

In the very large towns, control is stricter. DATAR, in liaison with the new Ministry of Regional Development, Housing and Public Works, has created small study groups, called OREAM, with the task of establishing a planning scheme for the metropolitan area under consideration (which often exceeds the geographical boundary of the principal conurbation and includes the neighbouring secondary conurbations). These schemes trace the broad outlines of development in the area being considered, in relation to the general perspectives of regional development policy.

It is interesting to note that the legal link between the metropolitan area schemes and the SDAU of the conurbations which they concern has never been specified. But since these schemes are subject to approval by the Cabinet, they are subsequently accepted as obligatory by the authors of the SDAU.

(b) Taking into account the more operational character of urban plans, DATAR also sought to exercise control over operational urban planning. It was therefore at its suggestion that an 'Interministerial Land-use Group' was created, in which it played an important role and whose function is to draw-up each year the list of urban planning schemes (industrial zones or housing zones) to benefit from public loans.

However, in the large regional cities the classical urban planning schemes were not up to the scale of the problems posed. A 'new towns' policy was undertaken, decided entirely at the central administrative level and in which DATAR played a predominant role. There again, the technique used is the same: the creation of a central group uniting the representatives of the different ministries and in which DATAR acts as the prime mover. Political decisions are taken either by the Interminsterial Committee for regional development policy, whose decisions are prepared by DATAR, or by the Cabinet.[7]

The creation of DATAR coincided with a change in direction of urban policy, very largely defined and implemented by central government. In this way, DATAR contributed to the accentuation of the centralised character of urban policy. It did this, however, in a less bureaucratic way than the traditional administration. What is more, it sought to give its policy a regional basis and in this way contributed largely, together with the national Planning Commissariat, to the establishment of regional institutions.

The national Planning Commissariat intervened in urban planning in two ways. On the one hand, with the creation of an Urban Investment Commission during the preparation of the Fourth Plan (which became the Towns Commission in the Sixth Plan), examination of urban development was initiated. On the other hand, it tried gradually to set up a process of public investment planning which began at the bottom, that is from the towns and the regions, and no longer came exclusively from above.

The Urban Investment Commission had, as its special initial mission, to work out the cost of infrastructure provision made necessary by the growth of urban areas, and to make good the accumulated short-fall, notably in sewage disposal and the provision of water. Thus it prepared the ground for governmental decisions by making recommendations. Some of these recommendations, notably on urban renewal, which had been accepted by the government, proved ineffectual because of a lack of sufficient examination of the social and economic conditions of urban development. Through this national programming of urban public services, a complete urban policy was being asserted, based on the peripheral extension of towns in specially planned zones, emphasising major 'structuring' public investments and renewal. Concomitantly, a certain number of recommendations for administrative reforms, which the application of this policy required, were made during the preparation of the Fifth Plan.

The Towns Commission, which replaced the Urban Investment Commission, marks a break similar to that which occurred in all the commissions for public sector functions, such as health and education. Stress is no longer laid first on investment (which is partially explained by the smaller place given to public investment in the Sixth Plan), but on a thorough examination of the problems to be dealt with. The new conception of urban planning developed by the Towns Commission was expressed in a call for decentralisation and by the abandonment of the idea that an urban policy can be worked out at the national level in as much detail as hitherto. This was not merely the lesson learnt from a certain number of previous failures. It also reflected the fact that the public authorities, henceforth, were obliged to compromise to a much greater extent with private actors, whose role was becoming predominant. Finally, it must be emphasised that, taking into account the priority given to industrialisation by the Sixth Plan, the Towns Commission placed much greater emphasis on investment in infrastructure which was necessary for industry, such as transport and telecommunications, while the preceding plans had stressed the necessity for developing public spending destined directly for the benefit of the inhabitants.

The attempts to decentralise the process of planning have aimed at the drawing up, at the level of the conurbations on the one hand, and at a regional level on the other, of documents which outline the perspectives of development, and decide the programme of public investment to be implemented, during the period of the Plan. At conurbation level, these documents, drawn up by the Planning Commissariat, are called Programmes of Modernisation and Investment (PME). They must, on the one hand, outline the general framework of the demographic and economic evolution of the agglomeration. They must, on the other, determine the public investment which will be achieved throughout the duration of the national Plan (five years) and the conditions of financing it. Ideally, they should allow choices and judgements to be made at the agglomeration level in conformity with the objectives of development fixed by the Urban Development Master Plan (SDAU); they thus constitute an extremely valuable instrument for the elaboration of regional and national programmes of public investment.

In fact, at the time of the preparation of the Fourth and Fifth Plans, it did not happen like this. The local representatives were excluded from the preparation of the PME, which prevented political choices being made. The PME were in fact no more than a catalogue of the schemes devised by the different administrative services of the central government. A greater effort at synthesis was attempted in certain towns during the preparation of the Sixth Plan. However, it does not seem that the PME have become useful instruments in the preparation of regional programmes. The latter have a direct effect on budgetary decisions, while the PME are simply working papers without legal or financial significance.

During the course of the Fourth and Fifth Plans it became clear that the plans established at a regional level ought to be based largely on the facts of urban development. The action of the Planning Commissariat, like that of DATAR, which played a decisive role in the setting up of new institutions at a regional level in 1964, has been in this direction. Examples of this have already been mentioned, notably in the Programmes of Modernisation and Investment. The Planning Commissariat has also asked that the hierarchical relationship and inter-dependence between towns should be taken into account through a regional 'urban structure scheme'.

However, if one sums up these various activities, it is clear that, throughout the sixties, the definition by central government of a new urban policy and the very strict control exercised over it has largely prevailed over the gestures towards decentralisation. In any case, the regions do not seem to have been capable of making the choices called for by very rapid urban development.

Planning: new way of life or compromise between conflicting interests?

In the end, urban planning appears to be a complex mixture of provisions with diverse effects. Some are norms of a general character, designed to guide the action of the public authorities over a long period, and therefore subject to revision (SDAU). Others are of an immediately binding nature (POS), still others are procedures proposed for a given type of scheme (ZAC). Finally, there are those which concern the financial aspects of urban policy (PME). A range of norms which differ not only in their function but also in the bodies they concern: sometimes public authorities (central or local), sometimes their most important private or semi-public 'partners' and sometimes the anonymous mass of property owners.

As it has been conceived, this type of urban planning stems from an excessively rationalistic and purposive conception of decision-taking. It is based on establishing a priority among objectives both as regards their importance and their time scale. The fundamental objectives determining the development of the agglomeration in the long term (thirty years) are spelt out in the SDAU. The more specific and shorter-term objectives are laid down in the POS or negotiated within the context of the ZAC; POS and ZAC at the same time giving the provisions of the SDAU their operational character. The place occupied by the PME is more ambiguous, since this document is integrated into two different hierarchies: on the one hand it is, or should be, an instrument for the application of the SDAU; on the other hand, it is the lowest level in the planning system which, at the higher levels consists of the regional programme and the national Plan.

This rational view of things is too far removed from the usual decision processes to be able to replace them. More seriously, it does not take account of the real basis of political intervention: this never occurs to achieve an abstractly defined scheme but to regulate the contradictions and conflicts which arise between social groups. This inherent function of the politician decides the way in which the politico-administrative apparatus is structured and the pattern of relationships which develop within it, and between it and its environment.

This may explain why the method of social control which a certain type of urban planning tried to apply has not been taken seriously by the various actors involved and that, as a consequence, it has not succeeded in having a direct impact on the implementation of urban policy. We shall try to demonstrate this first of all.

The first reason for the inefficiency of the mechanisms set up for the planning of urban development concerns the organisation of the political-administrative apparatus. Historically, the state has extended its social control, at least in France, by the creation of an administrative network covering in a close-knit fashion the whole of the country. Its officials, specialised in a given sector of activity, have developed privileged links with a well-defined clientele. Each of these administrative sectors is highly centralised, the field services set up at the local level acting according to detailed rules established by its ministry. Since the Second World War there have been, at the national level, an increasing number of attempts to establish better liaison between the activities of the different ministries (cf. the creation of the Planning Commissariat and DATAR). But real coordination still does not exist below the national level. The 1964 reforms began to give control over all the administrative services to the prefect of each *département*. But this control remains limited.

One of the objectives of the planning procedures created at regional or urban level was precisely to introduce a new rationality which would take into account the whole field of administrative action, thus breaking with compartmentalisation. But because they are in the habit of examining only those problems which are their or their clientele's direct concern, the local administrative services are ill-prepared intellectually to participate in the kind of urban planning which takes into account the multiple interactions of public and private interventions. Each ministry establishes its forecast according to its own particular time scale and criteria, which are decided, in all essentials, at the centre. When an Urban Development Master Plan (SDAU) or Modernisation and Investment Programme (PME) is being prepared, each field service makes great efforts to secure approval of the schemes which, following these criteria it has established for its own sector. Attempts to introduce techniques inspired by PPBS (the 'rationalisation of budgetary choices' or RCB) have generally got no further than taking into consideration the particular objectives of the ministry considered.

The information available about the way in which notably the PME have been worked out show that they tend to be an amalgamation of the intentions of each of the field services.

A more fundamental explanation of the limitations upon urban planning is the fact that the latter had been conceived more as a combination of technical solutions for the problems of urban growth rather than a political settlement between the social groups concerned. This is due especially to the fact that, in relation to central administration, municipal administration does not appear to be an autonomous regulatory entity. In the small communes, the local councillors have played scarcely more than the role of mediators on behalf of social demand, allowing the central government's actions to be modified and the inconveniences of a purely sectoral system of regulation to be corrected. In the larger towns, the local councillors are able to exert more influence with, however, two restrictions. On the one hand, they cannot, in practice, intervene in the productive sector while, on the other, with the central government retaining most of the technical expertise, it is difficult for the local councillors to develop conceptions different from those of the centre. This demonstrates how important it is for the councillors to master the language of the specialists and be able to have centres of expertise under their own control.

Required by function and vocation to consider all the interests and demands of social groups in a given area, the local councillors could, supposing that this problem of language were resolved, feel themselves directly concerned with urban planning. But owing to the way in which urban planning has been conceived, the behaviour of groups and of the private participants in urbanisation is precisely what is not taken into account. Now, the local councillor, who must submit to reelection every six years and because of this has a different time scale from that of the planner, pays special attention to public reactions, which the planner is not yet in the habit of doing. Consequently, the SDAU which, in the minds of the planners, was to be the centrepiece from which everything else derived, seems to the councillors a rather abstract exercise.

The specialist bodies responsible for working out the SDAU have sometimes been well aware of this; they have attempted to arouse popular support for the SDAU, to give it a more political dimension, and thus more legitimacy. By doing this they are competing with the local councillors in expressing the needs of the population. But their attempts involve a certain contradiction. In practice, this mobilisation of the population is sought for long-term objectives which are not divisive, reflecting the 'general interest' ideology characteristic of the administration, which the urban planners share. As for the inhabitants, they care more about resolving more immediate problems. Hence a certain dialogue of the deaf: the planners often come away with the disappointing impression that discussions with the population are limited to problems of crossroads and traffic lights. But this could also be a way of hiding from themselves the real conflicts of urban society experienced in everyday life.

The attempts made to involve the principal private-sector participants in urbanisation have not had much success either. They are only very rarely consulted, and in any case are only mildly interested by such long-term projections, which correspond to the period of depreciation of public investment.

Thus long-term urban planning is shorn of part of its political dimension: it is not the means for establishing an agreement between the different forces which confront each other in urban development and which urban policy has the function of regulating. The local representatives find themselves powerless in relation to the central government, or rather its various administrative services. A major uncertainty exists as to the policy variations of governmental action, as a function of variations in the circumstances. The state only defines its future policy for much shorter periods (the duration of the national Plan is five years) and its firm commitments are not even as long as that.

So, urban planning has not become, as intended, a consistent set of increasingly precise and legally binding norms. The progression from the SDAU to the norms establishing the legal control of land use, or to specific financial commitments, has not occurred.

As far as establishing the legal control of land use through the POS is concerned, difficulties have emerged which are both technical and political. Technical, because to the extent that one moves towards a more revolutionary conception of town planning, it becomes more difficult to draw up documents which establish in a rapid way the rules of land use for a fairly long period. Hence a very substantial delay has occurred in the preparation of the POS.[8] But the difficulty is also political. It appears that certain interest-group conflicts, which only partially emerged during the elaboration of the SDAU, became clearer and more acute during the preparation of the POS, upsetting the earlier agreements.

In fact, this phenomenon raises more fundamental issues concerning the conditions in which a land-use policy can be undertaken in France. After having, for a long time, favoured property owners, who are very numerous and form an electorally important clientele, central authorities are moving towards a more coercive policy as far as they are concerned, and one more favourable to property development. But the same is not necessarily true of the local councils on whom the influence of property owners can make itself felt much more directly. Given the difficulty of establishing the rules for land use unilaterally, rules have been negotiated between the public authorities and the developers through the ZAC procedure. This procedure, which was only suggested as a possibility in the Land Guidelines Act, has become a basic element in urban policy.

The link between physical planning, financial programming and budgetary decision has not been able, either, to be established in a clear manner, and urban planning has not resulted in decisions which are binding as far as local authorities are concerned. This is the case even though the final stage of planning, which gives it its executive character, provided for this: the Modernisation and Investment Programmes (PME) were intended to provide the link between the SDAU and national regional planning. It certainly seems that during the preparation of the Sixth Plan, the PME continued to be prepared in total separation from the regional programmes. Just as with the difficulty, already indicated, of translating the SDAU into the legal norms of the POS, there is also both a political and technical difficulty involved in translating the selfsame SDAU into financial programmes articulated with the national Plan. Added to which, even supposing the financial programmes for public services were effectively achieved, there still remains the problem of articulating them with budgetary decisions, one which has not been resolved despite the very timid attempt through the 'Plan contracts'.

Thus for local councillors, the complex and varied elements of urban planning have not added up to a way of assuring a satisfactorily rational consistency of their actions. Rather they represent the opportunity to gain acceptance for the schemes on which local councillors base their electoral position, without ever having the guarantee that this acceptance will result in the resources to implement them; a task which must thus always begin anew during the preparation of the SDAU, the POS, the PME and the regional programme, until the point where a sufficiently general commitment is reached which allows real hope of success.

The difficulties encountered by urban planning lead one to ask what its real social function is. It can be ascertained that, in the name of more realism and flexibility, a marked development has taken place in official conceptions. This development stands out notably in the report of the Sixth Plan Towns Commission. Urban planning is no longer considered there as a consistent and ordered whole, made up of objectives arranged according to a priority and the means of achieving them. It appears henceforth as a collection of procedures enabling each action of the urbanisation agents to be placed in an overall framework so that all the consequences of their actions can be grasped. One discovers that its most indubitable usefulness is less the *a priori* fixing of rational objectives than the analysis of the behaviour of all the agents of urban development. Only this analysis permits precise calculations to be made of the adjustments which the local authorities must undertake. In this sense, urban planning is not fundamentally different from a 'social forecast'. Like social forecasting, this analysis is not neutral: the various intellectual instruments used tend to define the norms, the development criteria, which already make a first choice between urbanisation's conflicting parties. For instance, the exclusive use of criteria of comfort and health in the analysis of slum dwellings directs public intervention as a matter of priority towards slum demolition and the transfer to the suburbs of the present inhabitants of these areas.

The lessening of the purposive character of planning, which is often combined with the technocracy and the idealism of the planners, signifies a greater subordination to the 'logic of development' or, in other words, to market mechanisms. So, it is easier to understand a return of the planners to more immediate schemes, more operational ones which can, more than long-term projects, be conceived in relation to the play of economic forces.

Alongside this, there is assigned to urban planning a certain pedagogical role: it is not content with simply registering tendencies, it also tries to direct them. Now, if this guidance depends in part on the consequences of such a public intervention on the existing play of forces, it also depends on the models of behaviour which the plan arouses in the different participants. Here one meets again the ideas developed by Lucien Nizard concerning the socialising function of national planning. In contrast to its initial function, urban planning produces fewer and fewer 'decisions' in the strict sense. Instead, it produces social norms, or, to borrow Lucien Nizard's expression, messages which aim to direct action by modifying the reciprocal expectations of the participants and their perception of the environment.

In this respect, town planning would tend to resemble national planning. But at the same time they are separated by important differences. In fact, national planning has dominant norms for which the Plan is the medium; these are notably the norms used in devising the model (FIFI) on the basis of which the Sixth Plan was prepared. No equivalent model of urban development exists which would be a vehicle for the dominant norms in relation to which the norms of other social groups would have to be defined. Urban planning still remains for the moment a more open field of encounter between several models of behaviour. Some of these behaviour models transpose the dominant norms of economic development to the problem of urban development. There is no doubt that the central authorities use urban planning, like regional planning, as a vehicle to communicate and to gain acceptance for the norms expressed by national planning. On the other hand, traffic requirements sometimes tend to become fundamental in planning practice at the urban level, just as the growth imperative dominates national planning. Such traffic imperatives in the end simply confirm the decisions of the dominant agents of urbanisation.

Doubtless, there will be seen developing, as against this economic rationality, demands of another type, reflecting the aspirations of certain social strata towards a different style of urban life. Urban planning can be a privileged link in the expression of social demands which would not be incorporated in national planning but would find their expression at this level.

All the same, and this is a second important difference between urban planning and national planning, these demands have at present, during the preparation of town plans, only the local councillors as their spokesmen. We have already seen that there is no consensus-building at this level comparable to that which, in the modernisation commissions of the national Plan, brings together representatives of the different socio-economic forces (especially employers and trade unions). Such consensus-building plays the role of a sort of model of political society, and would restore to urban planning the whole of its political dimension.

The fact that this consensus-building has not been established brings us to the more fundamental problem of the configuration of the forces involved. We have seen that the changes which have occurred in urban planning have as their principal cause the changes which have occurred in the way the town itself is developed. On the one hand, industrialisation and the concentration of the building and public works sector have given an increasing importance to property development, and have brought into commercial production public goods which until then had been excluded from it; on the other hand, the concentration of industrial production has given the industrialists a far greater freedom of choice in the localisation of their investments, making towns compete to attract them. But precisely because of this, these new participants who have a determining influence in urban growth have a basis which is much wider than the urban context. Their strategy, therefore, is not to try to influence the development of any particular town, but to choose the location of their industries according to the development decisions that the town has already taken.

To face these dominant economic participants, there have not as yet been established structured social forces capable of expressing a different urban rationality. The local councillors who attempt to express such a rationality still only very rarely find groups in France from which they can get support. It is difficult to set up 'public urban movements' comparable in scope to those which can be noted in certain foreign countries. The reason for this is, in part, the tardy awareness in France of urban problems. In the last few years, urban planning has brought about a certain reversal. It can even sometimes be the source of social aspirations contrary to the demands which it seeks to show as inevitable, precisely by bringing about an awareness of these requirements and their intolerable nature.

Yet another reason for this is the ambiguous position in which a public urban movement finds itself. In fact, neither the centres of economic nor political decision are to be found at town level and an attempt has to be made straight away to extend the action to a national level. This ambiguity can be seen clearly in the 'municipal action groups' (GAM) which were created in several towns to modify urban policy, as much in its content as in its form. These groups had, very quickly, to adopt a standpoint in relation to both municipal politics and national politics. It is only because the national political parties have for so long neglected local problems that the GAM were able to obtain certain electoral successes. As a result, one can see at present increasing attention being paid by the political parties to the problems of urban development.

Conclusion

Urban planning appeared at the beginning of the period as the expression of a way of civilised living which a state, acting as if it were above conflicts, could impose on the whole nation. In a certain way, Gaullism as an ideology had seen the state as the great architect of society. However, 'urban disorders' continue in spite of these grandiose pretensions, because the latter come into conflict with powerful interests within the coalition in power. The Bills dating from the beginning of this period have already been partially dismantled by the parliamentary majority.

The government's change of direction after 1968 no doubt explains why the legislation and recommendations previously prepared were only partially implemented. The strong conurbation authority endowed with an urban agency is, together with the property tax, among the stillborn offspring of the Gaullist era's urban policy.

Even so, urban planning has not disappeared. However, it expresses in its contradictory manifestations the difficult compromises made between the forces in power. In a way, the division between the zone of coordinated development (ZAC) and the areas left to spontaneous development expresses a certain compromise between the new producers on an industrial scale, the built-up environment and the property owners. Support for the former seems to be completely in keeping with the demands of the industrial imperative which dominates the Sixth Plan. But the coalition in power cannot neglect the importance of the property owners, especially in the rural areas, among its political following, or the anaesthetising effects of rising property values which are driving marginal farmers out of production. At the same time, bodies concerned with long-term studies gradually tend to become restricted to the analysis of the social effects of a growth over whose essential parameters they have no control.

While the state apparatus seemed to have won a certain autonomy at the end of the period of post-war reconstruction, it now appears, through the study of urban planning, to be an arena within which the conflicts and contradictions between the various forces in power are worked out.

NOTES

1 Club Jean Moulin, 'Le Plan, réponse aux besoins', in P. Viau (ed), *Démocratie, Planification, Aménagement*, Les Editions Ouvrières, Paris 1964.

2 'L'urbanisation', *Prospective*, No. 11, 1964, p. 19.

3 Atelier d'urbanisme et d'architecture, *Revue de l'Action Populaire*, No. 165, February 1963, p. 191.

4 See also the special number of Prospective, 'L'urbanisation'.

5 The division of 'agglomerations' into an often large number of communes has always been one of the obstacles to the control of urban planning by local councillors. Paradoxically, the latter have always opposed amalgamations proposed by the government. These proposals, which have attempted to give more and more responsibilities, notably in respect of planning, to bodies situated at the level of the agglomeration but based on the communes, have all experienced a relative failure (joint authorities, districts, urban communities). The July 1971 Act seeking to speed up amalgamations will not, perhaps, in its turn, have the hoped for result.

6 Cf. Christian Topalov, 'La Promotion Immobilière', *La Pensée*, No. 166, December 1972, pp. 109–41.

7 There exist in the provinces four types of 'new town' scheme. Originally this kind of scheme was conceived for the Paris region, to which the methods of urban planning set out in this paper do not apply. At the end of a long process, urban planning in the Paris region was placed under the responsibility of a high-ranking civil servant directly attached to the prime minister, the general delegate of the District of the Paris Region (1962), who later became the prefect of the Paris Region. The creation of an important research body (the IAURP), the publication of an urban development master plan in 1965, the decision to create new towns, have been the guinea pigs for the new urban planning in France. Note must be taken, however, of the fact that local authorities played a very limited role in this process. As for the city of Paris, which has its own plans, it must be remembered that it has an elected council but not an elected mayor like all the other French communes: the latter is replaced by a prefect, chosen by the government.

8 Cf. the declarations of the minister of housing and public works: 'We shall make every effort to ensure that the deadline of 1975 is met for the preparation of the POS...These urban development plans must be flexible if they are to be rigorously respected. It is necessary to carry out urban planning of a wholesale and not retail sort. It is necessary to have fairly precise rules for ordering development, but realistic enough to avoid exceptions.' (*Le Monde*, 21 July 1972.)

SELECT CRITICAL BIBLIOGRAPHY

There is no overall study of urban planning in France. Two special issues of the quarterly *Sociologie du Travail* (October–December 1969 and October–December 1970) provide a panorama of the varied sociological views on urban planning. Marxist views on the subject are frequently to be found in the journal *Espace et Sociétés*. The annual volume of *Aménagement du Territoire et Développement Régional* includes not only theoretical articles but contributions from planners, bibliographies and official documents. Recent research on French urban planning is published in the Mouton series 'Recherche Urbaine'. Finally, one may consult the special issue of *Projet* (April 1971) on 'Forces et stratégies dans l'aménagement urbain'.

16. Innovation and change in British land-use planning[1]

L. J. SHARPE

Over the past decade or so the British land-use planning system has been undergoing fundamental change both in its structure and its process. Some of these changes have yet to be fully adopted and the impact of others has yet to be felt, so that the system as a whole is still in a state of flux and uncertainty, and seems likely to remain so for some time ahead.

This chapter will focus mainly on three broad aspects of these changes. These are: (a) relations between the public and the planning authorities; (b) internal relationships within the planning authority; and (c) relations between levels of government in planning.

Since it is difficult to grasp these changed relationships without some understanding of what went before and some knowledge of the institutional and procedural changes which underpin them, we must begin with a brief historical assessment and a rough sketch of the main outlines of the new structure and the new planning processes. But before doing so a few preliminary cautionary comments are necessary.

The first is that, in making innovation the principal focus, there is always the danger that the defects of the system which innovation seeks to correct will be given undue weight and the overall picture thereby seriously distorted. In the circumstances this is unavoidable, but ought to be borne in mind throughout. Second, it is all too easy (particularly in the British context) to exaggerate the extent of change and to give a coherence and symmetry to the new order where in reality there is merely an inchoate mixture of the old and the new. This is especially true when discussing innovation in planning procedures. But even in the structural reorganization, where the chances of change might reasonably be expected to be greater, it is possible that many of the problems the innovation is supposed to alleviate will persist in the new order. Caution, then, is the watchword.

History

The planning system in Britain has evolved over a fairly long period and in so doing has gradually acquired new objectives. It had its origin in the link between public health and urban living, and especially housing conditions. As the minister said of the first major Town Planning Act in 1909, it 'aims in broad outline at, and hopes to secure, the home healthy, the house beautiful, the town pleasant, the city dignified and the suburb salubrious'.[2] The emphasis however, was on raising the standards of *new* development; little attention was given to the improvement of the existing pattern of development. Although planning theory began after 1909 to extend beyond a rudimentary and non-mandatory technique for controlling the layout and design of residential areas into wider questions of economic and social policy and there was a steady accumulation of legislation reflecting these changes, it was not until the 1947 Act that a fully integrated system covering the national and local level was finally established.[3]

The key features of the 1947 Act were as follows.

(a) Each local planning authority was required to draw up a concerted development plan which was to be the instrument through which it controlled virtually all forms of development.

(b) Central government took the responsibility for the overall coordination and oversight of land use throughout the country.

(c) The areas covered by the development plans were increased by making the counties and county boroughs the sole local planning authorities.

(d) Local planning authorities were given powers of compulsory purchase of land at existing use value.

(e) Development rights and development values were nationalized and, in a restricted number of cases, compensation to existing land owners for loss of development values was paid to them by a National Land Board at a proportion of 1947 values. With the exception of land ripe for development, those owners who were granted planning permission paid to the Board a development charge where the permission increased the value of the land.

With the exception of the last, these changes have remained permanent features of the planning system. During the 1950s the land value aspects of the 1947 Act covered under (d) and (e) were progressively dismantled so that development rights remained public, but development values were returned to private owners. Compensation for compulsory purchase by the planning authority also reverted to a market value basis. The effect of these changes was to make it more difficult for local planning authorities to plan effectively because of the high cost of land acquisition. Moreover, it meant that publicly created values accrued to private owners. Between 1967 and 1970 an attempt was made to overcome these deficiencies by the creation of a national Land Commission charged, first, with securing that the land was available at the appropriate time for the implementation of national, regional and local plans; and second, securing that a substantial part of the development value created by the community was returned to the community and that the cost of land for essential purposes was reduced. In order to achieve the first of the aims, the Commission was given wide powers to buy land either by agreement or compulsorily for disposal to developers, or for development by the Commission itself. Land for housing could be sold by the Commission at less than market price. In order to achieve this second objective, a betterment levy was introduced, to be levied on all land to be developed which in practice was equal to about 50 % of development value. The levy was deducted by the Commission on its own purchases of land, or levied by the Commission on private land sales for development.

With the return of a Conservative government in June 1970 the Land Commission and the betterment levy were abolished. The compensation problem, however, remains and it may fairly be said that the full potential of the existing planning system can never be fully realized until some form of control of development rights is reintroduced. The fundamental problem is one of equity and derives from the fact that government planning control discriminates between land owners. Those who are granted permission to develop can reap the full advantage of market values, whereas those who are denied it must be content with existing use value. Moreover, the community as a whole receives no benefit from the betterment created by the granting of planning permission to the fortunate land owner who alone benefits from society's deliberate rationing of supply.

This basic deficiency apart, how successful has the land-use planning system been? This is, of course, an impossible question to answer with finality because we do not know for certain what would have happened had there been no planning of land use. Nor have the general aims of the planning system had sufficient precision to make assessment very easy. Indeed, measuring success in planning of whatever kind is an elusive task: the more recalcitrant the society that is to be planned, or the weaker the planning authority, the greater the temptation to design the plan on the basis of what seems likely to happen anyway. Or, alternatively, to so revise the plan in the light of changing conditions as to achieve the same objective. There can be little doubt that the current fashion for 'flexibility', 'rolling programmes' and 'adaptable means' that seems to have overtaken the planning procedures of the industrial democracies, and is a strong feature of the recent changes in British land-use planning procedures just described, has at least some of its origins in the second method for ensuring success.

We may conclude that 'success' in planning rests as much on the objectives it initially sets itself as it does on the extent to which it meets these objectives. In one sense, the most successful planning is likely to be that which attempts to achieve least. Where more full-blooded attempts at planning are made – that is to say where the manifest purpose is to shape the development of the planned entity in accordance with a preconceived overall design drawn up on the basis of rational criteria – the likelihood of success is that much more problematic.

Nevertheless, in assessing the success of the British system, it can be said with some certainty that it has achieved one of its primary aims and one for which it has the strongest public backing. This is the rural preservation aim, or to put it in more positive terms, the management of urban growth. There can be little doubt that the planning system has slowed down the process of absorption of agricultural land for urban use. Between 1934 and 1939 the average annual rate of absorption of agricultural land for urban uses was 60,000 acres. In the period 1950–60 this average dropped to 36,000 acres per year.[4] And this contraction has been achieved despite a rising population and despite a rate of net household formation currently running at three times the rate of population growth itself. Over the period 1952–72 an annual average of 300,000 new dwellings have been built. There has also been a steadily increasing per capita use for land. In 1968, 88 acres of land were required per 1,000 persons, as compared with 50 acres in 1900, and it is estimated that 100 acres will be required per 1,000 population in the year 2000. The existing planning system has also played a major part in preserving areas of outstanding natural beauty adjacent to urban areas from being built upon, partly through the system of Green Belts and more decisively by the creation of ten National Parks, which in aggregate cover an area of 5,258 square miles.

The planning system has also been effective in combating the inevitable visual squalor generated by unrestricted market-determined urban expansion, and there can be little doubt that by the exercise of very strict controls on outdoor advertising, caravan sites and other forms of unsightly development, the visual character of new urban development is very much better than it might have been. At a broader level, the planning system has also improved the quality of urban living by segregating industry from residential areas, and in core city areas, lowering population densities and creating new recreational space.

Arguably the most notable and most widely known achievements of the land-use planning system in relation to the management of urban growth is the New Town. Nearly 1.7 million people now live in thirty-one New Towns, which in total represent a capital investment at 1972 values of over £1,092 million. More will be said about New Towns policy later.

The planning system

There are two land-use planning agencies in England and Wales in the sense that they alone exercise formal statutory authority.[5] The first one is the Department of the Environment (DoE) at the central government level. The DoE was created in 1970 and incorporates the old Ministries of Housing and Local Government, Transport, Public Building and Works, and the residual regional planning functions of the Department of Economic Affairs. As its title suggests, the DoE was created so as to achieve coordination for the whole range of public services that bear upon the physical environment, but it does not embrace distribution of industry and general aid to industry. The second agency is local government, and consists of the county councils and the district councils. London, which was reorganized in 1965, has a slightly different system consisting of the Greater London Council, which is the approximate equivalent of the county, and the thirty-two London boroughs, which correspond to districts in the other conurbations.

The two types of local authority work in partnership with the central department and the latter is the senior partner. The central government's responsibility is exercised by the minister, the secretary of state for the environment, who is responsible for 'securing consistency and continuity in the framing and execution of national policy with respect to the use and development of land throughout England and Wales'.[6] The county councils draw up the structure plan for their areas, which the minister has to approve after a public examination before the plan has legal status. He also approves periodic revisions to the structure plan.

The minister, or his inspector, is also the appellate authority for all aspects of development control. The minister exercises the appellate powers via the inspector, who presides at an inquiry into disputes or adjudges between written representations from potential developers, objectors and the local planning authority. The inspector then makes a report to the minister who, in making his final decision, may or may not accept the inspector's findings. About 14,000 of such disputes arise every year (out of a total of 615,000 planning decisions), and for about 50% of them (largely those involving straightforward cases of residential development on a small scale) the minister is not involved and the inspector makes the final decision. In recent years there has been a sharp increase in the number of disputes going to inquiry (over 50% increase since 1970),[7] and this led the government in 1973 to set up a committee of inquiry under Mr George Dobry to look at ways in which the appeals procedure can be speeded up.

In relation to inquiries and examinations affecting the formulation of the structure plan itself, the minister may restrict the kind of objections to be heard, and for developments with national implications (such as the third London Airport or the Greater London Development Plan) he may choose between an inspector or an expert panel to preside over the inquiry. The minister is also the confirming authority for the exercise by local planning authorities of the powers of compulsory land acquisition and comprehensive redevelopment. In practice, the regional administration of the DoE carries out most of the minister's quasi-judicial and confirming powers. The minister also has 'call in' powers whereby he can direct a local planning authority to remit to him particular planning applications, or major departures by the local planning authority from the development plan.

Every county council has to draw up a structure plan, there being no local discretion, so that the whole country is covered by a uniform system. But the structure plan is a very flexible instrument. It is not a zoning ordinance and, subject to its general outline, the county and the district councils do have wide discretion in its implementation, e.g. in exercising their development control powers. To call it a plan in the physical sense is perhaps a misnomer, for the structure plan is essentially a written statement of policy in relation to land use generally plus diagrammatic illustrations, rather than a detailed map of specific land allocations. It must also include policy statements in relation to traffic management and the improvement of the physical environment.

Below the county councils, the district councils are also planning authorities and in most instances they will be responsible for drawing up the *local plan*. These plans do not require any central government sanction and the county council is the sole approving authority. The local plan must, however, conform to the structure plan drawn up by the county council, or where there is conflict, the minister will arbitrate. These local plans are a detailed elaboration (including a map) of the implications of the broad policy outlined in the structure plan applied to a specific sub-community, usually smaller than the area of the district itself. The bulk of development control powers in relation to the local plan are exercised by the district councils. Local plans are of three types: *district plans* which cover areas within the structure plan area which demand comprehensive treatment; *action area plans* covering areas where major change (either in the form of new development or re-development over a relatively short time span) is expected or required; and *subject plans* which refer to specific types of land use such as mineral or gravel extraction.

In the six great urban concentrations around Birmingham, Manchester, Liverpool, West Yorkshire, South Yorkshire and Newcastle there is a slightly different system. The main difference is that the district councils – now called metropolitan districts – have a wider range of service responsibilities, including the whole of education and the welfare services on the London pattern. The counties in these areas – now called metropolitan counties – are therefore functionally weaker than the normal county, but they now have responsibility for the operation of the public passenger transport services (other than those run by British Rail), as does the Greater London Council.

The new structure

The planning system briefly outlined above is itself an innovation both as regards structure and process. The two-tier structure of county and district was established under the 1972 Local Government Act and did not come into operation until the spring of 1974. This new local government structure affects all local government services including planning, but it must be emphasised that one of the ostensible considerations underlying the change is to achieve more rational areas for land-use planning. The old system of local government that gave the county boroughs – roughly speaking most of the larger towns and cities – responsibility for all land-use planning within their areas was felt to be an anachronism. The new structure attempts to combine, where feasible, the larger urban centres with their service hinterlands while at the same time preserving the main outlines of the old county system. As the White Paper which preceded the 1972 Act puts it:

The areas of many existing authorities are out-dated and no longer reflect the pattern of life and work in modern society. The division between county and county borough has prolonged an artificial separation of big towns from the surrounding hinterlands for functions whose planning and administration need to embrace town and country.[8]

It must be added that this intention has only partly been fulfilled under the new system. The 'artificial separation' will persist in the planning of the metropolitan county areas, since they cover only the built-up core of the conurbations.

The effect of the new system is to replace the existing primary local planning authorities, comprising 58 counties and 82 county boroughs, by 53 new and in some cases enlarged counties, 6 of which became metropolitan counties. The two-tier system which operated in the old counties has been retained in the new, but the 333 new districts and the 36 metropolitan districts are now much larger than the 1,280 or so old districts (urban and rural) and municipal boroughs that they replace, and will have a population range of 40,000 to just over 1 million. Each of the new districts, unlike the old second-tier authorities they replace, is now a planning authority in its own right, so the number of planning authorities has been substantially increased. This means that whatever the spatial integration gain achieved by joining up town with country, it must be set against the functional disintegration in urban areas where there are now two planning authorities where previously there was one.

The new process

The land-use planning process is also of relatively recent origin: its main outlines were established under the 1968 Town and Country Planning Act. The new process was designed to achieve greater speed in decision-making, more popular participation and a more positive attitude to promoting a desirable environment overall. The White Paper which preceded the 1968 Act outlined the defects of the old system thus:

Three major defects have now appeared in the present system. First, it has become overloaded and subject to delays and cumbersome procedures. Second, there has been inadequate participation by the individual citizen in the planning process and insufficient regard to his interests. Third, the system has been built as a negative control on undesirable development rather than as a positive stimulus to the creation of a good environment.[9]

Besides correcting these defects, the other main objectives of the new planning process are to achieve greater flexibility in plan-making and greater recognition of the role of communications and market forces in determining the pattern of land use. The enquiry into the deficiencies of the old planning system summarized this last shortcoming thus:

It has proved extremely difficult to keep these plans not only up to date but forward looking and responsive to the demands of change. The result has been that they have tended to become out of date – in terms of technique in that they deal inadequately with transport and the interrelationship of traffic and land use; in factual terms in that they fail to take account quickly enough of changes in population forecasts, traffic growth and other economic and social trends; and in terms of policy in that they do not reflect more recent developments in the field of regional and urban planning.[10]

At the broadest level of generality, the aim of the new planning process is to shift the emphasis of land-use planning away from adherence to the relatively rigid development plan – the blue print – with its assumption that land-use planning is a transitional stage which will itself bring about by means of physical controls a very vaguely defined end-state: the preferable physical layout. The new system is intended to introduce a much more flexible approach which views planning as a continuous process in which objectives are much more clearly and explicitly defined but are also open to reformulation in the light of experience and changing circumstances. More concisely, it is a movement away from precise regulation of means leaving the ends unspecified, towards the specification of fairly precise objectives but allowing adaptable means.

The new process replaces the old development plan which was drawn up by all the counties and county boroughs. It had a twenty-year life with five-yearly revisions, and did not become operative until approved by central government. It consisted of a series of documents including an analysis of the pre-plan survey, a written statement summarizing very briefly the main proposals of the plan, plus detailed maps. One of the maps covered the whole plan area (the town or the county map) another was the programme map, and, in the case of the counties, more detailed maps were made for specific areas. The written statement did not contain any argument for or against the proposals, or any discussion of how the final choices were to be made, or the factual material on which the choices were made.

There are a number of features of the new land-use planning process which, to some extent, modify both its formal innovatory character and the extent to which comprehensiveness will in practice be achieved. The first is that in so far as the new process places emphasis on the need to formulate general principles and overall policy objectives, it is in fact reasserting what were the *intentions* of the 1947 Act. Somehow these intentions got lost in the practical application of the old process. One reason for this may be an inevitable tendency of the decision-making process of land-use planning (and possibly all decision-making with a planning intent in democracies) to become dominated by the control function; that is to say, for the individual, politically sensitive, short-term decision to prevail, irrespective of its implications for the synoptic strategy.

The second feature of the new process that requires qualification is that its insistence on flexibility should not be interpreted as implying that the old process involved a rigid adherence to a detailed physical plan. The old development plan was highly flexible in the sense that the local planning authority had a very wide area of discretion and could depart from the plan if it chose, provided it was not a major departure. Indeed, in the early phase of the old order, planning was conducted without a plan at all, since the development plan had yet to be formulated and then had to be approved by central government. Often the plan was out of date by the time it became operative. The first phase of the post-war planning process was not so much planning as interim development control. The defect of the old system was that at its worst it was flexible as to ends as well as means.

The third aspect of the new process that must be noted is that the intention to be comprehensive carries with it the danger of overambition – overambition in the sense that structure plans will attempt to lay down targets for aspects of the local economy such as employment and population movement over which the planning authority will have no, or very little, control. Moreover, even for public sector activities, the structure planning authority may have relatively little influence because government departments and statutory undertakers are largely immune from normal planning control.

The desire to state explicit aims that is an important feature of the new planning process also raises problems for, although the objective is to clarify the planning process and give it a greater precision of purpose, it may have the opposite effect and the new approach become just as remote from reality as the old. This is a danger that confronts all attempts to import management by objectives into government and derives from the fact that in practice such aims have to be pitched at a level of generality as to be literally meaningless so as not to invite more political conflict than is absolutely necessary. A high level of generality is also necessary to ensure that the aims are sufficiently drained of value content to place them safely within the province of the professional planner.[11]

Finally, from mid-1973, the new counties have been required to draw up a separate Transportation Plan – the Transport Policies and Programme (TPP). This will consist of a statement of the councils' transport objectives and strategy, and include a set of interlocking proposals for capital and current expenditures over the whole transportation field for a ten to fifteen-year period. The existence of such a plan is likely to encroach on the notion of the structure plan as the all-embracing framework, and will tend to perpetuate that division between transportation and land-use planning that the structure planning process was intended to overcome.

Regional planning

Other innovations in the planning process which must be noted centre on the creation of an intermediate layer of administration at the regional level between central government and the local planning authorities. Three innovatory regional agencies may be identified. These are: (a) Regional Economic Planning Councils and Boards (REPC and REPB); (b) Joint Regional Planning Teams (Joint Team); (c) Regional Standing Conferences of local planning authorities (Regional Conference).

The first agency was originally set up to form part of the central planning process and its primary task was to provide a regional component of the national economic planning process. As such it acted as the link between national economic planning – a process of resource allocation over time – and local land-use planning – the allocation of resources in space – to form a single national planning process connecting centre with periphery. It consists of two separate bodies, the *Council* (REPC) and the *Board* (REPB). The Council is an advisory body chosen by the minister, composed of three elements representing the local planning authorities within the region, the management of industry in the region and representatives drawn from the trade unions. There are, in addition, one or two members drawn from academic life. The REPC not only advises central government on particular aspects of economic planning policy concerning its region, but is also responsible for drawing up what in the early days of the REPCs were called regional economic plans and studies. In practice, the quality, scope and depth of these documents varied considerably. Their main function was to draw attention to the salient characteristics of their respective regions and their problems. Perhaps the best generic title for them would be draft strategies. All Councils have completed this aspect of their work since they were created in 1964. Their draft strategies have no statutory basis, and none has been adopted by central government, but they have been published and have been therefore the subject of considerable public debate in some regions. They have also provided the basis on which later plans could build.

The Board (REPB) is composed entirely of outstationed civil servants and is presided over by a director of under-secretary rank whose 'home' department is the Department of the Environment, which is responsible for land-use planning, local government generally, transportation and housing. The director acts as the principal adviser to the Council and below him are two regional controllers responsible respectively for planning and housing, and for roads and transportation. The office of director has only recently been designated and it marks an important shift in the tasks of the Board away from economic planning *per se* towards a much greater emphasis on land-use planning and transportation. This reflects a decline in central government interest in national economic planning and a much greater interest, both in the need to integrate the environmental public services at the regional level and the need to decentralize central government's quasi-judicial responsibilities for approving local structure plans. This change of emphasis is also reflected in the composition and character of the Board.

Its chairman is no longer drawn from an 'economics' department as

in the past, and although the members of the Board include representatives from other departments whose activities impinge on economic
planning including a representative from the current industrial planning ministry (the Department for Trade and Industry) the Board
appears to be much more an adjunct of a single department – the
DoE – than it was originally. This is a reflection of the fact that the
DoE embraces what had formerly been four separate ministries.

The second regional agency, the *Joint Regional Planning Team*, is not
a permanent body but a temporary partnership between local and
central government which is jointly sponsored by the DoE and the
respective REPC and Regional Conference (discussed below). The
chairman of the Team is a civil servant.[12] The task of the Team is to
draw up a land use strategy for each of the economic planning regions,
of which there are eight in England, with Scotland and Wales each
constituting an additional region. The content and character of these
regional strategies was delineated by the PAG Report cited earlier thus:

They will have to be concerned with physical planning issues which are of
regional significance, with the overall distribution of population and employment, green belt policy and other limitations on growth in the conurbations.
They must also encompass other physical factors of regional significance such
as projects; the economic implications of major development projects (motorways, docks, airports); and the impact of economic decisions on physical
planning.

In practical terms the strategies enunciate guidelines for the level of
future investment by central and local government, public corporations and private industry, that will provide the framework for the
structure planning authorities to fill in the more localized land-use
implications.

The Team itself is composed of civil servants (including economists,
sociologists and geographers) drawn mainly from the Department of
the Environment, but including officials of the Department of Trade
and Industry, planning specialists from local government and academics, comprising about thirty people in all. The work of each Team
is completed when the strategy has been drawn up. On the assumption
that Teams will be set up in every region we may assume that
eventually there will be an agreed strategy for each region. But it is
doubtful whether they will together constitute a composite national
strategy, since the process is likely to take a long time to complete for
the whole country. By the time it is complete the earlier individual
regional strategies will be out of date and will be in the process of
revision. In the current jargon there will be a 'rolling' national
strategy.

The regional strategies, when completed, are not adopted as government policy automatically but, since central government is intimately involved in their formulation, they are unlikely to diverge fundamentally from current government thinking although they may, of course, recommend fairly substantial departures from existing policy. Equally, they are unlikely to run counter to the interests of the larger constituent local planning authorities. A lot depends on the relative political weight of local political interests. The Team strategy, therefore, carries much greater weight than the wholly advisory draft strategies that have already been produced by the REPCs, and it seems likely that the Joint Teams have now entirely superseded them as plan-formulating bodies. In 1973 the only Team plan completed was that for the South-East (in June 1970) and was accepted with only minor modifications by the central government in the autumn of 1970. Joint Teams are at work producing strategic plans for all the regions except Yorkshire and Humberside, the East Midlands, and the South-West.

The third regional agency is the *Regional Conference* and, unlike the other agencies discussed, it is an entirely voluntary body and as such varies considerably both in title and in the scope of its activities. The Conferences have emerged initially in response to the inadequacies of existing local planning authority boundaries for certain key planning issues such as Green Belt extensions and the designation of growth areas, and later as an insurance by local authorities that land-use planning at the regional level would not pass out of the hands of local government to the REPCs. The Conference is, then, a part of local government and consists in most cases of all the planning authorities in each of the eight English economic planning regions. The primary function of the Conference is to act as a forum for the pooling of ideas about those aspects of land-use planning that transcend local planning authority boundaries. Some Conferences have a small professional planning staff drawn from the constituent member authorities. Like the REPCs, most of the Conferences have each produced their own regional document, but unlike the REPC draft strategies, less emphasis is given to economic factors and, with the exception of the South-East, they tend inevitably to comprise a collation of the existing or prospective statutory development plans of the constituent local planning authorities.

Probably the only Conference document that justifies the name strategy is that for the South-East. The South-East Conference also seems to have been the most active in producing technical analyses and surveys. The success of the Joint Team plan for the South-East owes a lot to this preliminary work. It is unlikely that the Joint Teams will supersede the Conference. Indeed, the latter is one of the sponsors of the Joint Teams and provides it with a direct link with the localities. The Conference – unlike the REPCs – is made up of the operational agencies which actually conduct the bulk of land-use planning, so cooperation and consultation between the individual Conferences and the respective Joint Teams is essential if only to ensure that the Joint Team strategy is realizable. As the terms of reference of the South-East Joint Team put it: the Team 'should arrive at recommendations for the future development of the Region which will be broadly acceptable to the authorities who will have to apply them – the government and local planning authorities'.

Relations with the public

As we noted at the outset, the first major theme of this chapter is the changing relationship between the public and the land-use planning authority. Before discussing this relationship, a few preliminary comments are necessary on the underlying characteristics of the land-use planning system and popular attitudes towards it.

The first point to note is that the land-use planning function in Britain is essentially that of *re-designing* the existing urban environment, whereas in Italy and in most of France, outside the Paris and the Lille regions, land-use planning is much more concerned with designing a new urban environment to accommodate the massive influx of population into urban centres from rural areas over the past twenty years or so. In Britain, population movement to the towns in now very small indeed and less than 3.5% of the employed population is engaged in agriculture. The overwhelming population movement is centrifugal from the urban centres to suburban and quasi-rural peripheries. After Holland and Belgium, Britain is now the most densely populated industrial democracy in the world.

This difference has two implications. The first is that land-use planning is more complex in Britain, since land for development in the place where it is needed is scarcer and the task of re-furbishing an existing urban area is both technically, and in some senses politically, more difficult to undertake.

The other implication of Britain being at another stage of the urbanization process is that public acceptance of land-use planning tends to be much higher in the British case, simply because the results of unrestricted industrialization and an unfettered market in land are only too visible to the average elector.

The greater public willingness in Britain to accept the restriction on individual freedom of action that a fully-fledged land-use planning system entails has a strong negative, preservationist tone. This is partly because of the sheer facts of urbanization and population density. Although only about 8.6% of the land surface of the United

Kingdom is actually developed, this development is heavily concentrated in the irregular oblong – the so-called 'coffin' – that includes the Merseyside and Manchester urban concentrations in the North-West and extends to the east to include the West Riding of Yorkshire and continues right down to the London region, embracing Birmingham and the Black Country on the way. Thus the warning 'If there isn't some control, then we shall have concrete from London to Manchester', although palpably implausible, appears as a very real threat to most people.

This popular support also reflects deeply held subjective attitudes, themselves of course linked to objective reality, about the superiority of rural life: what may be called rural nostalgia. For the upper classes this is axiomatic, and the ownership of land and a house in the country is almost an essential prerequisite of high social status. Similarly, the middle class, who tend to take their standards from above, have never been truly bourgeois in the continental sense; tending rather to reject the apartment in favour of the villa disguised as a cottage or manor house, suspicious of outward ostentation and favouring what by French or Italian standards is a distinctly non-urban, indefinably tweedy life style. The working class for their part have retained a very strong attachment to horticulture, particularly flower growing and public parks, together with an almost obsessional desire for keeping animals. The ideal English town life-style is, then, essentially suburban rather than urban: it is the encapsulation of rurality within the urban environment. This means that space standards both around and within the house tend to be important symbols of social status. Low density in urban areas is the unquestioned ideal. London, for example, has about the same population as New York City but covers twice the area, and less than 10% of the new building in Britain is in blocks of five stories or more. The comparable figure for West Germany is 78% and for France 60%.

In short, the ownership and nurture of open space has a particularly important place in English culture. It is possible that these attitudes will change over the next generation, given the forces working for metropolitanism in British society. But at the mass level the booming gardening supplies and pet food industries, continued public support for Green Belts, and a renewed hostility to flats suggests otherwise. Among the intellectual middle class what has been called the 'planning movement' remains, as it has in the past, a very influential force for maintaining and expanding the planning role of government.[13]

These popular attitudes have also affected another aspect of the British land-use planning system that must be underlined if its peculiar characteristics are to be properly understood. This is the distinction that has always existed between traditional land-use planning – town and country planning – and the various industrial location and employment policies that have been pursued by government, which may be called, for want of a better title, *economic* planning. One of the effects of this division is that, whereas land-use planning is a coherent centre-to-periphery decision-making process, industrial location and regional aid politics have always been firmly in the hands of a central department, and local planning authorities have had little or no power directly to determine industrial location and employment policy in their area.

The division has two aspects, one institutional, the other professional. Institutionally, the division has been the product of the rivalry between the central land-use planning ministry and the 'economic' ministry. Professionally, land-use planning has been the preserve of a quite distinct profession of planning officers at the local level, mainly drawn from architects, surveyors and engineers and later, after the Schuster Report,[14] of geographers and sociologists. These groups had little or no interest, or were hostile to, the economics of land use. There is, of course, no comparable profession for economic planning, and those economists who were interested in economic planning were not very concerned with land-use planning, but appeared to be content to leave locational economics (other than the effect of location on the firm) largely to geographers. This rigidity has been softening during the last decade: some economists have been taking an increasing interest in the spatial aspects of economic activity and the ambit of land-use planners has been significantly widened to include economic factors. Also, one of the institutional barriers was dismantled when the regional planning functions of the Department of Economic Affairs was absorbed by the Department of the Environment.

Nevertheless, the fact that industrial location and unemployment policies still remain the responsibility of a separate department (that for trade and industry) means that a key institutional barrier will remain. Moreover, it seems likely that there are probably severe limits in the extent to which traditional land-use planning can shuffle off its traditional concern with imprecise, non-measurable and essentially non-economic – not to say anti-economic – concerns, such as the preservation of amenity, environmental design and space standards, precisely because they have their roots firmly embedded in those British popular attitudes just described.

This brings us to the last distinguishing feature of the British system that needs initial emphasis: the relative independence of British local authorities. This has two aspects in relation to land-use planning: the first is that, unlike either France or Italy, the predominant weight of operational planning expertise lies with the local planning authorities and not with central government. This means that despite a highly developed system of regulatory, inspectoral and advisory powers exercised by the central department and, of course, the minister's quasi-judicial plan approval and legislative responsibilities, the operational heart of the land-use planning process lies in the localities. Policy change, therefore, usually begins in the localities, and the reality of the planning process – as opposed to the intentions of planning legislation – is ultimately largely determined by the local planning authority. Central–local relations are, then, highly complex, the locus of power labyrinthine and in mild but constant flux. As one foreign observer has put it:

Town planning proceeds so much from the bottom upwards in Britain that policy is often more fully expressed in reactions by the central government to specific proposals or decisions by local authorities – in the examination of development plan proposals, in passing on planning appeals, in suggestions during informal conferences, etc. – than in advance, general policy statements by central government. There is a sort of sidling sideways into policy rather than full advance head-on assertion of policy.[15]

The second consequence of local autonomy in planning is that despite the fact that the 1968 Act marks an important shift towards recognizing the importance of the economic dimension in land-use planning, the new system is not, as yet, integrated with economic or fiscal management at the local level. Still less does it form part of a national system aimed at integrating the allocation of land uses with resource allocation generally, which seems to be one of the objectives of parallel changes in the French land-use planning system. The local budget-making process remains almost wholly independent from central government in any case, and the control of investment exercised by the centre is either directed at restricting or expanding it (as part of the global tactics of the Treasury in relation to national demand management) or it is the normal control exercised over capital investment and grants by a specialist central department or sub-department in relation to a particular service such as education or highways. So, although there may be parallels in the change from blue-print planning to structure planning in Britain with the change notably to SDAU in France, the change does not seem to be anything like as all-embracing in Britain. Also, unlike the French situation, it is very much a change that is taking place *within* an existing, well-established professional setting. Because land-use planning does not impinge on the resource allocation processes of the local authority to any great extent, that setting is still a land-use one. This separation is reinforced by the departmental traditions of central government that were discussed a moment ago, and the separation could continue, despite the pressure for new coordinative resource-management techniques that are in the process of adoption for other service activities of local government.

The new participation

Interpreted in its broadest sense, the need to improve relations with the general public is one of the main objectives of the new planning system inaugurated by the 1968 Town and Country Planning Act. This is hardly surprising since land-use planning raises problems of public acceptability in a peculiarly sharp form. It is clearly a primordial function of government in the sense that, unlike, say, education or housing, it is not substitutable: it is either done by government or it is not done at all. Nevertheless, also unlike education or housing, it may have few tangible or visible outputs and operates on a lengthy time cycle. This severely diminishes its public appeal and makes it especially vulnerable to public displeasure. Whatever the cost, the public may appreciate the products of the public education or housing services because it can see them in the form of new schools and new housing. They appear after a fairly short time-interval between stated policy and its implementation. Planning outputs, by contrast, interfere with private property rights in dramatic and sometimes poignant ways that are immediately comprehensible to the general public and evoke considerable hostility towards the planning process: the aged widow dispossessed of her home to make way for a road widening; the small family shopkeeper driven out of the city centre to make way for a new shopping precinct whose rents will be far too high to allow him to return. The benefits that are to accrue from these changes – better traffic flows, a more congenial shopping environment – are problematic or too abstract to have a wide public appeal. Sometimes, they may be too technical and therefore incomprehensible, or so delayed in their ultimate fruition as to be to all intents and purposes unrealized.

This inherent handicap.was compounded by two basic weaknesses of the British system in relation to public participation. The first concerned public inquiries into objections to the draft development plan. These are a very important participatory feature of the system since they offer an opportunity for members of the public to voice their opinion on the draft plan and get it altered.[16] This potential gain for participatory democracy was, however, to some extent curtailed because at the inquiries the local planning authority was not required to state the explicit objectives of the plan. The validity of the planning authority's case was therefore very much more difficult to question. There was due process but not *substantive* due process. The new system, by requiring that the structure plan (that is to say the overall land-use plan for each local government planning area) consist of a statement of the plan objectives and the reasoning behind them instead of the detailed land-use map that was the 'plan' under the old system, may constitute an important gain for public participation at the plan inquiry, or to give it the new name, 'examination in public'. But the advantages gained by objectors from being given a clearer target to shoot at will almost certainly be outweighed by the fact that the general public are not normally interested in abstract objectives but in precise land-use changes, preferably set out in visual terms on a map so that the effect of change can be more easily judged.

In practice then, the new participatory arrangements will benefit those of the public who have the expertise to argue their case, or who can command such expertise, but it will not necessarily benefit the ordinary citizen. Indeed the ordinary citizen will have no automatic right to appear at the examination as he did under the old system. His automatic right to participate will be confined to the local plan inquiries and there will be no appeal from the local plan inquiry to the minister.

The second deficiency of the old system was the lack of consultation with the public in the early, formative stages of the plan-making process, when some of the key decisions which predetermine the ultimate character of the plan are inevitably made. Practice varied considerably up and down the country but, generally speaking, even when the plan was in its final form prior to ministerial approval, it was difficult to evoke public interest, and many planning authorities made little attempt to change the situation.

The broad proposals for enhancing public participation contained in the 1968 Act have been translated into processes by the Skeffington Committee.[17] As a result of their proposals, consultation with the general public can now take place at various stages of the planning process for both structure and local plans. Of particular importance in this context is the requirement that the planning authority put forward alternative proposals at the initial stage of the plan-making process.

In order to maximize public participation at each stage leading up to the local plan, three participatory instruments have been proposed. First, there is the *community forum* at which individuals and local groups can meet for discussion to learn from each other and to act as a focal point for receiving information on planning matters from the local planning authority. As the Skeffington Report puts it: 'the forum would also provide local organizations with the opportunity to discuss collectively planning and other issues of importance to the area'. Second, there is the possibility of a *community development officer* being appointed by the local authority, who would also provide a link between the planners and the planned and help the inarticulate and the unorganized to make their views known to the planning authority. It should perhaps be noted that the government's subsequent thoughts on community development officers were substantially less enthusiastic than those of the Skeffington Report.[18]

Finally, it is proposed that planning authorities should enlist the services of public relations experts to ensure the maximum publicity for all stages of the planning process. With the exception of the community development officer, each of these changes is being gradually adopted with varying degrees of enthusiasm, and subsequent legislation (The Town and Country Planning Amendment Acts of 1971 and 1972) has given the secretary of state for the environment the power to direct local authorities if he is satisfied that they are not providing adequate opportunities for public participation. What constitutes 'adequate' in this context, however, was not defined.

The precise reasons for these changes are difficult to unravel, but it has been alleged that one motive was a desire by the planning profession to bypass the elected councillors and generate a direct quasi-political relationship between the professional planner and the electorate. Whatever the truth of this interpretation, it is certain that these changes have the broad support of the professional land-use planners. Half of the members of the Planning Advisory Group, from whose report the 1968 Act stems, were professional planners working in local government. To some extent the profession's support for the new public participation procedures is hardly surprising since those of the procedures governing the preparation of the new structure plans prior to central approval, as we have noted, offer *less* opportunity for detailed criticism by the public. Greater participation at other stages of the planning process is seen as compensation for this loss.

It is also likely that the new participation procedures were seen by the profession as a gift offering to win back the waning support of the general public and so safeguard the future of planning as a public service. Whether they will succeed in doing so must be a matter of conjecture.[19] What cannot be denied is that these new opportunities for public participation have coincided with a sharp increase in public dissatisfaction with all aspects of environmental planning both for land use and for transportation. This may not necessarily be overtly expressed in relation to particular policies, but cuts deeper to the very basis of the service, to what may be called the operating ideology of planning. In a representative democracy where the bulk of decision-making has to be made at two removes from the electorate by full-time, non-elected professional specialists, the system can only work if there is implicit public trust of government. That is to say, however disagreeable particular policies pursued by government may be, there is agreement that collective action is necessary and agreement on the broad techniques and modes of operation employed. Thus, to take the example of public education, there may be political conflict about the location and the size of a school, but everyone – elector, representative and technocrat – is broadly agreed that there ought to be an institution called a school manned by people called teachers who take over the role of parents within its precincts, and that children within specified age groups should be compelled by law to attend it.

It is this agreement on the modes of operation of a public service that may be called its operating ideology. It is impossible for representative democracy to work if there is no accepted operating ideology because, without it, discussion on all policy issues other than the very minor ones has to go back to first principles. In this respect the relationship between the elector and the elected, on the one hand, and the full-time professional on the other, is no different from that between the client and his lawyer or plumber. It is essentially a principal and agent relationship, and for it to work there must be a firm foundation of agreed modes of operation if the agent is to be able to carry out this task, and this implies a sense of trust by the electorate. When this public trust collapses, public suspicion of the professional expert replaces it and the operation of the service is subject to continuous debate: all major decisions have to return to first principles and everyone becomes his own expert. Policy becomes the result of purely political forces. In short, the primacy of the electorate reasserts itself. In both land-use planning and in transportation planning something like this seems to be happening in Britain, and major planning decisions are much less likely than they were in the past to be accepted simply as the consequence of the planners' appraisal of a necessarily limited range of options and therefore as largely inevitable. Planning, then, faces a more critical and aggressive public and, together with traffic issues, has come to dominate local politics in many towns in recent years, often relegating the traditionally important housing and education issues into second place.

This is especially so in relation to urban road development where the Buchanan Report, published in 1963, seemed to be emerging as the basis for a new operating ideology for transportation planning.[20] Judging, however, by the stiff public resistance that has emerged in many cities to plans for building new urban roads to relieve inner city traffic congestion, there must be considerable doubt about this. These relief roads were based on the Buchanan redevelopment strategy which aimed at striking a balance between the needs of cars and pedestrians, and involved considerable expenditure for constructing new urban roads. But public opinion seems to be swinging towards a new *modus operandi* that seeks severe restraint on the use of cars in central urban areas rather than providing more road space to accommodate them.

Perhaps some of the public's disquiet concerning urban road building will be met by the Land Compensation Act of 1973. This provides compensation for the effect of highway construction in three ways: in relation to the actual value of the property affected; in relation to the costs of sound insulation; and in relation to the loss of the home i.e. the loss to the house-owner over and above the market value of the house and land.

Group politics

The clearest expression of the reassertion of the primacy of the electorate is the rapid growth of local group politics in addition to the normal producer groups such as Chambers of Commerce, teachers associations, trades councils and so forth. Over the past decade, there has been a remarkable flowering of voluntary group activity at the local level whose purpose is to complement, or improve, the quality of public services by representing the interests and opinions of those who consume the service, or are affected by it.[21] This growth forms part of a much wider change in British politics – the so-called consumer movement. This seems to have its origins partly in public dissatisfaction with the inevitable rigidity of the two-party system in urban areas, but it also seems to be derived from the increasing professionalization of the middle class. This has meant that the middle classes, who supply the bulk of political leadership, have become more critical of public services than in the past. The first reason is that they carry over into the public sector the professional norms they employ in their jobs. In some cases, these are not just norms but precise skills, so that the embarrassing situation can arise where the group is able to command greater expertise than the public authority. Second, the expansion of government responsibility in a wide range of services that previously were bought by the middle class in the private sector has brought them into the political arena. The third reason for the expansion of group politics seems to be the growth of formal education among the general public. All surveys show that it is the extent of full-time education that appears to have the closest link with the propensity to take an interest in, and to participate in, public voluntary activity.[22] More recently, group politics at the local level has developed in a new and more radical direction towards more explicitly egalitarian objectives which reflect an increasing concern about the perpetuation of poverty in central urban areas.[23] It is likely to have its greatest impact on planning in relation to the local plan process, which is directly linked to the growth of compensatory policies designed to combat multiple deprivation, of which more later.

If these are some of the non-planning reasons for the collapse of public faith in the operating ideologies governing the planning of the environment locally, there remain others that are more directly linked to the planning process itself. It is difficult to disentangle all of them but clearly one factor is sheer disenchantment with the results of the planning process that have emerged over the post-war period. In short, performance does not seem to have matched expectations. Whether it ever could is very doubtful since some of the apparent inability of the planning process to produce environments commensurate with the powers exercised is due to the fact that planners have control over only a tiny fraction of the process by which environments are changed. Moreover, the sheer financial costs, given that the planning authority has had to operate for most of the period in a free market for land, have also severely limited the ambit of the planning authority.

There seems to be the least public enthusiasm for one of the most visible products of the planning process, namely, the comprehensive redevelopment scheme, especially for central area shopping and offices where the high-density standardized buildings can reap enormous profits for the developers. At their worst, such schemes sweep away the seedy but unselfconscious spontaneity of the old centres only to replace it with a barrack-like and windswept symbolic environment that lacks any human scale, or any link with the local vernacular architecture. In some of the older towns the wholesale redevelopment of their irreplaceable medieval cores has become something of a national scandal. The other form of comprehensive redevelopment that has evoked strong public displeasure, at least from those most directly affected, is that which involves the destruction of whole neighbourhoods that are not slums but do not meet modern amenity standards. Part of the problem is that, once designated for clearance, the area becomes blighted, with disastrous consequences not just for house values but for the whole environment and the morale of its inhabitants – although the actual redevelopment may take many years to be implemented and may even be rescinded. The effects of blighting can be minimized by careful management; however, the destruction of homes whose occupiers consider them perfectly adequate poses profound problems of individual freedom and brings into question the whole purpose of planning of this kind. This is especially so when the dispossessed face the prospect of being moved to new, higher-rented housing estates remote from main shopping facilities, jobs and family networks.[24]

But whether the specific results of the planning process had been acceptable or not, it seems inherently likely that there would have been increasing public unease with planning generally. This is partly because there will always be a time-lag between new architectural forms and public acceptance of them, and partly because of the increasing tempo of new building and physical change. Not only has there been the new building to meet population growth, and the very long back-log accumulated from various past disinflationary cuts in capital investment, but there has also been the vast house building programme to meet the rapid growth in net household formation. To this must be added the very large number of slum clearance schemes, the widespread rebuilding of city centres and the piecemeal remodelling of the urban road system. All these changes to an urban fabric which has been familiar and evoked a sense of community to generations of inhabitants is bound to induce unease and insecurity, especially in a society that dislikes rapid change of any kind. Moreover, such alterations in land use widen the frontier of potential dissatisfaction precisely because every change afflicts someone and, as we have already noted, it is precisely the affliction of the individual – the widow or the small shopkeeper – that evokes the greatest public interest.

To these tendencies must be added what is perhaps the most decisive source of the public's critical interest in planning: the steadily rising proportion of the population who are owner occupiers. This is now over 50% and it means a growing public sensitivity to physical change, precisely because of the link between house values and alterations in the immediate environment in which the house stands.

Internal relations

Innovation in the internal relations of the planning authority have not been so far-reaching as those that have been made in its relations with the public. But before discussing these changes it might be helpful to briefly sketch in the way in which the local planning authority actually operates. Both the plan-making, and to a lesser extent the planning control processes, are conducted by a partnership of elected councillors and the full-time professional planner. The institutional instrument is the planning committee, which exercises planning powers delegated to it by its parent Council. Practice varies considerably, but usually the committee exercises autonomy for minor decisions and reports all of its major decisions to the full Council and they have to be approved by it before they can be implemented. The Council is the sovereign body and it can and does reject or modify committee decisions. The committee consists of elected councillors advised by the chief planning officer and his senior staff, and possibly other specialists such as the engineer and the town clerk as well. All of the full-time officials, it must be emphasized, are the employees of the

Council. The chief planning officer is usually allowed some discretion over routine decisions but in some councils he has power to decide as much as 50 % of decisions.

Each councillor has a vote in the committee and this means that he may take a direct hand not only in the plan-making process, but also in quite detailed matters of planning control as well. Such direct lay access and the fact that councillors are elected on a fairly small-scale, ward basis means that the councillor often acts as the spokesman for his ward or constituency and for voluntary groups. Most studies show that councillors have well-developed networks of contacts with the groups in their areas. On some committees, but not the planning committee, representatives of group interests are co-opted directly into the decision-making process as fully-fledged members of a functional committee.

Role of the councillor

There is some disparity in the commitment of elected members to their job as councillors, and there are a number of roles they can choose to play. The most obvious distinction that may be drawn, as with any representative assembly, is between those who settle for the role of representing the interests of their ward and individuals within it, and those who want a hand in major policy-making. The first group, the majority, may have an intense interest in particular cases but they are not interested in broad policy, nor in having close relationships with the full-time professional specialists. The second group are less interested in individual case-work and more interested in evolving policy objectives; of filling the executive role which, under the British local government system, has no formal constitutional existence and has to be created informally, mainly via the party system and through the budget-making and investment programming of the finance committee. The most important groups among the councillors who are mainly interested in high policy matters are the committee chairmen who direct the business of the committees and control their agenda.

Whatever labels one gives these two categories of councillor – parochials and metropolitans, or backbenchers and ministerialists – the distinction is an important one in planning for it is ministerialists who tend to take the most interest in the plan-making process, whereas the parochials' gaze tends to be firmly fixed on planning control. But this picture may be considerably modified by the type of authority under consideration. In the rural and semi-rural areas, the distinction is at its sharpest, because the settlement pattern is such as to powerfully underscore the back-bench or parochial role and detach most individual councillors, except committee chairmen, from broad policy-making except when it impinges directly on their own town or village. Moreover, their opportunities for making an impact on government generally are less because the distances to be travelled mean that the formal meetings of the committee and of the Council are necessarily much less frequent than in urban areas. However, the county ministerialists – who often form a kind of informal cabinet led by the chairman of council – maintain a much more continuous and direct hand in the decision-making process. In addition, the political system in rural areas is almost always non-partisan so that the ministerialist group can become an entrenched, self-perpetuating oligarchy whose position is reinforced in the deeply rural shires by the fact that elections are seldom contested. Such is the nature of rural society that this tends to ensure that those who enjoy a high social status – what has been called the squirearchy – dominate committee chairmanships.

The urban areas, by contrast, are usually rigidly partisan and are run along lines that mirror the two-party system nationally. Intra-party democracy requires that major policy issues are aired in party group meetings and possibly voted on, but once policy has been agreed, party discipline is usually enforced if the policy is opposed by the minority party. Without any formal institutional reinforcement, however, the party leadership performs an executive role by consent and this means that individual councillors always retain ultimate power. Their wish to do so has become more insistent in recent years because individual councillors have themselves become subject to the same grassroots pressures described earlier. Intra-party democracy has become, then, increasingly important in moderating the inclinations of the ministerialists for a more dominant role. The whims of the electorate, of course, can also have a similar, though more decisive, effect.

The autonomy of the full-time professional planner can be severely circumscribed by the elected element, especially by the ministerialists. The extent to which it is circumscribed will depend on a number of factors including the political strength of the majority party, its sense of purpose and the sheer personal will of the full-time professional. In so far as it is possible to capture the nuances of the relationship in a single word, it is essentially a partnership, and a partnership that is reinforced by two factors operating from opposite directions. First, the officer, like all professional experts in government, is subject to the law of anticipated reactions; he is bound to frame his advice within what he sees as the limits, both ideological and political, constraining the politicians. Second, the vertical character of the committee system, untrammelled as it is by any formal horizontal executive (like the French mayor) generates among politicians, and especially the ministerialists, a sense of corporate specialist identity with the full-time official which cuts across party loyalties. One of the tasks of the party as a collectivity is to ensure that this competing loyalty does not get out of hand. One way of achieving this is by allocating party members to more than one committee, occasional re-shuffling of the membership of committees and regular meetings of the party group.

There are fairly clear broad differences in party attitudes towards planning: the Labour party, for example, is much more sympathetic to the idea that governments should plan and especially that it should plan land use. The party has therefore always favoured the strengthening of the town planning powers of government and has been hostile to private profit in land values, particularly values generated by public policy. It is, indeed, the architect of much of the existing land-use planning legislation and of national policies such as those for New Towns and National Parks. The Conservatives, on the other hand, are much more reluctant to extend public power and have no hostility to private profit accruing from changes in land use. On the crucial question of land values they successively curtailed the powers of government during the 1950s, stopped the creation of any more New Towns until the 'return to planning' in the early 1960s, and rapidly dismantled the Land Commission which was the Labour party's second attempt to cope with the betterment problem.

This simple picture requires some modification, however. The effect of specialist loyalties generated by the committee system in moderating those of party has already been mentioned; to this must be added the strong preservationist attitudes which, as we noted earlier, cut right across British society and therefore the major parties. In rural areas the squirearchy, whatever their predilections about the role of government in other matters, will normally favour a draconian exercise of public power to curb the outward expansion of urban centres. Indeed, in the outer suburban and quasi-rural areas, a rigid application of planning control coincides with the preservation and enhancement of house values, if not land values: in these areas collectivism and self-interest may be happily joined.

Also, on aesthetic questions such as architectural design and unsightliness – which tend to dominate decisions in the day to day exercise of planning control on individual applications – the decision often turns on the visual consciousness and sense of aesthetic values of the politicians, and a middle-class Conservative may be just as likely to favour the maximum exercise of public control as a working-class socialist. Equally, in the socialist camp there has been a growing disillusionment with the actual outcome of the planning process which parallels the disillusionment among the public generally mentioned earlier. But socialist disillusionment has a sharper edge, precisely because what was supposed to have been the application of egalitarian principle to land allocation appears in practice to have lined the pockets of developers and broken up working-class communities. There is perhaps a certain naïveté about this reaction, since the instruments of control that the planning system places in the hands of government can be used just as easily for maintaining the *status quo* as for changing it; perhaps *more* easily, given the prevailing conservationist climate of opinion. At all events, socialist dissatisfaction with the existing system, particularly in relation to land values, is such that some form of out-right nationalization of land ripe for development is now canvassed as a serious possibility. In short, any discussion of party attitudes to planning has to take into account the fact that the land-use planning process in Britain has always had 'a streak of ambivalence' in the sense that it promises all things to all men – the preservation of the past and the control of the future.[25]

Status of professional planners

The new land-use planning system ushered in by the 1968 Act demands new skills, both in terms of techniques and in terms of supplementing the curriculum of traditional planning training with material drawn from the academic disciplines of sociology, economics and statistics. Another way of achieving the same objective is the direct recruitment of sociologists and economists into planning departments. Both approaches are being made, but it must be emphasized that they are organized from within the profession itself.[26] Because the local planning authorities are virtually the only operational planning agencies, the weight of planning expertise tends to lie with local government. The central government does have planning staffs of its own but they are relatively few in number and necessarily somewhat remote from the actual processes of planning 'at the coal face'. It has no outstationed planning staffs other than the inspectorate, who are of course an important factor in providing the centre with eyes and ears, and the small planning staffs of the Regional Economic Planning Boards at the regional level. This means that the planning profession as a whole is overwhelmingly dominated by planners working in local government. The profession, although not as powerful as some of the other local government professions is, nonetheless, a national special-ist community controlling via its national organization (the Royal Town Planning Institute) its own conditions of entry, and playing the predominant part in the character and extent of planning education and training. Its corporate strength is reinforced by the fact that, outside the very largest local authorities, there is a national career structure with planners moving up the ladder by moving from one local authority to another.

Central government can, of course, do a great deal to influence the speed and the direction of change since it determines the legislation which underpins the change. It can also assist by providing the money for setting up new training centres; it can mount official investigations, and it can cajole and persuade by ministerial announcements and departmental circulars. But it would find it extremely difficult to interpose a new agency at the local level, as seems to be the case in France, or create new professional cadres to achieve the desired effect. The nearest that the British system gets to such an approach is the Joint Team discussed earlier and the New Town Development Corporation. As we noted earlier, ultimately, change has normally to take place within the profession itself and within the local government system in which it works.

Planning as management

The broadening of the ambit of land-use planning under the 1968 Act so as to comprehend the given local area, not just as a mosaic of different land uses, but as a socio-economic process, inevitably projects it into the orbit of most of the other major service departments at the local level. This change coincides with another innovation that is gradually taking place within the general management structure of local authorities. This is the attempt to integrate all policy-making into a single coherent system of 'management by objectives' which entails the subordination of all the specialist departments to a single policy-making executive. This change has its origins in private business practice and theory that has acquired the generic title of corporate management. At its most extreme it entails the abolition of the committee system and the creation of a horizontal executive board which would make all major policy decisions at the apex of the decision-making structure.[27] This pure form of the model is unlikely to be adopted; first, because it would mean that the power of the individual backbencher would be severely diminished, and secondly, because the growth of grassroots pressures has already been undermining such centralized power as already exists. However, over the past five years or so there has been a growing recognition among some local authorities of the need for total resource allocation over a longer time-period than the fiscal year, for matrix management techniques – e.g. project planning that cuts across departmental boundaries – and for the strengthening of the position of the clerk as a generalist manager. These changes have entailed a reduction in the number of committees, some manipulation of the committee system so as to give it the semblance of a decision-making hierarchy, and the redesignation of the clerk as chief executive officer. The latest official report on these matters – the Bains Report[28] – makes detailed suggestion for this modified, and therefore more acceptable, centralization of the decision-making process. The greater opportunities for innovation afforded by the new structure of local government which came into force in April 1974 has given a strong impetus to this trend, and most of the new authorities seem to be establishing the institutional trappings of the Bains model. That it is only the trappings of the model that are being adopted must be emphasized. A complete adoption is impossible without a fundamental redistribution of political power such that a formal separate political executive is created which would give reality to the new role of the clerk as the chief executive heading up all the specialist chief officers, and coordinating the activities of the separate departments. The Bains model, in short, ignores the fact that it presupposes a political command structure. Great faith has therefore been placed in what has been called a community plan. This is an overall strategy in the corporate management style that attempts to look at the community embraced by the local authority as a total entity, involving all public services, and lays down a series of policy objectives to be achieved over a given time-span. The hope is, apparently, that the adoption of an overall strategy of this kind will by itself somehow invest the chief executive with the necessary authority and contain the tendency to departmentalism that is inherent in the present system.

Since one of the primary aims of the new planning process, as we noted earlier, is to achieve a much broader ambit and because land use underpins most substantive policy decisions taken by local authorities at some stage, there has been some speculation as to the proper place of land-use planning under a corporate management structure, especially one that attempts to formulate a community plan. In short, will the new land-use planning process remain as it is now, a distinct departmental line function like housing or highways, or will it become a staff element within some – as yet undefined – executive arm?

If we ignore for a moment the fact that no executive arm is likely within the foreseeable future, for the reasons touched on a moment ago, the answer to this question will depend to a very large extent on how far the synoptic function of the new planning process can be divorced from the substantive plan implementation process. At first sight such a divorce poses few problems, since the new county is now responsible for the overall structure plan and the new district now controls the vast bulk of the plan implementation process. The district is now also responsible for the more detailed application of the overall plan in particular localities via the local plans. However, experience in London (where the local government system was modernized on similar lines in 1965) suggests that divorcing plan-making from plan-implementation seriously undermines the ability of the plan-making authority to fulfil its task. There are a number of reasons for this, but primarily it is because the emphasis on the flexibility of means makes it essential that the implementation process should also be in the hands of the plan maker. In any case the immediate prospects for the full integration of land-use planning with some corporate management structure are problematic because there are strong professional rivalries involved, not merely between the planners and the putative chief executive, but also between him and other professional groups who feel similarly threatened.

There are, however, other potential threats to the autonomy of the land-use planner. One of the most important of these comes from the emerging profession of transportation planning. The traditional road engineers are acquiring new skills and a new role as the traffic problem bulks larger within the urban planning process. Transportation planning may have a potential advantage in relation to the politician, if not the public at large, because it has a more immediate, direct and more visible output. It may also have a vital intellectual advantage in inter-professional controversy over planning policy issues because it is able to frame its objectives in terms of ostensibly measurable effects. Traffic flows, congestion costs and modal splits can be quantified; amenity, bad layout and unsightliness cannot. The decision to require the new counties to draw up a separate transportation plan (the TPP mentioned earlier) may also tend to enhance the position of transportation. Official backing for the recognition of transport planning as having equal importance with traditional land-use planning within the environmental planning field was given in the Buchanan Report of 1962 and is explicit in the new structure planning process. It was also recognized institutionally when the central land-use and transportation functions were combined under the DoE in 1970. The latest and most extreme exposition of this view is to be found in the Sharp Report which stated:

Land use and transport planning are inseparable...Ideally the two should go hand in hand...the people engaged in transport planning should be interchangeable with those engaged in land use planning and that what is really at issue is the development of a corps of people with a wide variety of education, training and experience at work in the whole spectrum of environmental planning, and to be members of a single society in which all can meet to discuss their common problems.[29]

However, the rising star of transportation planning may be to some extent obscured by increasing public dissatisfaction with the current professional orthodoxies of the transportation planners derived from the Buchanan Report that was noted earlier. The Buchanan doctrine of meeting the growth of vehicular traffic by a balanced expansion of urban road space that at the same time maintained traditional town-planning notions of layout and design may give way to a policy of severe restraint on vehicle access to city centres and to the reassertion of the 'amenity' and the preservationist values of traditional town planning. Recent decisions by the secretary of state for the environment that severely curtail the London motorway building programme and the decision by a number of city councils up and down the country not to go ahead with plans to build inner city relief roads, suggest that this shift in emphasis is already happening. If this trend continues, the prospects of the land-use planners retaining their autonomy unimpaired are, of course, that much rosier.

Another problem the land-use planning profession faces in relation to its professional autonomy is linked to the new development just described in the field of corporate management and the community plan. This is the claim that the present planning process, even the new, more broadly based structure planning, should give way to an even more comprehensive approach that has been called social planning. Some of the discussion of the objectives of social planning is often of the haziest character and this may be due in part to the fact that some of its ideas have been borrowed from American experience where the context in which land-use planning operates and its historical development seem to be radically different. In their most banal form these objectives appear to be reducible to the maxim 'planning is for people' and, undoubtedly, good intentions have sometimes tended to obscure clarity of thought.[30] However, this does not apply to all the discussion of social planning and perhaps the best short definition has been given by Eversley who defines social planning as 'the total effort by all agencies to achieve changes in the physical environment and in the economic and social structure which exists within that environment, in pursuit of improvements in the living standards of an urban population'.[31]

The last line of this definition is important, for it reveals at least one of the main contributory threads that led up to the plea for social planning. Very briefly, this is the growing concern in Britain for the social problems of the inner city which dates from the Milner-Holland Report on London housing.[32] The particular focus of this concern is the continuing persistence in these areas of large concentrations of the poor, who have very narrow job opportunities and subsist in an outworn physical environment. Each aspect reinforces the other to perpetuate a society of multiple deprivation. In one sense the plea for social planning is also a plea for land-use planning to return to its conceptual origins, for it began very largely as an environmental response to the conditions of the urban poor at the end of the last century. The New Town concept is perhaps the most explicit manifestation of this aspect of the tradition, and on occasion land-use planners have been accused of being too interested in the social consequences of land-use planning. One example of this is the accusation that they have sometimes been seduced by a form of architectural determinism that sees physical layout as a means of changing social relationships. It may be concluded then, that in so far as the demand for social planning seeks to engage land-use planning more actively with the social consequences of the planning process, nothing fundamentally new is being demanded. What is perhaps more novel, at least in the British context, is the aspect of the demand for social planning that seeks to separate out the substantive, line aspects of land-use planning and make social planning a central feature of the overall policy process. Any kind of aesthetic design or amenity aims would be discarded, and the central objectives would be largely economic so as to root the planning process in measurable effects.

The cumulative result of the various encroachments so far described is that the land-use planning profession, which in any case has yet to achieve full recognition as a public profession of the first rank, has developed a certain sense of insecurity and may be even more sensitive than usual to any loss of professional autonomy. We have already discussed public disaffection with planning, which is probably a further factor affecting the profession's sense of security; another is that it has yet to develop either a very refined conceptual tool-kit or much in the way of a private language – the two essential elements for creating a professional 'mystery'.[33] Moreover, it has yet to wholly slough off its amateur origins. The demand for social planning is also motivated by a desire to cure these ills and there is another school of reformers who seek to achieve the same ends by pinning their hopes on the injection of systems analysis into the planners' technical equipment.[34] Hovering over most of these attempts to fully professionalize land-use planning is the belief that professional self-respect can only be achieved by freeing it from any value content. It is instructive, however, that one of the more influential groups in the planning world – the Town and Country Planning Association – remains obstinately open to outsiders and is still dominated by amateurs and academics.

The reason why land-use planning has yet to achieve first rank status in local government on a par, say, with the treasurer, or the education director, is that some local authorities have never acknowledged the need for a fully-fledged independent land-use planning department, and the land-use planning function is often in a subordinate position to other services. In some authorities under the old local government system, it formed part of the general policy-making functions, such as they were, of the clerk. In others, the planning function was absorbed by existing environmental specialisms such as those of the engineer or surveyor. In both cases this was made possible because planning is a relatively new major function, without any statutory requirement that a chief planning officer and committee be appointed, this being the traditional method whereby a new function establishes itself within the local government system and its practitioners acquire status. Even in the recent reorganization in London, only eleven of the thirty-three London boroughs created a separate planning department with its own chief planning officer.[35]

In these circumstances it seems likely that the planning profession would prefer to incorporate the need to integrate policy-making, and to recognize the transportation and social consequences of physical planning, into its own operating ideology rather than surrender ground to rival specialists. Certainly the attitude of the Royal Town Planning Institute with its insistence on maintaining a generalist education for planners supports this view.

Relations between levels of government

Central government

Undoubtedly the whole notion of planning, land-use or economic, has a centralizing effect on government. The more activities governments attempt to plan the more power they need. Under the existing land-use planning legislation, central government has clearly enhanced its planning role from the moment the present planning machinery was established during and after the Second World War. This is because it had to approve development plans and act in a quasi-judicial capacity while developing important national land-use policies in its own right, notably the New Towns and the National Parks. But the actual operational responsibilities are undertaken by decentralized bodies, in the case of the New Towns by public corporations and in the case of the National Parks by special *ad hoc* authorities or by local government.

Until the emergence of the Joint Team regional planning strategy,[36] the New Towns were by far the most important aspect of the central government's more direct role in land-use planning. Having decided on the site and having designated the area, central government hands over operational responsibility to a development corporation run by a board of up to seven members appointed by the secretary of state for the environment. The corporation owns the land and is responsible for the bulk of building and may sometimes undertake capital projects – such as water supply and sewerage – that are normally the responsibility of local government. Other than this overlap and the fact that the local authority may be responsible for some of the housing in the New Town, the corporation is wholly independent of local government. The corporation derives all its capital finance from central government in the form of loans at prevailing interest rates, and central government exercises close control over the corporation's development programme and has to approve all individual major development proposals. When the New Town reaches its target population, the corporation is wound up and its considerable assets, both in land and buildings, most of the value of which the corporation has created, are transferred to a permanent body (the New Towns Commission) which is part of central government. The Commission then undertakes the management of these assets.[37]

Both the New Towns and the National Parks reflect the application of the very broad national land-use planning objectives of preserving areas of outstanding natural beauty, decongesting major urban centres – especially London – rehabilitating obsolete industrial areas and, more recently, generating new economic growth centres. These policies apart, central government was very slow to develop its potential powers as a national land-use planner. Logically, of course, it should have developed its national planning capacities before land-use planning was established at the local level but, in practice, given the need to establish an effective planning machine throughout the country fairly rapidly, it tended to abjure logic in favour of the somewhat less demanding tasks of control, inspection and review. These functions comprise the traditional role of central government in Britain, which, in marked contrast to France, seldom takes operational responsibility for public services, relying instead on agents in the form of local government, public corporations or a myriad of quasi-independent boards and councils.

There were, however, sub-regional plans for particular areas that were adopted by central government before the advent of effective land-use planning locally. The most important of these was the Abercrombie plan for Greater London which was published in 1944. But other than in these areas, there has been no systematic attempt to provide a wider framework within which the local authority plans could be either determined or assessed until the Joint Team approach was established in the late 1960s. This meant that in its formative period land-use planning was mainly, as one observer has put it, 'a system hitched largely to local efforts involving manipulation of land uses on the basis of relatively cursory and intuitive information about the phenomena they were supposed to guide'.[38]

There is one new feature of central government's direct role in the planning field which perhaps deserves mention. It forms part of a broader trend in central government policy which has been called 'positive discrimination'. Broadly speaking, this policy, like the plea for social planning mentioned a moment ago, is mainly aimed at combatting the multiple deprivation of the inner city area inhabitants by channelling extra funds for a wide range of social and welfare services over and above that already provided by the existing public agencies, both central and local.

Positive discrimination has taken a number of forms and emanates from a number of central departments. The most extensive is the Education Priority Area Programme, which aims at improving the educational opportunities of school children mainly in inner city areas. There is also the Urban Programme, which is more directly related to planning since it seeks to provide for a whole range of public services and in 1973 had a budget of £10 million covering twelve Community Development Projects. Closer still to the environmental planning function is the Urban Studies Project which comes directly under the Department of the Environment. These are surveys sponsored by the Department that are being conducted by management consultants in six towns. The main aim of three of the surveys (those in Sunderland, Rotherham and Oldham[39]) is to provide guidelines for local authorities for the adoption of the 'total approach' to policy-making, and forms part of the shift towards the adoption of corporate management techniques in local decision-making touched on earlier. The other three studies (those in Lambeth, Birmingham and Liverpool) are more directly linked to the problem of multiple deprivation.

In so far as they have developed, neither the regional economic planning process (which began in 1964 and has remained dormant if not actually moribund since 1969) nor the regional-cum-national land-use planning process already described seem to have had any impact on traditional legislative and executive relations at the national level. This is partly because, in Britain, parliament has very little legislative power in the conventional sense, executive and legislative initiative being very largely concentrated in the Cabinet. But the main reason why the planning process has not affected legislative–executive relationships is that it has in no respect infringed the traditional role of parliament. Indeed, one of the problems of the land-use planning system at the central level is that the minister's quasi-judicial decision-making role in relation to planning appeals, the approving of plans and 'call ins' has meant that he is answerable for these decisions to parliament. The minister and parliament thus constitute an additional avenue for those objecting to local planning decisions to pursue their objections and obtain redress. The result of such centralization is long delays, possible frustration for the local planning authority, and above all, the clogging of the central government machine. With the translation of the Regional Economic Planning Boards into deconcentrated agents of the central planning department, some of the quasi-judicial functions at present exercised by the minister will be undertaken by the regional director in consultation with the Board. Other

more minor decisions will be settled by the inspector. In theory the
burden on central government will therefore be considerably eased. As
was intended, the new structure planning system should have a
similar result since a broad policy statement is easier to assess by the
centre than a detailed development plan, and the general public will
have no automatic access to structure plan examinations nor any right
of appeal to the minister from local plan enquiries. However, the very
rapid increase in planning appeals in recent years noted earlier has
swamped what gains might have been achieved by these institutional
changes, and despite an increase in the number of inspectors by 60%,
the delays in settling appeals are longer than ever.[40] In any case, it
would be imprudent to exaggerate the extent to which the new
planning process will speed up the system, since the first experiment in
structure planning – albeit one that was adapted from the old system –
has been excessively protracted. This is the Greater London Development Plan (GLDP) which began life in 1965, was completed in 1969
and has yet to be approved, if it is ever approved.[41]

At the local planning level quite significant changes in the relationships between levels of government may take place in the immediate
future. Once the Joint Team regional strategy is approved in each
region, the margin of choice open to the county planning authorities in
formulating their structure plans could be considerably narrowed, due
to the pre-existence of the Joint Team regional strategy. At the other
level of the local land-use planning system, the districts (which are now
fairly large and powerful authorities, usually with populations above
100,000) will, through the exercise of the bulk of planning control and
of the local plan-making function, be able to exert considerable
influence on the county over planning issues which the district considers are crucial to its own well-being. Experience of the London
system (which has been in operation for almost a decade) strongly
suggests that the combination of a regional strategy emanating from
above and a strong, assertive district planning authority below makes it
difficult for the intermediate authority to find a very effective place
within the planning system.[42] But whether the London experience is
relevant or not (and it is likely to be more relevant for the metropolitan counties than elsewhere), some price will have to be paid, in
terms of delay and caution by the county, for splitting land-use planning between the two authorities. The instrument designed to keep
this price as low as possible during the initial stage until the structure
plan is adopted is the Development Plan Scheme, which is a programme setting out the order and priority for drawing up and
implementing the local plans. It is formulated jointly by the county and
district, and submitted to the secretary of state for information. The
strong possibility of tension between county and district over the long

term will, of course, remain and is endemic to the new structure, hence the central government's strong emphasis on the need for cooperation between district and county.[43]

Regionalisation

The creation of regional economic planning bodies in 1964 reflected the need to integrate economic planning with land-use planning. It was at the level of the newly designated Economic Planning Region that the links had to be forged joining the vertical sector planning forming part of the National Economic Plan – the allocation of factors over time – with the horizontal planning of land use – the distribution of factors in space. The REPBs and REPCs were the first attempt to give this link comprehensive institutional expression. The abandonment of the National Plan in 1966 and the progressive decline in interest in national economic planning has meant that land-use plans have had little more than a ghost to integrate with. The only integration that has taken place since then is exemplified by the planning strategy expounded by the Joint Team for the South-East region. Obviously the economic content of each strategy will vary from region to region, but if the first is any guide, they appear to be mainly a broad gauge form of traditional land-use planning that has taken on board a much wider range of largely economic and transportation considerations in its rationale. It was still mainly concerned with the land-use question of decongesting Greater London by moving people and jobs to other areas in the South-East, but it did introduce the notion of zones of development which would exploit existing capital investment in rail and road communications, and it was related to economic factors external to the region.

There is another aspect of the planning system at the regional level that merits discussion in this context. This is the possibility of complementing the REPBs by some kind of representative body that would replace the REPCs and act as an executive agency for the regional strategy Teams. The minister for local government has already described the Teams as 'an interim administration of government' and a regional representative planning body was proposed by the Redcliffe–Maud Commission which was the most recent full-scale inquiry into the deficiencies of local government structure.[44] Any decision on this recommendation, however, was postponed until yet another official inquiry, the Commission on the Constitution under the chairmanship of Lord Kilbrandon, reported. This latter inquiry was set up in the wake of the upsurge in nationalist sentiment in Scotland and Wales in 1968–9. As a consequence, it saw its primary task as being to examine ways in which the existing unitary system of national government might be fundamentally changed so as to devolve power on a regional basis and thus assuage nationalist dissatisfaction. The Kilbrandon Commission published its report in November 1973,[45] and most of its members were agreed that some transfer of power to Scotland and Wales was desirable, but they differed as to the extent of such a transfer and to the extent of devolution within England. A majority of the eleven signatories of the majority report favoured the creation of legislative assemblies for Scotland and Wales and strategic planning advisory councils in the eight English planning regions. The powers of the latter follow closely the Redcliffe–Maud pattern. A minority report by two members of the commission is much more devolutionary in intent and advocates what amounts to the devolution of most of the day to day executive responsibilities of central government to seven directly elected regional councils (one each for Scotland and Wales and five for England) which would also have independent revenue-raising powers.

If either of these models is adopted, whatever their merits on other grounds, it would raise serious problems for any future regional economic growth policies. This is because one of the primary objectives of such growth policies is to formulate different priorities in each region to suit their varying economic circumstances. This must be a redistributive process, and it therefore demands an increase in the exercise of power at the centre in order to give it effect. The initial behaviour of the REPCs suggests, however, that a representative regional body in the prosperous regions would stoutly resist any attempt to siphon off investment that would have occurred in its region had there been no economic planning. The intermediate regions likewise would bend every effort to become designated as poor regions. Although naturally willing to be net gainers, even the poor regions would be very unlikely to accept without resistance the intra-regional pattern of investment that the central government might see as the most appropriate. In other words, regional growth policy attempts to achieve a more rational distribution of factors than would have been achieved by the market, but it also generates a sense of regional consciousness – a new and officially sanctioned focus for a latent sense of deprivation in the poorer regions. This has the effect of turning the original purposes of the exercise on its head, and regional policy becomes another political lever for channelling public and private investment to the poorer regions irrespective of its implication for promoting growth nationally.

If *elected* regional bodies are introduced, it seems likely that this process would be even more marked for, such is the geographical distribution of support for the two major parties, some regions are almost certain to have a well-entrenched majority of the party that is in a minority nationally.[45]

This leads us to one of the most interesting changes that regionalised economic growth policy is likely to have wrought on the political process. The introduction of a 'rational' policy designed to replace the 'irrationality' of the market may end up by supporting, and perhaps even generating, a new 'irrational' system; that of a regional politics which may in turn defeat the whole purpose of the exercise. This unintended effect is perhaps most evident in Scotland and Wales, but it could become important in the poorer regions of England. It is perhaps linked to the malaise that afflicts land-use planning and to the continued growth of government generally. Once planning becomes a public function it soon raises public expectations; what was designed to 'solve' a problem in practice generates a new set of problems for government to cope with. As the protagonists of the new land-use planning process never tire of reminding us, planning is a continuous process.

NOTES

1 The author wishes to express special thanks to Derek Senior and Dr Stanley Vince, who read this chapter and suggested a number of changes that greatly improved it.

2 Quoted in J. B. Cullingworth, *Town and Country Planning in England and Wales,* Allen and Unwin, London 1964, p. 18.

3 See W. Ashworth, *The Genesis of Modern British Town Planning,* Routledge, London 1954, for a discussion of the early development of town planning in Britain, and *Town and Country Planning, 1943–1951,* Cmd. 8204, HMSO 1951, for an account of the crucial post-war period.

4 P. Hall, 'Land Use – the Spread of Towns into Country' in M. Young (ed), *Forecasting and the Social Sciences,* Heinemann, London 1968, p. 95.

5 Scotland and Northern Ireland have different systems of local government, which are also in the process of reorganization; this paper will be confined to England and Wales.

6 *The Minister of Town and Country Planning Act (Transfer of Powers) Order,* 1943.

7 Circular 142/73, Department of the Environment.

8 *Local Government in England – Government Proposals for Reorganisation,* Cmnd. 4584, HMSO 1971.

9 *Town and Country Planning,* Cmnd. 3333, 1967.

10 *The Future of Development Plans: A Report of the Planning Advisory Group,* HMSO 1965. For a detailed description of the planning process inaugurated by the 1968 Act see *Development Plans: A Manual on Form and Content,* HMSO 1970.

11 See *Greater London Development Plan: the Report of the Panel of Inquiry* (Layfield), I, chapter 2, for a discussion of the problems of overambition and ambiguity.

12 The chairman of the West Midlands Team is not a civil servant, but this seems to be because combined operations between central and local government in pursuit of a regional strategy were begun before the Joint Team technique had been evolved.

13 See P. Hall *et al, The Containment of Urban England,* I, chapter 3, for a discussion of the importance of the planning movement in the emergence of land-use planning as a public function.

14 *The Committee on the Training of Planners: Report,* HMSO 1950.

15 Donald L. Foley, 'British Town Planning: One Ideology or Three' in A. Faludi (ed), *A Reader in Planning Theory,* Pergamon Press, Oxford 1973, p. 73.

16 There are also inquiries into appeals against refusals by the planning authority of individual planning applications. These are mainly designed to protect private interests, but they also

provide the opportunity for individuals affected (including third parties) to comment on and criticize a particular aspect of planning policy as it relates to specific applications.

17 *People and Planning*, HMSO 1969.

18 Circular 52/72. Department of the Environment.

19 See P. Levin and D. Donnison, 'People and Planning', *Public Administration*, XLVII, Winter 1969, for some suggestions on improving the Skeffington proposals.

20 *Report of the Committee on Traffic: Traffic in Towns*, HMSO 1963.

21 See M. Broady, *Planning for People*, Bedford Square Press, London 1968.

22 See *Report of the Royal Commission on Local Government in England*, III, appendix 7, Cmnd. 4040, HMSO 1969.

23 See D. Donnison, 'Micro-politics of the City' in D. Donnison and D. Eversley (eds), *London: Urban Patterns, Problems and Policies*, Heinemann, London 1973.

24 See M. Dennis, *Public Participation and Planners Blight*, Faber and Faber, London 1972 and J. Gower Davies, *The Evangelistic Bureaucrat*, Tavistock, London 1972, for highly critical accounts of the kind of comprehensive redevelopment in Sunderland and Newcastle.

25 Ruth Glass 'The Evaluation of Planning: Some Sociological Considerations', in A. Faludi, *A Reader in Planning Theory*.

26 See D. Diamond and J. B. McLoughlin (eds), *Education for Planning*, Pergamon Press, London 1973, for a discussion of the implications of the new planning process for the education and training of planners.

27 For example, the proposals in the *Report of the Committee on the Management of Local Government*, I, HMSO 1967.

28 *The New Local Authorities – Management and Structure*, HMSO 1972.

29 *Transport Planning: the Men for the Job*, HMSO 1970.

30 See, for example, J. A. D. Palmer's introduction to R. Goodman, *After the Planners*, Penguin Books, London 1972.

31 D. Eversley 'Problems of Social Planning in Inner London' in Donnison and Eversley, *London: Urban Patterns*, pp. 4–5. Also see D. Eversley, *The Planners in Society*, Faber and Faber, London 1973, chapter 6, for a more detailed elaboration of social planning.

32 *Report of the Committee on Housing in Greater London*, Cmnd. 2605, HMSO 1965.

33 See Lincoln Allison, 'Politics, Welfare and Conservation: A Survey of Meta-Planning', *British Journal of Political Science*, I, Part 4, 1971, for an interesting and original explanation of some of the underlying presuppositions of British land-use planning.

34 See G. Chadwick, *A Systems View of Planning: Towards a Theory of the Urban and Regional Planning Process*, Pergamon Press, Oxford 1971.

35 P. Self, *Metropolitan Planning*, Greater London Paper No. 14, London School of Economics, London 1971, p. 34.

36 *Strategic Plan for the South East*, Report of the South-East Joint Planning Team, HMSO 1970.

37 See F. Schaffer, *The New Town Story*, Paladin, London 1970, for an historical account of the New Towns policy.

38 L. Rodwin, *Nations and Cities*, Houghton Mifflin, Boston 1970, p. 120.

39 All three were completed in 1973 and are published by the DoE. The most comprehensive of the three is the Sunderland Study which appears in two volumes: *1. A Basic Handbook*, and *2. A Working Guide*.

40 Circular 142/73. Department of the Environment.

41 The Plan was reviewed by an expert Panel of Inquiry whose voluminous Report is remarkably outspoken about the shortcomings of the GLDP and also casts some doubts on the feasibility of the structure plan process as well. See *GLDP Report of the Panel of Inquiry*, I, HMSO 1973.

42 Self, *Metropolitan Planning*, chapter 7.

43 See Department of the Environment Circulars 131/72 and 74/73.

44 *Royal Commission on Local Government in England, Report*, I, chapter 10.

45 *Royal Commission on the Constitution Report*, Cmnd. 5460, HMSO 1973.

46 For a more detailed discussion of this problem see L. J. Sharpe, 'British Politics and the Two Regionalisms' in W. Wright and D. Stewart (eds) *The Exploding Cities*, Edinburgh University Press, Edinburgh 1972.

SELECT BIBLIOGRAPHY

Cullingworth, J. B. *Town and Country Planning in England and Wales*, 4th edn, Allen and Unwin, London 1972.
Faludi, A. *A Reader in Planning Theory*, Pergamon Press, Oxford 1973.
Hall, P. *et al*, *The Containment of Urban England*, II, *The Planning System: Objectives, Operations and Impacts*, Allen and Unwin, London 1973.
Schaffer, F. *The New Town Story*, Paladin, London 1970.

17. Land-use planning in Italy

ATTILIO BASTIANINI AND GIULIANO URBANI[1]

Land-use planning in Italy is extremely complex because the bodies involved are a mixture of the old and the new, because goals are confused and often overlap and because decision-making is often slow and unwieldy. The dynamic of the changes taking place and the importance of innovations can only be appreciated if one knows something of their history, and if one makes a clear distinction between urban planning and territorial or spatial planning. Clearly, there are close connections between urban planning and territorial planning and we are only emphasising this distinction for the purpose of examining the principal changes affecting land-use planning associated with the introduction of an economic planning policy. Nevertheless, territorial planning in the broad sense should be distinguished from urban planning in the strict sense in Italy. Urban planning means regulating the ways in which land can be used, with special regard to the problem of private and public land on the one hand and to town building programmes on the other. Territorial planning, however, is concerned with inter-city social and economic problems and with the spatial dimension as an element to be considered in economic planning.

Historically, territorial planning in Italy has been conditioned to a large extent by urban planning in the strict sense. This meant that a complex network of bodies were set up to decide on urban planning. They considered the more general problems of territorial planning to be secondary. Evidence of a change in tendency has been recent. Perhaps economic planning has been an important factor determining this change, but there are other important reasons. The rate at which land is being used up and the increased volume of inter-city communications have shown that land-use planning affects economic development, so territorial planning is now considered a fundamental element of national and regional economic planning. Naturally, for these innovations to become a proper policy, the public authorities must change both their attitudes and the laws about land.

This paper examines the problems connected with land-use planning in Italy and shows how and why it is difficult to change the

[358]

present situation. The first part concentrates on relevant institutions and procedures and the second part on how the planning process works in practice.

Institutional changes concerning land-use planning

The most significant change in the bodies concerned with land-use planning was brought about by the final establishment of the regions in May 1970. This reform, which we shall consider later, did not supplant the bodies already in existence and they are still in fact the dominant ones. There are two important points about land-use planning prior to the regional reform. Firstly, only urban planning was effective while territorial planning was almost completely absent. Secondly, land-use planning in Italy can only be understood if one bears in mind certain relevant laws, e.g. the laws favouring cheap popular housing. These laws have played a major part in determining planning in the country as a whole.[2]

The basic law of 1942, which with recent amendments still regulates land-use planning in Italy, was the first attempt to systematise relevant standards, institutions and financial procedures. Because of the war and the years of reconstruction this Act was not applied until 1954, when the first lists of boroughs which had to submit plans for the areas within their control were drawn up.[3] The setting-up of the regions has so far only meant that responsibility for supervising urban planning has been transferred, together with the relevant personnel, from central government while the provisions of basic urban planning law remain unchanged. The 1942 Act was designed to encourage both territorial and urban planning. It provides for a complex of plans with different controls according to size (from the neighbourhood unit right up to plans for the whole region) and according to content. Territorial planning is expressed in plans for coordinating spatial development (*piani territoriali di coordinamento*), which are made the executive responsibility of central government. These plans give wide-ranging general directives and coordinate local plans. The local authorities are obliged to observe these directives. To coordinate the development of neighbouring municipalities, the law provides for 'joint town plans' (*piani regolatori intercomunali*).[4] The procedures for joint town plans are very complex and none of these plans have ever been approved. Basically, plans are drawn up by each municipality and are then submitted to the Ministry of Public Works, which must approve them all as if they were a single plan. As regards urban planning in the strict sense, the law specifies three separate areas of responsibility: preparation of plans, checking, and final approval of plans. The local authorities are entirely responsible for preparation. The Ministry of Public Works and other interested ministries are responsible for checking the plan. Final approval belonged to the minister of public works or his representatives in the province, depending upon the importance of the plan, until regional reform led to the transfer of this function to the regions by presidential decree in January 1972.

The real basis of local planning is to be found in 'general urban plans' (*piani regolatori generali*). They try to establish rational urbanisation by dividing towns into zones and by fixing standards of population density and the provision of public services, as well as providing for an adequate road network. The local councils draw up plans which were until 1972 submitted to the Ministry of Public Works for approval and thereafter to the regional authority.[5] In the smaller boroughs, general urban plans are replaced by simple 'building plans' (*programmi di fabbricazione*). The content of these building plans is similar to that of the general plans, but they are much less complex and detailed and the checking and approval procedures are simpler.[6] The 1942 Act gave local government the exclusive right to control building development in their areas and also regulated urban building projects by 'executive plans' (*piani attuativi*). There are separate provisions for private and for public projects.[7] The proposal and approval procedures of public projects are the same as described above for urban plans submitted by local councils, and are not very different for private executive plans.

Two as yet unsolved problems dogged urban planning in Italy in the sixties, with serious territorial and social consequences. Firstly, urban growth often occurred where the necessary public services were not available, giving rise to congested and disorganised suburbs. Secondly, the laws governing expropriation for public use are more than a century old, and have favoured speculation in land and the unequal distribution of building land and land for public services.

The first problem has been tackled by a provisional Act of 1967 – until such time as a comprehensive law governing land-use planning could be passed – restricting the right to build, and forbidding the carrying out of private executive plans for urban building projects until the central, regional and local authorities have given their approval. Furthermore, the private builder must contribute towards the cost of all the 'primary' and 'secondary' urbanisation necessary in the new urban area.[8] This is a substantial modification of the 1942 Act. Previously, private executive plans for urban building projects were permitted, subject only to control by the town council. Now they are in principle forbidden and allowed only under certain conditions. Furthermore, the provisional 1967 Act makes a building licence necessary throughout the whole of the area controlled by the council and it is granted only on the condition that primary urbanisation exists or the developer promises to create it. Finally, the law greatly restricts building in towns where there is no general plan, and has fixed standards on building density, height, the ratio between industrial and residential quarters and the provision of areas for public services. The second problem, the high cost of land and the unequal distribution of building land and land earmarked by the plans for public services, was dealt with by the Constitutional Court in 1968. The Court declared some of the provisions of the 1942 Act unconstitutional in that they permitted the indefinite and uncompensated 'freezing' of private property rights. For a while it seemed that this decision would paralyse all planning, but a new Act was passed according to which projects involving expropriation are valid for only five years. If the plans have not been commenced within that time, the expropriation order lapses. In fact, the municipalities are at present so short of money that besides finding it difficult to pay for such projects, they could not even pay the compensation for land expropriated, except in a few exceptional cases.

How, then, has the system worked in practice? We shall consider this problem more fully in the second part, but here we should like to consider two matters. Although the 1942 Act deals with both urban and territorial planning, in fact it operated only in the case of urban planning and not at all in territorial planning. Secondly, in the vast majority of cases, the local authorities have not prepared executive plans and this had a considerable effect on the nature of urban planning as the law defined it. This is one of the main reasons why urban planning is in the lamentable state it is today. Because it was possible to build independently of an executive plan, so long as there were roads and no real clash between the projected building and the general urban plan, there are now innumerable cases of developments without even the most elementary public services. Thus private development of farm land into built-up areas was one of the greatest obstacles to land-use planning after the war. Widespread emigration from country to town has exacerbated the problems of planning in the areas of development and has increased the pressure on the local authorities to find money for infrastructures in the new housing estates.[9]

The building boom continued in full spate in Italy from 1950 to 1963. This was partly due to the widespread destruction and the halting of building programmes caused by the war. However, it was mainly due to the rapid migration from country areas to the densely industrial North. This expansion in the building industry increased the demand for building land, with the result that the price of land and therefore of houses increased enormously.[10] This laid the way open to speculation in land. When the results of urban concentration became obvious[11] and as it became more and more difficult to find building land, a new law was passed in 1962. According to this Act, municipalities had to draw up a 'plan for cheap housing' whose approval procedures were more or less the same as for the plans for urban development.[12] The land necessary for these plans, usually located in exclusively residential areas, was to be expropriated. The law also made special provisions for small rural municipalities (*piani consortili*): in these cases the plans were drawn up by the local authorities on the order of the Ministry of Public Works and returned to it for approval.[13]

The cheap housing programme was not very successful because the town councils did not have enough money to expropriate all the land the programme required.[14] It was necessary to solve this problem and to increase the amount of public building. After parliamentary debates and the collection of information, it was eventually decided in 1971 to change housing policy radically. Ever since 1969, the trade union movement has insisted that housing is one of the priority reforms for the seventies, and the pressure it brought to bear on the legislature played a major part in stimulating the housing reform movement.[15] The 1971 Act is extremely important in that it provides for a single body to decide on how and where funds are to be used in the public building sector. This body, the Housing Committee, works in close co-operation with the regions. Land may now be expropriated for public building, to carry out primary and secondary urbanisation programmes, to improve urban areas and to acquire up to 20 % of the expansion areas as well as to acquire land for the cheap housing programme. The town council has to grant ground rights of between 60 % and 80 % of the expropriated areas, to last not more than 99 years, so that popular housing can be built, the remaining areas being granted to co-operatives and to private owners.[16]

Territorial planning and economic planning

Ever since the war, the term 'land-use planning' has been changing in meaning. When the 1942 Act was passed, the term referred essentially to the control of building within the towns. From 1960 onwards, the term has come to mean the co-ordination of economic and urban planning and this is more or less its meaning in the Constitution.[17] Thus the practice of land-use planning, to be up to date with the new developments in land development, began to include territorial planning. At the end of the fifties, there was a great debate in Italy among intellectuals. The concept of the city as a static entity, and therefore of land-use planning as the control of building and road development, began to break down in the face of industrial development and

urbanisation. The industrial and population distribution was changing, movement becoming the chief characteristic of city life, traffic
being a spectacular example of this new dynamic. There was a more
open type of housing pattern involving adjacent municipalities. These
so-called metropolitan areas broke down the old insularity and at the
same time required greater areas of land to solve the problems they
created. The new concept of planning arising from these changes
included planning of the whole national territory. Planning had to be an
open and continuous process if it were to keep up with the changed
conditions, and it had to embrace all the problems ranging from urban
planning in the narrow sense to economic planning in general, e.g.
industrial and tourist development, commerce and traffic.

The Seventh Congress of the National Town Planning Institute
(INU) in 1959 provided the impetus for new planning legislation. The
Congress took the initiative in drawing up a new law, since the old 1942
Act could no longer cope with the new phenomena. Thus was born the
Urban Planning Code which was presented at the 1960 INU Congress
in Rome. For the first time, the concept of co-ordinating urban and
economic planning appeared in Italy.[18] The new ferment of ideas
created by this Code led to the setting up in the same year of a
National Study Committee under the auspices of the Institute, which
called for a single planning body with overriding powers in the
conurbations, generalised expropriation, compensation calculated
according to agricultural value, and state or town ownership of the
lands expropriated. However, the proposal was not even examined
by parliament. A new committee modified it in order to meet two
principal objections: the unconstitutionality of the transfer of property to municipal control, of generalised expropriation and of undifferentiated compensation. These new proposals were also ignored
and thereafter the Institute Committee has not considered the coordination of urban and economic planning but has been chiefly
concerned with the control of land speculation.[19]

The First National Economic Plan in Italy made no attempt to
co-ordinate the purposes, methods and procedures of territorial and
economic planning. At that time people were only beginning to
become aware of this problem and in fact the only part of the plan
which directly affected spatial problems was the concept of the city-
region as an alternative to the traditional conflict between metropolitan areas and predominantly rural non-industrialised areas. When
this plan was drawn up, the minister for the budget and economic
planning launched a research programme which examined territorial
planning on a national scale. This programme became the spring-
board for further studies into territorial planning as part of national
planning.[20]

Preliminary studies for the Second Plan finally included a land-use policy as an integral part of national planning. Thus the National Economic Plan for 1971-5 gave a new definition of metropolitan areas and issued instructions about the use of land, urban planning and infrastructures within these areas. The new definition of metropolitan areas implies different attitudes to industry, commercial concentration and urban development plans. The acceptance of the need to co-ordinate territorial and economic planning has also led to a change in the ways of arriving at decisions and implementing them in the different areas of the Second Plan. Briefly, in future, national planning will involve carrying out three different types of projects: sectoral, priority and pilot projects.[21] The pilot projects are particularly relevant to territorial planning and the five-year plan gives responsibility for these projects to the central planning bodies. However, it does not define the relationship between these bodies and the local authorities in spite of the fact that current legislation makes the local authorities the supreme executive land-use planning authority, so progress with the pilot projects has been paralysed.

The only body in Italy that has far-reaching powers for both land-use planning and controlling operations is the Cassa per il Mezzogiorno, which has independent control over its own spending. The 1971 Act on the Cassa orders it to carry out its programme through special projects covering infrastructures in general as well as support facilities for industry. There are to be other projects for protecting the countryside and natural resources as well as co-ordinated projects for services in the metropolitan and development areas. These projects should control the use of land according to the norms laid down for urban planning. Where there is no urban planning, then the norms laid down in the regional development programme should prevail.[22] Furthermore, the 1971 Act, for the first time in Italian history, establishes that permission must be obtained from the central planning bodies for the location of new industries.

Before the establishment of the regions, it was the responsibility of central government to supervise, and even sometimes initiate, urban and territorial planning. In other words the centre co-ordinated the urban planning of the different towns, bringing them into line with the policies of the various ministries. The main bodies involved were the Ministry of Public Works, which looked after the technical side of supervision, and the Higher Council for Public Works, which acted as a consultative body. There were other secondary bodies, like the Public Works Inspectorate and its town planning sections. These town planning sections were responsible for supervising planning at the local level and also served as a consultative body for the Inspectorate.[23] There were two main faults in this type of organisation: the continual conflict between local authorities and the central supervisory agencies and the slowness of the central bureaucracy in examining and approving any kind of plan.

Local authorities were, indeed still are, responsible for initiating the planning of town developments. The mayor controls local building by granting, refusing or annulling building permits. The actual technical side of planning is the responsibility of the local authority's specialist staff, but more often it is farmed out to specialised bodies, which can be public or private, and even to individual experts. Since the choice of plans has direct political consequences, the politicians themselves take a large part in selecting them. They look after all supervision apart from the purely technical aspects, so the plans often reflect the ideologies of the particular political group in power. The administrative bodies are not sufficiently strong or sufficiently independent to resist political pressure; but it is also difficult for them to realise the overall aims of the politicians. In fact this diffusion of power over planning and co-ordination frequently means that the proposals are superficial and contradictory, and the attempts of the administrative bodies to translate these proposals into concrete plans are not very successful.

In January 1972 the responsibility of central government for the supervision and approval of town planning was transferred to the regions.[24] This new responsibility is of great importance, since it means that the regions must establish plans on an inter-town or regional scale which will serve as a framework for smaller-scale plans. They now also have to supervise local development, including encouraging towns to form cheap housing consortia and playing a major role in carrying out the related public building plans. In addition, each region prepares a regional economic plan, in consultation with the local authorities and other interests. These plans pay particular attention to territorial planning, which can be an important factor when each region attempts to decide its development strategy.

Land-use planning: the policy process[25]

The decision-making process in urban planning

As we have seen, urban planning was formally effective but, generally speaking, territorial planning policy was a failure. Before examining the reasons for this failure, we should like to consider how urban planning worked. There were two main authorities involved: the local authorities and central government. The local authorities, generally speaking, made the decisions while the central government acted in a supervisory capacity.

Let us look at certain specific aspects of this decision-making by the councils: firstly, the political influences on decisions; secondly, relations between the local authorities and the public, organised in clubs or interest groups; thirdly, the changes in urban planning in recent years other than those concerning the bodies responsible for it. The councils' decisions concerning urban planning showed two main tendencies: they were based on what may broadly be called improvisation and aimed at expansion; they demonstrated a so-called rationalist approach to town planning, and because they sought perfection, they could not be implemented. We are concerned here with the general urban plans and the criticism is of the criteria used to arrive at such planning decisions. The decisions were imagined to be all-embracing and definitive, and they were to be applied rigidly. They were over-ambitious because it was considered necessary and possible to plan everything and to subordinate every other consideration to the desire for an immediate and simultaneous solution of even secondary problems. Being 'definitive', they did not allow for the inevitable adjustments that the future in a rapidly changing society would necessitate. There is an easy explanation for the defects in this kind of planning. The specialist urban planners, who generally created these plans for the council, had a theoretical education in urban planning and hence they were inclined to abstract philosophising. This education, and indeed the same is true of all politically relevant education in Italy, is based on ideology and the result is that the different sciences are little islands unto themselves without any intercommunication. The inevitable result was that the plans could not be implemented because it was impossible to reconcile such abstractions with practical needs.

A part from the technical problems arising from educational inadequacies, there was another difficulty deriving from the exaggerated tendency towards improvisation so marked in the decision-making processes of Italian politics. Decisions were often taken on a day to day basis and consequently were often contradictory. This is the logic of incremental adjustment. Why this should be true of Italian politics is a very complex question which we cannot explore here.[26] However, we might mention two factors which affect urban planning decision-making. The first reason is an economic one. The rapidity of Italian economic development – the 'incomplete miracle' – forced local authorities to act without making any of the necessary preparations. Day to day improvisation was the only way of solving the problems that arose from the disordered growth of the cities, e.g. the new housing necessary for industrial development.

The second reason is a political one, deriving from the characteristics and financial arrangements of Italian political parties. Parties in Italy have never had a very broad social base, at least not sufficient for a broadly based democratic system. Consequently, to be re-elected, the local councillors have used urban planning as a surreptitious way of securing funds for their party. By continually ignoring public projects in favour of speculative private projects, they have created very profitable pickings for private operators and financed their own political power, funds being channelled to the politicians through intermediaries. This obviously gives rise to improvised, absolutely unco-ordinated policies, which anyone looking at the chaos and degradation in Italian cities today will see to be true.

Naturally there are other reasons for the faults in the process of making decisions about urban planning, especially the disastrous financial situation of the town councils. This has systematically prevented any serious land-expropriation policy because there is simply not enough money to pay the compensation prescribed by law. There is another cause which we should mention, and that is the proportional representation system governing elections in the large and medium-sized towns. Given the extreme fragmentation of the party system in Italy, the proportional representation system is one of the main causes of executive instability in local government and stability is one of the main preconditions of genuine medium and long-term planning policy.

Let us now look at the relations between local authorities and the public with regard to urban planning. First of all, there have been very few opportunities for the public to participate in planning, and its contributions have been insignificant because they can only be made after the plans have been prepared. By law, trade unions, public bodies and interest groups as well as private property owners have the right to formulate observations and express their opposition to a plan, and the local authority is compelled to bring these criticisms to the notice of the supervisory authorities. However, only very rarely are the plans changed as a result. This is the formal, legal position concerning relations between local authorities and public. In practice, the only relations are those between the local authority and the interest groups. One can say generally that those groups most closely connected to the particular political parties forming the local government majority can bring the greatest pressure to bear. The bonds linking the two may vary from ideological to religious identification, from cultural to social affinity and from economic to ethno-geographic similarities.[27]

What changes have occurred in urban planning decision-making in recent years in Italy? We shall discuss institutional changes later. For the moment we shall look at some of the changes which are not strictly formal. Nowadays, the local authorities have largely abandoned the practice of drawing up improvised and un-coordinated plans which they used for political, electoral and financial advantage. The granting of permission for small building schemes has been cut back sharply, e.g. permits are now given for the building of whole blocks, not just single buildings.

The changed environment has led to a change in what people ask for politically from the local authorities. For instance, there has been a very important economic change in that the councils no longer have at their disposal the large tracts of land they once had. Thus one of the basic cornerstones of urban planning in the past has crumbled. The density of population in the large cities has made it impossible to plan in the old way for a small area, and consequently the old planning has given way to multi-town or at least inter-town planning. There has also been a change in the public's attitude to ecological problems and generally to what the quality of urban life should be. Ten years' work by organisations like Italia Nostra and the National Town Planning Institute has gone a long way towards creating this awareness of such problems by the general public.

The change in the attitudes of both the general public and the political elites to the social problems of land-use planning was due to the fact that groups of progressive intellectuals have ceaselessly sought to educate people. These intellectuals became aware of the problems long before the political parties. There are two ideological currents among these intellectuals. Firstly, there are the smaller elitist groups, associated with the liberal movement (Friends of *Il Mondo*) or the reformist socialists (especially from the Communità movement). Secondly there are the Marxist (PSI, PCI) and left-wing Christian Democrat intellectuals who see urban planning simply as a weapon with which to fight capitalism.[28] This is an important division because it explains the relative weakness of the innovators in the sixties and the divergences between the programmes of the parties interested in innovation. The innovators were very successful in publicising the defects and the cost, in social and environmental terms rather than in money terms, of traditional urban policy, but they could not agree on practical reform proposals. So, although there was pressure capable of bringing to an end an inadequate system of planning, no agreed policy of central and local authority intervention was attained. The major effect of these informal changes in decision-making for planning are in any case clear. The policy of the fifties and sixties has been almost completely abandoned. Although no real substitutes have yet been discovered, at least the old socially costly and inefficient system cannot carry on.

The decision-making process in territorial planning

Besides urban planning in the strict sense, it would be well to bear in mind what has been happening on the territorial planning front; or rather we should bear in mind what has not been happening, and the reasons for this, as well as what little has in fact happened or is slowly beginning to happen. To do this, we shall distinguish between territorial planning before and after the introduction of economic planning. Fundamentally, there was no territorial planning before economic planning. The 1942 Act had been passed in the war years and depended on a completely authoritarian executive. These were still the years of Fascism. Territorial planning had been left almost entirely in the hands of the central government while, as we have seen, urban planning was almost a monopoly of the local authorities. This corresponded with a real division of spheres of influence between two levels of power inside the governing Fascist party.

Recently in Italy there has been a lot of talk about the failure to enact measures enforcing the 1942 Planning Act. In fact, the real reason for this failure to apply the law is not a legal but a political one. With the end of the war and the advent of democracy, the two basic conditions for the success of the decision-making process provided by the Act disappeared. The first condition concerns the joint town plan which the one-party administration, in the shape of the Federale (the title of the Fascist governor of a whole province) could impose on the smaller towns in favour of the larger ones. Democracy ended this one-party system and at the same time removed the only power capable of coercing all the groups involved. Inter-town conflicts naturally sprang up and destroyed any hope of real joint town planning until such time as an overall urban authority was set up. The second condition concerns the co-ordination of plans. This was the responsibility of the central government and depended on the existence of a government sufficiently independent of local pressures and interests. Naturally, an authoritarian government meets this need. The advent of democracy destroyed the decision-making process set up by the Fascists. It is a fact that the new democratic governments were hardly ever sufficiently strong to impose their will on the local authorities, especially in the large cities. In these cases, electoral and party interests prevented the government playing too assertive a role in delicate local problems. In spite of all this, however, something was done about territorial planning during those years. But whatever was done occurred in spite of the decision-making machinery in existence and within the limits it imposed on the planners. Take, for example, the Milan Joint Town Plan. All attempts to rationalise and co-ordinate territorial planning foundered on the selfish shortsightedness of the different municipalities involved.

Doubtless the introduction of economic planning in the sixties gave grounds for hoping that things would also change in territorial planning. It seemed that, finally, here was a suitable means of tackling the problem. There were two reasons for this hopefulness. Attitudes

towards problems of land use had changed and there was an awareness of the fact that a territorially defined policy was an indispensable element in economic planning in a country where, among the
basic problems, were the imbalances of urban and industrial concentration between the North and the South, between town and country,
between industry, agriculture and services. With these problems in
mind, territorial planning became a very important element in economic planning. Proposals for reform of the existing laws on urban
planning were made and specific projects concerning particular
geographical areas were drawn up. However, in spite of this,
economic planning does not seem to have lived up to expectations.
Why not?

There are four main reasons why economic plans have been relatively unsuccessful in dealing with land use. Firstly, there were the
relationships within the bureaucracy. These relations have never been
good, at least as far as planners and senior civil servants are concerned.
The civil servants consider planners to be untrustworthy, perhaps
because planners and bureaucrats speak different languages, have a
different economic and planning education and come from different
socio-political backgrounds. This has resulted in a clear separation
between the overall plan for development and the separate policies
created by the different parts of the bureaucracy for different sectors.
The second reason concerns the general expropriation of land. All the
proposed urban planning reforms in the economic plan envisage this
happening in more or less the same ways. Very probably this provision is contrary to the present constitutional laws of Italy, and furthermore it has been the cause of real conflict within the groups forming
the government in existence at the time. Consequently, instead of
accelerating territorial planning policy, it has slowed down and impeded
it. The third reason is the education of the land-use planners, who are
not trained to see territorial planning as part of a general economic
plan capable of encouraging general development. In Italy today,
urban planning is still the preserve of architects, and architecture is
a science considered superior to all others, rather than as an interdisciplinary study in which all the modern social sciences should play a
part. The fourth and decisive reason is that there are no adequate
authority structures in territorial planning. Do the regions offer a
solution?

The possibilities opened up by the regional reform

The establishment of the regions was the real institutional innovation
concerning territorial planning and it coincided roughly with the
introduction of economic planning. We have already seen what it
meant formally: central government transferred some powers and

some functions to the regions. They have the power to legislate in matters of land-use policy and economic planning generally, and they supervise the urban planning decided by the town councils. For the first time, a single authority is responsible for some of the major questions in land-use planning and this authority seems to be adequate for the problems to be faced. Combining the supervisory role with the role of initiator and co-ordinator may mean that we are on the right road at last.

However, some doubts remain. The extent of the regions' powers is not yet clear. Moreover, the decision-making structure in the regions is somewhat ill-defined as yet. Still, some preliminary points can be made. Firstly, the regional assemblies are not very different from the other local authorities in form. For instance, the proposed electoral system is very similar to the proportional system for town councils and the national parliament. Consequently, in the regional assemblies there will be the same fragmentation of parties as at the national and the local council level.[29] Secondly, the leaders in the regions will be drawn for the most part from the old political class, whether it be local, provincial or national.[30] Consequently, the attitudes, links and methods of the regional governing class will be very much the same as in the past. This undoubtedly means continuity but it also means that it will not work very effectively. Thirdly, the support for regional politicians will be practically the same as for local or national politicians. This means that if they want to be re-elected, they will have to come to terms with the old ideological and electoral machine, which is one of the basic reasons why parliamentary and local institutions function badly.

It is easy to draw a conclusion from all this. If the principal elements in regional decision-making are going to be the same as decision-making in the local councils and in parliament, can we really expect them to make different decisions? Clearly, the answer is no, and this gives rise to another problem. It is certainly *possible* for the regions, in territorial planning, to be stronger and more independent of the local authorities than the central government was, but things being as they are, *it is not very probable that they will be.* Naturally, anxieties arise that full advantage has not been taken of the opportunity offered. Nevertheless, alongside these reservations, there may be cause for optimism. The regions have great powers for stimulating territorial planning because they are in a position to 'blackmail' the town councils. It is the regions that supervise projects in urban planning, and above all they can threaten to take over when the councils do not follow the precise policies laid down by the regional authorities. Furthermore, they are in a position to publicise territorial planning problems and can make the general public more conscious of them. The regions can thus instruct and inform because, more than any other institution, they can continually point out the connection between territorial planning and economic development.

The overall picture of the region as an adequate authority in territorial planning problems in the seventies is therefore a mixture of pessimism and optimism. We have seen that the main cause for anxiety is the inadequacy of the regions' decision-making structures. Consequently, the enthusiasm of those who considered the problem of territorial planning to be solved is not justified, because the regions may not be up to the task. In fact, from this point of view, the regions appear to be a two-headed monster, i.e. they have full supervisory powers, but as initiators as well as co-ordinators it remains to be seen how they will behave. In fact, they can only act as an effective territorial planning authority if their powers are expanded considerably and if their executive is assured stability and independence. On the first point, all that would be necessary would be national laws permitting them to function as an active planning body instead of just bureau-cratic supervisors of local government. The second point, perhaps, would require a different system of electing the presidents of the regional governments and a different relationship between the re-gional executives and regional legislative assemblies: namely the system which makes it impossible to get rid of the executive except by electing a new one. If these things do not happen, then we can easily imagine what the regions will be like in the future: the same old supervisory bureaucracy, with the only difference that it will be decentralised. Decentralisation alone will not be enough to create a structure capable of establishing a nation-wide territorial planning policy.

Politics, economic planning and land-use planning in Italy

Considering the problem as a whole, planning in Italy still generally follows a traditional pattern and is not a national strategy. Economic planning has indeed meant a move towards reform, but much less than the setting-up of the regions has done. This fact is very important if one tries to measure the impact of economic planning. Economic planning has had more influence on general attitudes to urban planning than it has had on the institutions governing it. We shall examine the way economic planning has affected territorial planning, and we shall try to forecast possible future developments.

We have already described the institutional changes at central government level. However, there are other important points to be considered.

(i) The changed relationship between the experts and politico-bureaucratic elites. The economic plan transfers some of the power over territorial planning from the latter to the former. However, what is transferred is the power to draw up plans and projects but this does not involve control over their application. Consequently, the plans have remained only plans and have not been implemented, so this transfer of power has been fruitless.

(ii) The role of the executive. Economic and territorial planning have meant neither greater centralisation nor any real decentralisation of government. Of course, there has been decentralisation in urban planning. The regions have taken over some of the authority of the state. There has also been centralisation in the economy. Economic planning has taken the place of the market in deciding certain things. But in these two cases, the decentralisation of one and centralisation of the other have been very uncertain and have produced their own contradictions. There is still no real concentration of responsibilities either in the hands of the central or the regional authorities. Functions and powers are still spread among many bodies and this is especially true with regard to economic affairs. The result has been a lack of interest in territorial planning.

(iii) Economic planning has had practically no effect on territorial planning. Why not? Briefly, the economic plan does not help solve practical problems. For instance the plan has never been related to the real possibilities of the national budget. The plan and the budget are based on two almost completely different types of logic. Consequently no one has any real faith in the economic plan, especially in that part of it dealing with territorial planning, simply because the big obstacle has always been the lack of money to pay for expropriation. Furthermore, the plan has never included a model of economic development inspired by a spatial orientation of policy, or, to put it in other words, the plan was not seen as a spatial development model. In considering territorial planning one must constantly bear this fact in mind. An economic plan that does not suggest an alternative to the unbalanced and socially wasteful territorial development decided by the market is worthless. This means that a large part of the failure of the plan derives from the fact that the economic planners did not try to overcome external resistance to it by explaining that it offered a more efficient and more rational spatial development than that decided by the market. Such planned development would gain the support of all those public and private operators whose job it would be to put it into effect.

(iv) The fact that planners and bureaucrats do not communicate with each other should also be borne in mind. The reason for this is certainly that they have two completely different conceptions of administration. The closed, hierarchical and traditionally minded structure of the bureaucracy has nothing in common with the planners, especially where territorial planning is involved. In fact, planning requires imagination, a solid interdisciplinary education, open-mindedness and flexibility. But it is for this very reason that an intelligent planning policy must systematically and increasingly involve the bureaucracy and make it amenable to a new method of spotlighting and working towards collective goals. Otherwise, there is no sense in complaining about the insensitivity of the bureaucracy; this only ensures the failure of all planning. This is a challenge that must be met. Instead the economic planners have locked themselves up in their little ministerial ivory tower and have failed to involve or win the co-operation of the rest of the central administration.

(v) The plan has had little effect on the relations between government and interest groups. Stemming from what has already been said, it is easy to understand why this should be so. It is obvious that the interest groups try to influence above all the most important centres in the decision-making structures. This explains why these groups were very interested in the First Plan (1966–70) but less so in the second one. They realised that the latter was not crucial to government decisions. During the First Plan some groups, especially house owners, organised both overt and covert opposition to generalised expropriation and the nationalisation of land. They openly declared that they wanted to stop this reform becoming law. They have not repeated this tactic because they realised that planning was still in a preliminary stage and did not yet involve the implementation of decisions. This was a very good reason for not exaggerating its importance.

Thus the plan did not greatly affect relations between interest groups and government. Neither the procedures governing these relations, nor the roles of the two parties changed. The plan did not even affect the groups' powers and organisation. There is one exception. The house owners' association – which in itself is not very popular – briefly enjoyed a lot of popularity at the precise time when the government proposed some urban planning reforms based on the nationalisation of land. The association became popular because the traditional, cherished dream of the Italian is to own his own house and the land it stands on. But even this popularity could not last because the plan had no continuous effect on things.

(vi) The relationships inside the government and citizen participation in politics. We should point out that in this case the innovations were greater and more significant than people imagine. Naturally the changes have not been formal and they will only show their importance over a medium and long-term period. With regard to relations inside the government, one may say that the plan started, or at least greatly speeded up, the process of making people aware of the absolute necessity of co-ordinating the activity of the decision-makers in the government and the bureaucracy if there was to be any chance of imposing some sort of integrated structure on national economic policy. With regard to the participation of the electorate, the plan encouraged large sectors of the educated public in the belief that the economic growth of a country depends on a 'policy of compatibility' or selection of priorities; which reforms should be made immediately and which could be postponed. Choices had to be made and some things sacrificed if development was to be assured. It is as yet too early to expect these informal changes to lead to institutional changes because the Italian political machine is too slow-moving.

Thus, the plan does not seem to have encouraged the very necessary co-ordination of budget and plan nor does it seem to have influenced the way the public judge the economic programmes of the political parties. Nevertheless, one can foresee a change in attitude on both these points judging from what the politicians, newspapers, intellectuals and interest groups are beginning to say. If this trend continues, it will be the most important, if the least evident, of the innovations brought about by economic planning in the sixties. This change in attitudes may be decisive in generating a genuine land-use planning policy.

NOTES

1 This paper was written by the two authors working together, but the first part is predominantly the work of Attilio Bastianini, and the second of Giuliano Urbani. The authors wish to express their thanks to Guerrino Savio for his invaluable help in the preparation of the text.

2 For an outline of the complexities in the system of land-use planning, see A. Bastianini, 'Il sistema di pianificazione del territorio operante in Italia', in *Biblioteca della Libertà*, Nos. 40–1, 1972, pp. xlviii–lxiii, which contain a more detailed study of the land-use planning process.

3 For the period prior to and for the implementation of the 1942 Act, see G. d'Angelo, 'Cento anni di Legislazione Urbanistica' in *Rivista Giuridica dell'Edilizia*, Nos. 4–5, Rome 1965; 'La disciplina e il controllo del territorio dall'unità d'Italia a oggi', in *Edilizia Popolare*, No. 86, Milan 1969. For a more general view of town planning in Italy before 1955, see G. Samonà, *L'Urbanistica e l'avvenire della città*, Laterza, Bari 1967. On the co-ordination of territorial plans see V. Testa, *Disciplina Urbanistica*, Giuffrè, Milan 1971, Part 2, chapter 7; and G. Furitano, *Istituzioni di dirritto urbanistico e edilizio*, Periodici Scientifici, Milan 1971, chapter 4.

4 For joint town planning, see G. De Carlo (ed), *La Pianificazione Territoriale Urbanistica Nell'Area Torinese*, *La Pianificazione Territoriale Urbanistica Nell'Area Bolognese* and *La Pianificazione Territoriale Urbanistica Nell'Area Milanese*, Marsilio, Padua 1964. For joint planning in Turin and Milan in particular, see *Urbanistica*, Nos. 50–1, Turin, October 1967, and for Bologna, *Urbanistica*, Nos. 54–5, September 1969.

5 For the legal aspects of the 'general urban plans' (*piani regolatori generali*), see Testa, *Disciplina Urbanistica*, chapter 6, and Furitano, *Diritto urbanistico*, chapter 6. The review *Urbanistica*, No. 38, March 1963, published an important inquiry into urban planning in Italy.

6 For the legal aspects of the 'building plans' (*programmi di fabbricazione*) and the distinction between them and the '*general urban plans*' see Testa, *Disciplina urbanistica*; Furitano, *Diritto urbanistico*, and A. Predieri, *Urbanistica, tutela del paesaggio, espropriazione*, Part 2, Giuffrè, Milan 1969.

7 See Testa, *Disciplina urbanistica*, chapters 8 and 23 and Furitano, *Diritto urbanistico*, chapters 7 and 11.

8 Law No. 847 of 29 September 1964 specified that 'primary' urbanisation involves roads, sewers, water mains, etc. 'Secondary' urbanisation covers facilities necessary in a particular inhabited area: schools, churches, social centres, hospitals, markets, local parks, sporting facilities.

9 On the problems of planning in Italian cities and on migration to the built-up areas, see F. Sullo, *Lo scandalo urbanistico*, Vallecchi, Florence 1964. On the allocation of land to private people, see *Indagine conoscitiva sulle lottizzazioni del terreno a scopo edilizio*, Ministry of Public Works, Rome 1968.

10 On the problem of land values and expropriation see A. Bastianini 'La rendita urbana in Italia' in *Biblioteca della Liberta*, No. 42, Turin 1973, pp. 69–90.

11 On economic and demographic concentration, migration and building development, see A. Villani, *La politica dell'abitazione*, Franco Angeli, Milan 1970.

12 See Law 167 of 18 April 1962: instructions for the acquisition of building land for cheap housing. On the legal aspects of 'cheap housing schemes' see Testa, *Disciplina urbanistica*, chapter 12; Furitano, *Diritto urbanistico*, chapter 9; G. Paleologo, 'I piani delle zone da destinare alla costruzione di alloggi a carattere economico e popolare', in *Il foro italiano*, Rome 1970. See Nos. 39, 40 and 41 of *Urbanistica*, 1963–4 for information about the plans of the main Italian towns. The article 'Esame e valutazione della Legge 167', in *Città e Società*, No. 1, Milan 1970, gives a good general description of the law providing for cheap popular housing.

13 The Town and Provincial Law No. 383 of 3 March 1934, subsequently revised (see arts. 156 sqq.) allows the municipalities to form consortia for the purpose of making plans together. The most important example of a consortium building cheap housing is the Consorzio Intercomunale Milanese per l'Edilizia Popolare. This was set up in 1965 and has sixty-five member municipalities in the Milan area. The plan drawn up was approved in 1971 and at present is being implemented.

14 For information about the cheap housing schemes in Rome, Milan, Turin, Geneva and Bologna, see V. Erba, 'Alcuni esempi di applicazione e attuazione della legge 167', in *Città e Società*, No. 4, Milan 1970. See also A. Bastianini, *La 167 a Torino*, APSU, Turin 1968.

15 For information about the housing problem in Italy, see Villani, *La politica dell'abitazione*; G, Cavalera, V. Intini, E. Tortoreto, *Italiani senza casa*, Nuovo Mercurio, Milan 1970; see also 'Discorso sulla casa', in *Vita e Pensiero*, No. 5, Milan 1970; the National Town Planning Institute's document published in *Urbanistica*, No. 57, Turin March 1970; the National Association of Builders' document, *Indicazioni per una politica della casa*, Rome 1971; *Edilizia Popolare*, No. 100, Milan 1971, which is entirely devoted to examining the housing problem.

16 For the legal aspects and the application of the law, see *La riforma della casa*, Rome 1971: a document by the Associazione Nazionale Istituti Autonomi Case Popolari (ANIACP); R. Pandini, *Nuova legge organica sulla casa*, Dets, Rome 1971; P. Bonaccorse, S. Lanzaro, *La legge per la casa*, Pastena, Rome 1972; the minutes of the Palermo Congress of ANIACP published in *Edilizia Popolare*, No. 104, Milan 1972, and also the minutes of the Tenth Congress of Associazione Nazionale Istituti Autonomi Case Popolari in *Edilizia Popolare*, Nos. 106–7, Milan 1972.

17 On the relationship between land-use planning and economic planning in the Constitution, see A. Predieri, *Pianificazione e Costituzione*, Communità, Milan 1963.

18 The Code as well as the minutes of the Congress are published in *Urbanistica*, No. 33, Turin April 1961.

19 The proposals were published in *Rivista Giuridica dell'Edilizia*, No. 1, Part 3, 1967. G. Samonà gives a more exhaustive study of reform attempts in his *L'urbanistica e l'avvenire della città*, Laterza, Bari 1967. See also Sullo, *Lo scandalo urbanistico*.

20 See the document of the Centro di Studi e Piani Economici, entitled 'Un primo schema di sviluppo regionale a lungo termine per l'Italia', published in *Urbanistica*, no. 49, March 1967. For an extensive bibliography on the problems of territorial planning in Italy, see A. Bastianini, *Conoscenza dell'attuale assetto territoriale dell'Italia nord-occidentale*, Centro Studi Confindustria, Milan 1973.

21 See *Documento Programmatico preliminare*, (Appendix IV), published by the Budget and Economic Planning Ministry, Rome 1971. The preparatory documents are *Progetto '80, rapporto*

preliminare al Programma Economico Nazionale 1970–75 (with appendix), Budget and Economic Planning Ministry, Rome 1969.

22 One of the 'special projects' concerns the tourist port system in the South and therefore coincides with a 'pilot project' provided for in the National Economic Plan.

23 On the administration of town planning in Italy, see Furitano, *Diritto urbanistico*, chapter 3.

24 On the powers of the regions, see M. Mazziotti, *Studi sulla Potestà legislativa delle Regioni*, Giuffrè, Milan 1961.

25 For a more detailed and exhaustive understanding of decision-making in the Italian political system, see G. Sartori (ed), *Il Parlamento Italiano, 1946–63*, ESI, Naples 1963; G. Galli, *Il bipartitismo imperfetto*, Il Mulino, Bologna 1966; Centro di Ricerca e Documentazione 'L. Einaudi', *Processo allo Stato*, Sansoni, Florence 1971; P. Farneti (ed), *Il Sistema Politico italiano*, Il Mulino, Bologna 1973; G. Ruffolo, *Rapporto sulla programmazione*, Laterza, Bari 1973.

26 J. LaPalombara's *Interest Groups in Italian Politics*, Princeton University Press, Princeton 1965, gives a good overall picture of the situation.

27 *Ibid.* chapters 3 and 7.

28 On the 'Comunità group' see the review of the same name first published in 1946. This has always dedicated a lot of space to the problems of territorial planning in general and urban planning in particular. See also A. Olivetti, *Città dell'uomo*, Comunità, Milan. For information about the Friends of *Il Mondo* which was a very important review in the fifties, see Autori Vari *I padroni della città*, Laterza, Bari 1957. For the Left Catholic position, see F. Sullo, *Lo scandalo urbanistico*, Vallecchi, Florence 1964. Finally for the Communist intellectual standpoint, see G. Campos Venuti, *Amministrare l'urbanistica*, Einaudi, Turin 1967.

29 See D. Fisichella, 'Conseguenze politiche della legge elettorale regionale', in *Rivista Italiana di Scienza Politica*, No. 1, 1971, pp. 145–57.

30 This is confirmed by all of the research done on regional governing classes. Some of this research has been published in Italian reviews. See, for example, A. Mastropaolo, 'Primi dati di una ricerca sull'assemblea regionale siciliania', in *Quaderni di Sociologia*, No. 8, 1969; P. Collina, 'Candidati eletti nella regione Emilia-Romagna', in *Il Politico*, No. 37, 1972, pp. 368–89; G. Riccamboni, 'Profilo di una classe politica regionale. Il Trentino-Alto Adige', in *Il politico*, No. 37, 1972.

SELECT CRITICAL BIBLIOGRAPHY

The formal organisation of Italian land-use planning in the sixties is delineated in G. Furitano, *Istituzioni di diritto urbanistico e edilizio*, Periodici Scientifici, Milan 1971, chapter 4. We find the most significant points of view of politicians in: F. Sullo, *Lo scandalo urbanistico*, Vallecchi, Florence 1964; G. Campos Venuti, *Amministrare l'urbanistica*, Einaudi, Turin 1967. Two general treatments are provided by AA.VV., *I padroni della città*, Laterza, Bari 1967, and AA.VV., *La politica del territorio: bilancio e prospettive*, Angeli, Milan 1973. Robert C. Fried, *Planning the Eternal City. Roman Politics and Planning since World War II*, Yale University Press, New Haven and London 1973, is an important study of land-use planning in Rome.

18. Urban planning and political institutions: an essay in comparison

BRUNO JOBERT

Even more than other planning practices, the analysis of urban planning runs up against the obfuscating language of the professionals of the art.[1] These see themselves all too often as new gods, as the inspired creators for whom politicians are merely necessary to provide the means, so that they can establish order in the chaos of urban development. So much so that the relations between urban planning and politics is for them a story of the back-slidings and betrayals, by political mediocrities, of creative genius...Nevertheless, it seems difficult to evaluate scientifically the development of this practice, using changing professional values as the sole criterion. It is through its own dynamic that the evolution of urban planning should be examined, rather than being content with crude judgements which sometimes envisage dismissing its practices, for example, as false and inauthentic. However, this approach involves abandoning the vision of urban planning as creator of the town.

It is the spatial interactions between groups and social classes which make up the town, which exists as a *social* space. Like all social development, urban development only occurs through clashes between these various groups. When these contradictions and conflicts of interest seem to threaten social cohesion, political intervention may occur, taking the form of urban planning. In other words, a complete reversal of perspectives must be made. Urban planning is not a science of the best urban layout, hovering above the battle. It is a form of political intervention which is prompted by these contradictions and conflicts. It is therefore with conflict that one must begin to understand the variations and the particularity of urban planning in the countries studied.

Urbanisation and industrial growth occurred at a very different rate and in very different ways in each of the three countries studied. While Britain was faced above all with the problems arising from changing an already fully urbanised country, the conflicts and contradictions resulting from the rapid influx into the town of rural migrants, and thus the problems of urban growth, were dominant in France and Italy. The international spread of the techniques and ideologies of urban

[378]

planning tend to mask these differences and emphasise the similarity of problems. However, analysis of the types of action characteristic of each planning practice and of their impact on the political system enables these developments to be seen in proper perspective.

The changing issues of urban planning

Two major trends can be detected in Western Europe. On the one hand, the industrial and market system each year conquers new branches of economic activity and leads gradually to the decline and demise of pre-capitalist forms of production. On the other hand, the industrial/market system of production is itself undergoing continuous reorganisation. Firms merge, the extent to which science is applied to production increases. As a result, the location of firms seems to be linked increasingly to the quality of the labour force and ease of access to multiple sources of information. Innovation affects not only the production conditions but the product as well. Private mass consumption, through the car and the dwelling, exercise a powerful influence over the shape of our towns.

The contraction of pre-capitalist sectors and the reorganisation of the factors of production have very different effects on urban development. The contraction of pre-capitalist sectors involves rural depopulation and therefore raises the problem of accommodating rural migrants in the urban areas. Reorganising the productive forces involves an intense restructuring of the towns inherited from the first industrial revolution and thus essentially raises problems of the re-utilisation of built-up areas, e.g. traffic and the town centre. In the sixties, these two trends did not affect the three countries in the same way. Although British society is characterised by an almost complete urbanisation, France and Italy have simultaneously to complete their transition from a rural to an urban society and reorganise the existing urban areas in accordance with recent economic changes. This results in very different situations as far as both urban expansion and restructuring are concerned.

Urban planning as a housing policy and regulation of urban growth

Industrial growth has for a long time been based on the attraction of rural labour to the towns and thus implies a very rapid increase in the towns' capacity to absorb this influx. So the central problem of urbanisation is the proliferation of residential areas. It implies the existence of a housing policy and of related policies providing the infrastructure and services to cater for this new work force. But this policy has to be carried out on land already owned and occupied on the rural fringes of the conurbations, such as smallholdings which are sometimes bought from the farmers by clever speculators. It implies the reservation of land for public services and council housing and their efficient connection to the local transport system. In these circumstances, a conflict of interest exists not so much between industrial firms and urban workers as between rural migrants and young workers looking for housing and rural land owners and private developers. It centres principally on the basic acceptance of the legitimacy of public intervention in the use of urban land and the transfer to public ownership of private land.

In this field, there appears to be a great contrast between the three countries. In Britain, it was at the beginning of this century that the problem of the legitimacy of state intervention was tackled, and since 1947 a system of planning based on the regulation of land use has covered the whole of the country. In contrast, these problems are still at the centre of political debate in France and Italy, the theme of 'a right to be housed' tending to be identified in both cases with that of 'a right to control over the town'. It is only in Italy, however, that social agitation on a large scale, launched by the trade unions, has centred on the issue of low-cost housing. The strength of the movement in Italy and its relative weakness in France can be explained, no doubt, by the fact that the workforce drawn to Italian towns is a national workforce, while it is foreign workers – without any political power – who make up the new work force in French towns.

Nevertheless, the possibility of having at one's disposal good land on which to build at the right moment remains an essential requisite for the planning of urban growth. A certain number of analogies between developments in the three countries may be noted, such as the separation of the forecasting and regulatory aspects of planning or the development of methods of consultation leaving a greater role to the discretionary judgement of the planning authority. The major phenomenon at a comparative level remains the contrast between the relative control over the land owner by British planners and the resounding failure of the French and Italian planners in this sphere. The legitimacy of public control of land use is much more easily admitted in a totally urbanised society than in societies where rural interests still weigh heavily in the balance of political forces. Also the survival in France of a large section of independent workers, artisans and shopkeepers, devoted to the institution of commercial property, gives added strength in the urban areas to the forces arrayed against any regulation of property. The development of large public and private housing combines can, however, counterbalance the influence of such groups within the framework of certain 'concerted actions': ZAC in France, agreements in Italy.

The planning of urban development: the structure plans

The need for a more comprehensive regulation of urban development became evident during the sixties with very varying degrees of intensity according to the country concerned. Undoubtedly, the internationalisation of the techniques and attitudes of the professional planners tends to blur the very great differences in the consciousness of the various contradictions generated by urban development. In France and Italy, the overall problems of urban development were approached during the sixties mainly by way of the inter-regional imbalances and the diseconomies which the growth of large urban conurbations produces. These problems are dealt with as part of general economic planning (Italy) or the national policy for regional development (France). But difficulties are encountered in these countries in implementing planning of adjacent urban areas and securing coordination with local planning. Equally, one may question the way in which the planning bodies established in the major French city regions have tended to blur the fundamental conflicts of interest which all urban growth provokes and have thereby made it more difficult to mobilise political support for their schemes.

In this respect, Britain seems to be more advanced. The towns, including the working-class districts, have undergone very profound internal transformations from the beginning of the 1960s, involving slum-clearance programmes, the rebuilding of shopping areas and town centres, or the construction of urban trunk-roads. All these types of intervention – which no doubt appeared necessary to ensure that the economic activity of the town continued satisfactorily – have increasingly been confronted, as these schemes were carried out, by very active resistance. It is here, finally, that planning seems to change fundamentally. Whereas in town planning based on housing it was the middle and working classes which provided some of the most active support for intervention, they are among the most vociferous opponents of a remodelling of the towns that has sometimes been conceived in too exclusively economic and functional a fashion. In the same way, property owners may become the spearhead of resistance against planning intervention. In other cases, the inner urban areas perform a reception and socialisation function for foreign migrants, and the partial destruction of these areas for reasons of public health, public order or traffic tends to increase the overpopulation of the remaining run-down districts. The renewal of urban-planning legislation in Britain seems, from this point of view, an attempt to fix arbitration and compromise procedures to settle disputes between the various interests involved. The effort to increase participation by and information for citizens, the attempt to coordinate traffic planning with

plans for built-up areas, appear to be attempts to make political
decisions take more note of the social interests of townspeople in
opposition to the excessively instrumental approach of certain planners. Britain appears to be a pioneer rather than simply out on its own,
and there would be no lack of points of comparison if it could be set
against the rebuilding of the large conurbations of France and Italy in
the 1970s. But one must stress here the astonishing vigour of urban
pressure groups in Britain. Even in the 1970s no pressure group of any
importance has succeeded in checking the accelerating destruction of
working-class Paris to make way for roads, tower blocks and prestige
buildings for the ruling classes.

Urban planning, therefore, embraces actions of very different range
and social significance according to whether it is a matter of accommodating a new workforce by extending the built-up areas or of restructuring the whole of the urban area in order to adapt it to the new
requirements of growth. These differences affect not only the pressure groups associated with it, but also the types of intervention which
urban planning involves and their relationship with the whole system
of state action.

Planning and the system of political intervention

Being new kinds of intervention, urban planning practices cannot be
analysed in abstraction from the system of political intervention of
which they are a part. Our analysis of their articulation with the whole
of this system of action will take as its starting point the Weberian
model of bureaucracy, defined as the existence of objective rules, of
impersonal norms established by superiors. We hypothesise that
the urban planning studied in the three countries has had to define
itself in relation to this type of hierarchical and compartmentalised
organisation.

The relationship to the system of bureaucratic action can be approached in two ways. Firstly, the nature of urban planning will be
emphasised, giving rise to three questions. To what extent is urban
planning a new type of state intervention? Is it simply a slightly
up-dated version of bureaucratic administration? Or is it a completely
new type of intervention? The problem of the compatibility of these
new interventions with the bureaucratic mode of administration
constitutes the second series of problems which must be dealt with in
this section. It is a matter of assessing how far this new style of action
involves and sometimes entails more or less large-scale reorganisation
of the whole system of political intervention.

From the production of rules to the production of influence

The instruments of state intervention vary to a considerable extent according to whether urban planning is concerned primarily with piecemeal proliferation or whether planning for comprehensive urban development dominates. Certainly, urban planning always shows up a major weakness of the bureaucratic model in so far as the latter is conceived simply as an instrument for implementing externally fixed objectives; so much so that the relationship between the bureaucracy and its socio-political environment is largely neglected.

However, in plans dominated by the problem of piecemeal urban proliferation of housing and its attendant services, the institutionalisation of the function of goal determination seems to be reduced to a minimum. Studies remain incremental and piecemeal. Consideration of objectives takes place mainly in working-out and applying professional norms. These norms then become instruments allowing regulation, in an objective and general way, of the relationship of the administration with its environment. It is through them that planning can become part of the system of bureaucratic action without substantially changing its structure. As a way of regulating land, these norms fix the use to which land can be put, the standards of use (densities, siting of buildings) and reservation of land for the provision of public services and roads. Furthermore, the application of all these provisions requires specific regulations for public acquisition of land, ranging from the right of first option to expropriation.

In such regulatory planning, the planning authority plays the role both of judge and architect. It sets itself up as the sovereign authority of an urban order on which it alone is qualified to pronounce. This order is expressed in a general system of regulation, the land-use plan, which the whole of existing legal and judicial sanctions is used to enforce. In practice, the solemnity of these plans and procedures conceals at best a multitude of marginal adjustments juxtaposed within a single plan (Britain) or ambitious schemes without the means to apply them, which exemptions soon undermine (France and Italy). Finally, these norms evaluate, in the light of professional practice, the public-service needs of any particular part of the town (x square feet of grass per family, y schools per thousand dwellings, etc...). All these rules constitute the basis of the piecemeal planning of new built-up areas that can be dubbed regulatory. In a way, this kind of planning appears to be an improved or modernised form of administration based on rational legal regulation, and conforms wholly with Weber's model of the bureaucracy. This cannot be said of the more comprehensive planning of urban development.

A bureaucratic type of planning reaches a certain level of instrumental efficiency as long as it is carried out on an urban structure which is relatively stabilised in its fundamental relationships, that is as long as urban development is conceived of as the enlarged reproduction of a scheme of spatial organisation. Bureaucratic administration presupposes not only that choices are made higher up but also that they can be specified in increasingly precisely defined tasks as one descends the hierarchy, overlapping of powers and conflicts of functions being regarded as exceptional. Consequently, activities are shared out between various authorities which each exercise a regulatory authority over a legally delimited area. This demarcation implies a relatively foreseeable relationship between public intervention and the social milieu for which each administration is responsible. It is only in such circumstances that the general objective norms of bureaucratic planning can mediate with maximum instrumental efficiency the exchanges between the administration and its socio-political environment. Conversely, when comprehensive urban development appears as a thorough structural reorganisation, the stability of the administrations' relationship with their specific environment is challenged. Overlapping, interaction between sectors, unforeseen effects of the measures taken, all these aspects which the bureaucratic administration had wanted to ignore and exclude from the formal organisation, appear with stark clarity. It is precisely these interactions and these side-effects of public intervention that the newest forms of planning are now trying to use for the purpose of regulating an urban development which is no longer merely the extension of an old model but a painful restructuring of the whole of organised urban space.

We turn to two other Weberian concepts in order to distinguish the bureaucratic mode of action from that which characterises structural planning. With Max Weber we can distinguish the authority concept of legitimate power (Herrschaft), which he defines as the probability of finding people ready to obey a specific order, from the notion of domination or influence which he defines 'as the probability of making one's own will triumph within a social sphere, even against resistance, no matter on what this probability is based'.[2] In bureaucratic planning for urban development, it is essentially the legal rational authority of the state which is involved and the debate about the *legitimacy* of its intervention in this sphere is at the heart of the conflict. In structural planning, political regulation is no longer content to juxtapose rules and services, but seeks to mobilise the influence of the state apparatus as an economic and social macro-actor to achieve its ends. It then appears, in its new practices, as the creation of intellectual instrumentalities in order to evaluate the respective interactions and their effects between functionally separated sectors and to combine their influence. Regulatory intervention and the new forms of planning should not be regarded as mutually exclusive, but regulatory intervention occurs in a new context, some of whose aspects can be indicated.

Public authority purports to descend from its pedestal and resort to all the instruments of analysis which enable it to assess the power relationships, the actions and the strategies of the various actors in urban development. This gauging of the power relationships and strategies, which certain types of consensus-building can simulate, should enable the planners to know the lie of the land and to select the place, the means and the moment when the effectiveness of public intervention will be maximised. Strategic action focussed on a limited number of structuring schemes, problems (e.g. traffic) or zones (e.g. secondary centres, run-down districts, renewal of town centres), seems to be a characteristic trait of the ambitions of new planning. Nevertheless, 'structuring action' does not eliminate the incrementalist regulations inherited from the traditional model. In Britain, the new planning tries to combine, for example, actions for structural reorganisations in the 'action areas' and the organisation of spontaneous development by traditional local plans. The same sort of articulation could be made between SDAU, POS, and ZAC in France. Classical negative control thus appears to be complementary to the strategic action at other points in the system.

The historical development of planning

In each country, planning was developed and modified at a very different rhythm and according to very different methods. Since 1947, an apparatus for planning has covered the whole of Britain whereas, at the beginning of the period under study, only small parts of Italy and France were subject to the regular supervision of a planning authority. Thus the agents of change in planning were to be different. In Britain the profession of planner, already well institutionalised at a national level, suffered competition from other groups of specialists: traffic engineers and general planners, as well as the ambition of the social services to develop social planning. It was also threatened by the growing dissatisfaction of the public. But it seemed to have a sufficiently broad institutional base to resist these competitors by integrating into its practice the new requirements on which the encroachments of the other professions were founded. In France and Italy, the profession of planner has not been recognised as such and the professional groups which have tried to win legitimacy for planning work differ. In France, it is the Ponts et Chaussées engineers who have assumed leadership and control over the new institution of urban planning.[3] As career civil servants, attached to a *grand corps*, they were able to link urban planning with the whole of the administrative apparatus.

Italian urban planners, architects for the most part, do not appear to have benefited from such integration within the administration. Besides this professional rivalry, innovation developed in a more diffuse way among British local authorities, whereas it is from the centre that the principal initiatives came in France, a centre which expands, moreover, to control and restrict innovations which do not originate from the centre.

Sectoralisation and structural planning

If, therefore, regulatory planning for piecemeal urban proliferation appears wholly compatible with a bureaucratic apparatus, the fragmentation of the administration into watertight and juxtaposed compartments constitutes a major obstacle to the development of structural planning. Of course this obstacle is clearly stronger in political systems where centralisation favours sectoral autonomy. For all that, it does not seem to be absent from a regime endowed with strong local government like Britain, since the potential integration is sometimes prevented by strong internal division of power. This sectoralisation results as much from the search by the professions for autonomy as from the local councils' specialist committee organisation. Thus the articulation of planning (control of the spatial allocation of resources) with programming (control of the temporal allocation of resources) seems in every country to face problems that are partially attributable to the sectoralisation of the traditional administration.

In a more fundamental way, does not the evaluation of needs, which the work of urban planning involves, entail a rather different logic to that which dominates economic and financial management? It is, in fact, at a local level that the social effects of economic growth emerge clearly, as well as the manner in which this growth is conditioned by non-market factors. Structural planning could, therefore, establish a set of priorities according to criteria which have very little in common with prevailing economic rationality.

Planning and the local authority structure

The consistency postulated by planning is threatened not only by internal administrative compartmentalisation. It is equally threatened by the multitude of separate local authorities within the same planning zone. The various planning instruments (structure plans, strategic schemes, land-use plans) are complementary in so far as they are included in the same development strategy. But they are the responsibility of different political authorities in the three countries. In Britain, the area to which the structure plan applies coincides at least with the largest local authority. But the local planning powers of the districts risk the reintroduction at this level of rural–urban cleavages (Conservative–Labour) which the structure plan precisely sought to overcome. Elsewhere, the structure planning bodies, SDAU or inter-communal planning bodies, often found themselves subject to the field services of central government or of a large town. In most cases, rivalry between centre and the periphery has combined with partisan rivalries to paralyse the application of structure plans, as much due to the incompatibility of plans as to piecemeal public intervention.

However, there is an undeniable contrast between the constancy with which the experts call for a unified planning and administrative body at the level of the city region and political indifference towards such proposals. Is this attributable simply to the lethargy of a basically conservative political class? Or should one conclude that the experts are neglecting the dangers of an excessively centralised management of the city region, with all the consequences of internal subdivision, social segregation and isolation from the population which charac-terise an outsize administration? Should greater attention not be paid to reform schemes which seek to create or strengthen new, smaller, administrative units which would not copy the old rural–urban divi-sions but would try to reconstitute the basic units of democratic oversight?

Local and national affairs

One of the most characteristic implications of the new form of planning appears to be the way in which it tends to blur the rigid distinction between local and national affairs. The construction of an underground, of an administrative centre, of a new town, the siting of a university or hospital, are so many vital elements in the organisation of an urban area. But dealing with these local matters requires resources which are often beyond the capacity of the largest local authorities to provide. Moreover, the consequences of such action often affect the whole of regional and interregional development. The classical hierarchy: national affairs being dealt with by the central government, local affairs by local government, is thus threatened in practice because these are local matters which have become 'affairs of state'. So the effects of this development upon the reality of local autonomy should be analysed. The germs of a national policy of urban development are already visible. They combine negative classical control, supervision of local plans and major development schemes: new towns, regional planning bodies, special intervention funds.

This raises the question of whether, in France at least, this policy does not lead to a further extension of state control over society. Conversely, the way in which the Joint Teams, a product of the local

planning authorities, have managed to become in Britain the chief
body concerned with preparing regional plans, seems characteristic of
the difference in power relationships between the two countries.
Consequently, the problem of local autonomy takes on a new form. It
is no longer a matter of maintaining independent control over a
limited number of local activities but of possessing a capability for
effective influence in an interdependent relationship with central
government.

Urban planning and public awareness

Attempts at developing citizen participation in urban planning seem to
have developed at very different rates in each country. They remain
rare in the context of the regulatory planning of growth. They only
become important when urban planning tries to analyse and, if
possible, influence, the strategies of the various agents of urban
development. Public participation has not developed significantly in
Italy outside the traditional channels of the political parties and
interest groups. However, at another level, the influence of the professional elite of planners is evident in the increasing public awareness
about urban and environmental problems. This socialising influence of
planning is also present in France, with the appeals to the public that
were a feature of the early sixties. It was then a matter of obtaining,
through the discussion of the plan as a social project, the public
legitimation of new professional teams caught in an ambiguous administrative position. In Britain, attempts to involve the public appeared to be linked above all to the search for a new definition of
the legitimate function of an already well-established profession that
felt its traditional norms threatened.

 With interventions producing opposition, which brings conflicting
interests and groups into the open, the creation of consultation and
information procedures seeks to re-establish a minimum consensus on
the role of the planner. These consultative procedures are integrated
within the planning apparatus. They represent very clearly the move
from a kind of planning in which the planner tries to impose his own
conceptions on the town, to a type of planning conceived more
explicitly as the search for criteria whereby group conflicts can be
arbitrated.

Conclusion

For a long time, the urban planning profession succeeded in getting an
active part of public opinion to accept the idea that every advance in the
development of planning activities represented a step in social progress. This assimilation was facilitated by the fact that urban planning

was concerned with specific and marginal aims: the preservation of green belts and the provision of low-cost housing. Significantly, it was at a time when planning has tended to embark upon a much vaster field of action that the divorce between urban planning and its erstwhile supporters gradually came about. This is because planning cannot itself modify in a significant way the power struggle between the various agents of urban development. As a result, planning's criterion of success loses its clarity. The plan which is most likely to succeed technically will be the one which conforms most closely to the dominant economic and social interests. To use Lucien Nizard's distinction, other types of urban organisation could be envisaged which would be compatible with the existing economic and social organisation, but their chances of 'success' would be that much weaker because they would serve the dominant interests less well. Here, as in other planning practices, the hopes for reform which urban planning once attracted have tended to evaporate, while the threats which the prevailing organisation of society pose for urban life become unmistakable.

NOTES

1 See H. Coing, 'La ville en Plan', *Revue Française de Science Politique,* February 1973.
2 Max Weber, *Economie et Société,* 1972, p. 56.
3 See Jean-Claude Thoenig, *L'Ere des Technocrates. Le cas des Ponts et Chaussées,* 1973, especially Part 2.

VI

Transport policy

JEAN-CLAUDE THOENIG AND NIGEL DESPICHT

At first sight, the transport sector seems to be rather unattractive, offering little by way of spectacular prospects for the study of social and political phenomena. Furthermore, during the 1960s in the three countries under consideration, transport was usually no more than a secondary claim on the attention of governments and planners relative to what were more generally considered to be the basic economic problems of those countries. In any case, there seemed, during that decade, to be something almost too obvious about planning a sector so visible, specific and technical as transport. At the same time, a closer examination of the reality of planning and transport policy leads us to wonder whether transport was not, in fact, one of those fields of action in which planners were at their most conservative and in which they failed to understand the full potentiality of the planning instruments they possessed for the organisation of spatial relationships between men and between human activities. We feel, in fact, that the successes and failures of 'planning', as it was conceived and practised in the field of transport policy, make this field an important test case in our study of planning and political institutions.[1]

Planning and transport policy

There is little in the transport sector itself, in the three countries under consideration, that would justify the planners in failing to give it the highest priority in their activities.

First, transport is quantitatively very important to national economies as an economic and social activity. In most western European countries, up to 10% of the total national labour force is employed in transport while between 15% and 20% of gross capital formation is annually devoted to transport. On a continental scale, trade links between national economies and the pattern of supply and marketing of commodities are largely determined by the state of development of the transport system.

Secondly, transport policy is the oldest and best-established field of regulation and state intervention in Europe. Shipping law and practice go back to medieval times; road and bridge planning have been major functions of modern (i.e. post-1450) governments, both central and local; the introduction of railway transport can be said to have created the earliest form of industrial technocracy. Since about 1820, technological advance in transport has been extremely rapid, and since 1945 quite phenomenal. The field of transport policy is, in fact, extremely well organised with strong tendencies towards technocracy. It presents planners with difficult problems when they try to justify innovations of policy of the sort associated with planning in the 1960s.

Finally, transport policy is a complex and uncertain concept which offers a great intellectual challenge to planners. While it is clear from an *operational* point of view what constitutes transport, it is anything but clear what should be regarded as the total transport context from a *planning* point of view. The examples of energy supply, telecommunications and urban transport, illustrate the challenge to planners.

(i) Energy supply used to be part of vehicular transport until the introduction of electric grids and pipelines. But solid coal remains an important element, both in energy supply and in vehicular goods transport, while petroleum and gas-based energy supply involves major maritime shipping activities.

(ii) Telecommunications are now a technical system of their own, whereas the 'mail' was simply one among many commodities for vehicular transport in the past. But telecommunications remain, to some extent, a substitute for vehicular movement and are becoming increasingly necessary to permit an optimum exploitation of new vehicular technologies (e.g. the transmission by telex and computer of the instructions and data needed to control the physical movement of goods across frontiers, and for the purposes of customs, insurance and financial clearance).

(iii) Urban transport had been regarded as part of the general transport system until motorisation created acute urban congestion (interfering with collection and delivery operations), and until special urban transport technologies began to be developed to conserve the environment. In modern conditions, it must be recognised that there are now at least *two* transport policies that need the benefit of the planning attitude: policy relating to trunk vehicular transport (of an inter-city/world-wide character) and policy relating to urban distribution systems, which are geographically isolated but require technical and operational standardisation to ensure world-wide compatibility.

Before considering the particular national experiences in France, Britain and Italy, it is necessary to consider the extent to which transport policy is the same, or a different, sort of activity in the three countries.

The composition of the national vehicular transport system

There are marked differences between the physical transport systems of the three countries. These influence national policy and attitudes towards transport planning.

Shipping. Both France and Italy are small maritime nations. Britain, on the other hand, has one of the world's largest merchant fleets, representing a stake in world shipping equivalent to that of the Six as a whole. British transport policy is, in fact, modelled on shipping policy. This is not the case in France or Italy.

Aviation. Britain and France are not only major world operators of aviation services, they are also major world producers of aircraft. British and French air operators are, of course, under pressure to buy national. Italy, on the other hand, has no aircraft industry and is a major world operator in a very commercial sense. Alitalia probably does make a profit!

Railways. The SNCF accounts for about half the goods carried in France, and in absolute terms French railway transport continues to increase slightly. In Britain and Italy, however, railway transport accounts for less than a quarter of national goods carriage, and is declining both absolutely and relatively. In France, the concept of the railways as a universal carrier continued throughout the 1960s. In Britain, the railways were deliberately reshaped from 1962 onwards as a specialised carrier, while moves towards an explicit specialisation of railway transport were also made in Italy from the mid-1960s onwards.

Waterways. France is planning major expansions of waterways transport (which takes about 12% of total inland goods), and has an operational stake in Rhine and European inland shipping. In Britain and Italy, inland shipping does not exist in any commercial sense.

Road transport. There is little to distinguish the three countries as regards bus transport. There is, however, a fundamental difference as regards commercial transport of goods. Both Britain and Italy are dependent on road haulage and can only envisage the future of inland transport in terms of the continued expansion of the transport of goods by road. In France, road haulage tends to be regarded simply as one of three modes, and the development of transport is conceived in terms of the coordinated expansion of several modes.

The stage of motorisation and urbanisation of the particular country

It is not sufficient to measure the motorisation of a country simply in terms of numbers of vehicles. As regards cars per thousand inhabitants, France is the most motorised of European countries, with Britain about next and Italy some way behind. All three countries can be said to be well along the road to a society in which each family has at least one car. But from the standpoint of planning and transport policy, it is necessary to pay equal, if not more, attention to the phenomenon of industrial urbanisation. In this case, the picture is very different. The dates at which the different national populations could be said to be predominantly urban and industrialised seem to be as follows: Britain, 1870; France, 1970; Italy, after 1980.

There is, therefore, a major disparity between the pace of industrial urbanisation in Britain on the one hand and that of the two continental countries on the other. This is reflected in political attitudes and administrative institutions concerned with urban planning and transport policy.

The tradition of state intervention in transport

In this book, the 1960s are generally regarded as a time when a new concept and practice of planning was introduced. In the case of transport planning, it would seem to be necessary to distinguish the national antecedents of transport policy by reference to their long histories.

France has had a centralised national state authority which has concerned itself with the regulation and planning of transport at least since Louis XIV. It is not an accident that the Corps des Ingénieurs des Ponts et Chaussées was a seventeenth-century creation, institutionalised in 1740. Neither Britain nor Italy has any comparable experience of centralised state regulation.

Italy was not a national state before late in the nineteenth century. It inherited the autarchic interventionism (as regards transport) of several small baroque states which continued to resist a more rational policy for Italy as a whole. One may say that a conflict between a centralising state power and centrifugal specialised or localised agencies still characterises Italian experience of transport policy. But in modern times this is less the inheritance of the past than the inevitable clash between an established central administration and new, emerging local forces created by industrialisation.

Britain tried every form of pre-industrial intervention (e.g. flag

discrimination, concessions, etc), and finally abandoned state intervention in transport altogether in 1849. The railways of Britain were
built with private capital and were never regarded as an instrument of
state policy. Modern attempts at persuasive coordination or at integration of road and rail transport were made as early as the 1920s, but
it was not until 1947 that the British state entered transport as an
operator through the instrument of nationalised industry.

It is easy to understand how these three national contexts gave rise to
very different historical and institutional processes and why the possibilities of making planning an integral part of governmental decision-
making were different in Britain, France and Italy.

The field of our study is the way in which transport policy developed in these countries during the 1960s. We are tackling it under two
lines of inquiry.

(a) To what extent did planning transform the conception of
transport policy? (By the term 'transport policy' we mean the acts and
omissions of the public authorities in respect of the transport sector.)

(b) In what ways did planning alter the political rules of the game for
making transport policy?

France: technocratic planning

In France, past and present, with or without planning, transport
represents a sector over which the state and officials exercise a
strong hold. This public control takes the form of the definition of
separate policies for each transport sector, even those like maritime
shipping in which private interests are relatively powerful and organised. The state employs a diverse and extensive set of means to exert
pressure on transport, such as tarification, quotas and subsidies. This
bureaucratic interventionism is justified by a long tradition which
regards transport as one of the special instruments of state action
aimed at ensuring at one and the same time economic development,
control of the country from Paris and military defence. In the
twentieth century the power of the state was increased by several
factors whose effects mutually reinforced one another: the nationalisations of 1936 and 1945, the economic crises of the thirties and
forties and the administrative centralisation carried out initially by
the Popular Front, increased under the Vichy régime and after the
Liberation and, as we shall see, by planning after 1960.

The state owns and manages, through powerful public enterprises,
the most important sectors of transport: the railways by the SNCF,
urban transport by the RATP, civil aviation by Air France and Paris
Airport. Similarly it is directly interested in maritime transport (Com-

pagnie Générale Transatlantique and others). Directly or indirectly, decisions taken by the government and its civil servants concern the whole transport system. Private interests, on the whole, have little power. For their part, local authorities are totally dependent on the state. This power of the state is evident for example in the field of financing investment. The Fifth Plan provided for the following investments: 10 billion [milliard] francs for the railways (provided by the SNCF); 26 billion francs for roads (of which 15 billions are provided by the state and the rest by local authorities, but under strict Paris control); 1.9 billion francs for navigable waterways (of which 1.5 billions by the state); 2.5 billion francs for the ports (of which 1.3 billions directly by the state).

A sectoral approach

Although French planning began in 1946, it was not until the 1960s that it was really extended to include transport. It is true that from the beginning the Planning Commissariat had a transport division, but for a long time it exercised only a minor influence. Certainly, the First Plan intervened in the railways, but this was to undertake a temporary task: the reconstruction of what had been destroyed in the war.

There were many reasons for this discretion on the part of the planners. They did not entirely understand the role transport could play in economic development. Above all, they found it difficult to penetrate into the closed world of transport. The Ponts et Chaussées service, which had the principal responsibility for transport, strongly resisted any outside interference in what it considered its own affairs. Moreover, the railway interests received privileged treatment at the expense of roads and waterways, based on the prestige (and financial appetite) of the railway administration. Everything concerning the railways came under the direct discretionary power of the government and its assessment of the political situation. Furthermore, a pressure group of Ponts et Chaussées engineers at the top of the government machine ensured the permanence of railway policy and resisted giving any attention to motor transport, which was treated as a luxury and hardly 'democratic'!

Transport planning, from the moment it was introduced in 1960, consisted, like many of the sectors coming under the Plan, of two main elements: a study of the market and a list of some desirable public investments. The Fourth and Fifth Plans studied prospective traffic flows and transport needs over the next five years. They calculated the funds required to meet the demand and drew up a list of the main investments called for, identifying the problems which might arise in their implementation. The Fifth Plan, stemming from the valuable experience and confidence acquired in the work on the Fourth Plan, introduced two or three more wide-ranging considerations. It paid attention not only to the building but also to management of infrastructures. In the name of price realism, it proposed that the public transport undertakings should aim at reducing their deficits. Similarly, it stressed the improvement of the quality of services provided (speed, comfort). It dealt with technical standardisation. It gave a place, finally, to the social and human problems of transport, such as working conditions. Moreover, during the preparation of the Fifth Plan, an effort was made to improve the coordination of the development of transport with industrial development. The geographic dispersal of investments was reduced and public money was concentrated on a few priority projects: electrification of some main railway routes, the improvement of the ports of Marseille and Le Havre and the construction of several nationally important motorways.

The policy of regional development[2] provides a good example of the sectoralisation of transport which the impact of planning scarcely affected. In contrast to British experience, French planning showed itself unable to establish a close relationship between public decisions concerning transport and those concerning regional development and urban planning. Transport policy was not really used at a local or regional level as an operational instrument. However from 1960 to 1970, France underwent a considerable acceleration in the urbanisation of its population. The town became a priority concern of the planners and the government. With regard to transport planning, the problem was solved very simply: urban transport was isolated from the rest of the transport system and entrusted to the Modernisation Commission for Towns. The Transport Commission itself had nothing to do with controlling the growth of towns.

The planners were certainly not blind to the problems this raised. For example, the Fifth Plan underlines the fact that 'transport must also be adapted to the economic development recommended by the policy of regional development and in certain cases even anticipate its achievement'. It states as a major objective the attainment of a sufficient level of investment in transport to enable a locality to be developed. In reality, only some particularly spectacular regional development operations, such as Fos-sur-Mer, really modified the content and approach of transport policy.

In general, those responsible for transport policy thought that in France transport was not a bottleneck for regional development. When circumstances made it really imperative, it was sufficient to react and make a slight adjustment in transport arrangements. At the same time, urban transport (i.e. transport as part of the essential process of urbanisation that underlay most regional development policies) was left on one side, in order to concentrate on trunk transport alone – the major lines of communication and the major ports.

This persistence of a sectoral approach represented a relative setback for planning. The weight of tradition, the resistance of the traditional administration and the demagogy of the transport interests partly explain why the planners remained prudent, even conservative, and hardly attempted to upset the established decision processes by imposing another approach. They contented themselves with flying a trial kite from time to time, but without following through. The Fifth Plan, for example, proposed for discussion a move from an investment policy to one of transport management, based on coordination of the different types of transport. This proposal was taken up again at the end of the Fifth Plan in the form of an experiment relating to travel between Paris and Lyon: rail, road and air interests were asked to participate in a working party established to compare the relative costs of the different forms of transport. This necessitated moving from an analysis based on the type of transport to one based on the market. Another attempt at a horizontal approach was made in the case of business trips. Finally, at the end of the Fifth Plan, the planners tackled the problem of container traffic, but this attempt to introduce criteria allowing a specialisation in the style of transport did not go very far.

In sum, the overall impact of planning appears feeble at first glance, despite a few isolated successes. In so far as certain innovations were introduced into transport policy, they seem, in fact, to owe very little to planning. An example of this amongst others was the decision to 'de-nationalise' the road network, particularly by granting to private companies the financing, construction and management of new motorways (such as Paris–Tours, Paris–Strasbourg). In fact, between 1960 and 1970 the planners followed a strategy of change which, even if it did not affect the approach to transport policy by those politically and administratively responsible, did yield some good results in other respects.

A reform of administrative practices

Transport planning was done by technocrats. The president, vice-presidents and the two rapporteurs of the Transport Commission of the Fourth Plan were senior civil servants. This situation reflected the state's hold over transport, but at the same time it conditioned and reflected the work of the planners who, by acting with the exclusive Parisian world of high officials, hoped, at the risk of becoming its prisoners, to modify its attitudes and gain access to the key-points at which the state's decisions were made. For them, it was a question of making the innumerable decisions taken within the governmental machine more rational. Such a way of going about things produced ambiguous and even contradictory results from the point of view of change.

By turning to planning, increased centralisation was brought about within the agencies in charge of transport. With regard to roads, maritime ports and navigable waterways, local state agencies lost their autonomy of decision in favour of the central administration. The ministries in Paris were strengthened, they were furnished with teams of economists and engineers. They usurped, thanks to their participation in planning, greater power to make the initial proposals and impose their decisions on the local agencies. This spectacular centralisation led to two consequences. On the one hand, administrative procedures became more bureaucratic; on the other hand, local authorities and local interest groups had even greater difficulty in exerting pressure on the decisions of the civil servants. Nevertheless, this was not the case in sectors where, as in the railways or aviation, the central administration already played the essential role because of the existence of public enterprises like the SNCF or Air France, which were themselves very centralised.

Planning did not upset existing institutions. The only pertinent innovation was the creation in 1960 of an Economic and International Affairs Service (SAEI).[3] Being an administrative unit composed of experts, this service fulfilled a horizontal task. It coordinated the plans of each type of transport, stimulated the ideas and action of the many bureaux which exercised this or that part of state control and advised the ministers concerned with transport. Provoking at first the hostility of certain of these bureaux, who were jealous of their autonomy, it was finally accepted as a valuable study centre and a modest-size coordinating body.

Apart from the SAEI, administrative institutions did not experience any innovation. Their compartmentalisation continued to reflect the sectoral division of the various types of transport: such as the Roads Division for roads, the Ports Division for maritime ports and navigable waterways. However, in order to avoid being superseded by the Planning Commissariat and by the SAEI, the officials in the ministries were led to take an interest in planning to such an extent that they took charge themselves, at least in certain cases, of the part of the Plan which concerned them. Their approach to transport certainly remained compartmentalised and traditional, but they were led to adopt the methods and to operate within the framework of planning. Above all, new inter-personal networks were set up between institutions. What until then had been done more or less secretly in the twilight of the separate ministries' offices, became located in the Planning Commissariat and was brought into the open. Competition with others had to be met. Face-to-face relations between the officials responsible for each kind of transport were strengthened, or even established for the first time.

Between the planners and the officials of the traditional ministries, an authentic planning network was created, over and above the hierarchical pyramids and divisions. Inter-personal communication was facilitated by the fact that the majority of the members of the network belonged to the same corps (Ponts et Chaussées). Similarly, contacts increased between the ministries responsible for transport and the powerful budget division of the Ministry of Finance. Budgetary negotiations were no longer confined to an infrequent and abrasive exchange between the spending ministries and the guardians of the public purse. More frequent discussions brought together officials at lower levels in the hierarchy. At the same time, a measure of agreement was reached between them to take account, in budgetary decisions, of the studies and medium-term objectives worked out in the planning process. This was noticeable, for example, in the case of roads. Previously treated as an 'electoral' concern, regularly sacrificed to the ups and downs of the annual financial situation, roads henceforth received more sustained attention and, above all, a guaranteed commitment of funds for the period of the Plan by the Ministry of Finance.

Although indicative, transport planning was progressively integrated into the budgetary process, to the point where it was one of the parts of the Plan whose implementation was most fully reflected in the government's financial decisions. The investment part of the Fourth Plan was fulfilled one hundred per cent. Several factors explain this harmony between the Plan and budget. Those who were responsible for transport planning were also those who participated in preparing governmental decisions, whether in the budgetary process or in day to day decisions recommended to ministers by their personal staff. To plan transport was to plan public decisions in transport matters. The dominance of the state was such that the application of the Plan was facilitated. The decisions concerning transport, at least those relating to investment, were of a medium-term nature and were insulated from short-term fluctuations.

It was only gradually and in the long run that such a process of change within the administration produced results in policy content. Although the sectoral approach remained the same, planning nevertheless slowly brought together the various policies through studies involving forecasts of traffic covering all types of transport. Unable to operate at the level of policy acts and omissions, the horizontal coordination of the various kinds of transport was achieved through the methods establishing the framework for decisions. Even within each type of transport, the impact of planning on policy was undeniable. The planners pushed their audacity so far as to cast doubt on the modernisation policy of the SNCF, which from 1946 had envisaged only electrification without giving serious consideration to the acceleration of the use of diesel power. At best they exercised a veto against proposals that were then considered impractical, such as the Rhône–Rhine canal project.

From 1960 to 1970, planning made procedures more explicit and arguments more rational within the little world of the technocrats. Dispersal of funds or incrementalism were questioned as budgetary principles. It was a very domestic change – within the family so to speak – but even so, a change which inhibited incest!

A transformation of the rules of the game

Between 1960 and 1970 transport policy was worked out in a political context characterised by two main features: a modification of the power relationships between those involved, and a transformation of the rules of the game. The central government technocrats strengthened their role and their capacity to intervene, thereby reducing the role of political debate as such. In fact, the alliance of engineers and economists, running like a seamless thread throughout the administration, held .two essential trump cards in the preparation of decisions: expertise and the ability to negotiate with the local and private interests concerned, choosing between their claims. With rare exceptions, the government ratified the suggestions of this alliance. Parliament played a small role, only intervening on points of detail, which was willingly accepted. Politicians in general accepted the 'rational' character and dominance of the experts in transport matters.

The influence of pressure groups and agencies representing the interests concerned differed widely according to their nature and the means at their disposal. Both sides remained about equally balanced in the sectors where government officials faced powerful and well-organised private interests (shipowners for example) or monopoly nationalised enterprises (such as SNCF, Air Inter). In such cases the planning alliance had to take notice of the opinions and wishes expressed by transport interests. Agreement with the nationalised enterprises and with the lobbies was an important pre-condition for the success of the planners. Agreement was much easier to achieve with the nationalised enterprises, because their directors were often former high-ranking civil servants and in particular former Ponts et Chaussées engineers. If the central administration imposed its viewpoint relatively easily when faced with not very well-organised or established interests, such as consumer associations, the situation was more delicate where it was faced with lobbies representing small or medium-size private road hauliers or boatmen. Politicisation of the issue was the most effective weapon which these lobbies possessed. Rather than accepting a more or less rational and undercover process of negotiation, they did not hesitate to employ extreme arguments and make the debate public. The willingness of these lobbies to sacrifice the public interest to their sectional aims succeeded in certain cases in obliging the planners and the government to give in. To take two examples: (i) a costly compromise between waterway and petroleum interests to share the transport of petrol between the waterways and pipelines, and (ii) the limitation of lorry axle weight to 15 tons, under the combined pressure of road hauliers and lorry manufacturers, a minor limitation in relation to the cost of road maintenance. This politicisation was all the more easy in that the sectoral approach in transport continued to be the norm. The planners' margin for manoeuvre was all the more reduced because very often the officials identified closely with the viewpoint of the transport interests they were supervising.

The other important innovation facilitated by planning was a transformation of the rules of the game. Transport planning provided an excellent illustration of the doctrine, worked out by Jean Monnet and re-affirmed by Pierre Massé, according to which one of the most important achievements the Plan can seek is to bring about a fundamental change of attitude, as a result of the participation in the work of planning of those involved (carriers, civil servants, experts and so on). While the Plan can be used by the carriers as a way of defending their vested interests and for commending the vital necessity of developing the mode of transport that they use, at the same time, and without any decisional constraint, it equally enabled questions to be raised. Waterways, for example, were a marginal, backward sector which, thanks to the Plan, acquired a renewed vigour. Similarly, rejected until 1960 as a useless gadget, motor transport achieved more equitable treatment thanks to the Plan. The road interests – officials, hauliers, car manufacturers – denounced the injustice done them in the interests of the railways and received satisfaction, for moral as much as 'rational' reasons. Road investment rose spectacularly but rail investment tended to stagnate. While railway freight traffic increased in the decade 1960–70 by some 20 %, that going by road more than doubled.

At the same time, genuine progress in the methodology and knowledge of transportation was achieved through the work of the Plan's Transport Commission. Statistical progress was as rapid as it was great, in the matter of traffic flows, studies of consumer preferences and so on. One technique developed rapidly: the cost-benefit analysis of investment schemes.[4] Ideas for new types of transport, such as hovertrains, were developed.

By the end of the decade, as a result of the impact of planning, the civil service had more or less carried out a major transformation of its interventionist activities. Step by step, it had moved from legalistic administrative regulation to economic and financial techniques. Its intervention had gained in flexibility and speed. By reducing the range of its instruments of intervention, which were previously as heterogeneous as they were oppressive, it had paradoxically gained in effectiveness.

For the transport industry, the Plan tried to be a kind of educator, dispensing both new information and a certain way of reasoning. The fact of analysing five years ahead, together with the mass of information passed on by the planners, put the representatives of the transport industry within a more rational and responsible framework. It became more difficult for the transport industry to insist on having its cake and eating it, for example to seek a large number of subsidies from the state *and* total freedom in setting prices. Even though conflicts of interest between government and transport industry were not eliminated, a common language for discussing their problems had emerged.

Britain: managing change

The tradition of state intervention in transport, against which the introduction of planning in the 1960s must be judged, is very complex in Britain. This is because the dimension of public policy which is *missing* in France and Italy (i.e. integrated planning of transport and urban development) was an established field in British administration at least a generation before the 1960s. At the same time, the British state had traditionally avoided ownership of any part of the transport industry, and nationalisation and state guidance of transport development had been one of the most controversial items in the Labour/Tory political debate since 1918. Economic planning, however, was of a limited kind even during the 1960s. A genuine forward look at transport in Britain was not contemplated until 1972. The result is that the 1960s, in contrast to the French and Italian experiences, represent a period in British administrative history which has a dual character.

(a) In its initial form, coordinated transport and urban planning had been instituted by the 1947 Town and Country Planning Act, which was part of the major reforming legislation emerging from wartime planning. A generation later, after a government enquiry in depth, the Town and Country Planning Act, 1968, turned it into 'urban structure planning'. This was based on the principle of transport planning and land-use planning being integrated to create a framework for urban development strategy.

(b) Economic planning of transport was still, at the end of the 1950s, a political battlefield in which the Tories defended Britain against the threat of Socialist planning. During the 1960s, however, economic planning ceased to be a hot political issue and became accepted as normal administrative practice in transport policy.

The effect of planning in the 1960s was to create situations and possibilities for reforms of the British state administration by political decision at government/parliament level. During the 1960s there was an effective political response to these opportunities as far as transport was concerned. First, fundamental improvements were made in the physical planning regime (both institutionally and conceptually). This improvement of an already well-developed physical planning regime can be compared to the impetus given by planning in France in the 1960s to the already well-developed economic and social planning regime. Secondly, institutions and practices were introduced which, although not always successful in themselves, created possibilities for a more effective economic planning of transport in the 1970s. This initiating or pioneering action can be compared to the Italian experience in the 1960s when the initial framework for *assetto del territorio* was created.

A radical transformation

In retrospect, the introduction of planning into British administration generally in the 1960s does not seem to have been solely a triumph of the Labour party's ideas of planning. First, the spadework epitomised by NEDC was done under the Conservatives. Secondly, the late 1950s and the early 1960s period was generally a time of agonising reappraisal, imposed on the government and parliament by the Suez débâcle, the reappearance of the depressed areas, the problem of 'entry into Europe' and so on. What is remarkable, however, is that there is strong evidence that planning would have been introduced *in any case* into physical planning and transport policy. This independent movement towards planning was a response to certain challenges specific to transport, such as motorisation and technological developments in distribution which, at about the end of the 1950s, began to change the traditional pattern of constraints as regards costs and physical possibilities.

The experience and forecasts of motorisation in the early 1960s confirmed the validity of visions like that of Buchanan's *Traffic in Towns* and of *ad hoc* practices of integrated transport and land-use planning by central and local government. The concept of urban structure planning that emerged from the 1964 PAG Report, the 1968 Town and Country Planning Act and subsequent transport planning regimes, were effectively an application of planning to physical planning problems, in response to an appreciation of the motorisation of British society.[5]

The technological developments in distribution indicated first, that railways could survive in the United Kingdom only as a specialised carrier, and secondly that only an 'intermodal' approach to transport policy would be adequate to take account of unit-load techniques, in particular containers. It was also urgent to speed up and rationalise the inevitably massive investment in roads and road vehicles. The Transport Acts of 1962 and 1968 represent a planning approach to transforming the commercial transport system in the light of these explicit appreciations.

The coincidence of a general move towards planning with a special move in the area of transport had the effect of permitting a great deal to be achieved in this special field. In the 1960s, British transport policy was radically transformed, not only in relation to its own past but also in relation to the development of transport policy in most other European countries. The legislation which is now the Transport Act, 1968, was heralded not by one White Paper but by three.

(a) In *1966*, a Transport Policy White Paper proposed a thoroughgoing reform on the lines of the typical 1960s' planning. This document showed signs of having been hastily put together and its doctrine was too novel to avoid causing confusion.

(b) In *1967*, the actual legislation (i.e. the Bill that finally became the Transport Act 1968) was preceded by two White Papers – the first dealing with the transport of goods and the second dealing with public passenger transport and traffic control. The publication of two White Papers indicated that, as a result of an application of planning, it was realised that modern industrialised and urbanised states need *two* transport policies, one, economic/commercial and the other, social/environmental.

The economic/commercial transport policy in Britain in the 1960s was a successful application of planning *within* a sector. It subordinated government intervention and regulation of transport to explicit appreciations of technological and economic realities. But the general economic planning machinery in Britain was not then able to digest this pioneer experience in transport policy, and its full significance was not apparent till the 1970s. On the other hand, the social/environmental transport policy was, from the start, part and parcel of the development of the urban structure planning regime in which the fundamental changes in the dynamic aspect of human life (i.e. transport) were a catalyst. Unfortunately, in both fields, planning failed to break the traditional conceptual framework of transport policy which treated vehicular transport, energy supply and communications as quite separate systems for the purposes of making public policy.

Institutional change and administrative practice

The 1960s were a period of remarkable institutional change in the British central state machine. To a great extent, the changes can be said to have been brought about by people imbued with the spirit of planning. There is, however, a contrast between the lasting achievement of the 1960s in physical planning institutions and the trial-and-error groping of economic planning institutions whose results were ephemeral.

(a) *Physical planning.* At the beginning of the 1960s, the Ministry of Transport and the Ministry of Housing and Local Government were separate Ministries which seldom concerted policy in advance. By the end of the 1960s, however, the two Ministries had been merged into one Department of the Environment. Concordance between transport and urban planning policies was ensured by the fusion of the former administrations down to divisional level. Furthermore, local authorities were already discussing the substance of their 'structure plans' with the central government prior to public debate about strategy.

(b) *Economic planning.* At the beginning of the 1960s, there were the Treasury, the NEDC and the Board of Trade. At the end of the 1960s, there was the Treasury, the NEDC and the Department of Trade and Industry. The DEA had come and gone.

The introduction of planning in the 1960s had two effects on administrative practice. First, it became necessary to 'have a plan' for any policy to have much chance of succeeding in political terms. Secondly, it became necessary to consult, or to possess within the administrative machine, 'experts' capable of ensuring that the plans were good ones. During the 1960s, however, the prototype of the expert was a self-conscious academic economist. By the end of the decade, most of these had resigned or had been promoted out of harm's way.

In physical planning, the British administration was already accustomed to 'having a plan'. It used the planning impetus of the 1960s to improve the type of plan to be made and the extent to which the plan committed public authorities to actual expenditure. This radical change in the quality of physical planning administration was brought about by the efforts of traditional types of civil servant in the ministries responsible for transport and town and country planning. The contribution made by the economic planners who had been brought in from outside was quite secondary. The political respectability of planning released forces under the state administration. At first, under the influence of the French model, the extra expertise needed was conceived in economic terms but, by the end of the 1960s, the general feeling was that the extra expertise needed for urban structure planning was not that of economists but that of sociologists.

In economic planning, the difficulty was to explain to the British administration what 'having a plan' meant in practice. The 1965 National Plan contributed nothing to transport policy. In this field, the new expert economists had a lot to say, but little of it was important because economic theory in the 1960s did not seem to have grasped the significance of the *technological* revolutions in transport. Instead, *de facto* 'planners' in the shape of dynamic managers within the transport industry (Dr Beeching was a prototype with his 'reshaping of British railways') applied planning from inside and carried out a major reorganisation of the transport system in spite of the National Plan and the government's economic advisers.

The success of planning in transport policy during the 1960s was due, in the main, to its catalytic effect in bringing about a closer link between the spending administrations (who conceive projects for investment) and the budgetary administrations (who are responsible for financial commitments). In practice, this was achieved in large measure by the forceful and tenacious activity of the Ministry of Transport. This ministry insisted to the Ministry of Housing and Local Government that urban structure plans must be a realistic first stage for commitments of investment money if the integration of transport planning and land-use planning was to mean anything in practice. Furthermore, it also insisted to the Treasury that, if the Ministry of Transport were able to produce a rational method of forward programming, the Treasury would have to be prepared to make forward financial commitments at the planning stage – a stage that corresponded to a very early, if not premature stage in traditional public finance practice. This activity of the Ministry of Transport was successful largely because, during the 1950s, the two types of civil servant concerned with transport – the professional engineers and the generalist administrative class – had succeeded in overcoming the barriers of professional jealousy and were working as unified Ministry of Transport teams down to sub-divisional level. The combined force of this administrative and technical expertise was greater than the force that any other ministry (including the Treasury) could muster. In the later 1960s, this experience of integrated administration in the Ministry of Transport was studied by the Fulton Committee[6] as a leading example of professionalism in public administration.

Less empiricism and more rationality

At the beginning of the 1960s, when planning became fashionable, the British transport system was, physically and commercially, very different from most of the transport systems on the continent of Europe. On the one hand, it had progressed very much further in motorisation. On the other, it had not been modernised after the war as the continental railway-dominated systems had been.

The administrative tools that were developed to implement the planning approach to transport policy – in particular to give effect to the reappraisal of traditional practice in the light of explicit objectives – altered the quality of transport policy. During the 1960s, it became more rational, more effective and more responsive to feedback from users of transport. Four examples will illustrate this.

(a) By defining the role of railways as 'commercial and not public service', analyses of existing practice revealed that 30% of the rail network carried only 1% of total rail traffic and cost benefit studies indicated that the best prospects lay in technical specialisation and intermodal ventures. The resultant reshaping during the 1960s brought British rail very near to solvency by 1970/1971.[7]

(b) In 1960, the roads programme was still limited to one year ahead. From 1961 onwards it was transformed by application of critical path analysis, by relating the long-term planning coefficients of traffic load/capacity to the criteria of investment programming priority and by the imposition of rational techniques for planning resource allocation. By 1970, the road programme was a five year 'rolling' investment programme linked to a ten-year project-preparation programme within the framework of a long-term network plan which was regularly updated by computerised methods.

(c) By the end of the 1960s, the central government was trying to arrive at a scale of levels of envisaged expenditure for assessing the realism of twenty-year-ahead urban structure plans. In 1960, such an exercise was regarded as foolishly academic, with the result that development plan approval was emotionally political.

(d) Types of regulatory regime were reappraised in the light of rational social and economic objectives and modified accordingly. As a result, road haulage licensing (both 'quality' and 'quantity' in the EEC jargon) including the juridical distinction between transport for hire and transport on own account was abolished. The separateness of traffic regulation, road building and public passenger transport provision was removed and new, interdependent institutions were created with powers, duties and financial possibilities that were designed to ensure *concerted* planning. At last, a large part of the inland waterway system was removed from the sphere of commercial transport and made exclusively available for water supply, drainage, pleasure-sailing and amenity.

Local and central government

The effect of planning on the role of local government in transport and on the relations between the centre and the provinces in transport was as far-reaching as its effect on central government institutions for transport policy.

(a) Technological advance in transport indicated the *possible* desirability of replacing multi-purpose local government administrations by single-purpose functional agencies which would not be democratic. The explicit planning of social/environmental strategy, however, indicated the need to retain an overall political planning authority, reinforcing the democratic process. These considerations were major factors in the proposals made for a reform in the structure of local government in England and in Scotland. They were also a source of criticism of the earlier proposals for the reorganisation of local authority areas in Wales.

(b) The need to plan transport investment as an integral part of environmental and economic development was a major factor determining the 1965 reform of the system for local government finance. It resulted in the retention of the specific 'capital' grant for transport infrastructure and traffic management, in the general context of an undifferentiated rate-support grant to local government revenue.

(c) Transport policy was one of the main concerns of the Regional Economic Planning Councils and Boards and the Ministry of Transport representative belonged to their small inner cores during the 1960s. The planning of transport development was one of the main factors leading towards the concern with so-called sub-regional plans, and the attempt to relate the development of certain regions not only to UK national development but also to European economic and social development.

In the United Kingdom, the experience of planning in the 1960s did not so much change the political framework, 'the rules of the game', as clarify and confirm the dual nature of the political framework peculiar to Britain. Many people in Britain felt that the experience of planning was very much an adoption of a French type of planning. This was an illusion. The French concept and practice of planning related to economic and social planning as one and the same activity. The problem in France has always been: how to fit in environmental planning? Despite the 1962 dictum of M. Claudius-Petit: 'l'aménagement du territoire est en réalité l'aménagement de notre société', the problem remained largely unsolved in France. *L'aménagement du territoire* had always to be a rival of the economic and social Plan, even though it was a weak rival that could be easily put in its place. In Britain, a single activity that could be called state economic and social planning would not really be a constitutional possibility. As the experience of the 1960s showed, there is one polarisation of British state planning towards *central* government (which is inherently commercial and economic) and another polarisation towards *local* government. This latter is essentially environmental and – if one may dare say so – in Britain, social as well. The introduction of the 1960s planning into transport policy (which was, as always, a very important function of *both* central and local government) was to enable the traditionally dualistic system to improve itself and in so doing to reinforce its duality. The dualism of the British system can be seen clearly in the attempts to bring transport policy matters effectively within the competence of Regional Economic Planning Councils and Boards. The result was political discussion without tangible results for transport policy. This was because the REPCs were monstrosities in Britain. They were an attempt by central government to invade the sphere of local government, a process which was vigorously rebuffed.

This striking 1960s planning experience makes it reasonable to suggest a comparative principle. In France and Italy, the 'region' represented a potentially beneficial level of decentralisation because the 'state' that did the planning in France and Italy had only *one* effective planning level: the central level. In Britain of the 1960s, the 'region' could only be a meeting point for harmonising the functionally different planning of the *two* planning levels in the state. Because the British region was not explicitly designed to perform this role, it was not able to be an effective force in transport policy, which had still to be carried out at both of the levels of state planning.

The consultation procedure

The making of transport policy in Britain both by central and local government, had long been a model for methods of public authority consultation with interest groups, lobbies etc.[8] This was one of the reasons why planning made such rapid progress in the 1960s. Planning can be said to have influenced the consultation procedure in two ways.

(a) The more rational and explicit method of making transport policy indicated that democracy would disappear unless the local government actors and partners represented much bigger, richer and more powerful local authorities. This was a powerful influence in proposals for local government reform.

(b) The attempt to make transport policy fall within the framework of wider national planning shifted the balance a little more in favour of the users of transport rather than the providers.

Planning certainly affected the relationship between the state authorities, the citizens and the carriers, i.e. the highly individualised interests. By the second half of the 1960s, 'participation' was the main theme of environmental/social planning. This was fully implemented in the transport aspect where, for the first time ever, the central government advised local authorities on the moral and political attitude which they should take towards objectors to proposed regulations of road traffic. In economic/commercial planning, there was a much greater involvement of the transport industry and the users of transport in the preparation of transport policy. The success of this involvement can be seen in the early 1970s when it was the CBI and the trade associations of the transport industry that were pressing the government to take a positive stand on the common transport policy of the European Community and not vice versa.

Italy: politicising the technicalities

In Italy, transport is a socio-economic sector in which strong intervention by the state is traditional. The Italian experience of state intervention is, however, different from that of France or Britain. Until the unification of the country only a century ago, her experience did not relate to the nation-state but to the small baroque state of the *ancien régime* and post-Napoleonic Restoration. Thus, in Italy, the tradition of state intervention in transport is a little paradoxical. It is, at one and the same time, an experience of centralising and *dirigiste* action by government and also an experience of centrifugal tendencies towards the autonomy of subnational structures.

The background

The present-day forms of Italian state intervention in transport did not crystallise until the twentieth century:

State ownership and regulation. The railways were nationalised in 1904. State responsibility for road building was nationalised in the 1920s with the creation of a managerially autonomous state agency (AASS and later ANAS).

Management by state enterprise. After 1945, the state enterprise IRI was entrusted with a substantial part of the merchant navy and the Italian civil aviation industry (merged into Alitalia). ENI had a large stake in the Italian tanker fleet as well as operating the pipeline network. In the mid-1950s, IRI also became the leading concessionnaire (and effective planner) of the motorway programme.

State concession. This particular form of administration, which was utilised in the nineteenth century for local and regional railways, remained a feature of the Italian system despite the bankruptcy of the concessionary railways and the need for the state to guarantee them. It was used for motorway building both under the Fascist regime and from the mid-1950s onwards. But, like the evolution of state railway concessions, it later became necessary to provide state guarantees for the finances of the private motorway concessionnaires.

Local authorities (communes, provinces and regions). These authorities were effectively excluded from conception and decision in policy for any transport except communal bus networks.

Three stages can be distinguished in the development of the Italian transport system during the post-war period.

1945–55. The transport system, which was almost totally destroyed by the end of the war, was rebuilt piecemeal by the uncoordinated efforts of the managers on the spot. This phase was the antithesis of any sort of planning. It lasted until the middle 1950s, when an attempt at national forecasting was made under the Vanoni Plan.

1955–65. The development of the transport system was primarily taken over by the State *enti* (IRI, ENI, etc) who were responsible for the industrial modernisation of the Italian economy and the change in the emphasis of the development programmes for the South. This phase can be regarded as an example of planning by autonomous and often competitive agencies without an overall national plan. It was during this period that a major challenge was made to the established bureaucratic mismanagement of transport development.

Since 1965. The introduction of the First National Plan can be regarded as an attempt by the central government to reassert political control over the development of the national economy, including the development of the transport system. As an instrument of government policy, the First National Plan had little effect upon the actual development of the transport system. As a stimulus to conceiving and planning for transport in a different way, however, it marked the beginning of explicit national objectives in harmony with the development of market forces and urbanisation.

In the Italian experience of the 1960s, planning in transport meant an increasing centralisation and coordination of decisions. It did not mean, however, that the central government administration actually acquired more power for itself at the expense of other major national agencies. Italian planning, in fact, brought about a reinforcement of rational processes and hence a concentration of power in the hands of those agencies, whether central government, regional government or *enti*, which were capable of implementing rational programmes. One can say that planning 'politicised' transport during the 1960s where it had been a 'depoliticised' subject previously.

The obligation to rationalise

It is doubtful whether planning was the cause of any specific institutional innovation in the Italian transport world. The major institutional innovation in transport policy was the creation of the national planning machinery itself. Transport policy was brought directly within the jurisdiction of the national planning process. Despite the theoretical nature of the First Italian Plan, transport policy was related, at least in principle, to the economic and social development of the country generally.

As regards administrative practice, it must be recognised that the concentration of government responsibilities in a single ministry, and the delegation to various *enti* of important transport policy functions, had taken place before the introduction of the planning peculiar to the 1960s. The planners were faced with an irreversible *fait accompli*. As a result, the First National Plan simply incorporated decisions made by previously established authorities in accordance with their own existing sectional criteria. At the same time, the planning process itself had certain successes. The planning of the 1960s introduced a forum where the proposals of the various authorities could be examined in the light of Italy's economic and social development as a whole. It also reinforced proposals for delegating much of transport policy and planning from central to regional governments (when the regions were set up). It also created a favourable climate for *contrattazione programmatica*[9] where transport infrastructure was concerned. Finally, the first attempt to produce a view of transport policy as an integral part of economic planning in Italy was made in *Progetto '80*, the scenario for the second Italian Plan.

On the other hand, the practical success of Italian planning in the 1960s was patchy.

(a) Coordination of decisions (particularly investment decisions) relating to different modes of transport was the dominant aspiration in transport policy. By the mid-1960s, however, there was little (if any) evidence in Italy that serious efforts had been made to take decisions concerning particular modes of transport in the light of decisions taken for other modes of transport. In any case, the characteristic of this sort of co-ordination was that the planning effort was turned inwards and related to problems within the transport system itself. The development of the transport system was still not considered, in practice, as a part of overall economic and social planning.

(b) The very successful motorway programme in Italy must be regarded as an application of rational planning systems to an individual sector. In this sense, it might appear not to be an example of planning in the 1960s sense at all. But the Italian motorway programme of the 1960s was clearly inspired by an explicit objective for future development, i.e. the economic and social unification of the country as a whole, overcoming the gap between North and South.

As a result of the technically unsuccessful experience of the First National Plan, various centres within the country (both regional and occupational interests) were beginning to make innovations in the concept and practice of transport policy. The two main examples of this were the concentration of research upon the problem of seaports and airports as the interchange points between different modes of transport, and the recognition of the need to plan metropolitan transport systems as systems in their own right, related to the regional and urban development of their locality, and not simply as extensions of the national transport system.

It was, however, only at the end of the 1960s that the basically economic bias of planning began to give way to more realistic and flexible concepts of *assetto del territorio*. The concept of planning and transport policy in *Progetto '80* was utopian as far as Italian political realities were concerned in 1969–70, but as a concept it was in tune with forward thinking in technology and planning in Europe and the USA. As a result, the developments of the later 1960s could not be said to have been an effective integration of decisional frameworks. They were, however, the first steps of a conceptual nature towards such an integration.

The region: a relevant framework

In itself, the introduction of planning in the 1960s had a limited effect on the political framework in which transport policy was made. This was because the state bureaucracy was quite unable to fulfil (as regards budgetary expenditure) the tasks imposed upon it. But this failure pointed a lesson for the future adaptation of the political system. It indicated that there was a potential role for the regions in the planning of the transport system. Such a lesson had a considerable political effect at a time when many people were beginning to wonder whether the revival of the regional aspirations of 1947 had any real meaning for the 1970s. The possibility of an effective regional function in transport policy seems to have been one of the reasons why a politician of the calibre of Bassetti chose Lombardy rather than the Italian parliament for his future career.

National planning in Italy was conceived from the outset as a process which involved a dialogue between regional and central public authorities. Regional Programming Committees were therefore set up, and these committees (together with the appropriate organs of the

Special Statute regions) provided the regional 'partner' in the planning dialogue. The question whether transport was in reality a matter capable of regional planning, or whether it was simply a convenient subject to give to the regional partners in the planning dialogue, was never fully answered in the 1960s. In the Italian case, it is probable that transport was originally conceived as a convenient item to put on the regional agendas. This move, however, had the effect of enabling a number of regions to commission studies, often by firms of consultants, which put a heavy emphasis on transport development. It can be said that the introduction of planning into transport policy provided the opportunity for new types of experts – in this case experts enthusiastic about ideas from America and Great Britain – to draw attention to a major gap in the traditional practice of Italian transport policy. It was realised towards the end of the 1960s that, within little more than a decade, Italy's population would radically change its character. Whereas in the 1960s, the urban population represented 40 % of the total, it was estimated that it would rise to 60 % of the total by about 1980, or, in more pertinent terms, the proportion of the population living in one of eight metropolitan areas was expected to rise from 28 % in 1961 to 37 % by 1981 and 45 % by 2001. As a result, the problem of the regulation of urban motor traffic, the provision of adequate public services for passenger movement and the creation of adequate infrastructures, in particular terminal facilities for supplying the rapidly growing urban areas, were seen to be urgent. During the 1960s, there was no success in defining new criteria for regional transport planning. But the emergence of the issue and its acceptance as part of planning represented a major shift in the balance of power between centre and regions as regards 'conception' in transport policy-making.

Change in habits of mind and practice

The First Italian National Plan must be regarded as 'declaratory' rather than 'indicative'. It cannot be said itself to have created new tools or given the state or public authorities greater power to influence the development of the economy or Italian society. The significance of the First National Plan was that it symbolised the acceptance by government and society of a change in the scale of values used to justify public action. In contrast to the traditionalist (even obscurantist) attitude towards public policy in the 1950s, it became necessary to present public policy in the 1960s with at least an appearance of the explicit rationality that characterises the planning outlook. At the level of general economic policy, it was difficult to distinguish the new planning outlook from the ethos of the swing to the Centre-Left. But at the mundane and technical level of transport policy, it was apparent that the change in the scale of values reflected more than a change in the political composition of the government coalition. The following are examples of the change in approach.

(a) Prior to 1963, the Italian authorities survived without any explicit concept of transport policy at all. During the 1960s, the relationships between the policies for different modes of transport and the role of transport in economic and social development were examined, openly debated and reappraised in the light of new criteria.

(b) Appraisals of the needs of urbanisation and economic development in the Mezzogiorno made in the context of Italian national planning were allowed to influence decisions about transport investment programmes, e.g. the road network for the industrialisation of the continental South. They were also instrumental in promoting widespread planning studies of transport, and proposals for new policy-making functions at the level of regional government.

This greater emphasis on the need for explicit rationality in policy proposals had some effects on the behaviour of pressure groups and politicians.

Publicisation and politicisation

Transport policy was quite orthodox prior to the 1960s. Decisions were made by a process of bureaucratic technocracy mitigated by parish-pump politics operating at the parliamentary level. In the absence of a specific programme established by law and a stable government coalition to implement it, concrete decisions were taken openly as part of the old established system of *clientilismo* or, if not openly, at least in tacit harmony, with the wishes of the major regional *notabili*. The planning of the 1960s altered the situation in certain important respects. First, the pressure of the *notabili* had to take forms that could be justified in terms of the explicit objectives of the National Plan. Secondly, the political force of the *notabili* could not be maintained without the help of experts with planning expertise. Both these factors must be regarded as initiating the process of weakening the historical, regionally based *clientilismo* as a determining factor in public policy for transport.

The imposition of the planning outlook on transport policy in the 1960s created a situation where the development of the transport system, both regionally and nationally – and on occasions internationally – became the subject of public debate. This was not the case before the 1960s. This opening up applied in particular to the following: (i) national plans for increasing the scale of inter-city and international transport, e.g. the scale and siting of airports; (ii) the development of adequate urban transport systems, i.e. the modal split between private motoring and public transport; and (iii) the provision of infrastructure ensuring that the various regions and cities of Italy were adequately linked with the rest of the country and the rest of Europe.

The opening of public debate took place both through the organisation of meetings where the studies and plans of public authorities were explained and discussed and through the introduction of transport planning themes into private conferences and seminars. Planning politicised transport policy.

One may therefore broadly summarise by saying that, in Italy, planning in the 1960s neither reinforced the role of the technocracies as in France nor promoted radical transformations in administrative institutions as in Britain. Nor can it be said to have created new types of decision-makers. What it did was to make transport policy a *political* matter. It revealed that transport policy can be – and, in contemporary Italian conditions, ought to be – a dynamic element in spatial planning (*assetto del territorio e sviluppo regionale*). In so doing, it revealed that transport policy reflected in miniature two major tendencies in post-war Italy: overcentralisation of political authority and the operational delegation of important public activities to functional *enti*. By bringing transport policy into the jurisdiction of the National Plan, planning in the 1960s can be said, firstly, to have given a powerful field of activity to the new regional authorities and, secondly, to have imposed a national *space-orientated* framework in the planning of separate subnational and function-oriented *enti*.

The sense and nonsense of 1960s planning in transport

Before talking about the sense that 1960s planning had for transport, it is essential to make a major distinction between France on the one hand and Britain and Italy on the other. French planning seems always to have been an affair of technocrats – a new instrument for *l'Administration* to use in its century-old task of managing France's transport system. *In the British and Italian contexts, however, planning is not a means of perfecting the state administration: it is a means of changing its character.* Such a thesis would seem to be confirmed by the following:

(a) the monotonous continuity of French transport policy from the 'coordination' of the 1930s to the 'coordination' of the 1970s;

(b) the backwards and forwards swing of British transport policy: 1947 nationalisation (Labour), 1953 de-nationalisation (Conservative), 1962 reorganisation (Conservative) and 1968 integration (Labour); and

(c) the absence of a coherent overall concept of Italian transport development before the Centre-Left political coalition of 1962–3 and the gradual application of planning rationality to transport problems thereafter.

In France, the political forces associated with planning have changed very little since Colbert. They have always been the ex-pupils of certain *Grandes Ecoles*. In their own way, they had already planned the development of French transport up to AD 2000 before the planning peculiar to the 1960s came on the scene. These same political forces are likely to endure at least until AD 2020 when, perhaps, the future ex-pupils of the newly decentralised ENAs may have seized all the important administrative posts as a prelude to ushering in the 'post-Colbert' era of French administration. Transport policy has been no exception to this generalisation.

In Britain, the political forces associated with planning took shape with the social reforms before the First World War. They achieved a lot between 1909, when they obtained the Road Fund, and 1947 when they forced through the nationalisation of inland transport. At the beginning of the 1960s, the younger generation of these political forces – a younger generation, it must be admitted, that was already approaching an average age of 50 – came to power in parliament, the civil service, local governments, universities, etc...The planning of the 1960s was introduced on their advice under the Conservatives and carried on by the Labour government of 1964–70. The Conservative government after 1970 continued the sort of transport policy that had been influenced by 1960s planning, and amalgamated transport and physical planning in the new Department of the Environment. In Britain, planning seems to be a matter of generations. But generations live and die. The political forces associated with the planning peculiar to the 1960s were, by the end of the decade, dead, retired or being a nuisance to a new generation of planners preoccupied with social and environmental criteria. Transport policy was already being influenced by new attitudes.

In Italy, the political forces associated with the planning of the 1960s seem to be a complex bridge across a generation gap. Their origins were in the embryonic technocracy of the first quarter of the twentieth century: the engineers and economists who launched the hydro-electric and irrigation schemes, pioneered civil aviation, electrified railways and built the first motorways. They were tolerated by the Fascist government. After the war and during the 1950s, they prepared the way for a second generation of Italian planners by pushing the Christian Democrat governments further than incrementalism and traditional economic reform, towards thorough-going modern industrialisation. By the 1960s, the main task of Italian planning had passed to younger men who had started their careers under the patronage of the old guard and were ready for nomination to high positions as soon as the Centre-Left came to power. Transport policy was one of the prizes.

One might summarise the historical reality of planning in the 1960s as follows:

(a) in France, it was little more than an episode in the perpetuation of Louis XIV's technocracy;

(b) in Britain, it was the swan song of the 'do-gooders'; and

(c) in Italy, it was a spontaneous and healthy reaction against the morbid condition of a divorce between state and society.

As a result, for the transport sector, planning in the 1960s was a traumatic experience for Britain and Italy. It caused governments and industries to examine critically the practices and attitudes of mind which they had previously accepted without question in transport policy. In many ways this sort of planning was alien to traditional British pragmatism and to the Italian *arte di arrangiarsi*. It was felt to be a conscious adaptation to a new rationality that had a wider than national significance. In this sense, it was a common European experience. It enabled the British and the Italians to talk to each other – and to the French – in an intelligible way. The French case, however, seems to have been quite different. Planning of the type practised in the 1960s was felt to be a typically French achievement. The European Community would do well to adopt it and the British and Italians did well to try to adopt it. It was a European experience for France in the sense that it was a victory for French concepts and practice.

It would however be wrong to think of planning in the 1960s only as an achievement of medium-term economic planning. It was also a transition from a compartmentalised approach to planning (based on defined sectors) to a new, integrated approach which endeavoured to tackle the problems of planning society in space–time. In this sense, the experience of the 1960s was a truly European experience for France and Italy, crystallising their recognition of planning problems at a time when Europe was becoming motorised and urbanised. The result was a concern with institutional reform to create 'regions' capable of integrating land-use and transport planning. The experience was similar in substance for Britain, but it was not recognised as a common European experience. It was felt to be the working out of a peculiarly insular achievement in physical planning – as the 1964 report to the Minister of Housing and Local Government put it – to make the world's best planning system of the 1940s into the world's best planning system of the 1970s.

For the reasons indicated above, it is extremely difficult, if not impossible, to speak of planning in the 1960s as an experience which had many common features in the three countries under consideration. It is not surprising that the differences between the national context of France, Britain and Italy should come out vividly where transport policy is concerned, because transport policy is one of the oldest and best-established spheres, not only of government intervention, but also of commercial law and practice. No one would in fact expect anything as new-fangled as 1960s planning – or as unfledged as the standard bearers of that particular form of rational analysis – to make much impact in ten years on a vast, complex sector of commercial and social operations such as transport. As a result, the planning of the 1960s in respect of the transport sector gives much more the impression of three national ritual dances rather than the introduction of any new universal method of policy-making. One runs up against this intractable disparity of national experiences as soon as one tries to make generalisations about the impact of the new planning techniques on actual transport policies. Following the characteristic illusion of the 1960s, one is tempted to take the institution of French economic and social planning as the general model, and to draw attention to the effect of planning in the 1960s substituting in many cases a medium-term (i.e. five to ten years) look ahead for a longer-term (twenty years or more) look ahead. But it would be quite wrong to extend this generalisation to the British and Italian experiences. Indeed, when the British and Italian experiences are taken as valid models in their own right, the change in planning period that one observes in the French case could well be ascribed to the relative failure of the French to develop a physical planning system equivalent to their economic and social planning system. It could be said, in fact, that one of the uses of studying the effect of 1960s' planning on the transport sector is to cast serious doubt upon the usefulness, let alone the validity, of using French planning experience as a model for understanding, let alone judging, planning experience in other European countries.

If the usual sort of generalisation and conclusion based upon cross-frontier comparisons of internal national developments do not seem to be as attractive as similar conclusions about other sectors of the economy – or so it would appear from other chapters in this book – it remains to decide in what ways the three national experiences of planning in transport policy could be compared. Our feeling on this subject is radical. We feel that the case-study of transport policy indicates that the only valid way to compare the experience of planning in the 1960s in France, Britain and Italy is by the establishment of *negative* limits.

(a) The identification of fundamental aspects of the national planning systems which are unique or peculiar to one country and hence throw light upon the different planning experiences of the other two countries.

(b) The convergence of the three quite different national planning experiences in what might be regarded as a common failure to grasp the essential basis for transport policy at a time of intense technological and social change.

We would like to end this study with a brief indication of what we regard as the common failure of planners in the 1960s in France, Britain, and Italy to grasp the challenge of transport policy. We are using the term 'common failure' in rather a special and limited sense. For our part, we would never have expected planners to have made much impact on the practices of such deeply entrenched administrations and commercial interests as those connected with the transport sector, and, indeed, the practical success which planning in the 1960s did have is a remarkable event. The real test of planning is not so much its immediate practical effect as the new perspective and new rationality which it succeeds in introducing into the process of policy-making. It is, therefore, in the context of perspective and rationality that we are considering certain common features of the planning experience in the three countries concerned as a 'common failure'.

In our view there were three major factors influencing the framework within which transport policy was being made that should have been major considerations even if they were resisted or even poohpoohed by the administrations and commercial interests traditionally responsible for transport policy and practice. These factors were the following:

(a) the effect of technological improvements on the commercial operations of transport;

(b) the European scale of transport development;

(c) the emergence of transport systems adapted to a high-quality urban environment.

As far as each of these factors was concerned, there seemed to be both a general and a particular reason why the planners of the 1960s failed to introduce new perspectives for transport policy based on a new insight into the significance of these three factors. The general reason stemmed from the limitations of the planning of the 1960s itself, while the particular reason stemmed from limitations in the planners' vision of the transport sector itself.

Technological development and commercial operation. There can be no doubt that the planners of the 1960s were aware of technological improvement and were eager to introduce this element into forward planning for the transport sector. But, in most cases, the planners tended to introduce technological criteria into transport planning in the same way as they had introduced technological criteria into industrial planning and general economic planning. They tended, in fact, to concentrate on those aspects of the transport system which were similar to phenomena in the secondary industrial sector, often to the exclusion of those aspects which differentiated the transport system and marked it as an extremely complicated tertiary service sector. It was a general limitation of the planners of the 1960s that they were planning for an economy which was assumed, almost without question, to be a production-oriented economy; as a result they pushed to one side the features of the transport system which later, in the 1970s, were seen to be of crucial importance for a services-oriented economy. This general limitation of planning in the 1960s was re-inforced, as far as the transport sector was concerned, by the lack of priority given to transport relative to other sectors in medium-term economic plans. As a result the planners tended to accept the estab-lished categories of previous transport policy, i.e. the formulation of policies limited to specific modes of transport and did not lead the way in the introduction of the intermodal concepts of transport and physical distribution that were appropriate to the new transport technologies.

The European scale. Although France and Italy were members of the European Community throughout the 1960s and Britain made no less than three attempts to join it during the decade, the planners of the 1960s had a geographical perspective that was national and not European. This remarkable structural bias in the thinking of the planners of the 1960s is clearly illustrated in most of the other chapters in this book. The studies of the other sectors take the form of separate national studies linked together by detached general com-ments of a comparative nature. As a result of this national perspec-tive, the planners of the 1960s saw no objection to applying to the transport sector the micro-economic criteria that had proved success-ful in dealing with certain national transport problems – for example inter-city and motorway road programmes and urban public pas-senger transport systems. The result was that medium-term economic planning in the European Community gave no help to the Common Transport Policy when its first proposals collapsed in 1966 and, at the European level, it was the experts responsible for transport who pointed to the deficiency of economic planning method rather than vice versa.

Urban transport systems. As the present study has shown time and time again, the planning of the 1960s was heavily biased towards medium-term economic planning, and no real attempt was made to integrate the vision and methodology of economic planners and physical planners. As a result, the planning of the 1960s had a blind spot for any problems of which the nature was as much commercial as it was environmental. As far as the transport sector was concerned, therefore, there was virtually nothing in the planning of the 1960s which heralded the almost universal concern with the 'urban transport interface' that became a preoccupation of commercial interests, policy-makers and planners thoughout the world by the mid-1970s. The blind spot in the planning of the 1960s, which arose from the lack of integration between economic and physical planning, was reinforced by the preoccupation of the physical and urban planners with the politically urgent, but essentially short-term, problems of passenger movement and private motoring in large cities. During the 1960s, the inflationary effects of increasing congestion and inefficiency in the distribution of goods, raw materials and energy supplies were neglected because these problems fell precisely in the difficult area where commercial criteria and environmental criteria were in fundamental conflict.

It can be said that all these three factors, where the planning of the 1960s failed to take the lead in transport policy-making, are interdependent, and that the planning of the 1960s would have had to invent a totally new concept of transport policy if it were to have avoided these failures. It is precisely this point which, we think, emerges as the general lesson from the experience of economic planning in transport during the 1960s. Its success lay in its effect upon method. Planning caused policy to be made more explicitly, and it obliged the various interests concerned in policy-making to consult one another and reach more rational common bases for their actions. But rational method does not in itself provide any substitute for knowledge and experience of the sectors in respect of which policy is being made. The planning of the 1960s did not in itself provide new insights into the nature of things. It was essentially conservative in that it accepted previously established concepts except for sectors which, unlike the transport sector, commanded high political priority for reasons unconnected with the planning of the 1960s.

NOTES

1 We would particularly like to thank Mr Rousselot (Planning Commissariat in Paris) and Mr Russo Frattasi (Turin Polytechnic) for their detailed comments and criticisms. The chapter remains nevertheless, the sole responsibility of its authors.

2 There is no exact equivalent to the French *aménagement du territoire*. In the 1960s, the English concept of 'regional development' came nearest to it.

3 See Jacques Lautman and Jean-Claude Thoenig, *Planification et Administrations Centrales*, 1966, Part 2.

4 See especially N. Thien Phuc, *Pour une politique économique des transports*, 1972.

5 See above, pp. 325, 336–7, 346–7.

6 Fulton Committee: The government committee of inquiry, under the chairmanship of Lord Fulton, charged with investigating the structure and management of the civil service, published its report on *The Civil Service*, Cmnd. 3638, in 1968.

7 The term 'solvency' is used here in the peculiar European railway sense of the term: 'in receipt of planned subsidies only'.

8 The force of British practice in consultation was evident when it was applied in 1962 to EEC Regulation No. 11 – an experience that was stimulating even if rather disconcerting for the Community institutions.

9 On 'planned bargaining' see above, pp. 134–5.

SELECT BIBLIOGRAPHY

Cheeseman, I. C. 'Transport Technology – Master or Servant', *Chartered Institute of Transport Journal*, XXXV, No. 2, 1973.

Commissariat Général du Plan, *Les Transports*, A. Colin, Paris 1972.

Despicht, N. S. *Policies for Transport in the Common Market*, 1964, Part 2: 'Transport Policy in the Six'.
    The Transport Policy of the European Communities, 1969, chapter 5: 'Transport Policy and Economic Union'.

Economic Survey of Europe in 1971, Part 1, 'The European Economy from the 1950s to the 1970s', 1972, chapter 7 on 'Perspectives and Policies in European Transport'.

Holland, S. (ed), *The State as Entrepreneur*, Weidenfeld and Nicolson, 1972, chapter 6.

Thien Phuc, N. (ed), *Pour une politique économique des transports*, Eyrolles, Paris 1972.

VII

20. The use of long-term studies in planning

BERNARD CAZES

Medium-term national planning (of the order of four to five years) can be considered as a method of overcoming the excessively restricted temporal horizon of the annual budgetary process. But the same assertion can be repeated *mutatis mutandis* for the medium-term horizon, which can fairly be considered insufficiently distant when decisions are taken whose consequences are felt over a period longer than five years. This is the justification for what is equivocally called long-term planning; equivocal because the word planning involves the idea of a consistent structuring of objectives and of the means for their implementation, and it is difficult to see how a public or private organisation could claim that it is pursuing objectives for the year 2000.

It would be better, therefore, to talk more modestly of futures research or long-term studies, while trying to establish what use government planners can make of them, something which presupposes that two conditions are fulfilled, neither of which can be taken for granted: firstly, that such studies exist; secondly, that they have practical validity.

The existence of long-term studies

While it is incontrovertible that 'futurology' has had a very great vogue over the last decade or so, it must be conceded that it is scarcely apparent when examining how planning works in the three countries considered. Its presence is particularly discreet in the case of Britain and Italy, which consequently leads me to concentrate, in what follows, on France, while hoping that the question will be taken up for the other two countries by British and Italian researchers better informed than I am.

To determine the areas where long-term studies have been carried out by or for the planners, it may be useful to begin by classifying these studies. Daniel Bell uses a tripartite classification, distinguishing the social structure (economy, technology, system of stratification), the political system, and the cultural order (into which he puts life-styles), and he associates a specific logic with each of these three spheres.[1] While recognising the analytical interest of such a method of classification, I am going to use a simpler one, which is based on the distinction between the 'vertical' prospective study covering a sector of economic or social activity and the 'horizontal' prospective study dealing with social processes or behaviour which might encompass several sectors at the same time. When it covers all sectors, it could just possibly be referred to as a 'synthetic' view, although the synthesis can never be a truly total one.

Long-term sector studies

The expression 'sectoral forward look' denotes all those types of studies which aim to represent a future state or, at best, the future states (generally up to 1985, but that will not remain valid for much longer) of an entity called a sector, understanding that word in a sense quite akin to that used by economists: a collection of private and/or public activities combining to produce a certain *output*. In fact there is no rigorous and agreed sector nomenclature, which, moreover, reflects the loose structure of the list of productive and collective functions that the planners use for convenience, although they have few illusions about its scientific validity.

We should note first of all that no sectoral prospective study was undertaken from the First to the Fifth Plan inclusive.[2] The genre only came into existence with the Sixth Plan (1971–5). Nine working parties were created, covering the following sectors: agriculture, cultural affairs, energy, health, housing, manufacturing industries, postal services and telecommunications, research, transport.

This list immediately allows one to identify some conspicuously absent sectors, the reasons for which vary in each case. The most astonishing omissions are natural resources other than sources of energy, as a long-term perspective is indispensable in dealing with them and there is no lack of specialists in this field. The absence of the pri.ate tertiary sector, on the other hand, is scarcely surprising, since until 1973 this disparate collection of activities, extending from the grocer to the lawyer, was virtually ignored by planning. In the public tertiary sector, national defence has not been altogether forgotten, but it is treated 'in house' by the ministry concerned. It is interesting to note the case of education. This is a sector like primary products, requiring very long-term but even more expensive investments, yet it has always been impossible to carry out prospective studies of education, at least within the framework of the official planning process. While there is a chapter in the report of the Sixth Plan Education

Commission dealing with the long-term future of education, it was compiled by a single rapporteur and was not discussed by the Commission.[3]

The form of organisation most widely used has been that of the 'closed' working party, i.e. composed entirely of civil servants and experts within the orbit of the administration. The only noticeable exception is that of the working party responsible for prospective studies of cultural development, whose membership represents an extremely wide spectrum of opinion.

Horizontal prospective studies

In one sense, the horizontal studies have a residual character: they are those which it is impossible to define as sectoral. In proceeding in this way, by elimination, the following six cases can be identified: population; old people; urbanisation; consumption and life styles; leisure activities; the mobility of workers. The problem of omissions is less significant than in the vertical cases because there is no finite set of constituent parts which make up the total social system. Nevertheless two major absentees from the list might be mentioned. The first is obvious, it is what can be called the international environment. If one excludes the 1985 synthesis report, the prospective studies carried out for the Sixth Plan are remarkably 'introvert', as if the only really important long-term future could be expected to occur within the six corners of the French 'hexagon'...The existence of the second omission, that of technological change, could be challenged for, after all, this question has been dealt with, often in a very detailed way, in several of the sectoral studies (agriculture, transport, telecommunications) quite apart from the other technological forecasting reports concerning the textile and food processing industries, undertaken for the Planning Commissariat by BIPE (Bureau of Economic Information and Forecasts). But the major defect of most of the studies devoted to the long-term technological future is that the innovations forecasted are only analysed for their *intra*-sectoral effects, while overlooking the negative or positive spill-over effects, which in turn are likely to affect the environment of the sector in which the innovation has occurred.[4]

At an organisational level, the working parties responsible for the horizontal prospective studies were much more open, in the sense that they included individuals belonging to a variety of socio-occupational categories, whose knowledge of the problem studied was often based upon practical experience rather than on technical or economic expertise.

This diversity of membership seems to have had an effect on the nature of the prospective studies carried out by the vertical and horizontal groups. According to a sociologist who has undertaken an evaluation of the activities of a certain number of the Sixth Plan long-term study groups, the individuals who made the sectoral forecasts were, for the most part, specialists familiar with projection techniques and economic reasoning. They were interested in questions capable of being formulated in quantitative terms, which led them to see the future as a matter of optimal adjustments between the supply and demand of goods and services subject to sources of change that were primarily of a demographic, economic and technological nature. Consequently, one gets the impression of 'more of the same' when examining the results of their work.

Without being radically different from the vertical groups the members of the horizontal groups were more suspicious of hard data and the technico-economic approach. They were justifiably inclined to believe that the long-term view is only valid if it encourages those concerned to go beyond the factors traditionally taken into account in medium-term planning. These groups have thus shown greater imagination than their sectoral counterparts, to the extent that they have sought to use extra-economic factors (structures and attitudes) in order to construct images of the future, and have thereby contributed to renewing the traditional approach to problems, e.g. in the study of the phenomena affecting the mobility of the workforce.[5]

'Synthetic' prospective studies

Synthesis appears to be the most difficult thing of all and normally has to come at the end. It is thus surprising that long-term studies began in France with the work of ten-year macro-economic projections (the projection for 1956–65 being undertaken as part of the preparation of the Third Plan, 1958–61). However, the paradox is more apparent than real. In the total absence of the necessary preliminary analytical studies, there was in reality nothing to synthesise...In the case of the Fourth Plan (1962–5) the same procedure was followed, the only difference being that the projection for 1975 was not published.

For the Fifth Plan, a 'Committee of Wise Men' was set up, which brought together leading personalities from various occupational groups and which derived its inspiration from a body of ideas worked out within the Association Prospective created a few years earlier by Gaston Berger. These ideas were: a refusal to consider the future as the simple result of the extrapolation of the most deep-seated tendencies; an attempt to perceive the change-about-to-come-about by the close observation of 'pregnant facts' which foreshadow a discontinuity in current tendencies; and a voluntaristic conception of long-term forecasting, which went hand in hand with the conception of planning as an instrument for collective control over change. All these ideas were expressed with talent and a certain optimism in the *Réflexions pour 1985*, published in 1964, just before the Fifth Plan (1966–70).

The implementation of this Plan was marked by rather spectacular 'accidents' en route, notably May–June 1968. Moreover, there occurred in France, as elsewhere, a noticeable transformation in atmosphere, which meant that the so-called synthetic prospective studies had to be approached in a less complacent state of mind. However, there are several ways of reacting against the optimistic mood of the 1955–65 period. The most fashionable consists of developing the theme that growth does not lead to happiness (this is the conservative version) or leads to inequalities and noxious side-effects (the radical version). The second generation '1985 Group' preferred not to follow these well-trodden paths and chose instead to explore the future starting from, on the one hand, the constraints arising from changes in the international context (a subject which had not previously ever been tackled prospectively) and, on the other, from the special features of the French socio-cultural model and the capacity of this model to meet future-shocks.[6]

Do the prospective studies have practical value?

It seems to me necessary to raise this question since the long-term studies which have just been discussed were not intended to push forward the frontiers of economic or sociological knowledge. They were part of a governmental planning process seeking to illuminate specific decisions or guidelines for action. Consequently, we must consider whether the studies carried out were what the planners generally expected them to be. It is not easy to answer this question since these features have nowhere been set down systematically. (It is significant that in this respect the expressions most often used are vague ones such as 'to stimulate the imagination', 'to clarify decisions', 'to see the problems in a new way'.) If one tried to spell out more precisely the ideas involved, one would perhaps end up with the following three propositions:

1. Long-term studies applied to national planning are not aimed at providing a vision of the 'good society' (that is an activity which belongs to political reflection) but that does not prevent them from trying to specify in each sphere the precise significance of the concepts by which the past, present or future state of society is interpeted.

2. Long-term studies have as their aim to research into what will change (and what will remain stable) in the environment within which a given policy operates, the reasoning being that if this environment is likely to change a lot, the corresponding policy must logically be

modified as well.[7] In other words, these studies are useful to the planners if they provide reasons for retaining a policy, or for modifying it more or less gradually. These reasons are drawn from a reflection on what might happen in the *future*, which distinguishes prospective from evaluative studies, since the latter draws on the same reasons in analysing the *past* results of a policy.

3. From this follows the third proposition, that long-term studies are not relevant in themselves, but must be supported by detailed research into the performance of public policies, both from the point of view of their effectiveness and of the equity with which their effects are distributed.

Let us try to apply these propositions to the three categories of long-term studies that we have identified, commenting briefly on each point.

First proposition. (a) For the groups engaging in sectoral prospective studies, the nature of the subject and/or the attitudes of the participants excluded the possibility of conceiving their work as the elaboration of the framework for an ideal society (apart from cultural affairs, a sufficiently imprecise domain in which the distinction between present and future has only a limited significance). As far as the search for precise concepts to describe the situation of each sector is concerned, it was hardly relevant to the activities mainly concerning intermediate consumption, such as energy. However, it would have been fully justified for the activities satisfying final demand, as their real effects are inadequately measured by the indicators normally used, namely the indicators of total expenditure or of investment expenditure. In fact, the sectoral prospective studies did not lead to any progress in the direction of arriving at adequate social indicators.

(b) As far as the horizontal prospective groups were concerned, they were less subject to economic constraints and as we have seen had a different membership. Therefore, the temptation to describe the desirable future (or to prognosticate a sombre future if one did not rapidly change direction) was stronger than in the sectoral case and this temptation did not encounter the same obstacles. Paradoxically, it is in this second category of studies that a serious attempt was made to improve the existing conceptual apparatus. CREDOC (Centre de Recherche et de Documentation sur la Consommation) tried to measure consumption in a broad sense, including private consumption, consumption financed by the community, and the divisible services furnished without charge by public social investment.

(c) While setting out to be as objective as possible the first *1985* Report, did not, in my opinion, succeed in avoiding being unconsciously normative; presenting as desirable a future society which, in the final analysis, was the enlarged projection of what the Fourth Plan was seeking explicitly to promote (the faster growth of public consumption) or of what it hesitated to specify too openly (continuous education, modernisation and humanisation of the administrative services in contact with the public). Conversely it could almost be said that the second *1985* Report has adopted the principle of rejecting any normative stance. It has expressed what others will regard as progress as being the consequence of quite substantial changes in the policies followed and in the implicit public preferences which underpin them. This judgement leads us quite naturally to discuss the next proposition.

Second proposition. To test the extent to which this second proposition can be applied, we must examine, firstly, whether serious consideration was given to a more or less drastic change of policies and, secondly, if the arguments advanced were supported by reliable evidence. On the first point, the answer is definitely in the affirmative, while making clear, nevertheless, that the working parties adopted different styles. In the field of housing, the forecasters established alternative projections of the needs and capacity to pay of households, which enabled them to show quite convincingly that it would be necessary in the first case, to intensify the building programme, and in the second, to retain the principle of financial assistance (if not in its present form). In the field of agriculture, the setting side by side of long-term perspectives of supply and demand for agricultural products led to the conclusion that it would be necessary to find another policy. The Commission drafted several strongly contrasting alternatives, ranging from the maintenance of the small family farm to the formula of capitalistic agriculture, with a number of more or less sophisticated variants in between. The third type of approach is the one that has been most commonly adopted in the sphere of social prospective studies. It lists in qualitative terms all the reasons (unsatisfied non-market needs, marked inequalities to be corrected) which call for increased public investment expenditure and transfer payments.

As far as synthetic prospective studies are concerned, the first *1985* Report adopted an approach fairly close to the third type, correcting it with an emphasis upon the principle of social marginal cost pricing, in the sphere of divisible public services. This corrective emphasis was repeated and further emphasised by the second *1985* Report, which stressed the need for a new approach to public services, which would seek to measure in a more precise way the cost and the results of their performance, instead of automatically considering as desirable all public spending which is good in intention.

Third proposition. This point can be quickly disposed of, for we find ourselves faced with a complete blank. The notion of evaluation is apparently unknown in France, except in the very embryonic form of the annual report on the implementation of the Plan. This omission compelled certain long-term study groups to devote part of their work to reconstructing past development as well as they could; this is what happened in the case of the 'Consumption and style of life' group, which brought together the existing statistical facts on income disparities for the period 1959–65. Curiously, its report is the only document connected with the preparation of the Sixth Plan in which these figures are mentioned.

The impact of long-term studies

In asking myself whether the long-term studies of the Sixth Plan contained useful characteristics in the eyes of the planners, I have hitherto examined the 'supply' of prospective studies. In considering the impact of long-term studies, I am led to enquire into the 'demand' expressed, explicitly or not, by the planning apparatus. Undoubtedly this demand exists, as shown by the considerable growth in the number of long-term studies which occurred during the Sixth Plan and which seems likely to continue, although at a reduced rate, for the preparation of the Seventh Plan. But it seems to me that there is a contradiction within the planning apparatus that weakens the impact of long-term studies. This contradiction can be described as follows: on the one hand, there are the problems that the Plan tackles from a decision-making standpoint, on which prospective studies have not thrown any light, e.g. the measures to encourage private saving. On the other hand, a number of questions tackled in the long-term studies, such as the various disparities between social categories, or the preparation of a new agricultural policy, were not politically 'ripe', so they were not taken up during the preparation of the Plan. Even in an area which appears purely technical, such as the measurement of consumption in the widest sense by CREDOC, it is only during the preparation of the Seventh Plan that this instrument will begin to be used seriously. Finally, the as yet very limited, tentative outlines of evaluation and analysis of alternative policies, which are to be found in certain long-term studies and in particular in the second *1985* Report, could scarcely have a great influence, since this type of approach is not used in medium-term planning, except in the very adulterated form of a 'spread' of growth rates or of the annual reports on the Plan's implementation.

A tentative conclusion might be offered. Prospective studies are more likely to have a positive influence if they are integrated in a continuum covering policy evaluation and analysis. Conversely, their impact will remain very limited as long as they are considered as a separate activity, because one can be that much more imaginative when no practical consequences are expected to follow from one's flights of fancy.

NOTES

1 See, for example, his 'The Post-Industrial Society: the Evolution of an Idea', *Survey*, Spring 1971.

2 There is an exception to this generalisation in so far as some consideration of the situation in 1985 can be found in certain reports of modernisation commissions of the Fifth Plan, particularly those dealing with crafts, energy, fuel, housing, postal services and telecommunications, transport, urban investment.

3 I shall deal later with the *1985* synthesis report in which long-term problems of the educational system were discussed using an approach which subsequently raised certain difficulties when the publication of the report was under consideration.

4 This is clearest in the case of transport and telecommunications.

5 B. Matalon, 'Les groupes de travail à long terme dans le préparation du VIᵉ Plan', April 1972, duplicated.

6 *1985: La France face au choc du futur*, A. Colin, 1972.

7 To take a simple example, any policy of vocational training occurs in an environment characterised, amongst other things, by a certain state of technology. If this changes and results in an industry such as textiles, which largely employed an unskilled work force, becoming capital intensive, the policy-makers should draw the necessary conclusions.

SELECT BIBLIOGRAPHY

Cazes, B. 'Applied Futures Research in France: Some Critical Views', *Futures*, v, No. 3, June 1973, pp. 272–9.

Commissariat Général du Plan, *Réflexions pour 1985*, Documentation Française, Paris 1964.

'Plan et Prospectives', eight reports, Librairie Armand Colin, Paris 1971 and 1972.

de Hoghton, C., Page, W. and Streatfield, G. ...*And now the Future*, PEP, London 1971.

de Jouvenel, B. *The Art of Conjecture*, English translation, Weidenfeld and Nicholson, London 1967.

VIII

21. Planning as the regulatory reproduction of the status quo

LUCIEN NIZARD

Planning and the market: a fallacious but significant opposition

One can demonstrate that there is a meaningful relationship between the various conceptions of the market and the various conceptions of planning, the latter often being conceived as antithetical to the market, at least as far as the means through which it is carried out. As far as the actual capitalist systems are concerned, an opposition between planning and market should be rejected even as an ideal point of reference. The crucial phenomenon is the appearance – induced by the increasing interdependence of social activities and the resulting multiple and partial socialisations of decisions – of an organised capitalism, indissolubly uniting features of the market and of planning. It is this fundamental unity which characterises organised capitalism, not the fictional opposition of contradictory elements, some derived from the market and others from planning. There are, nevertheless, some efforts to plan in the strict sense, i.e. as a governmentally differentiated and procedurally institutionalised activity, whose functions and innovative significance must be assessed.

The various conceptions of the market each emphasise a particular aspect of the ideal model. Let us consider their specific characteristics before showing what they have in common. Firstly, atomistic capitalism stresses the market's extreme multipolarity, which derives directly from the small scale of the firms and households which are its subjects. It implicitly or explicitly recognises the virtual equality of the competing subjects and their inability to influence the rules governing them. The emphasis is placed upon the profusion of decentralised individual decisions which are juxtaposed and not integrated. Overall equilibrium is their necessary but fortuitous consequence because it is not one of their motivations. Secondly, the market achieves an *ex post* adjustment of both the competing decisions of firms and of supply and demand. Equilibrium results from successive approximations involving marginal adjustments between incremental decisions that are not spontaneously harmonious. Not surprisingly, this interpretation came to the fore after the first crises of capitalist overproduction. It stressed the absence of a prior overview of the way the system worked and the time required for 'the invisible hand' to achieve equilibrium. Momentary disequilibria are necessary to the attainment of equilibrium. Thirdly, the market works for the most part outside institutional organisation and intervention. 'The institutionalisation of economic relations is negative, for while it allows freedom of action it creates a network of informal constraints. The movement "from status to contract" is in fact a transition from a positive to a negative status.'[1] Fourthly, the market is a *transparent system* in which information about prices is immediately available to all economic subjects, enabling *ex post* adjustment to take place. Fifthly, the market is restricted to the production of private goods, implying the need for a complementary public sector managing collective goods.[2]

What are the features common to these conceptions of the market economy that we have all too briefly mentioned? The inequality between 'economic subjects' – particularly as far as the appropriation of the means of production is concerned – is almost entirely passed over. This neglect is possible, in large measure, because the working of the market is presented as an encounter between flows of money and of goods and services. Human relations and social relationships underlying these flows, are mostly banished from the framework. *The state is excluded from the market.* It merely makes piecemeal corrections to some of the market's effects and is complementary to it. The state itself floats in the weightless world of conventional wisdom. The laws of its behaviour are either not sought or they lead through theories of 'constraint' or 'exchange' – even institutional theory – to singularly poor explanations of sovereign authority, conceived as above social relations and/or the source of the fortuitous character of state intervention.

The various conceptions of planning are the obverse of these representations of the market. To the decisional decentralisation of an atomistic capitalism, some conceptions of planning oppose the image of a macro-decision, choosing between decisions and arranging them in an order of priority. To *ex post* adjustment is opposed *ex ante* forecasting. The lack of institutional organisation is contrasted with the institutionalisation of bargaining. The postulated transparency of information is confronted with a transparency to be created. Lastly, the non-market economy is considered the best place to elicit public choices and organise them in a consistent manner. These conceptions can be reformulated around four alternative functions attributed to planning: the reduction of inconsistency, of uncertainty, of diversity and the management of the non-market sector.

As a reducer of inconsistency, planning subordinates competing wills to a unifying will, atomistic decisions to a macro-decision that fixes priorities.[3] The legitimacy of ends to be pursued is not questioned. Ends are given, the purpose of planning being to make decisions more efficient. Planning to reduce uncertainty is the counterpart of the market conceived as *ex post* adjustment.[4] This function stresses knowledge, not will; forecasting, not decision-making; the statistician, not the politician. The preparation of a unified frame of reference does not claim to integrate decisions within an order of priorities, but merely to give them a common expression. In any case, if such forecasting is able to exercise any influence, it is because action is conceived as adaptation to an environment whose constraints are both exogenous and reified rather than as uncertain change that has been chosen and willed.

The reduction of diversity is a response to the market's lack of institutional organisation. It recognises the diversity of the class and social group rationalities. Championed by some sociologists and politicians,[5] it stresses the organisation of consensus-building, performing an apprenticeship function that the market alone cannot undertake. It stresses the heterogeneity of the environment to be planned, not conceived as a single end–means system but as a plurality of actors with incompatible objectives. According to whether this heterogeneity allows for the structural inequality of social groups, confronted by change, planning will be castigated as an attempt at 'integration' or eulogised as consensus-building. Rejecting the notion of spontaneous market transparency, Claude Gruson attaches the highest importance to the development of a pluralistic information system and of economic and social indicators increasingly covering a growing number of interdependencies. Such transparency is ambiguous and appears to be both an attempt to reduce uncertainty through increased knowledge and the revelation of a common truth, precondition of a consensus and therefore an attempt at integration.

Lastly, some stress that because the logic of planning is fundamentally opposed to the market economy, it should rely mainly on the management of the public sector conceived as a non-market economy, the basis of the state's normative autonomy which planning would express in a programme.[6] However, the weakness of this thesis has been exposed by much contemporary research. A significant part of non-market production is directly necessary to the reproduction of an environment favourable to the development of the market economy. For most Marxists, the fundamental role of this sector is to make up for the falling rate of profit, an interpretation confirmed by empirical studies. Even those non-market goods that meet an apparently autonomous social demand are conceived and utilised in conformity with the logic of the market economy. Apart from this last conception, there is some truth in the various meanings of planning, but they are partial and one-sided. Furthermore, they are built on sand: an *imaginary market* which is to be organised. It is this latter point that we shall explore.

The dialectic between partial forms of regulation and comprehensive regulation in organised capitalism

Some preliminary remarks are necessary. The market economy has never conformed to the pure market model. However, it is not sufficient to say that the state has intervened increasingly. One must add that these interventions are neither autonomous nor discretionary. They are articulated around the dominant social groups who share in the regulation of the economy and society. Having distinguished phases of spontaneous and organised capitalism, the historic preconditions of the latter must be correctly grasped. To Nicolai's two conditions – increased group consciousness and greater knowledge of fundamental economic relationships[7] – we must add a third: the increasing socialisation of productive forces due to the increasing difficulties encountered by the holders of private power (whether or not this involves the legal ownership of the means of production) in exercising their power separately. There results a complex of regulations exercised concurrently by the various parts of the state apparatus *and* by the various dominant groups over the working and reproduction of contemporary capitalism. It is the dialectic of these regulations that will be examined to bring out that, far from being opposed to the market, a kind of planning has become an inherent part of the market economy.

Comprehensive planning is a systematic effort at medium-term regulatory reproduction of a social system. It is an attempt at overall regulation of the multiple forms of partial regulation. Planning should be apprehended through the specific forms of regulation that it promotes, the contents of this regulation and its dominant orientation. Like all regulation which is merely a secondary influence on the productive process, social relations and so forth, planning is both active will and passive reflection: will to act on a system to 'rationalise' its working and the behaviour on which it depends;[8] a reflection of the present state of structures and behaviour. This twofold dimension is to be found in the forms, content and orientation of planning regulation. However, at the risk of oversimplification, we are inclined to claim that the will to act is more evident in the forms and orientation of such regulation than in its content. We shall proceed from social reproduction[9] to planning regulation, to which in our opinion it gives its meaning.

A social system is a complex historical product, with sub-systems each partially conforming to a different and autonomous logic, increasingly tending towards fragmentation. Nevertheless, it survives to the extent that it has a dominant system capable of ordering the partial sub-systems that it includes. So the reproduction of a social system, such as a rapidly industrialising capitalist society, having in addition the cultural and specific features of France, is infinitely complex and contradictory. It cannot be the reproduction of an identical social system. It implies both persistence and change.[10] Each sub-system tends to perpetuate its own existence, even if this causes problems for the system as a whole. However, it remains subject to the capitalist mode of production and is shaped by its reproduction process. But the dominant process does not enjoy total control because it is itself the theatre of fundamental contradictions; the constituent sub-systems have very different reproduction rhythms and so time-lags occur; each sub-system has its own regulatory apparatus, which is far from being exclusively governmental. So change is clearly an essential concomitant of the dominant system's reproduction. Regulation is necessary to establish *cohesion*, not *consistency*, between these partial reproductions, relative to the dominant system as a whole. This has always been the essential function of political power and of the state apparatus. If this is so, what is the specific nature of planning regulation?

Three leading traits characterise French planning regulation: its horizon, its comprehensiveness and the non-bureaucratic character of the organisation from which it emanates. Its underlying conception of social reproduction is more ambitious than existed before planning. The medium-term horizon is necessary because the lengthy nature of reproductive processes and the irreversible character of the effects of many decisions must be anticipated on a longer than annual basis. Its effort at comprehensiveness has been partial and inadequate in practice but has been gradually extended. At first based essentially on the regulation of the economic system, it is now also concerned with social matters. This extension reflects both the attempt at greater comprehensiveness and its limitations, the regulation of the economic system controlling, indirectly, the whole social system. The third trait, the attempt to escape from the environment in which the traditional administration so often bogs down, is both possible and necessary for planners. Possible because, despite its growth and duration, the Planning Commissariat has not been transformed into a bureaucracy, doubtless mainly because it neither manages nor allocates resources. Necessary because, lacking the means – legal regulation, supervision, allocation of resources, etc – which the traditional administration possesses, it can only act by asserting the specificity of its approach, gradually gaining acceptance both for itself and its approach.

Three other significant traits that characterise planning regulation derive from the first three: control over the intellectual tools capable of constructing a symbolic environment (information system, model, social indicators); concern with consensus-building and how it is to be attained; the rejection of rules in favour of the enactment of norms. *Intellectual tools* are necessary both to assess the conditions of social reproduction in the medium term and to influence those who control in practice the various particular social reproduction processes. The planner does not have any direct control over the economic system. The fundamental precondition of its influence, therefore, is that it creates a specific symbolic representation of the medium-term constraints which cannot be ignored without serious risk. This is one of the few objectives it can attain and establishes the specificity of its role.[11] The planner's only mode of action is to interiorise in the decision-makers and social actors the medium-term constraints and collective objectives capable of counteracting both their individual purposes, which are under direct and more powerful short-term pressures, and their differentiated practices. To gain acceptance for their own conception of order, the planners must 'make absent things seem present' in day to day matters. The capacity to impose one's own language, and therefore to some extent one's own rationality, on others, is to be in rather a strong position.

Consensus-building is more complex. Firstly, it is an instrument of *simulation*, because it attempts to reconstitute in a distorted and simplified way the play of social forces, to assess their reaction to the government's scheme.[12] Next, it is a way of achieving *socialisation* or rather *acculturation* by subjecting groups having different values to apprenticeship in a common set of norms. Lastly, and perhaps to an increasing extent, consensus-building is an instrument of *legitimation* for the planning institution. The planners had to avoid appearing to the bureaucrats and citizens as 'cloud-cuckoo' technocrats. Planning had to forge its own legitimacy. By resorting to multilateral consensus-building, from which no group of any size was excluded, the planners were able to face the bureaucrats, backed by their clienteles, as the representatives of more numerous and less specialised interests. For the first time, outside the framework of political representation, a coordination structure sought a new legitimacy by having recourse to a system of social and economic representation aimed at beating the bureaucrats on their own ground.

The refusal to use rules, addiction to which is characteristic of bureaucracies, is to be accounted for not only by the specific nature of the planning institution but also by the generality and rigidity of rules. The latter are not suited to the increasing need for selective intervention. Furthermore, rules bind those who enact them as much as those for whom they are intended. However, the paradox of the non-bureaucratic Planning Commissariat is that it cannot manage without the help of the bureaucrats. They are indispensable if one is to act upon a society as penetrated by the various branches of the state apparatus as is France. This is evident in the forms of regulation, since consensus-building is applied with even more intensity to the public administration than to the private sector. It also has important effects upon the content of regulation.

If one accepts that the regulation of the comprehensive reproduction of the social system is an effort to achieve cohesion, regulation will aim at different ends according to the period and to the economic, social and cultural conditions that obtain. It would be necessary to distinguish various objectives of change: internal structure, increased contact with the environment, productivity and so on. For example (and oversimplifying), planning regulation might seek to accelerate change in a hitherto protected industry, slow it down in another, and abstain from interference elsewhere. The choice will depend on a comprehensive view of the compromise that it would be expedient to strike between the demands of economic consistency and the minimum of political cohesion below which one cannot go without serious risk. Each sub-system has its own regulatory structure, which is more or less organised, powerful and able to work out its own strategy. The planner must take cognisance of these factors, because he cannot, without running risks, suggest the same treatment for sub-systems with very different capacities for initiative and resistance. He cannot fulfil his task of comprehensive regulation without paying attention *both* to the state of the whole system to be regulated and of its heterogeneous constituent sub-systems. Planning regulation, therefore, tends to differentiate its intervention according to the nature of the adjustments and links that are desirable from the viewpoint of reproducing the whole social system. However, this is limited by the fact that the planner cannot avoid adapting the content of regulatory intervention to the differences in relative power and structural situations that it meets in each of the sub-systems.

The state apparatus also has to be regulated. Up to now, it seems to us that domination has been exercised in France by an alliance of classes, and not the fraction of one class or a single class. If the hegemony of industrial capitalism asserts itself clearly today, it is challenged.[13] Furthermore, it is a legalistic illusion to believe that the state apparatus is a single instrument wholly controlled by political power. The bureaucratisation process has its own laws. One of them is that an organisation becomes a power centre capable of pursuing its own ends. The various parts of the state apparatus were born at various times (especially in the latter half of the nineteenth century) to

meet the historically defined needs of particular social sub-systems and
to try to regulate new kinds of contradictions. We consider that, despite the fundamental structural changes that have since occurred in
the social system (involving the hierarchy of sub-systems, their functions, the new divisions between them), these features of the state
machine continue to reflect the time at which they were born. Administrative reforms which seek to adapt the state machine to the
changes that have occurred are powerless to efface these historical
residues and significantly reduce sub-system autonomy except in the
very long run. Our hypothesis is that each part of the administration
itself regulates the reproduction of a sub-system, of which it gradually
becomes a part by a sort of osmosis. It tends to perpetuate the
previous structure of the milieu it regulates, even if it is anachronistic,
because that is where it finds its social and political support and
because it has gradually come to represent and defend that milieu *vis
à vis* the government. The whole milieu – *including the administration* –
therefore tends to reproduce its previous functions and structures and
to resist changes that affect this threatened equilibrium.

The conclusion to which this analysis leads is that the state machine
is the focus of contradictions that should not be underestimated. They
often reflect – with distortions – real social contradictions and not
mere personal or functional rivalries. So, planning institutions, in
trying to regulate overall social reproduction, tend to modify the
administrative hierarchy and the political strength of parts of the
administration *at the same time* as that of their related sub-systems. They
modify the balance of power within the alliance of the component parts
of the ruling classes. But the planners need the help of these bureaucracies to exert their influence. Therefore, the planners can only count
on their support if they transform these bureaucracies or take their
standpoint into account. The role of the planners' language is important here because it tends to create uniformity in conceptual frameworks and so to unify the administrative apparatus, and through it
the social sub-systems which it manages. A greater flexibility of sub-
systems is a precondition of a more 'effective' overall regulation. This
is facilitated by influencing their rationality through a *rapprochement* of
their languages. But even if these efforts are effective, they will create
new problems because contradictions may persist despite the fact that
they have lost their means of expression.

At the risk of overemphasising the distinctions, we shall first briefly
illustrate the diversity of regulations brought about by the multiplicity
of types of adjustment and articulation between sub-systems, and then
those due to the structure or power of a given sub-system. The same
methods cannot be used, generally, in dealing with social tensions and
social contradictions. The former, as their name suggests, are mani-

fest; the latter may be latent or potential and are not empirically observable.[14] Tension expresses a conscious and exteriorised conflict of interests that may be ephemeral or fortuitous. Contradiction structurally opposes roles and processes that are both complementary and contradictory, whose joint reproduction is a permanent feature of a social system. Thus, the capitalist system requires the survival of the working class and the capitalist class. A social system might possibly reduce or eliminate certain social tensions and this is one of the essential functions of regulation. It cannot resolve a contradiction that is an inherent part of the system, but merely attempt to circumvent or reduce the political risks by dealing with some of the resulting tensions.

Nevertheless, we treat as social contradictions conflicts of interest that are objectively based upon contradictory roles but can be resolved. Such conflicts do not derive from an inherent contradiction of the capitalist system but from an opposition between capitalist development and social classes, such as landowners, who belong to an earlier mode of production but survive in a predominantly capitalist society. Land-use planning offers a good example of the various kinds of regulation that may be employed. It can attack the contradiction between landowners and industrial capitalists by contributing towards the expropriation of urban land, resolving this secondary contradiction at the price of potentially lively tensions. It might elude the contradiction by concerning itself primarily with reducing the consequent tensions. Comparisons show that this choice is not fortuitous, depending upon the level of industrial development and the political influence of the landowners.[15]

The diversity of content in planning regulation also takes other forms. Adjustment may seek to avoid excessive time-lags between reproduction processes. At various times, such regulation may seek to slow down the fastest processes (e.g. industrialisation and exodus from the rural areas), make up for the slowness of those processes that create bottlenecks or excessive social tensions (e.g. public services required by industrial growth and/or the satisfaction of certain social demands) or accelerate the rhythm of change, leading to debates about growth in the planning context. Furthermore, adjustment through planning regulation may try to reduce the autonomy of some processes, e.g. education, relative to the dominant system, or increase it, e.g. through regionalisation, to facilitate self-regulatory forms of behaviour that are considered necessary. Adjustment may also deal with dangerous tensions that arise owing to the rapid transformation of the economic system and the persistence of value systems and traditional political ways of handling conflicts. In these cases, it is necessary to act respectively on cultural norms – leading to the themes such as change, mobility, adaptability, dialogue, the style of social relations – or on the political system, for example, by developing the representation of economic and social groups, strengthening the executive, unifying the machinery of government.

The diversity of regulatory content is a function of sub-system structures and their own regulations. Planning regulation does not only depend upon the degree of interdependence of social activities in the whole social system. It also depends on two factors: the interdependence achieved within each micro-society making up the various productive sectors, hence the importance of the degree to which capital is internationalised, e.g. in the energy field; and the extent to which private control gives planning a particular form. Thus the oligopolistic structure and key role of the powerful trade association in the French steel industry has given planning in this sector a very specific style and content.

We refer to planning practices in the plural because the attempt by some state and non-state organisations to impart a dominant rationality to the conscious reproduction of the social system becomes meaningful only in relation to the diversity of situations with which it is confronted. Does the variety of forms of planning regulation involve a denial of the existence of a dominant orientation in planning? We do not think so. It would be to neglect the hierarchical character of the social system and the structuring role in social reproduction of the capitalist mode of production. The diversities and autonomies we have emphasised are only relative, remaining subordinated to the dominant logic even if they are not wholly mastered by it.

In a class-divided society, the pursuit of social cohesion is not an impartial function. It is motivated by the need to reproduce domination while seeking to make it compatible with social cohesion, by speeding up, slowing down or accepting changes arising within the productive process. Such changes concern, in particular, interconnected changes in the relative power of the various parts of the dominant class and the acceptance of new costs of social cohesion as well as the allocation of the burden which they involve. These changes must be carried out by a leading group, the part or whole of the class that is their main beneficiary. But it is not always able either to fulfil this role, owing to the inadequacy of its economic base, organisation or aptitude to work out its own collective interest, or to formulate a 'general interest' image of its sectional interest, ideological shortsightedness obscuring an understanding of its long-term interest. So, the permanance and change that social reproduction must dialectically achieve is variably attained according to the type of capitalist structure and the historical circumstances. Our hypothesis is that in France the balance of forces within capitalism was such that the cultural and political levels inhibited the shift in power that economic and social changes heralded, preventing the emergence of a group representing the new forces. An important role was played in this process by the trade associations and administration, who managed to hide their conflicts of interest.[16]

French-style planning was one of the ways of bringing about the changes necessary to the system's reproduction by hastening the birth of a real industrial management. This fundamental purpose can be detected more easily through the problems emphasised by the planners than in the measures that they recommended. It is revealed in various ways: the management of capital utilisation, the exposure of conflicts within business over conditions of growth and the nagging reiteration of the need for mergers, and the theme of ending protection from international competition, present in the early plans even if it became increasingly important. Continuous consensus-building, to reorganise business organisations and encourage them to become active over a wider field, was also emphasised.[17] The over-representation of large firms in the modernisation commissions was used to make up for the inadequacy of their sponsor Ministry of Industrial Development and because planning is only effective when the big firms control a large enough share of the market and plan themselves – Shonfield's '80:20 relationship'.[18]

By creating and diffusing social norms, by trying to ensure that the administration takes account of them, French planning tends to establish a new-style dominant ideology. It blurs the separation between public and private sectors which was fundamental both in French law and to the political ideologies of both the Right and the Left. Similarly, the notion of public service and its by-products disintegrate under the pressure of planning. In this way, it helps destroy the myth of the state as impartial referee, substituting for it social change, which is valued without regard to its content and whose bias is treated as an objective datum. The planner increasingly says 'one must' rather than 'we should'. The plan is less a demiurge than a classical chorus commenting fatalistically on the unfolding of destiny. This should not, however, lead us to overestimate the role of the planners. They have not created French neo-capitalism; they have been the catalyst that speeded up its emergence. They needed others to carry their message. It is significant that in the period when the employers, while supporting planning, were unable to give it the necessary support by imparting to it a decisive and comprehensive direction, its advocates were located in many parts of the political spectrum. The plan's emergence was at that time helped by its ambiguity, an ambiguity that we have attempted to dispel.

NOTES

1 A. Nicolai, *Comportements économiques et structures sociales*, 1960, p. 74. This book is of great interest, often ignored despite its pioneering character.

2 See A. Wolfersperger, *Les bien collectifs*, 1966. For a Marxist's critical analysis, see P. Herzog, 'A propos de la notion d'économie publique', *Revue Economique*, January 1973.

3 See P. Massé's preface to A. Shonfield, *Le capitalisme d'aujourd'hui*, 1967.

4 P. Massé, *Le plan ou l'anti-hasard*, 1965.

5 M. Crozier, 'Pour une approche sociologique de la planification', *Revue française de sociologie*, VI, 1965, p. 147. L. Hamon referred to the plan's role as a 'reducer of intransigence': 'Le plan et sa signification politique', in J. D. Reynaud (ed), *Tendances et volontés de la société française*, 1966, p. 197.

6 This viewpoint seems to be shared by Andrew Shonfield in his remarkable book on *Modern Capitalism*.

7 Nicolai, *Comportements économiques*, p. 75.

8 See L. Nizard's introductory article 'Planification et régulations bureaucratiques', in the *Revue française de science politique*'s special issue on 'Administration et Société', April 1973.

9 See Y. Barel, *La réproduction sociale*, 1973.

10 This analysis is further developed in L. Nizard, 'Théorie des systèmes: réproduction et mutation', *Cahiers internationaux de sociologie*, 1972.

11 L. Nizard, 'De la planification: production de normes et concertation', *Revue française de science politique*, October 1972.

12 L. Nizard, 'De la planification: socialisation et simulation', *Sociologie du Travail*, No. 4, 1972.

13 See the articles by A. Granou on 'Le VIe Plan et l'hégémonie du capitalisme industriel' in *Politique aujourd'hui*, July and August–September 1970.

14 See, for example, J. Habermas, 'Technique et science comme idéologie' in the UNESCO symposium on *Marx et la pensée scientifique contemporaine*, 1969, p. 569.

15 H. Coing, 'La ville en Plan', in the *Revue française de science politique*, April 1973, special issue on 'Administration et Société'. And see above p. 380.

16 J. Lautman, 'La construction de l'intérêt de la profession dans les syndicats patronaux', *Sociologie du Travail*, April 1967.

17 A. Jacob and J. Lautman, 'Roles du syndicalisme patronal et évolution économique', in J. D. Reynaud (ed), *Tendances et volontés de la société française*.

18 See Shonfield, *Le capitalisme d'aujourd'hui*, p. 141.

Conclusion

A comparative evaluation of planning practice in the liberal democratic state

MICHAEL WATSON

By the early 1960s the pre-war doubts about the viability of Western capitalism seemed to have been largely dissipated and those about its humanity assuaged. This is strikingly reflected in Shonfield's definitive work on political and economic trends in the fifties and early sixties, *Modern Capitalism*. Post-war capitalism worked; it had provided unheard of economic and social progress. Prosperity was general and increasing, full employment was being maintained, while the relative few who were less fortunate were decently provided for through social welfare arrangements. The key to *modern* capitalism, to successful capitalism, was the large part played by public power in social and economic affairs. Government had assumed extensive responsibilities for the level of economic activity and success had been achieved in keeping up demand. At the same time, a particular achievement was the reversal of pressures making for high consumption at the expense of investment. In this Shonfield already identified the role of a general economic planning, whether carried on primarily under the auspices of the state as in France, the banks as in Germany, or the public industrial and financial sector as in Italy. Its absence in Britain and the USA helped to explain their relatively poor growth performance.

For Shonfield the key to further economic and social progress lay in 'the management of the institutional apparatus which guides Western economic life'.[1] In this task, he attributed a central role to planning, as the way of ensuring the necessary 'explicitness and coherence' of economic decisions in the active, interventionist state of modern capitalism. Given its adoption, the future could be viewed with reasonable optimism. The main worry was whether a choice was not involved between material progress, assured in this way, and the liberties of the citizen as defended principally by parliamentary democracy. For planning turned largely on an exercise of executive power that was effectively out of parliament's reach. The only solution to the dilemma lay in new techniques of democratic control. The importance of Shonfield's assessment of economic planning in the context of the Western state necessarily makes it a backdrop for any conclusions a decade later. Without aiming at a treatment along the same lines, it is necessary to attempt a reappraisal which may be broadly played off against the earlier one. That this assessment turns out to be generally less favourable or optimistic is not to imply Andrew Shonfield was wrong about the 1950s and the early 1960s, only that times change and that we have had a further decade of experience.

An important element in the appeal of economic planning in the early 1960s was the acclaim given to the French model of the fifties. Not least, this model had demonstrated a type of government economic planning apparently compatible with the mixed economy, working effectively in the context of the continuing existence of a private sector accounting for some 65% of France's national product. A further decade of experience on a wider geographical front would seem to confirm this compatibility. Two basic questions, however, remain. Firstly, *in what sense* is it compatible? This involves examining the nature of the planning trend: the direction in which policy has moved during this period and the problems emphasised; the conception, not to say ideology, of planning that has gradually taken shape. Secondly, in what way and to what extent is the particular compatibility at a political and intellectual level reflected in decision-making practice? This involves examining the political relationships underpinning the dominant rationale of planning, with regard particularly to the difficulties in establishing the organisational and behavioural conditions for the ideological compatibility of planning and the mixed economy to be translated into an operational compatibility. Finally, the implications for the contemporary West European liberal democratic state of the preceding analysis will be assessed.

Problems and policies

We start from a recognition of the symbiosis that has occurred in this century between political and economic decision-making in Western Europe. This development was a response to the economic tribulations of the late twenties and thirties, as well as to the Second World War, and was, of course, associated politically with the rise of social democracy to power or significant influence for the first time. Planning subsequently emerged in this context. It has to be seen above all against the background of the problems arising in the functioning of the economy. These problems have basically been viewed as of two sorts: on the one hand, the obstacles to stability, growth, profitability; on the other, the various inequalities produced by the system. Underlying the problems emphasised, there is a difference in over-riding purpose between those wishing to change the existing structure of wealth and power in the interests of equality, and those seeking essentially to maintain it, while adapting society to new technological, economic, and political developments. This difference is politically expressed through the ideological division between reforming socialism and liberal conservatism. While planning has been regarded as characteristic of socialist reformism, only in the last two decades has it come to be recognised by liberal conservatives as capable of being an important *instrument of rationalisation* of the existing system, overcoming obstacles to its development and thereby helping it to work more efficiently.

Planning, it seems, can have a dual nature, either reforming or rationalising, according to who is effectively wielding power or major influence, within government, over the planning process. In this perspective, planning can involve the use of public power, coercively if necessary, to bring private sector behaviour into line with social purposes (e.g. regional equality), or it can be used to complement business behaviour in tackling imbalances and obstacles threatening industrial expansion and profitability, implying a degree of collaboration, if not always complete agreement, with the private sector. Both uses of public power can be combined, but an order of priorities tends in practice to impose itself. Is there, indeed, a pattern which emerges from the experience of the past decade indicating how realistic it is to believe that planning can assume either aspect equally well in the contemporary liberal democratic state? In this respect, the nature of planning is to be judged in the first place by its works. Such a balance sheet shows that the social reforming potential, which has not lacked government sponsors, has proved largely illusory, dominated by the preoccupation with management of the economic system of modern capitalism. This establishes the real sense in which planning is compatible with the mixed economy, in so far as it works for the maintenance of the social and political structure associated with it rather than for its change.

In the early and mid-1960s, however, the social democratic emphasis certainly appeared to be in the ascendancy. In France this was associated with the Fourth Plan, inspired not by the accession of the left to government but by the pre-eminence of certain reforming civil servants. The concern of the 1950s with economic modernisation seemed to have achieved as secure a basis as could be expected for medium, even long-term, growth. Thus, while not abandoning this concern, planning could turn more fully to consideration of the social and cultural dimensions of progress, and the Fourth Plan did, indeed, propose a remarked-on shift towards social priorities. This was epitomised in the talk of the creation of a 'civilisation of the cathedral' as opposed to a 'civilisation of the gadget',[2] a deliberate contrast with the USA's 'private affluence and public squalor'. In Britain, the return of a Labour government after thirteen years of Conservative rule was expected to give planning a much stronger social emphasis. This was notably signalled in the field of incomes where there was strong talk of planned growth ensuring a more equitable distribution of earnings. In Italy, the official adoption of planning resulted from the 'Opening to the Left', which led to the entry of the Socialists into the government coalition. The First Plan, as presented initially to parliament at the start of 1965, strongly emphasised social goals, involving notably a large rise in public investment and consumption as well as major reforms of the country's territorial structure, the bureaucracy, the fiscal system, and public enterprise. Associated with this approach was the view that planning should act as a counter-weight to the Bank of Italy and the Ministry of the Treasury, systematically pushing through medium-term objectives determined by the nation's representatives in parliament.

In the subsequent course of events, however, the social democratic aspirations, so strikingly heralded, failed to materialise. In Italy the First Plan was subjected to a concerted attack which, given the government's lack of control over parliament, seriously held up its ratification. Private industry and its supporters saw planning as a threat to the neo-liberal economic development on which, it was claimed, the 'economic miracle' of the previous decade had been based. Along with the nationalisation of the electricity industry, the effect was to reduce business confidence, produce a run on the lira and plunge the country into the worst recession since the war. Although, in the face of this situation, planning was not abandoned – this would have meant the end of the Centre-Left government – the proposed First Plan was shelved. A revised version was drawn up under a new, less radical planning minister. There was a fundamental shift from transformation towards rationalisation of the existing system, involving notably the coordination of public action to harmonise with the requirements of the private sector.

A similar pattern of events was repeated in Britain, notwithstanding the differing parliamentary situation. The British Plan was, in any case, less radical than the original Italian draft: it made social progress dependent on achieving economic growth. It is generally said that the Plan was overtaken by events, its effective abandonment forced on the government by the country's position as international debtor. The government certainly gave priority to the pursuit of economic and financial objectives over social ones. The resolution of economic problems was, in effect, accepted as a prerequisite for tackling social ones. Bankers, investors and industrialists had to be reassured and encouraged to have confidence in the nation's economy and contribute to its recovery, above all in terms of international competitiveness. Meanwhile, in France the aspirations of the Fourth Plan had already been at least partially shattered by the so-called stabilisation plan of 1963. After the planners had momentarily succeded in flirting with a 'less partial view of man'[3] – in more concrete terms, favouring a greater stress on social schemes – they were now brought back to the reality of the needs of the economy, to the recognition that these were still largely determined by the behaviour of private investors and industrialists. The change of emphasis was confirmed in the formulation of the Fifth Plan.

The revision of priorities is seen most clearly in Britain in the prices and incomes field. Here policy moved quickly from a concern with evening up the distribution of earned income, viewed as a benefit to be shared more equally, to an emphasis on wage restraint, concerned basically with relating income increases to productivity gains, with wages viewed as costs or price components. More attention was given to controlling incomes than prices, justified by the requirements of a simple market logic in the priority task of sustaining industrial investment. Moreover, while prices and incomes strategy was seen originally as inseparable from national planning, it soon became a dominant preoccupation in its own right, used as a means of restoring order in a wage-decision system which creates wider problems of economic disequilibrium as a result, in effect, of its 'high exposure to group conflict'.[4] Given the difficulty (exceptional short periods of total freeze apart) of controlling private sector decisions, greatest pressure was brought to bear on the public sector. The resort somewhat later to an attempt to legally regulate industrial relations confirmed the course embarked on, notably by seeking to circumscribe union power in strike action. Policy thus became focused, under a Labour government, on limiting not only the effects but the very source of organised labour's power in a full-employment economy. After 1970 a Conservative government simply extended the same policy further.

In France discussions on incomes policy in the early 1960s showed the planners to be sympathetic to the social dimension, but government actions soon revealed the real objective of public policy. Since then the same concerns as in Britain have been pursued, in fact by a rather different route. The most notable feature of this has been the policy of 'contracts', both for wages and prices. Under this, the emphasis, in return for a certain quid pro quo, is on restraint, but given the traditions of *étatisme* there has been a willingness to work through prices, the granting of excess wage rises under a 'contract' resulting in official price-freeze orders. However, as in Britain, the main effort has been directed at the public sector. Italy appears as the exception in the move to incomes and wage bargaining control. Nevertheless, increasing consideration has been given to the issue, and the principle of relating incomes to productivity was written into the revised First Plan. The policy has not been pursued, given the divisions in the coalition government and the priority which still has to be given to reducing unemployment and in particular underemployment, notably in agriculture. In this situation it has been difficult for government to stand against the spontaneous trend to the decentralisation of wage decisions, which in any case the large firms have believed they can control.

Incomes and wage bargaining policy, which seeks to restrain costs without interfering with investment, has been complemented by a growing stress on policies aimed at tailoring manpower as a resource more closely to the requirements of economic expansion, notably by industrial training and increasing mobility. In both Britain and France such concerns have been restricted to their narrowly economic aspect. In the field of higher and further education the same concern has manifested itself. Attention to improving working conditions has similarly been approached primarily from the perspective of simple return on capital. Again, Italy has lagged somewhat, with mobility and skills being less of a problem than increasing the proportion of the working population. As an increasing share of the economy becomes technologically advanced, this can be expected to change.

The preoccupation with policies aimed at servicing the economy within the terms of the system is well illustrated by developments affecting public enterprise. Social democrats have traditionally regarded public enterprise as a means *par excellence* for pursuing and enforcing social goals under planning. In fact, there has been a steady drive to apply commercial principles of performance, notwithstanding continuing *ad hoc* government interventions in the interests of maintaining employment or prices for the time being. The belief crystallised that 'public enterprise should be conceived primarily as a business'.[5] The few additional extensions of public enterprise in Britain and Italy have fitted into the mould of corporate, state-regulated capitalism. Activities that social democrats would have been expected to conceive as social services, e.g. railways, posts, saw their role, more or less gradually according to country, redefined as commercial. To this end, increasing importance has been attributed to the role of management *within* enterprises (not to say the public sector generally), viewed as comparable with that of private business. It could be said by the early 1970s, if not before, that the fact of public ownership in practice scarcely affected management behaviour. There was thus an extensive blurring of the distinction between the public and private sectors and although this represented in part, as we shall see, a growing involvement of government with private industry, it was essentially an alignment of public enterprise on the model of private corporate capitalism. What is particularly noteworthy politically is that this has been so no matter what the nominal political ideology of those shaping policy. In Italy, it is true, as in many things, it was more a question of government responding to a self-assigned role by those formally subject to its policies, in this case public enterprises, than of it playing a purposive role in forging a relevant policy. This only helps to confirm that what has been happening is a trend integral to the mixed economy system itself, rather than related to any specific political events.

In the industrial policy field as a whole – and a reflection of what has just been said about public enterprise is that policy for industry has increasingly been treated as a whole without reference to a public/private distinction – a number of concerns emerged as predominant in the 1960s and early 1970s. At the outset, with the social democratic influence running strong, planning was approached as a way of ensuring that industrial policy was not premised on the subordination of social action, notably in the matter of public investment priorities, but was itself to be made subject to certain social constraints, notably in the matter of location. In practice, the pressure to modernise has proved the continuing, overriding preoccupation. Consequently, the past decade has been characterised by policies in favour of industrial concentration, of investment in technical and commercial development, of identifying and tackling specific bottlenecks, and of improving the external economies of industry (signalling an emphasis on public expenditure most closely related to the needs of production). Priority has been given to the development of advanced or high technology industries, and the run-down, or conversion, of formerly major industries now regarded as providing too low a rate of return on capital. These aims have had a major underlying purpose: to strengthen the market position of industry, especially internationally. In other words, national industry was to be made as secure as possible from the vicissitudes arising largely from the development of the industrial process itself, not least given the increasingly huge and indivisible capital commitments involved. Industry was to be placed in a position, if not to control that process, at least to be able to meet its challenges.

The conception of the state's own role in the industrial development process itself changed as a result of these policies. From providing a general stimulus, largely through monetary and budgetary regulation, the notion of specific support for particular modernisation projects has been increasingly emphasised. According to this approach, government's main role is to provide technical and above all financial assistance. Contact with industry thus became more detailed, the relationship more symbiotic, involving direct dealings with particular firms. But this style of intervention has not, in general, sought to impose public control for ends opposed by industry. It has paid deference to the value of the (imperfect) market and given support to corporate development. In French terms, it has embodied a refusal of *dirigisme*. The watchword, then, is to leave management to the managers,[6] whether public or private, encouraging their initiatives. From this approach is expected to flow greater efficiency and a boost to industrial development, in particular by seeking to encourage pace-makers.

The resulting situation has, however, worked against a general industrial planning approach to policy. Policy is being fashioned inductively, with firms or branches supported in the pursuit of courses of action judged best within their own particular market context rather than set in a general industrial or national plan framework. There is certainly resistance to this amongst planners, especially in France, where the definition of industrial policy in as exhaustive and integrated a manner as possible in a medium-term perspective is still the model, with a view to establishing priorities for a discriminatory intervention. But cutting across this is the emphasis on support, based on a collaboration respecting managerial autonomy, rather than on constraint; the need for measures to have an effect *as intended* looms large here. Operational credibility implies that they are not judged as unrealistic by the industry envisaged. Thus many aspects of an integrated policy do not materialise. Perhaps particularly galling in this respect for social democratic aspirations is the general weakness of location policy.

What can arise is a certain competition between industries and even firms, especially, perhaps, between the public and private sectors, for the government's benevolence. In Italy, the success of public enterprise, through its closer, party-based relationship with government, in largely cornering the finance market from the late 1960s, produced some pain in the private sector. While selective intervention may work for given firms and industries, the *general* effect is to enhance uncertainty, above all since the grounds for such intervention are unpredictable, the obverse of planned. Intervention is not determined on the basis of a number of *explicit* clearly defined criteria, but turns essentially on relationships of influence and pressure and the conjunction of unforeseen events. It can be argued that non-discriminatory, selective action incorporates the worst of both worlds; purposive but more or less arbitrary intervention compounds the disequilibrating forces of the imperfect market. Not that the unintended consequences of the general approach in a broad policy area necessarily undermine all its more specific aims. In particular, one policy which has tended to thrive in such circumstances is that of concentration, especially in a financial rather than production sense. This acts as a safeguard for industry in two ways: it gives the firm greater control of its immediate market situation; and, at the same time, it is a greater guarantee, as events have proved, of government support.

Regional policy has changed little in its basic conception in the past decade, even though in reality it has produced few substantial dividends. Whereas industrial policy moved to an alignment with the pattern of a 'mature' (oligopolistic) market economy, regional policy has continued to set its face against the cumulative, centralising trends of market development. It has, however, the weakness of being by vocation a synthetic policy when the predominant conception of policy is sectoral. Regional planning has sought to make a strength of this weakness, but without much success, without the underpinning of a genuine budgetary function. So regional policy continues to seek to tidy over the troublesome social and political side-effects of a development stressing investment in capital returns rather than social returns. Its most positive approach is to try to bring backward and declining areas into the modernisation process by applying to them the same formula that spurs the development of the dynamic zones. This is particularly evident in the Mezzogiorno policy. Otherwise, an uphill struggle prevails to provide extra employment and income in response to new and old relative deprivations by the dispersal of a few factories or occasionally offices, or by undertaking some extra public works.

Land-use planning, on the other hand, is not intrinsically about reducing the centripetal tendencies or social side-effects of market development. A clear shift has occurred from the notion of blueprints establishing a preferred physical pattern to which development should conform, to a more flexible approach involving a greater recognition of the role of the market in determining the pattern of land use. Increasingly, blueprint planning proved to have been overtaken by events, or incapable even of establishing an effective regime of regulation due to political pressure either open or, most influentially, unavowed. What was demonstrated was that the liberal political process was not a matter of establishing a plan or particular policies according to the dictates of simple ideology or expertise, however well intentioned, and then imposing it ready-made on society. The main requirement in seeking credibility and operationality for regulating land use was to take account of the principal actors in the market situation – in other words to accept the criteria required by a commercial development logic. Land-use planning has thus responded to the challenge of the developer and industrialist with a wider base than the town, by seeking to provide for an orderly physical organisation of contemporary economic expansion, including the necessary supporting infrastructure, going beyond the traditional town boundaries. Sometimes, the planners have sought an alternative model as a basis for organising development; but primacy has had to be given to accommodating existing economic forces, given that these have been able in any event to circumvent alternative prescriptions. The shift in the approach to land-use planning has not occurred, however, without a major – and continuing – debate on ends and means, because at this level policy affects the public most visibly and, often literally, closest to home.

Altogether, in the policy sectors investigated, the emphasis in the past decade has been at variance with the priorities proclaimed at the outset, even where social democratic influence in government was nominally strong. The predominant concerns of policy have clearly been those related to eliminating imbalances and bottlenecks in the system and facilitating its continuing development in accordance with the existing socio-economic pattern. The fight against inflation became a constant, central preoccupation. But commitment to growth remained no less strong. Increasing the size of the cake has taken precedence over redistributing it, which has thus remained resolutely, at best, a promise for the future. While attention to easing the social side-effects of expansion has not been lacking and is even increasing (e.g. environment policy), public investment has generally, and often indiscriminately, been sacrificed to the requirements of the business cycle – even in France where, in the previous decade, priority had been given to sustaining it in periods of over-heating. It was to be expected that such crude Keynesianism would have been one of the first victims of planned policy-making.

Since policies have been geared to promoting industrial and commercial performance within the existing system, the most forceful control exerted by government has been aimed at the labour factor in production rather than the capital or land factors (contrast the approach to incomes and the labour market with that to industrial location and land use). This has occurred in response to a growing assertion by labour of its autonomous role rather than subordination to the other two factors as controlled by management. Indeed, in Italy, where government has not been in a position to intervene with a view to controlling this 'imbalance', the industrial process, dominated by a virtually unrestrained two-sided confrontation, becomes itself very largely an informal political process of settling conflict. Where government has intervened, its first priority has been to reassert a framework of authority based on a hierarchy of functions in which the management of capital predominates. Because the tendency of labour to become too intrusive has hindered the performance of this function, the unions have needed to be restrained.

The ideological presuppositions

The picture of policy developments presented in the preceding pages is reflected in the evolution that has occurred in the way planning is viewed and conceived. Alongside the view of planning as a single, organic whole, or even overtaking it, there has arisen the view of it as a set of practices which can find their application separately in different fields and levels of activity. Even in France, where national planning has remained the centrepiece of planning, there emerged a growing stress on the idea that it encompassed a number of partial types of planning and that a few even existed outside its increasingly sketchy overall framework. An ambiguity has thus been highlighted in the notion of planning, between what might be called its partial and comprehensive vocation. The decisional implications of this are examined in the next section.

As a pervasive, pluralistic phenomenon, planning is conceived of as decision-making technology embodying less a systematic approach seeking to combine all elements consistently in a broad forward flow of development, than a strategic one, in which attention is concentrated on a number of priority actions or schemes of a sectoral or territorial nature, in which aims are very closely linked with the ways and means of achieving them. Closely related to this is an emphasis upon operationality, the ingredients of which are: the subordination of intervention to the appreciation of technological and economic realities; the analysis and simulation of the behaviour of socio-economic actors; closer articulation with established decision circuits, involving if necessary more secretive methods; a more flexible and evolutionary approach to content, not attempting to fix policies too precisely in advance but to provide a framework to guide policy decisions.

The concern with operationality is reflected in the growing role of micro as opposed to macro-economists. Greater importance is attached to the pursuit of efficiency in given operations by various techniques associated with planning (cost-benefit, cost effectiveness, programme budgets, systems analysis) and the concern with macro coherences is de-emphasised. At this level Keynesian techniques, with their short-run applicability, have proved their durability though not their adequacy in relation to non-inflationary growth. Associated with this more micro-economic orientation is a growing concern with the problems of management of assets and not simply with their creation.

These developments are in keeping with a predominantly technical conception of planning as a process involving first and foremost the examination of *how* to secure further development rather than *what* development. The function of considering essentially second-order problems of efficiency, viewed basically as a question of management, has thus been elevated in planning practices above the primary political function of determining the pattern of development to be promoted. The conception of planning as a process representing an alternative avenue of democracy based on functional representation, in vogue in the early 1960s, has gone out of fashion. It is now regarded by some of its original political proponents, especially in France, as attendant on the demise of the existing system, in the belief that, to be valid, democratic planning has to be built on the practice of self-management (*autogestion*). The way the participation of interest groups is envisaged has not, in the end, moved very far from the traditional notions of consultation, namely as a specialist, advisory and discrete rather than deliberative and multilateral participation, representative perhaps, but only in the sense of opinion simulation with little serious suggestion that it be put on an electoral basis. Here the principle of parliamentary democracy has still held sway. It is assumed that the definition of ends is a matter for the government and not the planning process itself.

However, government or parliamentary control of the pattern of development to be promoted is, in any case, at least partly vitiated by the technical nature of the planning process. This involves an instrumental rationality of 'how best to', in the apparent belief that means can be clearly separated from ends. A major stress is placed on the role of expert knowledge in preparing decisions: these are to be underpinned by research, analysis, calculation. This establishes the parameters of the possible. Yet the 'facts' privileged in this way may be regarded as super-objectives specific to the given socio-economic system. The parameters which guide the choice of ends are themselves ultimately normative, since hard (economic, quantitative) data is sought and the harder the data the more it is tied to the current structural and behavioural pattern. But given the bias in favour of analytical empiricism, the economic specialists can scarcely be expected to regard data as perhaps including contingent socio-political facts; they have to work with what they have got.

The techniques thus work to ensure that the future is seen as an extension of the present and recent past. In effect, they enable the conditions to be stated for the reproduction of the system, but not for its transformation, and thus provide a distinctly conservative frame of reference for politicians to decide the preferred pattern of development. The crux of this is that the means to other ends are not seen as available. That this is, moreover, a major conceptual weakness in planning as it is practised is not to be doubted. When planning is not capable of being a projection and vehicle of socio-political change, but only of technico-economic change, it leaves itself wide open to being rapidly overtaken by political events. As it has been remarked: 'The shadow of politics silences the economists.'[7] Some small attempt at such projection has been tried in France in long-term studies, but it has effectively remained very much at the margins of the planning exercise as such. The inability to provide for socio-political change, whilst showing itself in a conceptual weakness, rests fundamentally on the existing structure of power relationships in society, of which experts are part, voluntarily or involuntarily.

The common thread running through both partial and comprehensive types of planning is an ideological one. Policies, as we have seen, have tended to serve a given purpose, which can be assimilated to a broad political ideology. Here, however, we are concerned with the message specific to, and apparently inherent in, planning practices as such. It is contained in the language and way of thinking. It can be summed up in the word 'rational'. A rational approach to decisions starts with the possession of expertise, primarily of an economic or even quantitative nature. It is a matter of understanding the logic of economic mechanisms and interdependencies, of establishing the necessary, politically neutral, criteria for action. The basis for these is information, mostly statistical, and calculation as against intuition or debate that is ideologically or interest-motivated. The task is to find the correct policy to solve a problem on the basis of a rigorous analysis of the facts. The politician's job is essentially to identify the problems worrying public opinion, and to implement the solutions.

The essence of the message coming from the specialists and planners is that decisions cannot be made without fear of contradiction, of producing opposite results to those intended, unless due cognisance is taken of the necessary relationships (or functions) underpinning economic activity. Overall, this means attention to the consistency of decisions. In terms of particular operations or activities having a practical purpose, it means a focus on efficiency in the use of resources. It should be noted that these requirements for rational action are those automatically fulfilled in the perfect market model, but which have in practice, it is accepted, to be achieved by the conscious, purposive action of *management*. What planning propounds through its 'language' is an objective rationality in pursuance of this. This approach can be regarded as technocratic. In its most extreme form, it seeks a definition of the public interest above the political fray: a refusal of the short-run compromises between the blinkered egoisms of individuals and groups and the commitment to a common, 'rational' recognition of how we can all be materially and socially better off. More practicably, perhaps, it is a matter of applying the knowledge and techniques developed by the social sciences (especially economics) with a view to improving the management of the system. Management is, in this perspective, taken to be a process analogous to steering. As such it fits well with the rationality that planning has propounded. Thus it is scarcely surprising that planning has not expressed a different regulatory logic. The expertise on which planning has been based requires that there be definite constants in the economic process, above all in its authority structure. Social science solutions rely on people behaving as their assigned role requires. In so far as planning has been a medium for propagating the reasoning underpinning such solutions, the circle involved has remained the very restricted one of those having a direct relationship to the management function, whether at the micro or macro level, since they are the ones on which successful steering is taken essentially to depend. The system is viewed as structured to permit management as a discrete, specialised and hierarchical function.

Planning is, however, particularly associated with the extension of this function into politics. It is not surprising that the application of many planning techniques has been developed in the industrial and military spheres, where goals and roles have traditionally been structured more tightly in a definite and integrated hierarchy. The techniques have subsequently been imported into government. In France their importation into central administration has been, rather, from those areas of the state concerned with the direct supervision of industrial and related public activities. In this perspective, planning is only a second-order phenomenon to the primary one of professional management.

The solutions specified by the rationality inherent in planning can be said to be objective only from a system or partial system maintenance point of view. The 'scientific' knowledge underpinning them is relative to the patterns of behaviour associated with the existing social and economic structures of a hierarchical nature. In other words, the solutions are set in a predictable framework only in so far as the professional managers – who are being actively brought on to the same wavelength by planning methods – remain firmly in control of the steering. How far the standardisation of steering techniques has succeeded in establishing the conditions for the consistency and effectiveness of decisions is a question for the next section. At this stage, however, one may doubt whether the rationality that planning propagates, with its managerialist bias, is appropriate for the political process, whose mainspring is the conflict of ideas and interests. Moreover, a potential discontinuity can be discerned between what is rational in particular management situations and what is rational in terms of the overall management function. It is not necessarily the inefficiency of particular activities which is the only source of overall incoherence and dysfunction. It can also arise if the aims of particular activities are not concordant. In fact, planning has generally attempted to achieve this by making the requirements of economic growth the yardstick and using this to establish a hierarchy of social and economic activities as the basis for the general allocation of resources. However, the efficiency of a particular activity in pursuit of its own aims may clearly involve lack of respect for the general hierarchy. And this is simply to assume divergences in the performance of the managerial function, whereas divergences of social and political interest have also to be reckoned with.

The development traced above in the conception of planning – and the ideology of rationality it propounds – in the end make sense as a powerful re-affirmation of the modern capitalist pattern of socio-economic development; a modified or mature market model allowing for, and indeed admitting, the benefits of oligopolies. Development is accepted as arising from the actions of more-or-less autonomous organisational hierarchies, including those within the state. The essential task is to overcome problems in their interactions which hinder or even threaten that development, to improve the overall and in some cases separate performance of the management function, especially in the matter of technological innovation and adaptation according to economic criteria. In this light, the key decisions of government impinging on development – supporting financial, infrastructural and even social action – need to be coordinated with those of industry and evaluated accordingly.

The nature of planning, as it has crystallised during the past decade, is thus that of being an instrument of rationalisation for the system rather than a process of socio-political change from within. Planning practices have functioned in various political settings as a support for a linear pattern of socio-economic development, integrated into a steering process of keeping the system on course without enquiring too closely into the ends it is serving. Attempts to map a different pattern were soon overtaken by the apparent imperative of managerial problem-solving. The next section, in examining the relationships between actors in decision-making, will help to account for this orientation, but principally will be devoted to examining how the necessary institutional and organisational modifications have worked.

Planning and decisions

As the Introduction underlined, it is not enough simply to produce
policies.[8] The effectiveness of policies depends not only on their
intrinsic quality for dealing with a problem, but also on a minimum of
consistency between policies, as well as, quite evidently, action taken in
accordance with them and on a coordinated basis. These are a matter
of the relationships amongst and between policy-makers and those on
whom policy implementation depends. Although there is a dominant
concern with working the system, the different components of it –
notably firms, government departments and trade unions – do so in
the way they think best in the light of their own particular aims. In fact,
the aim of some trade union participation, especially in France and
Italy, is to replace the system. But even if exception is made of trade
union activity, there remains the difficulty of ensuring that the immediate, specific interests of industry and government in producing
goods and services do not contradict the general interest of the
system's performance as a whole. Because the market does not suffice,
this remains primarily the responsibility of government. Planning
logically implies that rationalisation should begin with government
activities themselves. In practice, this has not always been the case and
has been a major weakness in national planning. This was particularly
true of the British 1960s experience and remains a primary stumbling
block in the progress of Italian national planning.

   Planning, then, involves not simply researching better policies but
also meeting certain organisational requirements, so that policies are
'better' in an applied and not just abstract sense. These requirements
are basically two: on the one hand, the *coordination* of policy so that
government action is consistent and integrated; on the other, to ensure
that public and private action are not contradictory. In keeping with
the emphasis of policy on rationalisation, the *dirigiste* approach to
aligning action by the extension and coercive use of public power has
been effectively discarded by government, at least in relation to
industry. It has been argued that '[direct] controls are extremely
difficult to administer', not least because 'the number of potential
violators is staggering'.[9] More broadly, there is plenty of evidence that
dirigisme is scarcely compatible with the mixed economy, given the
desire to sustain the economic performance of the system in which the
role of the confidence factor remains preponderant. The preferred
alternative has been the development of techniques of *concerted* action,
or consensus-building, based essentially on collaboration and financial
incentives. Referring to the pioneering effort of French planning in
this field in the fifties, Shonfield summed it up as a 'voluntary collu-

sion between senior civil servants and senior managers', producing, as he saw it, a 'conspiracy in the public interest',[10] although whether and why it is in the public interest he seems to take for granted.

As processes for improving the quality and consistency of decisions, coordination and concerted action place a special emphasis on the mutual exchange of knowledge and information, on sounding out proposals of government and the administration before they are cut and dried, and, not least, on explicitness: bringing arguments into the open, in particular to see how they stand up 'rationally'. Co-ordination within government is also regarded as a matter of hier-archical control, but this is where, in fact, it starts to run into trouble. For the final repository of overall control is the political executive, where it resides in perhaps just one man, at most a score. Even though backed by a secretariat or office, such control remains a matter inevi-tably of broad supervision and often, in practice, of 'crisis manage-ment'. Political control has proved, indeed, to have a greater affinity for injecting disjointed actions into the policy processes than for contri-buting to its thorough-going coordination. Political control itself needs to be set in a stronger framework of continuous, wide-ranging co-ordination at the level of detailed policy-making. Below the political executive, however, control splits into a number of bureaucratic compartments. While hierarchical coordination within each of these is more feasible, it leaves unanswered the problem of coordination on a broader front: indeed, it poses it more severely, in the light of the political executive's unsuitability for the task. It is thus at this level that the attempt to achieve greater coordination has been focussed, leav-ing the political executive to concern itself with the basic objectives of policy.

The political executive, then, can make little practical contribution to the coordination process in planning, other than to carry out the institutional and procedural changes considered necessary. Even in establishing the policy guidelines, it has been dependent on the researches and analyses of the planning specialists, which provide a frame of reference tied to the principal structural patterns of the existing socio-economic system. That political leaders have their own official expert advisers, separate from the administration's planning specialists, does not fundamentally change this situation. At most it means they reflect differences, essentially of a tactical nature, amongst official expert opinion, rather than other external grounds for argu-ment. It might be otherwise if a party or group possessed equivalent resources of expertise; but this is certainly not true in practice of the parties, and in the case of interest groups some – notably business organisations – are considerably better provided for than others. In this way politics can only effectively intrude into planning, as indeed it has done, disruptively, in the shape of short-term, *ad hoc* pressures. The difficulty, then, is that coordination cannot be hierarchical *and* general. In the pursuit of an alternative approach, important innovations and adaptations in the machinery of government have been undertaken in all three countries. The specific instances are detailed in the preceding chapters. We are concerned here with the general results and, although some changes have been more successful in achieving a certain permanence, every instance has shown an inability to sustain the requisite coordination of the policy process, often by giving rise to unforeseen side-effects.

In general, change has not involved a major re-shaping of the administrative structure; planning bodies have simply been added alongside, or inside, existing structures, and not substituted for them. The main original innovation was, of course, a central planning structure. The main problem in this respect was what position it should occupy in relation to the established administrative institutions. In Britain NEDO was placed outside the administration, while the DEA was established along the lines of a traditional department. As a result, the former had little hope of penetrating decision-making networks, while the DEA came into conflict with established departments, notably the Treasury. In contrast, the CGP in France has been able to walk the tightrope between these extremes, though its attachment to the prime minister's office has helped give weight to its role, especially at the more difficult times in its existence. The CGP approach has been to introduce the planning function almost by stealth, offering little direct challenge to established decision-making centres but, by participation in administrative and political decision circuits, working as an agent of change in decision-making practices. As for the BEP in Italy, while already a major, established ministry, its new planning office has had conflicts with existing services inside the ministry itself, as well as with other traditional ministries, notably the Treasury. In Britain, and to some extent Italy, a virtually separate decision-making system was created alongside the existing one in a short space of time, giving rise to a heterogeneous collection of planning bodies. This is the piecemeal pragmatism of setting up a separate body for each new task that is thought of, without enquiring too deeply whether it might not be closely tied to the performance of a wider function. Besides seeming to threaten established economic policy centres and therefore provoking their resistance, this proliferation can be seen to create further problems for coordination and indeed the more specialised bodies, such as the PIB and the Cassa in Italy, do complicate the criss-cross of responsibilities. This is the danger of the by-pass approach, intentional or not, in relation to the traditional administration. The frontal assault approach, however, is scarcely an alternative. Proposals for a 'super' economic planning ministry, absorbing the finance ministry, certainly keep coming up. But there is little chance that such a reform would enable the planners to impose their will on the administration. Even if undertaken, it would surely mean their submergence in the current preoccupations of financial administration. Whenever a finance ministry has been made the economic ministry as well, managing the government's purse strings has remained its dominant function. In the face of this problem, the CGP formula has undoubtedly been the most successful. Removed from getting too closely identified with day to day administration, it has nevertheless over the years been able to exert a diffuse influence over the conception of policy, particularly in matters of financial intervention. It has not, however, really succeeded in being the vehicle of a general economic policy coordination in a plan framework.

In fact, coordination has come to occupy a central place in the preoccupations of governments with their own functioning in the past decade, a trend with which the notion of planning is undoubtedly closely linked. But given the ambiguity of this notion as to whether the scope of its practical application should be partial or general, it is not surprising that the accompanying organisational developments have been diverse. Most noticeably, perhaps, there have been major concentrations of departments and services. Italy is an exception owing to the range of party interests to be satisfied with portfolios in the coalition, quite apart from bureaucratic resistances. Secondly, departments have created their own planning units, while budgetary programming has got under way. Thirdly, there has occurred the establishment of separate planning bodies in broad, cross-cutting policy areas: prices and incomes; regional development and land use; productivity and industrial rationalisation; scientific research and development.

These developments must be regarded as a very mixed blessing as far as the coordination of economic policy in a planning perspective is concerned. In fact, they reflect certain resistances to the drive to ever wider coordination. This is especially true of Britain, where the institutional provision for coordination in a general planning framework has ceased to exist. Even if departmental concentration has reduced the number of institutional barriers, in France and Britain this has probably gone as far as it can in respect of those policy responsibilities relevant to economic planning. Moreover, the barriers, though fewer, already appear higher. Larger ministries tend more readily to undertake their own planning and are more likely to establish their own medium-term policies. Yet they themselves face considerable problems in surmounting their own inevitably conglomerate nature,

itself a strong incentive to partial planning. Equally, budgetary programming may emerge as a competitor seeking to shape medium-
term policy orientations. The DTI was split up in 1974.

In these moves towards policy-specific planning, the micro-
economists have come to the fore. This has been reflected in a great
expansion in the past decade in planning-related specialists and
advisers in government. This raises the question of how they can
be inserted into the policy process especially when many of them,
notably in Britain, are 'irregulars' on a temporary or free-lance basis.
Undoubtedly, the dispersed nature of their involvement has created
further problems of coordination. It is, of course, not so surprising that
different parts of government should want to turn planning techniques to their own account, rather than leaving them to an overall
planning structure. But while this trend brings these techniques to bear
in a more directly operational way in the short term, it undoubtedly
represents a regression in terms of the search for overall coherence
and organising economic policy in an integrated developmental
perspective.

A crucial problem for putting government activity on a planned basis
concerns the relations between traditional bureaucrats and planners,
whether specialists or generalists. Often the two differ in educational
background and therefore intellectual approach, essentially a distinction between the law or arts man and the social scientist, the former
being more inclined to be guided by precedent and to treat each case
on its merits, in contrast to the latter's more systematic, analytical
approach, underpinned by theoretical reasoning. This distinction also
tends to be associated with different attitudes towards the government's role, the planners tending to favour intervention seeking to
achieve a substantive policy objective and not simply to arbitrate or
reconcile competing claims. These differences help to enhance departmental and service rivalries. They have been particularly nefarious for
planning's effectiveness in Italy, isolating the planners in their ivory
tower.[11] In France, it is true, the intellectual 'gap' has become less
pronounced as the graduates of the ENA have risen to occupy
leading posts in the administration; but this has itself been associated
with a new cleavage between the micro-oriented planners from the
Ecole Polytechnique and the more macro-oriented ones which the
ENA has tended to produce.

Rather than striving for coordination through a genuine cooperation between sectors, the tendency is to seek to expand the scope of
responsibilities of each. This does not generally mean the outright
substitution or subordination of one group of officials by another,
which is strongly resisted. It seems an unwritten rule that only new and
potential fields of activity are disputed, new, that is, for central

government, since this may well be attempted at the expense of lower-tier authority responsibilities. The creation of new structures is often only a means for leading groups of officials to maintain their position in the face of change. As a result, such changes scarcely contribute to a new disposition of forces in the civil service favouring the planners, which would enable them to play a leading role in coordination.

A second key problem for coordination in a planning framework arises from the division that can exist between policy conception and execution. Planners are mostly confined to the former. Is planning, as a result, caught in a vacuum? There is certainly a danger that it will lack applicability. But to confer the planning function on officials with executive powers leads to its degeneration into an attempt merely to secure smooth adjustments to events. This is the direction in which sectoral planning tends to go, with its closer identification of the planner and administrator. It is very doubtful, anyway, if an overall planning structure with executive powers could exercise effective operational control because the ramifications of policy implementation are so extensive. In fact, a main way to seek the alignment of action in keeping with planning prescriptions is through the association of planners with the executive coordinating bodies of the administration. On the whole, however, this has not proved too successful: such bodies are largely concerned with arranging things between departments in a short-term perspective. Any successes tend to depend on circumstances, not least the planners' skill, rather than the basic, continuing validity of a plan, which appears a less important factor for administrators to have to take into account than the immediate demands of group pressures and the political and economic situation generally.

Given a stress on coordination at the execution stage, the implementation problem often appears as one of the dispersal of executive responsibilities. This has been a main consideration behind departmental concentration, the defects of which have already been noted. In effect, whereas planning is totalising, policy application is inherently an activity in series. It was perceived, particularly perhaps in France, that coordination could not make a totality of policies at the execution stage; it needed to begin earlier, when policies were first under consideration. This meant the extensive and intensive participation of departments and services in planning work and the development of an inter-face network in the activity of policy conception. The failure to stress a large involvement of civil servants from executive departments directly in plan-making is undoubtedly a major explanation for some of the failures of national planning in Britain and Italy.

As France shows, however, progress in planned policy integration is a slow business, involving, as a first step, a socialisation process into new ways of reasoning. In this respect, planners represent a sort of intellectual task force. But, notwithstanding a certain broad conversion to the new rationality, substantive policy integration has remained more apparent than real, consisting for the most part of a juxtaposition of sectoral policies. The response in France has been to try to engineer a closer decisional integration in the definition of policies and not just in terms of the approach to defining them. The participation of bureaux has been more heavily emphasised and a deliberate effort made to investigate the inter-action of policies. In particular, a clearer guide to specific priorities has been given by the more strategic, more project-orientated approach to the Plan. This has been accompanied by a related hierarchical structuring of the system of modernisation commissions and working parties.

This experiment is relevant to the British and Italian planning experiences, in so far as little correlation has been achieved between planning intentions and policies actually pursued, or simply between policies in major sectors of intervention. The results, however, have been far from conclusively in its favour. Important aspects of major policy sectors have remained outside the Plan's policy definition activity; in other cases, the rigorous, detailed specification of relevant measures to put policies into effect has been lacking. There is a basic reluctance within ministries to accept inroads into their policy-making responsibilities, and they remain unenthusiastic participants in establishing inter-sectoral priorities. What is at stake is the avoidance of becoming too committed by a process which involves, at least potentially, a generalised redistribution of power, since ministries do establish close links, often informal and confidential, with particular planning bodies, as they do with particular interests. This can work quite well for a particular aspect of planning, but reinforces the obstacles to broader planning and policy integration. Moreover, proposals pre-established on a purely clientelistic basis can still be fed through the planning process relatively intact. A crucial factor in this situation is the reliance of planners on information from practitioners, public and private, in framing policies that can be expected to work because they are considered 'realistic'.

Planning has failed to break down sectoralisation in policy-making because it cannot effectively challenge the existing balance of forces in society. The attempt to limit and control the variability of departmental interests inherent in the integration approach really involves, at bottom, the impossible task of regulating the complex of societal interests, with their own separate power bases. What this means is that planning cannot be successfully a neutral, 'rational' activity, harmoniously elaborating the 'optimum' development. The planners have either to choose an alliance, or fall back on incremental adjustment simply in response to short-run party and group pressures. The planning experience is, indeed, at the most fundamental level of relationships, a further illustration that the state is not apart from society, least of all above it, but in it and, as such, the object as well as the subject of many, if not today most, of the great pressures that traverse society. It is by now a truism to say that the more planning fails to recognise and accommodate sectoral realities, the more it becomes an abstract and ineffective exercise. Thus the focus has come to rest on strategies and projects and sectoral planning, in the interest of operationality and of flexibility. In this way planning promotes the reflection by the government apparatus of the oligopolistic trend in the economy and society, the concentration into bigger units, even if of a rather conglomerate nature. In turn this enhances both the scope and the need for intra-sectoral planning and for associated specialist planning structures. In this situation overall planning appears increasingly incapable of reconciling relations between sectors in some overarching synthesis of policy aims and means. Planners are themselves drawn into closer, more structured, more permanent sectoral relationships. Thus the effort at the planned integration of government action on a broad front of socio-economic development has receded.

To stay in business, planning has forged an alliance involving a 'community of interest' in the rationalisation of the system. It has thereby found itself a more specific and clearly defined place and function within the state. This emerges more clearly when we turn to consideration of the problem of planning and the relations between government and groups. The central dilemma is to allow for the expression of interests while ensuring that economic decisions are consistent and purposive in serving the performance of the system as a whole, viewed over a period of years. Planning has sought the answer essentially in what was described in the mid-1960s as 'a step between exhortation and direct legal controls which is the object of great interest and experimentation',[12] namely concerted action or consensus-building (referred to in France as *concertation*). How, then, has the 'experiment' worked out?

Generally, the tripartite nature of consensus-building, between government, employers and unions, has been officially emphasised. France has put a greater stress than Britain and Italy on a continuous and wide-ranging participation of interests alongside planners and ordinary officials. In Britain and Italy tripartism has tended to be viewed as more a matter of 'summit' meetings; where participation has taken a more practical form, as in the 'little neddies' or through CNEL, officials from executive departments have not taken much part. In this situation, interests are expected to sort things out between themselves in the light of the government's main policy proposals, with the supporting help of the planner's explanations and expertise.

This broad portrayal of the nature of consensus-building scarcely represents the reality of the course of events in the past decade. There has been little 'sorting things out' between interests in Britain or Italy, or concerted action on a tripartite basis anywhere. A reluctance of interests to go beyond their immediate, particular preoccupations continued to cut across planning's requirements for a common approach to fundamental economic problems. Sectionalism, in fact, has remained predominant. Groups have maintained their action outside planning with no less vigour, and links between particular groups and particular ministries have not been weakened, a condition not only of concerting economic action but also of effective policy coordination in a planning framework within government. General commitments to a course of future action that have been agreed, e.g. George Brown's 'Declaration of Intent', proved essentially a matter of verbal formulae; it revealed the weakness of the peak organisations when it came to making commitments.

These setbacks undoubtedly add up to a major flaw in planning's general regulatory capability. Another aspect of consensus-building, no less significant politically, has been its biased nature. Notwithstanding the participation of a variety of interests, an established hierarchy has existed in the effectiveness of their contributions. A *de facto* convergence between planners, officials and industrial management has dominated the process since at least the mid-1960s in all three countries. In Britain, while this became evident in the 'little neddies', it has had perhaps its major expression in special instruments of intervention, the IRC and then IDE, and similarly in Italy with planned bargaining (*contrattazione programmatica*). In France it was most evident in the creation of the Industrial Development Committee and the subsequent reorganisation for the Sixth Plan of the modernisation commissions dealing with industry. Such an alliance has also been seen to blossom locally in land-use planning, in the collaboration of the authorities with commercial and industrial developers. Undoubtedly some planners and officials have regretted the extent of this alignment, but seen it as virtually inevitable, given the lack of organised support for consumers' interests and social needs, and given the lack of trade union expertise. Notwithstanding the great improvement that has occurred in national accounts and statistics, information from industry remains crucial for the planners' designs, especially when they are seeking to deal directly with specific problems, which the strategic, operational orientation of planning involves. Yet the reluctance of industrialists to disclose information, particularly to the unions, has not diminished. Here planning has signally failed to bring about explicitness in decision-making.

The failure of tripartism and broad-based participation goes deeper, however, than a question of information, expertise or even organisation. Indeed, the 'problem' of expertise is more a matter of differing rationalities than of lack of know-how. The bias, in fact, is inherent in the approach. The reliance on concerted action involves acceptance by government and planners of the prevailing authority structure with regard to the major economic decisions of industrial investment, production, marketing and employment. The logic of *effective* concerted action is thus to reproduce, in the deliberations, the authority structure in industry, privileging the role of those with management prerogatives, notably over investment and information.[13] In this situation, the participants are not equals and cannot be, partnership being a myth politicians and planners cling to and try to play on.

To have a consistent strategy for economic performance further requires that concerted action should not include the usual political practice of seeking to satisfy organised interests turn and turn about: an established hierarchy of 'partners' is the rule. Why, then, have the unions and the lesser organised interests as participants at all? The answer is primarily political: the need for legitimisation of the process and the hope of lessening eventual opposition. Moreover, union cooperation is important, perhaps crucial, for success in incomes and manpower policies. Most importantly, union participation may be expected to widen the circle of those initiated into the rationality of which planning is the medium. As Lucien Nizard has pointed out, this rationality – and the accompanying frame of reference for policy decisions – is not absolute but involves a choice.[14] It is a rationality compatible with the norms regulating the behaviour of the large corporation rather than with those traditionally guiding union or social service activity, or even those governing the political process itself. This is illustrated by the fact that the unions have generally been unsuccessful, in contrast with the employers, in getting their policy preferences adopted as 'technical' requirements of policy. To widen the circle of initiates, however, implies a lesser place accorded to such 'essentially ideological' divergences in the practice of economic decision-making.

It is not to be supposed that government and planners have adopted neo-liberal economic rationality as a result of direct business pressure, although this has played a role in Italy at least. Indeed, the need for such pressure may be regarded as reflecting the dysfunctionality of the Italian governmental system in so far as it lacks a structured ordering of political relations radiating from an established centre: the executive. Where the executive is able to ensure such control, the task of managing the mixed economy becomes an institutionalised function with the focus of attention displaced from ends to means. In this situation the choice of a neo-liberal economic rationality is assured. For the key to planning's effectiveness is seen to lie in speaking the same language as that of modern, large-scale management, given a prior acceptance by the political authorities of the prevailing authority structure in industry. The major industrial interests have thus little need to resort to pressure tactics on any scale. The terms of the discussion are inherently biased to serve their principal concerns, while pushing the unions and social interests, whose concerns are made to appear tangential if not hostile to the business of planning, into a reactive, defensive posture. The salience, since the mid-1960s, of the confrontation with the trade unions in government's relations with groups, is to be understood largely in the light of this situation. It further underlines the illusory character of a participatory process conditioned by a one-dimensional rationality whose basic norms coincide too closely with the interests of the authority structure in industry.

The impact of planning on the two principal 'partners' of government has not surprisingly differed, given the nature of consensus-building and its associated policy orientations. Any suspicions held by leading industrial organisations in the early or mid-1960s, whether about the principle of planning as in Italy, or about particular practices, faded. In Britain the IRC after all proved acceptable to business; while after the abandonment of the National Plan, the continuance of some of the EDCs and especially the NEDC was regarded with some benevolence. There has since been acceptance of prices and pay boards and a welcome for the IDE. In Italy, the fears of planning had largely evaporated by 1968, after important changes in the First Plan had been secured and any imperative element removed. Confindustria, as a matter of general policy, remains unenthusiastic, but there is, in practice, cooperation for a planning with basically 'technical' concerns (exchange of information, reduction of uncertainty, coordination of government policies in keeping with industry's development requirements, notably regarding finance and infrastructure). In France, the CNPF discarded its defensive anti-interventionist shell at the end of 1967 and launched its own model of development and planning. This coincided with growing doubts, not least amongst planners, about the effectiveness of the French planning process. An important modification of the apparatus of consensus-building was, therefore, undertaken for the Sixth Plan, largely in keeping with the requirements of the CNPF's conception. In effect, the CNPF was instated as principal architect of the Sixth Plan's industrial development imperative.

The *rapprochement* of industry and official planning practices has not occurred without changes inside the industrial lobby, characterised by the further ascendancy of the large corporations. This has been accompanied by increased tensions between big and small business – as in the case of the ITBs in Britain and planned bargaining in Italy – and reflected in the small business PMEs' continuing anti-interventionist faith in France. Small business has become more hostile to planning and generally alienated from government policy-making on a wider front. Only moves aimed at controlling trade union activity have produced support. Planning has undoubtedly encouraged the peak employers' associations to strengthen their organisation and resources, notably of expertise. Early in the 1960s they were still rather weak, umbrella organisations, considerably dependent on their constituent parts. Their role as privileged partners of the central planning bodies has enhanced their position of overall leadership. This has been reinforced by a burst of reorganising and renewing of the apparatus, both in the direction of centralisation and of developing their regional offices. Individual trade associations, however, have continued to develop their activities, as have major corporations, in those parts of planning relevant to their interests. The peak organisations' role is to coordinate and present the business case at the highest levels, if necessary putting alternative economic analyses to those of government experts. Confindustria's participation in the mid-1960s consisted largely in contesting and throwing doubt on the official figures and analyses. Finally, planning has encouraged large firms to bring their weight to bear in giving employers' organisations a more positive, purposive approach to public policy.

In the case of the trade unions, whereas there was support in the early 1960s for putting collective bargaining in a planning framework, their attitudes have progressively hardened against planning, at least in the mixed economy context and especially in so far as it relates to incomes. There has developed a suspicion that planning practices seek to involve them in at least tacit agreement on social peace, which is felt to be incompatible with their basic purpose. Thus a golden rule has emerged: undertake nothing through participation in planning that can compromise bargaining action elsewhere; use what information you can get from planning for such action. They are wary of getting involved in managerial problems for which, in industry, they have no formal responsibility or mandate. By the end of the 1960s the unions appeared to have lost interest in planning as a vehicle for their aims within the existing system. This contrasts with the relative ferment of interest that planning inspired in the early 1960s, especially in France.

The move in Britain to external legal regulation, with government impatient for results, has worsened relations and led to increased political activity by the unions as well as a growth in unofficial industrial action. Formal normative centralisation in wage determination proved repugnant at shop-floor level and, for the big unions, unacceptable. Similarly, the main union confederations in France have resisted being tied down too closely by 'contractual' arrangements. Both experiences have revealed the narrow limits of support such methods can give to mobilisation for planning objectives. In Italy the lack of an attempt to impose such frameworks has not, however, persuaded the unions to participate more whole-heartedly in consensus-building even though in respect of wage bargaining the government proved sympathetic in the late 1960s to a high wage policy, especially in public enterprise. Instead, they have pursued a campaign for social reforms in an overtly political manner. This was seen by them as compensation for the failure of planning to promote reform but it was also a response to pressures from the rank and file, which involved an increasing emphasis on 'qualitative' demands and in particular on the devolution of power to the industrial branch level and to works committees.

Unlike the employers, central organisation has scarcely been strengthened in the case of the unions. Indeed, the leaderships have increasingly been threatened in the 1960s with indiscipline by the rank and file. In the mid-1960s efforts were made (the TUC) or initiated (union of the Italian confederations) to bring greater cohesion and central direction. But the failure of planning, at least from the unions' point of view, not only weakened the impulse towards centralisation but brought new stresses. This was made worse in Britain by the legalistic turn policy took in respect of first wage and then strike restraint. Opposition within unions grew rapidly, leading to the very rare event of a defeat of the TUC. In France the union leaderships were also taken by surprise in 1968 at the extent of grass-roots dissatisfaction. In all three countries, militancy within the labour force was still running strong at the end of the decade and continued into the 1970s, so the prospect of stronger central control in the union movement receded.

What have been the general political consequences of the alignment of planning practices on the positions of large-scale industry? It has undoubtedly weakened government's possibility for effective discriminatory action between different sectors. This is reflected in the increasing favour that has been shown for sectoral plans and programmes and selective intervention projects. These accord with the vertical coalitions between parts of the administration and economic interests, which have finally foiled comprehensive approaches to a planned integration and coordination of economic policy. Moreover, difficulties in discrimination corrode the justification of planning as arbitration in the general interest. More important even than this, fundamental socio-economic divisions have been exposed and re-emphasised in the political process. Planning has fully demonstrated incompatible socio-political concerns resting on basic interest cleavages between 'partners'. Similarly, alternative models of development have been thrown into sharper relief.

These effects have been enhanced because continuing tripartite participation, even if a symbolic facade to real decision-making, has helped to ensure that the argument is articulated; the debate then goes wider than the specific content of plans. The concern with planning and controlling developments has thus increased the transparency of power relationships in socio-economic change. It has clarified the reality behind the woolly talk of liberals and state idealists alike concerning consensus politics and government's status as impartial mediator.

Tripartite consensus-building at the summit has been accompanied by a growing demonstration of the recalcitrance of those concerned to behave according to decisions authorised in this way. Individual firms, unions, plant committees, have continued to exercise or even newly assert their autonomy when and as they see fit. Elitist participation has increasingly been viewed negatively as mobilisation. One interpretation of the problem is that planning lacks agents of change capable of operating effectively at the lower levels. Italian planners, indeed, seem to have accepted this as an insurmountable obstacle in the major area of incomes. But planning at the regional and local levels, especially of land use, has also faced growing opposition, scarcely assuaged by official concern with consultation in the garb of participation.

In so far as the growing centralisation and concentration in the process of policy definition associated with planning practices has occurred, smaller and less economically powerful groups and lesser authorities have found it generally more difficult to participate through conventional channels. Planning has increasingly sought 'arrangements' with those exercising oligopolistic prerogatives. The decentralisation of policy implementation to administrative agencies or economic organisations hardly compensates a wide range of sectional and peripheral interests for their effective exclusion from policy conception. Furthermore, in forging a new framework of political discourse in terms of a technocratic economic rationality, planning doubly favours the large organisations employing experts versed in the appropriate techniques. While this may remove 'demagogy' and 'irrational' demands from the authoritative decision-making process, it tends to force them into unofficial expression.

Since at least the mid-1960s, planning has been associated with a strengthening of the professional managerial elite, both in terms of its role in the economy and, even more importantly perhaps, in terms of a *rapprochement*, if not conjunction, between the professional managers of the state and those of the large corporation. This is not to suggest a conspiracy. The key factor is the inability of the planning process to effect a shift in the balance of forces within the politico-economic system. In the name of effectiveness it therefore accommodates to this situation, and in so doing becomes a major instrument in an attempt to improve the system's functional efficiency viewed as a management problem. Whether or not there is a strong political executive, apparently able to impress a more programmatic mould on the planning process, does not seem to make any noticeable difference to this trend, which is characterised by the belief that the polity's destiny is hitched to that of the economy. However, planning emerged in the 1960s not only as a principal vehicle for the extension and concentration of the professional managerial elite, but also as an unintended source of an emergent challenge to that elite. National union leaderships have swung between closer assimilation with the managerial perspective and non-participatory opposition. On the whole they have increasingly tended to keep their distance from the state, doing deals on specific matters as it suits their purpose, but resisting being drawn into a system of reciprocity.

Whereas oligopolies may work to bring about relatively uniform economic behaviour, the political side-effects involve an increase in cleavages. Planning's problem is that it can only deal manageably with concentrated sectors. Planners thus deliberately seek a special *rapport* with the most dynamic major industrialists, knowing that the market will ensure that smaller firms and less dynamic firms will be swept along or swallowed up in the path of their progress. Such 'collusion in the public interest' is only politically stabilising, however, if it is acceptable to the public, or at any rate the most organised and articulate parts of it. Now 'collusion' implies secretiveness, and certainly if major decisions can be reached and implemented in this way the consequences will appear to the public as inevitable, as a matter of impersonal forces. Paradoxically, however, planning, while relying on collusion for managerial effectiveness, tends to make it visible. This arises, at the crudest level, from its purposive credo: that events are to be controlled rather than just happen without warning or forethought; some men *are* responsible. More specifically than this, the process of planning is too close to the political process to avoid participation and debate, unlike the planning done within a large corporation.

Moreover, the tendency to concentrate planning action on major projects, whether of development or of regulation, itself helps to focus public attention. Developments affecting groups and individuals are thus viewed as being determined 'on high'. Consensus-building practices – or for that matter parliamentary approval – do not necessarily make them more readily and generally acceptable as being in the public interest. This is even more likely to occur with planning than with traditional administrative processes of policy-making, for to be invited to take part in a wide-ranging and basic discussion of policies and then be largely frustrated is a surer way to politicisation. In the end, planning is caught in a contradiction between the managerial need for collusion and the need for the acceptance of its output as being in the public interest, especially by the mass-based organised groups. Pluralist politics is revealed as empirically antithetical to neo-liberal economics, whose rationality is scarcely compatible with the growing stress on participation by and within groups. How this conflict is to be resolved is thus a crucial question to the successful implementation of planned public policy.

Planning and power relations

For Shonfield, the achievement of government economic management was above all, as he vividly represented it, in keeping 'a good head of steam in the boiler at all times'.[15] In the past decade it has become clear that the really difficult task is controlling the head of steam. How to restrain the forces contributing to inflation has emerged as the major problem of modern capitalism. The 1973 report on the half-way stage in the Sixth Plan's execution in France underlined the critical nature of the problem in stressing the great risk of inflation 'sapping the very foundations of economic and social life' and leading 'to a profound modification in behaviour and to brutal reactions in the social system'. The implications of the way planning has worked is thus clearly of paramount importance for the problem of restraint. It is first necessary, however, to explore the basic elements in the problem.

The problem of restraint in dealing with inflation derives essentially from the fact that the behaviour of economic actors under oligopoly capitalism is regulated as much, or more, by relationships of power as by straightforward economic calculation. Galbraith recognised this over twenty years ago in his concept of countervailing power. As power became more and more concentrated in industry, it had become increasingly challenged by organised labour. But while this countervailence worked as a self-regulatory economic mechanism in resisting deflation – unions in effect helping to sustain demand – it encouraged inflation. This arose from the ability of management to raise prices in the imperfect market to at least compensate for any wage increases won by union action; the now familiar wage–price spiral. *Because of countervailing power it became impossible to keep up demand without producing inflation.* Thus Galbraith concluded that 'some slack in the economy is what keeps countervailing power from being converted into a coalition against the public', a coalition involving the complementarity of union and management action in fuelling inflation. Consequently, 'imperative efforts to increase production, far from being a cure for inflation, are a cause'.[16] In fact, modern capitalism is characterised by 'imperative efforts to increase production'. In the case of industry itself, they are the natural expression of the corporate drive for consolidation-through-expansion. Such efforts, however, dominate the polity no less than industry: growth comes before redistribution and social expenditure. Government intervention, in its complicity with management, becomes in effect an extension of the corporate planning of expansion. But the promotion of an oligopolistic pattern of industrial development – which is mirrored in the general weakness of anti-monopoly policy – only serves to oil the mechanism of countervailing power, ensuring the continuing build-up of steam.

To monetary, and especially Keynesian, techniques of economic regulation goes much of the credit for maintaining the level of activity, but they have proved inadequate for dealing with the problem of restraint. The strength of union, and especially management, complicity in inflation is such that when finally the government has been face to face with its responsibility for the general order of the system and in fact taken disinflationary action, this has effectively been short-circuited. In particular, the effects of tax increases have been neutralised by wage and salary increases. The financial sector has increasingly shown a multiform, not to say amoeba-like, character, in developing new forms of credit, even where a major part of it is state-run, as in France. The monetary mass has thus become extremely difficult to regulate, in the absence of a multiplication of direct controls amounting to a change in economic system. The level of activity can still, it is true, be reduced by cuts in public expenditure, but there is little evidence that this can be pushed to the point of so weakening the mechanism of countervailing power that the wage–price spiral is broken. Indeed, recent experience in Britain indicates that the real margin of autonomy that government possesses in limiting production is just sufficient to bring about stagflation: a levelling off in activity unaccompanied, even with unemployment reaching one million, by any significant slackening in inflation. The apparent view of some economists – that restraint is simply a matter of government deciding what should be curtailed – turns out to be decidedly simplistic.

What has to be recognised is that 'inflation is financially to the advantage of important groups in the community'.[17] These are the groups whose strategic position in the production of goods and services enables them to determine the distribution of wealth. They are first and foremost the large-scale industrial, commercial and financial groups, able to exploit simultaneously their market position and rising prices. Big farmers and unions are also favourably placed to hold their own in the play of producer groups through which the fruits of production are tapped at source; in effect, the cake is allocated as it is produced. Moreover, these categories help inflation along by anticipating it, further pre-empting the ultimate distribution of income. Thus periods of inflation are characterised by widening inequalities.

What, then, has been planning's contribution to this vital problem? Planning clearly represents a potential solution. Coordination and concerted action aim at establishing the consistency and rationality of decisions of economic actors, public and private. This involves the assumption by each of them of some of the general responsibility that the government has for the performance of the whole system. As we know, this has not happened. Industrialists, financiers, trade unions and government departments have continued to devote their single-minded attention to the pursuit of their own specific aims. The corollary of this has been the inability to attain or sustain comprehensive planning. Instead, planning has increasingly developed a piecemeal character, adapting to the contours of a capitalist neo-feudalism in which the state reflects a deeply segmented society dominated by large bureaucratic institutions and their manoeuvrings, often involving vertical coalitions of public and private power outside effective political control. It has thus been caught up in the contradictions of the system's evolving power relations – the play of corporative forces that largely creates the problem of restraint.

In coming to focus on a piecemeal rather than a comprehensive approach, planning experience confirms that liberal democracy cannot provide an autonomous and cohesive political power capable of controlling the oligopolistic pattern of development. In fact, by the basic acceptance of the industrial authority structure, planning has been associated with policies promoting such development. In so doing, it has contributed to maintaining the inflationary head of steam rather than its regulation. For the attempt to involve labour in corporate management's development problems has been altogether less successful, so that the effects of countervailing power have not been mitigated; indeed they have been enhanced by the extension and consolidation of economic and financial concentration. Moreover, a new manifestation of countervailing power has tended to emerge in the behaviour of labour at the decentralised level. Whereas the economic system has traditionally rested on the predictable and finally limited nature of workers' aspirations, there has developed a growing attempt at the grass roots to exert control over pay, employment and working conditions. This does not generally involve a formal demand for participation; it is, indeed, the *de facto* assertion of participation. As such it has become a principal element in the greater caution, if not antipathy, shown by union leaderships towards official consensus-building.

Although the mechanism of a decentralised countervailing power is clearly even less susceptible to centralised control than the original Galbraithian form, the pressures for government intervention have risen almost irresistibly, as Galbraith had forecast. The result has been a bifurcation of piecemeal planning in two distinct directions. Alongside the promotional aspect, allying government and large-scale industry, there has developed a narrow control aspect, seeking to circumscribe collective bargaining, either directly (incomes policy, contracts) or indirectly (price policy). Since this is a much more overtly political exercise than promoting industrial development – often involving confrontation with the unions – it requires an executive which is sure of its political position; hence the difficulties in Italy in launching such a policy. However, the attempt to limit the unwanted side-effects of the support for corporate expansion can scarcely be more than a short-term palliative, as has indeed proved to be the case. The worsening of inflation associated with this lack of success in tackling the problem of restraint has led to the resort, notably in Britain, to statutory control. This has occurred despite the fact that a key justification of planning has been the unsuitability of the law for dealing with complex economic problems. It is certainly true that its use against the private sector not only tends to undermine confidence but also to pose great difficulties of policing. Not surprisingly, therefore, it has been restricted largely to seeking to control, through the central union organisations, the behaviour of labour rather than capital and management.

The process of modern capitalist development tends constantly to weaken the market as a general regulatory mechanism, with the risk that the increasingly large-scale industrial operations will involve major miscalculations or inconsistencies. For, as Perroux has stated, these 'can no longer be evaluated by classical means, whether of profitability or even social productivity. They are *political works* [Perroux's italics] which directly or indirectly concern the mass of people.'[18] Piecemeal planning, however, does not provide the means of relating, ordering and controlling these 'political works' but rather, in contributing to their separate development, it strengthens the new feudalism. The continuing pre-eminence of Keynesian and monetary policy testifies to the inadequacy of planning, in practice, for making good the growing regulatory deficiencies of the market. But their chief advantage as regulatory techniques is their amenability to humdrum political and administrative decision-making. Because of this, and because they work largely through short-run aggregate responses, they do not serve to coordinate and control the 'political works' of the modern capitalist economy, necessarily a matter occupying a span of years.

It may be, however, that even now one has written off planning as an instrument of rationalisation too quickly. Although its immediate relationship with decision-making has proved at best uncertain in its effects, there is still its potential over the long term for the general inculcation of a new way of reasoning. The 'success' in this respect is much more difficult to assess. Planning rationality has undoubtedly taken hold to a substantial extent in French administration, to a lesser degree in Britain and really very little as yet in Italy. What, in any case, are the implications of the spread of this rationality? While it may help to ensure that those affected are pointing roughly in the same direction, it is already clear that it does not ensure that they are pulling together. Moreover, the question arises whether the direction in which it points is necessarily appropriate for post-industrial society, with its key and interrelated problems of inflation, resource diminution and preservation of the environment.

It is, in any case, an elite rationality, in the sense of only being available to those with the necessary training or substantial practical experience of it. It is increasingly doubtful, too, if even all elites in or closely proximate to the top managerial circle will fully assimilate it as their 'language'. This probably goes for the ordinary, non-ministerial political representative, but even more for many union leaders, for growing numbers of civic and consumer associations, as well as non-conformist political groupings. There is certainly a tendency, however, to drain of its substance the political function as performed classically by ministers. This does not so much involve a transference of power, defined by the roles performed, as the substantial acceptance by politicians in office, in day-to-day contact with senior officials, of the neo-liberal managerial rationality. A principal consequence is that a new concept of governmental responsibility has tended to emerge which stresses results rather than responsiveness. In this respect performance tends to become an end in itself and, even if profit is unavailable as a measure in most branches of government activity, effort is devoted to establishing other 'objective' yardsticks. Lucien Nizard has pointed to the danger this tendency poses for socio-political cohesion in so far as it weakens the representative function performed by ministries and services on behalf of group clients.[19]

Budgetary programming, in particular, has this potential by seeking to put expenditure allocation on a rational basis, involving a reallocation according to central criteria, so cutting across commitments to established group beneficiaries. Although the institutional obstacles to this coming about as a result of direct, central Treasury control are probably insuperable, the spread of planning rationality within the administration could have a similar effect in the longer term.

More important are the political implications of the convergence in the 'language' and methods of the public service – long considered a special political category of activity – with those of industrial management. One very important expression of this convergence occurs in the policy for structural change. The general managerial belief is in larger, more streamlined units. The response to overlaps, not to say interdependencies, is to promote coordination by greater concentration of responsibilities in a hierarchical framework. The fear of conflict is clear. Integration of clienteles through participation in the form of extended consultation is a prime objective. A closely related concern is the circulation of information among decision-making elites, since inadequate knowledge is considered a crucial factor in conflict. Procedures tending to politicise issues are generally in disfavour, or at least regretted as inimical to real problem-solving. This is particularly noticeable in matters of regional organisation, except for Italy, where a basic commitment to regional politics as opposed to regional administration was made in the highly politicised constituent assembly of 1946–7.

In attempting to encourage a broad consensus in policy conception, planning is associated with an increasing *centre–periphery cleavage*. Shonfield claimed that 'enhanced governmental power generates its own offset', while Galbraith referred to 'the tendency of power to be organised in response to a given position of power'.[20] There is no reason to think that this dialectical process stops with centralised union responses to industrial concentrations or centralised employer and employee responses to big government. This has been particularly evident in the cross-pressures to which union leaderships have been subject through the development of a more assertive rank and file. The centre–periphery cleavage is, as yet, a dispersed phenomenon, not clearly articulated in terms of social and political organisation. It arises both within functional structures and at a geographical level. It manifests itself through disruptiveness hampering the pursuit of 'centre' policies, although populist and regionalist-cum-nationalist tendencies have been on the increase. In industry, the substantial rise in absenteeism since the mid-1960s can be considered a manifestation of an associated alienation. It surely represents no less of a response than the militancy of decentralised leadership groups to the facts of a centre–periphery gap.[21] These facts are the raw material of a fully structured socio-political cleavage. They comprise, firstly, a gap that has widened between the language of government, including politicians, prone to increasingly didactic explanations of economic events couched in an esoteric terminology, and the language of everyday life which portrays the results of these events. Secondly, there is the increasing size and impersonality of industrial and governmental organisation, which stretches the links of responsibility. Thirdly, limitation of the alternatives effectively on the policy agenda for serious consideration within the system clearly encourages extra-system opposition, or at least frustration, leading to largely uncoordinated 'irrational' resistance to policy. It is clear that the recalcitrant behaviour of the periphery is increasingly becoming a key variable in policy implementation, yet it tends to be viewed by decision-makers in planning as a consequence rather than a cause of inadequate 'problem-solving', which is regarded as essentially a technical rather than a political matter.

The spread of planning rationality in elite decision-making circles is, then, no guarantee of a more effective solution of problems. The attempt to deepen and widen its penetration, which regional planning for example represents, is clearly two edged. The attempt can scarcely go far enough to include all lower-level leadership categories; while the further it goes, the greater is the possibility that it will actually contribute to the disintegration of the social regularities which give the reasoning much of its power, by encouraging a rejection of assigned roles – the strong tendency of participation in planning being to make relationships explicit. Moreover, although the effective decisional control is held by government in conjunction with industry, a wider awareness of what is involved is promoted by the discussions involving other interests in the course of the planning process. This can encourage criticisms, in some cases the presentation of alternative social aspirations and, at least, an inchoate resistance to the future portrayed. Such a reaction has been most visible perhaps in matters of land-use planning. Thus, rather than eliminating ideology, techno-managerialist planning has contributed dialectically to infusing it with continuing vigour. This is most evident in the growing, though as yet rather undefined, amorphous concerns such as the quality of life, control of life style and situation (e.g. place and hours of work), and a greater emphasis on ecological matters.

What lesson finally can be drawn from the planning experience? A key issue identified in the Introduction was the need for drastic institutional change to achieve the effective planning of economic and social development. A key issue stressed by Shonfield, as noted at the outset of this chapter, was that of democratic control. Our analysis strongly suggests these issues are interrelated. What has to be recognised is that the force of political rationality, involving the ordering and accommodation of power relationships, is a stronger determinant of decisions than economic rationality, with its stress on an impersonal, 'objective' efficiency and regulation. The modern economic process is a complex network of group interdependencies which are no longer susceptible to hierarchical control. Solutions to the problems arising in its spontaneous development increasingly involve the small group as well as the mass behaviour of workers; the human actor is replacing the human cog as the labour factor of production. Rather than seeking, therefore, to operate an economic rationality from above, attention should be focused on changing the structural conditions in which political rationality is applied.

We have argued that power relationships within the economic process cannot be harnessed constructively by the polity from outside. The conflict inherent in economic interdependencies requires the institutional recognition of role equalisation, so that solutions to problems may be evolved which have a greater chance of success because those within industry have a comparable – which of course does not necessarily mean direct – part in the solving process, rather than this being a matter solely for professional 'problem-solvers'. The development of a more democratic decision-making process in the economy could be expected to help free government in its planning endeavours from the dominance of a one-dimensional economic ideology sustaining modern capitalism in its frenetic course of expansion, concentration and therefore inflation – a dominance which is imposed, as we have seen, by the fact that senior management has sole responsibility for the key industrial and financial decisions. Of course, government itself would also need to have the will for an alternative rationality, such as a social and redistributive one. At least, the replacement of an absolutist system of industrial authority with a constitutional and representative one could be expected to provide a necessary internal check on corporate power.[22] More importantly, the democratisation, through an employee-elected board, of the major deliberations and information concerning corporate policy, would help to repair the structural weakness of labour's role in contributing to national economic policy-making, as manifested in planning.[23]

To re-equilibrate the role of government's major 'partners' is necessary if political rationality is to be embodied in a way conducive to the integration and coordination of action that planning requires, above all by restoring a greater autonomy to government as arbiter, and thereby in its strategic use of public power. The planning experience underlines the irreducibility of the political function, so that the pursuit of economic efficiency and development ignores it at its peril. At any rate, it is now clear that to identify the public interest in planning with the success of big business management and a bureaucratic state capitalism is to beg too many questions relative to the future of post-industrial society. In restricting itself almost exclusively to establishing the *economic* criteria and conditions of modern capitalism's progress, planning is paradoxically associated with a growing uncertainty about the political future, whereas a well-founded political order is the basis for any control over man's economic and technological future.[24] It is more and more evident that such a political order has to extend throughout the economy, where power relationships increasingly predominate in shaping decisions; otherwise, lacking a common legitimacy, they will continue to distort the operation of the existing political order, as the planning experience so plainly shows.

NOTES

1 A. Shonfield, *Modern Capitalism*, London 1965, p. 63.
2 P. Massé, *Histoire, Méthode et Doctrine de la Planification Française*, La Documentation Francaise, Paris 1962, p. 14.
3 Introduction to the Fourth Plan of Economic and Social Development (1961–5).
4 See above, p. 179.
5 See above, p. 97.
6 See above, p. 146.
7 'Veillée autour d'un Plan', *Le Monde*, 10 January 1973.
8 See above, p. 3.
9 M. Edelman and R. W. Fleming, *The Politics of Wage–Price Decisions. A Four Country Analysis*, Urbana 1965, pp. 284–5.
10 Shonfield, *Modern Capitalism*, p. 128.
11 See above, pp. 373–4.
12 Edelman and Fleming, *Wage–Price Decisions*, p. 302.
13 L. Nizard, 'Planification: Processus Décisionel et Changement', *Bulletin de l'Institut international d'administration publique*, October–December 1972, pp. 689–91.
14 *Idem*. 'La Planification: Socialisation et Simulation', *Sociologie du Travail*, No. 4, 1972, p. 379 and see pp. 373–5.
15 Shonfield, *Modern Capitalism*, p. 17.
16 J. K. Galbraith, *American Capitalism*, London 1957, pp. 210–11.
17 *Ibid.* p. 209.
18 F. Perroux, *Industrie et Création Collective*, II, Paris 1970, p. 111.
19 L. Nizard, *Sociologie du Travail*, 1972, pp. 376–7.
20 Shonfield, *Modern Capitalism*, p. 389, and Galbraith, *American Capitalism*, p. 127.
21 For a recent account of the situation, see a report by the ILO, *Human Values in Social Policy*, Geneva 1973, pp. 12–20, chapters 3 and 6.
22 On this see, for example, R. Dahl, *After the Revolution*, New Haven 1970, pp. 115–40.
23 See above, pp. 468–9.
24 B. de Jouvenel, *The Art of Conjecture*, London 1967, chapter 18.

Select General Bibliography

Far from trying to produce a long list of books and articles, many of which are now primarily of historical interest, we have been severely selective, using three main criteria. To qualify for inclusion a book or article should specifically provide either interesting theoretical insights into the problems of planning; or it should represent a challenging ideological interpretation of the planning phenomenon; or it should offer a relatively up to date description of planning in more than one of the countries concerned. Publications concerning particular countries or aspects of planning will be found at the end of the appropriate part of this book.

'Administration et Société à la lumière des Pratiques Planificatrices', special issue of *Revue Française de Science Politique*, XXIII, April 1973.

Benveniste, G. *The Politics of Expertise*, Croom Helm, London 1973.

Chamberlain, N. K. *Private and Public Planning*, McGraw-Hill, New York 1965.

Crozier, M. 'Pour une analyse sociologique de la planification française', *Revue Française de Sociologie*, June 1965.

Denton, G., Forsyth, M. and MacLennan, M. C. *Economic Planning and Policies in Britain, France and Germany*, Allen and Unwin, London 1968.

Dror, Y. *Ventures in Policy Sciences*, Part 3, American Elsevier, New York and Amsterdam 1971.

Faber, M. and Seers, D. (eds), *The Crisis in Planning*, 2 vols. Chatto and Windus, London 1972.

Faludi, A. *A Reader in Planning Theory*, Pergamon Press, Oxford 1973.

Gross, B. M. (ed), *Action under Planning: the Guidance of Economic Development*, McGraw-Hill, New York 1967.

Herzog, P. *Politique Economique et Planification en Régime Capitaliste*, les Editions Sociales, Paris 1972.

Jobert, B. and Revesz, B. *Représentation Sociale et Planification*, CERAT, Grenoble 1972.

Lutz, V. *Central Planning in the Market Economy*, Longmans, London 1969.

Nizard, L. 'De la planification française: production de normes et concertation', *Revue Française de Science Politique*, XXII, October 1972.

Osbekhan, H. 'Towards a General Theory of Planning' in E. Jantsch, *Perspectives of Planning*, OECD, Paris 1969.

Planification et Société, Colloque d'Uriage, Grenoble University Press, 1974.

Ruffolo, G. *Rapporta sulla programmazione*, Laterza, Bari 1973.

Schultze, C. L., *The Politics and Economics of Public Spending*, Brookings, Washington DC 1968.

Shonfield, A. *Modern Capitalism*, OUP, London 1965.

Waterston, A. *Development Planning: Lessons of Experience*, OUP, London 1966.

Wildavsky, A. 'If Planning is Everything, Maybe its Nothing', *Policy Sciences*, IV, 1973.

INDEX

Br = British; Fr = French; It = Italian

Abercrombie Plan 350
Adamson, Campbell 126
administration, *see* public administration
administrative justice 299, 320–1, 333–4, 352, 355 n. 16
advisory services, *see* technical assistance
agricultural interest organisations 26, 37, 50 n. 1, 106, 168
agriculture 99, 155, 168, 205, 430
alienation 187, 194, 480
allocation, resources and expenditure 11, 17, 194, 226, 231–2, 255, 256–7, 261–2, 270, 285, 288, 292–3, 332
aménagement du territoire, see regional development
American way of life 295–6
authority: governmental 231, 245, 259, 370–1, 384–5, 434; industrial 454, 469–70, 482

Bains Report 344–5
balance of payments 66–7, 71, 95, 180, 187–8, 190, 202
Banfield, Edward 3
banking and financial institutions and interests 33, 121, 476; Bank of England 193; Bank of Italy 84, 92 n. 27, 202, 448
Beeching, Dr Richard 406
Bell, Daniel 424
Berger, Gaston 427
Bloch-Lainé, François 12, 30
Board of Trade (BOT) 54, 58, 114, 123, 192, 237, 239, 259
Brown, Lord George 68 n. 8, 126, 241, 468
Brittan, Samuel 55, 126 n. 5
Buchanan Report 336, 346, 403

budgeting 35, 42, 44–5, 107, 109, 137, 255–7, 310, 373, 399, 406, 424
business, *see* employers

Cabinet 58, 81, 84, 96, 180, 184–5, 193, 304; *see also* political executive
Caisse des Dépôts et Consignations 297
capital, capital investment 131, 137, 159, 303, 450, 455
capitalism 55, 135, 146, 148, 150, 368, 433, 436–7, 439, 441, 445, 450, 459, 475–6, 478, 482–3
Cassa per il Mezzogiorno 14, 134, 210, 269, 270–2, 364, 462
CBI 63, 65–6, 68 n. 15, 121, 123, 125, 182, 186, 192, 194, 214, 251, 410
central government and administration 434, 454, 467; Britain 58, 238, 240, 249, 253, 262–3, 266, 291, 317, 320, 326, 328, 343–4, 349–51, 405, *see also* Whitehall; France 24, 93–4, 97, 104, 108, 170, 222, 225, 291, 306–7, 314, 398, 400; Italy 80, 83, 129, 135, 138, 209, 283, 364–5, 369, 374
central–local relations 219, 231, 238, 244, 255, 262, 277, 291, 331–2, 364, 387–8, 409–10
Central Policy Review Staff (CPRS) – Br 17
Central Training Council – Br 196, 198
centralisation 94, 98–102, 189, 198–200, 232–3, 237, 239, 255–7, 304, 349, 351, 373, 386, 396, 398, 411, 472–3
Centre-Left 15, 75, 79, 86, 91 n. 12, 128–9, 139 n. 1, 203, 212, 414, 416, 418
center–periphery 63–4, 179, 193, 200, 387, 480–1

[485]